The Rough Guide to Corsica

Written and researched by
David Abram

With additional contributions by
Theo Taylor, Geoffrey Young and Nia Williams

Help us update

We've gone to a lot of trouble to ensure that this third edition of *The Rough Guide to Corsica* is completely up-to-date and accurate. However, things do change: hotels and restaurants come and go, opening hours are notoriously fickle, and prices are extremely volatile. We'd appreciate any suggestions, amendments or contributions for future editions of the guide. We'll credit all letters and send a copy of the next edition (or any other *Rough Guide*) for the best.

Please mark all letters "Rough Guide to Corsica Update" and send to:
Rough Guides, 62–70 Shorts Gardens, London WC2H 9AB or
Rough Guides, 4th Floor, 345 Hudson St, New York, NY 10014.

Email should be sent to:
mail@roughguides.co.uk

Online updates about *Rough Guide* titles can be found on our Web site at *www.roughguides.com*

The Author

David Abram's first experience of Corsica was in 1986, during the sabbatical year of a French degree. The only thing he knew about the island then was that it had more green "*parcours pittoresque*" lines on its Michelin map than anywhere else in France. Fourteen years on, having visited Corsica annually since he became co-author of the *Rough Guide* in 1996, he has worked his way around nearly all of those wiggly lines, and remains amazed both by the island and his good fortune at being able to spend a month or two there each year. Piling on belt inches in Corsican restaurants, and trying to shed them afterwards in the mountains, provides the perfect foil for long research trips in India, where he spends most winters working on other Rough Guides. When at home in Barrow Gurney, near Bristol, UK, David likes to devote as much time as possible to pottering around the Mendips and playing his clarinet.

Readers' letters

Many thanks to all the readers who wrote in with comments on the last edition:

C.P. Aylott, Alex Bartram, Danièle Bourdais, Brian Catlos, Wim De Coninck, A.A. Cutts, Kristie Drummond & Ed Papworth, Olivia Eccleshall, Alex Fisher, K.B. Gilkes, Knut Hordnes, E. Hudson, Gordon Johnson, Andrew & Sarah Kenningham, Stephen Lamley, Brian McGarrigle, John Malloch, Audrey B. Moore, Susan Murray, J. Pagni, Colin Parker, Clare Partridge, Jim & Ann Skipper, J.H. Schultz, Peter Talbot, Steve Waring, Bill White.

The Rough Guides

Travel Guides • Phrasebooks • Music and Reference Guides

We set out to do something different when the first Rough Guide was published in 1982. Mark Ellingham, just out of university, was travelling in Greece. He brought along the popular guides of the day, but found they were all lacking in some way. They were either strong on ruins and museums but went on for pages without mentioning a beach or taverna. Or they were so conscious of the need to save money that they lost sight of Greece's cultural and historical significance. Also, none of the books told him anything about Greece's contemporary life – its politics, its culture, its people and how they lived.

So, with no job in prospect, Mark decided to write his own guidebook, one which aimed to provide practical information that was second to none, detailing the best beaches and the hottest clubs and restaurants, while also giving hard-hitting accounts of every sight, both famous and obscure, and providing up-to-the-minute information on contemporary culture. It was a guide that encouraged independent travellers to find the best of Greece, and was a great success, getting shortlisted for the Thomas Cook travel guide award, and encouraging Mark, along with three friends, to expand the series.

The Rough Guide list grew rapidly and the letters flooded in, indicating a much broader readership than had been anticipated, but one which uniformly appreciated the Rough Guides' mix of practical detail and humour, irreverence and enthusiasm. Things haven't changed. The same four friends who began the series are still the caretakers of the Rough Guide mission today: to provide the most reliable, up-to-date and entertaining information to independent-minded travellers of all ages, on all budgets.

We now publish 150 titles and have offices in London and New York. The travel guides are written and researched by a dedicated team of more than 100 authors, based in Britain, Europe, the USA and Australia. We have also created a unique series of phrasebooks to accompany the travel series, along with the acclaimed series of music guides, and a best-selling pocket guide to the Internet and World Wide Web. We also publish comprehensive travel information on our Web site: *www.roughguides.com*

Contents

List of maps

MAP SYMBOLS

Motorway
Major road
Minor road
Steps
Pedestrianised road
Footpath
Railway
Wall
Ferry route
Waterway
Province boundary
Chapter division boundary
General point of interest
Peak
Pass
Escarpment
Viewpoint
Cave
Tower
Lighthouse
Church (regional maps)
Convent/Monastery
Airport
Bus stop
Parking
Camping
Tourist office
Post office
Building
Church
Cemetery
Park
National park
Forest
Marshland
Beach

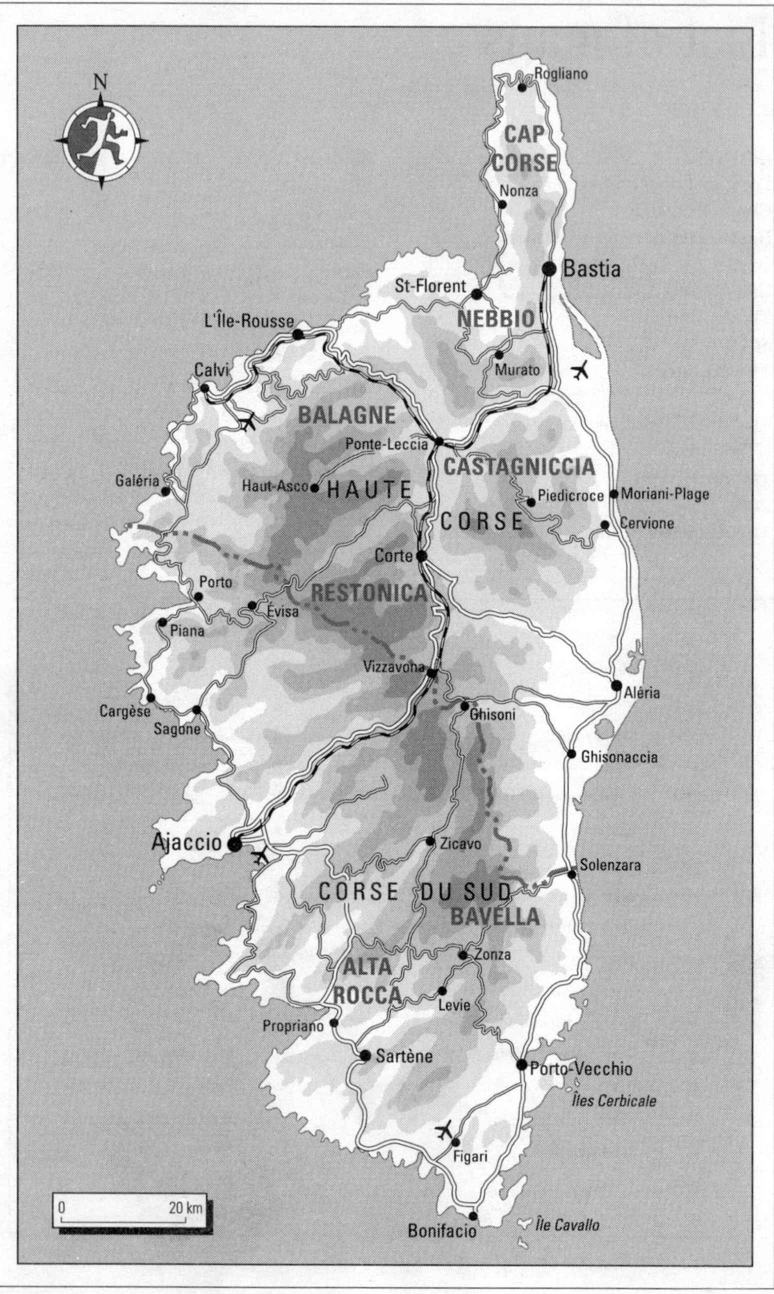
N
Rogliano
CAP CORSE
Nonza
Bastia
St-Florent
NEBBIO
L'Île-Rousse
Murato
Calvi
BALAGNE
Ponte-Leccia
CASTAGNICCIA
Galéria
Haut-Asco
HAUTE CORSE
Piedicroce
Moriani-Plage
Cervione
Corte
Porto
RESTONICA
Évisa
Piana
Vizzavona
Aléria
Cargèse
Sagone
Ghisoni
Ghisonaccia
Ajaccio
Zicavo
Solenzara
CORSE DU SUD
BAVELLA
Zonza
ALTA ROCCA
Levie
Propriano
Sartène
Porto-Vecchio
Îles Cerbicale
Figari
0
20 km
Bonifacio
Île Cavallo

Introduction

Around one and a half million people visit Corsica each year, drawn by a climate that's mild even in winter and by some of the most astonishingly diverse landscapes in all of Europe. Nowhere in the Mediterranean has beaches finer than Corsica's perfect half-moon bays of white sand and transparent water, or seascapes more inspiring than the mighty granite cliffs of Corsica's west coast. Inland, crystalline rivers cascade from the island's central peaks, rushing through dense forests of colossal pines that have been untouched for centuries. In the north of the island, exquisite Romanesque churches overlook olive groves and ranks of vines, while to the south prehistoric statues lurk on stark plains or amid green valleys cloaked in aromatic maquis shrubs.

Even though the annual influx of tourists now exceeds Corsica's population sixfold, tourism hasn't spoilt the island. There are a few resorts, but overdevelopment is rare and high-rise blocks nonexistent, thanks largely to local resistance – sometimes violent – to the approaches of foreign speculators. Although they are obliged to import practically every consumer durable from the French mainland, many Corsicans regard themselves as a people apart, and a history of repeated invasion has only strengthened their **self-identity**. Through the Saracen raids of the Middle Ages and the periods of Spanish, Italian and French rule, the Corsicans have tenaciously held on to their heritage, and continue to preserve their **ancient culture** in the face of the modern world. Unearthly choral chants sung in the native language can still be heard in some remote regions, and a belief in the supernatural remains a potent force. A continuing preoccupation with death is attested by the mausoleums that you'll see on hillsides all over the island, while the fierce sense of family pride preserves more than a vestige of the feeling which fired the notorious vendettas of the past. The code of honour that protected the island's bandits right into the present century persists in a culture that tends to regard collaboration with the police as something shameful. Yet the Corsicans' reputation for hostility to foreigners is largely undeserved. They might not be immediately approachable, but a deep hospitality is easily discovered if you make the effort – especially if you admire their island.

Where to go

Two hundred years of French rule have had limited tangible effect on Corsica, an island where Baroque churches, Genoese fortresses, fervent Catholic rituals and an indigenous language saturated with Tuscan influences show a more profound affinity with neighbouring Italy. During the long era of Italian supremacy the northeast and southwest of Corsica formed two provinces known as *Diqua dei monti* – "this side of the mountains" – and *Dila dei monti*, the uncontrollable "side beyond". Today the French *départements* of Haute-Corse and Corse du Sud roughly coincide with these territories, and remain quite distinct in feel.

Capital of the north, **Bastia** was the principal Genoese stronghold and its fifteenth-century old town has survived almost intact. Of the island's two large towns, this is the more purely Corsican, and commerce rather than tourism is its main concern, which makes it an attractive alternative to some of the southern towns. Also relatively undisturbed, the northern **Cap Corse** harbours inviting sandy coves and coastal hamlets such as Erbalunga and Centuri-Port – friendly fishing villages that provide hotel accommodation for the few tourists who make it up here. Within a short distance of Bastia, the fertile region of the **Nebbio** contains a plethora of churches built by Pisan stoneworkers, the prime example being the cathedral of Santa Maria Assunta at the appealingly chic little port of **St-Florent**.

To the west of here, **L'Île Rousse** and **Calvi**, the latter graced with an impressive citadel and fabulous sandy beach, are major targets for holidaymakers – and their hilly hinterland, the **Haute-Balagne**, offers plenty of hilltop villages to explore, as well as access to the northern reaches of the vast **Parc Naturel Régional**, an astounding area of forested valleys, gorges and peaks. The spectacular **Scandola** nature reserve, a part of the northwest coast that lies within the boundaries of the park, can be visited by boat from the tiny resort of **Porto**, from where walkers can also strike into the magnificently wild **Spelunca gorge** and **Forêt d'Aïtone** – where you might spot the island's delicacy, wild boar, if you keep your eyes peeled.

Climate chart – Ajaccio

	Jan	Feb	Mar	Apr	May	June	July	Aug	Sept	Oct	Nov	Dec
Average Daily Max Temperature (°C)	13	14	16	18	21	25	27	28	26	22	17	14
Average Monthly Rainfall (mm)	76	65	53	48	50	21	10	16	50	88	97	98

Sandy beaches and rocky coves punctuate the **west coast** all the way down to **Ajaccio**, Napoléon's birthplace and Bastia's traditional rival. Its pavement cafés and palm-lined boulevards are thronged with tourists in summer, most of whom take the opportunity to sample the watersport facilities of the expansive and beautiful **Golfe d'Ajaccio**. Slightly fewer make it to nearby **Filitosa**, greatest of the many prehistoric sites scattered across this, the most heavily visited, half of the island. Brash **Propriano** lies close to Filitosa and to stern **Sartène**, seat of the wild feudal lords who once ruled this region and still the quintessential Corsican town.

More megalithic sites are to be found south of Sartène on the way to **Bonifacio**, a comb of ancient buildings perched atop furrowed white cliffs at the southern tip of the island. Equally popular **Porto-Vecchio**, the spot that has perhaps suffered most from the tourist boom, provides a springboard for excursions to the amazing beaches of the south, or alternatively to the oak forest of **Ospédale**, or even to the astounding **Col de Bavella**, where flattened pines spring from the bald granite needles. The **eastern plain** has less to boast of, but the Roman site at **Aléria** is worth a visit for its excellent museum, while to the north of Aléria lies the **Castagniccia**, a swathe of chestnut trees and alluring villages.

Corte, standing at the heart of Corsica, is the best base for exploring the stupendous mountains and gorges of the interior, with the remote valleys of the **Niolo** and **Asco** a stone's throw away. Dominating these valleys, **Monte Cinto** marks the northern edge of the island's spine of high peaks: the experienced hiker could attempt the **GR20**, an epic trail that traverses this magnificent ridge, past Monte d'Oro and Monte Renoso, as far as Monte Incudine in the south.

When to go

Whatever kind of holiday you intend to take, the **best times of year** to visit Corsica are **late spring** and **late summer** or **early autumn**, when you're guaranteed sunshine without the stifling heat or crowds of July and August. The wild flowers carpeting the island in April and May make these delightful months to come, and autumn is just as good for scenic colour – the Castagniccia in particular is a riot of russet tones at this time of year. Beach goers will be ensured a tan as late as October, and even if you plan a visit in the depths of winter you're unlikely to encounter much rain, though snow on the high mountains can restrict driving through the passes in January, February and March, and visibility is often obscured by mists.

Crowds are only likely to be a problem in the major resorts such as Porto-Vecchio and L'Île Rousse, especially in August, when the whole of Italy and France take their annual holiday. In the more remote areas you should book **accommodation** in advance, for the simple reason that there is rarely more than a single hotel in any village. For most of the island, however, you can rely on finding a place to stay at any time.

ROUGH GUIDE HIGHLIGHTS

AUBERGES (COUNTRY RESTAURANTS)

A Pignata, near Levie. Definitive local cooking and a dream location. See p.252.

Ajgha, near Calvi. Superb Corsican cuisine with a Spanish twist. See p.125.

BEACHES

Plage d'Arone, near Piana. A perfect beach, as yet unspoilt. See p.177.

Plage de Loto, Déserte des Agriates. Pristine white sand, turquoise water and, best of all, a blissfully wild location. See p.109.

Plage de Rondinara, near Bonifacio. Like something out of the Maldives, despite being on the edge of the main tourist zone. See p.282.

FESTIVALS

U Catenacciu, Sartène. Hooded penitents reinact Christ's walk to Calvary in Sartène's flame-lit Good Friday procession. See p.266.

Rencontres de Chants Polyphoniques, Calvi. International singing festival with daily recitals by the island's top choral groups. See p.127.

HIKES

GR20, from Calenzana to Conca. Regarded as France's toughest long-distance hike: ten to twelve days of relentless gradient and jaw-dropping scenery. See p.144.

Martella tower, St-Florent. A wonderful coast walk to the watchtower that was blown up by Nelson. See p.103.

Trou de la Bombe, Bavella. The cream of the island's mountainscapes, the Bavella Needles, can be seen from this gentle path through giant Laricio pine forest. See p.259.

TRIPS

"U Trinighellu" Ajaccio to Calvi by train. Corsica's boneshaking narrow-gauge train rattles through the heart of the mountains and above the stunning Balagne coast. Unmissable. See p.213.

Calanches de Piana and **Scandola headland** Boat rides from Porto. Bob around at water level beneath the west coast's undisputed scenic highlights. See p.169.

Porto to Corte, by road. Arguably the most spectacular road journey on Corsica, through the Spelunca gorge and across the highest motorable pass on the island to the Niolu Valley. See p.179.

MEDIEVAL CHURCHES

La Canonica, near Bastia. The best-preserved and grandest of Corsica's Pisan cathedrals. See p.78.

San Michele de Murato, Nebbio. Late thirteenth-century, green-and-white-stone Romanesque church, straddling a windswept pass. An architectural gem. See p.106.

Museums

Musée Fesch, Ajaccio. One of Europe's finest collections of Renaissance painting. See p.208.

Musée Jérôme Carcopino, Aléria. Superb array of Greek and Roman artefacts unearthed in the adjacent ruins. See p.309.

Museu di a Corsica, Corte. Ethnographic museum in Corte's old citadel, housed in a recently converted, state-of-the-art complex. See p.347.

Period hotels

Castel' Brando, Erbalunga. Beautifully restored palazzo on the Cap Corse coast road. See p.83.

Le Monte D'Oro, Vizzavona. Late nineteenth-century mountain lodge that oozes atmosphere. See p.359.

Les Roches Rouges, Piana. A gorgeous *fin-de-siècle* hotel with original fittings and matchless sea views. See p.176.

Prehistoric sites

Filitosa, Golfe de Valinco. World-famous prehistoric site whose standing stones sport eerily carved faces. See p.232.

Pianu di Levie, Alta Rocca. Upstaged by Filitosa, but a far more impressive location. See p.252.

Rock formations

Calanches de Piana, near Porto. A vast mass of contorted red porphyry that's become Corsica's most photographed landscape. See p.175.

Campomoro coast path. Chaos of crystaline white granite smoothed into beautiful forms by the sea. See p.248.

Capu Tafonatu. The great "Pierced Peak" of Paglia Orba, visible for miles around. See p.341.

Viewpoints

Monte Rotondo, near Corte. Corsica's second highest peak overlooks the island's entire watershed – an unforgettable spectacle. See p.352.

Moulin Mattei, Cap Corse. Ruined windmill with a stone picnic table and breathtaking views over the Golfe de St-Florent. See p.91.

Tour de Turghiu, Capu Rossu. Stunning panorama of the Golfe de Porto from the ramparts of an old Genoese watchtower. See p.177.

Vineyards

Domaine de Toraccia, Lecci, near Porto-Vecchio. An idyllic vineyard whose "Oriu" red ranks among the island's top wines. See p.296.

Patrimonio, Nebbio. Heartland of Corsica's fragrant muscat, which you taste at the *caves* themselves. See p.104.

Part 1

The Basics

Getting There from Britain and Ireland

Flying is the fastest and most convenient way to reach Corsica. A direct flight to Bastia, Ajaccio, Calvi or Figari (near Bonifacio) – the island's four civil airports – takes between two and two-and-a-half hours from the UK. Fares vary according to the time of year, peaking in the Easter school holiday period and during July and August, but rarely cost more than the train and ferry journey. Travelling overland is only worth considering if you want to explore mainland France en route.

By Plane

The vast majority of British visitors travel to Corsica by direct charter flight – from the London airports of Gatwick, Heathrow or Stansted, and regional airports such as Birmingham or Manchester – with the air fare included in the price of a package holiday (see p.9). If you buy your own ticket, however, and arrange your own accommodation and transport on the island, you can save money.

Charter Flights

Operating from early April until mid-October, **charter flights** are run by specialist airlines such as Air 2000, Air UK and Monarch, who sell blocks of seats in advance to tour operators, who then combine them with accommodation and sell them on as packages. Any left-over unsold seats on the flights are cleared on behalf of the airlines by a consolidator called Holiday Options (see below). If during the weeks before the departure date the tour companies think they may have unsold seats, they may also offer discount "flight-only" deals. For this reason, the later you can leave buying a ticket, the more likely you are to come up with a cheap fare, although holding out for a last-minute bargain inevitably entails a degree of risk, particularly if you are travelling in high season. The only way to be sure of a seat on a charter flight, on the date you wish to travel, is to book well in advance, when tickets may be more expensive.

The best place to start looking for a charter air ticket is Holiday Options (☎01444/244411), whose published return fares (to Bastia, Calvi, Ajaccio and Figari) range from around £189 off season to £245 in mid-August. In addition, they frequently advertise "short-notice" or "late-availability" flights for as little as £100 (often with bargain fly-drive or accommodation options thrown in). If they are sold out, or only have standard fares on offer, try phoning around tour operators such as Voyages Ilena, Corsican Places, Simply Corsica, or others listed on p.10.

Charter flights to Corsica from the UK leave and return on Sundays; the ticket price should include all airport taxes. When booking, bear in mind which part of the island you intend to travel to first, and where any accommodation you may have pre-arranged is, or you could be faced with a long journey on arrival.

Scheduled Flights

Outside the tourist season, from November until March, and at times when the charters are sold out, your only option will be to take a **scheduled flight**. No scheduled carrier flies direct from the UK to Corsica. However, Air France, British Airways, British Midland and TAT all fly there, with a change of planes at either Paris, Nice or Marseille included in a single price. Of these, Air France offers the widest choice and best selection of discounts, with daily flights to three of Corsica's main domestic airports – Bastia, Ajaccio and Calvi - starting at around £199 for a return flight via Paris (Orly). BA offer comparable fares, routing you through one of the Riviera ports (Marseille or Nice).

The main disadvantage with scheduled routings compared with direct charter flights is that they take considerably longer. To the total flying time of around three hours (1hr 20min to Paris and 1hr 30min for the onward leg to Corsica, or 2hr to Nice and 45min to Ajaccio/Bastia), you have to add on another two or three hours (and sometimes more) for connections.

Aside for the annoying delays, the other downside with travelling scheduled is the extra **cost**. The cheapest scheduled tickets to Corsica start at around £200 return, rising to £440 in peak season (July and August). To cut costs, some travellers opt for a so-called **"double-ticket deal"**, buying a heavily discounted ticket from the London airports to Paris or one of the Mediterranean cities with an airline such as Easyjet, and the onward leg via a French domestic carrier such as Air Littoral, Compagnie Corse Mediterranée, Kyrnair, or Air Liberté. Most travel agents are happy to arrange this for you, but may point out that the typical £20–40 saving on the cost of a through-ticket with BA or Air France brings with it a greater risk of delay or inconvenience; on double tickets, the first carrier is not

AIRLINES AND AGENTS IN THE UK

Airlines

Air France, First Floor, 10 Warwick St, London W1R 5RA (☎0845/084 5111; *www.airfrance.fr*).

British Airways, 156 Regent St, London W1R 5TA (☎0345/222111; *www.british-airways.com*).

British Midland, Donington Hall, Castle Donington, Derby, East Midlands (☎01332/854274; *www.britishmidland.co.uk*).

EasyJet, Luton Airport, Bedfordshire LU2 9LS (☎0870/600 0000; *www.easyjet.co.uk*).

TAT, contact British Airways (see above).

Flight Agents

Holiday Options, Martlet Heights, 49 The Martlet, Burgess Hill, West Sussex RH15 9NJ; (☎01444/244411; *www.holidayoptions.co.uk*). *The UK's most promising source of discounted charter-flight tickets, often combined with unbeatable fly-drive and accommodation deals.*

North South Travel, Moulsham Mill Centre, Parkway, Chelmsford, Essex CM2 7PX (☎01245/492882). *Friendly and competitive agency offering discounted fares on scheduled airlines, with profits used to support sustainable tourism and projects in the developing world.*

Real Holidays, 101 Essex Rd, London N1 2SJ (☎020/7359 3938). *Extremely knowledgeable London-based Corsica specialists, dealing in charter and scheduled flights, as well as packages with most of the main operators.*

STA Travel, *www.statravel.co.uk*; 86 Old Brompton Rd, London SW7; 117 Euston Rd, London NW1 (☎020/7361 6262); 38 North St, Brighton (☎01273/728282); 38 Sidney St, Cambridge (☎01223/366966); 75 Deansgate, Manchester (☎0161/834 0668); 88 Vicar Lane, Leeds LS1 (☎0113/244 9212); 9 St Mary's Place, Newcastle-upon-Tyne (☎0191/233 2111); 36 George St, Oxford OX1 (☎01865/729800); *Discount fares with particularly good student and youth deals.*

Trailfinders, 215 Kensington High St, London W8 (☎020 7937 5400); 22–24 The Priory, Queensway, Birmingham B46 (☎0121/236 1234); 48 Corn St, Bristol BS1 (☎0117/929 9000); 58 Deansgate, Manchester M3 (☎0161/839 6969); 254–285 Sauchiehall St, Glasgow G2 (☎0141/353 2224). *One of the best-informed and most efficient all-rounders.*

Usit CAMPUS, National telesales and enquiries ☎0870/240 0101; *www.usitcampus.co.uk*; 52 Grosvenor Gardens, London SW1 0AG (☎020 7730 3402); 541 Bristol Rd, Bournbrook, Selly Oak, Birmingham B29 (☎0121/414 1848); 61 Ditchling Rd, Brighton BN1 (☎01273/570226); 39 Queens Rd, Bristol BS8 (☎0117/929 2494); 5 Emmanuel St, Cambridge CB1 (☎01223/324283); 53 Forrest Rd, Edinburgh (☎0131/225 6111); 105–106 Aldates Rd, Oxford OX1 (☎01865/242067); also at YHA shops and university campuses. *Student/youth travel specialists, with 49 branches on university campuses and at large YHA shops around the UK.*

contractually obliged to get you to your final destination, and will offer no compensation if a delay caused by them means you miss your connecting flight. Also, as Easyjet do most of their business over the Internet and telephone and do not pay agents' commission, it is worth bearing in mind that booking one of their tickets on the high street may incur a surcharge of around £20.

If you're offered a ticket to Corsica **via Paris** from a **regional airport in the UK**, check to make sure the onward leg to Corsica leaves from the same airport you arrived in. At the time of writing, only British Airways flew from Manchester and Birmingham to Paris Orly, which is where all domestic flights to Corsica depart from; fly with Air France via Paris and you'll land at Charles de Gaulle (CDG) airport, leaving you an inconvenient, time-consuming trip across the city to pick up your plane to Corsica.

By Train

The **Channel tunnel** has slashed travelling times between London and Paris, which in turn has led to a proliferation of cut-rate deals on regular train and ferry or hovercraft crossings. Given the low cost of charter flights, and the inconvenience and distances involved with travelling overland to Corsica, it is not surprising that very few British visitors approach the island by rail.

If you do opt for the train, you'll first have to choose between the tunnel and the sea crossing routes to Paris. From there, you can then take either a standard train south to Nice or Marseille, or the superfast, more expensive TGV (*Train de Grande Vitesse*). From both Nice and Marseille there is then a choice of slow and fast ferries to Corsica.

Eurostar

Eurostar's high-speed passenger service to Paris Gare du Nord via the Channel Tunnel departs seven to nine times daily from London Waterloo. Standard-class return fares for the three-hour trip range from £79 to £220, but special offers can bring prices down to as low as £50, even in the height of summer. Tickets can be bought directly over the phone from Eurostar; most travel agents; many rail stations in Britain; through SNCF (*Société Nationale des Chemins de Fer* – the French rail company) in London; from Waterloo International and Ashford ticket offices, and from the new Eurostar shop (see p.7 for details). Although ticketing is available if you travel on GNER or Virgin services from Manchester and Edinburgh, or the Alphaline Rail Service from South Wales, Avon and West Wiltshire, you'll be charged a hefty £30 supplement for the service. There is no sign as yet of the promised direct high-speed Eurostar services from the north of England, Scotland and the Midlands.

Rail and Sea

Crossing the Channel **by sea** instead of the tunnel can bring the overall cost of your train ticket to Corsica down slightly, but takes considerably longer. Services leave London Victoria at 7.15am to connect with the cross-channel ferries or hovercrafts at Dover or Folkestone, and onward trains on the other side from Calais and Boulogne, arriving in Paris Gare du Nord around 5.15pm.

Rather than purchase separate tickets for the London to Paris and Paris to Nice, or Marseille, legs of the trip, you can save money by booking the whole journey on a **Eurodomino Freedom pass.** These are particularly useful if you want to stop off en route, as they entitle you to unlimited travel through France, including travel on the TGV, on any three (£119), four (£139) or five (£169) days within a calendar month; under-26s pay £99, £119 and £139 respectively. You'll have to organize your own Channel crossing independently, but the pass also entitles you to reductions on rail and ferry links to France. In addition, periodic special promotions enable you to travel to Nice from London, for around £120 return, which includes crossing by a standard ferry, making this the **cheapest way** to travel as far as the French Riviera by train.

Also worth considering if you plan to travel around the continent on your way to Corsica is an **InterRail pass**, which offers unlimited use of almost all train services – not the TGV, though – within designated European "zones" for a period of 22 days or one month; you must have been resident in Europe for at least six months before you can buy the pass. France is in zone one, for which a 22 day pass will set you back £159 for under-26s, or £229 for over-26s. InterRail passes do not include travel between Britain and the continent, although pass holders are eligible for discounts on train travel in Britain and Northern Ireland, and on cross-Channel ferries.

Ferry Crossings from Britain

All the ferries listed below operate year round.

Route	Company	Frequency	Length of Crossing	Single Fare Car	Single Fare Passenger
Dover–Calais	Hoverspeed	11–17 daily	35–50min	£72–104	£25
Dover–Calais	P&O Stena Line	30 daily	1hr 30min	£62–110	£24
	Sea France	15 daily	1hr 30min	£73–95	
Folkestone–Boulogne	Hoverspeed	4 daily	55min	£70–94	£25
Hull–Zeebrugge	P&O North Sea Ferries	1 daily	14hr	£95–115	£36–45
Newhaven–Dieppe	P&O Stena Line	2 daily	4hr	£59–135	£24
Newhaven–Dieppe	P&O Stena Line	2–3 daily	2hr 15min	£59–135	£24
Plymouth–Roscoff	Brittany Ferries	1–12 weekly	6hr	£74–141	£31–37
Portsmouth–Caen	Brittany Ferries	1–3 daily	6hr	£70–135	£16–28
Poole–Cherbourg	Brittany Ferries	1–2 daily	4hr 30min	£70–135	£16–28
Portsmouth–Cherbourg	P&O European Ferries	mid May–Oct 2–3 daily	2hr 45min	£77–137	£15–30
Portsmouth–Le Havre	P&O European Ferries	2–3 daily	5hr 45min–7hr 45min	£77–137	£15–30

Cross-Channel Ferry Companies

Brittany Ferries ☎0990/360360.
Hoverspeed ☎0990/240241 or 0990/595522.
P&O European Ferries ☎0990/980555.
P&O North Sea Ferries ☎01482/377177.
P&O Stena Line ☎0990/980980.
Sea France ☎0990/711711.

By Car and Motorail

The most convenient way of taking your car across to France is to drive to the **Channel tunnel**, load your car on the train shuttle and be whisked under the Channel in 35 minutes, emerging at Sangette, France, just outside Calais.

The Channel tunnel entrance is off the M20 at junction 11A, just outside Folkestone, and the sole operator, **Eurotunnel**, offers a continuous service with up to four departures per hour (only 1 per hour midnight–6am; 24hr recorded departure info ☎0891/555566; 50p per minute). Because of the frequency of the service, you don't have to buy a ticket in advance – though this might be advisable in midsummer or during school holidays. You must arrive at least 25 minutes before departure, and the target loading time is just ten minutes. Once inside the carriages, you can get out of your car to stretch your legs during the crossing. Tickets are available though Eurotunnel's Customer Service Centre (see box opposite), or from your local travel agent. Fares are calulated per car, regardless of the number of passengers. Rates depend on the time of year, time of day and length of stay (the cheapest ticket is for a day-trip, followed by a five-day return); it's cheaper to travel between 10pm and 6am, while the highest fares are reserved for weekend departures and returns in July and August. For example, a fourteen-day trip at an off-peak time starts at £95 (per car) in the low season, rising to £135 in peak season. Alternatively there's a wide range of ferry/hovercraft crossings (see box above).

If you don't want to drive far when you've reached France, you can take advantage of SNCF's **Motorail** (☎0990/848848), putting your car on the train in Calais for Nice, Marseille or Toulon. This is a relatively expensive option: Calais–Nice, for example, costs £739 return for one car and one person, plus £238 for every additional passenger in peak season; dropping to £499 plus £204 for every additional passenger off-peak. Bookings and timetable information are available through the International Rail Centre in Victoria and Rail Europe (see box opposite).

By Bus

For any die-hard who might want to take a coach to Corsica, there is a direct service to Nice,

Crossing the Channel

Eurostar, Eurostar ticket office, 102–104 Victoria St, London SW1 (Mon–Fri 9am–5.30pm, Sat 9am–3.45pm; reservations ☎0990/186186; *www.eurostar.co.uk*); Waterloo International Station, London SE1 8SE; Ashford International Terminal, Kent.

Eurotunnel ☎0990/353535; *www.eurotunnel.co.uk*

Hoverspeed SeaTrain Express ☎0990/240241.

Rail Europe, 179 Piccadilly, London W1V (Mon–Fri 8am–8pm, Sat 9am-4pm; reservations ☎0990/848848; *www.raileurope.co.uk*).

UK Rail Enquiries ☎0845/748 4950.

which takes 24 hours and is operated by **Eurolines** (164 Buckingham Palace Rd, London SW1; ☎0990/143219; *www.eurolines.co.uk*), leaving once a week from London Victoria Coach Station from June through October. Fares are £115 return, with small reductions for under-25s and students.

Ferries to Corsica

Corsica has six **ferry ports** (Bastia, L'Île Rousse, Calvi, Ajaccio, Propriano and Porto-Vecchio), served by three ports on the French Riviera (Marseille, Toulon and Nice) and six in Italy (Savona, Genoa, La Spezia, Livorno, Piombo, and Santa Teresa in Sardinia).

From France, crossings take between 6hr (Nice–Bastia) and 13hr 30min (Marseille–Porto-Vecchio overnight) on regular ferries, and from 2hr 45min (Nice–Calvi) to 4hr (Nice–Ajaccio) on the superfast NGV hydrofoils (*Navire de Grande Vitesse*), which travel at a brisk 37 to 43 knots. Coming from the UK, Marseille is the obvious port to head for, but if you want to catch an NGV, you'll have to press on further up the coast to Nice. Both regular and NGV services are run by two companies: SNCM Ferrytérranée and Corsica Ferries (see p.9). Fares on their NGVs are the same as on regular ferries, with both varying according to whether you travel in a blue (off-peak), green (mid-season), white (high season) or red (peak season) period.

One-way tickets to all ports in Corsica for reclining passenger seats, for example, on services from Marseille and Toulon cost 256–292F, or 210–240F from Nice (return fares cost exactly double). Babies go free, while reductions of various degrees are available to children aged 4 to 12, young persons aged 12 to 25, senior citizens and for large families with four or more kids. You can also pay extra for a four-, two- or single-bed cabin (with or without shower and toilet). **Cars** are charged according to their length and height, with tariffs increasing dramatically (by around three times) in red periods. For a small car under 3.8m long and 2m tall, expect to pay around 160–510F from Nice and 215–615F from Marseille or Toulon; cars and passengers are charged separately. **Motorbikes** cost from 100F to 350F, and **bicycles** 91F any time of year.

On top of the advertised price of your ticket, note that you have to add on hefty **port taxes**, which vary from 53F to 72F per person per crossing, plus **vehicle tax** from 35F to 65F if you're driving.

Comparatively few British travellers approach Corsica **from Italy**, but ferry services from the six Italian ports are frequent throughout the summer and often less expensive (their red and white periods tend to be much shorter). Taking around 2hr 30min by NGV, the shortest, least expensive crossing is from Livorno to Bastia; tickets for foot passengers cost 90–160F one way, with a supplement of 50F if you opt for the NGV. Charges for (small) cars on the same route range from 250F to 450F. There is also a port tax for Italy: 40–44F per person, plus 23–30F for a car. Most of the companies (see box on p.8), do special offers that can bring the overall price down, particularly if you're travelling as a family or in a group. Look out for Moby Lines' bargain high-season, all-in fare of 1000F for a car and up to four passengers from Genoa to Bastia.

Bear in mind that during peak periods demand for ferry tickets to Corsica from both mainland France and Italy can far exceed supply. Book as far in advance as possible, particularly if you intend to take a car across, as vehicle places often sell out months ahead. **Reservations** can be made either through your local travel agent or, more reliably, directly with the ferry companies, over the telephone or Internet (their Web sites all

Ferry Crossings from France

Route	Company	Frequency	Length of Crossing	Single Fare Foot Passenger	Single Fare Small Car	Period of Operation
Marseille–Ajaccio	SNCM	3–7 weekly	11hr overnight, 4hr 30min (NGV) –7hr daytime	256–292F	214–612F	year round
Marseille–Bastia	SNCM	1–3 weekly	10hr overnight or daytime	256–292F	214–612F	year round
Marseille –L'Île Rousse	SNCM	1–3 weekly	11hr 30min overnight	256–292F	214–612F	June–Sept
Marseille –Porto-Vecchio	SNCM	1–3 weekly	14hr 30min overnight	256–292F	214–612F	June–Sept
Marseille –Propriano	SNCM	1–5 weekly	9hr 30min	256–292F	214–612F	March–Sept
Nice–Ajaccio	SNCM	1–6 weekly	12hr overnight	210–240F	161–509F	year round
Nice–Bastia	SNCM/ Corsica Ferries	3–24 weekly	6hr–6hr 45min	210–240F	161–509F	year round
Nice–Calvi	SNCM/ Corsica Ferries	2–5 weekly	2hr 45min (NGV) daytime	210–240F	161–509F	year round
Nice–L'Île Rousse	SNCM	4–6 weekly	7hr overnight, 2hr 45min (NGV) 5hr daytime	210–240F	161–509F	June–Sept year round
Toulon–Ajaccio	SNCM	1–4 weekly	10hr overnight	256–292F	214–612F	April–Sept
Toulon–Bastia	SNCM	1–3 weekly	8hr 30min overnight	256–292F	214–612F	April–Oct

Ferry Crossings from Italy

Route	Company	Frequency	Length of Crossing	Single Fare Foot Passenger	Single Fare Small Car	Period of Operation
Genoa–Bastia	Corsica Marittima	2 weekly	5hr 45min –11hr	116–170F	240–620F	June–Sept
	Moby Lines	2–4 weekly	6hr	190F	280–660F	April to mid-Sept
La Spezia–Bastia	Happy Lines	5–7 weekly	5hr	109–173F	271–481F	May–Sept
Livorno–Bastia	Corsica Ferries	1–3 daily	4–7hr	99–159F	250–450F	June–Sept
	Corsica Marittima	1–5 weekly	1hr 50min (NGV) 3hr 30min	96–156F	240–420F	April–Oct
	Moby Lines	2–5 weekly	4hr	180F	280–470F	April to mid-June
Livorno –Porto-Vecchio	Corsica Marittima	1–2 weekly	7hr 30min–10hr 30min	180–200F	470–610F	June–Sept
Piombino–Bastia	Moby Lines	daily	3hr 30min	180F		July to mid-Sept
Santa Teresa Di Gallura (Sardinia) –Bonifacio	Saremar	2–4 daily	1hr 30min	48–60F	140–194F	year round
Savona–Bastia	Corsica Ferries	1–3 daily	3hr	114–180F	250–630F	June–Sept
Savona–L'Île Rousse	Corsica Ferries	2–3 weekly	6hr	114–180F	250–630F	June–Sept

Ferry Company Addresses

For contact details of ferry company offices in their Corsican ports, see the relevant accounts in the guide section of this book.

Corsica Ferries, Port de Commerce, Nice 06300 (☎ 00 33 4 92 00 43 76; *www.corsicaferries.com*). In the UK their agents are Via Mare, Graphic House, 2 Sumatra Rd, NW6 1PU (☎ 020/7431 5456, fax 7431 5456; *www.viamare.com*).

Corsica Marittima, GSA/Cemar, via XX Settembre 2–10, 16121 Genoa (☎ 00 39 10 58 95 93; *www.corsica-marittima.com*).

Happy Lines, Via Maralunga, 45, 19126 La Spezia, Italy (☎ 00 39 187 56 45 30; *www.happylines.it*).

Moby Lines, 45 rue de Paradis, Paris 75010 (☎ 00 33 1 55 77 27 00; *www.mobylines.com*). UK agents: Via Mare (see Corsica Ferries) and Sarena, 40 Kenway Rd, London SW5 0RA (☎ 020/7373 6548, fax 7244 9829).

Saremar, Via G Mameli, 40, 09124 Cagliari (☎ 00 39 70 67 901, fax 00 39 70 66 32 94).

SNCM Ferrytérranée, 61 bd des Dames, Marseille 13002 (☎ 00 33 8 36 67 95 00; *www.sncm.fr*). UK agent: Southern Ferries, 179 Piccadilly, London W1V 9DB (☎ 020/7491 4968).

have English versions and you can pay by credit card; see box above for addresses). Most of the ferry companies also have **agents in the UK** whom you can contact for timetable information and bookings. If you do arrange your ticket through them, however, check at the outset for any additional charges: some levy a stiff booking fee for bookings under £100.

Packages

In its simplest form, a **package holiday** is a combination of an air ticket and accommodation, for which you pay a single all-in price. As tour operators block-book both flights and rooms at least a year in advance, they pay a lower rate than walk-in clients, which may – although not necessarily – mean better value for the customer. In Corsica, however, it invariably works out cheaper for you to make your own transport and accommodation arrangements. Going through a package specialist means you are basically paying for an organization to make the bookings on your behalf. However, with competition being as cut-throat as it is these days, the tour companies' mark-ups can be comparatively small and worth paying if you're short of time and/or not fluent enough in French to make all the phone calls yourself.

In addition to the flight and accommodation, most package operators offer **extras** such as car rental (aka "**fly-drive**"), sports facilities and flight upgrades. Again, it pays to compare their prices with those you can get if you organize everything yourself. Watch out for late-availability deals, however, which sometimes include such extras in a single (and invariably unbeatable) package.

The **cost** of package holidays varies enormously – from company to company, depending on the level of luxury offered and time of year you travel. The cheapest deals are usually for rooms in large holiday villages out of season. Self-catering chalets, with tiny kitchenettes, two bedrooms, living room and terrace, cost a notch more, followed by larger villas. A pool can double the cost of any place. If you're prepared to take the risk, **late-availability** deals can produce some superb packages, such as those offered by Holiday Options. Holiday Options are the sole consolidators for flights and packages to Corsica, and frequently offer amazing deals (see box on p.4).

It is not unusual to see late season fly-drive packages, offering a return air ticket and one week's basic accommodation including car rental for under £200 – impossible to match if you're booking independently.

The list of UK package tour companies in the box on p.10 includes all of the major British firms currently operating in Corsica, but smaller ones come and go. Apart from your local travel agent, the best places to hunt for their adverts are the travel pages of the Sunday newspapers, particularly the *Independent on Sunday*, the *Observer*, the *Sunday Times* and the *Sunday Telegraph*. Before booking with any travel company, ensure they are fully bonded – look out for the IATA or ATOL number given on the company's brochure.

Getting There from Ireland

No airline offers direct **flights** from Ireland to Corsica. From the **Irish Republic**, Aer Lingus

Package Tour Companies in Britain

Bladon Lines, 56/58 Putney High St, London SW15 (☎020/8785 3131). *Accommodation in beach hotels and catered villas. Tennis, sailing and water-skiing included in the price.*

Corsican Affair, George House, 5–7 Humbolt Rd, London W6 (☎020/8385 8438). *Fly-drive, hotel packages, self-catering and cycling holidays.*

Corsican Places Ltd, 16 Grand Parade, St Leonards on Sea, East Sussex TN37 (☎01424/460046; *www.corsica.co.uk*). *Experienced, knowledgeable Corsica specialists, offering tailor-made stays, mostly in gorgeous period properties, at very reasonable prices; flight-only deals too. Range of outdoor activities: sailing, windsurfing, diving, paragliding, horse riding and canyoning.*

Cresta Holidays, 32 Victoria St, Altrincham WA14 (☎0161/927 7000). *Basic hotel-and-flight deals.*

French Expressions, 13 McCrone Mews, Belsize Park, London NW3 (☎020/7794 1480). *Pricey upmarket holidays in four-star hotels, with scheduled flights.*

Mark Warner, 20 Kensington Church St, London W8 (☎020/7393 3131). *Watersports specialists, with accommodation in upmarket beach-club-style hotels and apartments. Adults only.*

Simply Corsica, 3 Chiswick Terrace, Acton Lane, London W4 (☎020/8995 9323). *Currently the UK's largest operator on the island, recently taken over by Thomson Holidays. Self-catering and hotel accommodation, with the full range of optional extras and good-value low season discounts.*

Vacances en Campagne, Bignor, near Pulborough, West Sussex RH20 (☎01798/869433). *Reasonably priced self-catering accommodation all over Corsica, from apartments and cottages to large mansions.*

VFB Holidays, Normandy House, High St, Cheltenham, Glos GL50 3FB (☎01242/240310). *Flexible fly-drive holidays with accommodation in various-star hotels and small resort complexes. They also have fifty charming apartments in the remote mountain village of Lama, all with access to tennis courts and a pool. Guided outdoor activities are extra.*

Voyages Ilena, 7 Old Garden House, The Lanterns, Bridge Lane, London SW11 (☎020/8924 4440; *www.voyagesilena.co.uk*). *Upmarket hotels and a wide range of attractive self-catering accommodation at particularly beautiful locations all over Corsica. This small firm is among the oldest-established and most knowledgeable operators on the island, offering consistently good value.*

operate **scheduled flights** direct from **Cork** and **Dublin** to Paris CDG (respectively 1 and 5 times daily), but you'll have to get from CDG to Orly airport on the other side of Paris to catch a flight to Corsica. The standard fare is £199 to Paris, though if you book early you may get one of the few seats at £129 return. Ryanair offer three flights daily from Dublin to Beauvais Tillé airport outside Paris for a little under £100 return. Budget Travel organizes **charter flights** from Dublin to Nice for £199 (May to mid-Oct), while Go Holidays arranges them (April–Sept) from Shannon, Cork and Dublin to Marseille and Nice. Alternatives via Britain are unlikely to be attractive, considering the additional time factor and the cost of a flight from Dublin to Britain.

From **Northern Ireland**, British Airways fly directly from Belfast City to Paris CDG. Otherwise, a routing through London to pick up a charter is the best option.

Airlines and Agencies in Ireland

Aer Lingus, 40 O'Connell St, Dublin (☎01/844 4777); 46 Castle St, Belfast BT1 (☎0645/737 747); 2 Academy St, Cork (☎021/327 155); 136 O'Connell St, Limerick (☎061/474 239); *www.aerlingus.ie*
Air Inter, 29–30 Dawson St, Dublin (☎01/677 8899).
British Airways, 60 Dawson St, Dublin (☎1-800/626 747); 9 Fountain Centre, College St, Belfast (☎0345/222 111); *www.british-airways.com.*
Ryanair, College Park House, 20 Nassau St, Dublin (☎01/797444 or 770444).

Discount Flight Agents

Budget Travel, 134 Lower Baggot St, Dublin (☎01/661 1866).
Joe Walsh Tours, 8–11 Baggot St, Dublin (☎01/876 3053); 31 Castle St, Belfast (☎028/9024 1144).
Trailfinders, 4 Dawson St, Dublin 2 (☎01/677 7888).
Usit NOW, 21 Aston Quay, O'Connell Bridge, Dublin 2 (☎01/679 8833); Fountain Centre, College St, Belfast (☎028/9032 4073); Ferryquay St, Derry (☎028/7137 1888); 10–11 Market Parade, Cork (☎021/270 900); Victoria Place, Eyre Square, Galway (☎091/565 177); 36–37 George St, Waterford (☎051/872 601); also branches in Athlone, Coleraine, Jordanstown and Maynorth; *www.usit.ie*

Getting There from North America

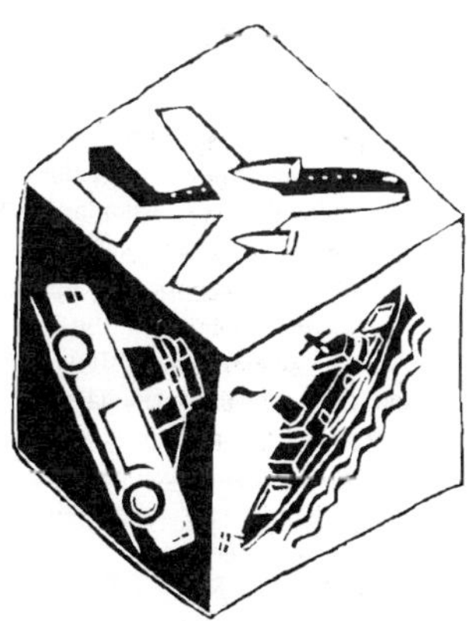

From North America, Corsica is one of your more obscure European destinations. Discount travel agents – normally the mainstay of budget travellers – concentrate on high-volume routes and are unlikely to be able to ticket you beyond Paris, or perhaps Nice. By all means give it a shot, but you'll probably end up paying a published fare to Corsica.

Scheduled Flights

Whichever company you travel with, flying to Corsica will involve at least one change of plane. Served by flights from over thirty North American cities, **Paris** is the most convenient gateway. It's also one of the Europe's cheapest destinations, thanks to stiff competition between the dozen or so companies who fly there. For the onward leg to Corsica, you'll have to purchase a second ticket to Ajaccio, Bastia or Calvi with Air Inter, Air France's subsidiary. This can be done before you leave, or more cheaply on arrival in France, although bear in mind that flights to Corsica from the mainland are heavily subscribed during the holiday season and should be booked months in advance.

Fares also fluctuate according to the season, and are highest from around early June to the end of August; they drop during the "shoulder" seasons (Sept–Oct & April–May); and you'll get the best deals during the low season (Nov–March excluding Christmas). Figure on the following approximate winter/summer Apex return to Ajaccio, Bastia or Calvi, based on mid-week travel (flying on weekends ordinarily adds about $65 to the return fare): New York, $745/$1129; Washington, $829/$1164; Miami, $865/$1179; Chicago, $845/$1168; Houston, $873/$1239 LA or San Francisco, $1140/$12750.

Air France offers the most frequent service to Paris, and has the additional advantage regular onward flights to Corsica on its domestic subsidiary, Air Inter, although its fares tend to be on the expensive side. Other airlines with non-stop services to Paris from a variety of US cities are United, daily from Chicago, San Francisco and Washington DC; Delta, daily from Cincinnati, Atlanta and New York; TWA, daily from New York and three times a week from St Louis; and AOM, three to five times per week from Los Angeles, depending on the season. With all these carriers, agents should be able to book you a through-ticket to Corsica that includes the onward flight from Paris with a domestic carrier.

Bear in mind, too, that several airlines fly non-stop from North America to **Nice** and **Marseille**. Air France, for example, has a daily service to Nice from New York. Routes to these southern French cities cost on average between $200 and $300 more than flights to Paris, but you save nearly that much on the onward flight to Corsica, which is considerably cheaper.

Shopping for Tickets

The cheapest scheduled tickets are **Apex** tickets. These carry certain restrictions: you have to book – and pay – at least 21 days before departure and spend at least seven days abroad (maximum stay three months), and you're liable to get penalized if you change your schedule. There are also winter **Super Apex** tickets, sometimes known as "Eurosavers" – slightly cheaper than an ordinary Apex, but limiting your stay to between 7 and 21 days. Some airlines also issue **Special Apex** tickets to those under 24, often extending the maximum stay to a year.

Discount outlets, advertised in Sunday newspaper travel sections such as the *New York Times*, can usually do better than any Apex fare to Paris or London. They come in several forms. **Consolidators** buy up large blocks of tickets that airlines don't think they'll be able to sell at their published fares, and sell them at a discount. Besides being cheap, consolidators normally don't impose advance-purchase requirements (though in busy times you'll want to book ahead just to be sure of getting a ticket), but they do often charge very stiff fees for date changes. Also, these companies' margins are pretty tiny, so they make their money by dealing in volume – don't expect them to entertain lots of questions. **Discount agents** also wheel and deal in blocks of tickets offloaded by the airlines, but they typically offer a range of other travel-related services such as travel insurance, rail passes, youth and student ID cards, car rentals, tours and the like. These agencies tend to be most worthwhile to students and under-26s, who can often benefit from special fares and deals. Some agencies specialize in **charter flights**, which may be even cheaper than anything available on a scheduled flight, but again there's a trade-off: departure dates are fixed, withdrawal penalties are high (check the refund policy), and the plane is likely to be packed.

An option well worth considering if you're on a tight budget is a **courier flight**, in which you deliver a package in exchange for a heavily discounted ticket. The disadvantage with these is that to get the best deals you have to book a maximum of three days before departure, but if you can be this flexible you stand to save a lot of money. Standard return courier flights to Paris go for around $350, while last-minute specials can cost as little as $150. For more information, contact The Air Courier Association, 191 University Blvd, Suite 300, Denver, Colorado 80206 (☎1303/279 3600), or consult *How to Travel Worldwide for Next to Nothing* by Kelly Monaghan ($17.50 postpaid from The Intrepid Traveler, PO Box 438, New York, NY 10034).

If you don't mind spending a few days in Paris or London first, or if you were planning to visit other parts of France anyway, you might consider nabbing a cheap transatlantic flight through a discount travel agent and sorting out your onward travel when you get there (see p.3 and p.5 for details of onward travel from the UK and mainland France).

From Canada

The strong links between France and Québec's Francophone community ensure regular air services from Canada to **Paris**, from where you have to change onto a domestic carrier for the onward flight to Corsica.

Air France, Air Canada and Canadian offer non-stop services to Paris from the major Canadian cities. You can also fly non-stop to Lyon from Toronto (from where Air Inter run scheduled flights to Corsica), and their fares (winter/summer) are very competitive (return to Paris from Toronto $825/$1210; from Vancouver $1115/$1639).

Package Tours

Corsica is way off the beaten path for most North American **tour** companies. Your choices basically come down to a couple of outfits that can arrange short-term rentals of villas ($5200 and up for a week for two people) and a couple of adventure-travel companies that do hiking trips in Corsica (about $1050 for a week's trek). If you're set on going with a package tour, you might want to consider contacting a tour

AIRLINES AND AGENTS IN NORTH AMERICA

Airlines

Only gateway cities are listed for each airline; other routings are always possible using connecting flights.

Air Canada (☎ 1-800/776 3000; in Canada ☎ 1-800/555 1212; *www.aircanada.com*). *Montréal, Toronto and Vancouver to Paris and Nice.*

Air France (☎ 1-800/237 2747; in Canada ☎ 1-800/667 2747; *www.airfrance.com*). *New York, Washington DC, Miami, Montréal, Toronto, Chicago, Houston, San Francisco and Los Angeles to Paris or Nice; connections to Ajaccio on Air Inter.*

American Airlines (☎ 1-800/433 7300; *www.americanair.com*). *New York, Miami, Dallas-Fort Worth, Chicago and Los Angeles to Paris.*

AOM French Airlines (☎ 310/338 9613; *www.aom.com*). *Non-stop from Los Angeles to Paris three to five times per week.*

British Airways (☎ 1-800/247 9297; in Canada ☎ 800/668 1080; *www.british-airways.com*). *Many North American cities to Paris and Nice (via London).*

Canadian Airlines (☎ 1-800/426 7000; *www.cd.air.com*). *Montréal, Toronto and Vancouver to Paris.*

Continental Airlines (☎ 1-800/231 0856; *www.continental.com*). *New York, Houston and Denver to Paris.*

Delta Airlines (☎ 1-800/241 4141; in Canada ☎ 1-800/555 1212; *www.delta.air*). *Atlanta, Cincinnati and New York to Paris.*

Northwest Airlines (☎ 1-800/225 2525; *www.nwa.com*). *Los Angeles, Minneapolis and Detroit to Paris.*

Tower Air (☎ 1-800/221 2500; *www.towerair.com*). *Daily non-stop from New York to Paris Charles de Gaulle.*

TWA (☎ 1-800/892 4141; *www.twa.com*). *New York, Boston, St Louis and Washington to Paris.*

United Airlines (☎ 1-800/538 2929; *www.ual.com*). *Chicago, Washington DC, Los Angeles and San Francisco to Paris.*

US Air (☎ 1-800/622 1015; *www.usair.com*). *Daily non-stop flights to Paris from Philadelphia.*

Flight Agents and Consolidators

Airhitch (☎ 212/864 2000; *www.airhitch.org*). *Standby seat broker; for a set price, they guarantee to get you on a flight as close to your preferred destination as possible, within a week.*

Air Brokers International (☎ 1-800/883 3273; *www.airbrokers.com*). *Consolidator.*

Council Travel (☎ 1-800/226 8624; *www.counciltravel.com*). Discount specialist with offices across the country.

Education Travel Center (☎ 1-800/747 5551). *Student/youth discount agent.*

Flight Centre (☎ 604/739 9539). *Discount air fares from Canadian cities.*

High Adventure Travel (☎ 1-800/428 8735; *www.highadv.com*). *Nationwide student travel organization with branches countrywide.*

Interworld Travel (☎ 305/443 4929). *Consolidator.*

Travel Cuts (☎ 416/979 2406). *A student travel organization with branches all over Canada.*

operator in Britain, where Corsica is a much more popular destination (see box on p.10). Alternatively, you could deal directly with Ollandini Voyages, Corsica's biggest tour operator – located at 3 place de Gaulle, BP 304, 20176 Ajaccio, France (☎104 95 21 72 21).

TOUR OPERATORS IN NORTH AMERICA

Adventure Center, 1311 63rd St, Suite 200, Emeryville, CA 94608 (☎1-800/227 8747). *Corsican village treks ($935 for 15 days).*

Himalayan Travel, 112 Prospect St, Stamford, CT 06901 (☎1-800/225 2380). *Trekking in the Corsican interior, from $1150 for 7 days.*

Vacances en Campagne, PO Box 299, Elkton, VA 22827 (☎1-800/327 6097). *Short-term rentals of châteaux and country houses, from around $570 a week.*

Getting There from Australia and New Zealand

There are no direct flights from Australia or New Zealand to Corsica – the best you can do is fly direct to Paris and change planes there for Ajaccio, Calvi or Bastia. If you qualify for student/youth discounts, it's best to book through an agent like STA (see box opposite). Fares tend to be cheaper from mid-January to the end of February and during October and November, increasing during high season (May–Aug and Dec–Jan). Some airlines, such as Alitalia and Air France, offer free transfer flights within Europe that can get you to Corsica. Others have competitively priced add-on fares from Paris and Rome from around A$370/NZ$440.

Air France fly from Sydney and Auckland **to Paris** (Charles de Gaulle) via Jakarta and Singapore at least once a week from around A$2000/NZ$2200, and will throw in a "side-trip" to Bastia or Ajaccio. Marseille and Paris can also be reached more cheaply on Aeroflot's bi-weekly service from Sydney via Moscow for A$1600, but you'll have to add on the cost of the onward flight to Corsica from there. The same applies to the dozen or so other international airlines that fly to Paris, and whose agents will gladly book a through-ticket to Corsica before you leave. Your best chance of finding out which one is currently offering the most competitive fares is to ring around the agents listed below, or to check the travel agents' ads in the travel sections of the weekend newspapers.

Some **round-the-world** routings allow Corsica as a side-trip, using a combination of airlines. Generally, six free stopovers are offered by participating carriers, with additional stopovers for around A$100 each in Australia and New Zealand. Fares start at A$2399/NZ$3380. Possibilities include UA's "Globetrotter", Air New Zealand/KLM/Northwest's "World Navigator", and Qantas/ British Airway's "Global Explorer".

AIRLINES AND AGENTS IN AUSTRALIA AND NEW ZEALAND

Airlines

Aeroflot, 88 George St, Sydney (☎ 02/9233 7911; *www.aeroflot.com*). No NZ office.

Air France/Qantas, 12 Castlereagh St, Sydney (☎ 02/9231 1000; *www.airfrance.com*); 2nd Floor, Dataset House, 143 Nelson St, Auckland (☎ 09/303 3521).

Alitalia, Orient Overseas Building, 32 Bridge St, Sydney (☎ 02/9247 1308; *www.alitalia.com*); 6th Floor, Trustbank Building, 229 Queen St, Auckland (☎ 09/379 4457).

British Airways, 64 Castlereagh St, Sydney (☎ 02/9258 3300; *www.british-airways.com*); Dilworth Building, cnr Queen & Customs streets, Auckland (☎ 09/3656 8690).

Singapore Airlines, 17–19 Bridge St, Sydney (local-call rate ☎ 13 1011; *www.singaporeair.com*); Lower Ground Floor, West Plaza Building, cnr Customs & Albert streets, Auckland (☎ 09/379 3209).

Thai Airways, 75–77 Pitt St, Sydney (☎ 02/9844 0999, toll-free 1-800/422 020; *www.thaiair.com*); Kensington Swan Building, 22 Fanshawe St, Auckland (☎ 09/377 3886).

Australian Agents

Brisbane Flight Centre, 260 Queen St, Brisbane (☎ 07/3229 9211).

Flight Centres, Level 11, 33 Berry St, North Sydney (☎ 131600 or 02/9460 0555); Circular Quay, Sydney (☎ 02/241 2422); Bourke St, Melbourne (☎ 03/9650 2899); *www.flightcentre.com.au*

Passport Travel, Kings Cross Plaza, Suite 11/401 St Kilda Rd, Melbourne (☎ 03/9867 3888).

STA Travel, 855 George St, Sydney (☎ 02/9212 1255 or 1300/360960); 256 Flinders St, Melbourne (☎ 03/9654 7266); *www.statravel.com.au*

Thomas Cook, 321 Kent St, Sydney (☎ 02/9248 6100).

New Zealand Agents

Budget Travel, 16 Fort St, Auckland, and at other branches around the city (☎ 09/366 0061, toll-free 0800/808 0040).

Destinations Unlimited, 3 Milford Rd, Milford, Auckland (☎ 09/373 4033).

Flight Centres, National Bank Towers, 205–225 Queen St, Auckland (☎ 09/209 6171); Shop 1m, National Mutual Arcade, 152 Hereford St, Christchurch (☎ 03/379 7145); 50–52 Willis St, Wellington (☎ 04/472 8101).

STA Travel, Traveller's Centre, 10 High St, Auckland (☎ 09/309 9995); 233 Cuba St, Wellington (☎ 04/385 0561); 152 Hereford St, Christchurch (☎ 03/379 9098); other offices in Dunedin, Palmerston North and Hamilton.

Specialist Tour Operators in Australia and New Zealand

The following companies offer a variety of package tours in Corsica, ranging from go-as-you-please accommodation and car rental deals to organized walking holidays.

Adventure Travel Shop, 50 High St, Auckland (☎ 09/303 1805).

France Unlimited, 16 Goldsmith St, Elwood (☎ 03/9531 8787).

French Travel Connection, Level 6, 33 Chandler St, St Leonards (☎ 02/9966 8600).

Thor Travel, 228 Rundle St, Adelaide (☎ 08/8232 3155).

YHA Travel, 422 Kent St, Sydney (☎ 02/9261 1111); 205 King St, Melbourne (☎ 03/9670 9611); 38 Stuart St, Adelaide (☎ 08/8231 5583); 154 Roma St, Brisbane (☎ 07/3236 1680); 236 William St, Northbridge, Perth (☎ 08/9227 5122); 69a Mitchell St, Darwin (☎ 08/8981 2560); 28 Criterion St, Hobart (☎ 03/6234 9617); *www.yha.com.au*

Red Tape and Visas

Citizens of EU countries, Japan, New Zealand, Canada and the United States do not need any sort of visa to enter France for a stay of up to ninety days. Nationals of all other countries, including Australia, must obtain a visa before arrival in Corsica.

If you do need a visa, you have a choice of three types (all of which are valid from date of issue): a transit visa (£5–8), which is valid from one to five days; a short stay (*court séjour*) visa (£15–20), valid up to thirty days after date of issue; and the long stay (£29–90), which allows multiple stays of ninety days over three years (maximum of 180 days in any one year). Prices vary according to the countries of issue and whether or not you ask for a single or (more expensive) multiple-entry visa.

To **obtain a visa** you'll need an application form (available from the consulate or embassy), a passport valid for at least six months from your intended date of arrival in France, a ticket or verification of travel, and the visa fee (see above). Obtaining a visa from your nearest French consulate (the addresses of the major French embassies and consulates are given below) is fairly automatic, but check the hours before turning up, and leave plenty of time, since there are often queues (particularly in London in summer). Australians can obtain a visa on the spot in London.

For stays longer than ninety days you are officially supposed to apply for a *Carte de Séjour*, for which you'll have to show proof of income at least equal to the minimum wage. However, EU passports are rarely stamped, so there is no evidence of how long you've been in the country, and if your passport is stamped you can legitimately cross the French border, to Italy for example, and re-enter for another ninety days.

French Embassies and Consulates Overseas

Opening hours for most French embassies and consulates are Mon–Fri 9am–1pm.

Australia 492 St Kilda Rd, Melbourne, VIC 3001 (☎03/9820 0921); 31 Market St, Sydney, NSW 2000 (☎02/9262 5779).

Canada 42 Promenade Sussex, Ottawa, ON K1M 2C9 (☎613/789 1795); 1 pl Ville Marie, Bureau 22601, Montréal, Québec, QC H3B 4S3 (☎514/878 4385); 25 rue St-Louis, Québec, QC G1R 3Y8 (☎418/694 2294); 130 Bloor St Wt, Suite 400, Toronto, ON M5S 1N5 (☎416/925 8041); 1201–736 Granville St, Vancouver, BC V6Z 1H9 (☎604/681 4345).

Ireland 36 Ailesbury Rd, Dublin 4 (☎01/260 1666).

Netherlands Smidsplein 1, 2514 BT Den Haag (☎070/312 5800); Vijzelgracht 2, 1000 HA Amsterdam (☎020/624 8346).

New Zealand 1 Willeston St, PO Box 1695, Wellington (☎04/472 0200).

UK 59 Knightsbridge, London SW1X 7JT (☎020/7201 1000); 7–11 Randolph Crescent, Edinburgh (☎0131/225 7954).

USA 4101 /Reservoir Rd NW, Washington, DC 20007 (☎202/944 6195); Park Square Building, Suite 750, 31 St James Ave, Boston, MA 02116 (☎617/542 7374); 737 North Michigan Ave, Olympia Center, Suite 2020, Chicago, IL 60611 (☎312/787 5359); 10990 Wilshire Blvd, Suite 300, Los Angeles, CA 90024 (☎310/235 3200); 934 Fifth Ave, New York, NY 10021 (☎212/606 3689); 540 Bush St, San Francisco, CA 94108 (☎415/397 4330).

Health and Insurance

No visitor to France requires vaccinations of any kind, and general health care in Corsica is of the highest standard. There are hospitals in all the main towns, and smaller places like Porto-Vecchio have clinics serving the surrounding area. EU nationals can take advantage of the French health services under the same terms as the residents of the island, as long as you're in possession of a form E111, application forms for which can be picked up at most major post offices. However, because the French health system provides subsidized rather than free treatment, travel insurance – covering health plus loss or theft of baggage – remains essential.

Health Problems

Under the French social security system, every hospital visit, doctor's consultation and prescribed medicine is charged – though in an emergency you won't be presented with the bill up front. Although all employed French people are entitled to a refund of 70–75 percent of their medical expenses, this can still leave a hefty shortfall, especially after a stay in hospital (accident victims even have to pay for the ambulance or helicopter that takes them there).

To find a **doctor**, stop at any *pharmacie* and ask for an address. Consultation fees should be around 110–150F, and after the visit you'll be given a *Feuille de Soins* (Statement of Treatment) for later documentation of insurance claims. **Prescriptions** should be taken to a *pharmacie*, which is also equipped, and obliged, to give first aid, for a fee. The medicines you buy will have little stickers (*vignettes*) attached to them, which you must remove and stick to your *Feuille de Soins*, together with the prescription itself. In serious **emergencies** you will always be admitted to the local hospital (*centre hospitalier*), whether under your own steam or by ambulance.

Insurance

As getting a refund for medical treatment entails a complicated bureaucratic procedure and in any case does not cover the full cost of treatment, it's essential before you leave to take out **travel insurance**, which generally allows full reimbursement, less the first few pounds or dollars of every claim, and also covers the cost of repatriation should this be necessary. In addition, most single-trip insurance policies cover you for personal liability, theft of valuables, loss of ticket or passport, and expenses incurred through curtailment of your trip.

When considering any insurance policy, find out first what you'll be covered for and what that cover consists of. Generally, skiing, climbing with ropes, diving and most other so-called "dangerous sports" require additional premiums. Let-out clauses on theft of money and possessions also vary greatly between companies, as do the levels of **excess** (the amount of any claim you have to pay yourself). With cheaper policies, there tend to be low ceilings on the sums paid out for any single item, as well as on the total amount claimable for valuables. It is a simple matter to extend cover for expensive equipment (such as cameras, musical instruments and bicycles), but, again, you'll have to pay extra. Note, too, that in standard policies you're unlikely to be covered for any expenses incurred in the treatment of **pre-existing medical conditions**.

Banks and **credit cards** often have certain levels of medical or other insurance included, especially if you use them to pay for your trip. This can be quite comprehensive, anticipating anything from lost or stolen baggage and missed connections to charter companies going bust. For example, Barclaycard automatically insures anything you've purchased with the card for 100 days, gives travel insurance for up to £50,000 if you pay for your package holiday with the card, and has free a International Rescue Service offering legal advice, translation assistance, money transfer, contact with relatives and accompaniment of children home. If you have a good "all-risks" **home insurance** policy, it may well cover your possessions against loss or theft even when overseas, and many **private medical schemes** also cover you when abroad – make sure you know the procedure and helpline number.

UK Cover

Nearly all travel agents and tour operators will offer you insurance when you book your flight or holiday, and some will insist you take it. However, you are probably better off shopping around with banks or **specialist insurance companies**. The best-value travel insurance policies, such as those offered by Columbus, cost from around £15 for two weeks in Europe, while ISIS policies, from STA Travel or branches of Endsleigh (see box below), are also usually good value.

While rates for annual **multi-trip** polices are enticing, they don't provide cover for extended trips: with each separate trip usually limited to a month, they are handy for frequent travel, though, and can usually incorporate married couples at a saving on individual rates. The annual multi-trip police offered by Worldwide is the least discriminatory, good for any couple, whether gay, straight, relatives or just flatmates, as long as they live at the same address, with unlimited trips of either 31 or 62 days' duration (single £69/£79 couples £89/£109). Columbus does an annual multi-trip policy with as many trips of up to sixty days as you like for £59 (Western Europe) or £82 (worldwide), while American Express has an annual travel insurance policy open to non-cardholders for an limited number of trips in Europe up to 31 days (£56), or worldwide cover for trips of up to 91 days (£94.95).

You may want to contact an even more specialized travel insurance firm to cover all your needs, like Snowcard Insurance Services, who specialize in mountaineering and activity holiday travel insurance, or Age Concern, who cover travellers over 65 (no upper age limit).

US and Canadian Cover

North Americans may find themselves covered for medical or other losses while abroad as part of a family or student policy. Many bank and charge accounts include some travel cover, and some credit cards offer insurance benefits if you use them to pay for your holiday tickets. Canadians especially are usually covered by their provincial health plans, and holders of ISIC cards are entitled (outside the USA) to accident coverage and hospital inpatient benefits – the annual membership is far less than the cost of comparable insurance.

If you do want a specific travel insurance policy, there are numerous kinds to choose from: short-term combination policies covering everything from baggage loss to broken legs are the best bet and cost around $48–70 for fifteen days (depending on level of coverage), $80–105 for a month, $149–207 for two months and $510–700 for a year. One thing to bear in mind is that none of the policies currently available covers theft; they only cover loss while in the custody of an identifiable person – and even then you must make a report to the police and get their written statement. Three companies you might try are: Access America (☎1-800/284 8300), Carefree Travel Insurance (☎1-800/323 3149) or, for Canada only, Desjardins Travel Insurance (☎1-800/463 7830). If transiting via Britain, North Americans might consider buying a policy from a British travel agent. British policies

Travel Insurance Companies in Britain and Ireland

Age Concern ☎01883/346964.
American Express ☎0800/700737.
Columbus Travel Insurance ☎020/7375 0011.
Endsleigh Insurance ☎020/7436 4451.
Frizzell Insurance ☎01202/292339.
Snowcard Insurance Services ☎01327/262805.
Usit CAMPUS, **STA** or **Trailfinders** in the UK (see p.4), and **Usit NOW** in the Republic of Ireland (see p.11).
Worldwide ☎01892/833338.

tend to be cheaper than American ones, and routinely cover thefts.

Australasian Cover

In **Australia** and **New Zealand**, travel insurance is put together by the airlines and travel agents' organizations such as UTAG (United Travel Agents Group) and AFTA (Australian Federation of Travel Agents), Cover More and Ready Plan, in conjunction with the insurance companies. Policies tend to be comparable in premium and coverage, though Ready Plan offer the best overall deals, costing A$196/NZ$220 for one month, A$271/NZ$320 for two months and A$335/NZ$400 for three months. Adventure sports are usually covered in standard policies, except mountaineering with ropes, and unassisted diving without an Open Water Licence. If you think you may need coverage for such activities, check the small print carefully before committing yourself. Low-cost companies in Australia and New Zealand worth telephoning for a quote include: UTAG, 347 Kent St, Sydney (toll-free ☎1-800/809462); AFTA, 144 Pacific Highway, North Sydney (☎02/9264 3299); Ready Plan, 141–147 Walker St, Dandenong, Victoria (toll-free ☎1-300/555017); Cover More, Level 9, 32 Walker St, North Sydney (☎02/9202 8000).

Money, Banks and Costs

Since January 1, 1999, it has been possible in France to make commercial transactions by cheque in euros, and prices are now widely given in both francs and euros. By the end of 2002, however, the euro will have replaced the franc completely, but until then the French franc remains the normal unit of currency in Corsica. 10F is worth the equivalent of €1.52.

Abbreviated as F or sometimes FF, the franc, which is subdivided into 100 centimes, comes in notes of 500, 200, 100, 50 and 20F, with coins of 20F, 10F, 5F, 2F, 1F, 20 centimes and 10 centimes. The exchange rate is prone to fluctuations, veering between 8F and 10F to £1, and between 3.50F and 5F to $1. For the most up-to-date exchange rates, consult the useful currency converter Internet site: *www.oanda.com*

Costs

With a cost of living only slightly higher than the UK's, Corsica is no longer the exclusive luxury destination it used to be. That said, it can be disconcertingly easy to spend more money on the island than you might have intended. Aside from the obvious fact that most commodities have to be imported by sea or air, the main reason for this is the island's economic dependence on tourism, which ensures that from June until September prices of almost everything in demand by visitors – principally rooms and restaurant meals – double or triple, allowing the locals to make enough cash during the short summer season to see them through the winter. However, your trip need not cost you a fortune, and throughout this book we highlight ways to help you enjoy the island on a minimum budget.

Accommodation will probably constitute your main expense during your stay, particularly if you come in July and August, when room tariffs soar. The majority of hotels charge 220–280F for a double room. As a rule of thumb, places on the coast tend to be more expensive, with the best-value deals in the mountains of the interior, where there's far less seasonal price variation. Luxury places and cheap *pensions* are rarer, and where this type of accommodation exists it is listed in the guide. Staying in campsites can be a money-saver as long as you stick to the basic sites found in rural areas (around 70–100F per day for two people, one tent and a car) and avoid the flashy three-star complexes along the coast, which can cost almost as much as a hotel. Travelling around the island out of season, you'll also find hoteliers ready to offer reductions, especially if you agree to stay for a couple of nights or more, so don't be afraid to haggle.

As for **food**, in any town you'll find restaurants with three- or four-course meals for between 75F and 120F, and the island is full of pizzerias where you can eat a filling hot meal for even less than that. Picnic fare, obviously, is less costly, particularly if you buy from small local shops or supermarkets rather than markets or specialist food outlets aimed at tourists. More sophisticated meals using takeaway salads and ready-to-heat dishes, bought in *rôtisseries* or charcuteries, can be put together without stretching the wallet too far. If you're on a tight budget, you need to beware of the expense of beer and coffee in bars, cafés and clubs – though cigarettes are thirty percent cheaper here than on the mainland. Also watch out for the cost of wine in restaurants, which can easily double your bill if you're not careful.

Public transport costs around 110F for 100km, whether you're travelling by buses or by the *micheline* train (Bastia–Ajaccio is currently around 120F). Petrol prices are amongst the highest in Europe, at just over 5F per litre for leaded and just under 5F for unleaded (approximately 25F per imperial gallon, 20F per US gallon). Car rental will set you back anything upwards of 1650F per week, depending on the season (see p.25 for more details). Bicycles cost about 150F per day, and motorbikes start at around 250F for a 50cc scooter.

Museums and monuments won't prove too much of a drain on your resources, for the simple reason that there are relatively few on the island. Most charge around 15F and give discounts for holders of ISIC cards or to under-26s on presentation of a passport.

Thus, a **minimum daily requirement** would be around 200F per person, if camping and doing your own catering; a couple staying in budget hotels could live comfortably on about 300F per person; and, in order to have no worries at all, count on spending around 600F per day. Finally, bear in mind local attitudes to money. Living on a rock-bottom budget – camping rough, eating nothing but bread and cheese, and avoiding bars and cafés altogether – is unlikely to endear you to the locals, who love to joke about *les mangeurs des tomates* – those die-hard backpackers and camper-van tourists that are so eager to save money they miss out on one of the things Corsicans are deservedly most proud of: their wonderful cuisine.

Changing Money

Standard **banking hours** are Monday to Friday 9am to 4pm or 5pm, with most branches closing at noon for a couple of hours; some are also open on Saturdays 9am to noon. All are closed on Sunday and public holidays. The usual commission rate is one to two percent on travellers' cheques and a flat-rate charge on cash transactions (a 30F charge for changing 200F is not uncommon). As a rule of thumb, the high-street banks – Crédit Agricole, Crédit Lyonnais and Société Générale – give much better value than the privately run **bureaux de change** around the island.

Travellers' Cheques

Travellers' cheques, one of the safest ways of carrying your money, are available from almost any of the principal banks, whether you have an account there or not. There's usually a service charge of one percent on the amount purchased, though some go as high as five percent (your own bank may offer cheques free of charge provided you meet certain conditions). Thomas Cook, Visa and American Express are the most widely recognized brands. In recent years, Thomas Cook travellers' cheques have been the best deal for British visitors to Corsica, as the Société Générale change them without charging commission provided they are in French francs. **Eurocheques** – formerly the cheapest and most convenient way to pay on the continent – are no longer widely accepted in Corsica, not even by the large banks.

Credit and Debit Cards and ATMs

All over Corsica the major **credit cards** are almost universally accepted, enabling you to pay for meals, hotel bills, shopping and petrol – just watch for the window stickers. Visa – known as *Carte Bleue* in France – is the most widely recognized, followed by MasterCard (sometimes called EuroCard), with American Express and Access ranking considerably lower – only the Crédit Agricole bank provides facilities for Access, and many restaurants and hotels won't accept it because of the huge commissions they have to pay. Whichever card you have, it's always worth checking in advance that the hotel or restaurant will accept it.

You can, of course, also use your credit card to withdraw money from banks, and **automatic cash dispensers** (ATMs or *distributeurs de billets*) during or outside normal banking hours. The commission tends to be higher – for example 4.1 percent instead of the 1.5 percent at home for Visa cards, but this can be well worth the convenience. The transaction itself takes a few seconds; your PIN number should be the same as the one you use for your bank at home, but check with your credit card company before you leave. Also, because French credit cards are smart cards, some ATMs refuse foreign plastic and may tell you that your request for money has been denied. If that happens, just try another machine. All ATMs give you the choice of instructions in French or English. Note that **post offices** in larger towns and villages tend to have ATMs these days, and that even the smallest post offices also give cash advances on Visa credit cards – very handy if you run out of money in areas such as Cap Corse, where there are no machines.

Debit cards can also be used in ATMs or to pay for goods and services if they carry the appropriate Visa symbol or there's an "edc" (European acceptance) sign. You will be charged around one percent or a minimum of £1.50 to use your debit card in an ATM.

If you intend to use your credit or debit card as your principal means of obtaining cash while you're away, check before you leave that your daily or weekly limits are adequate, and confirm your card issuer's transaction charges. You should also take along a supply of travellers' cheques or currency in case the card is lost or stolen. Bear in mind, too, that credit cards are essential if you intend to rent a vehicle, as you'll need one to fill out the mandatory deposit docket (*caution*).

Information and Maps

The foreign branches of the French Government Tourist Office give away maps and glossy brochures, including lists of Corsican hotels, campsites, sports facilities and public transport services. In Corsica every major town and large village has a tourist office, or *Office du Tourisme* (OT), addresses of which are detailed throughout this guide. Usually only open in summer (May–Sept), these offices give out specific local information, including free town plans, lists of leisure activities, bike rental and countless other things. Many tourist offices also

French Government Tourist Offices

Australia 25 Bligh St, 22nd Floor, Sydney, NSW 2000 (☎02/9213 5244, fax 9221 8682; *mfrance@mtl.net*).

Britain 178 Piccadilly, London W1V 0AL (premium-rate line costing 45p per min ☎0891/244123, fax 020/7493 6594).

Canada 30 St Patrick St, Suite 700, Toronto, ON M5T 3A3 (☎416/593 4717); 1981 av McGill College, Suite 490, Montréal, PQ H3A (☎514/288 4264, fax 845 4868).

Ireland 35 Lower Abbey St, Dublin 1 (☎01/703 4046, fax 874 7324).

USA 444 Madison Ave, 16th Floor, New York, NY 10022-6903 (☎212/838 7800, fax 838 7855); 9454 Wilshire Blvd, Suite 715, Beverly Hills, Los Angeles, CA 90212 (☎310/271 6665, fax 276 2835); 676 North Michigan Ave, Suite 3360, Chicago, IL 60611-2819 (☎312/337 6339).

publish hotel and restaurant listings, as well as driving and walking itineraries for their areas, and post daily weather forecasts, useful if you're hiking or sailing.

In addition to the various free leaflets – and the maps in this guide – the one extra map you'll definitely want is a detailed **road map**. The Michelin yellow map series 1:200,000 (no. 90) is the best map of the whole island for drivers. If you're planning to **walk or cycle**, check the three series of IGN maps: 1:100,000 (green), 1:50,000 (also green) and 1:25,000 (blue). The IGN 1:100,000 maps, the smallest-scale contoured maps available, are essential for cyclists, who tend to cycle off 1:25,000 maps in a couple of hours.

For advice on maps for the island's **long-distance footpaths**, see p.32.

MAP OUTLETS

Britain and Ireland

Hodges Figgis Bookshop, 56–58 Dawson St, Dublin 2 (☎01/677 4754).
John Smith and Sons, 57–61 St Vincent St, Glasgow G2 (☎0141/221 7472).
Stanfords, 12–14 Long Acre, London WC2; 29 Corn St, Bristol BS1. Mail order ☎020/7836 1321 or email *sales@stanfords.co.uk*
The Travel Bookshop, 13–15 Blenheim Crescent, London W11 (☎020/7229 5260; *www.thetravelbookshop.co.uk*).
Waterstone's, Queens Building, 8 Royal Ave, Belfast BT1 (☎028/9024 7355).

USA and Canada

The Complete Traveler Bookstore, 199 Madison Ave, New York, NY 10016 (☎212/685 9007); 3207 Fillmore St, San Francisco, CA 92123 (☎415/923 1511).
Open Air Books and Maps, 25 Toronto St, Toronto, ON M5R 2C1 (☎416/363 0719).
Rand McNally, 444 N Michigan Ave, Chicago, IL 60611 (☎312/321 1751); 1201 Connecticut Ave NW, Washington, DC 20003 (☎202/223 6751). For other locations, or for mail order, call ☎1-800/333 0136 ext 2111.
Ulysses Travel Bookshop, 4176 St-Denis, Montréal (☎514/843 9447).
World Wide Books and Maps, 736 Granville St, Vancouver, BC V6Z 1E4 (☎604/687 3320).

Australia and New Zealand

Map Land, 372 Little Burke St, Melbourne (☎03/9670 4383).
The Map Shop, 16a Peel St, Adelaide (☎08/8231 2033).
Perth Map Centre, 891 Hay St, Perth (☎09/9322 5733).
Speciality Maps, 58 Albert St, Auckland (☎09/307 2217).
Travel Bookshop, Shop 3/175 Liverpool St, Sydney 2000 (☎02/9261 8200).

Accommodation

At most times of the year accommodation is plentiful in Corsica. However, from June to August it's a good idea to book your room in advance wherever you're heading, and reservations are always advisable in the more remote parts of the island. August is the most problematic month, as the French and Italians take their holidays en masse at this time. The "Language" section at the back of this book (see p.393) should help you make your reservation, as few hoteliers or campsite managers speak any English. We've detailed a range of accommodation wherever such a range exists, but you'll find there are very few luxury places and only a couple of hostels in the whole of Corsica (both at Calvi).

Hotels

All French hotels are graded on a scale that rises to three stars, and the price of the room corresponds roughly to the number of stars, though unfortunately this system isn't very reliable in Corsica, as some hotels give themselves the stars regardless of whether they've been visited by inspectors. By comparison with the UK, however, hotel accommodation throughout the island represents extremely good value for money – at least outside the mid-July to August peak season.

Few places offer rooms for **under 200F**, and those that do tend to be basic; they'll probably have a washbasin (*lavabo*), and sometimes a bidet, but little else. The shower (*douche*) and toilets (WC) will be outside on the corridor (*palier*).

At the **one-star** level you can expect to pay 200–250F for a double, perhaps with a shower but probably not a toilet. **Two-star** places, with fully en-suite facilities and often a small balcony, charge around 250–350F for a double. **Three-star** hotels usually cost between 300F and 450F, for which you should enjoy a spacious double room with bathroom, television, large terrace or balcony, and access to a pool.

Breakfast can add 30–50F per person to a bill, though there is no obligation to take it and you will nearly always do better at a café. The cost of eating **dinner** in a hotel's restaurant can be a more important factor to bear in mind when picking a place to stay. Some places insist that you take at least one full meal with them (*demi-pension*), especially in the mountains, where food is usually of a high quality.

Single rooms are only marginally cheaper than doubles, so sharing always keeps down the cost. Some hotels will provide extra beds for three or more, charging around 25 percent per bed. Note that many hotels are **open only in summer**, usually from May to September – we've indicated in the guide those establishments that close for the winter. The ones that do stay open in winter often offer discounts to off-season visitors.

Chambres d'Hôtes and Ferme-Auberges

Some of the most congenial private accommodation in Corsica is offered in small, rural bed-and-breakfast establishments, or **chambres d'hôtes**. There are dozens of places dotted around the island where you can stay as a fee-paying guest in someone's home, usually in a newly converted wing or modern annexe of a farmhouse. As you'd expect, the experience is more personal, especially in those places where evening meals are offered, giving you a chance to get to know your hosts. Room tariffs are not cheap, averaging from around 230–280F for two, including breakfast, but for many visitors, particularly those keen to practise their French, the off-the-beaten-track locations and warm Corsican hospitality give *chambres d'hôtes* the edge over most hotels.

Ferme-auberges, literally "farm-inns", are similar to *chambres d'hôtes*, but with the emphasis being essentially on the food: classy Corsican speciality dishes, made from locally produced ingredients. The hosts may, or may not, offer rooms, but if they do you'll only be able to stay in one if you have dinner. For this reason, prices are given as half-board (*demi-pension*), which covers the room, breakfast and evening meal.

We've included some of the best *chambres d'hotes* and *ferme-auberges* in the guide, but for a full run-down of all the island's accredited establishments, pick up the leaflet entitled *Bienvenue à la Ferme* at a tourist office, in which you'll find the names, addresses and telephone numbers of hand-picked places across the island.

Rented Houses

If you're planning to stay a week or more in any one place, it might be worth considering **renting**

Accommodation Prices

Throughout this guide, hotel accommodation is graded on a scale from ① to ⑧. These numbers show the cost per night of the cheapest double room in high season, though remember that many of the cheap places will have more expensive rooms with en-suite facilities. In such cases we list two price codes, indicating the range of room rates offered.

① under 100F/under €15
② 100–200F/€15–30
③ 200–250F/€30–37.50
④ 250–300F/€37.50–45
⑤ 300–350F/€45–52.50
⑥ 350–400F/€52.50–60
⑦ 400–500F/€60–75
⑧ 500F and above/€75 and above

a house. The easiest and most reliable way of finding a property is to use **Gîtes de France**, the former French government letting service whose UK operations are now run by Brittany Ferries (enquiries ☎0990/360360), though you can still deal directly with Gîtes de France in Paris (59 rue St-Lazare, 75009; ☎01 48 70 75 75; Mon–Sat 10am–6.30pm). Call for a brochure or pick one up at a travel agent, then simply reserve a place for any number of full weeks over the phone. The excellent *Bienvenue à la Ferme* leaflet mentioned on p.23 (available from any Corsican tourist office) also gives details on ten or more gîtes around the island.

Another way of finding a place is to try one of the package holiday firms listed on p.10 (though these tend to be at the upper end of the market), or to look for properties advertised in the Sunday newspapers. Finally, you can wait until you arrive in Corsica and ask any local tourist office for a list of accommodation to rent in the region – these will work out less expensive, but there's obviously the risk that nothing suitable will be on offer.

Gîtes d'Étape and Refuges

Corsica has dozens of **gîtes d'étape** and **refuges** situated at crucial stages along the main hiking trails (see p.30). Although designed primarily for walkers, anyone can stay at them and in several remote villages of the interior and northwest coast they often constitute the only budget accommodation.

Gîtes d'étapes are essentially hikers' hostels offering basic accommodation, usually in four- to six-bunk-bed dormitories, with communal hot showers and toilets. When demand is high, you'll have to share the dorm with others, but during off-peak periods the wardens (*gardiens*) try to put clients in separate rooms for the price of a single bed (around 80F, many also offer four-course evening meals on request, for an additional 75F). It is rare to find a gîte that's not kept in immaculate condition, and many have attractive terraces or gardens. Self-catering facilities are always provided, and included in the cost of the bed, but most walkers opt for half-board, which can work out good value. As a rule, you can also **camp** in the garden for around the same price as a cheap campsite. Unlike hotels, the peak periods for gîtes are the walking seasons, from late May until early July and through September, when you should reserve a bed as far in advance as possible. At other times, you can usually secure a place by phoning ahead during the morning.

Situated in remote mountain locations, well away from roads, **refuges** are hikers' shelters, barely converted from shepherds' crofts or ancient stone dwellings. While some provide little more than a roof, others have primitive facilities: a simple gas stove, aluminium cooking equipment, dining room, common dormitory and toilets. Most also have a bivouac area nearby when you can bed down outdoors or pitch a tent. Along the GR20, the majority of the refuges are manned during the summer months by *gardiens* who also collect the daily fee (ranging from 25F to 45F depending on the level of comfort). Beds in refuges are allocated on a first-come, first-served basis, and cannot be reserved in advance.

All refuges and gîtes d'étape are marked on the large-scale IGN maps; we've also given the addresses and telephone numbers of all gîtes d'étape in our coverage of the island's six main long-distance walks (see p.30).

Camping

Practically every locality has at least one **campsite** to cater for the thousands of French, German and Italians who spend their holiday under canvas or in recreation vehicles. The cheapest – costing around 60–70F per night for a couple, tent and car – are small family-run farm campsites (known as **campings à la ferme**), which offer basic amenities in attractive settings. They tend to be a much more pleasant experience, and better value, than the superior categories of campsite dotted around the coast, where you'll pay prices similar to those of a one-star hotel for facilities such as bars, restaurants, tennis courts and swimming pools. People spend their whole holiday in these places – if you plan to do the same, and particularly if you have a caravan or a big tent, it's wise to book ahead. Throughout the guide, we've picked out the best sites in each area, basing our choices on the attractiveness of the setting (and cleanliness of the washrooms); standards of both can vary enormously, particularly during the congested summer months.

Lastly, a **word of caution**: never camp rough (*camping sauvage*) on anyone's land without first asking their permission. Beside the fact that it's illegal, you're liable to get a bullet flying your way. Camping on beaches is also illegal, though a lot of people do it. Wherever you camp, be careful with **fires**, as the maquis – which creeps down to the coast in many areas – burns quickly.

Getting Around

If you want to see a lot of Corsica in a fairly short time, the only way to do it is to drive; car rental firms are found in all the main towns and at the airports. This can add considerably to the cost of your holiday, but even if your budget will only stretch to a few days it's worth renting a vehicle of some kind. During the summer, bus services are adequate between the towns, but dwindle in the countryside, while in winter few routes have more than a skeleton service. Journey times and frequencies are given in "Travel details" at the end of each chapter, but bear in mind that timetables tend to change annually; you can always check schedules at a tourist office, or by phoning the transport company direct. As for the train, it's worth taking in order to admire the wonderful scenery it passes through, but don't take it if you're in a hurry.

Driving

For visitors used to the comparatively restrained roads and traffic manners of northern Europe, driving in Corsica can come as a rude shock. Once you're off the smooth national highways (*routes nationales*, prefixed with N), the constantly twisting *routes départementales* (prefixed with a D) present their fair share of hazards, not least of all **Corsican drivers** themselves, who race rally-style around the bends and habitually overtake in perilous situations. For this reason, expect to meet vehicles approaching at speed in the middle of the road, even on blind corners and brows of hills. If you find yourself with a local car breathing down your neck, pull over and let it pass at the first opportunity; nothing annoys Corsicans more than being held up by a cautious tourist in a rented car. Note, also, that the mountain and corniche roads are pitted with great potholes, while pigs or goats present further hazards.

EU and US **driving licences** are valid in France, though an International Driving Licence makes life easier if you get a police officer unwilling to peruse a document in English. If the vehicle is rented (see below), its registration document (*carte grise*) and the insurance papers must be carried (they are usually stored in the glove compartment of rental cars). In Australia, international drivers' licences can be purchased from the RAC (Royal Automobile Club) offices in most major towns and cities, and from the AA (Automobile Association) in New Zealand.

The French law of *priorité a droite* – **giving way** to traffic coming from your right, even when it is coming from a minor road – is gradually being phased out. It is sometimes respected in built-up areas of Bastia and Ajaccio, however, so you still have to be vigilant in towns, keeping a lookout for the yellow diamond on a white background that gives you right of way, until you see the same sign with an oblique slash, which indicates that vehicles emerging from the right have right of way. At **roundabouts** the cars on the roundabout have priority. *CEDEZ LE PASSAGE* means "Give way", a *STOP* sign means come to a complete halt.

Speed limits are 110kph (68mph) on two-lane highways, 90kph (56mph) on other roads in non-urban areas, and 60kph (37mph) in towns. **Fines** for exceeding the speed limit by 1–30kph range from 900F to 5000F, and are exacted on the spot, with only cash accepted. There are no toll roads in Corsica.

Car Rental

Given the competitive rates on offer (not to mention the high cost of public transport in Corsica), **renting a car** can work out cheaper than you think. In 1999, rock-bottom prices for a small hatchback were typically around £125–140 per week – not a whole lot more than two people might spend on buses, trains and taxis.

To rent a car in Corsica you have to be over 21 (and in some cases over 25) and have been in possession of a clean licence for at least one year. All the international rental companies are represented on the island, with branches at the airports and in major towns, and there are numerous local firms, too. Some of these offer better deals than their larger competitors, although it can sometimes be difficult for non-French speakers to obtain quotes and details in advance. One local outfit worth phoning, however, is Rent-a-Car, based at the *Hôtel Kallisté* in Ajaccio (see box, p.26), whose staff speak fluent English.

Another option is to look into the **fly-drive** deals offered by tour operators and consolidators (see p.9), who sometimes tack on a week's car rental to their discounted flights for as little as £70. Members of frequent-flyer clubs (such as British Airways' Executive Club) may also have access to special discounts, while passengers on British Midland are entitled to a ten percent discount on Avis cars.

When phoning a car rental company for a quote, ensure the price you're offered includes the following: unlimited mileage, collision damage waiver (check on the level of excess you are liable for if you cause any damage), theft protection, third-party insurance, licensing fee (aka "road surcharge") and airport surcharge. If you intend to share the driving with someone else, make sure they're eligible, and ask how much it will cost to name them as a second driver (usually around £15 extra per driver per week). Other points to clarify before booking might be whether or not it is possible to drop the car off in a different place to where you picked it up (and, if so, how much this costs), and whether you get a better deal by paying two or more weeks in advance.

If you **break down**, your only option is to hail a passing car and get them to take you to the nearest garage, so check that the cost of repairs is covered by your rental agreement (it nearly always is), or – if you're in your own vehicle – consider taking out **extra insurance cover** to meet this eventuality; in the UK, this typically costs around £40 for eight days. Look into the RAC's European Motoring Assistance (☎0800/550055; *www.rac.co.uk*), the AA's Five-Star Europe cover (☎0800/444500; *www.theaa.co.uk*), or Europ Assistance (☎0645/947000).

As in your home country, if you have an accident, exchange registration numbers (*numéros d'imatriculation*) with any other drivers involved. Break-ins should be reported to the local police

CAR RENTAL FIRMS

Britain

ADD Autos Abroad	☎020/7439 4068	**Europcar**	☎020/7834 8484; *www.europcar.com*
Avis	☎0990/900500; *www.avis.com*	**Hertz**	☎0990/996699; *www.hertz.com*
Budget	☎0800/181181; *www.budget.com*	**Holiday Autos**	☎0990/300404

North America

Avis	☎1-800/331 1084; *www.avis.com*	**Hertz (USA)**	☎1-800/654 3001; *www.hertz.com;*
Dollar	☎1-800/421 6868; *www.dollar.com*	**Hertz (Canada)**	☎1-800/263 0600; *www.hertz.com*
Europe by Car	☎1-800/223 1516; *www.europebycar.com*	**Holiday Autos**	☎1-800/422 7737

Australia and New Zealand

Avis	Australia ☎1-800/225533; *www.avis.com* New Zealand ☎09/525 1982	**Hertz**	Australia ☎13-1918; *www.hertz.com* New Zealand ☎09/309 0989
Budget	Australia ☎13-2848; *www.budget.com* New Zealand ☎09/275 2220	**Renault Eurodrive**	Australia ☎02/9299 3344

Corsica

Avis	☎04 95 23 56 90	**Rent-a-Car**	☎04 95 51 34 45
Budget	☎04 95 36 04 44		
Citer	☎04 95 70 16 95		
Europcar	☎04 95 30 09 50		
Hertz	☎04 95 23 57 04		

For further details of local car rental companies and franchises in Corsica, see the "Listings" section of the relevant accounts.

in order to make an insurance claim, and in the event of an accident you are also obliged to complete a *constat à l'aimable* (jointly agreed statement), which your car insurers or rental company should give you. As for **fuel**, note that in remote country areas – such as Cap Corse and the interior – petrol stations are especially scarce, so remember to fill up in the towns. Unleaded fuel (*sans plomb*) is available everywhere.

By Bicycle

Corsica is no soft option for cyclists, but if you're in good shape you'll enjoy the challenge of the island's convoluted routes and long climbs. The main disadvantage is the traffic, combined with the narrowness of the roads. In summer, you'll also have the fumes to contend with as well as the ferocious heat. All in all, it's a better idea to come in mid-season – May–June and Sept–Oct – and aim to avoid the traffic as much as possible.

If you want to **bring your bike** from home, flying is by far the easiest way; provided you box it in the prescribed way, most airlines will transport it free of charge. Car ferries also carry bicycles for free, but the French railway SNCF charges a flat fee of 150F for transporting your bike, which cannot be taken on the train you're travelling on; usually there's a three- or four-day time lag between your arrival at a given place and your bike's arrival. If you are taking your own bike from the UK, it's a good idea to join the **Cyclists' Touring Club** (Cotterell House, 68 Meadrow, Godalming, Surrey GU7 3HS; ☎01483/417217), which will suggest routes and supply advice to members; they also run a particularly good insurance scheme. The cost of membership is £25 a year (£12.50 for students, the unemployed and under-12s).

A handful of companies around the island rent **cycles**, usually mountain bikes, *vélos tous terrains* (*vtt*) in French. Rates are fairly standard, at 80–120F per day, or 450–500F per week, with small discounts of fifteen to twenty percent out of season. You're also usually required to leave a credit card docket or around 2000F in cash as a deposit (*caution*). For a full list of mountain bike rental companies around the island, see the box on p.28.

For more on **mountain biking** in Corsica, see "Outdoor Pursuits" on p.30.

By Motorcycle

Corsica is perfect **motorcycle** terrain, and during the summer its roads are teeming with tourers (most of them from Germany). If you've come without your own vehicle or can't afford to rent a car, you might consider **renting a bike**. This used to be relatively inexpensive compared to car rental, but today's high insurance premiums have pushed most of the smaller operators out of business, and forced prices to often prohibitive levels. Even so, it's well worth splashing out on a bike for at least a couple of days – the sense of freedom is hard to beat.

Bikes can be rented at various towns and resorts around the island, and the choice of vehicles on offer is pretty standard; only the prices vary. Cheapest of all, at around 250F per day, is a 500cc moped. While these are fine for nipping to and from the beach, they tend to struggle on the hills, which effectively writes off most of the island except the eastern plain. For a trip into the interior or around the coast, you'll need at least a Vespa-style 80cc scooter, preferably a new one. Starting at around 280F per day, these can comfortably carry a rider and pillion passenger on level ground, and will make it over even the highest mountain passes if you're riding solo. Trials-style 125cc bikes are also widely available, though they cost upwards of 350F per day; anything larger than that will set you back more than 400F.

In addition to the daily rental rate, you'll need to leave a hefty **deposit** (*caution*) of around 4000F. Rather than accept a cheque or cash, most companies these days prefer to swipe a credit card through their machine and keep the docket as security, tearing it up if you return the bike in a satisfactory condition.

Rental vehicles take some rough treatment, so check yours thoroughly before you ride off to make sure the brakes, lights and horn work. It's also a good idea to make a note of any scratches or bumps with the owner present. The cost of rental should include a helmet, and covers third-party insurance, but not damage incurred to the vehicle in any accident – another reason to ride defensively. Crash your bike, and you'll almost certainly have to foot the bill. Theft is another problem – every year, rented scooters are stolen from car parks above beaches. For this reason, owners should issue you with a strong D-lock (*anti-vol*) or chain, which you fasten around the front wheel.

Mountain Bike (VTT) Rental Companies in Corsica

Ajaccio BMS Location, Port Tino Rossi (☎04 95 21 33 75); Corse Évasion, Montée St-Jean (☎04 95 20 52 05); Locacorse, 10 av Beverini-Vico (☎04 95 20 71 20).
Bastia Objectif Nature, rue Notre-Dame-de Lourdes (☎04 95 32 54 34).
Calvi Location Ambrosini, rue Villa-Antoine (☎04 95 65 02 13).
Porto Porto Location, opposite Spar supermarket (☎04 95 26 10 13).
Propriano TCC Sarl, 25 rue Général-de-Gaulle (☎04 95 76 15 32); Location Valinco, 25 av Napoléon (☎04 95 76 11 84).

This, however, will at best only act as a deterrent, so be sure to use the steering lock as well each time you park up. If the bike does get stolen, notify the rental company and local police immediately. In theory, the company should be covered by their insurance for theft, but check this before you leave their office; some insist on retaining most or all of your deposit if a bike disappears.

By Bus

Buses are Corsica's principal form of public transport, but, as most Corsicans own at least one car demand outside the tourist season is minimal (for the most part, only visitors, students, pensioners and migrant workers use the buses). Even in summer, services on many routes are infrequent, to say the least, and if you rely purely on buses to get around your travels will be limited to a handful of arterial routes – between Bastia and Ajaccio (via Corte), Ajaccio and Porto-Vecchio (via Propriano, Sartène and Bonifacio), and Porto-Vecchio and Bastia (via Aléria) – along with a couple of routes in Alta Rocca and the northwest coast to and from Porto (via Cargèse).

In rural areas, the timetables tend to be constructed to suit working and school hours, which means there's often just one bus a day in any direction, departing at a dauntingly early hour. To confuse matters, virtually each route is covered by a different company, making it frustratingly difficult to obtain accurate timetable information. In theory, tourist offices should have up-to-date schedules (*horaires*) but you can't guarantee it.

The easiest way to work out which company serves which towns is to consult the "travel details" section at the end of each chapter; this will include a brief outline of the region's main routes and contact numbers for the bus operator. Most accounts in the guide section also list transport information.

Fares on Corsican buses are high – around 100F per 100km – though the vehicles themselves are comfortable enough and kept in good condition. Trunk routes are served by large coaches, while the mountain villages of the interior and the northwest coast are connected by modern minibuses.

By Train

Corsica's diminutive, bone-shaking **train**, the *micheline* or *trinighellu* (little train), crosses the mountains from Ajaccio to Bastia via Corte, with

Motorcyle Rental Companies

Ajaccio Locacorse, 10 av Bévérini-Vico (☎04 95 20 71 20); Corse Évasion, Montée St-Jean (☎04 95 20 52 05); BMS Location, Port Tino Rossi (☎04 95 21 33 75).
Bastia Plaisance Service Location, Port Toga (☎04 95 31 49 01).
Bonifacio Corse Moto Services, quai Nova (☎04 95 73 15 16).
Calvi Location Ambrosini, rue Villa-Antoine (☎04 95 65 02 13).
Porto-Vecchio Garage Legrand, route de Bonifacio (☎04 95 70 15 84); Corse Moto Service, Yamaha Garage, route de Bastia (☎04 95 70 45 51); Suzuki Garage, route du Port-de-Plaisance (☎04 95 70 36 05).
Propriano TCC Sarl, 25 rue Général-de-Gaulle (☎04 95 76 15 32); Location Valinco, 25 av Napoléon (☎04 95 76 11 84).

a subsidiary line running from Ponte Leccia, north of Corte, to Calvi. Constructed at the end of the nineteenth century, the line follows a rattling and precarious route across the mountains. Although slower than the bus (the 100km from Ajaccio to Bastia takes just under 4hr, as opposed to 3hr by road), it's an unmissable trip that you should try to do at least once, if only in one direction; the scenery is wonderful from start to finish, and there are plenty of tempting spots to get off and walk along the way. The line's most impressive feat of engineering is the famous pont du Vecchio at Vivario, designed by Gustave Eiffel in 1825. Crossing it, you get a matchless view across to the dizzying new pont du Vecchio road bridge, completed in 1999, with a span of 222m and a height of 137.5m.

Tickets cost about the same as the buses. If you can provide proof that you're a student, you get a discount on all tickets, and often if you're travelling to or from the university town of Corte you don't even need a card. Bicycles go for free.

Driving Vocabulary

to park the car	*garer la voiture*
car park	*le parking*
no parking	*défense de stationner*
petrol station	*la station-service*
petrol	*l'essence/le super*
fill it up	*faire le plein*
oil	*l'huile*
air line	*une ligne à air*
tyre	*le pneu*
wheel	*la roue*
puncture	*la crevaison*
to inflate	*gonfler*
battery	*la batterie*
plugs	*bougies*
to break down	*tomber en panne*
petrol can	*le bidon*
insurance	*l'assurance*
traffic lights	*les feux*
red light	*le feu rouge*
green light	*le feu vert*

Cycling Vocabulary

to adjust	*ajuster*
axle	*l'axe*
ball bearing	*le roulement à billes*
battery	*la pile*
bent	*tordu*
bicycle	*le vélo*
bottom bracket	*le logement du pédalier*
brake cable	*le cable*
brakes	*les freins*
broken	*cassé*
bulb	*l'ampoule*
chain	*la chaîne*
frame	*le cadre*
gears	*les vitesses*
grease	*la graisse*
handlebars	*le guidon*
inner tube	*la chambre à l'air*
loose	*dévissé*
to lower	*baisser*
mudguard	*le garde-boue*
pannier	*le pannier*
pedal	*la pédale*
pump	*la pompe*
rack	*la porte-bagages*
to raise	*relever*
to repair	*réparer*
saddle	*la selle*
spanner	*la clef*
to straighten	*rédresser*
stuck	*coincé*
tight	*serré*

Outdoor Pursuits

Corsica's varied landscapes and exceptionally mild climate make it ideal for outdoor pursuits of all kinds. Over the years the Parc Naturel Régional and numerous private activity centres have developed an impressive infrastructure for exploiting the island's potential as an adventure sports destination. Marked footpaths form an extensive network of long-distance trails across the most spectacular mountain areas, punctuated by well-maintained hiking hostels, and there are plenty of equestrian centres from where you can explore the countryside on horseback. For the more adventurous, mountain biking, climbing and canyoning are also well-established, with marked routes and guides on hand at several key locations. In addition, a string of diving schools around the coast offer the chance to sample the island's superb underwater life, which ranks among the most varied in Europe. The one catch with the Corsican adventure sport scene is cost. The seasonal nature of most outdoor pursuits on the island means that instructors and equipment providers tend to charge highly for their services; wherever possible, bring your own gear with you.

Hiking

Hiking (*la randonnée pédestre*, or *la rando* for short) is without doubt the best way to explore Corsica's amazing interior and remote stretches of coast, and there are nearly 1000km of marked trails to help you do just that. Ranging from two-week hikes over the mountainous spine of the island to leisurely half-day ambles across cool forests and stream valleys, these are maintained by the Parc Naturel Régional de Corse and municipal councils, and cater for all levels of ability.

Of the six main long-distance hiking trails in Corsica, the most famous is the **GR20** (covered on p.145), which crosses the island diagonally from Calenzana in the northwest to Conca in the southeast. Normally completed in ten to twelve days, it takes in the cream of Corsica's mountain scenery, with innumerable opportunities for side-trips to the surrounding peaks. However, the relentless series of arduous ascents and descents mean it's only suitable for experienced, fit and well-equipped hikers.

If you're keen to hike for a week or more but don't feel up to tackling the GR20, try one of the five other long-distance routes established by the Parc Naturel Régional. Designed to take in the most scenic and unspoilt corners of the island, these are consistently varied and well marked, and have the additional attraction of **gîtes d'étape** (see p.24) en route, where you can enjoy a hot shower, clean dormitory bed and self-catering facilities for around 80F; most also provide four-course evening meals on request, for a supplement of around 75F.

The five routes are covered in the Parc Naturel Régional's topo-guide, *Corse: Entre Mer et Montagne*, but we've included reviews of each, giving an outline of the route, advice on accommodation and details of how to get to the trail-head by public transport: **Mare e Monti**, from Calenzana to Cargèse in ten days, p.146; **Mare a Mare Nord**, Moriani to Cargèse via Corte in nine to ten days, p.320; **Mare a Mare Centre**, Ghisonaccia to Ajaccio in seven days, p.305; **Mare e Monti Sud**, Porticcio to Propriano in five days, p.219; and **Mare a Mare Sud**, Propriano to Porto-Vecchio in six days, p.243.

In addition to the long-distance paths, the Parc Naturel Régional has established a network of easier trails designed for day hikes. Known as **sentiers de pays**, these are waymarked, and a series of glossy leaflets (sold at park information counters and tourist offices throughout the island) indicate the route on black-and-white reproductions of the relevant IGN map.

Also featured throughout this book are descriptions of good walks and hikes not included in Parc Naturel literature. While many of these are gentle strolls between villages, some are hard climbs up the island's highest peaks, requiring experience and confidence at altitude. Before setting out on any such route, check the weather forecast (see box on p.32) and ensure you are properly equipped; an ice axe or snow poles can be useful on some ascents where sheltered gullies hold patches of eternal snow (*nevés*).

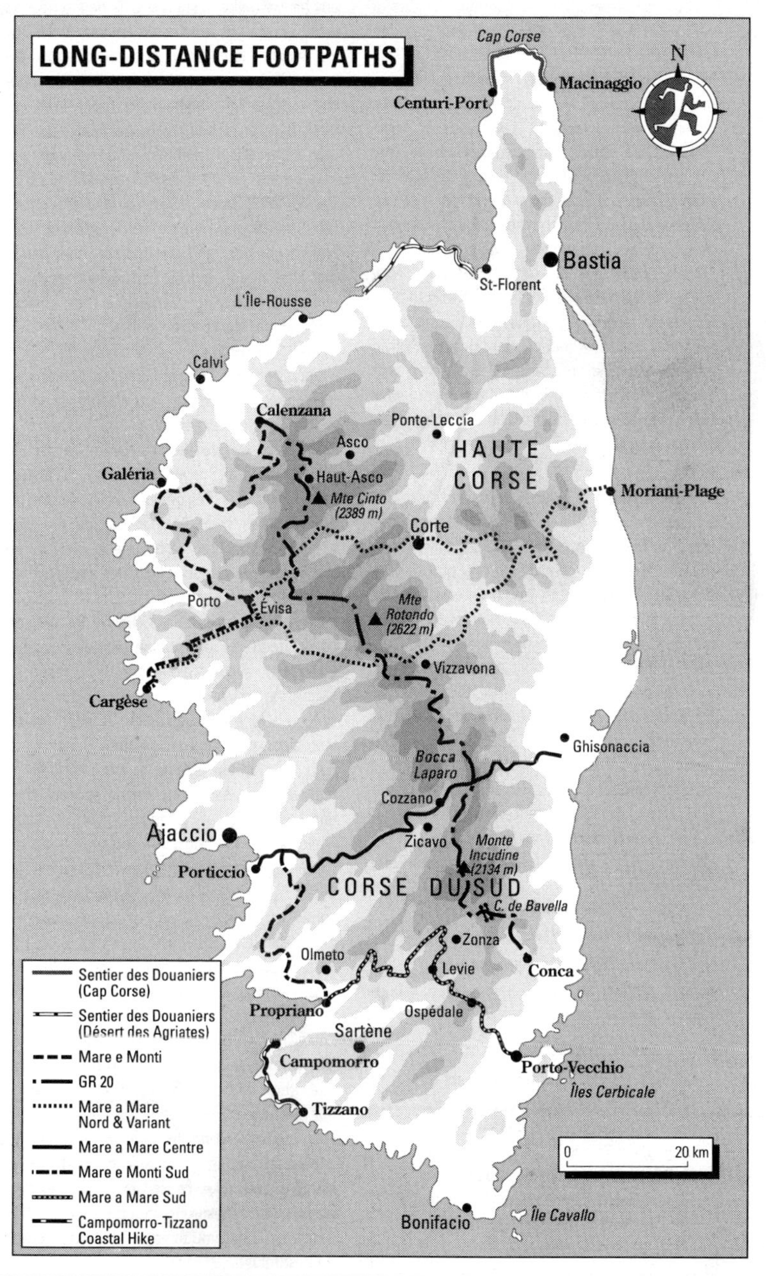

LONG-DISTANCE FOOTPATHS
N
Cap Corse
Macinaggio
Centuri-Port
Bastia
St-Florent
L'Île-Rousse
Calvi
Calenzana
Ponte-Leccia
Asco
HAUTE CORSE
Haut-Asco
Galéria
Mte Cinto (2389 m)
Moriani-Plage
Corte
Porto
Évisa
Mte Rotondo (2622 m)
Vizzavona
Cargèse
Ghisonaccia
Bocca Laparo
Cozzano
Ajaccio
Zicavo
Monte Incudine (2134 m)
Porticcio
CORSE DU SUD
C. de Bavella
Zonza
Olmeto
Levie
Conca
Propriano
Ospédale
Sartène
Campomorro
Porto-Vecchio
Îles Cerbicale
Tizzano
0
20 km
Bonifacio
Île Cavallo
Sentier des Douaniers (Cap Corse)
Sentier des Douaniers (Désert des Agriates)
Mare e Monti
GR 20
Mare a Mare Nord & Variant
Mare a Mare Centre
Mare e Monti Sud
Mare a Mare Sud
Campomorro-Tizzano Coastal Hike

Above all, never underestimate the **dangers** of walking in wilderness areas. Every year lives are lost on the mountains, usually because walkers fail to observe a few golden rules. First and foremost, be preared for sudden and dramatic changes in the **weather**, particularly at high-altitudes. Snowfalls are common from late October until early June, and during the summer violent storms frequently descend on exposed ridges and peaks, driving hikers off the mountain or into refuges, sometimes for days on end.

Many walks are best attempted from early spring through to late summer, principally to profit from the long daylight hours and also to avoid the mists and snow that descend over the hills in winter. From June until September, an early start is essential so as to arrive at the end of your walk before the afternoon heat becomes unbearable.

Maps

IGN publish the best contour **maps** for hikers (see p.22) and these – along with the walking guides listed in "Books" on p.390 – are strongly recommended if you are considering any of the long-distance walks. You can, however, save a lot of money if you buy the Parc Naturel Régional's excellent **topo-guides**, which contain the sections of the IGN maps pertaining to specific trails, plus a detailed description of the route (in French), along with lots of other indispensable information. Costing around 100F, they're sold at most good bookshops and large tourist offices on the island, and are essential if you're considering one of the long-distance footpaths outlined below. You can also buy them at Stanfords in the UK (see p.22), and through IGN's **Web site** (*www.ign.fr*).

Equipment

In the light of the potential dangers posed by the volatile weather and tough terrain of the mountains, it is essential to be properly equipped for any hike, whether a short *boucle de journée* (day walk) or *grande randonnée* (serious trek). Your top priority should be a good pair of **boots**, preferrably leather ones with plenty of ankle support. These days, lightweight boots made from synthetic waterproof and breathable fabrics are popular, especially in summer, and although they may be fine for Corsica's low-altitude hikes you should think twice about using them on the GR20, much of which crosses long expanses of broken boulders and granite scree that can be merciless on your ankles. Don't, whatever you do, attempt anything more ambitious than an hour-long amble along level ground in trainers, no matter how comfortable they may feel.

Unless you're planning some hard-core winter adventure sports activity, you won't need to hike with a **tent** in Corsica. All of the footpaths are well served by gîtes and refuges offering cheap shelter. It is technically forbidden to **bivouac** within the Parcs Régionaux (except in the purpose-built *aires de bivouac* outside the GR20 refuges), but in practice no one is likely to stop you as long as you don't light fires and leave rubbish behind. An army-style poncho or large plastic bivvy bag can come in handy for this, and you'll need a four-season sleeping bag to bivouac at altitude along the GR20, especially during the first and last months of the trekking season – June and September – when freezing temperatures are not uncommon.

As for **clothing**, expect to have to add and remove layers constantly. During ascents, shorts and vest are usually adequate, even at altitude, while on the way downhill you may need long sleeves and long trousers. A good fleece can also prove invaluable, as can a lightweight coat of some kind, ideally one made of waterproof breathable fabric such as Gortex© or Triple Point Ceramic©. Anyone attempting the GR20 might also consider shelling out on some kind of underwear made of wicking fibre such as Polartec©, which prevents the build-up of sweat that can cause sudden drops in body temperature when you stop moving; they're not cheap, but over a fortnight on the GR20 you'll easily get your money's worth. In summer, however, you should take along a sunhat and high-factor sun cream – sunstroke, caused by prolonged dehydration and exposure to strong sunlight, is a big problem if it hits you three or four hours from the nearest refuge.

Detailed recorded **weather forecasts for the Corsican mountains**, updated three times daily, are available (in French only) by telephoning France Météo (☎08 36 68 02 20; 2.23F/min). You should also be able to obtain reliable weather information at tourist and Parc Naturel Régional information offices across the island.

Water and Food

During a moderately strenuous walk in warm weather, you can expect to get through between three and four litres of water per day – or four to five on the GR20 in summer. Don't scrimp on liquid; it's heavy to carry, but the consequences of running out can be serious, especially in hot weather. On Corsica's low-altitude routes, you won't need to carry more than a couple of litres at a time, as the paths regularly cross villages, streams and springs where you can top up (note that "*Non Potable*" signs on fountains and springs mean they're not safe to drink). The IGN topo-guides also indicate the location of reliable water sources. Even at altitude, however, all torrents, streams and rivers in Corsica should be regarded as being contaminated with animal waste, or dead animals themselves, and treated accordingly; if you do need to drink any, boil or clean it first with water **purification tablets** (chlorine-based ones are fine, and healthier over long periods).

Food is likely to comprise most of the weight in your backpack, at least along the GR20, where opportunities to re-provision are less frequent than on the island's other long-distance footpaths. Aim to carry at least two or three days' worth of supplies with you on the GR20; during July and August, staffed refuges stock basic provisions (*revitaillement*), but you can't bank on them in June or September/October, and the food is always sold at grossly inflated prices. Where the path descends to road level (as at Haut Asco, Col de Verghio and Vizzavona), you'll always find a shop or bar selling supplies for hikers but, again, they'll be pricy. Dehydrated and dried food is obviously best: pasta, couscous, rice or "boil-up" powder meals (widely available in Corsican supermarkets, where they're much cheaper than at specialist outdoor shops). The one thing to definitely avoid while hiking strenuous routes is **alcohol**, which gives you a short burst of energy but will demand it back with interest the following day. As anyone who's nursed a hangover after a evening's premature celebrations along the GR20 will tell you, wait until you've finished before popping any corks.

Climbing

While not possessing the same allure as the Alps, Pyrenees or Gorges de Verdon in Provence, Corsica offers an impressive range of commendable climbing routes, from short cliff pitches to a number of classic *grandes voies*. Moreover, the **rock** – with a few exceptions (most notably the famous Bavella needles) – is solid.

For short climbs, the island's cream-tinted **chalk cliffs** are arguably the most rewarding. Dotted along a seam running from L'Île Rousse (on the northwest coast) to Solenzara (on the east coast), these are grouped in three main areas: the Nebbio, Ponte Leccia and Solenzara. Pick of the crop are the chalk escarpments at **Caporalino**, Pietralba (in the Ostriconi Valley near Ponte Leccia), but there are also some wonderful pitches around **Patrimonio** and in the **Désert des Agriates**. In the southeast, the **Falaise de Monte Santu**, just north of Solenzara near the hamlet of Penna, offers around fifty routes of varying degrees of difficulty, all of them with superb sea views.

The best known of the island's most demanding climbing sites, the *grandes voies*, are at **Bavella**, in south Corsica. However, you'll find less-frequented routes at several other sites around the island: **Bonifatu**, above the Carozzu refuge; around the lakes at the head of the **Restonica Valley**, near Corte; the famous north cliffs of **Capo d'Ortu**, rising sheer behind Porto on the west coast; and over the red flanks of **Paglia Orba**, the island's shark-finned peak.

To date, only one dependable **climbing guide book** to Corsica has been published in English: the excellent *Corsica Mountains* by Robin G. Collomb (West Co, UK), available through all branches of Stanfords in the UK (see p.22). Most of the classic routes are covered in detail, and there are plenty of technical tips for more proficient and adventurous climbers. In Corsica itself, you can pick up numerous climbing guides in French. Try *Les 100 Plus Belles Courses de Corse*, a good all-rounder by Henri Agresti and Jean-Paul Quilici (Éditions Danoël). For the three big cliffs of the south, *Sari, Conca et Zicavo* by Michel Charles and Jean-Paul Quilici (published and sold locally) is indispensable, while if you intend to tackle any of the *grandes voies* of the interior, around Paglia Orba or Monte Cinto, *Corsica: Escalades Choisies* by Pierre Pietri is the one to go for. Bavella, on the other hand, is best covered in Jean-Paul Quilici's definitive *Le Massif de Bavella* (published by Edisud).

Less confident climbers may wish to employ the services of a **qualified high-mountain guide**

Hiking Vocabulary

The following list is intended primarily as an aid to translating the Parc Naturel Régional*'s topo-guides, but it should also come in useful when asking directions.*

balisé (adj)	waymarked	*longer* (vb)	to follow (eg a river)
belvédère (m)	viewpoint	*météo* (f)	weather forecast
bifurquer (*à gauche/ à droite*) (vb)	to bear (left/right)	*montée* (f)	ascent
		névé (m)	patch of eternal snow
boussole (f)	compass	*passerelle suspendue (f)*	rope bridge
bergeries (f)	high-altitude shepherds' huts		
		pente (f)	slope
*bocca**(f)	pass	*piste* (f)	unsurfaced road
chemin (muletier) (m)	(mulepackers') path	*raide* (adj)	steep
		randonnée (f)/ *randonneur* (m)	hike/hiker
cascade (m)	waterfall		
courbe (f)	bend	*ravitaillement* (m)	provisions
crête (f)	ridge	*refuge* (m)	bothy, hikers' shelter
défilé (m)	gorge, ravine	*rive* (*gauche/ droite*) (f)	(left/right) bank (of a stream or river)
descente (f)	descent		
ébouli (m)	boulder choke	*ruisseau* (m)	stream
étape (f)	stage (of a hike)	*sac à dos* (m)	rucksack, backpack
fleuve (m)	river	*sentier* (m)	path
fontaine (f)	spring	*sommet* (m)	summit (of a mountain)
franchir (vb)	to cross		
gîte d'étape (m)	hikers' hostel	*torrent* (m)	mountain stream
hébergement (m)	accommodation	*vallée* (f)	valley
lacets	zigzags		

Checklist of Useful Items for Low-Altitude Hikes

- map/topo-guide
- compass
- day sack
- lightweight waterproof coat
- at least one pair of long trousers (for protecting your legs in the maquis)
- warm, fleece-style sweater
- money pouch
- change of clothes
- head torch or pocket flashlight
- sleeping bag
- survival blanket or bivvy bag
- whistle
- water bottles (2 x 1.5 litres)
- blister pads and/or surgical spirit, with plasters
- slippers or light sports shoes (for the evenings)
- corkscrew and penknife
- sunhat and high-factor sun cream
- pocket dictionary
- plastic bags (for keeping things dry in your backpack)
- telephone card (public phone booths in Corsica don't take small change)
- toilet tissue

Useful Contacts

Corsica Loisirs Aventure, rue Notre-Dame-de-Lourdes, 20200 Bastia (☎04 95 32 54 34). *Guided group expeditions.*

Move, 20214 Calenzana (☎04 95 62 70 83). *Small-group trips with qualified guides in northern Corsica.*

Muntagne Corse, 2 av de la Grande-Armé, 2000 Ajaccio (☎04 95 20 53 14). *Among the island's oldest-established walking holiday company.*

Muntagnoli Corsi, 20122 Quenza (☎04 95 78 65 19). *A small outfit based in Alta Rocca, run by Corsica's most famous hiker and mountaineer, the inimitable Jean-Paul Quilici.*

Parc Naturel Régional de Corse, 2 rue Sergeant-Casalonga, Ajaccio (☎04 95 51 79 10). *The best source of general information on all aspects of hiking in Corsica; and you can phone for the latest weather bulletins. It's also a good place to buy maps and leaflets for all the marked trails in Corsica.*

(*guide de haute montagne diplômé*). There are only three on the island, all of them well-known and thoroughly dependable: Jean-Paul Quilici, who lives at Quenza (☎04 95 78 64 33); Pierre Griscelli, *gardien* of the Carozzu refuge, Bonifatu, on the GR20 (☎04 95 30 82 51 or 04 95 44 01 95); and Pierre Pietri, expert on the Cinto massif and its environs (☎04 95 32 62 76).

Canyoning

An adventure sport that's been catching on fast in Corsica over the past three or four years is **canyoning**, which involves following the course of a river or stream (usually downhill) on foot. Where the water descends steeply, the route may require ropes and abseiling skills (and occasionally even toboggans). For anyone into climbing and swimming (at the same time), this offers the ultimate buzz.

Basic **equipment** for canyoning comprises a wet suit (*combinaison*), canoeing helmet (*casque*), wet sacks and training shoes (*des tennis*); for more challenging routes, you'll also need quality ropes, harnesses and karabiners. Given the potential dangers involved, it's better to hook up with a guide company, who can also rent out the necessary equipment. One proven outfit is Corsica Trek in Porto (☎04 95 26 82 02 or 04 95 26 21 21, fax 04 95 26 12 49), who offer a range of graded routes, from a leisurely half-day descent of the calanches de Piana (250F) to a ten-hour climb down the precipitous Faille de Revinda, between Piana and Cargèse (450F).

Other prime canyoning spots on the island include: the Falcone and Ladroncellu stream gorges around **Bonifatu** (southwest of Calvi); the **Fangu Valley**; the Spurtellu ravine near **Porto**; and the Fiumicelli and Polischello gorges in **Bavella**.

The greatest **danger** faced by canyoneers in Corsica are sudden and dramatic increases in water level caused by heavy rainfall. The non-porous granite rock drains water very quickly, and streams, particularly those in narrow defiles, can fill up at astonishing speeds. It is therefore not advisable to attempt severe routes in wet or unsettled weather.

Mountain Biking

Given the terrain and state of most of the roads in Corsica, **mountain bikes**, which the French call VTTs (*vélos tous terrains*), have the edge on standard touring cycles as the tool of choice, allowing you to sidestep the congestion and follow forest tracks and old mule paths into the interior. In recent years the island has become a Mecca for VTT enthusiasts of all abilities, and along the marked footpaths you're unlikely to encounter the disapproving looks reserved for off-road cyclists in Britain.

The most promising **routes**, which we've highlighted in the guide, are mostly in the south – around the Forêt de l'Ospédale, Bavella and the Coscione Plateau. The jeep tracks of coastal Sartenais, between Campomorro and Tizzano, also offer stunning rides, as do sections of the Mare e Monti Sud long-distance hiking path between Porticcio and Propriano (see p.219). In the north, the Désert des Agriates, between St-Florent and L'Île Rousse, has a rugged coastal path and network of tracks winding through some of the island's most memorable scenery. Serious mountain bikers should seek out Didier Richard's two VTT route guides (for North and South Corsica), which describe fifty of the island's best off-road possibilities, illustrated with reliable contour maps.

In view of the toughness of the trails (and the relative scarcity of shops supplying spares for bikes), you might prefer to **rent a bike** from one of the main towns and tourist resorts. A list of established rental firms appears on p.28.

Horse-Riding

The experience of riding Corsica's hidden bridleways and galloping across immense windswept beaches is one that few horse lovers should pass up. The island's old equestrian culture nearly died out after World War II, but has been revived over the past decade or two by the appearence of several excellent **centre équestres**, within reach of the main tourist areas, which offer half-day, full-day or even longer treks. Standards of horsemanship are consistently high, and you won't find an animal that's not in top condition. In fact few horses are ever sold; Corsicans pride themselves on keeping their horses at home until they die.

Diving

Thanks to a virtual absence of pollution and factory fishing, not to mention some enlightened marine-life management, Corsica's coastal waters rank among the cleanest and clearest in the

Accredited Horse-Riding Centres in Corsica

Jacques Abbatucci, "Fil di Rosa", 20150 Serra di Ferro (☎ 04 95 74 08 08, fax 04 95 74 01 07). Riding school on a beef and arable farm outside Porto Pollo, on the north side of the Golfe de Valinco. Lessons or longer rides at 55–110F per hour.

L'Albadu, Jean Pulicani, ancienne route d'Ajaccio, Corte (☎ 04 95 46 24 55). Half-day rides and bathing in the roadless Tavignano Valley, and longer routes into the centre (including to the exquisite Lac de Nino). Friendly, family-run place, which also offers inexpensive accommodation (see p.344). 400F per day for the rides.

Antoine de Rocca Serra, 20170 Levie (☎ 04 95 78 41 90, fax 04 95 78 46 03). Rides from the heart of Alta Rocca, in the forests and mountains around the prehistoric ruins of Pianu di Levie. 400F per day.

Arbo Valley, chez François Vascovali, Saleccia, Monticello, near L'Île Rousse (☎ 04 95 60 49 49). One of the island's top centres. Their *pièce de résistance* is a trip out to Saleccia, where you get to swim with the horses on one of the island's most beautiful and remote beaches. 450F per day.

Carole Leandri, Baracci, 20110 Propriano (☎ 04 95 76 08 02, fax 04 95 76 19 48). Day-trips or longer jaunts (3–15 days) from the Gulf of Valinco. Their speciality, unique to this centre, is the *traversée de la Corse*, which takes riders across the island's watershed in a fortnight. 500F per day.

A Madunina à Sartène, Sartène (☎ 04 95 73 42 89). Trips around the distinctive Cagna massif, across the vineyards of the Rizzanese Valley and to the remote beaches beyond Campomorro. 450F per day.

Pierre Milanini, Hameau de Jalicu, 20122 Quenza (☎ 04 95 78 63 21). One of the few centres at altitude, on the lower slopes of the isolated Coscione Plateau. 600F per day, includes bed and meals in a somewhat ropy gîte d'étape (see p.256).

L'Ostriconi, Pierre-Jean Costa, Lama, Balagne (☎ 04 95 48 22 99). Perfectly situated for stunning rides into the Désert des Agriates and around the dry east side of Balagne. 450F per day.

Christian et Claude Perrier, Domaine de Croccano, 20100 Sartène (☎ 04 95 77 11 37, fax 04 95 73 42 89; *christian.perrier@wandoo.fr*). Renowned stud farm 3km north of Sartène in the heart of the Rizzanese wine region. 70–130F per hour.

Mediterranean, supporting a profusion of underwater life that's matched by few other regions in Europe. Whether you're an experienced diver or a novice, you'll be spoilt for choice, both in terms of dive sites and schools. The island currently boasts nearly thirty accredited diving centres, where you can rent state-of-the-art equipment and boats, and gain expert advice on local sites and conditions.

Surface **water temperatures** fluctuate hugely throughout the year, from around 14°C in February to a balmy 25°C in August. September and early October are also good months for diving, with maximum water temperature rarely dipping below 20°C. **Visibility** varies according to the weather, but 25m is about average, rising to nearly double that in perfect conditions. Winds can prove problematic, whipping up choppy seas and swells at any time of the year around exposed headlands, particularly around the island's two most spectacular diving areas, the Réserve Naturelle de Scandola (on the northwest coast) and the Îles Lavezzi (near Bonifacio).

The island's underwater **landscape** mirrors that of its mountainous interior, with sheer drops plunging to depths of around 700m along stretches of the wild west coast. Coating the contorted granite rock formations underwater is a vibrant array of sea life: colourful anemones, vibrant gorgonian corals and an amazing wealth of fish. Among the many species unique to the Mediterranean is the **brown grouper** (*mérou* in French), whose characteristic fat lips and massive speckled body (which can grow up to more than 1m in length) are a common sight in the crystalline waters around the Îles Lavezzi. Other kinds of fish routinely spotted by divers off Corsica include moray eels, John Dory, forkbeards, damselfish, scorpion fish, and the exquisite turquoise-and-red **rainbow wrasse**.

Several **wrecks** lurk off the coast; among them an American B-17 bomber that crashed in Calvi bay after being shot down by a German fighter in 1944, and a Luftwaffe Heinkel-111, which lies just beyond the breakwater at Bastia harbour. The best source of information on **dive sites** are the staff at local **diving centres** (see box below), who can advise you on the most rewarding places to dive – given the prevailing weather conditions and your level of experience. They can also rent all the equipment you'll need, arrange transport and instruction, usually for an all-in package rate, and will refill your bottles for a fee if you've brought your own.

Typical **costs** for a single dive range from 140F to 250F; most centres also offer discount cards for three or more outings. After an initial, slightly more expensive introductory dive – or *plongée baptême* – beginners can also undertake **training courses** for the compulsory certificates required to dive, including the internationally recognized PADI qualification. Fees for the PADI open-water course, after which you're entitled to dive accompanied by an instructor to a depth of 20m, range from 2200F to 2500F and run for four or five days.

Whoever you dive with, be sure to respect the marine environment. Don't feed the fish (not even gouper, whom divers around Bonifacio have traditionally attracted with boiled eggs), as it can upset their metabolisms and make them sluggish. Try to keep your feet away from underwater plants while wearing fins: the sudden sweep of water caused by a flipper kick can be enough to destroy coral. And control the speed of your descent, because enormous damage can be caused to marine life by divers' landing hard.

Selected Diving Centres in Corsica

Atoll, *Auberge A Cheda*, 2km north of Bonifacio (☎04 95 72 03 83, fax 04 95 73 17 72)

Calvi Plongée Citadelle, Thalassa Immersion, 2 rue St Jean, Bastia (☎04 95 31 78 90).

CESM, Le Roya beach, St-Florent (☎04 95 37 00 61, fax 04 95 37 09 60).

École de Plongée de L'Île Rousse, Port de Commerce, L'Île Rousse (☎04 95 60 36 85, fax 04 95 60 45 21).

Génération Bleue, marina, Porto (☎ & fax 04 95 26 24 88).

Hippocampe, Plage de la Chiappa, near Palombaggia beach, Porto-Vecchio (☎ & fax 04 95 70 56 54).

Porto Pollo Plongée, Porto Pollo, Golfe de Valcinco (☎ & fax 04 95 74 07 46).

For details of other centres, consult the relevant section of the guide; most outfits can be contacted through their local tourist office. Note that **advance reservations** are essential during July and August.

Eating and Drinking

In common with their continental compatriots, Corsicans take their food and drink very seriously indeed. At 12.30pm sharp, a mini rush hour in towns across the island heralds the return of workers home, or to a local restaurant, for a leisurely three-course meal, whose dishes may well be the subject of avid discussions throughout the afternoon. The quality and authenticity of Corsican cuisine, in particular, can provoke passionate feelings: a former president of the Chamber of Agriculture was murdered recently for his stand against battery pig farming (see box on p.40), while a wine adulteration scandal at Aléria in 1975 led to a bloody armed siege (see p.309).

For some visitors, the islanders' attitude to food can seem obsessive at times, but it does ensure that standards in restaurants are generally high, and prices low. Even travellers on tight budgets should be able to afford to eat in pizzerias, and you'll be missing out on one of the region's undisputed highlights if you don't sample a full-scale Corsican speciality meal at some point.

Breakfast and Snacks

A typical café **breakfast** in Corsica consists of a croissant or *pain au chocolat* (the barman will usually leave a basket of pastries on your table and bill you according to how many you eat), served with hot chocolate or coffee. In coastal resorts, you'll find many places offering *petit déjeuner complet*, with half a baguette, butter and jam, fruit juice and a croissant for around 25–35F per person. Hotels invariably do set breakfasts for guests, too, but charge more and their dining rooms are often less appealing than a sunny café terrace.

At **lunchtime**, and sometimes in the evening, you may find cafés and small bistros offering *plats du jour* (chef's daily specials) from between 55F and 75F, or *formules*, a limited or no-choice menu. Croques-monsieur or croques-madame (variations on the toasted ham-and-cheese sandwich) are offered at cafés and street stands, along with *frites*, *paninis* (filled and toasted French sticks), *glaces* (ice creams), slices of pizza and all kinds of fresh sandwiches. Cafés in the mountains will make you up a *casse-croûte*, a huge sandwich often filled with a generous slice of *lonzu* (cured ham) or local *saucisse*, and *fromage corse* (local cheese). Most restaurants also offer a wide range of mixed **salads** from 25–55F, although the standard of these varies enormously. A much safer bet is generally a plate of Corsican charcuterie or cheese, served with fresh bread and a small *pichet* of wine for 55–65F.

Crêpes, thin pancakes with fillings, served up at ubiquitous *crêperies*, are popular lunchtime food – at least among tourists. The savoury buckwheat variety (often called *galettes*) provide the main course; the sweet white-flour ones, dessert. They taste nice enough, but are usually poor value in comparison with a restaurant meal; you need at least three, normally at over 25F each, to feel full. **Pizzerias**, serving pizzas usually *au feu du bois* (wood-fired) are also common. With most pizzas costing between 35F and 65F, they offer better value for money than *crêperies*, but quality varies greatly – look before you leap into the nearest empty seats.

For **picnics**, local shops and supermarkets can provide you with almost anything you need from fruit, avocados and tomatoes, to pâté, cheese, yoghurt and salad oils, and a visit to a *rôtisserie* or charcuterie is always rewarding. Cooked meat, ready-made dishes, quiches and assorted salads can all be bought by weight from the latter, or you can ask for *une tranche* (a slice), *une barquette* (a carton) or *une part* (a portion).

Salons de thé, though few and far between, serve cakes and ice cream and a wide selection of teas. They tend to be a good deal pricier than cafés, as you pay for the swish decor, and they generally have a more female clientele and ambience. **Pâtisseries** also do wonderful cakes and local sweet delicacies such as chestnut cake and *fiadone* (see box on p.46), as well as some savoury snacks like pizza and *tartelettes* (mini-quiches) and *canistrelli* (shortbread-style biscuits).

On the whole, **vegetarians** can expect an easier time than they might in mainland France. Several Corsican standards – including *omelette à la menthe*, stuffed aubergines and *cannelloni al brocciu* – are vegetarian dishes that you'll find on menus everywhere; and there are always plenty of meat-free options on offer in pizzerias. Remember the phrase "*Je suis végétarien(ne). Il y a quelques plats sans viande*?" ("I'm a vegetarian. Are there any non-meat dishes?". **Vegans**, however, should probably forget about eating in Corsican restaurants and stick to self-catering.

Full-Scale Meals

During the tourist season, when the island seems to sport as many **restaurants** as it does pleasure boats, there's no reason why you shouldn't eat consistently well for a fraction of what you'd pay at home. The only problem is knowing where to find value for money. The resorts, in particular, are littered with places churning out indifferent food for large groups of undiscerning tourists.

Throughout the guide, we've reviewed dozens of dependable restaurants and *auberges* (inns) to suit every budget. However, many change hands and have their ups and downs, and it's always worth asking locals or French people you meet for recommendations. This is the Corsican equivalent of commenting on the weather in Britain and may well elicit strong opinions. Above all, don't be afraid to take a chance on somewhere off the beaten track if it's been recommended. Many of the island's most acclaimed restaurants are lost deep in the maquis, without signs to show you the way. Dependent on word of mouth for their predominantly local custom, they are often classed as *ferme-auberges* (farm-inns), where top Corsican cuisine, made entirely from fresh, locally grown ingredients, is served in appropriately rustic surroundings.

With all *ferme-auberges*, and in touristy areas in high season, it's wise to make **reservations** – easily done on the same day. In small towns and villages, and during the winter, it may be difficult to find something open after 10pm, though in the larger resorts there's always at least a pizzeria open until midnight through the summer. Don't forget that hotel restaurants are usually open to non-residents, and are often good value.

Prices, and what you get for them, are posted outside restaurants. Normally there's a choice between one, or more, *menus fixes* – where the number of courses is predetermined and choice is limited – and choosing individually from the à la carte menu. The least expensive option is usually the **menu fixe**. At the bottom of the range, these revolve around standard dishes such as *cannelloni al brocciu*, lasagne, *steak frites* (steak and chips), *poulet frites* (chicken and chips), or fried fish of some kind (*friture du golfe* is common), and cost an average 70–90F. Further up the scale, there's usually a *menu Corse* that can by far the best value way of sampling regional cuisine, running to five or more courses that usually includes delicious local charcuterie and *fromage*.

The *plat du jour*, often a regional dish, might well be featured on the *menu fixe*, but for unlimited access to the chef's specialities you'll have to go **à la carte**, where you can expect to pay upwards of 65F for the main course. A perfectly legitimate tactic is to order just one course instead of the three or four. You can share dishes or go for several starters – a useful strategy for vegetarians. In Corsica, as in the rest of France, any salad (sometimes vegetables, too) comes separate from the main dish, and you will be offered coffee, which is also charged extra, to finish off the meal. Your Corsican hosts may also offer you a small glass of *eau de vie*, local firewater, on the house to round off your meal. Fish, incidentally, is sold by weight; the price quoted represents the cost per 100g, so check how much it will come to before the waiter disappears with it into the kitchen or you could get a nasty shock when your bill arrives.

Unlike most Mediterranean countries, Corsica has a fair selection of traditional **desserts**, the majority of them milk-and-egg-based concoctions such as *fiadone* (tart made with soft cheese) which locals love to soak in spirit and flambée. In more serious Corsican restaurants and quality pâtisseries, you'll also come across *beignets*, little doughnuts made from chestnut flour and often stuffed with ewe's cheese (*brocciu*). Run-of-the-mill French desserts – crème caramel, chocolate mousse or a piece of fruit – are also widely available, although rarely as good.

Service compris or *s.c.* means the **service charge** is included. *Service non compris, s.n.c.*, means that it isn't and you need to calculate an additional fifteen percent. **Wine** (*vin*) or a **drink** (*boisson*) is unlikely to be included, though occasionally it is thrown in with cheaper menus (*menus fixes*). When ordering wine, ask for *un quart* (0.25 litre), *un demi-litre* (0.5 litre), *une carafe* (a litre) or *un pichet* (a jug). You'll normally be given the house wine unless you specify otherwise.

It is regarded as self-evident that large family groups should be able to eat out together, and Corsicans are, on the whole, very well disposed towards **children** in restaurants, not simply by offering reduced-priced children's menus but in creating an atmosphere that positively welcomes kids. That said, you'll find locals intolerant of undisciplined behaviour; screaming children invariably provoke disapproving looks and gruff comments in Corsican if left unchecked.

Corsican Specialities

Whereas French cuisine traditionally relies upon complicated recipes and a large number of often unlikely ingredients for flavour, in Corsica freshness and simplicity are considered the essence of good cooking, with the emphasis more on quality than process.

For any important family meal, **meat** will invariably form the main course. Wild boar (*sanglier*) is probably the dish most closely associated with Corsica, whose forests remain well populated, despite the seasonal onslaught from camouflaged hunters (*chasseurs*). These days, however, if you see *sanglier* on a menu it's more likely to be free-range pork than real boar. Pigs, who feed on the chestnuts that were once the staple food in many regions such as Castagniccia, are reared in huge numbers to make **charcuterie**, which in Corsica has been elevated to an art form. Wherever you go you'll find a bewildering selection of cured meats on offer: *prisutu* (smoked ham), *figatellu* and *fitonu* (long liver sausages eaten chilled or grilled), *salamu* (spicy salami-style sausage), *valetta* (cheek), *boudin* (hard sausage) and *fromage de tête* ("head cheese", made from seasoned pigs' brains). Most *charcutiers* are happy for you to taste, and artisanal meat outlets are dotted all over the island where you can sample the full gamut before buying.

Other typically Corsican meat dishes include *cabri de lait* (suckling kid), veal (served with local olives) and, in the winter hunting season, slow-cooked game stew (*tianu*). At this time, many *auberges* will also feature locally shot **game** on their menus: roast woodcock (*bécasse*), partridge (*pédrix*) and blackbird (*merle*) pâté. To accompany a meat dish, you might be offered some kind of fresh pasta (tagliatelle is a favourite), or *pulenta* (polenta), a stodgy mash made from chestnut or maize flour, which can be fried or sweetened with caster sugar, and *eau de vie* or liqueur.

As you'd expect, **seafood** predominates on the coast. Reduced fish stocks in the waters around Corsica (the result of overfishing) mean that supplies are notoriously irregular and prices high. But you can bank on finding red mullet (*rouget*) and sea bream (*loup de mer*) during the summer, as well as a great variety of shellfish – the best crayfish (*langouste*) comes from around the Golfe de St-Florent, whereas oysters (*huîtres*) are a speciality of the eastern plain. **Trout** (*truite*) are fished from the unpolluted rivers and are popular alternative to meat dishes in inland areas.

Mountain cooking is dominated by dairy produce, particularly the soft ewe's cheese known as **brocciu** (pronounced "broodge"), produced only in the winter. You'll come across it stuffed into aubergines, *cannelloni* and omelettes with mint, or deep-fried in dainty little doughnuts (*beignets*). During the summer months, supplies of ewe's milk dry up and cow's milk is used instead: the result is an inferior product known as *brousse*, which doesn't taste nearly as good. In the high sheep-rearing Niolo and Asco regions, hard cheeses are also widely produced, and these can be excellent.

In addition to the desserts mentioned previously, look out for Corsica's wonderfully tangy **jams** (*confitures*), made from fig and walnut, fig and almond, lemon, clementine or chestnut. The island also boasts six varieties of AOC (*appellation d'origine contrôlée* – see box below) **honey**; those derived from the maquis flowers tend to be more subtly scented than the more full-on chestnut-flower honey, which you'll find on sale at roadsides in Castagniccia for a short period in late summer.

AUTHENTICA: THE REAL THING?

The cult of authenticity is something you'll encounter in different forms throughout Corsica, an island gripped by notions of regional and racial purity. In recent years, however, the struggle to define what is "pure Corsican" has spilt onto supermarket shelves. In the early 1990s, sales of that most Corsican of products – charcuterie (cured meats) – took a tumble when it was revealed that some seventy percent of the island's cured meat output came from factories that sourced their pork from Brittany and Spain.

Outraged by the revelation, around 250 farmers got together to form an organization called **Authentica**. In return for the right to use a special stamp of quality, its members agreed to conform to an exhaustive list of criteria guaranteeing that their primary ingredients were locally produced, their animals reared free-range and fed on organic feed (such as wild chestnuts), and their produce free of all artificial additives.

Visitors can purchase the results of Authentica's efforts through its chain of accredited **shops** on the island. Although far from cheap, their stock, sporting the sought-after stamp, ensures the highest standards:

Ajaccio, Délices et Santé, 7 cours Napoléon.
Calvi, A Casetta, 16 rue Clemenceau.
Porto, Hibiscus A Spusatella, La Marine.
Porto-Vecchio, L'Orriu, 5 cours Napoléon.
Propriano, Bocca Fina, rue des Pêcheurs.

FOOD AND DISHES

Basic Terms

Pain	Bread	*Poivre*	Pepper	*Verre*	Glass
Beurre	Butter	*Sel*	Salt	*Fourchette*	Fork
Œufs	Eggs	*Sucre*	Sugar	*Couteau*	Knife
Lait	Milk	*Vinaigre*	Vinegar	*Cuillère*	Spoon
Huile	Oil	*Bouteille*	Bottle	*Table*	Table

Snacks

Un sandwich/ une baguette . . .	A sandwich . . .
jambon	with ham
fromage	with cheese
saucisson	with sausage
à l'ail	with garlic
au poivre	with pepper
pâté (de campagne)	with pâté (country-style)
Croque-monsieur	Grilled cheese and ham sandwich
Croque-madame	Grilled cheese and bacon, sausage, chicken or an egg

Oeufs . . .	Eggs . . .
au plat	Fried
à la coque	Boiled
durs	Hard-boiled
brouillés	Scrambled

Omelette . . .	Omelette . . .
nature	plain
aux fines herbes	with herbs
au fromage	with cheese

Salade de . . .	Salad of . . .
tomates	tomatoes
betteraves	beets
concombres	cucumber
carottes râpées	grated carrots

Crêpe . . .	Pancake . . .
au sucre	with sugar
au citron	with lemon
au miel	with honey
à la confiture	with jam
aux œufs	with eggs
à la crème de marrons	with chestnut purée

Other Fillings/ Salads	
Anchois	Anchovy
Andouillette	Tripe sausage
Boudin	Black pudding
Cœurs de palmiers	Hearts of palm
Épis de maïs	Corn on the cob
Fonds d'artichauts	Artichoke hearts
Hareng	Herring
Langue	Tongue
Poulet	Chicken
Thon	Tuna

And Some Terms	
Chauffé	Heated
Cuit	Cooked
Cru	Raw
Emballé	Wrapped
A emporter	Takeaway
Fumé	Smoked
Salé	Salted/spicy
Sucré	Sweet

Soups (soupes) and Starters (hors d'œuvres)

Bisque	Shellfish soup
Bouillabaisse	Marseillais fish soup
Bouillon	Broth or stock
Bourride	Thick fish soup
Consommé	Clear soup
Pistou	Parmesan, basil and garlic paste added to soup
Potage	Thick vegetable soup
Rouille	Red pepper, garlic and saffron mayonnaise served with fish soup
Velouté	Thick soup, usually fish or poultry

Starters	
Assiette anglaise	Plate of cold meats
Crudités	Raw vegetables with dressings
Hors d'œuvres variés	Combination of the above, plus smoked or marinated fish

Fish (poisson), Seafood (fruits de mer) and Shellfish (crustaces or coquillages)

Anchois	Anchovies	*Daurade*	Sea bream	*Louvine, loubine*	Similar to sea bass
Anguilles	Eels	*Éperlan*	Smelt or whitebait	*Maquereau*	Mackerel
Barbue	Brill	*Escargots*	Snails	*Merlan*	Whiting
Bigourneau	Periwinkle	*Flétan*	Halibut	*Moules (marinière)*	Mussels (with shallots in white wine sauce)
Brème	Bream	*Friture*	Assorted fried fish	*Oursin*	Sea urchin
Cabillaud	Cod	*Gambas*	King prawns	*Palourdes*	Clams
Calmar	Squid	*Hareng*	Herring	*Praires*	Small clams
Carrelet	Plaice	*Homard*	Lobster	*Raie*	Skate
Claire	Type of oyster	*Huîtres*	Oysters	*Rouget*	Red mullet
Colin	Hake	*Langouste*	Spiny lobster	*Saumon*	Salmon
Congre	Conger eel	*Langoustines*	Saltwater crayfish (scampi)	*Sole*	Sole
Coques	Cockles	*Limande*	Lemon sole	*Thon*	Tuna
Coquilles St-Jacques	Scallops	*Lotte*	Burbot	*Truite*	Trout
Crabe	Crab	*Lotte de mer*	Monkfish	*Turbot*	Turbot
Crevettes grises	Shrimp	*Loup de mer*	Sea bass		
Crevettes roses	Prawns				

Fish Terms

Aïoli	Garlic mayonnaise served with salt cod and other fish	*Fumé*	Smoked
Béarnaise	Sauce of egg yolks, white wine, shallots and vinegar	*Fumet*	Fish stock
Beignets	Fritters	*Gigot de mer*	Large fish baked whole
Darne	Fillet or steak	*Grillé*	Grilled
La douzaine	A dozen	*Hollandaise*	Butter and vinegar sauce
Frit	Fried	*À la meunière*	In a butter, lemon and parsley sauce
Friture	Deep-fried small fish	*Mousse, mousseline*	Mousse
		Quenelles	Light dumplings

Meat (viande) and Poultry (volaille)

Agneau (de présalé)	Lamb (grazed on salt marshes)	*Foie*	Liver
Andouille, andouillette	Tripe sausage	*Foie gras*	Fattened (duck/goose) liver
Bœuf	Beef	*Gigot (d'agneau)*	Leg (of lamb)
Bifteck	Steak	*Grillade*	Grilled meat
Boudin blanc	Sausage of white meats	*Hâchis*	Chopped meat or mince hamburger
Boudin noir	Black pudding	*Langue*	Tongue
Caille	Quail	*Lapin, lapereau*	Rabbit, young rabbit
Canard	Duck	*Lard, lardons*	Bacon, diced bacon
Caneton	Duckling	*Lièvre*	Hare
Contrefilet	Sirloin roast	*Merguez*	Spicy, red sausage
Coquelet	Cockerel	*Mouton*	Mutton
Dinde, dindon	Turkey	*Museau de veau*	Calf's muzzle
Entrecôte	Ribsteak	*Oie*	Goose
Faux filet	Sirloin steak	*Os*	Bone
		Porc	Pork

Poulet	Chicken	*Steak*	Steak
Poussin	Baby chicken	*Tête de veau*	Calf's head (in jelly)
Ris	Sweetbreads	*Tournedos*	Thick slices of fillet
Rognons	Kidneys	*Tripes*	Tripe
Rognons blancs	Testicles	*Veau*	Veal
Sanglier	Wild boar	*Venaison*	Venison

MEAT AND POULTRY DISHES . . .

Bœuf bourguignon	Beef stew with Burgundy, onions and mushrooms	*Coq au vin*	Chicken cooked until it falls off the bone with wine, onions and mushrooms
Canard à l'orange	Roast duck with an orange-and-wine sauce	*Steak au poivre (vert/rouge)*	Steak in a black (green/red) peppercorn sauce
Cassoulet	A casserole of beans and meat	*Steak tartare*	Raw chopped beef, topped with a raw egg yolk

. . . AND TERMS

Blanquette, daube, estouffade, hocheôt, navarin, ragoût	All are types of stew	**For steaks:**	
		Bleu	Almost raw
		Saignant	Rare
Aile	Wing	*À point*	Medium
Carré	Best end of neck, chop or cutlet	*Bien cuit*	Well done
		Très bien cuit	Very well cooked
Civit	Game stew	*Brochette*	Kebab
Confit	Meat preserve		
Côte	Chop, cutlet or rib		
Cou	Neck		
Cuisse	Thigh or leg	*Beurre blanc*	Sauce of white wine and shallots, with butter
Épaule	Shoulder		
Médaillon	Round piece		
Pavé	Thick slice	*Chasseur*	White wine, mushrooms and shallots
En croûte	In pastry		
Farci	Stuffed	*Diable*	Strong mustard seasoning
Au feu de bois	Cooked over wood		
Au four	Fire-baked	*Forestière*	With bacon and mushroom
Garni	With vegetables		
Gésier	Gizzard	*Fricassée*	Rich, creamy sauce
Grillé	Grilled	*Mornay*	Cheese sauce
Magret de canard	Duck breast	*Pays d'Auge*	Cream and cider
Marmite	Casserole	*Piquante*	Gherkins or capers, vinegar and shallots
Mijoté	Stewed		
Museau	Muzzle	*Provençale*	Tomatoes, garlic, olive oil and herbs
Rôti	Roast		
Sauté	Lightly cooked in butter		

FRUIT (FRUIT) AND NUTS (NOIX)

Abricot	Apricot	*Brugnon, nectarine*	Nectarine	*Cérises*	Cherries
Amandes	Almonds			*Citron*	Lemon
Ananas	Pineapple	*Cacahouète*	Peanut	*Citron vert*	Lime
Banane	Banana	*Cassis*	Blackcurrants	*Figues*	Figs

Fraises (de bois)	Strawberries (wild)	*Myrtilles*	Bilberries	*Prune*	Plum
Framboises	Raspberries	*Noisette*	Hazelnut	*Pruneau*	Prune
Fruit de la passion	Passion fruit	*Noix*	Nuts	*Raisins*	Grapes
Groseilles	Redcurrants and gooseberries	*Orange*	Orange		
Mangue	Mango	*Pamplemousse*	Grapefruit	**Terms**	
Marrons	Chestnuts	*Pêche (blanche)*	(White) peach	*Beignets*	Fritters
Melon	Melon	*Pistache*	Pistachio	*Compôte de*	Stewed . . .
		Poire	Pear	*Coulis*	Sauce
		Pomme	Apple	*Flambé*	Set aflame in alcohol
				Frappé	Iced

Vegetables (légumes), Herbs (herbes) and Spices (épices)

Ail	Garlic	*Endive*	Chicory	*Petits pois*	Peas
Algue	Seaweed	*Épinards*	Spinach	*Pignons*	Pine nuts
Anis	Aniseed	*Estragon*	Tarragon	*Piment*	Pimento
Artichaut	Artichoke	*Fenouil*	Fennel	*Pois chiche*	Chick peas
Asperges	Asparagus	*Flageolet*	White beans	*Pois mange-tout*	Snow peas
Avocat	Avocado	*Gingembre*	Ginger	*Poireau*	Leek
Basilic	Basil	*Haricots*	Beans	*Poivron (vert, rouge)*	Sweet pepper (green, red)
Betterave	Beetroot	*verts*	string (French)	*Pommes (de terre)*	Potatoes
Carotte	Carrot	*rouges*	kidney	*Primeurs*	Spring vegetables
Céleri	Celery	*beurres*	butter	*Radis*	Radishes
Champignons, cèpes, chanterelles	Mushrooms of various kinds	*Laurier*	Bay leaf	*Riz*	Rice
Chou (rouge)	(Red) cabbage	*Lentilles*	Lentils	*Safran*	Saffron
Choufleur	Cauliflower	*Maïs*	Corn	*Salade verte*	Green salad
Ciboulettes	Chives	*Menthe*	Mint	*Sarrasin*	Buckwheat
Concombre	Cucumber	*Moutarde*	Mustard	*Tomate*	Tomato
Cornichon	Gherkin	*Oignon*	Onion	*Truffes*	Truffles
Échalotes	Shallots	*Pâte*	Pasta, pastry		
		Persil	Parsley		

Dishes and Terms

Beignet	Fritter	*Parmentier*	With potatoes
Farci	Stuffed	*Sauté*	Lightly fried in butter
Gratiné	Browned with cheese or butter	*À la vapeur*	Steamed
Jardinière	With mixed diced vegetables	*Je suis végétarien(ne). Il y a quelques plats sans viande?*	I'm a vegetarian. Are there any non-meat dishes?
À la parisienne	Sautéed in butter (potatoes); with white wine sauce and shallots		

Desserts (desserts or entremets) and Pastries (pâtisserie)

Bombe	A moulded ice-cream dessert	*Crème Chantilly*	Vanilla-flavoured and sweetened whipped cream
Brioche	Sweet, high-yeast breakfast roll	*Crème fraîche*	Sour cream
Charlotte	Custard and fruit in lining of almond fingers	*Crème pâtissière*	Thick, eggy pastry-filling

Crêpes suzettes	Thin pancakes with orange juice and liqueur	*Petits fours*	Bite-sized cakes/ pastries
Fromage blanc	Cream cheese	*Poires Belle Hélène*	Pears and ice cream in chocolate sauce
Glace	Ice cream	*Yaourt, yogourt*	Yoghurt
Ile flottante/œufs à la neige	Soft meringues floating on custard	**Terms**	
Macarons	Macaroons	*Barquette*	Small boat-shaped flan
Madeleine	Small sponge cake		
Marrons Mont Blanc	Chestnut purée and cream on a rum-soaked sponge cake	*Bavarois*	Refers to the mould; could be a mousse or custard
Mousse au chocolat	Chocolate mousse	*Coupe*	A serving of ice cream
Palmiers	Caramelized puff pastries	*Crêpes*	Pancakes
Parfait	Frozen mousse, sometimes ice cream	*Galettes*	Buckwheat pancakes
		Gênoise	Rich sponge cake
		Sablé	Shortbread biscuit
Petit Suisse	A smooth mixture of cream and curds	*Savarin*	A filled, ring-shaped cake
		Tarte	Tart
		Tartelette Sarrasin	Small tart

And one final note: always call the waiter or waitress *Monsieur* or *Madame* (*Mademoiselle* if a young woman), never *Garçon*, no matter what you've been taught in school.

CORSICAN DISHES

Starters

Cannelloni al brocciu	Pasta stuffed with *brocciu* and mint with tomato sauce	*Suppa di pesce/ soupe de poisson*	Fish soup served with toast and garlic
Omelette al brocciu	Omelette filled with *brocciu*	*Suppa Corsa/ soupe Corse*	Vegetable soup with beans

Charcuterie

Coppa	Smoked pork shoulder	*Lonzu*	Smoked pork fillet
Figatellu	Pork liver sausage	*Prisuttu*	Cured ham

Main Courses

Aziminu	Rich, heavily spiced, garlicky fish stew	*Stifatu*	A roll of stuffed meats – goat, lamb and sometimes blackbird – served with grated cheese
Bianchetti	Little fish fried in batter		
Cabrettu a l'istrettu	Strongly spiced kid stew	*Tianu d'agnellu*	Lamb stew
Formaghju di porcu	Pork brawn seasoned with onion, garlic, pepper and maquis herbs	*Tianu di cingale/ sanglier en daube*	Wild boar stew with potatoes
Fritelle di gaju frescu	Fritters made with chestnut flour and *brocciu*	*Tianu di fave*	Pork and bean stew
Lasagne di cignale	Wild boar lasagne	*Tianu di pisi*	Onion, carrot, pea and tomato stew
Pivarunata	Peppery beef and potato stew with pimentos	*Tripette*	Tripe in tomato sauce

Cheese and Puddings

Brocciu	Soft white cheese made with curds	*Fritelli/ beignets*	Small doughnuts, sometimes made with chestnut flour
Canistrelli	Soft shortbread-type biscuits made with white wine and honey	*Fromage Corse*	Uniquely flavoured indigenous hard cheese
Fiadone	Tart filled with *brocciu*		

Drinking

Cafés and bars line the streets and squares of Corsica's towns and tourist resorts, and these are where you'll likely do most of your drinking, whether as a prelude to food (*apéritif*) or as a sequel (*digestif*). Bars tend to be dark, functional places, whereas cafés are more open, often featuring a terrace where you can sit and watch life pass by. Every bar or café displays a price list with progressively increasing prices for drinks at the bar, at the table or on the terrace.

Wine (*vin*) is the regular drink, with rosé the type produced in greatest volume in Corsica. *Vin de table* is generally drinkable and always inexpensive; restaurant mark-ups for quality wines, on the other hand, can be very high for a country where wine is so plentiful. In bars, you normally buy by the glass, and just ask for *un rouge, un blanc* or *un rosé*; *un pichet* gets you a jug. For more on Corsica's wines, see the box opposite.

Belgian and German brands account for most of the **beer** you'll find. Draught beer (*bière à la pression*) is the cheapest alcoholic drink after wine – ask for a *demi* (25cl) _ while bottled beer is exceptionally cheap in supermarkets. A brand to look out for, both as *pression* and bottled in the shops, is **Pietra**, a delicious (purely Corsican) beer based on chestnut flour.

Strong alcohol is drunk right through the day, the most popular drink being strong aniseed-based pastis, especially the local brand, **Casanis**. Brandies and eaux de vie are always available – the latter comes in a variety of flavours, such as *prune* (plum) and *cerise* (cherry), and is usually distilled locally in the villages. In many small restaurants and bars you'll be offered these free. You may also be offered **Cedratine** and **Myrthe**, which are locally made, sickly sweet liqueurs.

On the **soft drink** front, you can buy cartons of unsweetened fruit juice in supermarkets, though in cafés the bottled nectars such as *jus d'abricot* (apricot) and *jus de poire* (pear) still hold sway. Some cafés serve tiny glasses of fresh orange and lemon juice (*orange/citron pressé*); otherwise it's the standard fizzy cans. Bottles of **mineral water** (*eau minérale*) and spring water (*eau de source*) – either sparkling (*pétillante*) or flat (*plate*) – abound, but you'll probably find yourself simply refilling your empty bottles from roadside springs (*fontaines* or *sources*), provided they don't carry the warning "*Non Potable*" (unsafe to drink). That said, that tap water (*eau du robinet*) is of a particularly good quality in Corsica, deriving originally from the fresh mountain streams.

Coffee is invariably espresso and very strong. *Un café* or *un express* is black, *un crème* is white, *un café au lait* (served at breakfast) is espresso in a large cup or bowl filled up with hot milk. Ordinary tea (*thé*) is Liptons' tea-bag tea nine times out of ten; to have milk with it, ask for "*un peu de lait frais*". Herb teas (*infusions*) are served in every café and can be a refreshing alternative. The more common ones are *vervaine* (verbena), *tilleul* (lime blossom) and *tisane* (camomile). *Chocolat chaud* – hot chocolate – unlike tea, can be had in any café.

Corsican Wines

The reputation of Corsican wine has, over the years, been dogged by scandal. In spite of optimum soils and growing conditions, the output at the top end of the m arket has lagged well behind the prodigious quantities of wine pouring from the *vin de table* vineyards on the eastern plain around Aléria. Of 25,000 acres under cultivation, only 2500 enjoy *appellation d'origine contrôlée* (abbreviated throughout this book as AOC) status, the international mark of quality.

Neverthless, several labels have gained a deservedly strong reputation over the past decade or so, and are well worth hunting out. Featured on the tourist office's much-plugged *Routes des Vins*, the best of them all cultivate traditional Corsican vine stock, or *cépage*: la **malvoisie**, responsible for the fine whites of Patrimonio; le **nielluccio**, which yields a deep red similar to Tuscan chiantis (try Antoine Arena or Yves Leccia in Patrimonio, Domaine de Toraccia in Porto-Vecchio; or clos Reginu in Calvi); and le **sciaccarello**, behind the pick of Ajaccio's reds (look out for domaine Comte Péraldi, or clos d'Alzeto).

Especially popular with foreign visitors (although often undeservingly maligned by some French wine critics) are the delicious **muscats** of Cap Corse. A rich, sweet, amber-coloured dessert wine that Corsicans love to offer as an *apéritif* (some also sing its praises as an accompaniment for strong ewe's cheese). Although it's grown in a relatively small area, with more or less exactly the same mix of *cépages*, the variation in soils ensures that no two are exactly the same. One of the great pleasures of touring the Cape and Patrimonio regions is tasting your way through them. Pick of the crop, however, are clos Nicrosi, clos Gentille and domaine de Gioielli – all small family-run concerns of under 75 acres.

Corsica has nine AOC regions; the most famous being Sartène, Patrimonio, Cap Corse and Ajaccio. Enthusiasts can pick up *Route des Vins* leaflets at any local tourist office, which lists the top *domaines* in each area. All of them welcome visitors and offer tasting (*dégustations*) sessions, when you can sample their range, beginning with white and rosé, and working through the reds to a end on a muscat (if they produce one). As Corsican wines are bottled following a short fermentation period in the barrels, the vast majority do not improve over time and are best drunk after a year or two. If you do taste a *vin de garde* ("wine for keeping"), you'll be advised of it at the time. There's no obligation to buy, but few visitors will leave a good vineyard without at least one or two bottles.

Post, Phones and Media

Post offices – *postes* or PTTs – are generally open Monday to Friday 9am to noon and 2 or 2.30pm to 5pm, plus 9am to noon on Saturday. However, don't depend on these hours: in the major towns you might find the main office open through the day, whilst opening and closing times vary enormously in the villages.

Mail Services

You can have letters sent to you by **Poste Restante** at any main post office on the island. The addresses of the principal offices are: cours Napoléon, Ajaccio 20000, and av Maréchal-Sebastiani, Bastia 20200. To collect mail you'll need a passport, and should expect to pay a charge of a few francs. If you're expecting mail, it's worth asking the clerk to check under *all* your names, as filing systems tend to be erratic. The quickest international service for **sending letters** is by *aérogramme*, sold at all post offices. You can get ordinary **stamps** (*timbres*) at any *tabac* (tobacconist). If you're sending **parcels** abroad, try to check prices in the various leaflets available: small *postes* may need reminding of the huge reductions for printed papers and books, for example.

Telephones

To make domestic and international phone calls from any telephone box (*cabine*), you'll need a **phone card** (*télécarte*), available for 49F (for fifty call units) and 97F (for a hundred units) from post offices and most *tabacs*. By pressing the button showing two little flags joined by an arrow, you should be able to get English instructions – when the option is given. In the majority of Corsican call boxes, however, the LCD displays still only give instructions in French: *décrochez* (pick up the receiver); *introduite votre carte ou faire numéro libre* (insert your card or dial freephone number); *patientez SVP* (please wait); followed by *numérotez* (dial). From the moment the call goes through, the window shows the number of units remaining on your card. When these run out, it will read *crédit épuisé*, at which point you can either end your call or **insert a new card**. To do this, press the green button and wait for the message *retirez votre carte*, at which point you should withdraw the used card; you should only insert your new one when the display reads *nouvelle télécarte*.

For **domestic calls** within Corsica and France, whatever the distance, you should dial all ten digits. Charges vary according to the time of day and day of the week, with the cheapest times Monday to Friday 9.30pm to 8am, and Saturday 12.30pm to 8am, or any time on Sunday.

For **international calls**, dial 00, wait for a tone, dial the country code (see box below), then the area code (minus its initial 0), and finally the subscriber number. By far the cheapest way to call abroad is with a standard French **télécarte**, which allows you to call any EU country for 1.85F per minute or 1.45F off peak (Mon–Fri 7pm and 8am, or 8pm Fri until 8am Mon). Calls to the US cost around 2F per minute, or 1.6F off peak.

To make a **reverse-charge international call**, dial 00 33 followed by your country code (see box below), which will put you through to the international operator. You can also make international calls using a **calling card**, opening an account before you leave home; calls will be billed monthly to your credit card, to your phone bill if you are already a customer, or to your home address. Note, however, that the charges for these are considerably higher than calling from a standard call box (90p per minute for BT in the UK).

An alternative to dialling internationally from a *cabine* is to use the booths at main post offices, where you pay after making the call. If you do this, make sure you count your units, which are clearly displayed – mistakes can made in calculating the bill.

Telephones

To call **Corsica from abroad**, dial ☎00 33 plus the nine-digit number (omit the first 0).

To call **abroad from Corsica**, the country codes are as follows:

Britain ☎00 44
Ireland ☎00 353
USA and Canada ☎00 1
Australia ☎00 61
New Zealand ☎00 64

Time

Corsica is one hour ahead of Greenwich Mean Time, six hours ahead of Eastern Standard Time, and nine hours ahead of Pacific Standard Time. This also applies during daylight saving seasons from the end of March to the end of September.

Useful Telephone Numbers within Corsica

Ambulance ☎15
Fire ☎18
Police ☎17
Weather For the coast ☎08 36 68 08 20; for the mountains ☎08 36 68 04 04; calls are charged at 2.23F per minute.
Time ☎36 99
International Operator For Canada and the US ☎00 33 11; for all other countries ☎00 33 followed by the country code.
International Directory Assistance For Canada and the US ☎00 33 11 12 ; for all other countries ☎00 33 12 followed by the country code.
French Directory Assistance ☎12

Useful Web Sites

http://perso.wanadoo.fr/euromail/cormed01.html
A gateway to more than 600 Corsica or Corsica-related sites, with an exhaustive subject directory and some snappy graphic hotlinks. The most comprehensive information bank on the island currently online.

www.internetcom.fr/corseweb
Corseweb's well-integrated site is essentially a platform for booking accommodation (hotels, gîtes and summer lets), accessed through a glossy region-by-region overview of the island.

www.corsematin.com
Extracts – in French – from Corsica's best-selling daily paper.

www.napoleon.org
Everything you ever wanted to know about Napoléon (and a lot more besides), with plenty of juicy links for Bona-philes.

www.chez.com
Corsican folk-dance gigs and festivals, entered via a burst of hellish electronic oompah music.

www.sitec.fr/iledebeaute
Myths and legends of the island, along with profiles of some of those who've shaped its history.

http://membres.tripod.fr/polog2marco
Published by a hiking fanatic, this small but interesting site focuses on the prehistoric, religious and mysterious geological hot spots of the deep south.

www.sitec.fr/imuvrini
This site, devoted to Corsica's most popular music group, the staunchly nationalist *I Muvrini* ("The Mouflons"), includes interviews with co-founders the Bernardini brothers, and audio snippets from their 1999 "Leia" tour.

www.caladisole.com/giramondu
The Web site of pop polyphony group Giramondu features extracts from the best-selling latest album in RealAudio or (less troublesome) MP3 format.

http://perso.wanadoo.fr/d.aubin/cpa.htm
An astonishingly comprehensive collection of old postcards from 1900 to 1940 showing everywhere from Ajaccio to Zicavo as they haven't looked for decades, as well as some fine portraits of local bandits and village characters.

Newspapers and Magazines

The Corsican newspapers with the widest circulations are the two **local dailies**: *Corse-Matin*, printed by Nice-Matin, and *Le Corse-Provencal*, which is more of a tabloid. These usually feature reports of gruesome shootings or hold-ups, which tend to be given greater prominence than news of the wider world, and are really more useful for listings. Of the **national dailies** *Le Monde* (daily except Mon) is the most intellectual and respected, with no concessions to entertainment (such as pictures), but written in an orthodox French that is probably the easiest to understand. *Libération* (daily except Mon) is moderately left-wing and colloquial, with good selective coverage; *L'Humanité* is the Communist Party newspaper, with a constantly diminishing readership. All the other nationals are firmly on the Right. British newspapers and the *International Herald Tribune* are intermittently available in the larger resorts, and in Ajaccio and Bastia.

Weeklies, on the *Newsweek/Time* model, include the wide-ranging, Left-leaning *Le Nouvel-Observateur* and its Rightist counterweight, *L'Express*. The best and funniest investigative journalism is in *Le Canard Enchaîné*, but it's almost incomprehensible to non-natives. Corsican nationalists are represented by the weekly political magazine *Aritti*, with articles in French and Corsican, and there's also a general-interest Corsican monthly called *Kyrn*, which has some articles in Corsican.

TV and Radio

You get both **French and Italian television** in Corsica. French is slightly better quality, featuring a range of programmes from trashy quiz shows to intellectual discussions about wine. The third channel – **FR3** – features Corsican regional programmes, with a local news bulletin every lunchtime and evening and a sporadic schedule of documentaries. Italian television is less widely available; the RAI channels are the best, featuring documentaries and good news coverage. Many hotels also have **satellite** channels, which include at least one English-speaking station.

There are a few local **radio** stations in Corsica, many of them broadcasting within a tiny area.

The best of these is Bastia's RCFM (Radio Corse Frequenza Mora; 103FM), broadcasting in French and Corsican and playing a good variety of music, including the traditional folk music and modern Corsican bands.

The **BBC World Service** broadcasts around the clock, but for best reception in Corsica tune in on short wave from 7pm on 6195kHz or 9410kHz. Atmospheric conditions permitting, you can also pick up the World Service on FM, via Radio Riviera in Monaco, on 106 and 106.5.

Email and the Internet

The Internet revolution has yet to hit Corsica in a big way, partly due to the fact that ownership of personal computers is very low on the island, but also because of the predominance of English on *Le Net*, as it's known in French. It is, however, considered pretty chic to have an email address and increasing numbers of hotels and other businesses are online.

In the guide, we list details of places offering **Internet access**, but cybercafés are still pretty thin on the ground and you'll more often than not have to rely on your hotel's connection, if it has one. Opening a **free Internet account** for use while you're away is easy: head for *www.hotmail.com* or, better still, *www.yahoo.com*. For a rundown of recommended Corsica-related sites, see the box on p.49.

Business Hours and Public Holidays

Basic hours of business are 8am till noon and 2pm till 6pm; almost everything in Corsica – shops, museums, tourist offices, most banks – closes for a couple of hours at midday. In remote parts of the island, lunch breaks tend to be lengthier and opening times less reliable. Food shops all over the island often don't open until midway through the afternoon, closing around 7.30pm or 8pm, just before the evening meal.

The standard **closing days** are Sunday and Monday, and in small places you'll find everything except the odd boulangerie shut on both days. **Museums** are not very generous with their hours, tending to open around 10am, close at noon until 2pm or 3pm, and then run through until 5pm or 6pm – opening hours from mid-May to mid-September are generally slightly longer than during the rest of the year. Museum closing days are usually Monday or Tuesday; sometimes both. Most churches are open all day; if you come across one that's locked, you can ask for the key at the local mairie (town hall).

Festivals and Events

Aside from the nationally celebrated **religious festivals**, such as the Assumption of the Virgin Mary, local saints' days are celebrated in Corsican towns throughout the year, and often include fireworks and processions. Many events are music- and arts-based affairs, with outdoor concerts and film festivals boosting the local tourist industry. There are also a few local **country fairs**,

Public Holidays

There are twelve national holidays (*jours fériés*), when most shops and businesses, though not museums and restaurants, are closed.

January 1 New Year's Day
Easter Sunday
Easter Monday
Ascension Day (forty days after Easter)
Pentecost (seventh Sunday after Easter, plus the Monday)
May 1 May Day/Labour Day
May 8 Victory in Europe Day
July 14 Bastille Day
August 15 Assumption of the Virgin Mary
November 1 All Saints' Day
November 11 Armistice Day
December 25 Christmas Day

Calendar of Events

March 18 – **Ajaccio** *Notre-Dame-de-la-Miséricorde* (see p.203).
March (first fortnight) – **Bastia** English film festival (see p.73).
Good Friday – **Erbalunga** *La Cerca* (see p.82); **Sartène** *U Catenacciu* (see p.266); **Calvi** *La Granitola* (see p.126).
May 3 – **Bastia** *Fête du Christ Noir* (see p.70).
June 2 – **Bastia, Ajaccio** and **Calvi** *St-Erasme* Fishermen's festival celebrated with a mass and firework displays in the harbour (see p.66).
June (third week) – **Calvi** Jazz festival (see p.126).
July (first and second week) – **Calvi** *Festivoce* music festival.
July (third and fourth week) – **L'Île Rousse** *Fête du Livre Corse*: Corsica's only literature festival.
August (first week) – **Lama** Wonderful open-air film festival held in the most unlikely setting of an idyllic Balagne village. The theme is always "*Le cinéma à la campagne, et la campagne au cinéma*", with all the films set in rural societies.
August – **Ajaccio** *Fêtes Napoléoniennes* Son et lumière in the Jardin du Casone.
August 15 – **Bastia, Ajaccio** and **Calvi** *L'Assomption*. Son et lumières in the citadels.
September 8 – **Lavasina** *Notre-Dame-de-Lavasina* (see p.82).
September 8–10 – **Casamaccioli** *Santa di u Niolu* (see p.340).
September (around 14–18) – **Calvi** *Rencontres de Chants Polyphoniques* (see p.126).
October (last week) – **Calvi** *Festiventu* Hundreds of kites and twenty thousand visitors attend Calvi's fastest-growing festival, held on the beach (see p.126).
November (third week) – **Bastia** Mediterranean film festival in various languages (see p.73).

where you can hear traditional Corsican singing and purchase regional specialities.

Of the innumerable Catholic feast days, the most fervent are the **Easter** celebrations, almost invariably featuring a parade across town bearing a statue of the Virgin or of Christ, followed by Mass and a street party with fireworks and music. Many of these rituals also include a procession called a *granitola*, an ancient rite whereby a line of penitents forms a spiral as it moves through the town. The most intense of all Corsican religious ceremonies is the **Catenacciu** in Sartène, an Easter procession led by a penitent who drags a cross through the streets in imitation of Christ's walk to Golgotha.

Of the island's plethora of **folk festivals**, one that is definitely worth attending is the September *Santa di u Niolu* in Casamaccioli, a riotous event involving much drinking, singing and gambling. Corte's *Ghjurnate di u Populu Corsu* summer festival brings together nationalist separatists from all over Europe for a week of concerts and political speeches, although its place as the island's top choral festival has been lost to Calvi's excellent *Rencontres de Chants Polyphoniques*, featuring a cappella groups from all over the world. Mediterranean folk **music festivals** take place at various locations throughout the summer, and there's a two-week jazz festival at Calvi every June.

The box above gives a rundown of the main annual events, with cross-references to the places in the guide where you'll find more details. For further information, ask at local tourist offices.

Trouble and the Police

Despite Corsica's reputation for violence and extremist politics, you are unlikely to encounter any trouble during your stay on the island, provided you keep within the law. Petty crime is minimal, though it makes sense to keep a close eye on your valuables in the crowded tourist resorts. If you should get robbed, hand over the money promptly and start dialling the cancellation numbers for your travellers' cheques and credit cards. Vehicles are rarely stolen, but tape players and luggage left in cars are more vulnerable to thieves. Try not to leave any valuables in sight, and make sure you have insurance (see p.17).

There are two main types of French police (popularly known as *les flics*): the **Police Nationale** and the **Gendarmerie Nationale**. For all practical purposes, they are indistinguishable; if you need to report a theft, or other incident, you can go to either. A noticeable presence in Corsica are the **CRS** (*Compagnies Républicaines de Sécurité*), a mobile force of heavies posted here to handle demonstrations and the terrorist threat, with whom you should have no contact unless you inadvertently get caught up in a riot.

The police have the right to demand identification from any citizen, so if you want to avoid all possible hassle, make sure you're able to produce your passport, or something equally incontrovertible, on the spot. For driving violations such as speeding, the police also have the right to impose on-the-spot fines (see p.25). Should you be arrested on any charge, you have the right to contact your nearest consulate, which is likely to be in Marseille (see box below). People caught smuggling or possessing **drugs**, even a few gram of marijuana, are liable to find themselves in jail, and the consulate will not be sympathetic.

Sexual and Racial Harassment

Women are less likely to experience **sexual harassment** in Corsica than in mainland France or Italy. Men do tend to stare, but they rarely approach or pass audible comment. An in-built "respect" for the opposite sex means that men will never take advantage of a situation – if a woman is in any trouble, she can rely on a Corsican (male or female) to help out. It's not unusual to be offered a drink in a bar, and accepting doesn't leave you open to any harassment – rather it's a case of people not liking to see you paying as a guest in their country. Walking around at night is usually safe, especially in mountain villages and major towns. You're more likely to encounter trouble from foreigners in tourist resorts.

You may, as a woman, be warned about *les Arabes*, a standard instance of French **racism**. If you are Middle Eastern or black, your chances of avoiding unpleasantness are unfortunately slim. Empty hotels claiming to be full, police demanding your papers and sometimes abusive treatment from ordinary people are all commonplace.

Emergency Numbers

Ambulance ☎ 15
Fire service ☎ 18
Police ☎ 17

Consulates in Marseille

Britain ☎ 04 91 53 43 32
Canada ☎ 04 91 37 19 37
Ireland ☎ 04 91 54 92 29
Netherlands ☎ 04 91 25 66 64
USA ☎ 04 91 54 92 00

Disabled Travellers

France has no exceptional record for providing facilities for disabled travellers, and Corsica lags far behind other regions in this respect. Accessible hotels do exist in the major resorts, and ramps or other forms of access are gradually being added to museums, but the situation is far from satisfactory. The organizations listed below can provide various forms of useful information.

TRAVELLING WITH A DISABILITY: USEFUL CONTACTS

France

APF (Association des Paralysés de France), 17–21 bd Auguste-Blanqui, 75013 Paris (☎01 40 78 69 00). *A national organization with regional offices all over France, which can provide lists of accessible accommodation.*

CNFLRH (Comité National Française de Liaison pour la Réadaption des Handicapés), 236 bis rue Tolbiac, 15013 Paris (☎01 53 80 66 66). *Information service for disabled travellers, with details of accessible accommodation, holiday centres, etc. Also distributes various useful guides, including one to Corsica.*

Handi Cap Evasion *http://handy.univ-lyon1.fr* *An organization set up to aid disabled hikers, with the help of an ingenious wheelchair called "Joelette". Check out this French-language Web site for news, views and info on forthcoming trips into the Corsican mountains.*

Britain

Access Travel, 16 Haweswater Ave, Astley, Lancashire M29 7BL (☎01942/888844, fax 891811). *Tour operator that can arrange flights, transfers and accommodation. This is a small business, personally checking out places. ATOL bonded.*

Holiday Care Service, 2nd Floor, Imperial Building, Victoria Rd, Horley, Surrey RH6 7PZ (☎01293/774535, fax 784647; Minicom ☎01293/776943). *Information on all aspects of travel.*

RADAR (Royal Association for Disability and Rehabilitation), 12 City Forum, 250 City Rd, London EC1V (☎020/7250 3222, fax 7250 0212, Minicom ☎020/7250 4119). *A good source of advice on holidays and travel.*

TRIPSCOPE, The Courtyard, Evelyn Rd, London W4 5JL (☎020/8994 9294). *Phone-in travel information and advice service.*

USA and Canada

Twin Peaks Press, Box 129, Vancouver, WA 98666 (☎206/694 2462 or 1-800/637 2256). *Publisher of the* Directory of Travel Agencies for the Disabled ($19.95), *listing more than 370 agencies worldwide;* Travel for the Disabled ($19.95); *the* Directory of Accessible Van Rentals ($9.95); *and* Wheelchair Vagabond ($14.95), *loaded with personal tips.*

Australia and New Zealand

ACROD (Australian Council for Rehabilitation of the Disabled), PO Box 60, Curtin, ACT 2605 (☎06/682 4333); 24 Cabarita Rd, Cabarita, NSW 2137 (☎02/6282 4333). *Provides lists of travel agencies and tour operators for people with disabilities.*

Disabled Persons Assembly, PO Box 10, 138 The Terrace, Wellington (☎04/472 2626). *New Zealand's equivalent of ACROD, offering all-round support, advice and information for disabled travellers.*

Directory

BEACHES are public property within 5m of the high-tide mark; it's illegal to camp on them, however. Some beaches are protected areas, where you are prohibited from climbing on the dunes. And beware of goats – an aggressive hazard in many spots.

CHILDREN are adored in Corsica and welcome in bars and restaurants. Hotels charge a small supplement for an extra bed or cot. Bus and train travel is free for the under-4s, half-fare for 4–12s.

CIGARETTES are the only consumer items cheaper than in mainland France, selling at 7–9F per packet.

CONTRACEPTIVES Condoms (*preservatifs*) are prominently displayed on pharmacy counters, and there's an increasing number of dispensing machines in public places. You need a prescription for the Pill (*la pilule*).

ELECTRICITY is 220v, using plugs with two round pins.

LAUNDRY Self-service laundries in Corsica are thin on the ground; details are given in the "Listings" sections of the relevant accounts. You could discreetly do your own in your hotel room, though technically it's forbidden to wash clothes in hotels.

LEFT LUGGAGE *Consignes* are found in the ports and train stations, charging around 10–25F per item per day.

PHOTOGRAPHIC FILM is slightly more expensive in Corsica than the UK, so bring as much as you'll need. Slide (*diapositif*) and professional films such as Astia, Provia and Velvia are only available in Ajaccio and Bastia. Processing of both is done on the mainland within 24hr on weekdays.

TIME French summertime begins on March 28 and finishes on September 26, and is therefore an hour ahead of Britain for most of the year, except in October, when times are the same. It's 6hr ahead of Eastern Standard Time, 9hr ahead of Pacific Standard Time.

TOILETS Toilets, usually found at the back of bars, can be primitive, hole-in-the-floor affairs, tending to lack paper. Outside public toilets are virtually nonexistent. This can be especially awkward for women travellers, who should feel free to use those in bars or cafés; ask for *les toilettes*, or *le WC* (pronounced "vay-say").

Part 2

The Guide

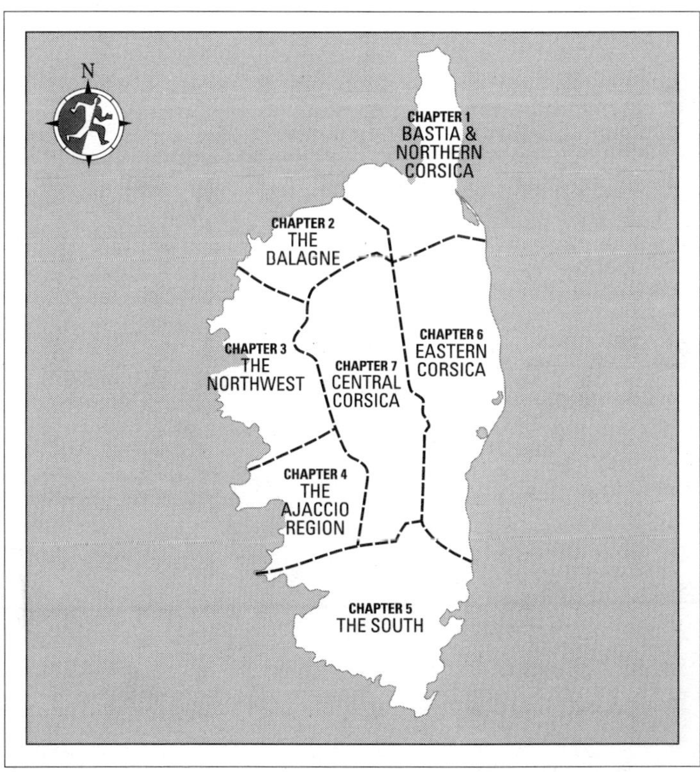

Chapter 1

Bastia and northern Corsica

Bastia, nowadays capital of the département of Haute-Corse, was the capital of the entire island under Genoa's colonial administration, and it was the Genoese who laid the foundations of northern Corsica's prosperity by encouraging the planting of vines, olives, chestnut trees and other more experimental crops – there's a village called Sparagaghjiu (Asparagus) in the hills above St-Florent. The long-term result of this development was that the peasant farmers of the north tended to be not just better off than their southern counterparts, but also politically more ambitious. Thus, when Pascal Paoli recruited his rebel armies it was on this region's downtrodden rich that he concentrated his efforts, rather than on the downtrodden poor of the south. Even today there's a palpable difference in the political climate of the island's two halves, with northerners tending to see themselves as more radical, energetic and enterprising.

A thriving freight and passenger port, **Bastia** is the point of arrival for many visitors, and it can be a rather depressing experience at first, with industrial sprawl on the way into town from the airport, high-rise blocks stacked up the hillsides above town, and no decent beaches. Yet, while Bastia lacks the appeal of sleek Ajaccio, this is the town to visit if you want to get to grips with modern Corsica, for

Accommodation Price Codes

Throughout this guide, hotel accommodation is graded on a scale from ① to ⑧. These numbers show the cost per night of the cheapest double room **in high season**, though remember that many of the cheap places will have more expensive rooms with en-suite facilities. In such cases we list two price codes, indicating the range of room rates offered.

① under 100F/under €15	⑤ 300–350F/€45–52.50
② 100–200F/€15–30	⑥ 350–400F/€52.50–60
③ 200–250F/€30–37.50	⑦ 400–500F/€60–75
④ 250–300F/€37.50–45	⑧ 500F and above/€75 and above

N
Île de Giraglia
Tollare
Barcaggio
Îles Finocchiarola
SITE NATUREL DE LA CAPANDULA
Ersa
Rogliano
Centuri-Port
Macinaggio
Meria
Pino
Tour de Sénèque
Luri
Santa Severa
LIGURIAN SEA
Marine de Porticciolo
Canari
CAP CORSE
D80
Marine de Pietracorbara
Punta di Canelle
Monte Stello (1307 m)
Marine de Sisco
Nonza
Castello
Erbalunga
Lavasina
Plage de Saleccia
Punta di Curza
Plage de Loto
Golfe de St-Florent
Punta Mortella
Lisciu
Patrimonio
D81
Bastia
Désert des Agriates
Mte Genova
Mte Revincu
St-Florent
Bocca di Vezzu
Casta
NEBBIO
Pineto
Mte Ambrica (1063 m)
Oletta
Biguglia
Olmeta-di-Tuda
Défilé de Lancône
Etang de Biguglia
Santo-Pietro-di-Tenda
Bevincu
Rapale
D162
San Michele
N193
La Marana
Mte Asto (1535 m)
Sorio
Pieve
Murato
D5
La Canonica
Mariana
San-Parteo
Golo
0
5 km

a quarter of the island's population lives and works here and in the immediate surroundings. Moreover, despite suffering considerable damage in World War II, the city has retained its Italian character, especially around the **Vieux Port**, a horseshoe of vertiginous buildings dominated by the towers of the Église St-Jean-Baptiste and bulk of the Genoese citadel.

The nearest beaches are to the south along the unremarkable stretch of coast known as **La Marana**, which adjoins the **Étang de Biguglia**, a huge lagoon that's a haven for migrating birds, and the beautiful Pisan church of **La Canonica**. To the north of Bastia, a single road follows the shore of the long rocky peninsula of **Cap Corse**, giving access to some exceptionally beautiful and unspoilt stretches of coast, as well as a string of diminutive ports, of which **Erbalunga** and **Centuri-Port** are the pick. At the base of the cape's finger, on the western side, lies **St-Florent**, a smart sailing centre and fishing village with most of the north's accommodation outside the capital. The hinterland of St-Florent, the **Nebbio**, is famed for the wines produced near **Patrimonio**, for dramatically sited upland villages such as **Oletta** and **Santo-Pietro-di-Tenda**, and for the finest Romanesque churches on the island – Santa Maria Assunta, on the outskirts of St-Florent, and the chapel of San Michele, near Murato. West of St-Florent lies the uninhabited **Désert des Agriates**, a vast semi-barren expanse covered in massive clumps of rock, stands of cactus and the ruins of ancient stone dwellings. The coast here is generally wild and inaccessible, though the beaches of **Saleccia** and **Loto** are amongst the finest in Corsica.

Public transport in the region is generally better than elsewhere on the island, but that isn't saying much. Corsica's train, the *micheline*, threads south from Bastia a little way, passing the Étang de Biguglia, but doesn't serve anywhere else covered in this chapter. Buses aren't common, but you can get one up into Cap Corse or the Nebbio at certain times of the week, and daily to St-Florent, while during the summer services run along the north coast to Calvi, skirting the southern fringes of the Désert des Agriates.

Bastia

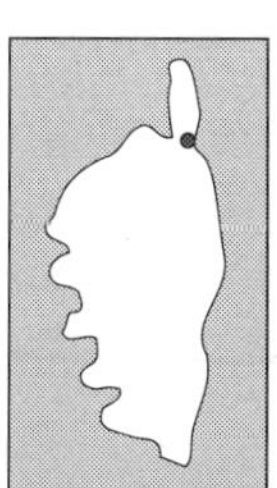

Paradoxically, the dominant tone of Corsica's most successful commercial town, **BASTIA**, is one of charismatic dereliction, as the city's industrial zone is spread onto the lowlands to the south, leaving the centre of town with plenty of aged charm. This charm might not be too apparent from the vast **place St-Nicolas** and the two boulevards parallel to it, which, though flanked by faded Art Deco shop fronts, are choked with expensive cars and busy shoppers. But to the south of here lies the old quarter known as the **Terra Vecchia**, a tightly packed network of haphazard streets, flamboyant Baroque churches and lofty tenements, their crumbling golden-grey walls set against a backdrop of maquis-covered hills. **Terra Nova**, the historic district on the opposite side of the old port from Terra Vecchia, is a tidier zone that's now Bastia's yuppie quarter, housing the island's top-flight architects, doctors and lawyers.

Young upper-crust Bastiais always used to be sent to Italian universities for their education, a traffic that has had a marked effect on the city's tradition of professional success and on its cultural life – it's here that you'll find Corsica's only purpose-built theatre. Modelled on Milan's La Scala, it was regularly visited by the great Italian opera stars, and nowadays, even though some of the gloss has gone, the place fills up for occasional concerts by touring companies from Italy, or for one of Bastia's film festivals. Nothing packs in the crowds quite like the recurrent nationalist rallies, however, for Bastia is something of a centre for dissidence. Discontent with the way the city is run is a constant feature of life here, as highlighted in 1989, when Bastia's civil servants rioted over the mysterious disappearance of local government funds – the disturbances culminated soon after with the razing of the local tax office by a nationalist-terrorist bomb. Highly politicized and busily self-sufficient, Bastia may make few concessions to tourism, but its grittiness makes it a more genuine introduction to Corsica than its longtime rival on the west coast.

A brief history of Bastia

In the twelfth century, when Corsica was under Pisan control, wine was exported to the Italian mainland from **Porto Cardo**, forerunner of Bastia's **Vieux Port**. Moorish raids made the area too vulnerable to inhabit, however, and it wasn't until the Genoese ascendancy that the port began to thrive. At first the Genoese governed from the former Roman base at Biguglia, to the south, but in 1372, when the fort was burned down by Corsican rebels, the Genoese governor abandoned the malarial site in favour of Porto Cardo, a spot close to Genoa and within easy trading distance of the fertile regions of the eastern plain, Balagne and Cap Corse. Before the end of the decade the governor, Leonello Lomellino, had built the *bastiglia* (dungeon) which gave the town its name; ramparts were constructed high on the escarpment above the port, and Genoese families, attracted by offers of free building land, began to settle within the fortifications in an area which became **Terra Nova**.

The sixteenth century saw the rise of a new class of merchants and artisans, who settled around the harbour on the site of Porto Cardo, the area now known as **Terra Vecchia**. The boom lasted until 1730, when Bastia was raided by an army of four thousand peasants, following similar attacks on Aléria and the Balagne settlements. Provoked to desperation by the corrupt despotism of the Genoese republic, the *paesani* went on the rampage for three days, annihilating most of the population of Terra Vecchia, who lacked the protection of the upper-class inhabitants of Terra Nova. Peace was finally restored by the intervention of the bishop of Aléria, but the remaining Genoese merchants promptly left for the safer ports of Bonifacio and Calvi, and Bastia went into decline.

During the **Wars of Independence** (1729–96) Bastia became a battleground. Pascal Paoli coveted the town for its strong position facing Italy, but it took two attempts and the efforts of the British fleet to take the town – the second assault was led by Nelson and Hood, who, though outnumbered by two to one, overcame the defenders in a long and difficult siege. In 1794, in the wake of this victory, Bastia became home for English viceroy Sir Gilbert Elliot, who lived here for the two years of the Anglo-Corsican alliance. Bastia's hour of glory was short-lived, however, as the French finally gained full control of Corsica in 1796, and the island was divided into two *départements*.

Despite the fact that in 1811 Napoleon appointed Ajaccio capital of the island, initiating a rivalry between the two towns that exists to this day, Bastia soon established a stronger trading position with mainland France. The **Nouveau Port**, created in 1862 to cope with the increasing traffic with France and Italy, became the mainstay of the local economy, exporting chiefly agricultural products from Cap Corse, Balagne and the eastern plain. During **World War II** Bastia's economic prominence made it an obvious target, and it was the only town on Corsica to be severely bombed. A German division based here caused much of the destruction, but it was the Americans who caused the most damage, launching an attack as the people came out to celebrate their liberation. Many buildings were destroyed, including much of the old governor's palace, and the consequences of the bombing can still be seen in Terra Vecchia.

Today Bastia's population has grown to fifty thousand, with the long-standing industries of freight handling and small-scale manufacture providing most of the employment, augmented by the burgeoning bureaucracies of local government. The city has also become a hotbed of nationalist activity, with more than its fair share of political assassinations and bombings in recent years; among these was the explosion in July 1996 in the Vieux Port, which killed a prominent Cuncolta leader. However, the worst tragedy since the war occurred on May 5, 1992, when a stand in the **Furiani stadium**, home of Corsica's top football team, Sporting Club de Bastia (SCB), collapsed during a European Cup tie with arch rivals Olympic de Marseille (OM). Seventeen supporters died in the disaster and more than 1300 were injured. Those responsible have yet to be brought to justice, while the issue of compensation for the victims has become embroiled in scandal and protracted legal cases.

Arrival and information

Bastia's Poretta **airport** is 16km south of town, just off the Route Nationale (N193); **shuttle buses** (*navettes*) into the centre coincide with flights, and enter town via Terra Nova, dropping passengers at the north side of the main square, place St-Nicolas, for 50F (one way). **Taxis** from the airport cost around 200F.

Terminus for the *micheline* from Ajaccio, Corte and Calvi (via Ponte Leccia) is Bastia **train station** on the north side of town off the rondpoint Leclerc (gare SNCF; ☎04 95 32 80 60); the pricey *consigne*, where you can leave luggage for 30F per article, is behind the computerized ticket counter.

Ferries dock at the **Nouveau Port**, a short way north of place St-Nicolas, which has two terminals – North (Nord) and South (Sud) – roughly 200m apart. Both have exchange counters (July–Sept 11am–5pm) and ticket hatches for the various ferry companies; only the south terminal building (also known as the gare maritime) has a left-luggage room (daily 8–11.30am & 2–7.30pm; 15F per article).

Bastia doesn't have a proper **bus station**, which can cause confusion, with services arriving and departing from different locations around the north side of place St-Nicolas. Rapides Bleus (☎04 95 31 03 79) services from Bonifacio and Porto-Vecchio via the east coast stop outside their travel agents opposite the post office (PTT) on av Maréchal-Sébastiani, whereas Beaux Voyages' (☎04 95 65 11 35) buses from Calvi pull in outside the train station (gare SNCF), as do Autocars Cortenais' (☎04 95 46 02 12) three-weekly buses from Corte, via Ponte Leccia. Eurocorse Voyages (☎04 95 21 06 30) twice-daily services from Corte and Ajaccio arrive at a small square on the opposite side of av Maréchal-Sébastiani from the tourist office (see map) – which, confusingly, is referred to as the gare routière, even though it's little more than a lay-by. This is also the arrival point for suburban services, and for buses from Cap Corse, the Nebbio (including St-Florent) and Castagniccia. The shuttle service from the **airport** approaches town via the citadel and bd Paoli, dropping passengers outside the Préfecture building, on the opposite side of the roundabout from the train station. For a full rundown of Bastia's bus routes and companies, see "Travel details" at the end of this chapter.

Drivers should head for one of the two large **car parks** in the centre – beneath place St-Nicolas, and in the citadel, on the right as you enter the main town from the south. Parking around town is expensive on weekdays, but free after 7pm, and all day on Sunday.

The **tourist office** is at the north end of place St-Nicolas (☎04 95 31 81 34; June–Sept 15 daily 8am–8pm; Sept 16–May Mon–Sat 8am–6pm, Sun 9am–1pm). In addition to the usual range of glossy leaflets, they hand out useful summaries of **bus timetables** for services to and from Bastia, and free fold-up **maps** of Corsica.

Accommodation

Bastia's passenger port receives twice as many visitors as Ajaccio's, but few linger in the city, preferring to head straight off to quieter

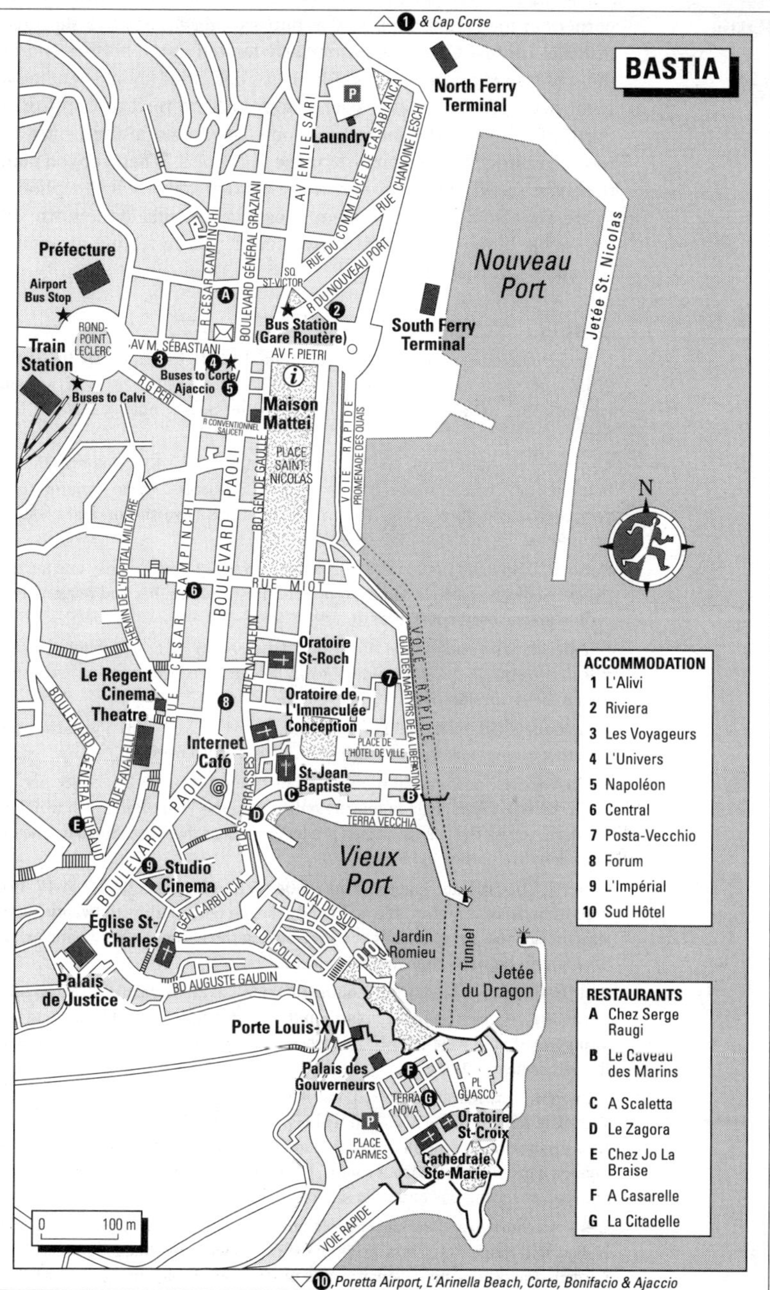

BASTIA
1 & Cap Corse
North Ferry Terminal
Laundry
Nouveau Port
Jetée St. Nicolas
South Ferry Terminal
Préfecture
Airport Bus Stop
Train Station
Bus Station (Gare Routère)
Buses to Corte/Ajaccio
Buses to Calvi
Maison Mattei
PLACE SAINT-NICOLAS
Oratoire St-Roch
Oratoire de L'Immaculée Conception
St-Jean Baptiste
Le Regent Cinema Theatre
Internet Café
Vieux Port
Studio Cinema
Église St-Charles
Palais de Justice
Jardin Romieu
Tunnel
Jetée du Dragon
Porte Louis-XVI
Palais des Gouverneurs
Oratoire St-Croix
Cathédrale Ste-Marie
PLACE D'ARMES
ACCOMMODATION
1 L'Alivi
2 Riviera
3 Les Voyageurs
4 L'Univers
5 Napoléon
6 Central
7 Posta-Vecchio
8 Forum
9 L'Impérial
10 Sud Hôtel
RESTAURANTS
A Chez Serge Raugi
B Le Caveau des Marins
C A Scaletta
D Le Zagora
E Chez Jo La Braise
F A Casarelle
G La Citadelle
0 100 m
10, Poretta Airport, L'Arinella Beach, Corte, Bonifacio & Ajaccio

corners of the island. This may in part explain the relative shortage of **hotel rooms**. Choice is particularly limited at the bottom end of the scale, so if you're on a tight budget think twice about spending a night here. Most of the classier places line the road to Cap Corse north of the port; the more basic ones are found in the centre of town, within striking distance of place St-Nicolas. Wherever you plan to stay, it's advisable to reserve a day or so in advance by telephone. There are also a handful of **campsites** located outside the town, all accessible by bus. The most convenient if you're relying on public transport is *Les Orangers*.

Hotels

L'Alivi, route du Cap, Ville Pietrabugno (☎04 95 31 61 85, fax 04 95 31 03 95). Large, swish, seaside three-star hotel, 3km north of the city, with a pool, car park and private access by elevator to the beach. Among Bastia's top hotels. ⑥.

Central, 3 rue Miot (☎04 95 31 71 12, fax 04 95 31 82 40). Well-maintained hotel just off the southwest corner of place St-Nicolas. Clean, comfortable, very central and good value. Their pricier options have air-con and en-suite bathrooms; the rest share toilets. ④–⑥.

Forum, 20 bd Paoli (☎04 95 31 02 53, fax 04 95 31 65 60). Cosy and attractively chic, with spacious rooms, repro antique furniture, bar and relaxing terrace in an enclosed courtyard. ⑦.

L'Impérial, 2 bd Paoli (☎04 95 31 06 94, fax 04 95 34 13 76). Slightly overpriced two-star on the south side of town. Recently redecorated, but its rooms are on the small side. ⑥.

Napoléon, 43 bd Paoli (☎04 95 31 60 30, fax 04 95 31 77 83). Plush two-star with tiny rooms (few with air-con). Central and efficient. ⑥–⑦.

Posta-Vecchia, quai-des-Martyrs-de-la-Libération (☎04 95 32 32 38, fax 04 95 32 14 05). Large, chic hotel (the only one in the Vieux Port) with wonderful views across the sea from the (pricier) rooms at the front. Smaller, cheaper options are in the old block. ④–⑦.

Riviera, 1 bis, rue du Nouveau-Port (☎04 95 31 07 16, fax 04 95 34 17 39). Well-established, comfortable and handy for the ferry port, with twenty good-sized, clean and airy rooms (some overlooking the harbour). Very popular, so book ahead between June and Sept. ③–⑤.

Sud Hôtel, av de la Libération, Lupino (☎04 95 30 20 61, fax 04 95 30 53 85). Charming, recently renovated place on the south edge of town (1km along the airport road, and west off RN193), with its own car park, sociable patio and friendly owners. ③–⑤.

L'Univers, 3 av Maréchal-Sébastiani (☎04 95 31 03 38, fax 04 95 31 19 91). Variously priced rooms in an old tenement opposite the post office. Their no-frills options on the top floor (no lift) are frayed around the edges, and traffic noise is a problem in the front rooms, but this is the cheapest place in town and convenient for the bus and train stations. ②–③.

Les Voyageurs, 9 av Maréchal-Sébastiani (☎04 95 31 08 97). Recently refurbished mid-range hotel in a prime location. Their three budget rooms are a bargain; the others, much smarter and pricier. Good value in its class. ④–⑥.

Campsites

Esperenza, Plage du Pinède, route de Pineto (☎04 95 36 15 09). About 19km south of Bastia, beyond *San Damiano* (see below) and with fewer facilities, but cheap and within easy reach of the beach. Hourly buses in summer from the gare routière.

Les Orangers, Miomo, 5km north along the route to Cap Corse (☎04 95 33 24 09). Shady well-equipped site near the sea; any of the half-hourly buses to Erbalunga will drop you there.

Les Sables Rouges, 4km south, just beyond the turn off for L'Arinella beach (☎04 95 33 00 65). Grotty and small, and for much of the year next to a noisy fairground, but slap on the beach and easily accessible by bus. Security could be a problem.

San Damiano, Pineto, 10km south of Bastia (☎04 95 33 68 02). Huge, pricey 200-place site with top facilities, including a pool and Jacuzzi; take the road to the left across the bridge at Furiani roundabout (5km south on the N193). Buses as for the *Esperenza*, or you can jump on the train (the nearest station is Rocade). Open April–Oct.

The Town

Bastia is not a large town, and all its sights can easily be seen in a day without the use of a car. The spacious **place St-Nicolas** is the obvious place to get your bearings: open to the sea and lined with shady trees and cafés, it's the main focus of town life. Running parallel to it on the landward side are **boulevard Paoli** and **rue César-Campinchi**, the two main shopping streets, but all Bastia's historic sights lie within **Terra Vecchia**, the old quarter immediately south of place St-Nicolas, and **Terra Nova**, the area surrounding the **Citadelle**. Tucked away below the imposing, honey-coloured bastion is the much-photographed **Vieux Port**, with its boat-choked marina and crumbling eighteenth-century tenement buildings. By contrast, the **Nouveau Port** area, north of the *place*, is bland and modern, with little of interest other than restaurants and bars.

Place St-Nicolas

The most pleasant spot to soak up Bastia's Mediterranean atmosphere is **place St-Nicolas**. Lined by palms and leafy plane trees, the long rectangular square is the social hub of the town. During the evening, with the Nouveau Port's gigantic white ferry boats forming a surreal backdrop, its cafés fill up with snappily dressed young Bastiais on their way home from work, while pensioners take leisurely promenades under the trees. Apart from the camp marble statue of Napoléon in Roman emperor's garb, the square's only real sight is the wonderful Art Deco façade of the **Maison Mattei**, on the north-west side. This old-established wine merchants (July & Aug open till 10pm) sells liqueurs from all over the island, including the famous local quinine-based aperitif, Cap Corse.

Terra Vecchia

From place St-Nicolas the main route south into Terra Vecchia is rue Napoléon, a narrow street with some ancient offbeat shops and a pair of sumptuously decorated chapels on its east side. The first of these, the **Oratoire St-Roch**, is a Genoese Baroque extravagance, built in 1604 and reflecting the wealth of the rising bourgeoisie. Particularly remarkable are its walls, which are covered with finely carved wooden panelling. The chapel also possesses a magnificent organ decorated with gilt and wooden sculpture; hardly altered since it was built in 1750, it is played on religious festivals and in special concerts.

A little further along stands the **Oratoire de l'Immaculée Conception**, built in 1611 as the showplace of the Genoese in Corsica, who used it for state occasions such as the inauguration of the governor. In later years, the English viceroy, Sir Gilbert Elliot, held parliamentary sessions here during the brief Anglo-Corsican alliance. Overlooking a pebble mosaic of a sun, the austere façade belies the flamboyant **interior**, where crimson velvet draperies, a gilt and marble ceiling, frescoes and crystal chandeliers create the ambience of an opera house. The unusually narrow nave terminates at an elaborate polychromatic marble altar, over which hangs an unimpressive copy of Murillo's *Immaculate Conception*. On the left stands a **statue of the Virgin**, which, on December 8, is paraded through the streets to the Église St-Jean-Baptiste. The sacristy houses a tiny **museum** (daily 9am–6pm; free) of minor religious works, of which the wooden statue of Erasmus, patron saint of fishers, dating from 1788, is most arresting.

If you cut back through the narrow steps beside the Oratoire de St-Roch, a two-minute walk will bring you to **place de l'Hôtel-de-Ville**, commonly known as place du Marché because of the half-hearted **farmers' market** that takes place here each morning (8am to 1pm). At the south end of the square is the **Église St-Jean-Baptiste**, an immense ochre edifice that dominates the Vieux Port. Its twin campaniles are Bastia's distinguishing feature, but the interior is less than impressive – built in 1636, the church was restored in the eighteenth century in a hideous Rococo overkill of multicoloured marble. Decorating the walls are a few unremarkable Italian paintings from Napoléon's uncle, Cardinal Fesch, an avid collector of Renaissance art (see p.208).

Around the church extends the oldest part of Bastia, an oppressively secretive zone of dark alleys, vaulted passageways and seven-storey houses locked in isolation from the rest of town. Hidden among them, on the rue Castagno, is one of Corsica's few remaining synagogues, the **Beth Meir**. A plaque on its wall alludes to the anti-Semitism that was rife in Bastia during World War II, after which all but a handful of the town's Jewish population left. Since then, families of Moroccan immigrants have moved in to take their place as the district's much-disparaged underclass, lending a distinctly North African feel to this former Jewish ghetto.

By turning right outside the Église St-Jean-Baptiste and following rue St-Jean, you'll come to **rue Général-Carbuccia**, the heart of Terra Vecchia. Pascal Paoli once lived here, at no. 7, and Balzac stayed briefly at no. 23 when his ship got stuck in Corsica on the way to Sardinia. Set in a small square at the end of the road is the **Église St-Charles**, an august Jesuit chapel whose wide steps provide an evening meeting place for locals; opposite stands the **Maison de Caraffa**, an elegant house with a strikingly graceful balcony.

The Vieux Port

The **Vieux Port** is the most appealing part of town: soaring houses seem to bend inwards towards the water, peeling plaster and boat hulls glint in the sun, while the south side remains in the shadow of the great rock that supports the citadel. Site of the original Porto Cardo, the Vieux Port later bustled with Genoese traders, but since the building of the ferry terminal and commercial docks it has become a backwater, deserted by day, when the clinking of yacht masts echoes around the marina. It's livelier at night, with the glow and noise from the harbourside bars and restaurants. These continue round the north end of the port along the wide quai-des-Martyrs-de-la-Libération, where live bands clank out pop classics for the tourists in summer.

The best view of the Vieux Port is from the **Jetée du Dragon**, the quay that juts out under the citadel. To build it, engineers had to destroy a giant lion-shaped rock known as the Leone, which formerly blocked the entrance to the harbour, and which featured in the foreground of many nineteenth-century engravings of Bastia. To reach the citadel from the quai-des-Martyrs, you can walk through the **Jardin Romieu**, an eighteenth-century terraced garden adorning the cliff on this side of the harbour. Despite the elegantly sweeping stone steps, the gardens are dusty and unremarkable and are a notorious hangout for dubious characters – and certainly not the spot for a picnic.

Terra Nova

The military and administrative core of old Bastia, **Terra Nova** (or the **Citadelle**) lords it over the old port from its perch atop a sheer-sided rocky promontory. Beautifully restored over the past couple of decades, the quarter has a distinct air of affluence, and its lofty apartments and pastel colour-washed houses are now largely the preserve of Bastia's affluent set. The area is focused on **place du Donjon**, which gets its name from the squat round tower that formed the nucleus of the town's fortifications and was used by the Genoese to incarcerate Corsican patriots – Sampiero Corso was held in the dungeon for four years in the early sixteenth century. Next to the tower, a strategically placed terrace **bar** commands a magnificent view which, on a clear day, extends across the Tyrrhenian Sea to the Tuscan island of Elba.

Facing the bar is the impressive fourteenth-century **Palais des Gouverneurs**, Terra Nova's most prominent landmark. With its great round tower, arcaded inner courtyard and pristine peach-coloured paintwork, this building has a distinctly Moorish feel.

The Moor's Head

You can't travel far in Corsica without coming across the island's ubiquitous national symbol, the **Moor's head**. Depicting the profile of a young black male with a white scarf, or *bandeau*, tied behind his head, this enigmatic image crops up everywhere, from car stickers to key rings, postcards to football pennants. Yet its origins are obscure, shrouded in a mixture of myth and historical fact.

The first concrete associations of the Moor's head with Corsica date from the early seventeenth century, when it featured on German maps of the island. This inspired Théodore von Neuhof to use the image on the single silver coin he had minted to mark his short reign as king of Corsica. Not until November 24, 1762, however, was it declared the official symbol of Corsican Independence, at the instigation of Pascal Paoli.

The choice of the Moor's head seems somewhat strange, given the fact the symbol was known to have originally come from Spain and was at one time synonymous with the threat of colonial rule. It first came to the region on the battle standards of the Crown of Aragon, who ruled neighbouring Sardinia following the expulsion of the Saracens during the Crusades. Indeed, the white *bandeau*, which on Aragon standards was drawn covering the eyes rather than the forehead, is believed to symbolize the defeat of the Muslims and their forced conversion to Christianity, while the four heads featured on the dragonese arms refer to the legend of the four Muslim chiefdoms killed in the **Reconquista** of Spain.

The association of the Moor's head emblem with the defeat of the Saracens during the Middle Ages finds echoes in an old Corsican legend. In the story, a young woman named Diana from Aléria, on the east coast, was abducted by Moorish pirates and taken to Grenada. However, her fiancé, Paoli, managed to free her and, after crossing the Sierra Nevada, returned safely to Corsica. The king of Grenada, Mohammed Abdul Allah, was furious at being outwitted by a peasant and instructed his top general, Mansour ben Ismail, to recapture the fugitives dead or alive. After landing at Piana on the west coast, the Moors are then said to have raped and pillaged their way across the mountains to Aléria, where they were engaged, and eventually defeated by, a courageous Corsican army. In the course of the battle, Paoli avenged Diana's abduction by slaying Mansour and parading his disembodied head at the end of a stick around the entire island – whence the now famous image.

In more recent times, the Moor's head has been appropriated by the nationalist movement as the unofficial emblem of the Corsican Independence struggle. Wherever you find a French *tricolore*, you're almost certain to see a black-and-white Moor's head flag flying provocatively nearby.

During the Genoese heyday, the governor and the local bishop lived here with an entourage of seventy horsemen, entertaining foreign dignitaries and hosting massive parties. When the French transferred the capital to Ajaccio, it became a prison, and was then destroyed during Nelson's attack of 1794. The subsequent rebuilding was not the last, as parts of it were blown up by the allied bombardment (see box on p.370) in 1943, and today the restorers are trying to regain something of the building's former grandeur.

Part of the palace is given over to the **Musée d'Éthnographie Corse** (currently closed for renovation, but from 2001 will be open daily: June 9am–6.30pm, July & Aug 9am–8pm, Sept–May 9am–noon & 2–6pm; last entry 45min before closing time; 15F), which presents the history of Corsica from prehistoric times to the present day. Its vaulted chambers contain a motley collection of exhibits from rare rock specimens to Pascal Paoli memorabilia, an array that at first sight seems rather tired yet does include a handful of fascinating historical titbits. In amongst the geological specimens are some rare minerals, including the unique greenish ring-patterned diorite found in Ste-Lucie-de-Tallano, and a sample of the orangey-brown sulphurous arsenic which the Germans used to make gas bombs in World War I.

The museum's archeological exhibits include some of the few remaining Roman artefacts left in Corsica, among them a diminutive **sarcophagus** decorated with hunting scenes. Thought to have belonged to a child, it was discovered in Bastelicaccia, near Ajaccio, where it was being used as a horses' drinking trough. The remaining exhibits illustrate the island's history with old maps, engravings and indecipherable documents, along with cases relating to key figures such as Sampiero, King Théodore and Nelson. On your way around, look out for Napoléon's uncannily realistic death mask, and for the original **flag of Independence**, an emblem of obscure origins (see box).

Most visits to the museum wind up with a guided tour (price included in admission fee) of the renovated Genoese **dungeons** below the governor's palace. Although of little interest in themselves, the damp stone chambers are well worth a look if you can follow the French commentary, which describes in gruesome detail the conditions endured by the 350 or more inmates incarcerated here, many of them chained for days on end to the wet walls. Particularly poignant is the cell in which resistance fighters were held and tortured by the Nazis during World War II; one actually cut out his own tongue rather than divulge the whereabouts of his comrades.

On the terrace of the museum stands the conning tower of the submarine **Casabianca**, which played a pivotal part in the liberation of Corsica (see box on p.70).

Back in place du Donjon, if you cross the square and follow rue Notre-Dame you come out at the **Église Ste-Marie**. Built in 1458 and overhauled in the seventeenth century, it was the cathedral of Bastia until 1801, when the bishopric was transferred to Ajaccio. The over-restored façade is an ugly shade of peach, and there's nothing of interest inside except a small silver statue of the Virgin, which is carried through Terra Nova and Terra Vecchia on August 15, the Festival of the Assumption. Virtually next door, in rue de l'Evêché, stands the **Oratoire Ste-Croix**, a sixteenth-century church decorated in Louis XV style, all rich blue paint and gilt scrollwork. It houses another holy item, the **Christ des Miracles**, a blackened oak crucifix which in 1428 was discovered floating in the sea surrounded by a luminous haze. A festival celebrating the miracle takes place in Bastia on May 3.

Beyond the church, the narrow streets open out to the tiny **place Guasco**, a delightful square at the heart of the citadel that typifies the exclusivity of Terra Nova. A few benches offer the chance of a rest before descending into the fray.

For more on the Casabianca and the Liberation of Corsica in 1943, see "Corsica in World War II" box on pp.370–371.

The Casabianca

The 1500-tonne submarine, the **Casabianca**, whose coning tower now dominates the courtyard of Bastia's Palais des Gouverneurs, was named after 12-year-old Giocante de Casabianca, who died at Aboukir in 1798 when he refused to leave his father's ship after it had been attacked by Nelson's fleet (giving Felicia Hemans her inspiration for the poem beginning, "The boy stood on the burning deck"). Commanded by the redoubtable **Capitaine l'Herminier**, the submarine was used to supply Maquis fighters in Corsica with weapons, ammunitions and secret agents (including a number of British SOE – Special Operations Europe – operatives) during World War II.

The audacity with which the Casabianca regularly approached beaches under cover of darkness, hiding until the dead of night on the sea bed and resurfacing to dispatch the supplies, soldiers or radio operators, made l'Herminier a war hero (you'll come across streets and harbourfronts named after him all over the island). In all, the Casabianca completed seven successful rendez-vous with the Corsican Resistance, mostly in isolated bays on the west and north-west coast (see "Plage de Saleccia", p.109). Her greatest hour, however, was on September 14, 1943, when she successfully transported a rapid response, or commando unit of 109 crack troops from Algeria to Corsica overnight, landing them in the Golfe d'Ajaccio. For the next month, the highly trained soldiers of the company harassed occupying Italian forces and, after the Italian armistice, formed the spearhead of attacks on the German army as it retreated along the east coast and to Italy via Bastia. A memorial to the many North and West African soldiers who died liberating Corsica in 1943 stands on the **Col de Teghime**, between Bastia and St-Florent, where some of the most ferocious fighting took place.

Bastia's beaches

Crowded with schoolchildren in the summer, the pebbly **town beach** in Bastia is only worth visiting if you're desperate for a swim. To reach it, turn left at the flower shop on the main road south out of town, just beyond the citadel. A better alternative is to head 1km further along the same road to the long beach of **L'Arinella** at Montesoro, the beginning of a sandy shore that extends along the whole east coast. A **bus** to L'Arinella leaves from *Café Riche* at the top of boulevard Paoli every twenty minutes; get off at the last stop and cross the railway line to the sea. There are a couple of sailing and windsurfing clubs here, plus a bar.

Leaving Bastia in the other direction, you will find sandy beaches about 1km along the road to **Cap Corse**, but these are rather polluted and the sea tends to be choppy.

Eating, drinking and nightlife

Lively place St-Nicolas, packed with cafés, is the place to be during the day, particularly between noon and 3pm, when the rest of town is deserted. For a more sedate atmosphere, head along bd Paoli and rue César-Campinchi, which are lined with chichi salons de thé offering elaborate creamy confections, local chestnut cake and doughnuts. Late-night clubbers can revive themselves with an early coffee and a pain au chocolat at one of the three cafés in place de l'Hôtel-de-Ville, which open at 4.30am for the market traders. You'll find that most cafés serve croque-monsieurs at exorbitant prices, but for better-value **snacks** try the offbeat retro **kiosks** on place St-Nicolas, which sell hot dogs, crêpes, *paninis* and tasty *casse-croûtes* for a few francs. Numerous **pizza vans** are scattered about town until about 9pm (there's usually one outside the train station), evidence of a strong Italian influence that's also apparent in the predominance of pizzerias and pasta places crammed into the narrow backstreets behind the quai-des-Martyrs. The town also boasts some excellent yet inexpensive **restaurants** serving Corsican specialities, and fish is inevitably prominent: the posh places on the quai-des-Martyrs do the best *aziminu*, a Corsican version of bouillabaisse. Most of the good restaurants are to be found around the Vieux Port and on the quai-des-Martyrs, with a sprinkling in the citadel. The establishments listed below are open daily unless specified.

Drinking is serious business in Bastia. The **Casanis** pastis factory is on the outskirts of town in Lupino, and this is indisputably the town's drink – order a "*Casa*" and you'll fit in well. There are many bars and cafés all over town, varying from the stark, bright bars of Terra Vecchia that are the haunt of old men, to the elegant, dimly lit cafés on place St-Nicolas, where you can sip hot chocolate on low leather seats. The best place to buy wine is *Grand Vin Corse* at 24 rue César-Campinchi; the obliging proprietor will fill up plastic bottles of muscat from the barrels for you, at 5F per litre.

Bastia

Bastia doesn't offer much in the way of **nightlife**. There are a couple of cinemas, the island's only good theatre and a couple of cheesy clubs. The best source of information about all events is the daily local paper *Corse Matin*, produced in Nice.

Bars and cafés

Bar de la Citadelle, in front of the Palais des Gouveneurs, Terra Nova. Basically a sandwich and ice-cream bar that would have little to recommend it were it not for the superb location overlooking the Vieux Port.

Gigatec, 8 rue Fontaine-Neuve, just above the Vieux Port. One of Corsica's only Internet cafés; low light and high prices (minimum 40F/hr).

Café des Palmiers, pl St-Nicolas. One of the few along this stretch with comfy wicker chairs that catch the sun at breakfast time. Delicous fresh *pâtisseries* and attentive service.

Le Pub Assunta, 5 pl Fontaine-Neuve. Large, lively bar with a snooker table on its mezzanine floor and a terrace opening onto the old quarter. A good selection of draught beers, and live-music nights with local bands on Thursdays. Serves fast-food indoors or on a shady terrace outside.

Restaurants

A Casarelle, 6 rue Ste-Croix (☎04 95 32 02 32). Innovative Corsican-French cuisine served on a terrace on the edge of the citadel. The chef's specialities are traditional dishes of the Balagne, such as *casgiate* (nuggets of fresh cheese baked in fragrant chestnut leaves) or the rarely prepared *storzzappretti* – balls of *brocciu*, spinach and herbs in tomato sauce. À la carte only; count on around 150F per head. Closed Sat & Sun lunchtimes.

Le Caveau du Marin, 4 quai-des-Martyrs-de-la-Libération. Welcoming little place decked out like a fishing hut, sharks' teeth and all. Seafood pasta a speciality. Menus from 95F.

Chez Jo La Braise, 7 bd Hyacinte-de-Montrea/bd Général Giraud (☎04 95 31 36 97). Authentic Corsican pizzeria, decked out like the interior of a Castagniccian *séchoir*, whose succulent meat dishes and pizzas, cooked over wood grills with maquis herbs, have made its owner a local celebrity. The *tarte aux herbes* is a must for vegetarians, and the charcuterie's wonderful, while the banana flambé is a must. Bank on around 100F for the full works. Closed Aug & Sun.

Chez Serge Raugi, 2 bis, rue Capanelle, off bd Général Graziani, at the north end of place St-Nicolas (☎04 95 31 22 31). Arguably Corsica's greatest ice-cream maker, from an illustrious line of local *glaciers*. In winter, they also do a legendary chickpea tart to take away.

La Citadelle, 6 rue du Dragon, Citadelle (☎04 95 31 44 70). Gorgeous gourmet restaurant at the heart of Terra Nova. Mostly classy French cuisine (*magret de canard en orange* is one of the chef's top dishes), served inside a vaulted cellar with mellow lighting and an old olive press in the corner. Prices are top-rate (180F *menu fixe*, or around 220F per head à la carte without wine), but this is simply one of the finest places to eat on the island. If you're splashing out, try one of their to-die-for desserts (the *mille-feuille aux fruits rouges* is sublime).

A Scaletta, Vieux Port, entrance on the steps leading from the port to Église St-Jean-Baptiste. Fresh fish is served on a precarious balcony overlooking the boats (reserve early if you want to sit here). The generous Corsican speciality menu is 85F, and there's a good range of inexpensive à la carte options; if you're lucky, you may get eau de vie on the house.

Le Zagora, 4 rue des Terrasses, Vieux Port (☎04 95 34 12 01). French-style Moroccan restaurant, with tables either in a tastefully ethnic interior or on a tiny balcony overlooking the harbour. Try their delicious *tagines*, veal with plums and almonds, or chicken in olive sauce, washed down with mint tea. Around 130F per head. Closed Sun.

Nightlife

What there is of Bastia's **nightlife** centres around the bars, cafés and restaurants of the Vieux Port and place St-Nicolas. A couple of discos and cinemas add some variety to an evening, but you'll have to search hard for a crowded venue, as the preferred entertainment of Bastiais seems to be a quiet night in front of the television.

If there is a concert in Bastia it will almost certainly be held in the **theatre** in place Favalelli (☎04 95 34 98 00; tickets 100–150F; box office Mon–Sat 9am–noon), west of rue César-Campinchi. Concerts of traditional Corsican singing and nationalist rallies are also regular events at the theatre and at the Chambre de Commerce off place de l'Hôtel-de-Ville – check out the fly posters scattered around town.

Of Bastia's two **cinemas**, the triple-screen *Le Regent*, just off the south side of rue César-Campinchi, shows new films, always dubbed into French, whereas the *Studio*, in nearby rue Miséricorde (see map for both), is a small outfit showing mostly subtitled foreign and art movies. The week-long Festival du Film et des Cultures Méditerranéennes takes place in the third week of November at the cinemas and the theatre, showcasing films, backed up by exhibitions, from all parts of the Mediterranean region. There's also a British film festival in the first two weeks in March, featuring fairly recent releases with French subtitles.

Nightclubs are few and far between. In the centre of town, the best is the long-established *St Nicolas*, underneath the *place* at 14 bd Général-de-Gaulle, whose music is more varied than the usual endless Europop. Out of town, *L'Apocalypse*, 10km along the La Marana stretch south of Bastia, is *the* disco to be seen at, but it attracts a mainly teenage crowd, and you'll need a car to get there. Entry is free and drinks extortionate at both, which keep going till dawn (closed Mon & Tues).

Summer firework displays are a regular occurrence, with the most spectacular show happening in place St-Nicolas on **Bastille Day** (July 14), when street parties are held all over town. A solemn procession heralds the **Fête de l'Assomption**, or le Quinze-Août (August 15), after which the Vieux Port becomes overrun by revellers. Other annual events include the **Fête du Christ Noir** on May 3 (see p.70), a **regatta** in June and the **Foire de Bastia** in July, which has stalls – mainly promoting local businesses – and live music in the evenings.

Listings

Airlines Air France, 6 av Émile-Sari (☎04 95 32 10 29 or 04 95 54 54 95); Air Inter, 6 av Émile-Sari (☎04 95 31 79 79). Both companies also have branches at Poretta airport.

Airport enquiries ☎04 95 54 54 54.

Banks and exchange Most of the main banks and automatic cash dispensers are on place St-Nicolas, at the bottom of bd Paoli, and on rue César-Campinchi. The main branch of the Société Générale (best for changing Thomas Cook travellers' cheques) is at the bottom of the square on rue Miot. American Express travellers' cheques are best changed at Crédit Agricole, who have a foreign-exchange counter in the arrivals hall of the gare maritime (terminal sud) in the Nouveau Port. One place to avoid is the Change at 15 av Maréchal-Sébastiani, opposite the post office (July & Aug Mon–Sat 9am–7pm), which charges a very stiff commission fee.

Bicycle and motorbike rental Locacycles, behind the Palais de Justice (☎04 95 32 30 64), rent bicycles by the day or for longer periods, as do Objectif Nature, rue Notre-Dame-de Lourdes (☎04 95 32 54 34). The only place in Bastia offering motorbike rental is Plaisance Service Location, Port Toga, at the north side of the Nouveau Port (☎04 95 31 49 01), which has bikes from 50cc to 400cc. Rates start at 250F per day.

Bookshops The best-stocked bookshop and stationer is L'Île aux Livres, at the top of rue César-Campinchi, which has a great selection of titles on Corsica.

Car rental Avis (Ollandini), 40 bd Paoli (☎04 95 32 57 30), airport (☎04 95 54 55 46); Europcar, 1 rue du Nouveau-Port (☎04 95 31 50 91), airport (☎04 95 30 09 50); Hertz, square St-Victor (☎04 95 31 14 24), airport (☎04 95 30 05 00). For central reservations of these and the island's other main rental companies, see "Basics", p.25.

Diving Thalassa Immersion (☎04 95 31 78 90), 2km north of the centre (head past the marina and turn left at the Elf petrol station), or book through the shop of the same name, on rue Napoléon, just behind the Vieux Port; Club Plongée Bastias, Vieux Port (☎04 95 33 31 28), works from their boat, moored on the north side of the harbour. Both outfits run trips to the famous Heinkel-111, just beyond the sea wall, and to the wreck of *La Cannonière*, about an hour's ride up the coast off Pietracorbara. Rates are around 180F per dive.

Email *Gigatec*, 8 rue Fontaine-Neuve, just above the Vieux Port, offers Internet access for a minimum charge of 40F – for the first hour – and 20F every subsequent hour.

Hospital Centre Hôpitalier de Falconaja, rue Imperiale, Lupino (☎04 95 55 11 11).

Laundry Lavoir du Port (7am–9pm), two doors down from the big Esso petrol station, opposite the ferry dock's north terminal, charges 34F for a machine load (plus 8–10F for drying); cycles last around 40min.

Left luggage In the arrivals hall of the gare maritime at the Nouveau Port (daily 8–11.30am & 2–7.30pm; 15F per article, per day), or at the train station (7am–10pm; 30F per article, per day).

Pharmacies Plenty on bd Paoli, or try Ricci-Luciani, at the top of place St-Nicolas, near the tourist office (8.30am–12.15pm & 2.30–7pm). In an emergency, call ☎ 04 95 31 99 17.

Post office The central post office is on av Maréchal-Sebastiani, between the train station and place St-Nicolas.

Taxis There is a taxi rank at the southern end of place St-Nicolas (☎04 95 34 07 00).

Travel agents Corse Eurotours, 14 rue César-Campinchi (☎04 95 32 52 22); Corse Voyages, 2 av Émile-Sari (☎04 95 34 12 59).

Moving on from Bastia

As Corsica's busiest passenger ferry port, with road and rail connections to most parts of the island, Bastia is the north's main transport hub, and if you're travelling without the luxury of your own vehicle you're bound at some stage to pass through here. Obtaining information about departure times and points can sometimes be difficult, mainly because most services are run by private companies with offices scattered across town. The only place that keeps up-to-date timetables for all public transport services operating out of Bastia is the tourist office on place St-Nicolas, where you can also get advice about onward journeys from other parts of the island, and towns and cities on the continent.

By plane

Bastia's Poretta **airport**, 16km south of town, is served by direct flights from London (Gatwick and Stansted), Birmingham and several major French cities; a full list of destinations appears on p.110. The cheapest way to get there from the town centre is on the beige-and-blue shuttle bus, or *navette*, which departs seven times daily from the Leclerc roundabout, in front of the train station. For precise times of the service, which costs 50F each way, call ☎04 95 31 06 65.

By ferry

Regular car and passenger **ferries** operate all year round between Bastia and the French ports of Nice and Marseille, with a less frequent service to Toulon. Also served in the summer months are the Italian ports of Genoa, La Spezia, Livorno, Savona and Piombino. In summer, be sure to reserve a place, especially if travelling by car; vehicle supplements on all services during high season are around 280F. The fares quoted below apply to a single foot passenger travelling in July and August; children can normally travel for half the adult fare. Tickets are sold through the ferry operators' offices listed below, and at travel agents across the city (see "Travel agents" above).

Corsica Ferries, 5 bis, rue Chanoine-Leschi (☎04 95 32 95 95, fax 04 95 32 14 71), or at the gare maritime (☎04 95 32 95 94, fax 04 95 32 95 55). To: Livorno (June–Sept 1–3 daily; 4–7hr; 99–160F); Nice (year round 1–2 daily; 6hr–6hr 45min; 114–180F); Savona (June–Sept 1–3 daily; 3hr; 114–180F).

Corsica Marittima, 15 bd Général-de-Gaulle (☎04 95 32 69 04, fax 04 95 32 69 09). To: Genoa (June–Sept 2 weekly; 5hr 45min via NGV –11hr;

116–170F); Livorno (April–Oct 1–5 weekly; 1hr 50min via NGV–3hr 30min regular ferry; 96–156F).

Happy Lines gare maritime, Nouveau Port (☎04 95 55 25 52). To: La Spezia (May–Sept 5–7 weekly; 5hr; 109–173F).

Mobylines, Sarl Colonna D'Istria & Fils, rue Luce de Casablanca, Bastia (☎04 95 34 84 94, fax 04 95 32 17 94). To: Genoa (April to mid-Sept 2–4 weekly; 6hr; 190F); Livorno (April to mid-June 2–5 weekly, mid-June to Sept 1–2 daily; 4hr; 180F); Piombino (July to mid-Sept daily; 3hr 30min; 180F).

SNCM, Nouveau Port, BP 57 (☎04 95 54 66 88, fax 04 95 54 66 69). To: Marseille (year round 1–3 weekly; 10hr overnight/daytime; 256–292F); Nice (year round 3–24 weekly; 6hr–6hr 45min; 210–240F); Toulon (April–Oct; 1–3 weekly; 8hr 30min overnight; 256–292F).

By train

Corsica's famous narrow-gauge train, the **micheline** (see p.28), terminates in Bastia, and there are regular services from the town to stations along both branches of the line. During the summer (July 1–Sept 23), four trains run each day between Bastia and Ajaccio (120F), via Corte (60F), while for the rest of the year (Sept 24–June 30) only two services operate Monday to Saturday, with an additional two trains on Sunday. The schedule for the line connecting Bastia, L'Île Rousse and Calvi (90F) remains the same all year round, with two services running per day. Timetables (*horaires*) are available from the train station and tourist office. For information, call ☎04 95 32 80 60.

By bus

Bastia is better connected by bus than any other town on the island, but finding out when and from where the services depart can be problematic (ask at the tourist office for their bus service resumé). Roughly speaking, buses to **Ajaccio**, and to smaller, rural destinations – including Patrimonio, Nonza, Cap Corse, Nebbio, St-Florent and Castagniccia – tend to operate out of the so-called gare routière, at the north end of place St-Nicolas behind the Hôtel de Ville, whereas services to the main towns start from less obvious spots. For **Bonifacio**, **Porto-Vecchio** and buses to the east coast, you pick up the bus from the roadside opposite the main post office on av Maréchal-Sébastiani. Services for **Corte** only, and **Calvi** (via **L'Île Rousse**), depart from outside the train station.

For a complete rundown of destinations reachable by bus from Bastia, see "Travel details" on p.110. Tickets for all services are available on the bus from the driver.

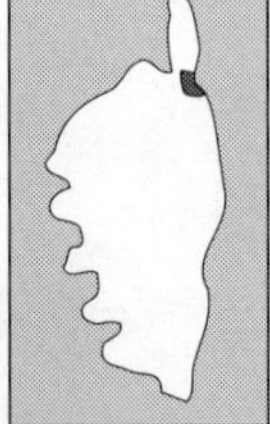

South of Bastia

It's easy to be put off by the industrial sprawl **south of Bastia**, but amidst the built-up areas there are some hidden sights ideal for a half-day excursion. At the Furiani junction, about 3km along the N193, you can turn off the main road to follow the stretch of coast known as **La Marana**, where holiday villages and villas back a sandy beach lined with pine woods. Between this strand and the N193 lies the **Étang de Biguglia**, a wildlife-rich **lagoon** named after the ancient capital of Corsica, now an unremarkable village on the slopes above the main road. The lagoon stretches as far as the **Roman site** of **Mariana**, 25km south of Bastia, where you can see the remains of a twelfth-century basilica and the superb **Pisan church** of La Canonica.

South of Bastia

There is no public transport direct to Mariana. **Buses**, which leave from opposite the Bastia gare routière at 11.30am and 6pm in summer, take you along La Marana as far as Pineto. From here it's a good three-kilometre walk to the Roman site.

La Marana and the Étang de Biguglia

Traditionally the summer haunt of prosperous Bastia families, the sixteen-kilometre *littoral* known as **La Marana** (pronounced "la-mar*an*") is the beginning of the sandy stretch that continues more or less uninterrupted all the way down to Porto-Vecchio in the south. Largely the preserve of joggers, rollerbladers and windsurfers, the beach offers shady pine woods, restaurants and bars and, even though the sea is quite polluted due to boat traffic and the proximity to the town, it makes an agreeable excursion from Bastia when the heat gets too much. All this part of the coast is divided into holiday residences or sections of beach attached to bars, the latter freely open to the public.

Fed by the rivers Bevinco and Golo, the **Étang de Biguglia** is the largest lagoon in Corsica and one of its best **birdlife** sites, thanks largely to the reed beds bordering the water. Of the birds that nest in the reeds, various species of warblers are most common – in summer you'll find reed warblers at the southern end of the lagoon, as well as moustached warblers and cetti warblers, with their distinctive loud repetitive cry. In winter, Biguglia is a stop-off point for migrating grey herons, kingfishers, great crested grebes, little grebes, water rails and various species of duck, such as the spectacular red-crested pochard, identifiable by its red bill, red feet and a bright-red head.

Mariana

The Roman town of **Mariana**, just south of Étang de Biguglia, can be approached by taking the turning for the airport, 16km along the N193, or the more scenic coastal route through La Marana.

Founded in 93 BC as a military colony, Mariana had become a Christian centre by the fourth century, when its basilica was built. The settlement was damaged severely by the Vandals and Ostrogoths in the fifth and sixth centuries, and by the time of the Genoese occupation Mariana had become so waterlogged and malarial that it had to be abandoned. Now the ruins and old Pisan church form an incongruous counterpoint to the space-age architecture of Poretta airport across the fields, whose constant traffic – both overhead and along the road – detract somewhat from the forlorn beauty of the place.

The houses, baths and basilica are now too tumbledown to be of great interest, but the square **baptistry** has a remarkable mosaic floor decorated with dancing dolphins and fish looped around a bearded Neptune – Christianized pagan images representing the Four Rivers of Paradise.

Adjacent to Mariana stands the church of Santa Maria Assunta, commonly known as **La Canonica**. Erected in 1119 close to the old capital of Biguglia, it is the finest of around three hundred churches built by the Pisans in their effort to evangelize the island. The perfectly proportioned edifice, modelled on a Roman basilica, is decorated outside with Corinthian capitals plundered from the main Mariana site and with plates of Cap Corse marble, their delicate pink and yellow ochre hues fusing to stunning effect. Carvings of animals and Celtic-like geometric bands also embellish the arch above the door. The interior has been recently restored in a very plain style, and is used for concerts and for Mass on religious festivals.

Marooned in muddy fields about 300m to the south of La Canonica stands **San Parteo**, built in the eleventh and twelfth centuries over the site of a pagan burial ground. A smaller edifice than La Canonica, the church also displays some elegant arcading and stone sculpture – on the south side, the door lintel is supported by two writhing beasts reaching to a central tree, a motif of Oriental origins.

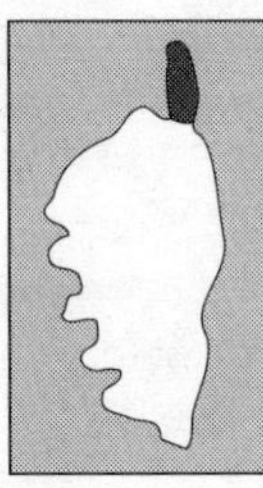

Cap Corse

Until Napoléon III had a coach road built around **Cap Corse** in the nineteenth century, the promontory was effectively cut off from the rest of the island, relying on Italian maritime traffic for its income – hence its distinctive Tuscan dialect. Ruled by feudal lords who retained substantial independence from the island's governors, it maintained a peaceful existence that greatly influenced the character of the Capicursini, or **Cap Corsins**. For all the changes brought by the modern world, Cap Corse still feels like a separate country.

Forty kilometres long and only fifteen across, the cape is divided by a spine of mountains called the Serra, which peaks at **Cima di e Folicce**, 1324m above sea level. The coast on the **east side** of this divide is characterized by tiny ports or *marines*, tucked into gently sloping river mouths, alongside coves that become sandier as you go further north. The villages of the **western coast** are sited on rugged cliffs, high above the rough sea and tiny rocky inlets that can be glimpsed from the corniche road. Cap Corse remains virtually untainted by tourism: wild flowers grow in profusion on the mountainsides in spring, goats graze freely, fishing villages are quiet and traditional, and many of the inland slopes are occupied by vineyards,

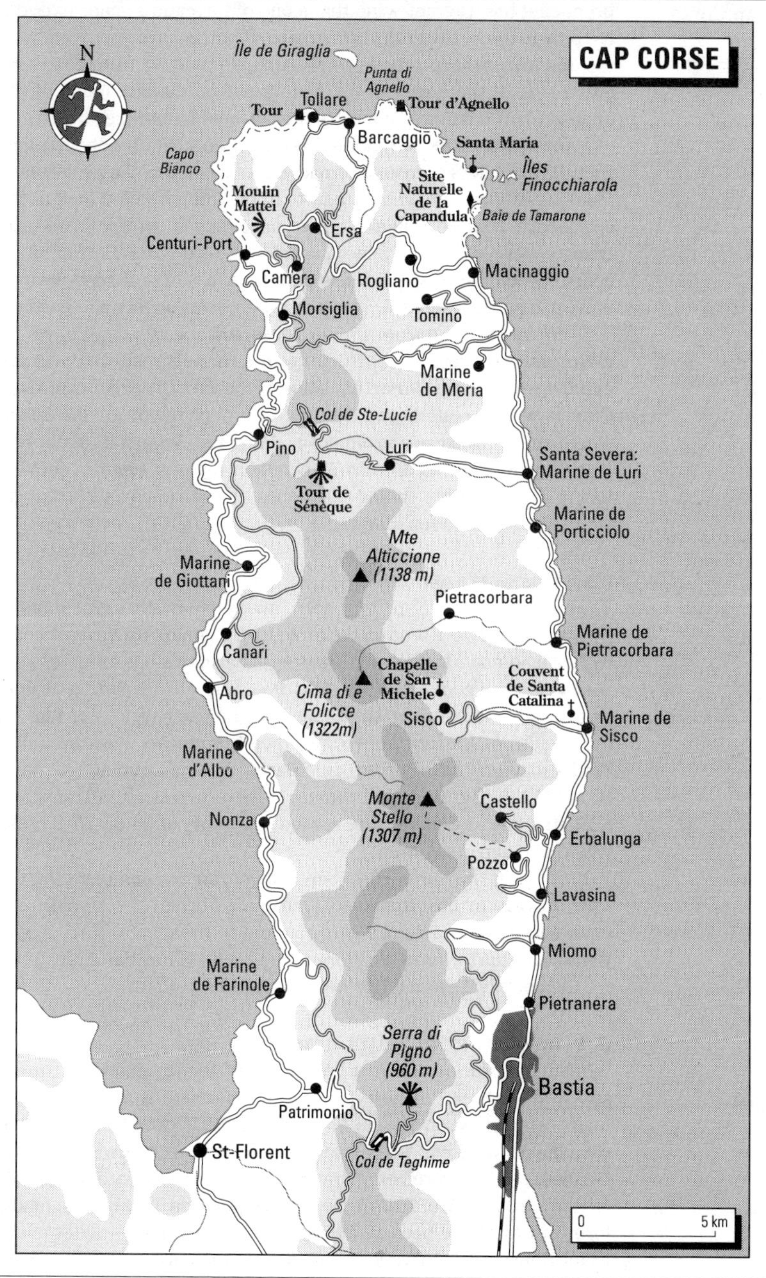
CAP CORSE
N
Île de Giraglia
Punta di Agnello
Tollare
Tour
Tour d'Agnello
Barcaggio
Santa Maria
Îles Finocchiarola
Capo Bianco
Moulin Mattei
Site Naturelle de la Capandula
Baie de Tamarone
Ersa
Centuri-Port
Camera
Rogliano
Macinaggio
Morsiglia
Tomino
Marine de Meria
Col de Ste-Lucie
Pino
Luri
Santa Severa: Marine de Luri
Tour de Sénèque
Marine de Porticciolo
Mte Alticcione (1138 m)
Marine de Giottani
Pietracorbara
Marine de Pietracorbara
Canari
Chapelle de San Michele
Couvent de Santa Catalina
Abro
Cima di e Folicce (1322m)
Sisco
Marine de Sisco
Marine d'Albo
Monte Stello (1307 m)
Castello
Nonza
Erbalunga
Pozzo
Lavasina
Miomo
Marine de Farinole
Pietranera
Serra di Pigno (960 m)
Bastia
Patrimonio
St-Florent
Col de Teghime
0
5 km

producing the fragrant **wine** that's one of the cape's major exports. It's only in the last twenty years or so that hotels have appeared, with the highest concentration at **Macinaggio** and **Centuri-Port**, on either side of the northern tip. Unfortunately, though, much of the once verdant countryside has been blackened by fire (see p.115).

Many people tackle the hundred-kilometre corniche in a one-day tour from Bastia. A less arduous alternative is to cut across the peninsula at Santa Severa, thereby getting a taste of the interior and a look at the spectacular **Tour de Sénèque**, where, according to popular legend, the Roman poet-philosopher Seneca spent his exiled years. Best of all, of course, would be to spend a few days here. If you're driving, bear in mind that petrol stations are few and far between, so fill up in Bastia.

Even more conspicuous than these towers are the **convents**, **churches** and in particular **Romanesque chapels** scattered over the cape; it was on Cap Corse that some of the first Christian centres in Corsica were created, and this was the only region of the island where the Franciscan movement had any real influence. Elaborate marble **mausoleums** are also a common feature, often occupying lonely places on the inland hill-slopes and standing out strikingly white in a sea of green maquis.

Cap Corse transport

The main villages on Cap Corse are connected to Bastia's gare routière by **bus**, but services tend to be infrequent. Running up the east coast to Rogliano and Macinaggio, Transports Saladini's bus operates year round (Mon, Wed & Fri; 40F; ☎04 95 35 43 88), departing at 4pm from Bastia and arriving 1hr 15min later in Macinaggio. For Luri, in the middle of the northern cape, there's Autocars Pavarini Jules' Wednesday-only bus (departs 4pm Bastia, arrives 4.50pm; 35F; ☎04 95 35 00 11). The other year-round service on Cap Corse is Transports Saoletti's bus to Canari (Mon & Wed; 1hr; 45F; ☎04 95 37 84 05), which also departs at 4pm.

From early July until early September, you can complete the full *tour du Cap* by bus, thanks to Transports Micheli's convenient circular service from Bastia's gare routière to Erbalunga, Macinaggio, Centuri, Canari, Nonza, St-Florent and Oletta (Mon–Sat daily; 110F for the complete circuit, 40F to Centuri, 30F to Nonza).

A brief history of Cap Corse

Inhabited by various ancient civilizations – the Phoenicians, Greeks and Romans were all here – Cap Corse became significant in the tenth century, when the da Massa lords came over from Pisa and established fiefdoms across the region. By the following century Genoese settlers were being drawn to the cape's vineyards, and after Genoa's trouncing of Pisa at the Battle of Meloria in 1284, the feudal lords of Cap Corse became important – if intermittent – allies of the island's new rulers. Two local families shared most of the cape from this time – the da Mare clan held the north, whilst the da Gentile ruled the south, a situation that lasted into the late eighteenth century, when the French gained control of the island.

Although subject to the Genoese, the lords of Cap Corse were allowed a certain autonomy: largely ignored by the rest of the island, and well positioned for trading with the French and Tuscan ports, they were able to control their profits to a greater extent than their compatriots in the south. By the seventeenth century, Cap Corse was economically more successful than any other region in Corsica, but **piracy** was a huge problem for the cape's tiny ports, which is why the coast is dotted with some thirty fortified towers, built as refuges for the local villagers in times of trouble (see the box on p.100).

The late eighteenth and early nineteenth centuries saw an upsurge in emigration from the cape, as a shortage of agricultural land (brought about by a sharp rise in population) forced thousands of Capicursini to seek their fortunes in the colonies of South America and the Caribbean. Many of the emigrants grew rich on gold prospecting and coffee or sugar planting, and in time returned home to live in large villas, or *palazzi*, erected on their ancestral land. Known as *les maisons d'Américains*, these ostentatious country mansions, with their colonial-style colonnades and arches, lend a distinctively Central or South American feel to villages such as Rogliano, Morsiglia and Pino. Most are still in use, and during the summer welcome families from Puerto Rico or Venezuela, where Corsican colonies still exist – indeed, one former Venezuelan president was a Corsican.

Today, though wine continues to be a major export and nationalist politicians are promoting exploitation of the indigenous cedrat fruit, from which a liqueur and jam are made locally, tourism has become the only way to make real money. So far, however, it has been slow to develop on the cape, and there are few spots where concrete spoils the view.

The eastern cape

The **eastern coast** of the cape progresses from tightly packed villas immediately outside Bastia to lonely *marines* such as **Pietracorbara** in the north, via fishing villages such as **Porticciolu** and **Erbalunga**. The D80, which follows the coast all the way around Cap Corse as far as St-Florent, is mostly built up within a short radius of Bastia (about the first 5km), so it's a good idea to leave the main road at the roundabout a couple of kilometres out of town, taking the turn-off signposted as the "**Route de la Corniche**". This loop bypasses the worst of the developed strip, gives a good panorama from the mountains and, on a clear day, the Tuscan islands of Elba and Monte Cristo.

Lavasina

LAVASINA, 5km north up the coast from Bastia, grew up around a sanctuary created in the sixteenth century by one Danesi, who was given a painting of the Virgin which he donated to the sanctuary in lieu of payment for some merchandise. It became a place of pilgrimage in 1675, when a nun called Marie-Agnès, having disembarked from a boat to take shelter from a storm, prayed at the sanctuary and was promptly cured of her paralysis of the legs. Within two years the **Église Notre-Dame-des-Grâces** had been built to house the miraculous painting. An ugly rectangular grey clock tower, surmounted by a stiff statue of the Virgin, was added to the large pink building in the nineteenth century and effectively ruined the classical lines of the church. Inside, however, you might as well take a look at the famous **Madone de Lavasina**, which hangs above the great black-and-white altar. The painting, a melancholy work from the school of the Umbrian artist Pietro Perugino, is still believed to perform miracles and is the focus of a **festival** on September 8, involving a candlelit procession on the beach and a midnight Mass.

Next to the church, a granite panel indicates the head of the trail to **Monte Stello** (5hr); if you have a car, you can cut out the first part of this route (and save 2hr) by driving up to Pozzo, above Erbalunga. An account of the hike appears on p.84.

Erbalunga

Built along a rocky promontory 3km north of Lavasina, the small honey-pot port of **ERBALUNGA** is the highlight of the east coast, with its old stone buildings stacked like crooked boxes behind a cosy harbour and ruined Genoese watchtower. A little colony of French artists lived here in the 1920s, perhaps drawn by the fact that the ancestors of the poet Paul Valéry came from the village, which has continued to attract a steady stream of admirers ever since. During the winter, well-to-do Bastiais frequent the harbourside restaurants, while in summer Erbalunga is transformed into a veritable cultural enclave, with concerts and art exhibitions adding a spark to the local nightlife.

A port since the time of the Phoenicians, Erbalunga was once a more important trading centre than Bastia or Ajaccio. With the increasing exportation of wine and olive oil in the eleventh century, it became the capital of an independent village state, ruled by the da Gentile family, who lived in the *palazzo* that dominates **place de Gaulle**. Its ascendancy came to an end in the 1550s, when long-running conflicts within the da Gentile camp finally broke the family's hold on this part of the cape, and in 1557 French troops destroyed the port, reducing the fifteenth-century tower to the ruined state it's in today.

Erbalunga is famous for its **Good Friday procession** known as the **Cerca** (Search), which has evolved from an ancient fertility rite.

Starting at Église St-Érasme, at the entrance to the village, a procession of hooded penitents covers a distance of 14km, passing through the hamlets of Pozzo, Poretto and Silgaggia in the mountains and picking up people on the way. At nightfall, back in Erbalunga, the penitents form a spiral known as the *Granitola* (Snail); candles held high, they move to place de Gaulle and the spiral unwinds, while a separate part of the procession forms the shape of the cross.

Practicalities

Most of the village is closed to vehicles, but there's a **car park** on the left-hand side of the main road from Bastia, where the regular **bus** from place St-Nicolas stops. From here, the harbour is reached through place de Gaulle, where the mairie and the *palazzo* Gentile stand side by side. On the quayside, a couple of **bars** shaded by an enormous chestnut tree look out across the water to the tower.

The one **hotel**, the congenial *Castel' Brando* (☎04 95 30 10 30, fax 04 95 33 98 18; ③; April to mid-Oct), stands at the entrance to the square, shaded by a curtain of mature date palms. It's an elegant, old, stone-floored building with a lovely pool and its own car park. Period furniture and antique Corsican engravings fill the rooms and apartments, which are all air-conditioned; those on the top floor have great views. Rates soar in July and August, but at other times you can spend the night here for under 400F. Breakfast is served in the courtyard.

Pick of the harbourside **restaurants** is the long-established *Le Pirate* (☎04 95 33 24 20; Easter–Oct), which specializes in fresh seafood. It has a 130F menu featuring local fish dishes, but vegetarians will do better with entrées from the *carte* – aubergines baked in parmesan or grilled vegetables with mozzarella. A less expensive option is *A Piazzetta* (☎04 95 33 28 69), in the tiny square behind the harbour, which does acceptable pizzas and has a great selection of fresh pasta dishes from 60F to 85F. In a similar price bracket, *Chez Antoine*, three minutes' walk north of the *Castel Brando* on the main street, does delicious *moules marinières* (55F), as well as pizzas (from 45F) and a good selection of *grillades* on their budget menu.

Castello

The thirteenth-century castle at **CASTELLO**, one of the many bases of the da Gentile family, stands 2km inland from Erbalunga, beyond the hamlet of Mausoleo. This ghostly village, dominated by the now-ruined castle, was the scene of a family feud that lasted a hundred years and split the da Gentile family into two factions. The strife began in 1450, when the lady of the castle, known simply as *La Sposetta* (The Little Wife), began an affair with one Guelfuccio, cousin of her husband Vinciguerra da Gentile. On discovery of this deception, Vinciguerra stabbed his errant wife to death, chased his

Monte Stello

The starting point for the climb up **Monte Stello** (1307m), the second-highest peak on Cap Corse (the highest is neighbouring Cima di e Folicce, 1324m), is the medieval hamlet of **Pozzo**, 3km from Erbalunga. From the summit, a superb panorama extends west across Golfe de St-Florent to encompass the island's main peaks, and east across the sea to the Tuscan coast. To enjoy the views, though, you'll have to set off early in the morning, as cloud invariably obscures the top of Monte Stello from 11am onwards. Allow around five hours for the round-trip.

In Pozzo's square, a sign marked "Monte Stello 3h" points the way through the houses into the maquis, where the trail starts off clearly marked by arrows and daubs of blue paint. The first section of the hike climbs steeply west into the deep Arega stream valley, via the **Bergerie de Teghime**, reaching the windswept **Bocca di Santa Maria** pass, a distinctive niche in the Cap's watershed where you get your first hard-earned glimpse of the Golfe de St-Florent, after around 1hr 30min. From here it's another 1hr 40min and 169m haul to the summit. Return by the same route.

For this walk we strongly recommend you take along IGN map #4347 OT Cap Corse. While most of the path is well waymarked, or cairned towards the summit, the maquis has overtaken some stretches, making it hard to follow in places.

cousin out of the castle and stormed off to settle with his brother in nearby Erbalunga. Here he built a new castle, which was wrecked in 1556 by the French, supported by members of the Castello branch of the da Gentile clan. Quick to retaliate, the Erbalunga side of the family, supported by the Genoese, launched an attack against Castello, an action that resulted in the total devastation of the port when the French struck back the following year. *La Sposetta* is generally thought to haunt Castello – presumably she also drops in on the da Gentile family's house, built in 1602 at the entrance to the hamlet.

Fifteen minutes' walk south of the village along the road to Silgaggia, you come to the well-preserved little chapel of **Notre-Dame-des-Neiges**, which dates from the tenth century and houses the oldest known **frescoes** in Corsica. Dating from 1386, they depict several saints, including Christopher, Catherine and possibly George.

Sisco

Beyond Erbalunga the landscape takes on a more desolate aspect and the road gives an ever clearer view of the rocky coast. After 6km you reach **Sisco**, a *commune* made up of several hamlets scattered over the mountainside and the tiny seaside village of **MARINE DE SISCO**. The latter comprises a small sandy beach, and a cluster of restaurants and hotels, making it a pleasant stopover. If you decide to **stay**, a dependable mid-range option is the *Hôtel de la Marine*, the first hotel you come to on the right (☎04 95 35 21 04; ③–④; no credit cards; Easter–Sept), which consists of rooms in terraced chalets that open onto a quiet garden behind the beach. There's no restaurant, but breakfast is served on the stone-floored verandah of the main house. If this place is full, try the swisher *U Pozzu*, opposite (☎04 95 35 21 17, fax 04 95 35 27 19; ④): it's a bit bland, but the rooms are comfortable enough, and the welcoming proprietor speaks fluent English. The restaurant's not bad, either, with a choice of two *menus fixes* (80F/100F), and lots of fresh seafood à la carte (best accompanied by a bottle of rosé from the Lina Pieretti vineyard at nearby Luri). By far the best-value budget accommodation in the village is the four simply furnished en-suite rooms (half-board only in July & Aug) at the *Auberge A Stalla Sischese*, 200m along the road leading inland from *U Pozzu* (☎04 95 35 26 34; ⑤; May–Oct). The little restaurant on the ground floor serves authentic Corsican food (*ravioli al brocciu*, *ratatouille* and *fiadone*) in unpretentious surroundings; set menus start at 80F, rising to 120F for an eight-course feast.

There are two churches in Sisco worth visiting. The most striking is **San Michele**, a beautiful Romanesque chapel, which can be reached from **CHIOSO**, the *commune*'s principal hamlet, 7km via the D32, which leads off from the coast road at the centre of the *marine*. Just beyond the large, unremarkable Église St-Martin, take the right-hand track signposted to San Michele, and after a couple of minutes you'll see a rocky track leading uphill on the left; you can leave the car here and climb the last 200m to San Michele. The elegant chapel, built in 1030 by Pisan masons, occupies a spectacular windswept hillside overlooking the Marine de Sisco, with Pietracorbara a misty ridge of buildings stretching to the north. On September 29, the Festival of St Michael brings pilgrims up from the surrounding hamlets to celebrate Mass here.

The Couvent de Santa Catalina

Back on the main coast road, the huge **Couvent de Santa Catalina** stands on a hillside high above the corniche, about 500m beyond Marine de Sisco. The convent is now an old people's home, but you can visit the church, which is reached by turning left off the main road, along a hairpin bend that doubles back to the building. (Ignore the turning next to the large stone statue of St Catherine, some 200m before, which leads to a dead end.) Built in the twelfth century, the graceless church, overshadowed by an ugly tower, was enlarged in the fifteenth century, when the hulking buttresses were added and the entrance widened to receive the pilgrims who came to see its famous relics. Comprising a piece of the clay from which Adam was made, an almond from Paradise, and one of Enoch's fingers, the relics were enshrined here in the thirteenth century by fishermen who, caught in a storm off Cap Corse, vowed to bring their holy cargo to the first church they came across if they were saved. This happened to be Santa Catalina; unfortunately, the relics are now kept in the mairie at Chioso and are not accessible to visitors. Perhaps the most impressive feature of the church's bare interior is the round crypt, dating from the 1200s and based – like nearly all round churches – on the Holy Sepulchre in Jerusalem.

Pietracorbara

Heading north, the next village along the cape is **PIETRACORBARA**, 18km north of Bastia, whose beautiful beach marks the end of a broad river valley carpeted in shimmering reed banks. Overlooked by a ruined Genoese tower are a handful of houses, among them several worthwhile **restaurants**. The most sophisticated of the group is *A Lumbrina* (☎04 95 35 26 17), on the beach itself, which offers imaginatively prepared local seafood such as sardine and soft-cheese (*brousse*) tart or grouper (*mérou*) simmered in muscat. Their three-course menu is a reasonable 85F, but doesn't feature the best of the chef's fish dishes – sampling these will set you back 180–200F à la carte. For a cheaper meal, try the nearby *Restaurant des Chasseurs* (☎04 95 35 21 54), which does succulent pizzas for under 50F and has a couple of simple 60F *menus fixes* (salad, calamari and dessert).

Porticciolo

PORTICCIOLO appears after another 7km of winding corniche, which passes directly beneath the dramatic **tour de l'Osse**. Porticciolo village is attractively compact and crumbling, with a tiny mooring for fishing boats jutting into the green sea. Its white-sand beach is rather marred by the proximity of the road, but the two **hotels** here offer peace and quiet, and make good bases for forays into the interior of the cape. The welcoming *U Patrïarcu* (☎04 95 35 00 01; ④–⑤; open year round) is a stalwart period building with immaculate rooms overlooking the sea or the hills behind; half-board (around 250F per person) is obligatory in July and August. An equally good choice with comparable tariffs is the nearby *Torra Marina* (☎04 95 35 00 80; ④–⑤; open May–Sept), swathed in greenery and boasting an excellent little restaurant with exposed stone, wood beams and a terrace overlooking the water. The accent is squarely on seafood here (all caught by the *patron*'s neighbour): if you're lucky they may have *langouste* (crayfish) as the *plat du jour*, although the *menu fixe* (120F) has plenty of choice, including a couple of meat dishes such as *escalope à la crème*.

Santa Severa and Tomino

At the little *marine* of **SANTA SEVERA**, 2km north of Porticciolo, the D180 cuts across the cape to Luri and the Tour de Sénèque (see p.93). The village has a few hotels, but as it doesn't ooze character you're better off pressing on to Macinaggio (see opposite).

Six kilometres beyond Santa Severa lies **Marine de Meria**, a collection of pastel-shaded cottages scattered around the base of a well-preserved watchtower. From here it's 2km inland to the little *commune* of **Tomino** (Tuminu), dubbed "the cradle of Christianity in Corsica" because the island's earliest Christians hid in caves on its hillsides during the Saracen raids of the sixth century. Sited on a windy, rocky spur, the *commune*'s main hamlet, **STOPIONE**, was once a serious rival to commercial Rogliano (see p.90), producing an excellent muscat wine. These days it lies boarded up and virtually deserted, but the **view** alone is worth the steep drive up the D353 from the *marine*. Following the hairpin road, which emerges on the left just before you enter Macinaggio, you'll soon come to the crest of the hill, where a Baroque chapel and a Genoese tower face each other before a tight cluster of houses. In the near distance, the Îles Finocchiarola and the Tuscan island of Capraia are visible across the vast expanse of deep-blue sea.

The northern cape

Macinaggio, northern terminus of the road along the east side of the cape, is also the largest settlement due north of Bastia, with a handful of hotels and restaurants, and one of the cape's few petrol stations. The only **bus** service to this somewhat isolated resort runs three times weekly (Mon, Wed & Fri) from Bastia's gare routière, and is operated by Transports Saladini (☎04 95 35 43 88).

The land between Macinaggio and **Barcaggio**, at the very tip of Corsica, forms part of a protected zone called the **Site Naturelle de la Capandula**, and is a wonderful area to explore on foot, boasting some glorious **beaches**. Known as the "holy promontory" in Roman times because of its Christian settlements, the tip of the cape also has many ruined chapels, such as **Santa Maria**, near Macinaggio. Inland, the eight hamlets of **Rogliano**, spectacularly spread out over the slopes 5km inland, were for a few centuries the fief of the da Mare family, whose castles and towers lie dotted over the hills. On the western side of the northern tip, the chief focus of interest is picturesque **Centuri-Port**, where the colourful horseshoe-shaped harbour shelters several attractive hotels.

Macinaggio

A port since Roman times, well-sheltered **MACINAGGIO** was developed by the Genoese in 1620 for the export of olive oil and wine to the Italian peninsula, and in later years played its part in the wider history of the island. Pascal Paoli landed here in 1790 after his exile in England, whereupon he kissed the ground and uttered the words "O ma patrie, je t'ai quitté esclave, je te retrouve libre" ("Oh my country, I left you as a slave, I rediscover you a free man") – a plaque commemorating the event adorns the wall above the ship chandlers. Napoléon also stopped here on his way to Bastia as he fled from the

Paolists in 1793, and in 1869 the empress Eugénie was forced by a storm to disembark here on her way back from the opening of the Suez Canal, before taking refuge in Rogliano – the road from Macinaggio to Rogliano has been called the "Chemin de l'Impératrice" ever since. There's not much of an historic patina to the place nowadays, but with its turquoise marina, its line of colourful seafront awnings and its end-of-the-world feel, Macinaggio has a certain appeal; it also lies within comfortable walking distance of some of the island's most beautiful coastal scenery.

The best place to **stay** is the recently renovated *Hôtel des Îles*, opposite the marina (☎04 95 35 43 02, fax 04 95 35 47 05; ④–⑤), which also has a good restaurant. The tiny rooms at the front of this old building overlook the port but get noisy at night, being above the most popular bar in the resort, so if you're a light sleeper ask for a room at the back. Otherwise your best bet is *U Libecciu*, down the lane leading from the marina to the Plage de Tamarone (☎04 95 35 43 22; ⑤; May–Sept, with obligatory half-board July & Aug); it's a modern building with no view to speak of, but the rooms are spacious. *U Ricordu*, on the south side of the road to Rogliano (☎04 95 35 40 20, fax 04 95 35 41 88; ④–⑤; March–Sept, with obligatory half-board Aug), is along the same lines as the *U Libecciu*, but with a swimming pool and a sauna. Macinaggio's only **campsite**, *U Stazzu*, lies 1km north of the harbour and is signposted from the Rogliano road (☎04 95 35 43 76; May–Oct). The ground is hard, but there's ample shade and easy access to the nearby beach; they also do particularly fine breakfasts for 25F.

Besides the hotel **restaurants** above, you could try the *Pizzeria San Columbu*, at the end of the port facing out to sea, which does a passable seafood pizza, or, for a gourmet Corsican meal, *Les Îles*, one of a string of places with tables under awnings on the quayside, which does good fresh fish dishes, cocktails and ice creams. Set menus start at 100F, so count on around 150F for a four-course meal with wine. At the far north of the village a short way beyond the marina, *Chez Bellini* (☎04 95 35 40 37) is the other established favourite, whose 135F menu is a slap-up seafood supper *par excellence*; they also have a good range of inexpensive pasta dishes à la carte.

Site Naturelle de la Capandula

Macinaggio's town beach is seaweed-strewn and dirty, but you can get to some stunning stretches of white sand and clear sea by following the track at the north end of the marina to the **Site Naturelle de la Capandula**. Covering 930 acres of windswept maquis and pristine coast between Macinaggio and Bracaggio, the reserve, which encompasses the deserted Îles Finocchiarola and the Île de la Giraglia, can only be crossed on foot, via a coastal path that takes you through some wonderful scenery.

Although Capandula is off limits to motor vehicles, it is possible to drive the 2km from Macinaggio to the **Baie de Tamarone**, whose deep clear waters make this a good place for diving and snorkelling. The car park here also marks the start of the popular **coastal walk** through the reserve, known as the *Sentier des Douaniers* after the Genoese customs officials who originally cut the path. Clearly marked with yellow splashes of paint, it winds via a series of exquisite coves and ruined watchtowers all the way to Barcaggio – a return trip of around six to seven hours. Note that there are no springs along the way, so carry plenty of drinking water. For the less adventurous, there's a shorter circular route (1hr 30min–2hr), which begins at the Baie de Tamarone and takes in most of Capandula's highlights. From the car park, follow the Sentier des Douaniers along the line of the bay and around the headland to a second beach, **Plage des Îles**.

The sprinkling of barren islets offshore are known as the **Îles Finocchiarola**, after the wild fennel that grows in abundance over the rocks in the area. Hundreds of gulls and cormorants haunt this strip of coast, which, during March and June, is a stopoff for migrating **birds** from North Africa. If you're here at this time, look out for the elusive Audouin's gull, with its distinctive red bill encircled by a black band. Only 2500 pairs still survive in the Mediterranean, and they are a protected species here. Other types you might expect to see are the more common herring gull, large with grey upper parts, black wing tips and a yellow bill; the black-headed Mediterranean gull; and perhaps a Manx shearwater or Cory's shearwater. Though similar in appearance to gulls, these last two brown-backed species are distinguished by the way they glide low over the sea with straight, stiff wings. The islets are a nature reserve, only visitable between March and August, and fires and camping are strictly forbidden. **Boat excursions** run in July and August from the marina in Macinaggio; tickets cost 75F. The round-trip includes a stop on the largest islet so that enthusiasts can do a spot of birdwatching.

Half an hour after leaving the Baie de Tamarone, you arrive at a stunning arc of turquoise sea known as the **Rade de Santa Maria**, site of an isolated Romanesque chapel. Raised on the foundations of a sixth-century church, the **Chapelle Santa Maria** comprises a tenth-century and a twelfth-century chapel merged into one, hence the two discrepant apses.

This bay's other distinctive landmark is the huge **Tour de Santa Maria**. Dramatically cleft in half and entirely surrounded by water, the ruined three-storeyed building was one of three *torri* built on the northern tip of the cape by the Genoese in the sixteenth century (the others are at Tollare and Barcaggio) as lookout posts against the increasingly troublesome Moorish pirates (see box on p.102). As Macinaggio grew in importance, the towers were also used by health and customs officers, who controlled the maritime traffic with

Genoa. Pascal Paoli established his garrison here in 1761, having failed in his attempt to take Macinaggio, and contemplated building a rival port. Six years later, to undermine Genoa's position in the area, Paoli sent two hundred men under the command of Achille Murati to capture the neighbouring island of Capraia, which had belonged to Genoa since 1507. Murati's relatively easy victory marked the beginning of the downfall of the Genoese in Corsica.

If you turn south from the Chapelle Santa Maria and follow the track past a vine-covered hillside for around thirty minutes, you'll eventually arrive back at the Baie de Tamarone. Note that this circular walk can also be done in a clockwise direction by turning left out of the Tamarone car park instead of right at the start of the hike, and following the track inland to the chapel, and thence around the coast.

Rogliano

A cluster of schist-tiled hamlets scattered in a lush valley below the jagged grey crags of Monte Poggio make up the *commune* of **Rogliano** (Ruglianu), 7km up a series of hairpin bends from Macinaggio. This is one of the oldest and most picturesque settlements in Corsica. The constituent hamlets – Bettolacce, Olivo, Magna, Soprana, Vignale, Sottana and Campiano – were the base of the da Mare lords from the twelfth to the sixteenth centuries, and the ruins of their convents, towers and castles are distributed among them. However, the village's name, derived from the Latin *Pagus Aurelianus*, dates from the Roman era, when Rogliano presided over a busy trade with the Italian coast, while the oldest vines on the hillside are known to be of Carthaginian origin.

The easternmost and largest hamlet, **BETTOLACCE**, is dominated by the privately owned **Tour Franceschi**, an enormous round tower in remarkable condition. It also boasts a **post office** and an excellent **hotel**, the *Auberge Sant'Agnellu*, opposite the pleasantly proportioned church of Sant'Agnellu (☎ & fax 04 95 35 40 59; ③–④; mid-April to Oct, with obligatory half-board July & Aug), which has large, comfortable rooms and a magnificent restaurant terrace overlooking the valley. At 90F, the set menu of mainly Corsican specialities is good value, and the views are superb.

Isolated in the valley some 500m beneath Bettolacce stands the ruined sixteenth-century **Église St-Côme-et-St-Damien**, accessible via the path leading opposite *Auberge Sant'Agnellu*. A curious rectangular bell tower stands separated from the nave, which is the oldest part of the church. **VIGNALE**, the hamlet above Bettolacce, is dominated by the crumbling ruins of the **Castello di San Colombano**, from which there's a magnificent view across the valley to Macinaggio. The castle was built in the twelfth century and became known as *U Castelacciu* (The Bad Castle) in the sixteenth, when Giacomo Santa da Mare abandoned the Genoese cause, switched his allegiances to Sampiero Corso and defected to the

Franco-Turkish army. In 1553 the Genoese retaliated by destroying the castle, which was later restored then burned down in 1947.

From here a track leads 300m to **OLIVO** and the **Couvent St-François**, an imposing vine-covered building straight out of a Gothic romance. The convent and adjoining church, surmounted by a spindly clock tower, were built in 1520 by the Franciscans, who also restored them in 1711. They are now private property and closed to the public.

Barcaggio and around

To get to the very tip of Corsica, continue west along the D80 for about 5km, until you reach **Ersa**, where the D253 twists off northwards to **BARCAGGIO**, giving breathtaking views of the Île de la Giraglia. The *marine* (harbour settlement) is tiny – just a jetty, a couple of restaurants and a dozen houses built from the greenish local schist – but the setting is sublime and the **beach** wild and windswept. Curving east of the village to a headland crowned by a Genoese watchtower, it is set against a backdrop of austere, maquis-covered hills that are oddly reminiscent of the Scottish Highlands. You can leave your vehicle in the village **car park** (also a park for camper vans), from where a track leads through the dunes to a crystalline sea. The *La Giraglia* **hotel** (☎04 95 35 60 54, fax 04 95 35 65 92; ⑦; April–Sept) occupies a fantastic location at the north end of the village overlooking the tiny harbour (rooms 25 and 26 have the best views), though it's expensive for what it offers and doesn't accept credit cards. Nor does it have a restaurant, so if you fancy a **meal** your only options are *U Pescadore*, an ugly prefab hut on the jetty serving pricy fresh seafood dishes, or the better-value *Chez Néné*, 7km south of Barcaggio along the D253, which has a single set Corsican speciality menu at 100F, served on a small terrace.

The northern extremity of Corsica is marked by the **Île de la Giraglia**, a green islet whose bare, rocky slopes sport a lighthouse and a sixteenth-century Genoese tower.

About 2km west of Barcaggio lies **TOLLARE**, a neglected little coastal village of squat grey fishing cottages. Apart from the handful of holidaymakers who rent houses in the summer, hardly anyone ventures out here, but you can park up and paddle on the hamlet's tiny pebble beach.

Centuri

From Tollare, a potholed road loops back up the valley to rejoin the D80, close to the turn-off for Barcaggio. If you continue west on the main road you'll go over the **Col de Serra** (365m); for a fantastic **view**, walk from the col up to **Moulin Mattei**, the round building with the coloured tiled roof on the hill above the road. Some considerate soul has installed a stone picnic table in the lee of this former windmill (restored by the Maison Mattei as tasting place for their famous aperitif, Cap Corse), from whose terrace you can admire an impressive panorama along the peninsula's north and west coasts.

Once over the col you soon come to **CAMERA**, the first hamlet of the *commune* of **Centuri** (pronounced "Chen*to*ri"), where the bizarre cylindrical turrets of the **Château de Bellavista** peer from the woods beneath the road. One of many so-called "Maisons d'Américains" in this area, the castle (closed to the public) was built in the nineteenth century for Count Leonetto Cipriani, a mercenary in the service of the Duke of Tuscany, who later became a close friend of Napoléon. The smaller hamlet of **Canelle**, overlooking Centuri-Port and accessible from Camera along the road heading north or on foot from the port, is renowned for its enormous fig trees, whose drooping branches overhang the houses and shadow the road.

When Boswell arrived here from England in 1765, the former Roman settlement of **CENTURI-PORT** was a tiny fishing village, recommended to him for its peaceful detachment from the dangerous turmoil of the rest of Corsica. Not much has changed since Boswell's time: Centuri-Port exudes tranquillity despite an influx of summer residents, many of them artists who come to paint the fishing boats in the slightly prettified harbour, where the grey stone wall is highlighted by the green serpentine roofs of the encircling cottages, restaurants and bars. The twenty or so boats are evidence of the village's still thriving fishing industry, and lobster-potting provides an important income for its handful of permanent residents. The only drawback with the settlement from the tourists' point of view is that the small pebble **beach** to the south is disappointingly grubby and not ideal for sunbathing.

Practicalities

Centuri-Port has more **hotels** than anywhere else on Cap Corse. The best value among them is the *Hôtel-Restaurant du Pêcheur*, the pink building in the harbour (☎04 95 35 60 14; ④; April–Oct), which is also the most pleasant and fills up quickly in high season; its rooms are agreeably cool, with thick stone walls and green shutters, and it has a popular **restaurant**. The *Vieux Moulin*, in a prime location behind the harbour on the right as you enter the village (☎04 95 35 60 15, fax 04 95 35 60 24; ④–⑥; open March–Oct), has a marvellous terrace, but the rooms are rather stuffy. The *Hôtel La Jetée*, at the far end of the jetty (☎04 95 35 64 46; ④–⑤; Easter–Sept), is well situated and has a good fish restaurant with a 95F menu and a choice of inexpensive pizzas; its rooms are pretty ordinary and don't have sea views, but they're the cheapest in the village during high season. For **campers**, the only option is the uninviting *Camping l'Isolettu*, 400m south along the D35 (☎04 95 35 63 63; May–Oct). The only place to **change money** is the tiny post office up in Camera (Mon–Fri 9.30am–noon & 2–4pm), where you can make cash withdrawals against Visa and MasterCard.

The western cape

South of Centuri the corniche cuts through villages stacked up the cliffsides above small *marines* that are often masked from the road by rocky outcrops. At **Pino** you can take a detour inland to see the **Tour de Sénèque**, while further south **Canari** offers another remarkable Romanesque church. Just a few kilometres north of St-Florent lies **Nonza**, perhaps the most spectacular of all the cape villages, perched on the edge of the cliffside above a black sandy beach.

Morsiglia

The change of scenery south of Centuri is striking and sudden: gentle green slopes give way to chalky cliffs that plunge down from the high corniche road, deep indents punctuate the coast and the sea is a dark peacock-feather blue.

After 6km the three towers of **MORSIGLIA** (Mursiglia) come into view: six of these enormous structures were originally built here to defend against Moorish pirates in the sixteenth century (see p.102). A few kilometres further lies the **Golfe d'Aliso**, a small cove where the sea has an incredible depth and colour, and the red sand makes a dazzling contrast. There's access to the shore from the road, though not much room to park.

Tour de Sénèque

A short distance north of Pino (see p.94), a turn-off in the direction of Luri will take you winding through pine woods to the Col de Ste-Lucie. If you take the steep turning on the right at the pass, then head along a badly potholed lane through the forest, you'll soon come to an abandoned school, above which looms the **Tour de Sénèque**. Set atop a pinnacle of black rock, the impressively forbidding tower was built in the fifteenth century by the da Mare family, on the spot where Seneca is said to have lived from 41 to 49 AD, having been exiled for offending Emperor Claudius and accused of seducing the emperor's niece. His rampant misconduct didn't stop there. During his exile, Seneca reputedly once came down from his rock in an attempt to ravage the Corsican women, for which he was attacked with nettles – hence the profusion of the plants around the base of the tower. Whilst here he wrote a few bitter verses about the place:

Oh Corsica whom rocks terrific bound
Where nature spreads her wildest deserts round
In vain revolving seasons cheer thy soil
Nor ripening fruits, nor waving harvests smile.

It's a thirty-minute climb through the woods to the tower – well worth the effort for the views, which extend to both coasts of the cape and over the Monte Stello massif (see box on p.84). To pick up the trail, follow the motorable dirt track from the deserted school towards the radio transmitter above you in the woods, then bear left along the path that peels from it after about five minutes. From here, it's a stiff ten-minute climb through the trees to the top, with the last 20m or so over exposed rocks.

Luri

Passing over the Col de Ste-Lucie, you soon come to the *commune* of **Luri**, an unexceptional place surrounded by a delightful landscape of lemon trees and vineyards. At **PIAZZA**, Luri's central hamlet, you might take a look at **Église St-Pierre**. Dating from the seventeenth century, it houses a late sixteenth-century painting that represents the life of St Peter against a background showing the local castles in the fifteenth century – the one on the left is the Tour des Motti, a precursor of the Tour de Sénèque, and on the right is the Castello di San Colombano, at Rogliano (see p.90).

Pino

A sense of the tropics pervades the air at **PINO** (Pinu), some 2km south of the turning for Luri. Palm trees grow up the cliff, and the houses, coloured pale pink, orange and yellow, feature turreted roofs and verandahs. The grander ones are "maisons d'Américains", one of which was built by Antoine Liccioni, who, like many of his generation, left the village vowing not to return until he was rich. Liccioni struck lucky, discovering seams of gold in both Venezuela and Brazil, and when he died it is said he owned half of Guyana. You could stop in the village for a drink under the shade of the chestnuts and plane trees, or follow the steep road from just outside the village down to the *marine*, where a fifteenth-century **Franciscan convent** lies half-hidden amongst a jungle of bamboo. Although its outward appearance is grim, try to get inside for a look at the faded fifteenth-century frescoes above the entrance, featuring the Virgin flanked by saints Francis and Bernard. If the convent is locked, ask for the key at Église Ste-Marie, in the centre of the village.

Canari and around

South of Pino, the high corniche road winds past rocky inlets for several kilometres through Barretali and **Marine de Giottani**, where there's a small pebbly beach. Some 5km further, you come to **Canari**, a large *commune* with a couple of notable churches, which is served by buses from Bastia (daily in summer, with Transports Micheli ☎04 95 35 64 02; or Mon & Wed year round, with Transports Saoletti ☎04 95 37 84 05).

Right on the main road in Canari's chief hamlet, **MARINCA**, stands the Romanesque **Santa Maria Assunta**. Built at the end of the twelfth century and attractive chiefly for the quirky sculpture that decorates the cornice beneath the roof – weird mask-like faces alongside strange beasts and stylized patterns. The gloomy Baroque **Église St-François**, formerly attached to a Franciscan monastery, is situated a little way up the road in **PIEVE**. The highlight here is a fifteenth-century gilded panel of St Michael, on the left as you enter; a panel from the same altarpiece is set into the sacristy cupboard door. Also of interest is the sixteenth-century *Assumption of the Virgin* on the right of the nave, above the tomb of Vittoria da Gentile, who died in 1590 at a convent, no longer in existence, in Canari.

A gentle fifteen-minute walk from here along a marked path up to **EMISA** brings you to the tiny fifteenth-century **Chapelle Ste-Catherine**, which houses two faded panels from that period. Alternatively, you could descend to the tiny *marine* of Canari, where the **restaurant** *U Scogliu* (☎ 04 95 37 80 06; April to mid-Oct), overlooking the rocks, serves some of the tastiest fish on Cap Corse. The chef only does à la carte dishes, and a four-course meal with wine will set you back around 200F per head.

South of Marinca, the road cuts across a sheer mountainside horrendously disfigured by the workings of an **asbestos mine**, whose closure in 1966 resulted in the dumping of untold quantities of toxic dust on the surrounding beaches. The mine has also been blamed for the premature deaths of many ex-employees.

Nonza

Set high on a black rocky pinnacle that plunges vertically into the sea, the village of **NONZA** is one of the highlights of the Cap Corse shoreline. The village was formerly the main stronghold of the da Gentile family, and the remains of the **fortress** still cling to the furthest rocks of the overhanging cliff. Nonza has a shady square, behind which you twist your way through stone-tiled houses and bougainvillea bushes to reach the ruined fortress and the more impressive green **watchtower** nearby. In 1768 the tower, one of the few on the island built in Paoli's time and not by the Genoese, witnessed one of the greatest con tricks in military history. The French, having succeeded in taking over all of Cap Corse, closed in on the Nonza garrison, which was under the command of one Captain Casella. Fearing that Casella's tenacity would lead them to their deaths, the Corsican troops absconded, leaving him to defend the tower single-handed. This he did, using a system of cables to maintain constant fire from a line of muskets and a single cannon, until the disheartened French offered a truce. Old Casella demanded that his army be allowed to parade out in dignity, and duly emerged alone and on crutches, brandishing his pistol, to the amazement of the besieging army.

Nonza is also famous for **Santa Julia**, patron saint of Corsica, who was martyred here in the fifth century. The story goes that she had been sold into slavery at Carthage and was being taken by ship to Gaul when the slavers arrived. A pagan festival was in progress, and when Julia refused to participate she was raped, tortured and crucified; the gruesome legend relates that her breasts were then cut off and thrown onto a stone, from which sprang two springs, now enshrined in a chapel by the beach. To get there, follow the sign on the right-hand side of the road before you enter the square, which points to the **Fontaine de Ste-Julie**, down by the rocks.

Reached by a flight of six hundred steps, the long grey **beach** is thus coloured as a result of pollution from the asbestos mine up the coast. The local council has banned bathing here (allegedly because of the undertow). However, it's worth the walk down to the beach for the view of the tower alone, which looks as if it's about to topple over into the sea. The only **accommodation** in the village is the *Auberge Patrizi* (☎04 95 37 82 16; ④), attached to the big restaurant below the church. Made up of two houses (the one with rooms to let is a 5min walk down the track towards the beach), the *Auberge* is an old-fashioned place where half-board is obligatory, but the food is good and plentiful.

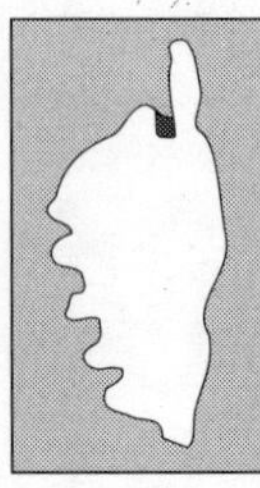

The Nebbio

Named after the thick mists that sweep across it in the spring and autumn, the **Nebbio** (Nebbiu) has for centuries been one of the most fertile parts of Corsica, producing honey, chestnuts and some of the island's finest wine. Officially, the region includes the barren **Désert des Agriates**, further west, but essentially Nebbio comprises the amphitheatre of rippled hills, vineyards and cultivated valleys that converge on St-Florent, a region nicknamed *A Conca d'Oro* (The Golden Shell) by Pascal Paoli because it encompassed all the wealth of the region. Nourished by the headwaters of the **Aliso River**, its many beautiful villages, perched on pale-green bluffs of schist that jut from the gently sloping sides of the basin, are swathed in greenery, with finger-thin bell towers pointing from their midst. In spite of their proximity to the coast, tourism has made little impact on these scattered settlements, which remain largely dependent on agriculture and EU subsidies. The one major development in recent times has been the shift to **viticulture**: some of the wines produced around the *commune* of **Patrimonio** rival those of Sartène, and *caves* offering wine tastings (*dégustations*) are a feature of the whole region.

St-Florent at the base of Cap Corse – a bishopric until 1790 and now a chic coastal resort – remains the Nebbio's chief town and best base, while villages such as **Olmeta-di-Tuda** and **Oletta**, being close to Bastia, are lively and well-populated places, especially in the summer, when families move up to the cooler mountains from the city. The two most notable historic sites in this part of the island are the Pisan church of **Santa Maria Assunta**, just outside St-Florent, and the diminutive **San Michele de Murato**, close to the chapels strewn across the valley between **Rapale** and **Santo-Pietro-di-Tenda**.

The principal **public transport** serving the Nebbio is Transports Santini's bus from Bastia to St-Florent (see p.99 for details).

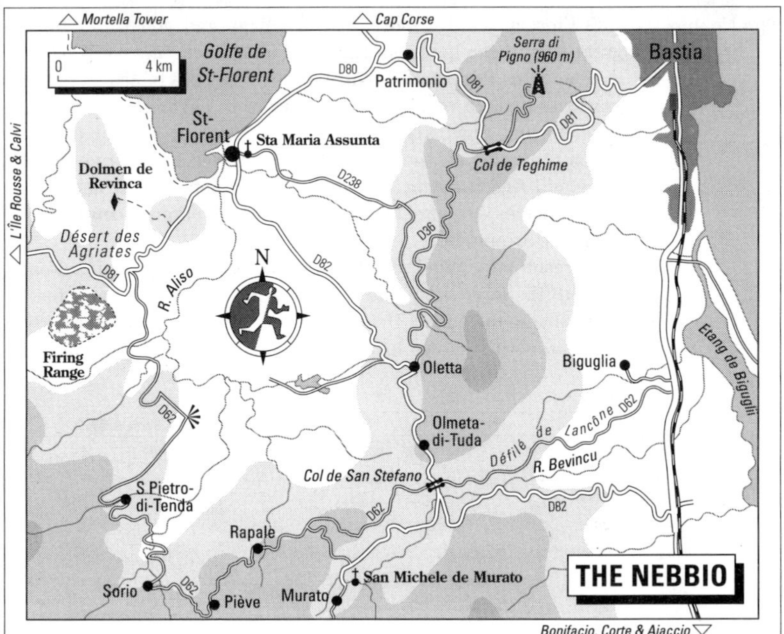

St-Florent

Viewed from across the bay, **ST-FLORENT** (San Fiurenzu) appears as a bright line against the black tidal wave of the Tenda hills, the pale stone houses seeming to rise straight out of the sea, overlooked by a squat circular citadel. It's a relaxing town, with a decent beach and a good number of restaurants, but the key to its success is the **marina**, which is jammed with expensive boats throughout the summer. Yet, despite the seasonal influx of well-heeled yacht-owners, the place remains relatively unspoilt for the time being, and its position next to the Désert des Agriates lends it a pleasant air of isolation.

In Roman times a town called **Cersunam** existed on the site where the Santa Maria Assunta stands today, 1km east of the present village. Few traces remain of the settlement, which in the mid-fifteenth century was eclipsed by the port that developed around the new Genoese citadel. St-Florent proceeded to prosper as one of Genoa's strongholds, largely through the export of olive oil produced in its fertile hinterland, but later went into decline as its population – ravaged by malaria, Moorish pirates, and continual battles between the Corsicans, the French and the Genoese in the mid-sixteenth century – dwindled to 65. The town was also fought over during the struggles for Independence in 1769; and it was from here that Paoli set off for London in 1796, never to return.

St-Florent is little more than a village and you won't find a great deal to see here, but there are lots of relaxing cafés to laze in. **Place des Portes**, the centre of town life, has tables facing the sea in the shade of plane trees, and in the evening it fills with strollers and nonchalant *pétanque* players. In **rue du Centre**, which runs west off the square, parallel to the seafront and marina, you'll find a string of inviting restaurants, shops and wine-tasting places – be sure to sample the sweet, maquis-scented muscat made around here.

To reach the **citadel**, climb to the end of rue du Centre and pass through the large wire gate – it looks like private property but is accessible to the public. Unique in Corsica for its circular shape, the *torrioni*, as it's known locally, was built in 1439 for the Genoese

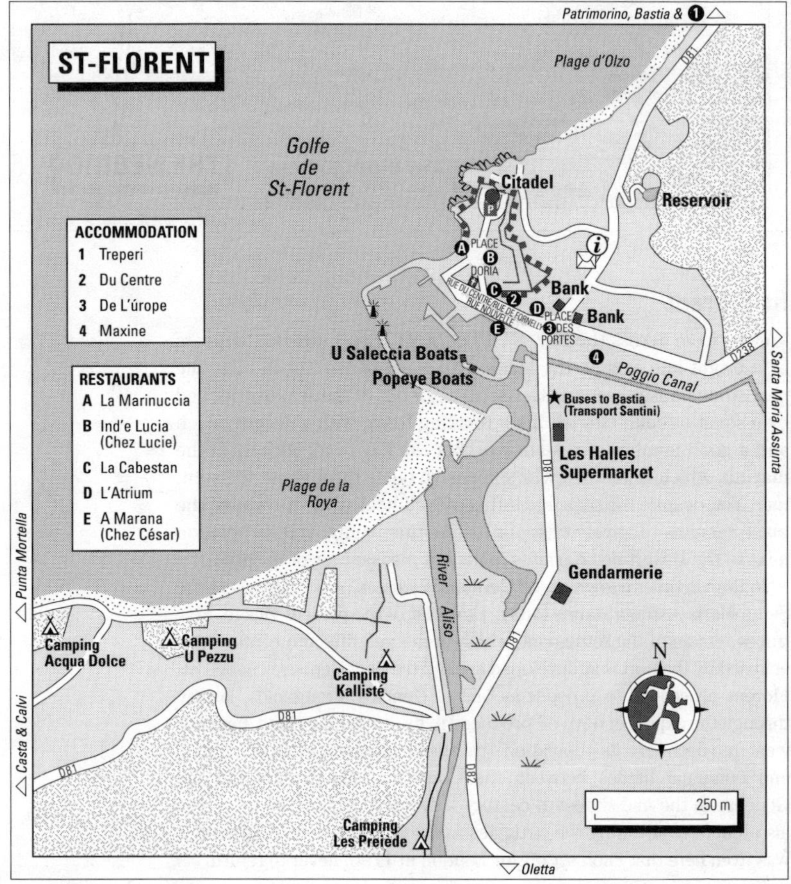

governors, but was bombarded for two days by Nelson's fleet in February 1794 and reduced to a virtual ruin. During World War II, the British took it over again, this time to house secret supplies for Resistance fighters on the island. Substantially renovated in 1998–99, the citadel is today worth a visit primarily for the beautiful views of the hills of the Nebbio and the mountains of Cap Corse, disappearing into mists up the coast.

The nearest **beach**, Plage de la Roya, is a windy stretch of sand and mud flats to the west of the village, fine for windsurfers but less than ideal for bathing, as the sea is rather murky due to sewage from the town. To get there, cross the bridge to the south of place des Portes.

Practicalities

Transports Santini **buses** (☎04 95 37 04 04) run from Bastia's gare routière to St-Florent twice daily – except Sundays – leaving at 10.30am and 5.30pm between June and September, and at 11am and 6pm during the rest of the year (except Oct–May Wed & Sat, when they leave at noon & 5.30pm), pulling into the village car park, behind the marina. This is also the departure point for the return buses to Bastia, which from June to September leave at 7am and 2pm, and at 6.50am and 1.30pm from October until May. The journey takes one hour. Bus times vary a little from year to year, but can be checked at the **tourist office**, at the top of the village (July & Aug daily 9am–noon & 2–5pm; Sept–June Mon–Fri 9am–noon & 2–5pm, Sat 9am–noon; ☎04 95 37 06 04), where you can also get free **maps** of St-Florent and its environs, as well as the usual range of glossy leaflets on the area. The **post office** next door will change travellers' cheques (for a 1.2 percent commission) if they are in French francs or dollars, but not if they are in sterling. Both the Société Générale and Crédit Agricole **banks**, off place des Portes (Mon–Fri 9–11.45am & 2–4.30pm), have bureau de change counters and hole-in-the-wall cash dispensers that accept MasterCard and Visa.

Les Halles de St-Florent, on the bridge, is the best **supermarket** for a long way, and is open on Sundays in the summer. There's a **pharmacy** two minutes up the small unmarked road leading east off place des Portes towards the Santa Maria Assunta cathedral. You'll find a cluster of **telephones** in the marina car park in front of the square. **Motorcycles** are available for rent from Sun Folies, at the far west end of Plage de la Roya (☎04 95 37 04 18) and Corse Plaisance, just across the bridge on the south side of the village (☎04 95 37 00 58); both charge around 270F per day.

Accommodation

St-Florent is a popular resort and **hotels** fill up quickly, especially in the height of summer when prior booking is essential. A fair number of **campsites** are dotted about the coast, most of them large two-star places in the pine trees behind the beach, which are packed in August and closed out of season. Closest to town is *Camping U Pezzu*, route de la Plage d'Ozo (☎04 95 37 01 65), 3km west on the small road that backs the beach. The three-star *Camping Kalliste*, 2km further on the same road (☎04 95 37 03 08), is larger and marginally posher, with its own beachside bar and restaurant.

Du Centre, rue du Centre, 100m up the main street from *de l'Europe* (☎04 95 37 00 68). Nothing special, but well established and a good fall-back, with modest, clean rooms, en-suite showers and toilets. ⑥.

De l'Europe, place des Portes (☎04 95 37 00 33). An old-fashioned place in a prime location with comfortable rooms (ask for one facing the sea) and a lively local bar downstairs. The most attractive option around the square. ⑥.

Maxime, route d'Oletta, just off place des Portes (☎04 95 37 05 30, fax 04 95 37 13 07). Modern hotel in the centre. The rooms, all with TV and en-suite bathrooms, are immaculate, although those at the back suffer from their proximity to the open drain running below them. ⑤.

Treperi, 1.5km northeast on the Bastia road, just past the Elf petrol station (☎04 95 37 40 20, fax 04 95 37 04 61). Smart, vine-covered roadside motel overlooking the beach and gulf, whose large ground-floor rooms have terraces and bathrooms. Generous off-season discounts. March–Oct. ⑤.

Eating and drinking

St-Florent is renowned for its crayfish (*langouste*) and red mullet, but be careful when choosing your **restaurant** – the tourist places displaying menus in every language along the quayside tend to be mediocre. Of the cafés and bars, the *Europe* is the most popular **café** in place des Portes, while *Bar du Passage*, opposite, attracts a younger clientele, partly on account of its jukebox, and *Bar de Col d'Amphore*, on the north side, has stylish 1930s decor.

L'Atrium, place des Portes (☎04 95 37 06 69). Currently the classiest address in St-Florent, run by an inspired young chef who's fast gaining a reputation among sybaritic Bastiais. The menu features delights such as duck liver and dried figs in flaky pastry with port sauce, or more traditional beef *al brocciu* and wild mushrooms. Most main dishes around 100F. Count on 250F per head with wine. Open all year.

Cabestan, rue de Fornellu (☎04 95 37 05 70). A reasonably priced place serving quality seafood – it has a large *vivier* (lobster tank) – and Corsican specialities such as stews and rich game dishes. The *menu corse* (90F) offers the best value for money, but they also have plenty of fresh pasta options à la carte.

Ind'e Lucia (Chez Lucie), place Doria (☎04 95 37 04 15). This cosy, unpretentious bistro, opening onto a small square below the citadel, is hard to beat. The menu is dominated by mountain dishes (such as wild boar terrine and rabbit stew), but they serve some seafood specialities (including wonderful sardines stuffed with *brocciu*). Go for the good-value 100F set menu; carafes of quality local AOC wine cost just 20F.

A Marina (Chez César), rue Nouvelle, on the harbourfront (☎04 95 37 15 33). Consistently good pizzas *au feu de bois*, grilled fish dishes from 45F, lasagnes, copious salads and several filling pasta options from around 50F. A sound budget choice.

La Marinuccia, place Doria, below the citadel (☎04 95 37 04 36). Topnotch seafood served in optimum surroundings: a terrace jutting out into the sea off place Doria. *Menus fixes* around 100F.

Around St-Florent

The area around St-Florent offers plenty of opportunities for short excursions: the cathedral of **Santa Maria Assunta** is only a fifteen-minute walk from the town centre; also within walking distance are the **Tour de Mortella**, the creepy **Dolmen de Monte Recincu**, and the wonderful beaches of the Agriates coast.

Santa Maria Assunta

Situated in a lonely spot 1km east of St-Florent on the original site of the Roman settlement of Nebbium, **Santa Maria Assunta** – the so-called "Cathedral of the Nebbio" – is a fine example of Pisan Romanesque architecture, rivalled only by La Canonica at Mariana, its exact contemporary (see p.77). To reach it, head down the road running due east off place des Portes. In theory the cathedral should be left open all day, but frequently isn't and you should check at the tourist office, where the key is kept, before leaving St-Florent.

Deprived of its bell tower, which was knocked down in the nineteenth century, and set among pastures next door to a farmyard, the cathedral has a distinctly barn-like appearance. Built of warm yellow limestone, it's a superlatively elegant barn, though, and a close look soon reveals an unexpected wealth of harmonious detail: gracefully symmetrical blind arcades decorate the western façade, and at the entrance twisting serpents and wild animals adorn the pilasters on either side of the door.

The interior, too, is deceptively simple. Carved shells, foliage and animals adorn the capitals of the pillars dividing the nave where, immediately to the right, you'll see a glass case containing the mummified figure of **St Flor**, a Roman soldier martyred in the third century for his Christian beliefs. Found among the catacombs of Rome with a vial of blood, signifying martyrdom, the soldier's remains were donated by Pope Clement XIV to the Bishop of the Nebbio in 1771, and a gilded wooden statue stands as a further commemoration in the apse. The spacious nave also holds the tomb of **General Antoine Gentili**, a supporter of Pascal Paoli during the struggles for Independence.

Dolmen de Monte Revincu

One of the Nebbio's few surviving ancient monuments, the **Dolmen de Monte Revincu**, lies ninety minutes or so by foot southwest of St-Florent, lost in a scrub-covered gulley in the Désert des Agriates. The path starts around 2km out of town on the D81; cross the bridge over the Aliso River and follow the main road as it bends southwards through the hamlet of Fromontica. Just 250m beyond the second crossroads (roughly 3km out of St-Florent), a track zigzags downhill through the *maquis* to cross a stream, after which it climbs a steep spur, which it then follows before dropping into a gulley on the far side. When you reach the point, 1.5km further on from the ridge, where two paths cross, turn left (southwest) and follow the way marks to the dolmen, which crowns a rocky hillock. Once again, you'll find the going a lot eas-

Pirates and Watchtowers

Crowning rocky promontories and clifftops from Cap Corse to Bonifacio, the 91 crumbling Genoese watchtowers that punctuate the Corsican coast have become emblematic of the island's picture-postcard tranquillity. Yet they date from an era when these shores were among the most troubled in Europe. During the early fifteenth century, some five hundred years after the Moors had been ousted from the interior, Saracen **pirates** from North Africa began to menace the coastal villages, descending suddenly from the sea and making off with any valuables – including people – that could be shipped back to the Barbary States.

Held for ransom or sold as slaves, Christians were prime plunder for the pirates, and hundreds of islanders were abducted each year. Some did eventually return to their homelands, though not to resettle. Taking advantage of a law that allowed a slave to claim his freedom if he converted to Islam, former captives would set themselves up as traders in their new countries, or, more often, turn to piracy as a means to amass a fortune. For some reason, the latter vocation appealed particularly to Corsicans: records illustrate that, of the ten thousand or so pirates operating out of Algiers in the mid-sixteenth century, some six thousand were from the island. It is a little-known fact that most of the raids on Corsica during the Genoese era were perpetrated by former natives. Among these were such notorious figures as Mammi Pasha, the scourge of his birthplace, Cap Corse, and Piero Paolo Tavera, better known as Hassan Corso, one of two Corsicans who actually rose to become kings, or deys, of Algiers.

Pirate raids became so common by the end of the fifteenth century that many Corsicans left the coast altogether, retreating to villages in the hills. To protect those that remained, as well as the threatened maritime trade, the Genoese erected a chain of **watchtowers**, or *torri*, at strategic points on the island. Comprising one or two storeys, these squat, round towers measured 12–15m in diameter, with a single doorway 5m off the ground reached by a removable ladder. The towers were paid for by local villagers and staffed by watchmen, or *torregiani*, whose job it was to signal the approach of any unexpected ships by lighting a fire on the crenellated rampart at the top of the tower. In this way, it was possible to alert the entire island within an hour.

Piracy more or less died out by the end of Genosese rule in the mid-fifteenth century, but the *torri* remained in use long after, proving particularly effective during the Anglo-Corsican invasions 250 years later. The British were so impressed with the system that they erected similar structures along the south coast of England and Ireland to warn of attacks by the French. Named after the first Genoese watchtower ever built in Corsica – on the Pointe de Mortella, protecting the port of St-Florent and the Nebbio – these **Mortello towers** were later used as lookout posts in World War II.

ier with a copy of the IGN topo-map for the area, #4348 OT "Bastia and St-Florent" (available from the bookshops in town).

This megalithic tomb, made up of three roughly hewn stone slabs, is popularly known as the **Casa di u Lurcu** (House of the Ogre), after a gigantic creature with the head of a man and a wolf-like body that allegedly used to terrorize the locals by sucking the blood out of their cattle. One day, so the legend goes, the people decided to strike back. Gauging the monster's shoe size from his footprints, they made him some huge boots, which they filled with tar and left by his drinking place. Duly ensnared, the *Lurcu* tried to bribe the villagers with a special recipe for *brocciu*, a Corsican cheese, but the people suspected a trap and threw him into a ditch and buried him. Though it's not clear exactly when the stones were placed here, the legend dates them around 1500 BC.

Tour de Mortella

The ruined **Tour de Mortella**, isolated on the coast 7km west of St-Florent, is the most impressive piece of Genoese architecture hereabouts. Built around 1520 as an anti-piracy measure, the tower fell into disuse over time due to its inaccessibility, until the Corsican wars of Independence, when it was reoccupied by French soldiers to guard the sea approach to the gulf. In February 1794, the British navy sailed in to blockade St-Florent, and were amazed when their two ships – a 74-gun and a 32-gun – were beaten off by the tower's three cannons, sustaining severe damage and suffering some sixty casualties. Only after two days of continual pounding from four guns placed on land (at a mere 137m from the tower), did the 38-strong French garrison surrender. As a result of the British bombardment, the tower was cleft in half, but its renovated ochre-washed walls still strike an impressive profile.

The Tour de Mortella may be accessed via a superb coastal hike. For details, see p.104.

A tour of inland Nebbio

St-Florent may attract the bulk of visitors to the Nebbio, but the picturesque **villages** of its **hinterland** form the real heart of the region. Backed by a wall of sheer granite mountains, they cling to the sides of the spectacular **Aliso basin**, overlooking a vista of undulating vineyards that tumble to a deep cobalt-blue sea. Graffiti scrawled over any exposed rock face reminds you that this is a staunchly nationalist area; the Nebbio witnessed some of the fiercest fighting during the wars of Independence against the French in the eighteenth century, and the spirit of resistance has never diminished.

Strung together by the winding D62, the villages of inland Nebbio can be visited in an easy day's drive from St-Florent. Aside from a handful of churches and **statue-menhirs**, they harbour few sights, but the constantly changing **views** make this round-trip one of the most rewarding forays from the coast. Most people follow a loop from St-Florent, climbing the **Col de Teghime** and dropping down through

Walk to the Tour de Mortella and Plage de Loto

Mortella point and its famous tower can be reached on foot from St-Florent – a wonderful, mostly flat walk (2hr 30min–3hr) along some of the island's most scenic coastline. Set off early enough, and you can continue past the tower to Plage de Loto in the Désert des Agriates. The path is easy to follow, but you may want to take along IGN's Top 25 #4348 OT (available at the Maison de la Presse newsagents on the place des Portes in St-Florent).

The route begins at the far (west) end of Plage de la Roya, from where you follow the surfaced lane running behind the beach. With transport, it is possible to cut short the dull first stretch of this walk (2km) by driving or cycling as far as **Anse de Fornali**, a narrow inlet overlooked by a cluster of luxury villas where there's a small car park (note that the last 2km of the drive is via a severly rutted *piste*). From the car park, a sign points the way through the maquis to the start of the **Sentier des Douaniers** (Custom Officers' Path). This hugs a highly convoluted, rocky coastline, studded with a string of tiny bays below the Domaine de Fonaverte, to round the **Punta di Cepo** headland fifty minutes further on from the car park. From here onwards, the coast is very beautiful, with plenty of idyllic coves for swimming. The IGN map implies the river mouths are open, but you can cross them easily on seaweed-covered sand bars. Winding due north, the final stretch from the crystal-clear, white-bottomed **Fiume Santu bay** to the tower takes around thirty minutes.

Most walkers turn around at the **Tour de Mortella**, but you can continue onto Plage de Loto by heading around the next promontory and following the path west as it cuts inland beneath the lighthouse. At the top of the rise, just after the trail starts to give ground, another path peels right, but you should ignore this and go straight on. **Plage de Loto** is reached after another good hour from the tower. Time your arrival well, and you might be able to catch a ride back to St-Florent on one of the two excursion boats than run here daily – ask at the marina before setting off. Two companies, U Saleccia (☎04 95 37 19 07) and Le Popeye (☎04 95 36 90 78), run **boat trips** from St-Florent marina to Plage de Loto. Tickets cost 55F (return) and should be booked the day before from June to September (when there are two departures daily).

Oletta to the **Col de San Stefano**, then up to **Murato**, and down again to **Santo-Pietro-di-Tenda** before heading back to St-Florent. If you're driving into the Nebbio from Bastia, you can join this loop at Col de Teghime or Col de San Stefano, the latter approached by the dramatic **Défilé de Lancône**; driving from St-Florent, the circuit may be shortened by taking the road straight up to Oletta. The Bastia to St-Florent bus, run by Transports Santini (☎04 95 37 04 04), follows the direct route over the Col de Teghime, stopping at Patrimonio on the way.

Patrimonio

Leaving St-Florent by the Bastia road, the first village you come to, after 6km, is **PATRIMONIO**, centre of the first Corsican wine region to gain *appellation contrôlée* status. Apart from the famous local muscat, which can be sampled in the village or at one of the *caves* along the route from St-Florent, Patrimonio's chief asset is the sixteenth-century **Église St-Martin**, occupying its own little hillock and visible for kilometres around. The colour of burnt sienna, it stands out vividly against the rich green vineyards, but the interior was effectively ruined in the nineteenth century, when an elaborately painted ceiling and overdone marble altar were installed.

In a small clearing 200m south of the church, reached via the lane that drops sharply downhill from the crossroads, stands a 2m-tall **statue-menhir** known as *U Nativu*, a late megalithic piece dating from 800–900 BC. The only limestone menhir ever discovered in Corsica, it was ploughed up in four fragments by a local farmer in 1964, restored and placed here under a small shelter. A carved T-shape on its front represents a breastbone, and two uncannily life-like eyebrows and a chin can also be made out.

Patrimonio's only other claim to fame is its annual open-air **guitar festival**, held in the last week of July, when performers and music aficionados from all over Europe converge on the village.

Col de Teghime to Oletta

From Patrimonio the road climbs in a series of sharp switchbacks to the **Col de Teghime** (548m), where a memorial recalls the intense fighting that took place here prior to the withdrawal of the German army from Bastia in October 1943, and commemorating the troops who died here.

For more on the dramatic events of 1943, see p.370.

From the col, it is possible to see the coastlines of both sides of the cape (when it's not swathed in fog), with a stunning panorama of St-Florent and Patrimonio spreading out to the west, while to the east you'll see Bastia, with the glistening Étang de Biguglia stretching south. It's not unusual for the weather to be entirely different on either side. For an even better view, follow the Bastia road for another kilometre and turn left onto the D338, which leads to the **Serra di Pigno**, a gentle climb of about 45 minutes – a massive television antenna marks the summit.

The road south of the Col de Teghime will bring you after 10km to **OLETTA**, where faded multicoloured houses are stacked haphazardly against each other up the hill, and vegetation springs from cracks in the walls. The eighteenth-century **Église St-André**, in the centre of the village, has an ancient relief of the Creation (symbolized by a tree of life) embedded in its recently renovated façade, a relic from the church that occupied the site in the twelfth century. Inside, there's a graceful triptych dating from 1534, portraying the Virgin and Child flanked by SS John the Baptist and Reparata. This used to reside in a local peasant's house until the Madonna allegedly called out to the mother of the household to warn her that her baby's cot had caught fire. Thereafter the triptych was transferred to the church, and has been venerated as miraculous ever since.

The **square** outside the church witnessed one of the more gruesome episodes in the Paolist insurrections of the eighteenth century, when a daring rebel plan to seize Oletta from the French backfired. Eager to make an example of his Corsican prisoners, the French commander condemned the rebels to a horrible death. After having their fingers crushed in a metal vice, they were led naked to the square carrying torches of flaming wax, and forced to plead forgiveness. The executioner then tore out their arms and kidneys, gashed open their thighs, and finally tied them face upwards on a cartwheel, where they were left to die.

If you can keep this grizzly episode out of your mind and choose to **stay** in Oletta, try *A Maggina*, at the entrance to the village (☎04 95 39 01 01; open April–Sept, with half-board obligatory in July & Aug; ③), which has three cosy en-suite rooms with superb views over the Nebbio to the sea. Their **restaurant**, whose terrace also enjoys a fine panorama, is worth a stop too, serving a good selection of local dishes such as duck and olives, roast lamb and veal *sauté*; their set menus range from 110F to 140F, including wine.

Olmeta-di-Tuda to Murato

If you continue along the D82 you come to the hamlet of **OLMETA-DI-TUDA**, which rises abruptly from the rocky slopes. Huge elm trees dominate the foreground, and the distant peaks of Monte Asto create a forbidding backdrop.

A further 3km along, the crossroads at the **Col de San Stefano** (349m) marks the entrance to the **Défilé de Lancône**, an exhilarating, precipitous descent that hits the main coast road 9km south of Bastia. Hewn out of the black rock, with nationalist graffiti adorning the rock face at every lurching bend, the road winds far above the River Bevinco, from whose bed the serpentine for the church of San Michele de Murato was quarried. The Défilé is a road to be treated with respect – numerous little shrines along the way testify to the fatal smashes that have occurred here.

If you continue along the D5 instead of taking the Défilé, you'll soon pass the Pisan church of **San Michele de Murato**, which sits gracefully on a grassy ledge high above the hazy mountainous landscapes of the Nebbio. Built around 1280, this late Romanesque building is notable for its asymmetrical patterning of dark-green serpentine and off-white marble, a jazzy counterpoint to the simple lines of the single-naved church, though these were damaged in the late nineteenth century, when the disproportionate bell tower was added. Outside, there's some sophisticated carving on the arches of the blind arcades and immediately beneath the roof, depicting gargoyles, wild beasts and human figures – look out for a relief on the north wall, showing an ashamed Eve reaching out to take the huge apple proffered by the serpent. Within the church you'll find less to catch the eye, although there's a faded fifteenth-century

Annunciation frescoed on the arch of the apse. The church is always open to visitors.

The village of **MURATO**, a short distance beyond the church, has a good, inexpensive **restaurant**, *Le Monastère*, which serves delicious roast kid and lamb in maquis herbs at tables on a grassy terrace overlooking the village. Murato is also renowned for its crusty round bread (*miches*) and plaited loaves (*scaccies* and *scacettes*), which you can buy in the boulangerie just down the road from *Le Monastère*. For a gourmet meal, try the *Ferme-Auberge Campu di Monte*, a wonderful farmhouse restaurant perched on the mountain on the outskirts of the village (☎04 95 37 64 39; reservation essential; June 28–Sept 15 daily; Sept 16–June 27 Fri & Sat evening, Sun lunchtime). At around 200F per head for the full works, it's not cheap, but the views are great (especially at sunset) and the food sublime, with traditional soft-cheese doughnuts (*beignets de fromage*), veal stews and fresh trout among their specialities. Finding the place is something of a challenge: turn left at the *Victor Bar* in the village, and follow the road down to the river at the bottom of the valley; shortly after the bridge, an unsurfaced track (indicated with a sign for the auberge) turns right off the road, heading 1.5km to the farm.

On from Murato

To continue the Nebbio tour, backtrack to the D162, which hugs the side of the Tenda massif as it runs west, snaking through villages built precariously on the lip of a shadowy forested valley. At **RAPALE**, a tiny ancient hamlet with castle-like houses built of schist stone, you can see the Romanesque chapel of **San Cesareo**, a green-and-white ruin hidden in the woods south above the village – it's a fifteen-minute walk.

Back on the main road, another 2km will bring you to **PIÈVE**. Set on a plinth in front of the church in the heart of this village are three well-preserved **stone menhirs**. Carved in the same minimalist style as the monolith at Patrimonio (see p.104), the 3000-year-old family group gazes out across the Aliso basin to the forbidding wall of cloud-fringed peaks to the west.

From Pième, the road twists through valleys along the River Aliso through Sorio and on to **SANTO-PIETRO-DI-TENDA**, an attractive red-stone settlement spread out under the shadow of the Mount Asto massif (1535m). An ancient chronicle recalls that a fierce battle took place on the mountain above the village some time in the tenth or eleventh century, when four thousand Moors were killed by a combined army of Spanish and Corsican troops, led by the Count of Barcelona. This defeat heralded the end of Muslim occupation of the island in the medieval era, but no traces of the momentous battle have ever come to light. These days the village's main point of interest is the tall Baroque **Église St-Jean**, joined by a bell tower to the contemporaneous Chapelle Ste-Croix. The latter is closed to the public, but inside the church you'll find the most lavish decor in the Nebbio – elaborate trompe l'œil painting on the walls and a gloomy seventeenth-century *Descent from the Cross* above the altar, which has a wooden tabernacle displaying some fine marquetry on its pedestal.

If you follow the road for 12km until it joins the D81, it's only 7km further to St-Florent.

The Désert des Agriates

Bordered by 35km of wild and rugged coastline, the **Désert des Agriates** is a vast area of uninhabited land, a rocky moonscape interspersed with clumps of cacti and maquis-shrouded hills. The desert's limits extend eastwards to the Golfe de St-Florent, stretch west to the mouth of the Ostriconi River and down as far south as Santo-Pietro-di-Tenda. Although it might appear inhospitable, the desert has a long agricultural history, as its name implies – *agriates* means "cultivated fields". During the time of the Genoese, it was a veritable breadbasket: the Italian occupiers even levied a special wheat tax on local farmers (most of whom came from Cap Corse) to prevent any build-up of funds that might have financed an insurrection in the area. Every winter until the early years of this century, shepherds from the mountains of Niolo and Asco would move down with their flocks to the desert for the annual bartering of goat's and ewe's cheese, which they exchanged for olive oil and wheat cultivated on the Agriates. The grain was stockpiled in square stone storage huts known as *pagliaghju* or *paillers*, about twenty groups of which still exist and are nowadays used by hunters for shelter.

In the course of the eighteenth and nineteenth centuries, fires and soil erosion reduced the region to desert, and it was a total wilderness by the 1970s, when numerous crackpot schemes to redevelop the area were mooted. These included a proposal to convert it into a test zone for atomic weapons, and a plan to transform the entire coast into a purpose-built Club-Med-style tourist complex, complete with concrete holiday villages and a giant marina. In order to block these schemes, the government gradually acquired the Agriates from its various owners (among them the Rothschild family), designating it a protected site. Wildlife, however, remains under threat, not least from trigger-happy hunters. Various ecologically sound projects are currently under discussion, such as plans to introduce controlled breeding of the Agriates's **wild boar**, the purest type on the island due to the isolation of the area, but now endangered by illegal hunting. Other rare species, such as the huge orange-and-brown Jason butterfly, are also under threat of extinction, largely due to the fires that increasingly devastate the maquis (in September 1992, 7500 acres went up in smoke in a single day, fanned by a mistral blowing onshore at 150kph). The maquis also harbours many species of rare birds, including bee-eaters, red-backed shrikes and various kinds of warbler.

Marked footpaths are being established around the coast of the desert, but it remains a difficult area to penetrate by motor vehicle. Only one of its many beautiful **beaches** is accessible by car. **Plage de Saleccia**, 10km west along the coast from St-Florent by the Punta di Curza, is among the most exquisite beaches in Corsica. A glistening stretch of silver sand lapped by translucent green sea, it was among the favoured landing sites of the submarine *Casabianca* (see p.70). This historic connection, and the picturesque setting, was doubtless why Saleccia was used as a location in the World War II epic, *The Longest Day*.

The beach is most easily reached by heading 12km west from St-Florent on the main Calvi road, which passes through the hamlet of **CASTA**. A short way beyond Casta you reach the *Hôtel Le Relais de Saleccia* (see below), from where a very rough dirt track drops down into the desert. Before venturing any further, enquire at the hotel about the state of the track, which even when it's in good condition can only be attempted by 4WD vehicles and motorcycles. After 11km of relentless ruts, the *piste* passes Corsica's most remote campsite, *U Paradisu* (see below), and ends at a car park. This is a great base from which to explore the desert on foot, with paths leading in both directions up the coast. Head east around the maquis-covered headland for an hour and you'll arrive at the sheltered cove of **Plage de Loto**. This beautiful beach can be reached by boat from St-Florent (see box on p.104).

Practicalities

There's just one major road in the desert, the D81, which cuts across its south side and passes through the **Bocca di Vezzu** (312m), a mountain pass where fabulous views extend across to the Nebbio. Any of the buses running between Calvi or L'Île Rousse and Bastia will drop you at Casta, where *Le Relais de Saleccia* (☎04 95 37 14 60; ④; Easter–Oct) is the only **hotel** in the area. Run by a welcoming young couple, the hotel, which boasts a fine view of Monte Genova and the surrounding desert, has ten rooms (three of them with terraces). A meal at their small restaurant will set you back a little under 100F. **Mountain bikes** can also be rented from here for the trip to Saleccia, costing 90F for a full day.

Campers should press on along the track from the hotel to Saleccia, where the *U Paradisu* **campsite** overlooks the beach from the brow of a shady hill (☎04 95 37 82 51; May–Oct). The ground is stony, but they have a bar, restaurant and café, and even change travellers' cheques.

For more **information** about the area, visit the Syndicat Mixte Agriate, in Santo-Pietro-di-Tenda (Mon–Fri 9am–noon & 2–4pm; ☎04 95 37 72 51), or the tourist office in St-Florent (see p.99).

Travel details

TRAINS

Bastia to: Ajaccio (2–4 daily; 3hr 40min); Algajola (2 daily; 2hr 40min); Aregno-Plage (2 daily; 2hr 40min); Belgodere (2 daily; 2hr); Biguglia (2–4 daily; 10min); Bocognano (2–4 daily; 2hr 25min); Calanzana (2 daily; 2hr 50min); Calvi (2 daily; 3hr); Casamozza (2–4 daily; 25min); Corte (2–4 daily; 1hr 30min); Francardo (2–4 daily; 1hr 5min); Furiani (2–4 daily; 10min); L'Île Rousse (2 daily; 2hr 30min); Mezzana (2 daily; 2hr 55min); Ponte Novu (2–4 daily; 50min); Ponte Leccia (2–4 daily; 1hr); Sant'Ambrogio (2 daily; 2hr 40min); Ucciani (2 daily; 2hr 30min); Venaco (2–4 daily; 1hr 45min); Vivario (2–4 daily; 2hr); Vizzavona (2–4 daily; 2hr 10min).

BUSES

The acronyms featured below refer to the following bus companies. For precise timetable information in English, telephone Bastia tourist office (☎04 95 31 81 34; see also p.62).

AF = Autocars Figarella (☎04 95 31 07 80).
APJ = Autocars Pavarini Jules (☎04 95 35 00 11).
BV = Autocars Les Beaux Voyages (☎04 95 65 11 35).
EV = Eurocorse Voyages (☎04 95 21 06 30).
RB = Rapides Bleues (☎04 95 31 03 79).
TM = Transports Micheli (☎04 95 35 64 02).
TS = Transports Saoletti (☎04 95 37 84 05).
TSD = Transports Saladini (☎04 95 35 43 88).
TST = Transports Santini (☎04 95 37 04 04)
TT = Transports Tibéri (☎04 95 57 81 73).

Bastia to: Ajaccio (EV; 2 daily; 3hr); Aléria (RB; 2 daily; 1hr 30min); Algajola (BV; 2 daily; 1hr 55min); Bonifacio (RB; 2–4 daily; 3hr 50min); Calvi (BV; 2 daily; 2hr 20min); Canari (TS; 2 weekly; 1hr 30min); Centuri (TM; 1 daily Mon–Sat in summer; 2hr); Corte (EV; 2–3 daily; 1hr 50min); Erbalunga (municipal buses 1 hourly; 30min); L'Île Rousse (BV; 2 daily; 1hr 40min); Luri (APJ; 1 Wed; 50min); Macinaggio (TSD; 3 weekly in summer; 2hr); Moriani (AF; 2–3 daily; 3hr 45min); Nonza (TM; 1 daily Mon–Sat in summer; 1hr 15min); Olmeta-di-Tudi (TS; Mon–Sat 1 daily in summer; 1hr); Patrimonio (TS; 2 weekly in summer; 30min); Porto-Vecchio (RB; 2 daily; 3hr); St-Florent (TS; Mon–Sat 2 daily; 1hr); Santo-Pietro-di-Tenda; (TS; 3 weekly in summer; 2hr); Solenzara (TT/RB; 2–3 daily in summer; 2hr 30min).

FERRIES

For ferry details, see p.75.

FLIGHTS

Bastia to: London (March–Oct 2–4 weekly; 2hr); Lyon (April–Sept 5 weekly; 1hr); Marseille (April–Oct 3–4 daily; 45min); Nice (April–Oct 3–4 daily; 45min); Paris (April–Oct 3–4 daily; 1hr 35min).

Chapter 2

The Balagne

Much of Corsica's northwest is taken up by the **Balagne**, a region divided into Haute-Balagne – the coast between Calvi and L'Île Rousse, and its hinterland – and Balagne Déserte, the area south of Calvi. In the past the Haute-Balagne was the most fertile region of Corsica, famous for its prolific production of honey, fruit and wine, but nowadays – though it has its patches of lushness – a stark brightness characterizes the fire-devastated landscapes of the interior, with acres of gnarled olive trees and wavy vestiges of dry-stone walls intermittently breaking the pattern of pale orange rock. If you're approaching this region from the east, the first glimpse of its coast is an arresting sight, the turquoise-and-white stripes of sea and sand making a vibrant contrast with the mottled land.

Calvi, the Balagne's largest town and Corsica's third largest port, is also one of the most attractive places in Corsica, with its medieval citadel rising majestically from a stark granite promontory. Six kilometres of sandy beach, backed by a dark ribbon of pines, ensures its popularity as a summer resort, the seasonal influx being served by numerous hotels and a string of campsites. Tourist development has got a little out of hand to the east of Calvi, where private marinas and expensive holiday villages occupy much of the Haute-Balagne coast, but the beaches are outstanding, none more so than at the former Genoese stronghold of **Algajola**. A stunning white strand also forms

Accommodation Price Codes

Throughout this guide, hotel accommodation is graded on a scale from ① to ⑧. These numbers show the cost per night of the cheapest double room **in high season**, though remember that many of the cheap places will have more expensive rooms with en-suite facilities. In such cases we list two price codes, indicating the range of room rates offered.

① under 100F/under €15	⑤ 300–350F/€45–52.50
② 100–200F/€15–30	⑥ 350–400F/€52.50–60
③ 200–250F/€30–37.50	⑦ 400–500F/€60–75
④ 250–300F/€37.50–45	⑧ 500F and above/€75 and above

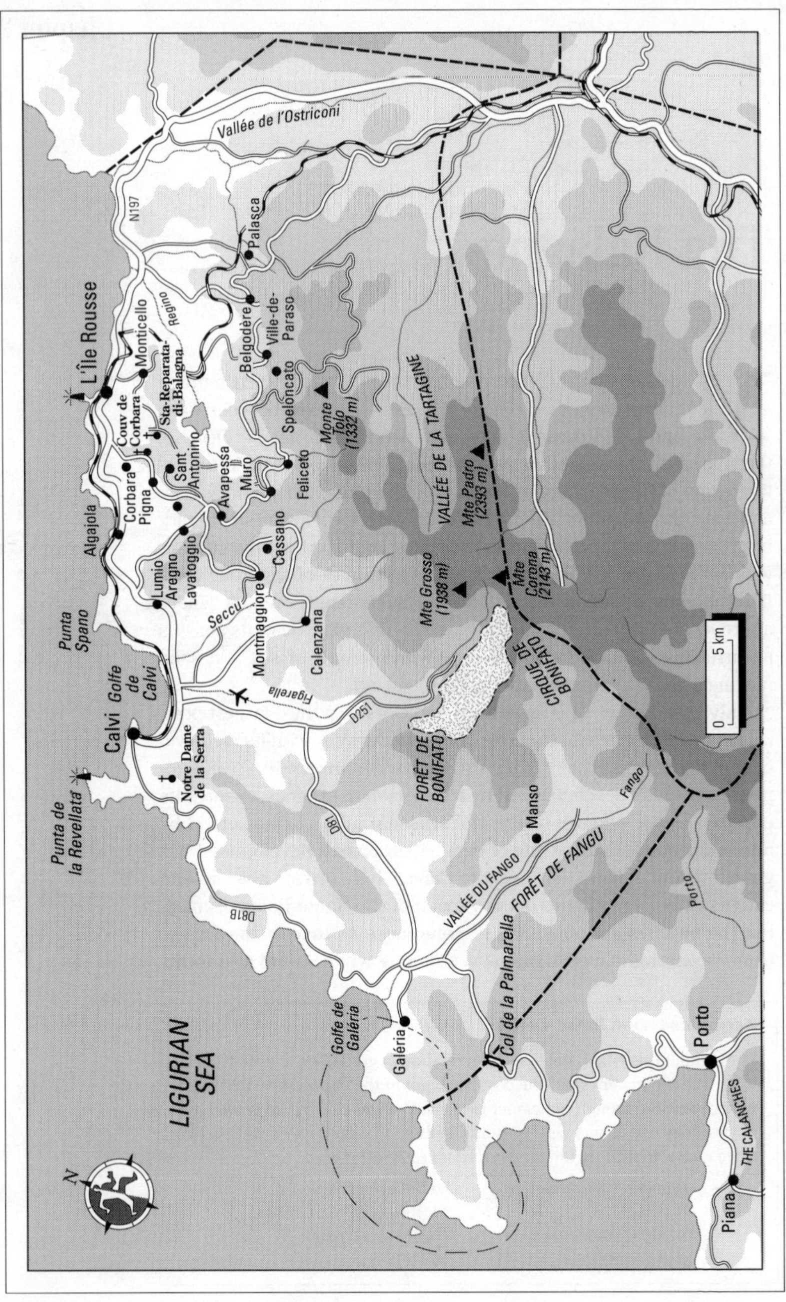

LIGURIAN SEA
L'Île Rousse
Calvi
Golfe de Calvi
Punta de la Revellata
Punta Spano
Algajola
Corbara
Pigna
Couv de Corbara
Monticello
Sta-Reparata-di-Balagna
Sant Antonino
Lumio
Aregno
Lavatoggio
Avapessa
Muro
Feliceto
Cassano
Montmaggiore
Calenzana
Seccu
Speloncato
Belgodère
Ville-de-Paraso
Palasca
Regino
N197
Vallée de l'Ostriconi
Monte Tolo (1332 m)
VALLÉE DE LA TARTAGINE
Mte Padro (2393 m)
Mte Grosso (1938 m)
Mte Corona (2143 m)
CIRQUE DE BONIFATO
FORÊT DE BONIFATO
Figarella
D251
D81
D81B
Notre Dame de la Serra
Manso
Fango
VALLÉE DU FANGO
FORÊT DE FANGU
Col de la Palmarella
Golfe de Galéria
Galéria
Porto
Piana
THE CALANCHES
0
5 km
N

the focal point of nearby **L'Île Rousse**, a beguilingly faded port built in the eighteenth century as a rival to Calvi.

The hinterland of Haute-Balagne is a glorious landscape, with thousands of abandoned olive trees swathing the rocky slopes, and fortress villages such as **Sant'Antonino** and **Speloncato** crowning the hilltops, each one embellished with a Baroque bell tower. Many of these settlements are at the receiving end of government programmes aimed at reviving ancient industries and crafts, so you'll see functioning workshops in various places – indeed **Pigna** and **Feliceto** are practically run by their artisan communities. The area tourist office has included most of them on the so-called **Strada di l'Artigiani**, or route des Artisans, which you can follow in easy day-trips from the coast; ask at any tourist office for the colour catalogue outlining the route.

The Monte Grosso massif, whose sheer granite spine dominates the horizon south of the Haute-Balagne, divides the coastal strip from the secluded **Vallée de la Tartagine**, a region of landlocked pine and chestnut forest known since ancient times as the **Giussani**. With only a handful of depopulated villages hemmed in by towering peaks, this isolated valley system harbours some the best hiking routes on the island. Its highest ridges are accessible via sections of the infamous **GR20**, which skirts the Giussani and presses southeast along the Corsican watershed towards the interior (see p.143). Most walkers, however, start the arduous ten- to fourteen-day route at **Calenzana**, in the hills southeast of Calvi. The village also marks the start of the more gentle ten-day **Mare e Monti** trail, which zigzags south to Cargèse through some of the Mediterranean's most dramatic scenery.

More detailed descriptions of both these walks feature on pp.144 and 146.

South of Calvi the terrain becomes increasingly grandiose, and the isolated coastal settlement of **Galéria** is well placed for excursions

Walks and Hikes in the Balagne

In addition to the two major long-distance hikes originating in the Balagne (the GR20 and Mare e Monti; see pp.144 and 146), a network of **footpaths** has recently been established between the region's three *communes*. Following the old mule tracks, or *chjappate*, that formerly linked villages, these wind across 200km of sea-facing hillsides, cloaked in beautiful olive groves and almond orchards; they're easy to follow and broken into manageable chunks (1hr 30min–3hr 30min), with a couple of longer routes connecting larger settlements. The paths are well marked with specially erected posts displaying the Balagne development council's cherry symbol, but you'll need a good map to make sense of them. In theory, the Pays Côtier leaflet, showing the trails on a monochrome map, should be available at local tourist offices, but they're like gold dust these days and you'll probably have to shell out for the more detailed **topo-guide** *Balagne* if you plan to do more than one of the hikes. The latter not only gives full-colour maps with the routes, but also good descriptions of the paths themselves. For more information, contact SIVU du Pays Côtier de Balagne, at the mairie in Avapessa (☎04 95 61 74 10 or 04 95 75 61 72).

into some memorable landscapes. Inland, there's the **Vallée du Fango**, whose dense forests track the river to the base of towering Cinto Massif, or the spectacular **Cirque de Bonifato**, a ridge of jagged peaks (among them the red shark's fin summit of **Paglia Orba**) encircling another forested valley.

Transport in the Balagne

The Balagne has scarce **public transport**. **Buses** from Bastia (with Beaux Voyages; 2 daily; ☎04 95 65 15 02 or 04 95 65 11 35) serve just the main coast towns, and a minibus (operated by SAIB; May 15–Oct 10 daily Mon–Sat; Aug daily; ☎04 95 22 41 99 or 04 95 21 02 07) runs along the coast from Calvi to Porto, via Galéria.

The **train**, operating all year round, hugs the Haute-Balagne coast northeast of Calvi, veering inland beyond L'Île Rousse to Belgodère, before continuing on to Ponte Leccia, which has connecting services to Bastia and Ajaccio. It's a memorable journey from start to finish, rattling past a succession of turquoise bays and red-roofed hill villages, with the grey cliffs of Monte Tolo (1332m) as a dramatic backdrop. The last stretch before Ponte Leccia traverses the desertified, empty Ostriconi Valley, before passing through a long tunnel to penetrate the heart of the island at the confluence of the Tartagine, Asco and Golo rivers. Two train services per day leave Calvi for Ajaccio (140F) and Bastia (92F); they run year round, but on Sundays and public holidays a slightly different timetable applies. Check departure times at any gare SNCF, or call ☎04 95 65 00 61. In addition, a slower, even more rattly **tramway** train operates along the Balagne coast between Calvi and Île Rousse (mid-April–Oct), stopping at all the resorts, campsites and *villages de vacances* en route.

A full run-down of travel services in and around the Balagne region appears on p.162.

A brief history of the Balagne

Archeological digs in the Balagne have yielded evidence of settlements dating back to the sixth millennium BC. Early Neolithic peoples hunted and gathered along the coast, moving gradually inland during the late Neolithic period; by the Bronze Age, most settlements occupied more easily defensible hilltop sites. Tools and bones discovered in these suggest that their inhabitants both hunted (mainly a now-extinct species of mountain goat) and reared sheep for milk, establishing an agro-pastoral economy that would endure more or less unchanged for more than four thousand years.

Sweeping economic changes occurred in antiquity with the arrival of technologically advanced Phoenician and Etruscan traders, but the Balagne's agricultural potential was only fully exploited by the **Romans**, who began the cultivation of olives here in the fertile volcanic soil. Known since these times, and in various languages, as the "Pays de l'Huile et du Froment" (Land of Oil and Wheat), the region became the richest on the island, and a prime target for the Saracen raiders who menaced the Mediterranean in the medieval era. The attacks subsided under the rule of the **Pisans**, who constructed forts along the coast to keep the marauding Moors at bay. They also erected dozens of beautiful churches and chapels, whence the popular nickname "Ste Balagne". After the **Genoese** takeover in the thirteenth century, the citadels at Calvi and Algajola were built, and these new ports did a steady trade with Tuscany, the chief cargo being the local olive oil, which for hundreds of years enjoyed a reputation as the best in the

For more background on piracy in Corsica, see p.102.

Bushfires and the Bovine Connection

Each year, between 25,000 and 50,000 acres of land are devastated by fire in Corsica (one fifth of the total surface area burned annually in France). All kinds of people have been blamed for starting the blazes – from lone pyromaniacs to cigarette-butt-chucking tourists – but the real culprits have only recently been singled out: **cows** or, more accurately, their owners.

The link between the annual infernos and the skinny cattle roaming the island's interior leads back to Brussels and the European Union's Common Agricultural Policy. In the late 1970s, the EU, attempting to reduce its milk lakes and butter mountains, introduced grants for dairy farmers to convert to beef and veal. Although they had never in fact produced much milk, the Corsicans responded by developing a sudden passion for cattle husbandry: within twenty years, the number of cows on the island nearly tripled from 29,000 to 80,000, bringing in a shower of lucrative **subsidies** from Brussels. Ironically, few of the recipients of EU money actually own any land – proof that you possess cattle is enough to secure entitlement. The cows, meanwhile, wander freely across communal areas of maquis, which the *faux éleveurs*, or "fake cattlemen" (also dubbed "the subsidy hunters"), routinely burn so that fresh shoots of grass will grow to feed their neglected animals. This technique has been used by pastoralists for centuries to provide food for cattle in long, dry summers, but their careful control of the fires meant that the amount of land damage was always sustainable.

That local cattle owners are behind the majority of bushfires has long been common knowledge in Corsica. However, it took a Fire Service study to bring the issue into the open. Dividing the island into blocks of one thousand acres, the *pompiers* kept detailed records of all fires reported and cross-referenced their findings with livestock ownership statistics. Soon patterns emerged, and it became possible to predict to within eighty percent of certainty when, where and in what weather conditions fires were most likely to occur.

In September 1994, when the bureaucrats in Brussels finally got wind of what was happening in Corsica, all EU aid to the island was suspended. The effects of the move were dramatic: bushfires fell to one tenth of the normal level that summer. Solving the problem in the long term, however, may be more difficult. EU subsidies bring in large sums of money for cattle owners, and any threat to their livelihood is bound to come up against stiff resistance. Nor is it only the farmers who benefit from the fires, but also builders (who restore damaged houses), foresters (to replant the trees) and, of course, firefighters (who welcome the overtime pay). Combine the financial disincentive with the customary Corsican mistrust of outside interference, and the future for the maquis looks black indeed.

Mediterranean. Under the Genoese, the region was divided into semi-autonomous cantons ruled by the local nobility or **Sgio**, many of whom were highly cultured men who had been educated in Italy – a remarkable contrast to the wild *Sgio* of Sartène (see p.260). Furthermore, although class divisions were as strong as elsewhere in Corsica, the peasants of the Balagne were distinguished by their versatility, with many working as tailors or cobblers as well as farmers, and by their greater independence from their lords, in that they were allowed their own flocks. The result of this comparatively enlightened rule was that the people of the Balagne remained loyal to Genoa well into the eighteenth century.

The Balagne reached its apogee in the nineteenth century, but decline set in when emigration began in the early twentieth century and the small oil mills in the depopulated villages could no longer compete with industrialized producers. It wasn't until the 1950s, when Calvi and L'Île Rousse became popular tourist spots, that the local economy began to pick up, and hotels and holiday complexes mushroomed along the Balagne coast. More recently, the new D8 road, linking Calvi to Bastia via Ponte Leccia, has improved communications with the rest of the island, while maritime traffic and flights to mainland France have increased in the last couple of years. Nevertheless, the economy of rural areas continues to struggle, in spite of attempts to develop small-scale wine and olive oil production with a modern irrigation programme; a telling fact is that the expensive new **Codole Dam**, inland from L'Île Rousse, has remained full to the brim since it was built because there has been so little demand for its water; the planned resorts hereabouts, for which the reservoir was constructed, have failed to materialize due to unwieldy local bureaucracy and the complexities of nationalist politics. Further setbacks to rural development have been the fires that have repeatedly devasted the countryside in recent years (see box on p.115), and an increasing number of nationalist-terrorist bombings such as the blast that destroyed Calenzana's main wine cave in 1987.

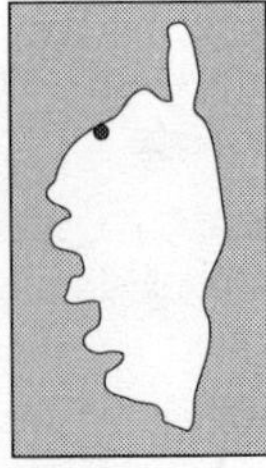

Calvi

Seen from the water, **CALVI** is a beautiful spectacle, its three immense bastions topped by a crest of ochre buildings, sharply defined against a hazy backdrop of snow-capped mountains. Below the citadel, a much-photographed strip of pastel-painted, red-roofed houses, belfries and spidery palm trees delineate the *basse ville*, with its yacht-crammed marina, from where the town beach sweeps in a graceful semicircle around the bay. Add a perpetually mild climate and convivial atmosphere, and you can see why Calvi has been attracting tourists for quite a while.

A popular hangout for European glitterati since the 1950s, when *Tao's* nightclub kept the tangos playing till dawn (see box p.126),

Calvi

Calvi in high summer has the ambience of a ritzy Côte d'Azur resort, with expensive quayside cafés whose clientele wouldn't look out of place at Cannes. A more down-to-earth holiday culture is never far away, though, thanks to the huge campsites that sprawl under the *pinède* (pine forest) to the east of the town, and the backstreets have their fair share of tacky souvenir boutiques.

Over the past few years, Calvi's cultural life has been considerably enriched by the numerous **festivals** that take place here. The best established of these is **Calvi Jazz**, which fills the bars lining the marina with big names from the international scene. September's **Rencontres Polyphoniques**, when traditional Corsican singers play host to some of the world's finest a cappella groups, also draws big crowds, **Festiventu**, in late October, sees the beach filled with hundreds of colourful kites and bizarre wind-powered contraptions. The town also hosts more authentic Balagne customs, principally Easter's **Granitola** procession of hooded penitents, and the October 12 celebrations for **Christopher Columbus** Day. Calvi is widely believed in Corsica to have been the birthplace of the great navigator, a debatable assertion proclaimed through a plaque in the citadel and various statues scattered about town.

For more on the annual festivals and events held in Calvi, see p.125.

A brief history of Calvi

Calvi began as a fishing port on the site of the present-day *basse ville*, but like many of Corsica's coastal towns it was victim to relentless Vandal, Ostrogoth and Saracen raids between the fifth and tenth centuries. Until the Pisans conquered the island, no more than a cluster of houses and fishing shacks existed on the site. Only with the arrival of the Genoese did the town become a stronghold when, in 1268, **Giovaninello de Loreto**, a Corsican nobleman, built a huge citadel on the windswept rock overlooking the port and named it Calvi.

The republic of Genoa granted the town special privileges, such as freer trading rights and tax exemptions, in order to ensure the fidelity of the population who, in any case, were for the most part Genoese. This fidelity was tried in 1553 by a terrible combined siege of the Turks and French, earning Calvi its motto: *Civitas Calvis Semper Fidelis*. In 1758 Calvi refused to become part of independent Corsica, a stand for which it suffered in 1794, when Paoli made an alliance with the British. A fleet commanded by Nelson launched a brutal two-month attack, bombarding the walls from all sides and eventually forcing surrender. Nelson left saying he never wanted to see the place again, and nearly didn't, for during the attack he lost his eye.

The nineteenth century saw a decline in Calvi's fortunes, as the Genoese merchants left and the French concentrated on developing Ajaccio and Bastia. One Victorian traveller described it as "a frowning fort with cracked, tottering ruins, worn and wasted by the rain". Later Calvi became primarily a military base, used as a point for smuggling arms to the mainland in World War II, and has been a base of the **Legion Étrangère** (Foreign Legion) since 1962 (see box on p.123); you're bound to see groups of cropped-haired legionnaires in their characteristic white peaked hats (*képis*) and immaculate khaki uniforms strolling up and down the marina, watched by couples of similarly attired military police. Tourism, however, is now the essence of Calvi: the town became fashionable right after the war and has done good business as a holiday resort ever since.

Arrival and information

More transport details are listed in "Moving on from Calvi" on p.129, and in "Travel details" at the end of this chapter.

Ste-Catherine **airport**, served by daily flights from mainland France and weekly charters from the UK and other northern European countries during the summer, lies 7km south of Calvi (☎04 95 65 08 09); **taxis** provide the only public transport into town, and fares shouldn't cost more than 70F during the day (or 90F in the evening and on Sundays). The **train station** is on av de la République (☎04 95 65 00 61), close to the marina and the air-conditioned **tourist office** on quai Landry (June 15–Sept 30 daily 9am–7pm; Oct 1–June 14 Mon–Fri 9am–noon & 2–5.30pm, Sat 9am–noon; ☎04 95 65 16 67), whose staff are very helpful.

Beaux Voyages' **buses** from Bastia and towns along the north coast stop outside the train station on place de la Porteuse d'Eau, whereas SAIB's minibuses from Porto pull in at the marina.

Ferries dock at the Port de Commerce, immediately below the citadel. For details of companies offering **car** and **motorbike rental** in Calvi, see "Listings" on p.128.

Accommodation

There are a vast number of beds for tourists in Calvi, and **accommodation** is easy to find except during the jazz and choral festivals (see p.117), when you should book at least a fortnight ahead. Hotels range from inexpensive *pensions* to luxury hotels with pools and sweeping views of the bay. Prices are generally reasonable, apart from during high season, when they go through the roof. If you're on a tight budget, take your pick from the town's two excellent **hostels**, or the dozen **campsites** within walking distance of the centre.

Hotels and pensions

Les Arbousiers, route de la Pietra-Maggiore (☎ 04 95 65 04 47, fax 04 95 65 26 14). Large, fading pink place set back from the main road, 1km south of town, with rooms ranged around a quiet courtyard. Good value (200F for doubles) outside July & Aug. ④.

Le Belvédère, rue de l'Uruguay, off place Christophe-Colomb (☎04 95 65 26 95, fax 04 95 65 33 20). Large, simple rooms, in a good location between the citadel and *basse ville*. Open all year. ④.

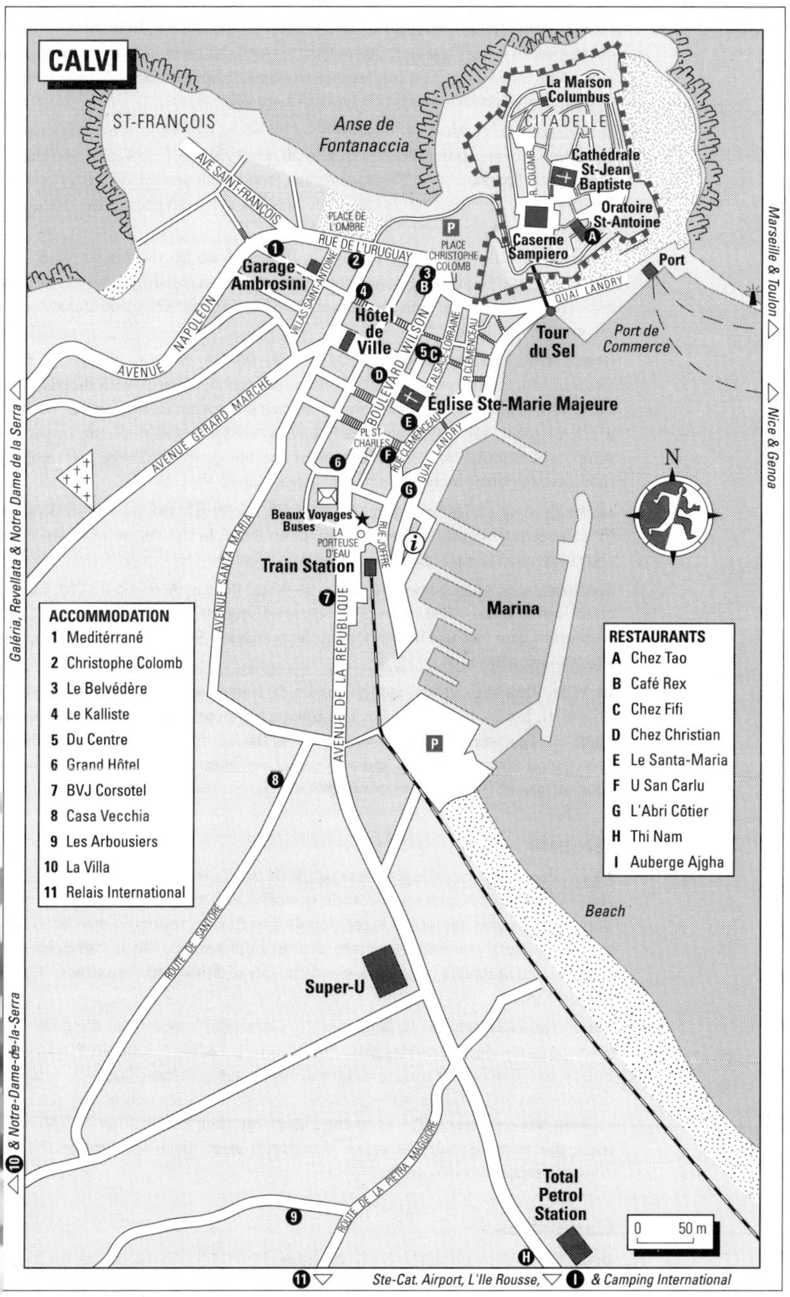
CALVI
ST-FRANÇOIS
Anse de Fontanaccia
La Maison Columbus
CITADELLE
Cathédrale St-Jean Baptiste
Oratoire St-Antoine
Caserne Sampiero
R. COLOMB
Port
QUAI LANDRY
Tour du Sel
Port de Commerce
Marseille & Toulon
Nice & Genoa
AVE SAINT-FRANÇOIS
PLACE DE L'OMBRE
RUE DE L'URUGUAY
PLACE CHRISTOPHE COLOMB
Garage Ambrosini
VILLAS SAINT-ANTOINE
Hôtel de Ville
BOULEVARD WILSON
R. ALSACE-LORRAINE
R. CLEMENCEAU
AVENUE NAPOLEON
AVENUE GERARD MARCHE
Église Ste-Marie Majeure
PL ST CHARLES
RUE CLEMENCEAU
QUAI LANDRY
Beaux Voyages Buses
LA PORTEUSE D'EAU
RUE JOFFRE
Train Station
AVENUE SANTA MARIA
AVENUE DE LA RÉPUBLIQUE
Marina
N
Galéria, Revellata & Notre Dame de la Serra
ACCOMMODATION
1 Mediterráné
2 Christophe Colomb
3 Le Belvédère
4 Le Kalliste
5 Du Centre
6 Grand Hôtel
7 BVJ Corsotel
8 Casa Vecchia
9 Les Arbousiers
10 La Villa
11 Relais International
RESTAURANTS
A Chez Tao
B Café Rex
C Chez Fifi
D Chez Christian
E Le Santa-Maria
F U San Carlu
G L'Abri Côtier
H Thi Nam
I Auberge Ajgha
Beach
ROUTE DE SANTORE
Super-U
ROUTE DE LA PIETRA MAGGIORE
10 & Notre-Dame-de-la-Serra
Total Petrol Station
0 50 m
11
Ste-Cat. Airport, L'Ile Rousse, I & Camping International

Casa Vecchia, route de Santore (☎ 04 95 65 09 33, fax 04 95 65 37 95). Small chalets set in a leafy garden, 500m east of town, and a stone's throw from the beach. In May, June and September doubles drop to 170F. A safe budget option, though book ahead. Closed Oct–April ③.

Du Centre, 14 rue Alsace-Lorraine (☎04 95 65 02 01). Old-fashioned *pension* ccupying a former police station in a small, pretty street near Église Ste-Marie-Majeure and harbourside. Pleasant rooms (most with shared WC) overlooking a garden. The cheapest option after the hostels, although prices rise sharply in July and August. Open June–Oct. ②–④.

Christophe Colomb, rue de l'Uruguay (☎04 95 65 06 04, fax 04 95 65 29 65). Comfortable and spacious rooms, most with expansive views across the bay. There's also a bar and restaurant. The best upmarket option this close to the centre. April–Oct. ⑦.

Grand Hôtel, 3 bd Wilson (☎04 95 65 05 74, fax 04 95 65 37 69). Characterful *fin-de-siècle* luxury hotel in the centre of town, with mostly period furniture and fittings. The rooms, though somewhat dowdy and in need of a lick of paint, are huge, and many have good views (as does the breakfast salon, which looks over the rooftops of the old quarter). There are smaller-than-average tariff increases in high season. April–Oct. ⑤–⑦.

Le Kallisté, 1 av Gérard-Marché (☎04 95 65 09 81, fax 04 95 65 35 65). Medium-sized, slightly airless rooms, all en suite, in the centre of town. Own restaurant and terrace garden. Closed Apr–Oct. ⑤.

Meditérranée, 45 av Napoléon (☎04 95 65 02 08, fax 04 95 65 37 75). Clean, comfortable rooms, 500m out of the centre along the D81 towards Porto. Own restaurant, and free use of the pool in the upmarket *St-Christophe* hotel opposite. Closed winter. ⑤.

La Villa, 2km out of town along Chemin de Notre-Dame-de-la-Serra (☎04 95 65 10 10, fax 04 95 65 10 50). The town's top hotel is a tastefully furnished, luxurious four-star with panoramic views of the bay from its large pool and terrace. Good sports facilities and a gourmet restaurant, though all at expense-account prices (600–4300F per night). ⑧.

Hostels

BVJ Corsotel, 43 av de la République (☎04 95 65 14 15, fax 04 95 65 33 72). Huge youth hostel in prime position opposite the station and facing the sea. Very clean rooms for up to eight people (no double rooms), some with balconies, at 120F per bed. A superb deal in high season, but no off-peak discounts. Inexpensive meals served in an institutional canteen. Open March–Nov.

Relais International de la Jeunesse "U Carabellu", 4km from the centre of town on route de Pietra-Maggiore (☎04 95 65 14 16, fax 04 95 80 65 33). Follow the N197 for 2km, turn right at the sign for Pietra-Maggiore, and the hostel – two little houses with spacious, clean dormitories only at 75F per bed looking out over the gulf – is in the village another 2km further on (along a track that's impassable for cars). Wonderful views from the terrace. Phone ahead to make sure it's open.

Campsites

Bella Vista, 2km along the N197 from Calvi (☎04 95 65 11 76, fax 04 95 65 03 03). A large, quiet and friendly three-star site, popular with bikers. To get here, turn right at the sign to Pietra-Maggiore, and the campsite's another 1km along on the right-hand side. April–Oct.

Camping International, 1km along the N197 near Prisunic supermarket (☎04 95 65 01 75). Well situated and shady, with more grass than most. The site's café is really lively on weekends (see "Cafés and bars", p.124). May–Oct.

La Pinède, 2km east of Calvi between the beach and N197 (☎04 95 65 17 00, fax 05 96 65 19 60). Popular site in a pine forest, with bar, restaurant, supermarket, tennis courts and telephones. Catch the train out here, and ask the guard for two stops after Calvi. Open April–Oct.

The town

Social life in Calvi focuses on the restaurants and cafés of **quai Landry**, a spacious seafront walkway linking the marina and the port. This is the best place to get the feel of the town, but as far as sights go there's not a lot to the *basse ville*. At the far end of the quay, under the shadow of the citadel, stands the sturdy **Tour du Sel**, a medieval lookout post once used to store imported salt. If you strike up through the narrow passageways off quai Landry, you'll come out at rue Clémenceau, where restaurants and souvenir shops are packed into every available space. In a small square opening out onto the street stands the pink-painted **Église Ste-Marie-Majeure**, built in 1774, whose spindly bell tower rises elegantly above the cafés on the quay but whose interior contains nothing of interest. From the church's flank, a flight of steps connects with bd Wilson, a wide, modern high street which rises to **place Christophe-Colomb**, point of entry for the *haute ville* or **citadel**.

The citadel

Beyond the ancient gateway to the **citadel**, with its inscription of the town's motto – *Civitas Calvis Semper Fidelis* (see p.117) – a narrow alleyway twists past the enormous **Caserne Sampiero**, formerly the governor's palace. Built in the thirteenth century, when the great round tower was used as a dungeon, the castle was recently restored and is currently used for military purposes, therefore closed to the public. The best way of seeing the rest of the citadel is to follow the **ramparts**, which connect three immense bastions. From each one the views across the bay to the mountains of the Balagne and Cinto massif are magnificent.

Within the walls the houses are tightly packed along tortuous stairways and cobbled passages that converge on the diminutive **piazza d'Armes**, next to the Caserne Sampiero. Dominating the square is the **Cathédrale St-Jean-Baptiste**, set at the highest point of the promontory. This chunky ochre edifice, founded in the thirteenth century, was partly destroyed during the Turkish siege of 1553 and then suffered extensive damage twelve years later, when the powder magazine in the governor's palace exploded. Rebuilt in Greek cross form and surmounted by a black-tiled octagonal dome, the church became a cathedral in 1576, as the reconstruction was drawing to a close. **Inside**, to the left of the entrance, are three elaborate alabaster fonts, which date from 1568. Beside the ostentatious marble altar stands a finely carved eighteenth-century wooden pulpit, while beneath the dome lies the tomb of the Baglioni family, an illustrious Genoese clan who made their money from trade in the fourteenth century. In 1400 the hot-headed Bayon Baglioni is said to have saved the town from a treacherous pair who were plotting to hand Calvi over to the Aragonese. As he stabbed the traitors, he screamed "Libertà! Libertà!", a cry that became part of the family name and eventually, by a circuitous line of descent, the name of one of London's most famous stores, *Liberty*. If you look up, you'll see a line of theatre-like boxes screened by iron grilles under the roof of the cupola; built for the use of the noblewomen of the town, the grilles acted as protection from the commoners' gaze. In the apse there's a seventeenth-century wooden statue of John the Baptist, framed by a solemn triptych dated 1498 and attributed to the obscure Genoese painter, Barbagelata. The church's great treasure is the **Christ des Miracles**, which is housed in the chapel on the right of the choir; this crucifix was brandished at the marauding Turks during the 1553 siege, an act that reputedly saved the day.

North of the piazza d'Armes, in a small patch of wasteland off rue du Fil, stands the shell of the building that Calvi believes was **Christopher Columbus's birthplace**, as the plaque on the wall states. The claim rides on pretty tenuous circumstantial evidence. Columbus's known date of birth coincides with the Genoese occupation of Calvi, at which time a weaving family by the name of Columbo lived in the town. Papers left by Columbus's son state that Christopher was the son of weavers, that he had two relations in the navy (there was indeed a Corsican sea captain named Columbo), who "came from the sea" (which could be interpreted as coming from the island of Corsica). What's more, Columbus is said to have taken Corsican dogs on his voyage, and he placed his first New World ports under the protection of popular Corsican saints. Believers claim that the Genoese deliberately burned the town archives in 1580 and renamed the street, formerly rue Columbo, in order to cover up the truth. The house itself was destroyed by Nelson's army during the siege of 1794, but as recompense a statue was erected on May 20, 1992, the 500th anniversary of his "discovery" of America; his alleged birthday, October 12, is a now a public holiday in Calvi celebrated with fireworks and speeches.

On the east side of the citadel, it's a quick walk along the ramparts to Maison Pacciola, where Napoléon spent a night in 1793. Close by, the **Oratoire St-Antoine** is an unremarkable building dating from the early sixteenth century, but look out for a graceful grey granite **relief carving** above the door, featuring Anthony, patron saint of Calvi, flanked by St John the Baptist and St Francis.

White Képis and Winged Daggers

Each year on April 30, ranks of immaculately dressed legionnaires from Calvi's Camp Raffali parade through town to celebrate "Camerone Day", commemorating a battle that, ironically, was among the worst defeats in French military history. Trapped in a cannon-scarred farmhouse on the road between Vera Cruz and Mexico City in 1863, a company of 63 men held out against an army of nearly three thousand, long enough for an important arms column to reach their besieged comrades in the capital. Only three came out alive. The Camerone parade is the public face of a very private army unit: the enigmatic **2e Régiment Étranger de Parachutistes** of the **Légion Étrangère**.

The French Foreign Legion was formed in 1831 at the behest of King Louis Philippe as a means to gainfully employ the potentially troublesome hordes of economic migrants and excitable revolutionaries collecting in Paris at that time. Enticed by the promise of French citizenship in exchange for five years' service (an incentive that still exists today), the recruits were promptly packed off to fight in France's North African colonies. Expected to march 30km per day across soft sand carrying full packs, the first legionnaires were just as likely to perish from heat exhaustion and dysentery as battle wounds.

It was during this era that many of the clichés surrounding the Legion were coined; deserters were indeed buried up to their necks in sand to face the Saharan sun with their eyelashes sewn open, or dragged for days tied to mule carts. But in spite of the inhumane conditions, recruits continued to pour in. Many – like the American songwriter Cole Porter, English philosopher Arthur Koestler and the young Prince Aage of Denmark – did so for pure adventure; many more signed up to flee debt, prison or unhappy love affairs. Then, as today, the legion offered **anonymity** for its recruits. For the first year of service, legionnaires are given a false name and there's an unwritten law that no one should be forced to answer questions about their past. Today, the Légion Étrangère comprises 8500 men from more than one hundred countries. The selection process they have to endure is among the toughest of its kind, beginning with an arduous three-week physical fitness ordeal at the Legion's headquarters in Aubagne on the mainland, after which recruits are assigned to units all over the world.

The muscle-bound, crew-cut Rambo lookalikes you'll see swaggering around Calvi's quai Landry in their knife-edge creases and white *képis* are members of the Legion's elite force, hand-picked from the cream of the recruits. Based at Camp Raffali, on the southeast edge of town, the 2e REP earned its fame with a daring raid on Kolwezi, Zaire, in 1978, when three thousand expatriate civilians were rescued with ruthless efficiency from the midst of a communal massacre. Training of today's 1300 crack paras exploits the mountainous terrain of the Corsican interior and the varied coastal terrain near Calvi, where month-long courses culminate in 72-hour missions, during which recruits carry out high-altitude parachute drops, amphibious landings and simulate hostage rescues. Anyone who survives this basic training gets to wear the coveted green beret bearing the famous winged-hand-and-dagger emblem of the 2e REP. More often than not, however, it is the distinctive *képis* you'll encounter on the quai Landry, pulled more steeply over the eyes by Calvi's notoriously arrogant legionnaires than by those from regular regiments.

The beach

Calvi's spectacular **beach** sweeps right round the bay from the end of quai Landry. Most of the first kilometre or so is owned by bars, which rent out sun loungers for a hefty price, but these can be avoided by following the track behind the sand to the start of a more secluded stretch. The sea might not be as sparklingly clear as at many other Corsican beaches, but it's warm, shallow and free of rocks. You can also swim and sunbathe off the rocks at the foot of the citadel, which have the added attraction of fine views across the bay.

Eating, drinking and nightlife

Eating is a major pastime in Calvi and you'll find a wide selection of restaurants and snack bars catering for all tastes, though few offer outstanding value for money. This is particularly true of the **fish restaurants** lining the marina, where a three-course seafood supper fresh from the bay can cost upwards of 250F. As a rule, it's cheaper to eat in the backstreets of the *basse ville*, whose stairways and cramped forecourts hide a host of buzzing, inexpensive pizzerias and Corsican restaurants.

Cafés, complete with raffia parasols, are strung along the marina, becoming more expensive the nearer they are to the Tour de Sel. The best places are those closest to the beach, which also get the sun all day.

Calvi's **nightlife** is livelier than you might expect, with discos opening up all over town in the summer; the best of the marina's discos is *Le Calypso*, at the far end of quai Landry under the citadel (summer only). There's also a summer open-air cinema, *Le Pop Cyrno*s, next to the Rallye supermarket on the N197, 1km out of town towards L'Île Rousse, which screens new releases (dubbed in French).

For **food shopping**, Calvi's two largest **supermarkets**, Prisunic and Super U, are both south of the centre on the main road (av de la République). You can also buy groceries at the small self-service *alimentation* on the corner of rue Joffre and rue Georges, above quai Landry (open Sun during the tourist season), or at the daily fruit and vegetable **market** in the hall between rue Clemenceau and boulevard Wilson.

Cafés and bars

Café International, in the campsite of the same name, 1km south of town on the main L'Île Rousse road. The most happening café-bar in Calvi, open daily but liveliest on Friday and Saturday nights in summer, hosting live rock and local jazz-funk bands. Drinks at regular prices, and a refreshingly relaxed, mixed-nationality crowd. Open till late.

Café Rex, top of bd Wilson on the corner of place Christophe-Colomb. An old-fashioned, smoky French-style café that's a good spot to kill time while waiting for a bus. Popular with locals and visitors alike.

Restaurants

L'Abri Côtier, on the quay, but entrance on rue Joffre. Mostly seafood dishes (fish and *langouste* from the gulf) and pizzas (from 45F) served on a terrace looking out to sea. Their set menus (100/165F) and *suggestions du jour* are invariably the best deals; for vegetarians, there's a delicous *millefeuille concombre à la mozzarella*. Closed in winter.

Auberge Ajgha, 5km south of town (☎04 95 65 35 15). Head for Ste-Catherine airport and look for the sign on the right of the road a short way after the turn off the N197; the *auberge* lies 1km further down a rutted (but motorable) track. Set on a hillside, with its own picturesque garden, this is the most congenial restaurant in the area, run by a warm Corsican-Spanish couple. Starters include calamari and melt-in-the-mouth dates stuffed with *brocciu*, and there's usually a choice of four main courses (mostly grilled meat or fish), washed down with AOC Balagne wine. Five-course menu from 150F. Advance (same-day) reservations essential. No credit cards.

Chez Christian, place Maréchal. A good option if you're on a tight budget, with a filling 69F three-course menu, served in a small square beneath the mairie. As an accompaniment, try their light French cider.

Chez Fifi, place du Marché (☎04 95 65 39 16). Unpretentious place with small inner courtyard that's deservedly popular with cost-conscious tourists for its good-value set menus (75–125F). The house wine (40F per litre) is local AOC quality, and a resident guitar duo adds to the atmosphere in summer (music on Fridays from 8pm).

Chez Tao's, rue St-Antoine, in the citadel (☎04 95 65 00 73). Legendary nightclub (see box on p.126), now turned into an expensive piano bar with fussy nouvelle cuisine and local fish dishes, ranging from 100F to 150F à la carte. Outstanding view of the bay. June–Sept 7pm–midnight.

U San Carlu, place St-Charles, off rue Clemenceau (☎04 95 65 92 20). Fine seafood and moderately priced French-Corsican cuisine served in a former (sixteenth-century) Genoese hospital in the old quarter. Choose from five *menus fixes* (from 85F to 130F) and sixty à la carte dishes, served in a colonial-style garden terrace, shaded by palm trees and bougainvillea bushes. Closed Nov–March.

Le Santa Maria, next to the Église Ste-Marie-Majeure, rue Clemenceau (☎04 95 64 04 19). Popular four-course tourist menu (89F), and particularly good paella (100F), served in an atmospheric little square in front of the church; the AOC house wine (35F) is excellent.

Thi Nam, opposite Total petrol station, 1km east of town on the main road (☎04 95 65 38 62). Authentic, spicy Vietnamese main dishes (duck, chicken, prawn and beef) from 40F to 55F. The interior's uninspiring; you'd do better to take away.

Festivals and events

Over the last decade Calvi has sought to reinvent itself as the island's culture capital through hosting a string of lively music **festivals** and **arts events**, over the summer and in the early autumn. One of the chief instigators of this renaissance was Jean-Témir Kéréfoff, son of the famous nightclub impressario, Tao, who saw a festival scene as the ideal way to assert a new identity for a town

Tao

A rare Dionysiac interlude in Dorothy Carrington's classic but rather staid portrait of Corsica, *Granite Island*, occurs in a club in Calvi in the late 1940s:

> *The night was gathering impetus ... it carried us with the rising moon into dark, unexplored, fathomless places. The music was hypnotic. No-one resisted it; the dancers moved with a taut, controlled violence, the men crouching over their partners as if kindling a fire.*

When Lady Carrington was being whisked off her feet by dashing legionnaires and "unnaturally quiet men from Calenzana", *Chez Tao's* (see p.125) was still owned and run by its founder, Tao, a charismatic Russian whose life story reads like the plot from a lurid Picaresque novel. A handsome Tcherkess Muslim from the Caucasus, Tao came to Calvi via a convoluted odyssey that began with him fleeing slaughter following the defeat of his White Russian cavalry regiment in the Crimea. He escaped to Constantinople and scraped a living as a dancer, performing for the sultan and his harem. From Turkey he danced through the vaudeville theatres and ballrooms of Europe to Paris and eventually New York where, in 1928, he met **Feliz Youssoupof**, a rich Russian nobleman believed to be one of Rasputin's murderers. The two became firm friends and together decided to return to Paris, and then to Calvi.

The arrival of the exotic pair, together with their musical entourage, must have cut a dash in the (then) sedate Corsican town. Before long, peasants and fishermen from all over the island were flocking in to watch Tao's show, and to dance with the foreign thespians on the quayside (at that time women dared not venture out at night, so men danced with them "sailor style", as Dorothy Carrington puts it). His popularity was still running high when his benefactor left, and the resourceful Tao, now married to a local woman, was able to open a nightclub in the former chapel of a bishop's palace in the citadel.

Now run by Tao's son, *Chez Tao's* occupies the same sixteenth-century vault and still does a brisk trade during the season, but it's no longer a place where, in Dorothy Carrington's words, "masks and attitudes slip away". Far from it: posing and star-spotting these days preoccupy the majority of *Chez Tao's* summer punters. The local contingent, however, remain as "unnaturally quiet" as ever.

whose inhabitants feel perennially outnumbered – by tourists in the summer, and legionnaires in the winter months. The festivals generally don't pay performers, but instead offer a week's expenses-paid stay in a local hotel. Specific dates and details, for all the events listed below, are available through the Calvi tourist office (see p.118).

La Passion, Good Friday, Calvi. One of the island's most sombre Easter celebrations revolves around a procession of hooded penitents called *La Granitola* ("The Snail" in Corsican), which takes place on Good Friday. Starting at 9pm in Calvi's *basse ville*, the line of penitents, barefoot and carrying simple wooden crosses, winds and unwinds itself through the streets to the citadel, accompanied by an eerie chanting from the onlookers.

Festival du Jazz, third or fourth week of June, Calvi. One of the highlights of France's packed jazz calendar, featuring headline acts from all over the world. Tickets for the formal evening gigs (available at the marquee on the north side of the marina, immediately below the citadel) cost around 150F, but you can catch spontaneous free jam sessions, or *bœufs*, in the bars on quai Landry afterwards.

Citadella in Festa, Ascension Day, 15 August, Calvi. A lively celebration of Corsican culture, with conferences, exhibitions of local crafts, and concerts culminating with a firework-spangled *son et lumière* at the citadel.

Rencontres d'Art Contemporain, mid-June to early August, Calvi. Exhibitions by local artists at various galleries in the citadel.

Rencontres de Chants Polyphoniques, mid-September, Calvi. Corsica's principal festival of song is hosted by renowned Corsican singer Jean-Claude Acquaviva and his wonderful polyphonies group, A Filetta, who share the stage with top a cappella performers from around the world. Regular workshops run throughout the fortnight.

Festiventu, late October, Calvi (☎04 95 65 06 67; *www.festival-du-vent.com*). Calvi psychs itself up for winter with a feast of kite flying and microlight aircraft displays on the beach, as well as other weird attractions loosely connected to the theme of wind. Perfect for children.

Around Calvi

Even without your own vehicle, you can take in some interesting sights around Calvi. For an unrivalled view of the town you could walk, drive or ride to the **Chapelle de Notre-Dame-de-la-Serra**, situated high on a cliff overlooking the bay. An easier walk goes along the **Punta della Revellata**, the rocky peninsula that shelters Calvi to the west. Great views of this headland may also be had on the **boat excursions** down the west coast to the isolated village of **Girolata**, via **La Scandola** nature reserve.

Chapelle de Notre-Dame-de-la-Serra

Surveying Calvi and its mountainous hinterland from a picturesque hilltop south of the town, the **Chapelle de Notre-Dame-de-la-Serra** is a popular picnic spot, and an obvious target if you fancy a short hike inland. If you're travelling by car, follow the Ajaccio road for 3km, then take the left turn up the hill. An alternative route is the steep and rather slippery path that starts above *La Villa* hotel (see p.120): following the signposts off the main Calvi to L'Île Rousse road, drive or hike to the end of the lane running past the hotel, and follow the well-worn track that peels off left through the maquis for about twenty minutes until you see the chapel above you, set amid bulbous clusters of pale-pink granite.

Built in the 1860s over the site of a fifteenth-century sanctuary, the building boasts a fine parchment painting of the Immaculate Conception, but it's essentially the view that draws visitors – the great bastions of Calvi presiding over the perfect curve of the bay.

Punta della Revellata

To reach the **Punta della Revellata**, the long rocky headland forming the west arm of Calvi bay, follow the Ajaccio road (D81) from place Christophe-Colomb for 500m past *Camping Les Tamaris*. Just beyond the entrance to the site, a lane runs off to the right; head down this, bearing left at the fork further on, until you reach the arched gate to *L'Oasis*, where you should take the unsurfaced track off to your left. This becomes a gentle, shingly path that crosses the Punta Vaccaja peninsula before dropping down to sea level and a group of houses on the east slope of the Punta della Revellata. From here you can head uphill to join the trail leading north along the headland to the **lighthouse** at the wave-lashed tip of the *punta*. Return by the same route rather than via the D81, which lacks pavements and can only be reached on a rough, zigzagging and often steep road. This is a particularly fun route to do on a **mountain bike** (for details of cycle rental in Calvi, see "Listings", opposite), but is impossible by car.

Listings

Airport enquiries General information: Air France or Air Inter Europe (☎0802/802802 or 04 95 65 88 88); Compagnie Corse Mediterranée (CCM) ☎09 36 67 95 20.

Ambulance ☎04 95 65 11 91.

Banks and exchange All main banks and cash distributors are on bd Wilson. The bureau de change on place de la Porteuse d'Eau, at the bottom of bd Wilson (June–Sept 9am–noon & 3–7pm), is one of several such places that change money outside normal banking hours (for a hefty commission fee).

Bookshops Halle de la Presse, at the top of bd Wilson on the left as you're heading towards the citadel, stocks a good selection of English titles.

Bus information Agence les Beaux Voyages, Résidence Le Vieux Chalet, place de la Porteuse d'Eau (☎04 95 65 11 35 or 04 95 65 15 02). Departure times can be checked at the tourist office (see p.118).

Car rental Avis, 6 av de la République (☎04 95 65 88 38); Budget, at the airport (☎04 95 65 88 34); Citer, l'Orée des Pins (☎04 95 65 29 99), or at the airport (☎04 95 65 16 06); Hertz, 2 av Maréchal-Joffre (☎04 95 65 06 64), or at the airport (☎04 95 65 02 96).

Diving Calvi is one of Corsica's diving hot spots, with a wrecked American B17 bomber from World War II at the mouth of the harbour (only 30m down), and more challenging underwater corridors full of marine life around the Punta della Revellata. The town's five diving centres are: Calvi Plongée Citadelle, in the marina (☎04 95 65 33 67); Club de Plongée Castille, marina (☎04 95 65 14 05); Hippocampe, at the foot of the citadel next to the fishing outfitters (☎04 95 65 46 66); École de Plongée Internationale de Calvi, next to the marina car park (☎04 95 65 42 22); JMB Diving, route de Donateo #42, Lot les Collines 9 (☎04 95 65 87 59).

Doctors Dr Michel Fade and Dr Brigitte Malter-Fade, 6 rue Joffre (☎04 95 65 03 20).

Laundry The most accessible self-service laundry is in the car park of Super U supermarket, av Christophe-Colomb (daily 8am–9pm).

Left luggage Bags can be left at the train station for 20F per article per day (6am–7pm).

Motorbike and mountain-bike rental Location Ambrosini, rue Villa-Antoine, on the left just west of place Christophe-Colomb (☎04 95 65 02 13). Well-maintained motorcycles (500–125cc; around 250F per day) and mountain bikes (100F per day). Take along your credit card, which they'll need for the deposit (1500F).

Pharmacy Pharmacie Centrale, next to the *Rex Café*, bd Wilson, opens on Sunday during the tourist season.

Police Av de la République (☎04 95 65 33 30).

Post office At the lower end of bd Wilson.

Taxis At the airport and place de la Porteuse d'Eau (☎04 95 65 03 10).

Train information Gare de Calvi ☎04 95 65 00 61.

Travel agents Agence les Beaux Voyages, Résidence Le Vieux Chalet, place de la Porteuse d'Eau (☎04 95 65 11 35 or 04 95 65 15 02); Agence Corse Voyage, 6 bd Wilson (☎04 95 65 00 47, fax 04 95 65 26 71); Corsica Touring, route de l'Aéroport d'Eau, right opposite the airport (☎04 95 65 20 70).

Moving on from Calvi

Calvi is a busy air and ferry port during the summer, as well as a year-round terminus for the *micheline* train, and is thus fairly well connected to mainland France and the rest of Corsica. Daily buses run along the recently revamped N197/193 road link to Bastia via Ponte Leccia; transport services down the west coast from Calvi to Porto and beyond are less dependable. However you travel, check departure times and points in advance with the tourist office, or directly with the operator by telephone if your French is up to it, as these tend to alter slightly from year to year. Bear in mind that timetables change during the off-peak period (late Sept–early June).

By plane

Daily flights to Paris and Nice with Air Inter and Compagnie Corse Mediterranée (CCM) leave from Calvi's Ste-Catherine **airport**. Tickets for these may be booked at any of the travel agents mentioned in "Listings" above. Weekly charter flights from the UK (Gatwick and Stansted) also leave from here during the summer, and you can sometimes pick up one-way tickets on these through local agents, or by telephoning one of the charter operators in England, listed on p.4, who might offer you a fare for one of their unsold seats.

By ferry

Superfast Corsica Ferries and SNCM **navettes** to and from Nice run five times per week in each direction from July until mid-September, three or four times per week in April and May, three times a week in June, and twice each week or less from mid-September through the winter. The journey on the new NGV boats takes a mere 2hr 45min

Boat Excursions from Calvi

Catamarans, run by Colombo Line (☎04 95 65 32 10), leave Calvi marina every day during the tourist season for Girolata, on the west coast, calling at **La Scandola** nature reserve and the **Calanche** rock formations of Piana en route (see pp.174 and 175). Much of this beautiful coast is off limits to visitors and can only be seen close up from the sea, which justifies the somewhat hefty ticket price. Full-day excursions, leaving at 9.15am and returning at 4pm, cost 270F (children aged 4–10 half-price, babies free); the 2pm trip (return at 5.30pm) will set you back 220F (95F for kids). Along the way, the boat chugs into gulleys, or *failles*, in the stark red cliffs, and you can occasionally glimpse marine life through the glass floor of the boat. It's a good idea to book the day before, and be prepared for last-minute cancellations if the weather looks unstable.

and costs 250F–710F per vehicle, plus 210F–280F per person depending on the time of year. To make a reservation (essential in peak season), go to SNCM's office in the port opposite the excursion boat stalls, or Corsica Ferries' agent, Les Beaux Voyages, in place de la Porteuse d'Eau (☎04 95 65 11 35 or 04 95 65 15 02).

By train

Two **trains** leave Calvi for Bastia daily – one early in the morning and the other in the afternoon – taking around three hours to wind along the Balagne coast via L'Île Rousse. You catch the same trains to get to Ajaccio, but have to change at Ponte Leccia onto one of the services running south from Bastia through Corte and Vizzavona – a spectacular journey that takes around four hours. Timetables (*horaires*) are available at the tourist office and the SNCF train station in Calvi.

By bus

Buses from Calvi run throughout the year to Bastia with Les Beaux Voyages (Mon–Sat depart 6.45am; ☎04 95 65 11 35 or 04 95 65 15 02), stopping at Lumio, Algajola and L'Île Rousse along the route, and there's a quicker *navette* service to L'Île Rousse only from mid-May through October (July & Aug hourly, May–June & Sept–Oct every two hours; 50min). Beaux Voyages buses also run to Calenzana (July to mid-Sept Mon–Sat depart daily 2pm & 7pm; Sept 16–June timetables co-incide with school terms only; contact the company for exact times), trailhead for the GR20 and Mare e Monti hikes, and to Galéria (July to mid-Sept Mon–Sat depart 3pm; mid-Sept to June Mon, Tues, Thurs & Fri depart 5.30pm, Sat depart 11.30am). Ajaccio is more difficult to get to – you can either take a bus from Port de Plaisance to Porto (May 15–Oct 10 Mon–Sat depart 3.30pm) and then another bus from there the following day to the capital (both legs are operated by Autocars SAIB; ☎04 95 22 41 99 or 04 95 21 02 07), or take Beaux Voyages' Bastia service as far as Ponte Leccia, from where a connecting bus runs the rest of the way.

DAVID ABRAM

Nonza, Cap Corse

DAVID ABRAM

Tour Santa Maria, Site Naturelle de la Capandula

DAVID ABRAM

San Michele de Murato, Nebbio

DAVID ABRAM

Tour D'Agnelo, Cap Corse

T. WHY/TRIP

Quai Landry, Calvi

GREG EVANS

Plage de Perajola, Ostriconi, with Désert des Agriates in background

MICHAEL BUSSELLE/CORBIS

Plage de Verghia, near Porticcio

GREG EVANS

Road through Les Calanches de Piana

SANDRO VANNINI/CORBIS

Nationalist graffiti

DAVID REED/CORBIS

Pétanque

DAVID ABRAM

Plage d'Arone, near Piana

The Haute-Balagne coast

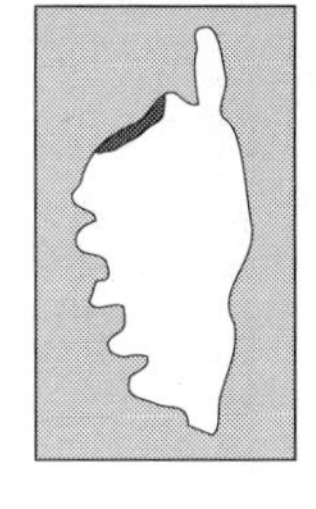

The **Haute-Balagne coast** may have been developed in recent decades, with purpose-built holiday villages and private marinas, but there are many unspoilt places to spend a pleasant few days in this corner of the northwest. East of Calvi, the N197 cuts inland through **Lumio**, a terraced village overlooking the gulf that boasts both an exceptional Romanesque church and the fascinating Centre d'Ethnographie et de Recherche Métallurgique, where you can watch steel being smelted and forged by traditional Corsican methods. One of the most pleasant places to stay in the area, is **Algajola**, a few kilometres further along the coast road, a compact, relaxed resort with a golden half-moon beach. Beyond here, the distinctive red-tinged headland of La Pietra shelters the rather overrated and overrun town of **L'Île Rousse**, and a couple of outstanding beaches.

At regular intervals along the coast road, you can turn inland to visit the beautiful Haute-Balagne hill villages, the pick of which are covered in the section beginning on p.141.

Lumio

Lining a sun-drenched hillside above the Golfe de Calvi, **LUMIO** was in ancient times the centre of a sun-worshipping cult, and was known to the Romans as *Ortis Culis* or "Where the Sun Rises". The proximity of the busy Route Nationale, however, combined with the absence of a decent hotel, makes this a less than promising place to stay, though the views over the gulf are wonderful (particularly at sunset) and there are couple of sights worth pulling over for.

One kilometre south of the village, on the N197 you'll pass the pale granite **Chapelle San Pietro** standing amidst a monumental cemetery. Founded in the eleventh century and rebuilt in the eighteenth, it retains some of its original Romanesque features, notably the palm-shaped capitals and geometric windows at the eastern end of the apse. The most outstanding feature, however, is the pair of grinning **lions** jutting from the façade above the door; it's thought they were originally intended to support a porch.

Just before you enter Lumio from Calvi on the Route Nationale you'll see a small sign marked "C Moretti, Couteaux d'art", which leads through the outskirts of the village to the **Centre d'Éthnographie et de Recherche Métallurgique** (Mon–Fri 11am–noon & 5–6pm; ☎04 95 60 71 94; free). A team of young craftsmen, led by founder **Christian Moretti**, mine ore by hand in the mountains of Cap Corse and refine it through an extraordinarily involved process, replicating the methods used in Corsica from the late Iron Age to the end of the last century. A video illustrates the various stages, and you can watch the smiths in the forge. A selection of their work is on sale, from pocket-size pieces (700F) to long blades worked into olivewood or bone handles (upwards of 7000F) – not as expensive as they

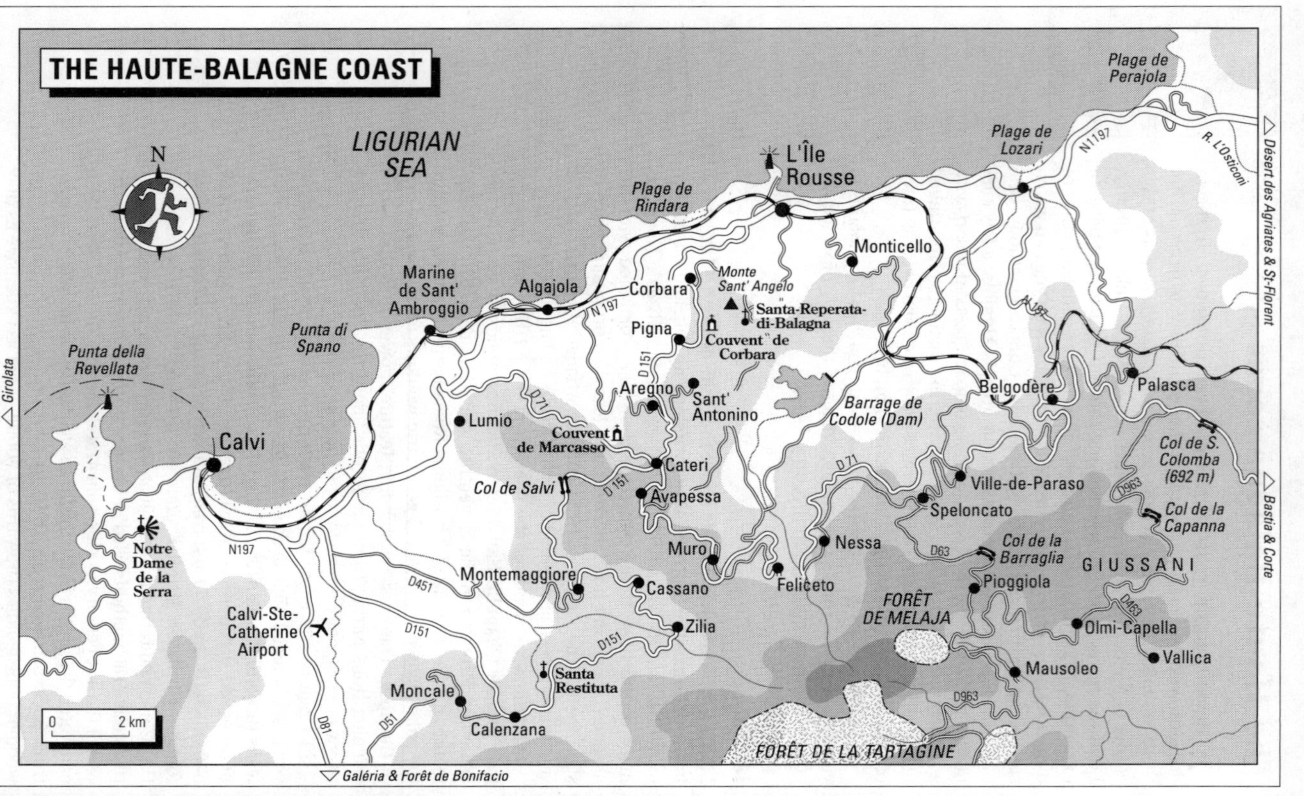
THE HAUTE-BALAGNE COAST
LIGURIAN SEA
N
Désert des Agriates & St-Florent
Bastia & Corte
Galéria & Forêt de Bonifacio
Girolata
0
2 km
Plage de Perajola
Plage de Lozari
R. L'Osticoni
N1197
L'Île Rousse
Plage de Rindara
Monticello
Marine de Sant' Ambroggio
Algajola
Corbara
N 197
Monte Sant' Angelo
Santa-Reperata-di-Balagna
Couvent de Corbara
Pigna
Punta di Spano
Punta della Revellata
D 151
Aregno
Sant' Antonino
Belgodère
Palasca
Barrage de Codole (Dam)
Lumio
D71
Couvent de Marcasso
Calvi
Cateri
Col de Salvi
D 151
Avapessa
Col de S. Colomba (692 m)
Ville-de-Paraso
D963
Speloncato
Col de la Capanna
Notre Dame de la Serra
N197
Nessa
Muro
D63
Col de la Barraglia
Montemaggiore
Feliceto
GIUSSANI
D451
Cassano
Pioggiola
FORÊT DE MELAJA
Calvi-Ste-Catherine Airport
Zilia
D151
D463
Olmi-Capella
Vallica
Santa Restituta
Mausoleo
Moncale
D963
D51
D81
Calenzana
FORÊT DE LA TARTAGINE

sound when you consider it takes the team a total of two and a half weeks to make a single small blade.

Algajola

Roughly midway between Calvi and L'Île Rousse, **ALGAJOLA** is Balagne's third largest resort, but a considerably quieter and less pretentious place than either of its more famous neighbours. Although the village gets as swamped as anywhere else along this coast during July and August, out of season you can expect to have the beach, Aregno-Plage, a kilometre-long curve of coarse sand beneath a picturesque Genoese citadel, pretty much to yourself.

Because of its exposed situation, Algajola has suffered the frequent attentions of hostile forces: in 1643, the Turks devastated the Genoese citadel, and in the 1790s Nelson assailed the town as a preliminary to the great Calvi siege. Despite such setbacks, the village did a steady trade in oysters and olive oil, and continued to be a major port on this part of the coast until L'Île Rousse developed towards the close of the eighteenth century. Its status was temporarily revived early in the twentieth century, when hotels were built over the old port, transforming it into a small but smart resort. However, decline set in after World War II, fuelled by the growing popularity of Calvi and L'Île Rousse.

Algajola consists of just one street, which begins alongside the beach, **Aregno-Plage**, and leads up to the **Citadelle**. Beyond the gates, the dominant building is the **Castello**, raised on its small promontory in the thirteenth century then heavily restored in the seventeenth, when the fortifications were added after the Turkish attack. For a hundred years, the fort served as the Genoese lieutenant governor's residence, and it is still an administrative building, so closed to the public. However, you can walk around the ramparts behind the castle, from where a path leads back down to the beach.

Algajola lies on the main bus and train routes between Bastia and Calvi, and is thus well served by **public transport**, with regular services in both directions throughout the year. Unless you're pushed for time, travel here by train, as the journey along the coast is highly memorable.

Accommodation

Virtually every **hotel** in Algajola overlooks the sea. Although none can claim to be anything special, their rates are competitive, especially between Easter and June and from mid-September through October. **Campers** can stay at *Camping de la Plage*, at the north end of the beach (☎04 95 60 71 76 or 04 95 60 72 12), or the more attractive *Camping Panoramic*, 4km west on the N197 (☎04 95 60 73 13), which is well managed and has wonderful sea views.

Le Beau Rivage, on the main street behind the beach (☎04 95 60 73 99, fax 04 95 60 79 51). The same view as *L'Ondine*, but at a more reasonable price.

Light, airy and modern rooms with tiled floors; those on the second storey have more spacious balconies. Cheaper options in the hotel's annexe. Obligatory half-board (⑧) peak season. ⑤.

De la Plage, on the beach (☎04 95 60 72 12, fax 04 95 60 64 89). An old-fashioned place, caught in a 1950s time warp, slap on the beach. Very good value given the size of the rooms and the views, but often booked (by groups of pensioners) in May, June and September. Peak season half-board is obligatory (⑧). ⑤.

L'Esquinade, next door to the post office by the citadel gates (☎04 95 60 70 19). The best budget choice: clean en-suite rooms (ask for one on the *côté jardin*), with tariffs dropping to 170F off season. No restaurant, but the bar's cheery enough. ⑤.

L'Ondine, on the beach (☎04 95 60 70 02, fax 04 95 60 60 36). A luxurious place boasting a garden, swimming pool and a panoramic view of the bay. Pricy half-board (860F per head) July & Aug. ⑧.

Saint-Joseph, at the entrance to the village if you're coming from Calvi (☎04 95 60 73 90, fax 04 95 60 64 89). Good-value, modern chalet-style rooms with turquoise shutters opening onto a breezy courtyard-terrace with sun loungers. ⑤.

Eating

L'Ondine, see above. This place has Algajola's most adventurous chef, who prepares traditional Corsican dishes with a dash of something unusual: lamb-and-chestnut stew or trout stuffed with *brocciu*. Set menus from 130F, or à la carte at around 175F per head.

U Castellu, in the little square behind the castle. Superb local specialities (such as red mullet with fennel and *herbes du maquis*) are served in a stone-vaulted room or on a cactus-lined terrace next to the citadel. Good-value *menu corse* for 110F, and a handful of *suggestions du jour* that often include "fish and chips" (sic). Alternatively, chose from the à la carte menu (dominated by seafood), with salads at around 50F.

U Furnellu, on the lane running between the main street and citadel. Inexpensive pizzas (45F) and a range of budget set menus from 85F, served in a pleasant square.

L'Île Rousse

Developed by Pascal Paoli in the 1760s as a "gallows to hang Calvi", the port of **L'ÎLE ROUSSE** (Isula Rossa) simply doesn't convince as a Corsican town, its palm trees, neat flower gardens and colossal pink 1930s hotel creating an atmosphere that has more in common with the French Riviera. Yet, for all its artificiality, the place has become unbearably popular in recent years, receiving more ferries and packing in more tourists than the larger port of Calvi. The proximity of three large white-sand beaches is the main reason for the resort's enduring popularity, together with its ultra-mild microclimate; thanks to the amphitheatre of hills that shelter the town from the cool winds blowing off the Haute Balagne's mountains, temperatures here average two degrees higher than Bonifacio and Porto-Vecchio, making this the hottest place in Corsica.

The Haute-Balagne coast

Pascal Paoli had great plans for his new town, which was laid out from scratch in 1758. He needed a port for the export of olive oil produced in the Balagne region, since Calvi was still in the hands of the Genoese, whose naval blockade was stifling the economy of the fledgling government. Originally the place was to be called Paolina, but the *Rubica Rocega* (Red Rocks) label had stuck from Roman times and L'Île Rousse it became. A large part of the new port was built on a regular grid system, featuring lines of straight parallel streets quite at odds with the higgledy-piggledy nature of most Corsican villages and towns. Thanks to the busy trading of wine and oil, it soon began to prosper and, two and a half centuries later, still thrives as a successful port. These days, however, the main traffic consists of holidaymakers. That the only town intended to be a Corsican success story makes its living from tourism as a classic French-style resort adds an ironic twist to Paoli's dream.

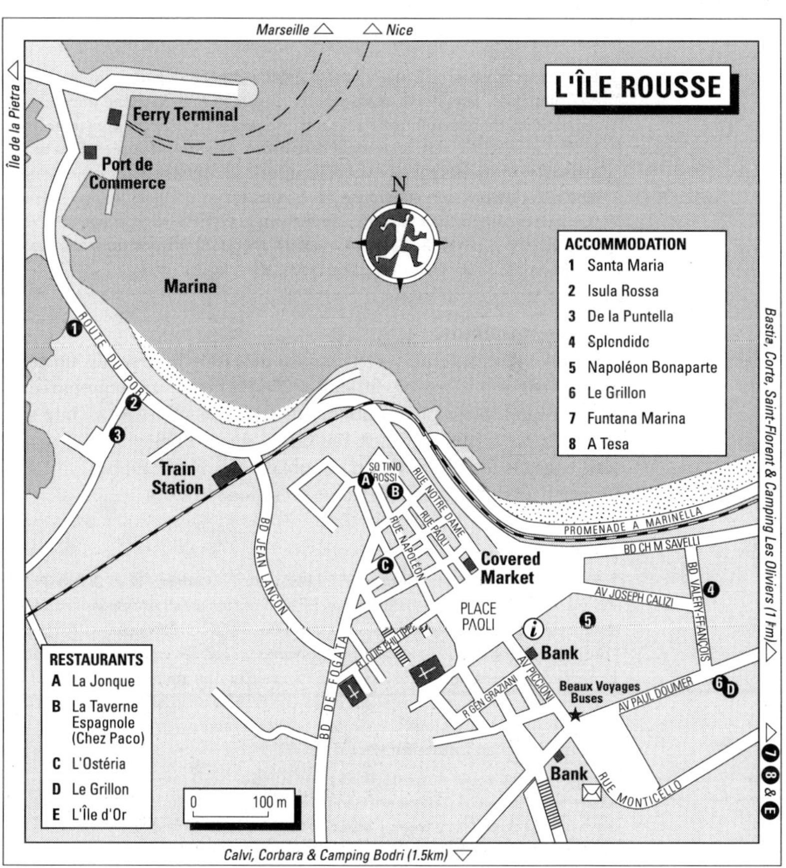

L'Île Rousse is connected by year-round **bus** services to Bastia and Calvi, with Autocars Les Beaux Voyages (☎04 95 65 15 02). The narrow-gauge **train** also stops here en route between Calvi and Ponte Leccia, where you can pick up connecting services to Ajaccio, via Corte and Vizzavona.

Arrival and information

The **train station** is on route du Port (☎04 95 60 00 50), 500m south of where the ferries arrive. Beaux Voyages's Bastia–Calvi **bus** stops in the town's main thoroughfare, **avenue Piccioni**, just south of place Paoli. The **tourist office**, on the south side of place Paoli (April–June & Sept–Oct Mon–Fri 9am–noon & 2–5pm; July & Aug daily 9am–1pm & 2.30–7.30pm; ☎04 95 60 04 35), hands out ferry and bus timetables. The **post office** is situated a five-minute walk to the east, in rue Monticello.

Ferries

Ferries between L'Île Rousse and mainland France depart from the Port de Commerce, 1km north of the centre. Between mid-June and the end of September, there are four to six daily crossings to Nice on the superfast NGV (2hr 45min), with additional departures on slower boats to Nice and Marseille (the overnight ferries taking up to 11hr 30min to reach the mainland). **Tickets**, which should be booked as far in advance as possible if you're travelling with a vehicle, can be bought from the SNCM agent, CCR (aka Tramar), on av Joseph Calizi (☎04 95 60 09 56), or from the gare maritime (☎04 95 60 11 30). For **fares**, see "Basics", p.8.

Accommodation

Such a long season (May–Oct) means that L'Île Rousse fills up early in the year and it can be difficult to find a **hotel**, so be prepared to hunt around. Most places double or triple their prices in July and August (the period to which the tariffs quoted below apply), when half-board is more often than not obligatory. For **camping**, you've a choice between two equally good sites close to town.

Hotels

A Tesa (**"Chez Marylène Santucci"**), Lozari par Belgodère (☎04 95 60 09 55, fax 04 95 60 44 34). The principal attraction of this small *auberge*, lost in the countryside near the Barrage de Codole, is the topnotch Corsican cooking (see "Eating and drinking" p.138), but Mme Santucci has seven comfortable, neatly decorated en-suite rooms, at 300F, and offers an unbeatable value 550F half-board deal (for two people). Follow the N197 towards Bastia for 7km and turn off onto the unnumbered lane running southwest from Lozari; the *auberge* is 2.5km further on your right. ⑤.

De la Puntella, route du Port (☎04 95 60 04 34, fax 04 95 60 40 87). Offering smart little "studios" (rooms with four beds, kitchenette and bathroom), which are usually booked on a weekly basis during August; particularly good value for families. There's ample parking, and a 10am checkout. ⑥.

Funtana Marina, route de Monticello (☎04 95 60 16 12, fax 04 95 60 35 44). A modern hotel, 1km south of L'Île Rousse, with a pool and better-than-average views of the town and bay from its rooms. Reasonable rates out of season, but very expensive in July & August. March–Dec. ⑦.

Le Grillon, 10 av Paul-Doumer (☎04 95 60 00 49, fax 04 95 60 43 69). The best budget hotel in town, just 1km from the centre on the St-Florent/Bastia road. Nothing special, but quiet and immaculately clean. Half-board in August (540F), but at other times rates fall to 250F per double. April–Oct. ⑤.

Isula Rossa, route du Port (☎04 95 60 01 32, fax 04 95 60 57 32). Smallish, tiled rooms with en-suite bathrooms, in a modern block on the seafront. Garden-side rooms are the least expensive. ⑦.

Napoléon Bonaparte, 3 place Paoli (☎04 95 60 06 09, fax 04 95 60 11 51). Converted *palazzo*, built in the eighteenth century, renovated in the 1930s, occupied by the King of Morocco during his exile in the 1950s, and garishly refurbished (in ice-cream pink) a decade ago. Now falling apart at the seams and undeserving of its three stars and high-season tariffs. That said, some rooms in the original (cheaper) wing have a certain faded charm; ask for no.225, whose room-service bell has a button for the wine-cellar man. There's also a huge pool. April–Sept. ⑥–⑧.

Santa Maria, route du Port (☎04 95 63 05 05, fax 04 95 60 32 48). Next to the ferry port, this is one of the larger and best-value three-star places. Rooms have air-con and overlook a small garden and pool. Open all year. ⑧.

Splendid, 4 bd Valéry-François (☎04 95 60 00 24, fax 04 95 60 04 57). Well-maintained, 1930s-style building with a small swimming pool and some sea views from upper floors; very reasonable tariffs, given the location. Half-board available. April–Oct. ⑥–⑦.

Campsites

Camping Bodri, 1.5km west on the Calvi road (☎04 95 16 19 70). Separated from the beach by the train line, and well equipped with laundry and a small pizzeria. It's also marginally less cramped in peak season than others in the area. You can get here direct by train (ask the conductor for "*l'arrêt Bodri*"). June–Sept.

Les Oliviers, 1km east of town (☎04 95 60 19 92, fax 04 95 60 30 91). Situated on a low hill overlooking the town, 1km towards Bastia on N197. Open all year.

The town

All roads in L'Île Rousse lead to **place Paoli**, a shady square that's open to the sea and has as its focal point a fountain surmounted by a bust, *U Babbu di u Patria* (Grandfather of the Nation), one of many local tributes to Pascal Paoli. There's a Frenchified covered market at the entrance to the square, while on the west side rises the recently restored façade of Église de l'Immaculée Conception.

From place Paoli, the three parallel streets of the **old town** run north to square Tino Rossi, where the Hôtel de Ville, formerly a military headquarters, displays the Corsican flag. Opposite stands a **tower** dating from before Paoli's time, but a plaque commemorating the Corsican hero has recently been placed on the wall.

To reach the **Île de la Pietra**, the islet that gives the town its name, continue north, passing the station on your left. Once over the causeway connecting the islet to the mainland, you can walk through the crumbling mass of red granite as far as the lighthouse at the far end. From here, the **view** of the town is spectacular, especially at sunset, when you get the full effect of the red glow of the rocks. Heading back along **promenade A Marinella**, which follows the seafront behind the town beach, a ten-minute walk will bring you to the town's main sight, the **Musée Océanographique aquarium**, situated at the far eastern end of the beach (April–Oct Mon–Fri 10.30am–1pm & 2–7pm; 45F). It publicizes itself as the "*Grotte aux Requins*", though the only members of the shark family on display are some timid dogfish. Nonetheless, the guided tour of tanks full of lobsters, conger eels, rays, octopuses and scores of other aquatic species is interesting, especially at feeding time. The owner, Pierre Pernod, knows everything there is to know about fish behaviour.

The beaches

Immediately in front of the promenade, the town beach is a crowded, Côte d'Azur-style strand, backed by a row of lookalike restaurants. If you have your own transport, you're better off heading 3km west, where a signpost reading "Roc e Mare" points the way down an unsurfaced track to the other most popular beach in the vicinity, **Plage de Rindara**. The track ends at a fee-charging car park, but you can actually park for free across the train line in the field that backs onto the beach (keeping off the dunes). A snack bar serves refreshments for the crowds in high season; outside August, you can usually rely on relative peace.

Eating and drinking

Tourism has taken its toll here, hence the abundance of mediocre eating places. However, a few **restaurants** stand out, most of them in the narrow lanes of the old town. With your own transport, you might also consider heading inland to eat in one of the hill villages (see pp.141–154).

The best **cafés** are those lining the south side of place Paoli, under a canopy of shady plane trees.

A Tesa (**"Chez Marylène Santucci"**), Lozari par Belgodère (☎04 95 60 09 55). Wonderful *ferme-auberge* inland from L'Île Rousse that's among the top Corsican speciality places hereabouts. All the ingredients are fresh and locally produced, and the portions copious. Their 180F fixed menu includes an aperitif, five courses, wine, eau de vie and coffee. Advance reservation is essential. (You can also stay here: see "Hotels", p.136.)

Le Grillon, 10 av Paul-Doumer (☎04 95 60 00 49). High-ceilinged, blissfully cool air-conditioned hotel dining hall with a limited, but consistently good menu of mainly French dishes. Their *steak au roquefort* and cod in spicy creole sauce are perenially popular, while for vegetarians there's a delicious courgette and basil pâté, rounded off with home-made honey-and-almond ice cream. Count on 110–150F per head.

La Jonque, rue Paoli. One of only a handful of Chinese/Vietnamese restaurants on the island. Drab, formulaic decor, but the food is fresh and spicy, and they do a good-value set menu for 95F.

L'Ostéria, place Santelli. Tucked away on a quiet square in the old quarter, this is the town's best Corsican speciality restaurant, serving good-value set menus (117F), including delicous *beignets de courgettes*, in a vaulted room adorned with farm implements. Closed Wed.

La Taverne Espagnole (Chez Paco), rue Paoli. Copious portions of tasty Spanish food (including paella, at 170F for two) and spicy fish dishes (including bouillabaisse, for 90F), served under awnings in a quiet backstreet in the old town. Aperitifs and digestifs are often on the house.

Listings

Banks Several large banks are scattered around place Paoli, but the Société Générale, which charges no commission for changing Thomas Cook French franc travellers' cheques, is on av Piccioni.

Bicycle rental Mountain bikes (VTT) are available for rent (100F per day) at La Passion en Action, av Paul-Doumer (☎04 95 60 15 76), along with advice on the most rewarding routes in the area.

Bus information Autocars Les Beaux Voyages (☎04 95 65 15 02 or 04 95 65 11 35) operates a year-round service connecting Calvi and L'Île Rousse with Bastia and Ajaccio, via Ponte Leccia (Mon–Sat 1 daily). Buses depart from in front of the *Bar Sémiramis*, on the junction of av Paul-Doumer and av Picconi, at 7.10am, or at 6pm heading in the opposite direction to Calvi. In winter, the timetable changes slightly, so check with the company or at the tourist office (see p.136) before you leave.

Car rental Europcar, place Paoli (☎04 95 60 30 11); Filippi Auto, route de Calvi (☎04 95 60 12 63); Hertz, place Marcel-Delanney (☎04 95 60 12 63).

Diving One of Corsica's best-known dive sites, a colossal rock draped in colourful corals, lies in the bay. Known as Le Naso, it's a prime spot for moray and conger eels. The town has two dive schools: recommended for advanced divers is Beluga, at the *La Pietra* hotel near the ferry dock (☎04 95 60 17 36); and the École de Plongée de L'Île Rousse, in a Portakabin near the ferry building (☎04 95 60 36 85), which caters particularly well for beginners and children.

Horse riding Arbo Valley, 4km east (singposted off the main Bastia road, N197), is an accredited riding centre offering short hacks and longer expeditions (☎04 95 60 49 49 or 06 12 06 34 38).

Laundry Rue Napoléon, one block down from *L'Osteria* restaurant (7am–midnight).

Left luggage You can leave luggage in the gare SNCF for 16F per article per day (6am–7pm). The *consigne* at the ferry terminal has been closed for the past couple of years for security reasons.

Pharmacy There's a huge pharmacy on the corner of av Piccioni and rue Monticello.

Post office rue Monticello, on the south side of town (Mon–Fri 8.30am–5pm, Sat 8.30am–noon; ☎04 95 63 05 50).

Taxis The tourist office keeps a list of private rental companies, or you can telephone direct on ☎04 95 60 04 35.

Train information gare SNCF, route du Port (☎04 95 60 00 50). L'Île Rousse is on the main *micheline* line, and connected by two daily services to Calvi (30min; 30F) and Bastia (2hr 15min; 70F), via Ponte Leccia, where you can pick up *correspondances* to Ajaccio (3hr 20min; 120F). In summer, the tramway train also shuttles five times daily to and from Calvi.

Travel agents Ferry and air tickets are available from: Corse Voyages, place Paoli (☎04 95 60 11 19); and CCR (aka Tramar), av Joseph Calizi (☎04 95 60 09 56), is the agent for SNCM and CMN ferry companies (both are open Mon–Fri 9am–noon & 2–6pm, Sat 9am–noon). Alternatively, ferry tickets can be purchased at the gare maritime (☎04 95 60 11 30).

East of L'Île Rousse

Two excellent **beaches** indent the wild coastline **northeast of L'Île Rousse**. The first, the **Plage de Lozari**, is a long semicircular sweep of pure white sand, 7km out of town along the N197. A surfaced road signposted "Lozari" leads down to the shore and a discreet holiday village that attracts huge crowds in summer.

For more on the extraordinary Désert des Agriates region, see p.108.

Even more spectacular is the much-photographed **Plage de Perajola**, at the mouth of the Ostriconi River, where the rocky hills of the Désert des Agriates ripple north against a backdrop of turquoise sea, forcing the Route Nationale east up the depopulated, denuded Ostriconi valley. To reach it, you have to turn north off the N197, 10km east L'Île Rousse, and join the old corniche road (D81); head past the campsite and *village de vacances* (see below) and continue for around 500m until you see a couple of lay-bys on the right of the road where you can leave your car. From here, a steep path cuts down through the maquis to the southwest side of the beach. Tourists from the holiday village spill over it in summer, but off season this is a remote and windswept spot. The wilderness immediately to the north offers plenty of potential for **hiking**, although you'll definitely need an IGN map of the area (#4249OT, ref C3/D3), as the main path does not follow the coast; instead, it cuts inland at the first inlet you come to after Perajola (a narrow bay called **Anse de Vana**, where there's a pretty sandy beach), and follows the north side of a scrubby stream valley towards the Baie de l'Acciolu. This forms the concluding part of a superb three- to four-hour round route particularly favoured by equestrian centres in the area (see p.139), who lead horse treks into the heart of the desert from here.

Practicalities

The whole stretch described above is covered by Les Beaux Voyages's daily Calvi–Bastia–Calvi **buses**; ask for a ticket to Lozari or the village de l'Ostriconi.

Inexpensive **accommodation** is available at the *Village de l'Ostriconi* itself, 1km inland from Perajola beach (☎04 95 60 10 05, fax 04 95 60 01 47; ④), where simple bungalows cost 260–390F peak season, dropping to 170–295F in April, May and October (the pricier ones have bathrooms and kitchenettes). The same owners also have a large, well-shaded campsite (same phone; Easter–Oct), within walking distance of the beach, but you can easily camp wild in the dunes behind Perajola – if you do, bring plenty of mosquito repellent, as the beach is backed by a brackish lagoon.

Inland Haute-Balagne

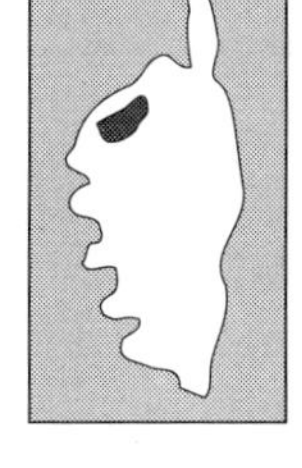

The fortress villages of **inland Haute-Balagne** are among the most picturesque on the island, their higgledy-piggledy terracotta rooftops and belfries presiding over an idyllic Mediterranean landscape of cypress-studded olive groves, backed by a dramatic wall of pale-grey mountains. Many of the settlements are nearly a thousand years old, having developed from the time of the Pisan occupation, when **Romanesque churches** such as the churches of San Trinita at **Aregno** and Santa Restituta at **Calenzana** were built. The rash of **Baroque churches** in the region emerged during the prosperous years under the Genoese, and some of them, such as the church at **Corbara**, warrant a visit for the sheer flamboyance of their decoration, even if Baroque isn't your thing.

A recent government redevelopment programme for the Balagne has meant the regeneration of certain traditional practices, including the production of olive oil using old presses. Young people are being encouraged to settle in the villages by the introduction of special grants for artisans willing to live and work here, and several places have their own musical and crafts societies – look out for posters advertising summer concerts in villages such as **Pigna** and **Belgodère**.

The only **buses** in the area run daily between Calvi and Calenzana (with Les Beaux Voyages – see p.162). The train stops near Belgodère, but to make the most of this beautiful area you need to have your own vehicle and be prepared to walk. Belgodère has some hotel accommodation, and there are more hotels at **Speloncato** and **Feliceto**.

Calenzana

Overshadowed by the great bulk of Monte Grosso and encircled by a belt of olive trees, the village of **CALENZANA** overlooks some of the most fertile land on the island. Historically an economic rival to Calvi, it's still a thriving agricultural centre, renowned for its wine and honey, plus the village speciality, a little dry cake blessed with the tongue-twisting name of *cuggiuelli* (pronounced "koo-joo-*ell*-ee"), which you dunk in white wine. There's a less pacific side to Calenzana as well. In the eighteenth century it was known as a refuge for Paoli's freedom fighters, who weren't welcome in the Genoese stronghold of Calvi, and this century it gained a reputation for harbouring French gangsters; with Marseille a quick hop across the water, many high-ranking mob members retired here in the 1960s.

Lying close to the borders of the national park, Calenzana is renowned among hikers as the point of departure for the infamous **GR20 hike** (see box on p.144), whose ten- to fifteen-day haul through the island's mountain spine starts just above the village. It's also the trailhead for the shorter **Tra Mare e Monti** walk, which traverses a section of the national park as far as Cargèse.

The lively core of the village, the **Piazza Communa**, is a pleasant tree-lined square dominated by the heavily Baroque **Église St-Blaise**. Founded in 1691, the church boasts a sumptuous but dusty interior. Its centrepiece is a marble altar (1750), to the right of which stands a seventeenth-century tabernacle with a particularly ghoulish painted border.

The bell tower beside the church, built in the 1870s, stands on the "**Cimetière des Allemands**", the burial place of five hundred Austrian troops dispatched by their king, Charles VI, to help his allies the Genoese quell an uprising in January 1732. With no artillery to hand, the villagers are said to have hurled beehives, tiles and boiling oil from their windows, set flaming cattle loose in the alleyways, and then used makeshift weapons to pick off the Austrians as they fled through the old town. Only one hundred of the soldiers survived the massacre – a turnabout that played no small part in forcing the Genoese to capitulate at Corte the following May, three hundred years before the island's eventual independence.

Practicalities

Run by Les Beaux Voyages (☎04 95 65 15 02), **buses** between Calenzana and Calvi operate throughout the summer (July to mid-Sept Mon–Sat 2 daily); off season, you can reach the village (in term time only) via the school bus – but this tends to run at inconvenient times (schedules available from the Calvi tourist office) – or by telephoning the above number. Most hikers walk or hitch the 12km of flat road from Calvi along the Bartasca river plain.

There are only two **hotels** in Calenzana: the *Monte Grosso*, at the bottom of the village, on the left as you arrive from Calvi (☎04 95 62 70 15; ④), which has ten basic en-suite rooms; and the *Bel Horizon*, opposite the church (☎04 95 62 71 72; ③–⑤; May–Sept), which is also fairly basic, but comfortable enough and popular with hikers. Most long-distance walkers, however, head for the congenial gîte d'étape *municipal*, a short walk off the D151 on the edge of the village (☎04 95 62 77 13), which charges 60F per night for a place in its clean eight-bed dorms. The gîte also has tent space for campers (self-catering facilities included in the 25F per-person fee), and serves simple evening meals if you order in advance the morning before.

A handful of **restaurants** in the village cater for the constant stream of hungry hikers pouring through. Best of the bunch is the

English-run *A Stazzona* (☎04 95 62 80 44), opposite the *Monte Grosso* hotel, which does a filling 90F Corsican speciality menu and a generous selection of fresh pasta dishes, tasty stuffed aubergine, omelettes and salads. A cheaper option closer to the square is the *Pizzeria Prince Pierre*, which serves pizzas from 35F on a pleasant terrace next to a fountain. To sample the famous *cuggiuelli* (see p.141), hunt out the Corsican speciality patisserie, *E Fritelle*, up a narrow alley called U Chiasu on the left of the road as you leave Calenzana in the direction of Calvi, just past the pizzeria.

The best restaurant in the area, however, is an upmarket *ferme-auberge* called *A Flatta* (☎04 95 62 80 38; ⑧), tucked away 3km above the village in a hidden side-valley. To find it, bear right at the church and follow the signs. Their two set menus (100F or 140F) are both dominated by local meat, which is grilled over a wood fire and accompanied by traditional sauces (veal in olive, wild boar marinated in red wine, lamb with parsley and garlic). For continental gastronomes, they also offer a selection of fussier French dishes (such as *salade à la mousse de canard*), changed monthly; count on spending 200–250F (plus wine) for five courses à la carte. **Rooms** are available, but at 600F for a double and 1100F for the luxury suite they're far from cheap. The location, however, overlooking the valley with the GR20 and Monte Grosso trails only a stone's throw away, can't be beaten.

Church of Santa Restituta

One of the most important places of pilgrimage in Corsica, the church of **Santa Restituta**, is set beside a shady grove of olive trees to the north of Calenzana, about 1500m along the D151. Dedicated to the martyred St Restitude, who in 303 AD, during the reign of Diocletian, was decapitated in Calvi for her Christian beliefs, the Romanesque church has been rebuilt many times but retains its attractive eleventh-century single nave. In the crypt you can see the fourth-century **sarcophagus** of the martyr. Discovered in 1951, it's a magnificent marble tomb, decorated with a figure of Christ and adorned at each end with strikingly human faces. During the thirteenth century, the sarcophagus was covered by a cenotaph decorated with **frescoes** depicting St Restitude and her fate against a tableau of Calvi, which are displayed nearby. The key to the church is kept by the owner of the *tabac*, just down from the village square, behind the church hall (*cazzasa*).

Calenzana to Cateri

The D151, which winds beyond Calenzana across a spur of the Monte Grosso massif to **Cateri**, strings together several of the region's prettiest villages, in particular **Cassano** and **Montemaggiore** with superb views of the mountains to the south. Moving on northwest from Calenzana a little over 1km past Santa Restituta, is an essential stop

The GR20

Winding some 200km from Calenzana (12km from Calvi) to Conça (22km from Porto-Vecchio), the **GR20** (pronounced "jay-air-*van*") is Corsica's most demanding long-distance footpath. Only one third of the hikers that start it complete all sixteen stages (*étapes*), which can be covered in ten to twelve days if you're in good physical shape – if you're not, don't even think about attempting this route. Marked with red-and-white splashes of paint, it comprises a back-to-back series of harsh ascents and descents, sections of which exceed 2000m and become more of a climb than a walk, with stanchions, cables and ladders driven into the rock as essential aids. The going is made tougher by the necessity of carrying a sleeping bag, all-weather kit, and two or three days' food with you. That said, the rewards more than compensate. The GR20 takes in the most spectacular mountain terrain in Corsica, from the shattered granite peaks of the central watershed to the fragrant pine forests and flower-spotted slopes of the island's highest valleys. Along the way you can expect to spot the elusive mouflon mountain goat, glimpse eagles wheeling around the crags, and swim in ice-cold torrents and waterfalls.

The first thing you need to do before setting off is get hold of the Parc Naturel Régional's indispensable **topo-guide**, published by the Fédération Française de la Randonnée Pédestre, which gives a detailed description of the route, along with relevant sections of IGN contour maps, lists of refuges and other essential information. Most good bookshops in Corsica stock them, or you can call in at the office of the Parc Naturel Régional de Corse in Ajaccio (see p.199).

The route can be undertaken in either **direction**, but most hikers start in the north at Calenzana, tackling the toughest *étapes* early on. These first few days are relentlessly tough, but the hardship is alleviated by extraordinary mountainscapes as you round the Cinto massif, skirt the Asco, Niolo, Tavignano and Restonica valleys, and scale the sides of Monte d'Oro and Rotondo. At Vizzavona on the main Bastia–Corte–Ajaccio road, roughly the halfway mark (seven to nine days to this point, depending on your level of fitness), you can call it a day and catch a bus or train back to the coast, or press on south across two more ranges to the needle peaks of Bavella. With much of the forest east of here blackened by fire, hikers in recent years have been leaving the GR20 at Zonza, below the Col de Bavella (served by daily buses to Ajaccio and Porto-Vecchio), and walking to the coast along the less arduous Mare a Mare Sud trail (see p.242).

for wine buffs – the **Domaine d'Alzipratu** – where you can taste and buy some the island's finest wines (daily 8am–noon & 2–7.30pm; ☎04 95 62 75 47). However, it is olive cultivation that provides the staple income for this area, centred on the photogenic village of **ZILIA** (Ziglia). The other chief source of employment is the unsightly **mineral water** plant on the outskirts, from where some eleven million bottles of naturally sparkling Zilia water are exported annually.

Cassano and Montemaggiore

The most worthwhile stop along the D151 is **CASSANO** (Cassanu), which boasts a unique village square in the form of a star and has an

Accommodation along the route is provided by **refuges**, where, for around 50F, you can take a hot shower, use an equipped kitchen and bunk down on mattresses. Usually converted *bergeries* located hours away from the nearest road, these places are staffed by wardens during the peak period (July & Aug), when up to one thousand people per day may be using the GR20 at any one time. Advance reservation is not possible: beds are allocated on a first-come, first-served basis, so be prepared to bivouac if you arrive late. Better still, set off as early as possible to arrive before everyone else. Another reason to be on the trail soon after dawn is that it allows you to break the back of the *étape* before 2pm, when clouds tend to bubble over the mountains and obscure the views.

The **weather** in the high mountains is notoriously fickle, with extreme and sudden changes. A sunny morning doesn't necessarily mean a sunny day, and during July and August violent storms can rip across the route without warning, confining hikers to the refuges or sheltered rock crevices for hours or even days. It is therefore essential to to take good wet-weather gear with you, as well as a hat, sun block and shades for the baking heat that is the norm in summer. In addition, make sure you set off on each stage with adequate **food** and **water**. At the height of the season, many refuges sell basic supplies (*alimentation*), but you shouldn't rely on this service; ask hikers coming from the opposite direction where their last supply stop was and plan accordingly (basic provisions are always available at the main passes of Col de Vergio, Col de Vizzavona, Col de Bavella and Col de Verde). The refuge wardens (*gardiens*) will be able to advise you on how much water to carry at each stage.

Finally a word of **warning**: each year, injured hikers have to be airlifted to safety off remote sections of the GR20, normally because they wandered off the marked route and got lost. Occasionally, fatal accidents also occur for the same reason, so always keep the paint splashes in sight, especially if the weather closes in – don't rely purely on the many cairns that punctuate the route, as these sometimes mark more hazardous paths to high peaks.

For more general tips on hiking and climbing in Corsica, see "Basics", p.30. Advice on getting to the trailheads by **public transport** is given above (for Calenzana), p.363 (for Vizzavona), p.300 (for Zonza and Bavella) and p.296 (for Conça).

outstanding triptych (1505) in its seventeenth-century **Église de l'Annonciation**.

Fountains, arcaded houses and ancient streets characterize the village of **MONTEMAGGIORE**, which occupies a rocky pinnacle 3km north of Cassano. The **Église St-Augustin**, in the main square, has some interesting seventeenth-century paintings and an impressive organ dating from the 1700s, but can't compete with the view from **A Cima**, the rocky outcrop at the eastern end of the village – from here you can see the ruins of the old village of Montemaggiore and right across to Calvi, with the gigantic granite cliffs of Monte Grosso on the opposite side of the valley.

The Tra Mare e Monti Trail

The **Tra Mare e Monti** is the longest, oldest and most varied long-distance trail in Corsica, zigzagging down the northwest coast from Calenzana to Cargèse via Galéria, Porto and Evisa. It's also one of the few hiking paths on the island that rarely strays far from the sea, so the views are superb from start to finish. Chief among the highlights of the route is the beautiful Scandola nature reserve, with its outlandish red cliffs and deep, cobalt-blue coves, and the San Petru ridge, above Ota, which overlooks both the Spelunca gorge and the dramatic gulf of Porto to the west. Elsewhere, you get to traverse old-growth Laricio pine forests, cross original Genoese stone footbridges, and swim in some of the best natural river pools in Corsica.

Waymarked with orange splashes of paint, the Mare e Monti is broken into ten stages (between 3hr 30min and 6hr 30min), which take between nine and ten days to walk. A couple of these *étapes* are longer than usual, which, together with the overall length of the trail, puts many people off, but there's no reason why you can't break the hike for a couple of days in one or more of the idyllic coastal villages along the way.

The Mare e Monti can be undertaken at any time of year, though spring and autumn are best. If you do it during the height of summer, set off very early in the morning so as to arrive before the heat of mid-afternoon. In July and August, it's also advisable to reserve your bed in the **gîtes d'étape** that punctuate most stages. Note, too, that more comfortable hotel accommodation is available at several villages, including Calenzana, Galéria, Serriera, Porto, Evisa, Ota and Cargèse; for further details, consult the relevant accounts, using the index on pp.400–403. Information on **transport** to the trailheads is given on p.144 (Calenzana) and p.184 (Cargèse). Detailed contour maps and descriptions of each stage (in French) are featured in the Parc Naturel Régional de Corse's invaluable **topo-guide**, available at most good bookshops and from the organization's office in Ajaccio (see p.199).

Mare e Monti gîtes d'étape

Calenzana M. Isnard	☎04 95 62 70 13
Bonifatu Mme Baron, *Auberge de la Forêt*	☎04 95 65 09 98
Curzu M. Colonna	☎04 95 27 31 70
Galéria M. Rossi	☎04 95 62 00 46 (see also p.160)
Girolata *Le Cabane du Berger*	☎04 95 20 16 98
and M. Teillet, *Le Cormorant*	☎04 95 20 15 55
Ota M. Ceccaldi, *Chez Félix*	☎04 95 26 12 92
Marignana M. Ceccaldi	☎04 95 26 21 21
Tuarelli M. Mariani	☎04 95 62 01 75
E Case M. le Gérant, *Le Refuge*	no phone

The Romanesque church of **San Raniero**, one of the Balagne's most enchanting buildings, is best approached by the rough track that begins 2km along the D151 from Montemaggiore. Constructed by Pisan stoneworkers in the eleventh and twelfth centuries, the church has an intricate multicoloured façade topped by two heads flanking a little cross. Inside, three hideous sculpted faces look out from the cylindrical stone font.

In the third week of July each year, Montemaggiore plays host to the **Fiera di l'Alivu**, which brings together the *commune*'s olive producers (*oléiculteurs*) for a weekend of exhibitions and tasting. The proceedings are brought to a close with a prize-giving ceremony for the region's best oil of that year. For precise dates of the festival, contact the Calvi tourist office (see p.118).

Cateri

Three winding kilometres after Montemaggiore, the road crosses the **Col de Salvi** (509m), from where the seaward view is superb. Another 2km and you need to turn left along the D71 to get to **CATERI**, which straddles the crossroads of the Balagne's principal routes. Tiny streets with overgrown balconies surround the requisite Baroque church, **Église de l'Assomption**, a seventeenth-century edifice dedicated to the martyr St Bernin, whose tomb is the principal feature inside. The hamlet of **SAN CESARIU**, just below the village, is worth visiting for its Romanesque sanctuary, while 1km west of the village lies the oldest functioning Franciscan convent in Corsica, the **Couvent de Marcasso**, dating from 1621.

Cateri's only **hotel** is the *Auberge Chez Léon-U San Dume* (☎04 95 61 73 95, fax 04 95 61 79 31; ④–⑤), a modern building whose rooms have en-suite showers and toilets and wonderful views. Their restaurant, *U San Bume*, is commendable too, serving mainly seafood dishes on a terrace that makes the most of the location. This village is renowned as a cheese-making centre, and the best place to sample local dairy specialities is the excellent *La Lataria*, on the left of the crossroads as you leave the village (☎04 95 61 71 44), where you can round off a meal of grilled veal and olives or *lasagna au brocciu* with home-made *fiadone*, a delicious cheesy cake; the terrace affords a beautiful view over the Calenzana valley, and they do a choice of two set menus (90F or 130F).

Moving on from Cateri you have three possible routes: the D71 down to the sea, passing through **Lavatoggio** (which offers a brilliant view from the terrace of its church); the D151 north towards Sant'Antonino and Aregno; or the D71 south to Muro, Feliceto and Speloncato (see p.153).

Sant'Antonino to Monticello

The hazy silhouette of the oldest inhabited village in Corsica, **SANT'ANTONINO**, is visible for kilometres around, its huddle of orange buildings clinging like an crow's nest to the crest of an arid granite hilltop. The village was occupied in the ninth century, when the Savelli counts ruled from the now-ruined castle, and its circular layout of narrow cobbled lanes, vaulted passageways and neat stone houses has changed little over the past three hundred years. Recently voted one of France's most picturesque villages, Sant'Antonino has become something of a honey-pot destination, famed for its unrivalled 360-degree view of the Balagne. Out of season, however, the place has a folorn air, with most of its houses locked or boarded up; the 110 permanent residents are mostly retired smallholders or artisans.

You can't drive up into Sant'Antonino, but there is a **car park** at the end of the road, just below the village. After a quick look at the sixteenth-century church, **Sant'Annunziata**, which boasts some attractive Baroque decor and a late eighteenth-century organ, head uphill into the warren of alleys above, where sooner or later you'll stumble across the wonderful A Stalla shop, which sells local produce; in addition to the pungent charcuterie and cheeses hanging from its rafters, there's olive oil, eggs, raisins, almonds and the delicious *cucciole* biscuits, made with chestnut flour.

For a substantial **meal**, try *La Taverne Corse* (☎ 04 95 61 70 15), overlooking the car park, whose 120F Corsican speciality menu is rounded off by fresh *fiadone*, served on a shady terrace with fine views of the hills inland. On the opposite side of the village, the more modest *La Bellevue* (☎ 04 95 61 73 91) lives up to its name: the dishes on their good-value 85F menu (cured ham starter, lamb stew with beans to follow, and ewe's-cheese cake for dessert) are all traditional and made with local ingredients, although for vegetarians there's little on offer beyond *omelette à la menthe*.

For picnic food, call at Olivier Antonini's little produce stall, at the entrance to the village just off the car park, where you can buy local wine, and citrus-fruit jams that are made according to recipes devised by the proprietor's mother twenty or more years ago.

Aregno

A kilometre further down the D151 lies the village of **AREGNO**, set amidst a blanket of olive, orange and lemon orchards that stretch down to the sea. The chief attraction here is the graceful Romanesque **Église de la Trinité et San Giovanni**, dating from the twelfth century and constructed, like San Michele de Murato in the Nebbio (see p.106), of chequered green, white and ochre stone. The triple-decker façade displays a fascinating diversity of stonework: an arch above the door is framed by two primitive figures; over these is a blind arcade decorated with geometric patterns and fantastic creatures; and right at the top there's a window surmounted by a couple of intertwined snakes and a crouching man holding his foot (believed to symbolize man paralysed by sin). Inside, on the north wall of the nave and to the right of the altar, are some arresting and well-preserved frescoes: the portraits at the top of the wall are the four Doctors of the Church, painted in 1458, and below them is St Michael lancing a dragon, from 1449. Since 1997, this village has played host to Corsica's only almond festival, **A Fiera di l'Amandulu**, which takes place at the beginning of August. Nut farmers and their families travel from all over the island to take part in cooking competitions.

Pigna

The tiny village of **PIGNA**, a compact cluster of orange roofs and sky-blue shutters set beneath the road 2km from Aregno, is home to one of the most successful restoration projects in the region. Combining the practical refurbishment of buildings with a revival of traditional culture, the project's achievements so far include the building of a new mairie out of earth, and the transformation of an old animal shelter into a lively theatre. Several **artisans' workshops** (open summer 10.15am–noon & 3–7pm) are good for browsing, with various craftworks for sale, including ceramics, engraving (*gravure*), musical boxes and instruments (namely flutes and the rare sixteen-stringed Corsican cistern), furniture and traditional woodcarvings.

The village follows an architectural plan typical of the Balagne, known as a *chjapatta* (hedgehog), whereby the streets branch out from the centre like spines. Pretty piazza d'Olmu and piazza Piazzarella provide glorious views of the sea, but your first visit will probably be to the central **Église de l'Immaculée-Conception**, built in the eighteenth century on a Romanesque base. A squat building with a giant façade flanked by a pair of stumpy campaniles, the church houses a magnificent organ that was restored in 1991 by local craftsmen.

In summer, the nearby open-air theatre hosts **concerts**, often featuring the ancient Moorish dance, the Moresc, which was traditionally performed to celebrate victory over the Saracens. Pigna is especially lively in early July when the **Festivoce** festival provide a forum for long nights of traditional a cappella singing in the outdoor amphitheatre, made from a renovated goat's shed. Concerts run by E Voce di U Comune, an association of artists and musicians dedicated to the promotion of Corsican literature, singing and art, are also held every Tuesday night in summer (or on Saturdays in winter) at the Casa Musicale (☎04 95 61 77 31 or 04 95 61 76 57, fax 04 95 61 74 28), an old house that has been turned into a kind of musical inn at the edge of the village. These generally start at around 10pm and feature recitals by *polyphonies* singers, violins, harpsichord, citterns, and traditional percussion and wind instruments made from goats' horns. Admission is free, but most of the audience is drawn from Casa Musicale's restaurant, where you can enjoy quality Corsican charcuterie and main dishes such as *cabrettu a l'istrettu* (a kind of spicy kid stew) or delicious roast lamb and mutton, rounded off with home-made chestnut-flour cakes. Their terrace, with its panoramic view of the Balagne, is also an ideal spot for breakfast; non-residents pay 30F for a *petit déjeuner complet* of coffee, fresh bread, *canastrelli* biscuits, local honey and home-made fig-and-walnut jam. If you feel like **staying** the night, you can do so in the Casa's attractively decorated en-suite rooms (④–⑤); they are all very pleasant, but "Sulana", on the first floor, has the added attraction of a huge terrace.

Couvent de Corbara and Corbara

One kilometre down the road from Pigna stands the little chapel of **Notre-Dame-de-Latio**, which houses a beautiful painting of the Virgin dated 1002. Opposite, a steep road leads up to the austere **Couvent de Corbara**, attractively framed by olive trees at the foot of Monte Sant'Angelo (see below). Founded as an orphanage in 1430, it was transformed into a Franciscan convent in 1456, badly damaged during the revolution of the 1750s, abandoned soon after, then restored in 1857 by the Dominicans. During World War I the place was used as a prisoner-of-war camp. The Dominicans returned in 1927 and remain there today, running the place as a spiritual retreat. Inside the adjoining white church, of which the oldest part is the eighteenth-century **choir**, you can see the **tombs** of the Savelli family (see below) bearing the family arms – two lions holding a rose.

A mule track behind the convent leads to the summit of Monte Sant'Angelo (560m), a stiff one-hour walk. From the top you can see for kilometres across the Balagne and over the Désert des Agriates to the west coast of Cap Corse – on extremely clear days, it's possible to see the Alps. Descend either by the same route, or by heading south to Sant'Antonino or east to Santa Reparata di Balagna.

Fanning out over the Colline de Monte Guido, 2km beyond the convent road and 2km inland from the coast road, **CORBARA** is a quintessential Balagne town of small cubic houses clinging to a steep hillside. It served as capital of the region before the Genoese took over and founded the citadel at Calvi, and it still boasts the largest of Balagne's parish churches, the **Église de l'Annonciation**, a glitzy Baroque edifice built in 1685. Inside, the most overblown feature is the enormous swirling main altar flanked by two cloud-borne angels, which was constructed from Carrara marble brought over in the 1750s. The painted panels and carved furniture in the sacristy date from the fifteenth century and are relics of the church that occupied this site before the present structure. Two doors down from the church stands a grand house bearing the arms of the Franceschini family, who owned the village from the ninth to the nineteenth centuries. Known as the **Casa di Turchi**, it was built by Marthe ("Davia") Franceschini while she was married to the Sultan of Morocco (see box).

Occupying a rocky pinnacle below the village, the craggy ruin of **U Forte** was once the seat of the Savelli clan, the former overlords of this region. Founded in 1292 by Aldruvando, a vassal who had rebelled against Count Arrigho Savelli, the castle was completed in 1375 by Savelli's son, Mannone Savelli de Guido. When the castle was dismantled by the Genoese in the early sixteenth century, following a battle between the feudal lords and the republic, Savelli de Guido's descendants restored the nearby **Castel de Guido**, a fort founded in 816 by Guido de Sabelli, who was made Count of the Balagne by the pope after a victory against the Saracens. Here the

More background on the pirate raids on Corsica appears on p.102.

Davia Franceschini: Queen of the Moors

Corbara's Casa di Turchi is associated with the extraordinary story of **Davia Franceschini**, a member of the local ruling family who, in the late eighteenth century, rose to become Queen of Morocco. According to the local version of events, Davia was the daughter of a poor charcoal-burner and his wife, who decided to seek their fortune on the mainland. Shortly before leaving Corsica, the girl came across a destitute old woman, half-dead with cold and hunger, to whom she gave food. The beggar returned the kindness by giving her a talisman, "La Main de Fatma", which she said would bring luck on her journey. In the event, the voyage to Marseille turned into a disaster as a storm broke the mast of the boat and swept it south to the Moorish coast, where the passengers were promptly imprisoned. It was at this point that the talisman came to Davia's aid: struck by the beauty of both the object and its wearer, the jailer took the young Corsican woman to meet his sultan, who immediately recognized the pendant hanging around her neck. It had belonged to a long-lost sister who had run away years ago to escape an arranged marriage with an ugly old merchant, never to been seen or heard of again. The sultan was smitten with Davia and they were married soon after. Her family was allowed to return to Corbara, where they lived in a grand house on the square.

This epic, however, is more fairy story than historical truth. In fact, the real Davia did not come from, and never even visited, Corsica. Born Marthe Franceschini in Tunis, she was the daughter of a couple abducted from Corbara by pirates in 1754 – an all-too-common occurrence at the time. Mother and child were both freed, only to fall into the hands of pirates a second time, and ended up in the Marrakech slave market. Eventually, Marthe, or **Daouia Lalla** as she was later known, entered the Sultan of Morocco's harem and grew to become the ruler's favourite and most influential wife. After her death in the plague of Larache in 1799, her story was taken up and embellished by writers of exotic Oriental fiction, whence the more colourful Cinderella-syle yarn still spun by locals in Corbara's village bar.

Savellis ruled in an uneasy coexistence with the Genoese for two hundred years. Then, in 1798, this castle too was wrecked, on the orders of a political adversary of the Savelli family, one of whom was Paoli's chief administrator for the new town of L'Île Rousse.

Santa Reparata di Balagna and Monticello

From Corbara you can head back inland by the D263, which climbs up the side of the Regino valley for 3km before reaching **SANTA REPARATA DI BALAGNA**, a terraced village of ancient crumbling buildings and arcaded streets that give you spectacular glimpses of the sea. The best viewpoint is the terrace of Santa Reparata, from where L'Île Rousse occupies the foreground. The church was built over a Pisan chapel and retains the eleventh-century apse, though the façade dates from 1590.

Four kilometres higher up the D263 lies **MONTICELLO**, fief of the great warlord Giudice della Rocca, whose thirteenth-century

Castel d'Ortica sits on a rocky hillock to the north of the village, surrounded by a belt of olive trees. In the centre, the sole sight is the imposing **Maison Malaspina**, formerly owned by descendants of Pascal Paoli's sister, and yet another house in which Napoléon once spent a few days. One other famous former resident of Monticello was the English writer and comedian Frank Muir, who bought a house here called "A Torra" ("The Tower") with his wife, Polly, in the 1950s. In his autobiography, *A Kentish Lad*, Muir recalls many happy memories of the Balagne, among them "going on a tour and finding that we would rather be in Monticello than anywhere else on the island".

Cateri to Belgodère

To the south of Cateri the D71 swings through a region that's received a lot of government money to attempt to reverse the effects of the Balagne's recent dramatic depopulation (see p.377). Smaller-scale initiatives are in place, too, as you'll see at **AVAPESSA**, whose ancient watermill produces an olive oil that you can sample at *L'Alivu*, a restaurant set up by a community of young people trying to revive the local economy. Gîtes have also been opened in the vicinity – the mairie in the village square has full details (☎04 95 61 74 10).

Muro

The next village along the route from Avapessa is **MURO**, once a hive of artisans, blacksmiths, silk-weavers and wheelwrights. Nowadays it's part of the programme to revive old industries in the region, hence the two olive oil mills straddling the river are working once again. Further evidence of former prosperity are the village's three churches. An elegant bell tower and an imposing façade decorated with statues distinguish the eighteenth-century **Église de l'Annonciation**, on the right as you enter the village. Inside, the usual profusion of marble surrounds a **Crucifix des Miracles**, which in 1730 allegedly started bleeding during Mass and now attracts a steady trickle of penitents and pilgrims. The church opposite, **Santa Croce**, is much older, dating from the fourteenth century, and even more ancient is nearby **San Giovanni**, a partly ruined eleventh-century church, one of the oldest in Corsica.

Feliceto

Glass, wine and olive oil are the chief products at **FELICETO** (Filicetu), a village scattered over the banks of the River Regino, 2km east of Muro. The village is also famous for the purity of its water – a couple of sources 200m west of the centre provide a refreshing halt along the way. The inevitable Baroque church is **Église St-Nicolas**, its crypt containing the lavish tombs of local bigwigs; the next-door **Chapelle St-Roch** has a beautiful seventeenth-century wooden statue of Roch, patron saint of shepherds and horsemen, in a chapel beside the altar. If you're in the mood for a brisk walk, head for the building known as the **Falconaghja** (Eagle's Nest), an hour's climb along the footpath on the left as you leave the village heading north. A mayor of the village constructed this in the last century so he could keep an eye on his citizens with a telescope; later it became a hideout for passing outlaws, hence the alternative name *Maison des Bandits*.

In the village, next to the hotel, is the **Domaine Renucci cave** (June–Oct daily 9am–noon & 2.30–6pm), where you can taste a highly perfumed rosé and one of the best-value AOC reds on the island, made from grapes grown in vineyards spread out below Feliceto.

Practicalities

Feliceto has one of the few **hotels** in these parts, the *Mare e Monti* (☎04 95 63 02 00, fax 04 95 63 02 01; ⑦; April–Oct), an enormous nineteenth-century building with a faded façade and plain stone-floored interior. Its rooms are of modest size and have good views over the valley, although the adjacent restaurant lacks character. A better place to **eat** is the *Osteria U Mulinu* (☎04 95 61 73 23; May–Oct daily except Tues), a restored olive-oil mill at the eastern end of the village. This inn is renowned throughout France thanks to the plate-throwing, whip-cracking and gun-firing antics of its eccentric *patron*, Joseph Ambrosini, and gets booked out weeks in advance during the summer, though it's still worth phoning ahead to see if they have a table free. Set menus start at around 160F, which includes an aperitif, a choice of desserts and as much of the house wine as you can drink.

If Ambrosini's somewhat ostentatious style sounds too much for you, try the more sedate *Osé Fina*, at nearby **Nesa** (☎04 95 61 78 69), 2km east, where excellent-value Corsican speciality dishes à la carte are served in a beautifully restored eighteenth-century house with views. Main courses here cost around 60F, and are usually salmon, grilled *au feu du bois* with local honey and lemon, or fresh meat *aux herbes du maquis*. They also offer baked aubergines for vegetarians (34F), and delicious *bastelles d'oranges* (orange pastries) as dessert.

Speloncato

Named after the caves and cavities that riddle the rocky prominence on which it sits, **SPELONCATO**, 6km from Feliceto and 33km east of Calvi, is one of the most appealing Balagne villages. A tight cluster of terracotta-red roofs crouched in the shadow of the Monte Grosso massif, it's dominated by the ruins of a convent of Santa Maria di a Pase, while the core of the place is the delightful market square, **place de la Libération**. Opposite its café stands the massive **hotel** *Spelunca* (☎04 95 61 50 38, fax 04 95 61 53 14; ④–⑤; April–Oct), former residence of Cardinal Savelli, an eighteenth-century papal

Speloncato marks the start of a twisting mountain road into the Tartagine Valley, covered on p.155.

The Speloncato "Eclipse"

The best known of Speloncato's many caves is the **Pietra Tafonata** (literally "Pierced Stone"), a barrel-shaped grotto 2km up the mountain from the village. Open at both ends, the 8m tunnel has for centuries been used by shepherds for shelter, and may have been enlarged by prehistoric hunters, whose remains archeologists have unearthed amid the detritus littering the cave floor. It is also responsible for an extraordinary "**eclipse**" that takes place here twice each year. At precisely 6pm on April 8 and September 8, the sun sets behind the ridge to the west of the village, only to reappear moments later as its rays shine through the Pietra Tafonata, briefly illuminating the square.

minister whose corruption earned him the nickname *Il Cane Corso* ("The Corsican Dog"). The hotel doesn't have a restaurant, but you can **eat** well at the *Auberge de Domalto* (☎04 95 61 50 97; advance reservation essential), 6km below the village off the D71, which serves attentive and imaginative cuisine in a stylish eighteenth-century house. At 160F for a *menu fixe* plus wine, this isn't a cheap option, but quality is guaranteed.

Belgodère

BELGODÈRE, fourteen winding kilometres northeast of Speloncato, lies at the junction of the main inland routes and provides a possible base for the beaches around L'Île Rousse (see p.138), 15km northwest. The main Calvi–Ponte Leccia train also stops here, though the distance between the station and the village is too great to be covered on foot, and there are no taxis on hand. You can **stay** at *Hôtel Niobel*, 400m from the square on the edge of the village (☎04 95 61 34 00, fax 04 95 61 35 85; ⑥; April–Oct), a modern but cosy hotel with a good **restaurant**, whose large windows offer breathtaking views of the Balagne coast. Local specialities here include pork in chestnut sauce, veal stew and Niolo cheeses.

There are a couple of churches in and around the village worth a look: the **Église St-Thomas** (San Tumasgiu) dates from the sixteenth century and houses a magnificent painted panel of the Virgin and Child (ask for the key in the café opposite); and the **Oratoire de la Madonuccia**, 500m from the square along the Speloncato road, harbours Corsica's oldest statue of the Madonna, placed here in 1387 to seal a reconciliation between Speloncato and the rival villages of San Columbano. Legend has it that the site was chosen because two bullocks who were transporting it between the opposing settlements stopped here and refused to move, which local people took to be a sign.

The best **views** of the surrounding area are to be had from the ruined **fort** on the edge of the village; to reach it, head through the archway between the two cafés on the square.

The Giussani

The Giussani is a spectacularly isolated part of the Balagne, enclosed by Monte Grosso (1938m) and Monte Padro (2393m), the northernmost high peaks of Corsica's mountainous spine. Rising in the cirque of Monte Corona, just south of Monte Grosso, the **River Tartagine** flows through its heart, fed on its northern flank by tributaries whose ravines are overlooked by four high-altitude villages and a scattering of more remote hamlets. Swathed in deep-green chestnut and oak forest, these are exquisitely picturesque but see surprisingly few visitors considering their proximity to the coast; most people who come here do so only for a day to take advantage of the **hiking trails** that thread around the lush sides and floor of the valley.

There are two **approaches** to the region. The first, giving an absolutely amazing view over the entire Balagne, is via the D63, which begins about 500m south of Speloncato, climbs up a high open route to the windswept Bocca di a Barraglia pass, and then plunges south, coming to a dead end in the base of the valley. The other route is along the D963, which branches off the N197 6km east of Belgodère, then drops down into the Tartagine Valley from the Bocca Capanna pass. If you're visiting the area as a day-trip from the coast, you could travel in on one road and out on the other, completing a loop that strings together the main settlements.

Pioggiola

Following the D63/D693 route in an anticlockwise direction, the first place you'll come to is **PIOGGIOLA**, a crown of yellow buildings nestled in a fold of hundred-year-old chestnut trees at an altitude of 1000m – which makes it one of the highest villages in Corsica. **Accommodation** is available in the ten-roomed *Auberge l'Aghjola*, just above the village proper (☎04 95 61 90 48, fax 04 95 61 92 99; obligatory half-board in July & Aug; ⑥), whose prices drop to a very

---

Theatre in the Giussani

One of the Balagne region's most commendable attempts to revitalize the cultural life of its outlying villages has to be the annual drama festival held every summer in Giussani: the **Rencontres Théâtrales Internationales de Haute-Corse**. Organized by acclaimed Corsican actor, **Robin Renucci**, the festival holds six weeks of workshops facilitated by performers from all over Europe, which culminate in a week of performances (in French), held at various locations in the Giussani area. With the help of government grants, costs are kept to a minimum and this extraordinary event looks set to become one of the highlights of the island's cultural calendar.

Over the past few years, the festival has kicked off on the second weekend in August. For more information, contact the organizers on ☎04 95 61 93 97.

---

good-value 160F per double room off season. The building has retained its original rustic feel, and the food in the **restaurant** downstairs (open to non-residents by reservation) is excellent, with local game and other mountain specialities providing the staple fare on a top-quality 160F menu.

Roughly midway between Pioggiola and its neighbour, Olmi-Capella, *A Tramula* (☎04 95 61 93 54; ⑤), a huge new building faced with local stone, is a newer hotel-restaurant that's fast developing a strong reputation for its comfortable en-suite rooms and fine Corsican speciality cooking, served on a spacious terrace overlooking the valley.

Olmi-Capella

Beyond Pioggiola the road divides, one branch of the D963 descending to the region's principal village, **OLMI-CAPELLA**, a cluster of sharp red roofs and mellow stone overlooking the Tartagine. In past centuries, many of the inhabitants of this village used to make their living as itnerant traders, selling topnotch Giussani olive oil and leather shoes throughout the island; apparently their customers regarded them as *unti e fini* (unctuous and fine) – as much, presumably, for their slippery salesmen tactics and slick attire as their good manners and greasy mule packs. There's nowhere to stay here, but you can **eat** definitive Giussani cooking at the *Auberge La Tornadia*, 2km east of the village in the direction of Pioggiola (☎04 95 61 90 93; April–Oct). Frequented as much by locals as visitors, this is a lively place that's full of atmosphere, with low wooden ceilings and old farm implements on the walls.

Walks in the Giussani

Cut off by two of the highest motorable passes on the island, the **Giussani** is a walker's and mountain biker's paradise, with an extensive network of well-marked and well-maintained trails leading through acres of pristine pine, chestnut and oak forest. The Parc Naturel Régional has produced a leaflet entitled *Giussani: Oasis de Verdure*, detailing the routes on a monochrome section of the area IGN map, which you should be able to pick up at a tourist office, otherwise, get hold of the IGN topo-map for the area (#4249OT).

Eight different **round-walks** are featured in the leaflet, marked every 10m or so with splashes of orange paint. For a day-hike, try the five-hour route from Olmi-Capella to Vallica, which takes in a water mill, a Genoese bridge and bathing spots along the Tartagine River; or the five-hour loop from Pioggiola to Forcili and back, which skirts the cirque below Monte Tolu before dropping down to the Bocca di a Scoperta pass above Mausoleo. This latter hike can be extended by an hour to take in the San Parteo peak (1680m); an unmarked mountain path scales the east flank of the cirque and follows the ridge to the summit, from where you follow the spine of another ridge west to rejoin the waymarked trail to Mausoleo. The maison forestière marks the start of another great five-hour loop that hugs

Specialities include roast lamb, fresh pasta made with chestnut flour and, during the autumn, wild forest mushroom sauces; their home-baked biscuits and cakes are great, too. Expect to pay 120–160F per person.

Vallica and Mausoleo

Carry on 3km further east from Olmi-Capella and you'll come to **VALLICA**, a sleepy village swamped in greenery that looks out to Monte Padro on the other side of the valley. Apart from the spectacular views, there's little of note here other than the nineteenth-century church and, just beyond it, a decent restaurant, *U Monte Padru* (☎04 95 61 92 77). Owned by the mairie, this place is run by a young chef from Castaniccia who's particularly proud of his home-made charcuterie; island cuisine dominates the 160F set menu, which includes a local AOC wine. If you want to stay after a meal at *U Monte Padru*, ask for one of the **rooms** in the same building (④–⑤).

The other branch of the D963 from Pioggiola descends to a junction for the ancient village of **MAUSOLEO**, the last of the Tartagine quartet, which boasts a fifteenth-century church containing an olive-wood statue of John the Baptist. Past the Mausoleo turning, the D963 twists through the spectacular gorges of the River Melaja to the banks of the Tartagine, terminating at the maison forestière and the **Forêt de la Tartagine-Melaja**. For a brief taste of the forest, you can follow various short marked paths from here; the principal major hikes are detailed in the box below.

the true right bank of the Tartagine, then climbs up to Mausoleo, before winding up the awsome Melaja Valley. After crossing the stream, you follow the path down until it meets the D963, which you keep to for the remaining 45 minutes back to the maison forestière.

In addition to these relatively easy *sentiers du pays*, Giussani offers several more challenging hiking trails that give access to the high ridges and peaks surrounding the basin. Affording superb panoramic views of the Balagne, the most popular of these is the six-hour climb up the Tartagine valley to the **Refuge d'Ortu di Piobbu**, springboard for the ascents of Monte Corona and Capu a u Dente, and an important étape on the GR20 (see p.144), for which you'll need to carry all-weather gear, a sleeping bag, and a day's food and water. To pick up the equally demanding trails to **Col de la Tartagine** (1852m), 15km southwest, and **Col de L'Ondella** (1845m), 10km south, follow the waymarks from the maison forestière along the south side of the river until you reach signposts indicating the way. The routes to both these passes are ancient transhumance arteries used by shepherds and traders to reach the pastures of the west coast and upper Asco valley. They're fairly straightforward, though you definitely need to take a **topo-map** (see above), as well as adequate clothing and supplies.

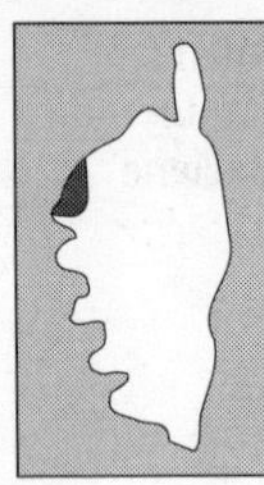

South of Calvi: Balagne Déserte

From Calvi, two routes run south down to **Galéria**, a tiny fishing settlement and summer resort situated about 25km down the coast. If speed is your main concern, the inland D251/D51 is the better option, a well-maintained road that cuts through the **Balagne Déserte**, a region of deep-red rocks studding kilometres of empty maquis. This is one of the most sparsely populated corners of the island, largely due to the ravages of Muslim pirates in the fourteenth and fifteenth centuries, who burned some ninety villages to the ground and carried off their inhabitants as slaves to ports of North Africa; later, a succession of malaria plagues took their toll, while fierce fighting with the Genoese during Paoli's war of Independence ensured the area's terminal decline by wiping out virtually all of its few remaining menfolk.

The D51 separates from the D251 about 10km out of Calvi at **Suare**, from where the latter road continues to the **Cirque de Bonifato**, a luscious forest of Laricio pines and evergreen oaks bordering some of the highest mountains in Corsica. The alternative route to Galéria is the D81, a sinuous corniche bordered by gigantic boulders that looks down on a rock-strewn sea. This road rejoins the D51 at the Cinque Arcate bridge, where a right turn brings you to Galéria and a left leads to the **Vallée du Fango**, one of the least-traversed areas of Corsica, worth visiting for its dramatic combination of old-growth forests and barren ground scattered with great orange rocks.

Public transport along this route is limited to Autocars Les Beaux Voyages's minibus from Calvi to Galéria (July–Sept 15 Mon–Sat; ☎04 95 65 11 35), and Autocars SAIB's service between Calvi and Porto (May 15–Oct 10 Mon–Sat, Aug 1 daily; ☎04 95 22 41 99). Cycles and scooters can also be rented from Calvi (see p.129) and Porto (see p.167), though these are more expensive than those available in Ajaccio. If you have the time, however, the best way to explore this beautiful stretch of coast is on foot, via the Tra Mare e Monti long-distance **footpath**, which runs from Calenzana, just south of Calvi, to Galéria, Porto and across the hills to Cargèse. For a fuller description of the trail, see p.146.

Cirque de Bonifato

An immense basin of forested land encircled by a ring of orange crags, the **Cirque de Bonifato** is a 20km drive along the D251 southeast of Calvi, plus a further 8km on foot. The adjacent forests of Calenzana and Bonifato are magnificent hiking terrain, and the best place to start exploring them is from the maison forestière, a foresters' hut located in the heart of the woodland, where the road ends. If you just want to take a look around, leave the car in the nearby car park and retrace your approach as far as the **Chaos de Bocca Rezza**, a viewing point on the north side of the road, less than 1km away. From here you can see across the forest as far as the immense granite pinnacles enclosing the cirque to the east. If you're going to tackle anything more ambitious, you'll probably want to check into the large *Auberge de la Forêt*, by the car park (☎ & fax 04 95 65 09 98; ③; April–Oct); catering mainly for hikers and backpackers, it also offers dorm beds in more basic gîte accommodation (65F, optional half-board 180F). You can also camp or bivouac here for 35F, which includes hot showers.

South of Calvi: Balagne Déserte

The most obvious walk is the one up to **Spasimata** (1190m), a row of disused dry-stone huts in the core of the cirque, marking the spot where shepherds once rested on their journey down to Calenzana. It's a relatively easy-going five-hour hike from the auberge, initially following the forest trail that skirts the nearby waterfall and then tracks the River Figarella, which courses through great hollowed-out slabs of pink granite. After thirty minutes you'll come to the confluence of the rivers Melaja and Figarella, from where a path marked with red and white paint ascends to Spasimata, a route that crosses several streams and intersects with the GR20 mountain trail at the top. Here you'll find the *Refuge du Carozzu*, the only refuge in the vicinity, run by the garrulous Pierre Griscelli, one of only three Corsican high-mountain guides, and his German partner.

For more on the GR20, see p.144.

Galéria

Isolated amid a somewhat austere landscape of red rocks and straggly eucalyptus trees, **GALÉRIA** is believed to have been first settled by the Phoenicians in the sixth century BC, possibly even before the rise of Aléria on the east coast. Numerous Roman artefacts found in the vicinity – including fragments of a Roman anchor discovered by divers here during summer of 1992 – have also helped archeologists identify this as the site of ancient Kalaris, named on Ptolemy's map of the Mediterranean and a key port in classical times. Later, the anopheles mosquito ruled supreme, ensuring that the village remained malaria-ridden until the advent of DDT in the 1930s. More recently, Galéria has turned its relatively remote location to profit, becoming a popular summer resort and sailing centre. Its handful of hotels and restaurants back onto a jetty and surround a small semicircle of sand spreading from the foot of a Genoese tower, while 500m north out of the village lies Plage de Riciniccia, a vast red-shingled cove that's been adopted by nudists.

Practicalities

Galéria's **tourist office** is at Maison a Torra, a hut located 4km away from the village, at the junction of the D81 and D351 by the Cinque Arcate bridge (June–Sept daily 9am–noon & 2–6pm; ☎04 95 62 02 27). The office carries useful information for hikers, including a list of mountain gîtes d'étapes, and sells route leaflets and topo-maps of the area. A **bus** stops at this junction twice daily, one coming from Porto and the other Calvi; for timetable information, contact SAIB or the Calvi tourist office on ☎04 95 65 16 67.

South of Calvi: Balagne Déserte

The Galéria to Girolata Hike

The hike from **Galéria** to **Girolata**, a tiny fishing village at the east edge of the Scandola reserve that can only be reached on foot or by boat (see p.174), is the fourth and most impressive stage of the ten-day Mare e Monti trail. Winding from sea level up the Tavulaghu ravine and over the Capu Licchia ridge (700m) to the Gulf of Porto, the route takes in some of the wildest scenery on the west coast, including the red volcanic crags of Scandola and the sugar-loaf Capu Rossu cliffs, 6km south across a deep-blue bay. You can do this hike at any time of year, though spring and autumn are best; if you attempt it in high summer, set off early in the morning, as much of the path is exposed.

The trail, waymarked with orange splashes of paint, is signposted from Galéria's gîtc, from where you head up the surfaced road 200m, turning left again when you see a sign pointing through the maquis. After passing a small stagnant reservoir (30min), the footpath climbs the Tavulaghu, crossing from one side of the stream bed to the other as it makes for the head of the valley. The going gets tougher towards the top, with the trail zigzagging through dense vegetation and evergreen oak forest to the ridge, reached after three hours. From here the views are breathtaking as you follow the rocky spine due west, ascending to a maximum height of 784m at the **Bocca di Fuata pass** (4hr 40min). The round walk to the col and back takes between 2hr 30min–3hr, but most hikers continue downhill from the col to a fork, where you bear right and wind along the base of the Cavone ravine to Girolata village, visible below. For details of **accommodation** in Girolata, see p.173.

Return by the same route (6hr 20min) or else follow the Mare e Monti trail for another hour and a quarter until it reaches the D81 at **Col de la Croix**, from where you can hitch back to Galéria. **Buses**, run by Autocars SAIB, also stop here at 9am en route between Porto and Calvi (May 15–Oct 10 Mon–Sat 1 daily; Aug 1 daily; ☎04 95 26 13 70).

Accommodation

Galéria has plenty of places to **stay**, ranging from dormitory accommodation for walkers in a pleasant gîte d'étape to swish self-catering chalets. There are also a couple of small hotels 1km east of the village in the lower Fango valley (see opposite), and a well-equipped **campsite**, *Les Deux Torrents* (☎04 95 62 00 67; June–Sept), 5km north on the Calvi road. Most of the mid-range places offer optional half-board and have adequate restaurants.

L'Auberge, opposite the school in the village centre (☎04 95 62 00 15 or 04 95 62 03 00). Simple rooms above a restaurant. Inexpensive, but in the centre of the village with no views to speak of. ③.

Auberge Galéris, just behind the *Filosorma* (☎04 95 62 02 89). Half a dozen modest rooms with terraces in a modern concrete house, tucked away off the road. Breakfast available on request. Good value and friendly. April–Oct. ④.

E Cinque Arcate, 4km east at the Cinque Arcate crossroads (☎04 95 62 02 54). Run-of-the-mill mid-range hotel that's handy if you're travelling by bus (it's next to the bus stop), but otherwise inconveniently far from the village. May–Sept. ③.

Filosorma, on the beach road in the centre of the lower village (☎04 95 62 03 45). Galéria's poshest hotel has comfortable sea-facing rooms, all with showers and toilets en suite. ④.

Gîte d'Étape, 1km out of the village on the Mare e Monti trail (☎04 95 62 00 46). A well-equipped gîte with thirty dorm beds (70F), hot showers, good self-catering facilities and a resident duck called Sidone. Half-board costs 200F and 270F, for off peak and peak season; campers pay 35F, which includes the use of a gas ring in the garden. Advance reservation (by postal payment of fifteen percent) recommended in May, June and September – the height of the hiking season.

L'Incantu, route de Calca (☎04 95 62 03 66). An unobtrusive complex of spacious studios and chalets with mezzanine floors, kitchenettes and sea-view terraces. Excellent value, particularly during the week. A good option for divers and watersports enthusiasts. ④–⑤.

La Martinella, behind the beach, near the *Loup de Mer* (☎04 95 62 00 44). Five immaculate rooms (all en suite and with fridges), some for up to four persons, opening onto a small garden with tables and views of the bay. Good off-season discounts. ④.

Stella Marina, opposite the *Loup de Mer* (☎04 95 62 00 03, fax 04 95 64 02 29). A dozen large, light rooms in a block behind restaurant (of the same name). The top-floor rooms have the best views. ③.

Restaurants

L'Alivu, at the bottom of the village, where the road bends towards the marina. The best option if you're on a budget. Three course for 85F, or a fish of the day dish, served under an old olive tree at the roadside.

L'Auberge, opposite the school in the village centre (☎04 95 62 00 15 or 04 95 62 03 00). Mountain charcuterie and meat dishes; also fresh lobster and crayfish (which you have to order a day in advance). Menus at 85F and 120F.

Stella Marina, on the beach (see "Accommodation"). Wood-grilled cuisine served in a modern building above the bay. *Langouste* is the chef's big speciality, but his apple pie *flambée à l'eau de vie* is to die for. Count on 120–150F per head.

Vallée du Fango

The road into the **Vallée du Fango** follows the Fango River for 15km as far as the base of the Paglia Orba mountain. A forest of pines, chestnuts, beeches and eucalyptus carpets the valley slopes, providing excellent picnic spots and walking possibilities. A couple of villages scattered over the slopes of the valley do little to disperse the desolate feel of the place, and few people venture up the mountain unless it's for trout fishing or hunting, for which the area is renowned.

About 1km from the Cinque Arcate bridge, the D81 along the river becomes the D351 for 13km as far as Barghiana. At this wild junction there are two **hotels**, the *Fango* (☎04 95 62 01 92; ③–④) and *A Farera* (☎04 95 62 01 87; ④), the only places to stay in the valley; also useful if Galéria is overcrowded. Of the pair, the former is the larger and more welcoming, with a bar and restaurant. The shark's fin of Paglia Orba, visible for most of the onward drive, can be seen to especially good effect 6km along the road from the junction at **Tuarelli**, where a short walk down a track to the left of the road leads to a bridge over the Fango.

Keep heading along the main road and you'll soon come to the turning for the village of **MANSO**, which spreads out over the mountainside. A terrace at the entrance to the village affords a glorious view over the valley: a low screen of olive trees strung across the base of Paglia Orba and Capo Tafonato looming up to the southeast. After Manso the D351 road deteriorates as it comes to an end amidst the chestnut trees at the hamlet of **Barghiana**. A 2km walk up to the **Pont de la Rocce**, a bridge over a tributary of the Fango River, leads off to the right, from which point there's a breathtaking panorama of Capo Rossu and Capo Tafonato, belonging to the Cinto massif.

Travel details

TRAINS

Algajola to: Ajaccio (2 daily; 4hr 15min); Bastia (2 daily; 2hr 45min); Belgodère (2 daily; 35min); Corte (2 daily; 2hr 10min); L'Île Rousse (2 daily; 15min).

Calvi to: Ajaccio (2 daily; 4hr 40min); Algajola (2 daily; 25min); Bastia (2 daily; 3hr 15min); Belgodère (2 daily; 1hr); Corte (2 daily; 2hr 30min); L'Île Rousse (2 daily; 40min); Ponte Leccia (2 daily; 2hr).

L'Île Rousse to: Ajaccio (2 daily; 3hr 30min); Algajola (2–5 daily; 10min); Bastia (2 daily; 2hr 15min); Belgodère (2 daily; 20min); Corte (2 daily; 2hr 15min).

BUSES

AS = Autocars Santini (☎04 95 37 02 98 or 04 95 37 04 01).
BV = Autocars Les Beaux Voyages (☎04 95 65 15 02 or 04 95 65 11 35).
SAIB = Autocars SAIB (☎04 95 22 41 99 or 04 95 21 02 07).

Calvi to: Ajaccio, via Ponte Leccia (BV; Mon–Sat 1 daily; 3hr); Bastia (BV; Mon–Sat 1 daily; 2hr 15min); Calenzana (BV; July to mid-Sept Mon to Sat 2 daily; mid-Sept–June timetable coincides with school terms; 30min); Galéria (BV/SAIB; Aug 2 daily, mid-May to July & Sept to mid-Oct Mon–Sat 1–2 daily; 1hr); L'Île Rousse (BV; Mon–Sat 2 daily; 40min); Lumio (BV; Mon–Sat 2 daily; 10min); Porto (SAIB; Aug 1 daily, mid-May to July & Sept to mid-Oct Mon–Sat 1 daily; 2hr 30min); St-Florent (AS; July to mid-Sept Mon–Sat 1 daily; 3hr).

Galéria/Fango Crossroads to: Calvi (BV/SAIB; Aug 2 daily, mid-May to July & Sept to mid-Oct Mon–Sat 1–2 daily; 1hr); Porto (SAIB; Aug 1 daily, mid-May to July & Sept to mid-Oct Mon–Sat only 1 daily; 50min).

L'Île Rousse to: Ajaccio, via Ponte Leccia (BV; Mon–Sat 1 daily; 2hr 30min); Algajola (BV; Mon–Sat 1 daily; 10min); Bastia (BV; Mon–Sat 1 daily; 1hr 50min); Calvi (BV; Mon–Sat 1 daily; 25min).

FERRIES

For ferry details, see pp.118 and 136.

Chapter 3

The northwest

For sheer diversity of landscapes, nowhere else on the island compares with Corsica's **northwest** – the giant amphitheatre of mountains and valleys rearing up behind the gulfs of Porto and Sagone. Ringed by high peaks, this whole region – from the Palmarella pass in the north and the Col de Verghio in the east, to the Golfe de Sagone in the south – is believed to have been formed by lava flows from the Cinto massif, and its contorted rock formations retain a distinct air of cataclysm. The wild feel of the northwest, however, can be somewhat tempered by the volume of tourists who pour through from June until mid-September. Most of Corsica's one and a half million annual visitors will spend a day or so here at some stage in their holiday, and your enjoyment of the scenery will probably depend on the extent to which you are able to escape the crowds.

Thanks largely to its proximity to the Calanche, **Porto** village, at the easternmost extremity of the **Golfe de Porto**, has become the epicentre of the region's tourist scene, with a crop of hotels, campsites, restaurants and shops lining the narrow floor of a deep valley. Although a peaceful enough place out of season, traffic congestion and overcrowding at the height of the summer can make it a much less appealing base than some of the smaller villages dotted around the gulf. Reached via the breathtaking D81 corniche road, the **Col de la Croix** pass, northwest of Porto, marks the start of the well-trodden

Accommodation Price Codes

Throughout this guide, hotel accommodation is graded on a scale from ① to ⑧. These numbers show the cost per night of the cheapest double room **in high season**, though remember that many of the cheap places will have more expensive rooms with en-suite facilities. In such cases we list two price codes, indicating the range of room rates offered.

① under 100F/under €15	⑤ 300–350F/€45–52.50
② 100–200F/€15–30	⑥ 350–400F/€52.50–60
③ 200–250F/€30–37.50	⑦ 400–500F/€60–75
④ 250–300F/€37.50–45	⑧ 500F and above/€75 and above

trail to the most picturesque of these, **Girolata**, the only permanently inhabited settlement in Corsica still unreachable by road. West of here stretch the spectacular cliffs of the **Scandola Nature Reserve**, a pristine red-granite promontory that supports a wealth of wildlife (both above and below the water level). The reserve is strictly off limits, but you can approach its fringes by boat or on foot, along one of the superb marked paths that wind high above the headland.

The region's principal attraction, however, has to be the **Calanche de Piana**, west of Porto on the opposite side of the gulf from Scandola. Made famous by the drawings of Edward Lear, this vast mass of twisted red- and green-tinged pinnacles, ravines and

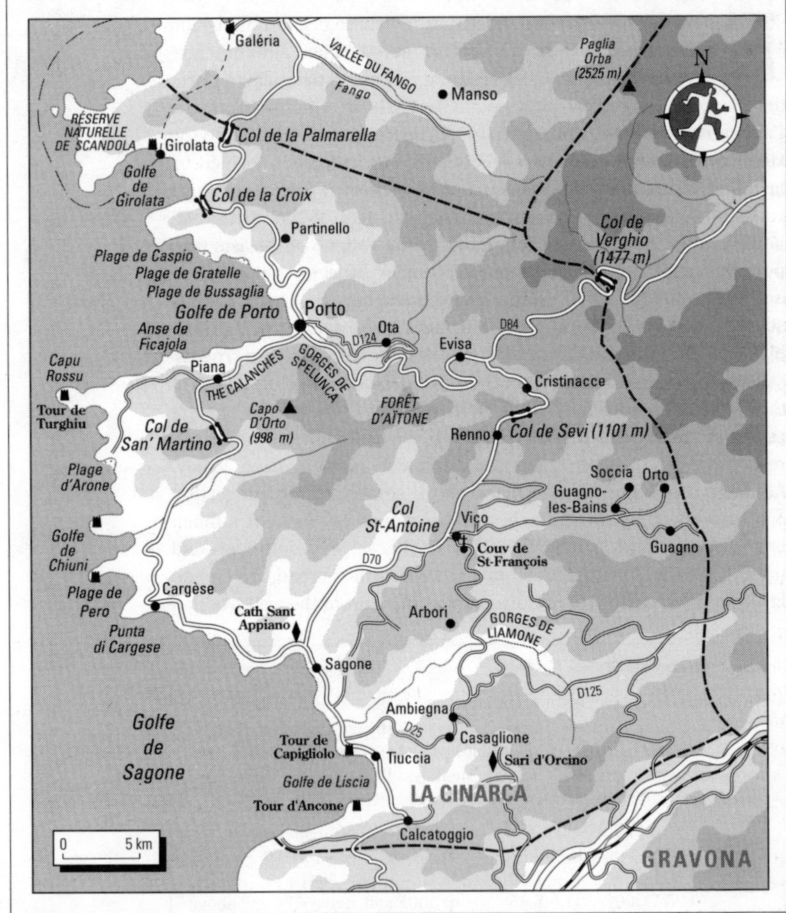

cliffs lies midway between Porto and its more sedate neighbour, **Piana**, whose pretty stone houses stand on the lip of a sheer drop with stunning views across the bay. Beyond it, the *falaises* of the westernmost Calanche peak at **Capu Rossu**, a vertiginous lump of pink rock crowned by a solitary watchtower, which overlooks the least-exploited beach hereabouts, **Plage d'Arone**.

Inland from Porto, the D84 and an old paved Genoese mule path wind through the towering **Gorges de Spelunca** to **Evisa**, a compact hill village and hiking centre clustered on a spur below the huge **Forêt d'Aïtone**. The Genoese shipbuilding industry nearly finished this forest off four centuries ago, but the woodland has recovered and huge Laricio pines still loom over the main road to Corte, roamed by herds of semi-wild pigs. Temperatures drop as you approach the **Col de Verghio** via the highest motorable road on the island – gateway to the hidden Niolo Valley.

A full account of the Niolo Valley appears in Chapter 7, on pp.334–341.

Back on the coast, the corniche road climbs high above Piana to the Col de Lava, then cuts inland to enter the **Golfe de Sagone** at **Cargèse**, an enchanting village with an unusual history of conflict and immigration from Greece. Lying within easy reach of the gulf's best beaches and coast walks, Cargèse makes a much better base than either **Sagone** or **Tiuccia**, two resorts further down the coast that boast a good range of amenities but little character. In this area, the gloomy mountain village of **Vico** and its surrounding hamlets, scattered over the steep slopes inland from the Golfe de Sagone, are the most promising targets for day-trips to the interior, offering glimpses of the watershed peaks between forests of chestnut and pine trees. Another possible diversion, which you could take en route to or from Vico, is a tour of to the wine-growing (and bandit-plagued) **Cinarca** district.

Getting around the northwest

Public transport in the northwest region is limited to SAIB's daily **bus** service between Ajaccio (July & Aug 2 daily; rest of year Mon–Sat 1–2 daily; 1hr), Cargèse, Porto and Ota (July & Aug 2 daily; rest of year Mon–Sat 1–2 daily; 1hr; ☎04 95 22 41 99), and Autocars R Ceccaldi's daily bus from Ajaccio to Vico, via Sagone and Tuiccia (Mon–Sat 1 daily; extra departures in term time; ☎04 95 21 38 06). In summer, SAIB run an additional service beyond Porto to Galéria and Calvi (mid-May to July, Sept & Oct Mon–Sat 1 daily; Aug 1 daily), and you can catch buses inland from Porto over the Col de Verghio to Niolu and Corte with Autocars Mordiconi (4 daily Mon–Sat July to mid-Sept; ☎04 95 48 00 04).

Barely a straight stretch of road exists in this area, and surface qualities can vary as wildly as the scenery, so if you're driving take extra care, especially on the corniche road between Porto and Col de Palmarella, which sees more than its fair share of accidents.

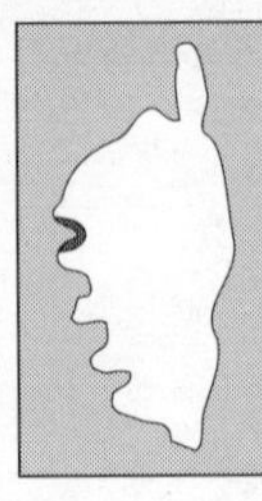

The Golfe de Porto

The coast of the **Golfe de Porto** is one of Corsica's classic landscapes, famed above all for the corroded beauty of its crimson cliffs. Soaring sheer from a lapis-blue sea, the famous red-granite escarpments give way to layer upon layer of shadowy ridges that culminate in the shark's-tooth peak of **Paglia Orba**, dominating the horizon to the east. On a clear day, the gulf presents a simply unforgettable panorama, and one that tempts many visitors to forget their tight itineraries.

Porto, hidden in a niche at the end of the gulf, serves as the area's main resort. Although rather boxed in and cut off from the best of the views, the village does boast plenty of amenities, and is perfectly placed for day-trips. Northwest along the corniche road, a string of secluded coves punctuate the route to **Col de la Croix**, jumping-off place for wonderful walks to **Girolata**, an isolated fishing village on the edge of the **Scandola Nature Reserve**. Highlight of the southern gulf are the **Calanche**, 12km of dizzying pinnacles and ravines, ideally explored on foot, or at sea level by launch. A couple of superbly situated hotels make the nearby village of **Piana** a good alternative to Porto as a base, lying close to one of the island's most outstanding beaches, **Plage d'Arone**.

Porto

Before the tourist boom of the 1950s, virtually the only building in **PORTO** was an old Genoese watchtower, erected in the sixteenth century on an outcrop of granite where the river debouches into the gulf. Now the tower presides over a straggling rash of hotels, restaurants and shops, serving the hordes of visitors who pass through en route to or from the nearby Calanche. Overdevelopment, however, has been effectively held in check by the steep mountain slopes that hem in the village, and it is still the dramatic landscape of the gulf and its hinterland, rather than traffic congestion and jammed campsites, that leave the most lasting impressions. That said, you'd do well to time your visit carefully. Porto is so small that it can become claustrophobic in July and August, when overcrowding is no joke. Off season, the place becomes eerily deserted; the best months are May, June and September.

For details of accommodation around Porto, see "The northern gulf" (pp.171–174), Ota (p.179) and Evisa (p.179).

An avenue bordered by stately old gum trees, **route de la Marine**, links the two parts of the resort. A strip of supermarkets, boutiques, cafés and hotels 1km from the sea makes up the end of the village known as **Vaïta**, but the main focus of activity is the small **marina**, located at the avenue's end. Until the end of the nineteenth century Porto was used for exporting Laricio pines from the inland forests, and the route de la Marine was built to accommodate the great carts that used to haul the timber down from the mountains. Clustered around the great red rock that supports the tower, a nucleus of hotels

The Golfe de Porto

and restaurants vie for views of the sea, while the rest of the buildings are crammed into what little space remains.

It's about a fifteen-minute walk from the marina up to the recently restored **Genoese Tower** (May–Sept daily 9am–8.45pm), a squat, square, chimney-shaped structure, built in 1549, that was cracked by an explosion in the seventeenth century, when the construction was used as an arsenal. Renovated in 1993, it offers the village's best view of the churning sea.

The **beach** consists of a pebbly cove south of the massive rock supporting the tower. To reach it from the marina, follow the little road that skirts the outcrop, cross the wooden bridge over the River Porto on your left, then walk through the car park under the trees. Although it's rather exposed and the sea is very deep, the great crags overshadowing the shore give the place a vivid edge, and there's some great snorkelling to be had from the rocks to the south of the cove.

Arrival and information

Autocars SAIB's **minibus** from Calvi (May 15–Oct 10 Mon–Sat 1 daily, Aug 1 daily; ☎04 95 22 41 99) stops in front of the Banco supermarket car park at Vaïta, but leaves for the return journey from in front of the tourist office. Coaches to and from Ajaccio, also operated

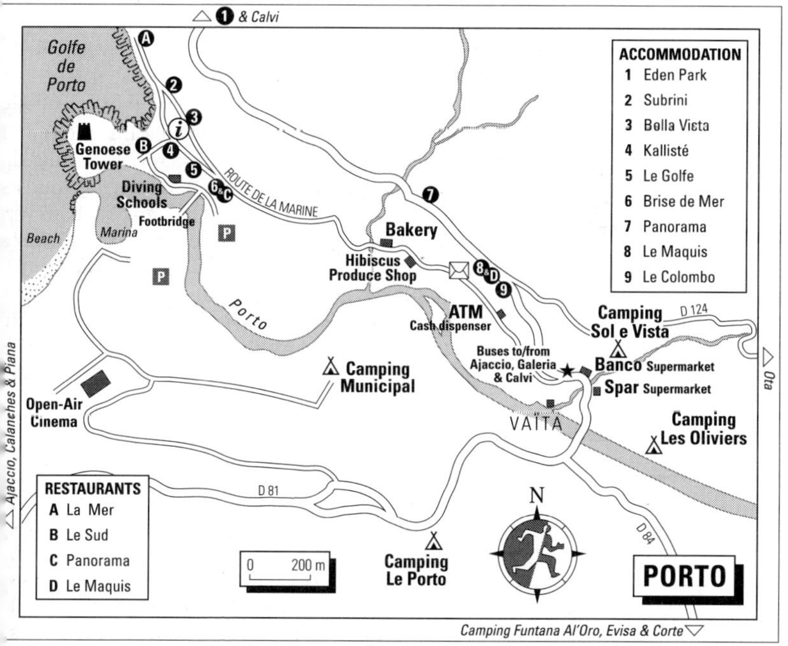

by Autocars SAIB, run all year round (Aug to mid-Sept Mon–Sat 2 daily, Sun 1 daily; rest of year Mon–Sat 2 daily; 2hr), stopping at the marina and opposite Banco supermarket; note that the afternoon departure to Ajaccio leaves two hours earlier (ie at noon) on Saturdays. Tickets can be bought on the bus and cost 65F one way. From July until mid-September, an additional service runs to Corte, via Evisa, with Autocars Mordiconi (☎04 95 48 00 04), costing a stiff 110F one way.

The well-organized **tourist office** is down in the little square behind the tower (May, June & Sept daily 9am–noon & 3–7pm; July & Aug daily 9am–7pm; Oct–April Mon–Thurs 2–6pm; ☎04 95 26 10 55, fax 04 95 26 14 25). Among the many publications on sale here is a particularly useful one for hikers, *Balades & Randonnées dans le Golfe de Porto*, detailing the best day-walks (*boucles de journées*) in the area, with extracts from the relevant topo-maps – a bargain at 15F.

Unless you can use ATMs to withdraw cash (see below), changing money in Porto can be a problem, largely due to the absence of a year-round bank. During July and August, a temporary branch of the Crédit Agricole opens on route de la Marine, just beyond the **post office**, opposite *Hôtel Cala di Sol*, but the transaction will cost less at their year-round **cash dispenser** outside. Otherwise, the only alternative is the small bureau de change at the Spar supermarket up in Vaïta (daily June–Sept 9am–noon & 2–5.30pm), whose commission charges are steep.

Accommodation

Competition between **hotels** is more cut-throat in Porto than any other resort on the island. During slack periods towards the end of the season, most places engage in a full-on price war, pasting up cheaper tariffs than their neighbours to entice the straggling tourists – all of which is great for punters. In late July and August, however the normal sky-high rates prevail. At this time, queues for the three main **campsites** often trail along the main road, forcing many visitors further north along the gulf, where a string of quieter villages and beaches – notably Bussaglia and Partinellu – harbour a handful of smaller hotels and campsites. All the places listed below are marked on our map of Porto; the rates quoted apply to peak season

Hotels

Bella Vista, above the village on the Calvi road, just past *Le Maquis* (☎04 95 26 11 08, fax 04 95 26 15 18). Pleasant, well-furnished rooms in an old pink-granite building with outstanding views of the mountains and sea. Also fully equipped studios, and a good restaurant. Obligatory half-board in August. April to mid-Oct. ④

Brise de Mer, on left of route de la Marine as you approach tower from the village, opposite the telephone booths (☎04 95 26 10 28, fax 04 95 26 13 02). A large old-fashioned place with very friendly service and a congenial terrace restaurant. Rooms at the back have the best views. April to mid-Oct. ④.

Adventure Sports and Boat Trips

The clear waters of the gulf offer superlative **diving** possibilities, with a string of outstanding sites along the Golfe de Porto from Capu Rossu to the tip of Scandola. Moreover, these are only explored by two schools, both working out of the marina next to the footbridge: the École de Plongée Sous-Marine "Genération Blue" (☎04 95 26 24 88) and the Centre de Plongée du Golfe (☎04 95 26 10 27). Both run courses for beginners and will take out more experienced divers with their own equipment for 180–220F; you can also fill your gas bottles here. The Centre de Plongée du Golfe also offers good-value guided **snorkelling** trips around the base of Capu Rossu and Scandola (150F per person), and they have unsinkable **canoes** for rent (150F per half-day, 220F per full day), ideal for paddling into the hidden coves around Porto.

For trips along the corniche or up to Ota and beyond, **mountain bikes** and **scooters** are available to rent at the café opposite the Spar supermarket (90F per day for a mountain bike, 300F for an 100cc step-through).

Porto is perfectly placed for the increasingly popular sport of **canyoning** (see p.35), with a range of descents of varying difficulty down the steep stream gorges of the Spelunca valley. Corsica Trek, based at Marignana, 17km east of Porto (☎04 95 26 82 02), run guided half- and full-day trips.

Tickets for the daily **boat excursions** to the Réserve Naturel de Scandola via Girolata, and to the Calanche de Piana, are available in advance direct from the operators (not from the tourist office), who run stalls outside their associated hotels in the marina. Working out of the *Hôtel Monte Rossu*, just off the square, JB Rostini's Porto Linea carries only twelve people (April–Oct: for Scandola and Girolata, daily departures 8.45am and 2pm, 190F; Calanche de Piana evening cruises daily 6pm, 100F; ☎04 95 26 11 50). The rival Compagnie Nave Va, operating from the *Hôtel Cyrnée*, just behind the tourist office (April–Oct: Scandola and Girolata daily departures 9.30am and 2.30pm, 160F; Calanche de Piana daily 1.30pm, 100F; ☎04 95 26 15 16), has a much larger boat, which accommodates up to 180 people. Compagnie Nave Va also run longer excursions that take in both the Calanche de Piana and Réserve Naturel de Scandola (daily 2.30pm; 5hr; 230F).

Le Colombo, at the top of the village opposite the turning for Ota (☎04 95 26 10 14, fax 04 95 26 19 90). An informal, sixteen-room hotel overlooking the valley, imaginatively decorated in sea-blue colours with driftwood and flotsam sculpture. ⑥.

Eden Park, 4km north of Porto on the Calvi road (☎04 95 26 14 74). Porto's most luxurious hotel is set in its own grounds above Busaglia beach, with a palm-lined pool, piano bar and swish restaurant. April–Oct. ⑥–⑦.

Le Golfe, at the base of the rock in the marina (☎04 95 26 13 33). Small and cosy; every room has a balcony with a sea view. Among the cheapest at this end of the village. May–Oct. ④.

Kallisté, in the marina (☎04 95 26 10 30). Despite its ugly exterior, this three-star is the swishest hotel in the village centre, with spacious rooms and a relaxing bar. April–Oct. ⑦.

Le Maquis, at the top of the village just beyond the Ota turning (☎04 95 26 12 19). A perennially popular, recently renovated budget hotel; rooms are simple, but comfortable enough. There are very good off-season discounts. Advance booking recommended; half-board obligatory July and August. ②–④.

Panorama, route de la Marine (☎04 95 26 11 05). The most pleasant option in this row of hotels backing the marina, offering competitive rates and sea views from most rooms; their terrace restaurant is a great venue for breakfast. April–Oct. ④–⑤.

Subrini, opposite the tower (☎04 95 26 14 94, fax 04 95 26 11 57). A very comfortable three-star right in the centre of things, but with peaceful, air-conditioned rooms. Ideally placed for the sunsets behind Scandola. April–Oct. ⑧.

Campsites

Camping Funtana al'Oro, 2km up the Evisa road (☎04 95 26 15 48). Too far from the village if you're travelling without your own vehicle, but a shady, well-managed site close to some quiet bathing spots in the river.

Camping Municipal, behind the beach (☎04 95 26 17 76). The one to avoid unless you're counting every franc: stony ground and grubby washrooms.

Camping Le Porto, on the right as you approach Porto from Piana (☎04 95 26 13 67). Further out of the village than the other sites, but smaller, and with plenty of shade.

Camping Sol e Vista, at the main road junction near the supermarkets (☎04 95 26 15 71 or 04 95 26 10 79). A superb location on shady terraces ascending a steep hillside with a small café at the top. Great views of Capo d'Orto cliffs opposite, and immaculate toilet blocks.

Eating and drinking

With a few notable exceptions (see below), the overall standard of restaurants in Porto is pitiably poor, with overpriced food and indifferent service the norm, particularly during high season. There are, however, a handful of exceptions, notably *Le Sud*, which serves some of the most succulent seafood in Corsica. If you're here during the summer and fancy eating somewhere less hectic than the busy pizzerias in the marina, head for *Chez Félix*, 4km up the road at Ota (see p.179). Porto also boasts one of the island's top artisanal food outlets, Hibiscus, on route de la Marine, where you can taste and buy a range of authentic charcuterie, cheese, jams and alcohol.

Le Maquis, see hotel, above. Honest, affordable home cooking in a warm bar or on a tiny terrace that hangs over the valley. Their good-value 90F menu includes delicious scorpion fish in mussel sauce.

La Mer, opposite the tower. One of the finest seafood restaurants in the area, with fish fresh from the gulf, imaginatively prepared and served in an ideal setting beside the tower. Set menus from 90F.

Panorama, see hotel, above. Recommended for its fine views and authentic Corsican specialities, such as pigeon in eau de vie and lasagne with wild mushrooms (in season). Set menus range from 80 to 100F.

Le Sud, along the walkway leading from the square to the marina. Arguably the best restaurant in Porto, thanks to their strict policy of serving nothing except the freshest local food – hence the limited menu (if the local fishermen haven't landed anything, you won't find fish on the menu). Simple and delicious cooking, and a stylishly designed terrace overlooking the marina. Menu at 150F, plus wine.

The northern gulf

The D81 north of Porto, a 30km sequence of hairpin bends around the base of **Monte Manganello**, provides breathtaking views across the gulf to the Calanche, plus the opportunity to swim or dive at a string of tiny coves along the way. Autocars SAIB's Calvi bus travels this route daily, but hitching is fairly reliable in season, with droves of visitors driving from Porto to the two viewpoints at **Col de la Croix** and **Col de la Palmarella**. Alternatively, you could also **cycle** up to these passes, or ride by scooter (see box on p.169 for bike rental details).

Bussaglia

An abrupt left turn off the D81 about 5km west of Porto leads to **Plage de Bussaglia** (Bussaghia), the longest strand on this side of the gulf and the first you can get to by car. A sheltered swathe of grey pebbles hemmed in by scrubby headlands, it's flanked by a pair of seasonal pizzerias – the one on the left as you face the sea is among the best places in the region for seafood and pasta, popular with locals and visitors alike.

You can also **stay** in Bussaglia, at the very pleasant *Hôtel L'Aiglon* (☎04 95 26 10 65, fax 04 95 26 14 77; ③; April–Oct), a large building with a relaxing terrace, restaurant and comfortable rooms that overlook the valley; their tariffs and half-board deal represent excellent value for money for this area, especially in July and August, when, unlike most hotels hereabouts, they do not increase their prices. Further down the road towards the beach, the more upmarket *Stella Marina* (☎04 95 26 11 18, fax 04 95 26 12 74; ⑤; May–Sept) boasts a small pool. For **campers**, there's the self-contained but rather exposed *Camping Bussaglia* (☎04 95 26 15 72), complete with supermarket and pricy snack bar.

Partinello

Beyond the turning for Bussaglia beach, the corniche road crosses a dry stream bed (site of a famous roadside spring) and snakes up the folds of the scrub-covered hillside to sleepy **PARTINELLO**, set high above the shore under a carpet of green woodland and maquis. A quiet and friendly place to **stay** here is *Aria Marina* (☎04 95 27 30 33; ③; June to mid-Sept), below the café-bar in the village centre, where half a dozen immaculate, inexpensive rooms (with showers and shared toilets) overlook the vegetable garden to the sea. There are also a couple of interconnecting family suites on the lower floor that are great value if you're travelling in a group of four or more. On the south side of the village, *Le Clos des Ribes* (☎04 95 27 30 36;

4500–5600F per week) is a posher option, whose luxurious studios (which can comfortably accommodate a family of four) have kitchenettes and verandahs; these are normally rented on a weekly basis, but you may be able to fix a rate for a night or two out of season – if you call in person, ask at the newsagent on the west side of the main road.

Plages de Caspio and Gratelle and cols de la Croix and Palmarella

A left turn along the D324 from Partinello takes you down a broad valley to the popular **Plage de Caspio**, a steeply shelving mix of pebble and sand backed by a bar, 3km from the main road. The sun disappears behind the cliff in the afternoon during the summer, so arrive early if you want to catch some rays.

A more enticing cove along this stretch is shingly **Plage de Gratelle**, just north of Caspio, accessible via a narrow signposted road at a point where the road widens, about 10km on from Partinello. The deep translucent sea and superb views of the Calanche and Capo d'Orto make this one of the most attractive beaches in the area, though it's far from a well-kept secret and gets crowded in summer with campers from the site behind it.

An account of Galéria and the region beyond Col de Palmarella appears on p.159.

A short distance beyond the Gratelle turning, the **Col de la Croix** (272m) has a strategically placed drinks hut from which to enjoy the views westwards towards Scandola and southwards to the chaos of the Calanche. It also marks the start of the footpath to Girolata (1hr 15min), via Cala di Tuara (see box). **Col de la Palmarella** (374m), a further 10km north, gives more glorious vistas across the Scandola headland and distant hills, and is a popular target for cyclists.

Girolata

Connected by a mere mule track to the rest of the island, the tiny fishing haven of **GIROLATA** has a dreamlike quality that's highlighted by its proximity to the sea and the vivid red of the surrounding rocks. For hundreds of years its few inhabitants lived a reclusive life, surviving on fishing and hardly communicating with the rest of the island. Then, in 1530, drama struck, when the notorious corsair Dragut was taken prisoner here by the Genoese general, Andrea Doria, who captured nine galleys. Dragut managed to bribe his way out of trouble, though, and returned eleven years later to get his revenge by razing Girolata to the ground.

A sleepy place of only fifteen permanent inhabitants, Girolata comprises a short stretch of stony beach and a handful of houses overlooked by a stately seventeenth-century Genoese **watchtower**, built high on a bluff above the cove. For much of the year, this ranks among the most idyllic spots on the island, with only the odd yacht and party of hikers to disturb the settlement's tranquillity. From June through September, however, daily **boat trips** from Calvi (see p.130)

A Round-Hike from Col de la Croix

Col de la Croix is a key landmark on the Mare e Monti trail from Calenzana to Cargèse (see p.146), a section of which makes a superb six-hour round-hike that you can attempt at any time of year. Incorporating a couple of lengthy climbs, it's a strenuous walk, but the scenery is wonderful all the way, with ever-changing panoramic views of the gulf and its mountainous hinterland. Water is in short supply along the route, so carry plenty with you; we also recommend you take along the IGN **topo-map** of the area, or the Parc Naturel Régional de Corse's topo-guide *Corse – Entre Mer et Montagne*, both available at shops and the tourist office in Porto (see p.168).

From the car park at the pass, head down the signposted path to Girolata, which after around forty minutes ends at a grubby, flotsam-covered cove known as **Cala di Tuara** (30min). If you're only hiking as far as Girolata, the more rewarding of the two marked routes that wind onward is the one peeling left around the headland, from which you get a series of wonderful sea views. To continue the round-walk, follow the path to the right, which begins at a breach in the maquis a little way up the Tuara stream bed, and from there zigzags up to a pass. Once at the ridge (1hr), follow the right fork further up the hill and keep heading northeast until you reach the **D81** (2hr 15min), where you should turn right. After 300m, a track on the left strikes east up the ridge to **Punta di u Muntitoghju** (640m; 3hr), bending gradually southwards as it skirts the west face of Punta di u Tartavellu (825m) en route to the Bocca Ascenso pass. A short ascent from here, with the crags of Punta Salisei to your left, is followed by a drop down to the **Salisei spring** (4hr), where you can refill your bottles for the steady descent southwest along the Salisei ridge to **Capu di Curzu** (852m; 4hr 50min). The path continues to give ground as it approaches a final pass, marked with an orientation table. Either head due south from here down a series of steep switchbacks to rejoin the main road at the village of **Curzu** (5hr 50min), where there's a gîte d'étape (see box on p.146), or else continue along the right fork from the pass and follow the north face of the ridge past Capu di Linu (622m) and back down to Bocca a Croce, which you should reach after around six hours.

From mid-May until the end of August, it is possible to pick up Autocars SAIB's **bus** back to Porto at 5.10pm from Col de la Croix, or from Curzu at 5.30pm (May 15–July Mon–Sat 1 daily; Aug 1 daily). Check the times before you set off, as they tend to change slightly from year to year.

and Porto (see p.169) ensure the village is packed during the middle of the day, so if you want to make the most of the grandiose scenery, and peace and quiet, walk here and stay a night in one of the gîtes.

Though obliged to travel across the bay by boat to Porto to do their shopping, Girolata's few residents nevertheless enjoy the luxury of hand-delivered mail: each day, a **postman** hikes here and back from the nearest roadhead at the Col de la Croix, distinguished from amateur ramblers by his thick white beard, Lacoste sweatband and zealous pace.

There are no hotels in Girolata, but you can stay at one of two **gîtes** that cater for the steady flow of hikers through here in the summer.

Located on the beach, *La Cabane du Berger* (☎04 95 20 16 98; 50F per person for dorm bed, ② cabin, ③ with half-board) offers a choice of accommodation in dorms or small wood cabins in the garden behind (these accommodate two people); you can also put your tent up here. Meals are served in their quirky woodcarved bar, but the food isn't up to much. The other gîte is *Le Cormorant*, amongst the houses at the north end of the cove (☎04 95 20 15 15; 50F per person, 170F half-board), which has eighteen dorm spaces and a small restaurant overlooking the boat jetty.

Réserve Naturel de Scandola

The 700-square-kilometre **Réserve Naturel de Scandola** (Scandula) takes its name from the wooden tiles (*scandule*) that cover many of the island's mountain houses, but the area's roof-like rock formations are only part of its amazing geological repertoire. The stacked slabs, towering pinnacles and gnarled claw-like outcrops were formed by volcanic eruptions 250 million years ago, and subsequent erosion has fashioned shadowy caves, grottoes and gashes in the rock. Scandola's colours are as remarkable as its shapes, the hues varying from the charcoal grey of granite to the incandescent reds and rusty purples of porphyry, striking a vivid contrast with the deep greens of the maquis and the cobalt-blue sea.

The headland and its surrounding water were declared a nature reserve in 1975, so **wildlife** is as varied here as anywhere in Corsica. Dolphins and seals thrive in the area, which also supports more than 450 types of seaweed and other subaquatic plants – including a rare type of photosynthesizing grass that grows at a depth of 35m due to the exceptional clarity of the water here – as well as some remarkable fish, such as the grouper, a species more commonly found in the Caribbean. Colonies of giant gulls and cormorants inhabit the cliffs, and you might see the odd **peregrine falcon** preying on the **blue rock thrushes** that nest on the bare rock ledges. Ospreys, extremely rare in the Mediterranean, are also found here, their huge nests of twigs crowning the pinnacles; there used to be only seven pairs, but careful conservation has increased the number to 24. Rare plants native to Corsica grow freely, such as the sea daffodil (*Pancratium maritimus*) and the *Senecio cineraria*, with its distinctive furry silver leaves.

For more on boat trips to Scandola and Girolata, see p.130 (for Calvi) or p.169 (for Porto).

Unfortunately for flora-spotters, however, the entire reserve is off limits to hikers, and can be viewed only from the sea, which for tourists means taking one of the daily **boat trips** from Calvi and Porto.

Starting the return-trip from Calvi, the first port of call is the **Baie d'Elbu**, last refuge in Corsica of Europe's largest bat. Two kilometres south of here lies the **Punta Palazzu**, so called because of the soaring rocky towers that spring from the sea like a giant palace. Over the course of the last thousand years or so, the seaweed here has formed a thick white band around the base of the cliffs just above the surface of the water – a rare phenomenon that provides invaluable information about the changing sea level.

Beyond this point the boat weaves through the narrow straits by **Île de Gargalo**, an islet created from volcanic lava where the most westerly point on Corsica is marked by a lighthouse. Excursion boats from Calvi and Porto stop for two hours (the later boat from Porto stops for 45min at Girolata before turning round).

The southern gulf

South of Porto, the sinuous D81 winds gently through the Piana pine forest before entering the spectacularly eroded terrain of the **Calanche**. The village of **Piana** itself, 12km along the route, has this area's main concentration of cafés, restaurants and hotels, and lies within easy reach of several rewarding day-hikes, among them the ascent of **Capo d'Orto**, the mountain whose sheer northern crags tower above Porto, draped in vegetation. On the seaward side of Piana, the panoramic **route de Ficajola** connects with the D824, a refreshingly smooth road leading to **Plage d'Arone**, the finest beach in the vicinity. En route, you pass the start of the footpath leading to **Capu Rossu**. Crowned by a Genoese watchtower, this distinctive sugar-loaf lump of pink granite marks the southernmost extremity of the Golfe de Porto, of which its summit affords a sweeping view.

The Porto–Ajaccio **bus** stops at Piana (SAIB; Aug to mid-Sept Mon–Sat 2 daily, Sun 1 daily; rest of year Mon–Sat 2 daily; 2hr).

The Calanche

The UNESCO protected site of the **Calanche** takes its name from *calanca*, the Corsican word for "creek" or "inlet" (in French, *calanque*), but the outstanding characteristics of the Calanche are the vivid orange and pink rock masses and pinnacles crumbling into the sea. Liable to unusual patterns of erosion, these tormented rock formations and porphyry needles, some of which reach 300m above the sea, were described by Maupassant as a "nightmarish menagerie petrified by the will of an extravagant god", and have long been traditionally associated with different animals and figures, of which the most famous is the **Tête de Chien** at the north end of the stretch of cliffs. Other figures and creatures conjured up include a Moor's head, a monocled bishop, a bear and a tortoise. An old local legend holds that these fantastic forms were the work of the Devil, who created them in a fit of rage after a shepherdess refused his amorous advances. Unable to punish her pure soul, he conjured the shapes of his enemies from the fiery rocks, among them the giant representations of the shepherdess and her fiancé that tower above the corniche road to this day.

The Calanche has long been the west coast's top tourist site, and the road that winds through its granite archways en route to Piana gets clogged solid with cars, coaches and camper vans during July and August. One way to avoid the jams is to view the cliffs on a **boat excursion** from Porto (see p.169). Alternatively, head for the *Roches Bleues* café, 8km along the road from Porto, from where a network of marked trails fans through the cliffs, crags and pine trees.

Piana

For some reason, **PIANA**, in a prime location overlooking the Calanche, does not suffer the deluge of tourists that other such picturesque places endure. Retaining a sleepy village feel, it comprises a cluster of old stone houses ranged around an eighteenth-century church and square, from the edge of which the views over the Golfe de Porto are sublime.

If you want to **stay** here, consider splashing out on a night at *Hôtel les Roches Rouges*, at the entrance to the village on the Porto side (☎04 95 27 81 81, fax 04 95 27 81 76; ⑤; April–Oct); built in the 1930s, this wonderfully dated building lay empty for nearly twenty years, but was reopened with most of its original fittings and furniture intact. The rooms are huge (make sure you get one facing the water), and there's a gorgeous restaurant terrace – menus at 120F and 150F, featuring mostly seafood cooked in herbs – that juts out

Calanche Walks

Several routes, varying from easy to strenuous, can be followed in the environs of the *Roches Bleues* café (see above), marked at regular intervals with splashes of paint. A monochrome **topo-map** of the area is featured in the local council's free *Piana Randonnées* leaflet, available at local tourist offices, and the staff at the café are helpful sources of advice on the state of the trails.

The most popular short walk in the Calanche is the round-hike to the **Château Fort** (1hr 15min), a large square chunk of granite resembling a ruined fort from which an impressive view extends along the coast to Capu Rossu. Waymarked with blue spots, the trail starts 700m north of the café at a car park on the right of the Porto road.

The **corniche** walk (about 50min), also marked in blue, starts on a well-worn track, east off the road directly in front of the *Roches Bleues* before the bridge. The track, signposted "Corniche", climbs in a loop around to the main road, coming out a few kilometres down from where you started.

For a more demanding three-hour ramble, another path, beyond the corniche track and signposted "Châtaigneraie", follows a pleasant shady trail through the **chestnut forest**, indicated by blue-painted marks all the way.

A shorter walk (1hr 30min) begins by the **Oratoire de la Vierge**, a little chapel 500m south of the *Roches Bleues*, west off the road where two lay-bys provide parking. A mule track (*chemin des muletiers*) marked by blue paint leads off to the north of the road. Beginning with a steep ascent between two massive rocks, the track then follows the coast for an hour, affording fabulous views over the gulf, before regaining the road.

over the cliffs, affording a magnificent view of the Calanche and the sea. Their tariffs are exceptionally low, too, considering the hotel's situation and character; even if you can't afford to stay here, drop in for coffee and a game of chess on the terrace. A cheaper alternative is *Hôtel Continental*, on the right as you leave Piana (☎04 95 27 89 00; ②–③); it's an old house with high wooden ceilings and a leafy garden. The *Mare e Monti*, between the two (☎04 95 27 82 14; ②–④; April–Oct), also offers fine views from its sea-facing side, though the "mountain view" rooms actually overlook the road.

Around Piana

If you've only got time for a very short trip from Piana, head 2km south of the village along the D81 to the **Col de Lava**, a famed viewing platform for the gulf. Rather more rewarding, though, is the **route de Ficajola** (D624), a short steep road that loops down to the shore from the central junction in Piana. Stunning views of the gulf make it a lovely drive in itself, and ten minutes' walk away from the road's end, accessible via a stone stairway, there's the bonus of the **Anse de Ficajola**, a small cove of red rocks and limpid sea.

Best of all, though, is the drive along the **D824**, which leaves the route de Ficajola a short way outside Piana. About 6km along the road, there's the option of a walk along the marked trail to the **Tour de Turghiu**, a Genoese watchtower occupying the extremity of **Capu Rossu**, the finger of red rocky land that marks the southern boundary of the Golfe de Porto. The headland is a dramatic sight from afar, its sharp point dwarfed by a great tooth-like spur, and the view at the end is even more remarkable, extending south to Cargèse and north as far as the Golfe de Girolata. Indicated from the road by a blue-and-yellow Parc Naturel Régional panel, the walk to the tower and back takes about three hours and is hard going on the final stretch. Along the way, you pass ruins of old cottages, terraces and animal enclosures dating from an era when the area was intensively farmed. The tower itself has recently been renovated and contains a small fireplace, which means you can bivouac in it and thus be up here for sunset, when the views of the red rocks tumbling down the coast in both directions are unforgettable.

Continue along the D824 for another 6km and you'll reach another exceptional beach, **Plage d'Arone**, where there's a congenial and clean campsite (☎04 95 20 64 54; June–Sept) and a pleasant pizzeria, the *Casabianca* (whose manager allows clients to camp for free in a small grove behind the restaurant). The beach can get crowded in summer, but tracks lead through the rocks on either side of it to secluded coves. Snorkellers and anglers should head right, where the surfaced road leading down to the sea forks, then follow the dirt track that plunges into the maquis at a sharp left-hand bend; ten minutes' walk further down this path brings you to a rocky promontory where the water is crystal clear and the sea bed shelves steeply down, giving glimpses of many kinds of fish and underwater plants.

Inland from Porto

The coast around Porto may be spectacular, but it's positively tame in comparison with the jaw-dropping scenery immediately **inland**. Slicing into the craggy spine of the island, the Spelunca valley snakes from sea level to the **Col de Verghio**, draped in thick pine forests. Its great feature, however, is the breathtaking **Spelunca gorge**, whose colossal granite cliffs can be approached either by the D84 or along the smaller D124, via the attractive village of **Ota**, the administrative centre for the area and the best base for hiking in the valley. From here you can walk up through the gorge along an ancient mule track, pausing at the elegant Genoese bridges and crystalline bathing pools, to **Evisa**, a resort situated in the lap of the mountains. Evisa is also well placed for a visit to the fragrant **Forêt d'Aïtone**, which borders the route to the windswept Col de Verghio, the highest point in Corsica traversable by road.

For those without transport, the Ajaccio–Porto **bus** passes through Ota (SAIB; Aug to mid-Sept Mon–Sat 2 daily, Sun 1 daily; rest of year Mon–Sat 2 daily; 2hr). During July and August there's also a daily service to Corte that calls at Evisa before scaling the pass into the Niolo; timetables for these are available from tourist offices, or you call the companies direct with the phone numbers listed in "Travel details" at the end of this chapter.

A Walk to Capo d'Orto

The ascent of **Capo d'Orto**, the colossal domed mountain looming above Porto, ranks among Corsica's classic hikes. The 10km walk should take between five and six hours and is accessible to anyone in reasonably good shape, but should not under any circumstances be attempted in wet conditions, as the granite can be lethally slippery when wet. If you're at all prone to vertigo, this route may also cause a few heart-stopping moments, as certain stretches of it are very exposed. Ensure you take the right footwear for the rocky terrain.

The track begins 2km north of Piana. Follow the D81 halfway, then take the little road on the right just before the bridge. After another 1km this stops at a fork, where you can leave the car. Take the right-hand track of the fork and continue alongside the river. After 3km the track gives way to a path marked with flashes of orange paint, which ascends east through a pine wood. The orange paint, ends at the mountain pass of **Foce d'Orto**, a huge gap between giant mounds of rock, two hours into the walk. For Capo d'Orto, head north along the left path (which soon peters out) and the way to the summit becomes marked by stone cairns. A corridor of rock overgrown with scrub leads up to a plateau, from which point it's an easy scramble to the top and a truly glorious view.

The Spelunca gorge

Spanning the 2km between the villages of Ota and Evisa, the **Spelunca gorge** is a formidable sight, its bare granite walls, 1000m deep in places, plunging into the green torrent created by the confluence of the rivers Porto, Tavulella, Onca, Campi and Aïtone. The sunlight, reflecting off the rock walls, creates a sinister effect that's heightened by the dark, jagged needles of the encircling peaks. Not surprsingly, local legend has it that the gorge was hewn by the Devil in a terrible rage.

The most dramatic part of the gorge is best viewed from the road, which hugs the edge for much of its length, but you can explore some beautiful side-valleys and riverbanks by striking out on foot along the old path between Ota and Evisa (see box overleaf).

Ota

Isolated on a verdant ledge 5km east of Porto, **OTA** is dominated by **Capo d'Orto**, a colossal dome of a mountain whose overhanging summit looks like it's about to topple onto the village. Generations of kids here have grown up believing that the only reason it doesn't is because the rock is held in place by monks tugging on long chains. As a ploy to get them to eat their greens, the children are also told that the ecclesiastical strongmen are sustained in their task by spinach *bastelles*, or pasties, delivered to them each week by an old lady on a donkey.

If you're in the area to hike, this village makes a much better base than Porto. An overnight stage on the Mare e Monti trail, it boasts two excellent **gîtes d'étape**: *Chez Félix* (☎04 95 26 12 42), where you can bed down in clean and cosy dorms for 60F per night, and *Chez Marie* (*Le Bar des Chasseurs*), just down the road (☎04 95 26 11 37), which is equally well maintained. Given the choice, however, the former has the edge thanks to its wonderful **restaurant**, whose terrace affords a sublime view of Capo d'Orto on the opposite side of the valley. The food is great, too – ranging from local specialities such as lamb stew and grilled veal or wild boar (featured on the 110F *menu corse*), to more adventurous couscous dishes – and their deliciously cool draught beer is more than welcome if you've just hiked up from the river.

Evisa

The bright-orange roofs of **EVISA** emerge against a lush background of chestnut forests about 10km from Ota, on the eastern edge of the gorge. Situated 830m above sea level, the village caters well for hikers and makes a pleasant stop for a taste of mountain life – the sky is blue, the air crisp and clear, and the food is particularly good.

Buses to Evisa leave Ajaccio up to three times daily except Sunday, via Sagone and Vico; the service runs year round, with a slightly reduced schedule outside school terms. Timetables can be consulted at most tourist offices in the area, or by telephoning Autocars R. Ceccaldi (☎04 95 21 01 24 or 04 95 21 38 06).

The best place to **stay** is the rambling *La Châtaigneraie*, on the west edge of the village on the Porto road (☎04 95 26 24 27, fax 04 95 26 23 11; ③; year round). Set amid chestnut trees, this traditional schist and granite building has a dozen cosy rooms with pine furniture and en-suite bathrooms, and they do good-value half-board deals. *Hôtel du Centre*, opposite the statue in the centre (☎04 95 26 20 92; no credit cards; ③; closed 15 Oct–Jan), is a pleasant fall-back, with small rooms but an excellent Corsican speciality restaurant on its ground floor; the 130F menu features the chef's renowned *sanglier* (wild boar) steak in chocolate sauce, and a melt-in-the-mouth chestnut *parfait*. Half-board (480F for two) is obligatory here from June through September; if you plan just to eat here, be sure to reserve a table before 5pm. At the other end of the village, *Hôtel l'Aïtone* (☎04 95 26 20 04, fax 04 95 26 24 18; ③–⑧; year round) is a large country hotel with a wide range of differently priced rooms, swimming pool, and relaxing bar-restaurant that enjoys a reputation both for gastronomic prowess and its fine views; the atmosphere here is best around early evening, when you can watch the sun set behind the gorge from their terrace. Otherwise, there's the more modest *U Pozzu*, opposite (☎04 95 26 22 89; ④), run by the same family, which has a handful of light and airy rooms. For an inexpensive meal, *U Mulinu*, downstairs, is the best option, serving mainly pizzas from around 45F. Finally, *Café di a Posta*, in the middle of Evisa, serves delicious chilled draught Pietra beer and plates of local charcuterie.

Forêt d'Aïtone

Thousands of soaring Laricio pines, some of them as high as 50m, make the **Forêt d'Aïtone** the most beautiful forest in Corsica. Incorporating the mountainous Forêt de Lindinosa, it reaches 1391m at its highest point – the **Col de Salto** – and extends over ten square kilometres between Evisa and the Col de Verghio. Well-worn tourist paths cross the forest at various points, but human disturbance is not yet great enough to upset the balance of local **wildlife**, even if the Aïtone foxes have become quite tame owing to visitors feeding them. Wild boar and stoats thrive here, while, high up in the remoter parts of Lindinosa, mouflon are sometimes seen. Birds sighted in the forest include eagles, sparrowhawks and goshawks, and if you're lucky you may spot a Corsican nuthatch, a unique species distinguished by a black crown and a white stripe over the eye. The most exotic creature to haunt these parts is a rare, large and savage cat known as a **ghjattu volpe** – literally "cat-fox". A few years ago, a haul of illegal game from Corsica was uncovered by French customs, amongst which one of these cats was discovered. However, sightings of the creature in the wild are extremely rare.

Walks from Evisa

An enjoyable short walk from Evisa runs down to the local **chestnut wood** (*châtaigneraie*) beneath the village. About 250m west of the village square, a stone gateway leads into the wood, from where you soon emerge into a field of bracken. The view here embraces the Golfe de Porto, the Spelunca gorge and Ota. This is a good walk to do at sunset, when the colours can be amazingly vivid.

The three-hour walk from **Evisa to Ota**, which drops down to the Spelunca gorge via dense deciduous and evergreen woodland, is an immensely popular hike, in spite of the fact that for most of the way the views of the gorge are obscured by trees. Cobbled centuries ago by the Genoese and now clearly marked with orange splashes of paint, the route is basically easy-going, though from Ota you may prefer to hitch back to Evisa rather than climb back up the valley. Less experienced walkers may also prefer to skip the steep descent from Ota to the first of the two Genoese bridges, in favour of the more rambling, scenic stretch along the Spelunca valley floor (see the end of this account).

To pick up the trail, follow the road west of the village as far as the **cemetery**, where a path marked "Ota–Evisa" descends into the gorge, through maquis interspersed with pines and evergreen oak. Continue through the mossy trees, past precipitous walls of bald grey rock, and follow the steepening path as it plunges into the valley. About one third of the way down, you pass an eternal spring on the left, where you can fill your bottle; from here, the trail descends through an endless series of sharp switchbacks, emerging after around an hour and a half at the picturesque Genoese **Pont de Zaglia**, a row of alders leaning across the confluence of the Aïtone and Tavulella. This is a good place for a swim, and a side-track heads northeast up the Spelunca from the bridge, giving access to less-frequented bathing spots. Hugging the left bank of the stream, the path cuts through the rocks below the most spectacular cliffs in the gorge to the confluence of the Onca and Spelunca, reached after around two hours. You can either cross the road bridge here and head up the Onca Valley to a chain of beautiful deep-green pools that are perfect for swimming, or else turn left onto the road, follow it for five minutes, and then skirt the village football pitch on your right to pick up the onward trail to Ota. This keeps to the left bank of the river until it reaches another beautiful Genoese bridge, the **Ponte Vecchiu**, from where the path gradually ascends the north flank of the valley to the village. This last section of the walk, between Ota and the Pont de Zaglia, is the most scenic, and makes a very pleasant, undemanding two- to three-hour round-hike from Ota.

You can park 7km along the road from Evisa by the **Maison Forestière d'Aïtone**, the forest headquarters and information centre (daily June–Sept 9am–noon & 2–6pm), and a starting point for walks in the area. In this part of the forest grow the oldest Laricio pines in Corsica, some of them clocking up five hundred years. Fine-grained, strong and very resistant to weathering, the Laricio was highly valued by the Genoese for ships' masts and furniture, and it was they who first built a road down the valley to the coast, later upgraded by the French using convict labour. Throughout the nineteenth century, forests all over Corsica were regularly decimated, as the island has the very best specimens of this species, which only grows in forests higher than 1000m. When the British artist and poet Edward Lear came here in the 1860s, he noted with regret "the ravages of [the] hatchets: here and there on the hillside are pale patches of cleared ground, with piles of cut and barked pines . . . everywhere giant trees lie prostrate".

One of the most popular short walks goes to the **Belvedère**, a great projecting rock 5km north of Evisa. To reach it, follow the signposted track leading into the forest, from beside a wide lay-by on the left-hand side of the road. The magnificent **view** across the valley takes in the rivers Aïtone and Porto, which rush between high walls of copper-tinted rocks down to the Spelunca gorge.

Another well-trekked route leads to the multiple **Cascades de la Valla Scarpa**, where the crystalline waters of the Aïtone crash into a pool hollowed out by the falls. It's just fifteen minutes' walk from the maison forestière, signposted "Piscines/les Cascades", and thus it does become overcrowded in summer – though you don't have to walk much further along the river to find more tranquil spots for a picnic and a swim.

If you want to reach the higher slopes, an hour's walk from the maison forestière will bring you to the **Col de Salto**, and a further three hours' heavy climbing along the same rocky track will bring you to the **Col de Felce**, for a fantastic vista of the Golfe de Porto. For the more ambitious, the **Col de Cuccavera** – above the tree line at 1500m – can be attained by cutting north before the Col de Felce, striking right up the mountainside. Once you're this far up, you can make out hazy distant views of the Gorges d'Asco.

For more on the Niolo, see p.334.

The Corsican origin myth relating to this unusual geological formation is described on p.338.

Just 4km beyond the maison forestière, the road, strewn with pine cones and foraged by herds of semi-wild pigs, runs over the **Col de Verghio** (1477m), gateway to the remote district of the Niolo and the limit of the Forêt de Valdo-Niello. You can park up here and strike out on foot along the marked mountain trail leading north towards the Bergeries de Radule, roughly an hour away. Minutes into the walk, the views improve dramatically, with vistas of Punta Licciola and the lower slopes of the red, wedge-shaped **Paglia Orba** opening up to the north. Keep going long enough and you'll eventually hit the GR20, which winds up to the **Refuge Ciuttulu di i Mori**, springboard for the ascent of Paglia Orba and the adjacent giant rock archway, Capo Tafonata. As long as you overnight in the refuge and set off at dawn, the peak is technically straightforward; don't, however, attempt it without adequate clothing, footwear and maps (see box on pp.144–145).

Immediately below the Col de Verghio is one of Corsica's few **ski stations**, an incongruously grim concrete edifice that sees few visitors even in winter, as these days there's rarely enough snow to keep it in use. Desperate for some customers, the entrepreneurial owner

Théodore Poli: Roi des Montagnes

Théodore Poli was twenty years old in 1817, at a time when the French administration was conscripting young men all over the island in an attempt to curb banditry. A brigadier from Poli's village of Guagno, in an act of spite, neglected to inform Poli that he was due for national service, thereby making him a deserter – an offence on which the French were especially harsh. Poli shot the man in revenge and, in true outlaw tradition, took to the maquis, where his confederation of some 150 bandits soon elected him "Roi des Montagnes". A bandit constitution was drawn up, whereby Poli was named Théodore II, after Théodore I, who had briefly ruled Corsica some sixty years earlier. Hiding out in the Aïtone forest, Théodore and his gang proceeded to terrorize the neighbourhood, imposing a heavy "tax" on the rich and the clergy, while exempting the poor. Becoming ever more ambitious, these self-styled champions of the downtrodden poor whipped up anti-French feeling wherever they could, raiding the gendarmeries for arms and even gunning down the local executioner of Bastia when he refused to participate in anti-French demonstrations. In 1827 the Roi des Montagnes' rule came to an abrupt end – lured into a forest glade by a beautiful woman, he was shot dead by one of his many enemies.

"re-directed" the GR20 through his establishment some years back with a couple of tins of red and white paint bought from the local store. His bar and extortionately pricy provisions counter thrived briefly until the Parc Naturel Régional got wind of what he'd done and removed the misleading marks. The road is extremely rocky along the last stretch up to the building, where a café is usually open from May until September.

The Golfe de Sagone

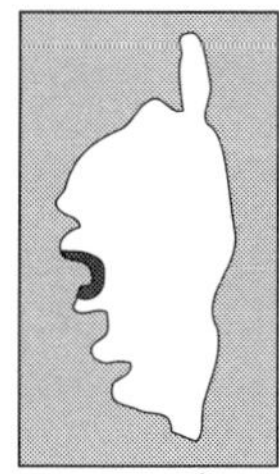

Long curves of sandy beach characterize Corsica's largest gulf, the **Golfe de Sagone**, which stretches 40km from Capo di Feno up to the Punta di Cargèse. The gulf lacks the wild allure of much of the west coast, with new holiday villages, bungalows and campsites springing into existence every year, but its resorts make acceptable bases for a few days if you have your own transport. Tucked into the Golfe de la Liscia at the easternmost indent of the gulf, **Tiuccia** occupies the most sheltered spot, with a fine golden beach close by. North of here, **Sagone** thrives as a centre for scuba diving and watersports, but it can't match the appeal of **Cargèse**, a lovely and increasingly chic clifftop village at the northern tip of the bay.

Cargèse

Sitting high above a deep-blue bay on a cliff scattered with olive trees, **CARGÈSE** (Carghjese) oozes a lazy charm that attracts hundreds of well-heeled summer residents to its pretty white houses and hotels. The locals, many of them descendants of Greek refugees from

Cargèse marks the end of the popular Mare e Monti long-distance footpath, which starts in Calenzana, see p.146.

the Peloponnese in the seventeenth century (see box on p.187), seem to accept this inundation and the proximity of a Club Med complex with generous nonchalance, but the best time to visit is September, when Cargèse empties and you can enjoy its distinctive qualities in peace.

Two **churches** stand on separate hummocks at opposite sides of the valley head: one Catholic and one Orthodox, a reminder of the old antagonism between the two cultures. Built for the minority Corsican families in 1828, the **Catholic church** is one of the latest examples of Baroque in Corsica and has a trompe l'œil ceiling that can't really compete with the view from the its terrace. The **Greek church**, however, is the more interesting of the two – a large granite neo-Gothic edifice built in 1852 to replace a church that had become too small for the congregation. Inside, the outstanding feature is the **iconostasis**, a gift from a monastery in Rome, decorated with **icons** painted by monks from Mount Athos and brought over from Greece with the original settlers in the late seventeenth century. Behind it, the graceful *Virgin and Child*, to the right of the altar, is thought to date from as far back as the twelfth century. The frescoes lining the side walls were recently restored, giving the church a rather too vibrant look.

You can swim off the rocks beneath the hotel *Bel'Mare* (see p.186), if you climb down the cliff through the gate just past the hotel. There's also another quieter sand and gravel beach 2km south; head towards Ajaccio and turn off along the track where you see the Hertz sign, leading to a small marina. However, by far the best beach in the area, **Plage de Pero**, is 2km north of Cargèse – walk up to the junction with the Piana road and take the left fork down to the sea. Overlooked by a Genoese tower, this white stretch of sand has a couple of bars and sailboard stalls, but it's large enough to absorb the crowds that descend here in summer. **Plage du Chiuni**, a further 2km along the same road, is much busier thanks to its full-on watersports scene and the high profile of the Club Med resort that backs the beach. A more secluded spot lies 1km south of the village at **Plage du Monachi**; this small, sandy cove is reached by climbing down the track at the side of the road and past the little chapel on the cliff side.

Practicalities

There's an unusually helpful **tourist office** on rue Dr-Dragacci (daily: July–Sept 9am–noon & 4–7pm, Oct–June 3–5pm; ☎04 95 26 41 31), which can provide you with a map of the area and will help you find accommodation; it also sells tickets for the boat trips up to the Calanche and Girolata (see p.169), leaving at 9am daily in summer and costing about 200F for the day.

Buses running between Ajaccio and Porto pull in for a ten-minute pit stop at the *Bar des Amis*, in the village centre. Two services a day operate all year round from Monday to Saturday in

Casabianca and the "Pearl Harbour" Landing

On December 14, 1942, the 1500-tonne submarine **Casabianca**, commanded by captain l'Herminier, arrived from its safe haven in Algeria and made a daylight periscope reconnaissance of Chiuni bay, just north of Cargèse. It then submerged to hide on the bottom until darkness fell – a dangerous technique requiring expert knowledge of local currents and the sea bed's topography. Having remained underwater until just after midnight, the sub resurfaced and, barely breaking the waves, put ashore three crew members and a team of four secret agents: one Englishman codenamed "Tommy", and four Corsican patriots. Equipped with wireless sets, French francs, Italian lire, food, supplies and forged papers, the four-man team were to become the first agents to infiltrate enemy-occupied territory in Europe.

After seeing them safely ashore, the *Casabianca* retreated back underwater, but came back up again thirty hours later to ferry one further consignment of provisions and US-dispatched arms to the beach. On this occasion, however, one of the rubber dinghies capsized, forcing the two Free French sailors to help the agents to swim ashore, where they remained stranded for two months. "Tommy", on the other hand, swam through the darkness for two and a half hours until the sub found him.

Over the following months, the wireless operators, aided by Corsican partisans, were able to crisscross the island and broadcast valuable information regarding Italian and German troop movements in Corsica; their radio link with the Allies in North Africa also enabled military chiefs to co-ordinate Resistance operations prior to a possible full-scale invasion. In all, the unit, codenamed "**Pearl Harbour**", sent 202 messages before the chief radio operator was captured, tortured and killed in the summer of 1943.

Aside from the messages "Pearl Harbour" sent from Corsica, the successful landing in the winter of 1942 was of huge significance, as it provided a model for all further liaisons between the *Casabianca* and the Corsican Maquis. However, several months later it transpired the mission had, unbeknown to the captain and his crew, nearly floundered at the first hurdle. Instead of landing on Chiuni beach, as planned, Captain l'Herminier, who could not see clearly through his periscope in the darkness, accidentally put the agents ashore on the next cove north, known to local fishermen as crique de Topitti. The error proved a miraculous reprieve. Had the agents landed on Chiuni beach, they would have walked straight into a battalion of 1500 enemy soldiers camped in the dunes.

A fuller account of the Liberation appears on p.370; you can also read more about the *Casabianca* in our description of Bastia's museum (see p.70), where its coning tower is housed today.

either direction, with an additional departure on Sundays during the summer. Timetables can be consulted at any tourist office, or telephone Autocars SAIB (☎04 95 22 41 99 or 04 95 21 02 07); note that services on Saturdays leave one hour earlier than during the week.

All the best **hotels** are located within a few minutes' walk of the centre, with the budget places at the top end of the village. The least expensive is the *Continental*, on the left as you descend into the main square from Porto (☎04 95 26 42 24; ②), which is a bit dingy but clean and comfortable enough. If you can afford a little more, head for the characterful *Bel'Mare*, 400m south of the centre on the Ajaccio road (☎04 95 26 40 13 or 04 95 26 48 24; ③–④), which occupies a great location overlooking the bay. The rooms in both the main building and annexe below are en suite and spacious, and have sweeping views from their balconies; the restaurant here is also pleasant, with a breezy terrace and a varied, good-value set menu that changes daily. If it's full, ignore the overpriced *Spelunca*, an ugly modern building directly opposite the *Bel'Mare*, and head to the top of the village where the *St Jean*, overlooking the crossroads (☎04 95 26 46 68, fax 04 95 26 43 93; ④–⑦), offers more luxurious rooms, some of them with mezzanine floors and self-catering facilities; ask for one at the front with a sea view. For a room directly on the beach, however, you'll have to drop down the road leading north off the crossroads at the top of the village to the *Thalassa* (☎04 95 26 40 08; ④), 1.5km from the centre. Among the oldest-established places in the area, this is Cargèse's most attractive hotel, an intimate place swathed in bougainvillea, right behind the sands, and with friendly owners; it's also extremely popular in season, when advance booking is essential.

The only **campsite** within easy reach of Cargèse is *Camping Toraccia*, 4km north along the main road (☎04 95 26 42 39; May–Oct). Well shaded under olive groves, the site's best pitches are at the top of the hill, looking inland towards Capo d'Orto; they also have simple wood cabins that can be rented on a daily basis out of season, or for 2500F per week from late June through August.

There are a fair number of **restaurants** scattered about the village, as well as the standard pizzerias. *A Volta*, next to the Catholic church, offers a good-value 110F menu featuring seafood, game and pasta served on a spectacular terrace jutting out over the sea. Cargese's best, and most expensive, restaurant, *Chez Antoine*, is located down in the marina. Don't be fooled by its rustic fishing-shack appearance: the food is delicious, particularly the legendary bouillabaisse, and the place draws yachtsmen from the moorings opposite and well-heeled Ajacciens in equal numbers. For a **drink**, go no further than the main square, where you can watch all the action from *Bar des Amis*, which has a pool table, or *Bar Chantilly*, which commands the best vantage point for people-watching.

The least expensive places to change money are the **banks** along the main street, just up from the *Bar des Amis*, two of which have cash machines.

Sagone

SAGONE, 13km east of Cargèse, was a bishopric and important fishing port until marauding Saracens destroyed the town in the sixteenth

The Greeks of Cargèse

Some 730 Greek settlers from Mani, in the southern Peloponnese, originally landed on Corsica in 1676, fleeing the Muslim attacks and persecution that followed the conquest of Crete seven years earlier. They came as part of a Genoese plan to weaken Corsican resistance by colonizing the island with different nationalities; the deal involved the payment of a large sum of money in return for guaranteed protection from any hostile Corsicans who might object to their presence. The Greeks were allowed to maintain their own customs, including their Orthodox religion (though they had to recognize the supremacy of the pope), but were forced to Italianize their surnames: thus Papadakis and Dragakis became Papadacci and Dragacci, two prominent names in the village to this day.

The first settlement was 4km northeast of Cargèse at a place they called **Paomia**. Within a year they had built five hamlets, proving so successful as farmers that they began to incur the wrath of the locals, who resented Genoa's patronage. Peace came to an abrupt end in 1715, when Paomia was ransacked by Corsican patriots enraged by the Greeks' refusal to take up arms against their Genoese benefactors. After much bloodshed, the Greeks were forced to take refuge in Ajaccio, where they remained for forty years until the arrival of the French brought temporary peace to the island.

Their deliverance came in the form of **Count Marbeuf**, an ambitious French nobleman who in 1773 attempted to integrate the communities by forming a united regiment of Greeks and Corsicans, and offered the Greeks Cargèse as compensation for the loss of Paomia. Unfortunately, the building of 120 family houses and a castle for Marbeuf again provoked the locals, who in the same year descended from the hills to burn the castle and drive the Greeks into hiding in the towers of Plage de Pero. In 1793 the Greeks were attacked once more: their village was burned to the ground and they had to flee to Ajaccio. Four years later, only two-thirds chose to return. Gradually the Corsicans came to join them in their reconstructed village, marking the beginning of an uneasy coexistence which, largely through intermarriage, eventually led to integration. In the nineteenth century the Corsicans built their own church, after which the Greeks built one opposite and adopted some Catholic rites as a gesture towards integration.

There are still three hundred Greek families in Cargèse, well assimilated into the Corsican way of life but still observing the Greek liturgy and conducting weddings in the traditional Greek style, with the bride and groom crowned with vine leaves and olive branches. Also distinctively Greek are the **festival** of St Spiridion on December 12, when fireworks light up the village, and the Easter Monday blessing of the village, when all the women dress in black, the lights in the village are extinguished and the villagers form a candlelit procession to the church.

century. Today, however, the only evidence of its past glory is the cathedral of **Sant'Appiano**, a crumbling medieval ruin 1km north of the village. The settlement proper comprises a string of tired-looking hotels and restaurants, slightly redeemed by **Plage du Liamone**, a long sandy beach to the north of the resort. Despite its minimal charm, Sagone gets pretty crowded in high season, principally on account of the watersports facilities offered along the beach. The town is served by Autocars SAIB's buses between Ajaccio and Porto (see p.194 for details).

Accommodation is strung out along the main road through the centre of the village. *Hôtel Cyrnos*, next door to Immeubles les Mimosa in the centre (☎04 95 28 00 01; ④), is functional but nothing special – it is, however, the base for the Centre Subaquatique (same phone number), whose staff can guide you to the excellent **dive** sites around the Ponte Leccia, a headland with a sheer underwater drop of 80m. Alternative hotels, just beyond the village, are *La Marine*, an attractive stone building on the left of the road to Ajaccio (☎04 95 28 00 03, fax 04 95 28 03 98; ④–⑤; closed Jan), whose terrace jutting into the sea gives it the edge on other hotels in the vicinity; and the *Motel Funtanella*, 4km along the road to Cargèse (☎04 95 28 03 36; ④), which is shady and secluded but doesn't have a restaurant. The best **campsite** in the area, *Camping Sagone*, lies 3km inland on the road to Vico (☎04 95 28 04 15, fax 04 95 28 08 28; May–Oct), and offers riding, tennis and underwater fishing. The only commendable **restaurant** in the area is the *Kallisté*, an inexpensive pizzeria on the beach that serves a good range of seafood dishes, including anemone soup (*soupe d'oursin*).

The Scandola nature reserve and Girolata, an isolated fishing village, are located along one of the most dramatic stretches of the coast in Corsica *(see pp.172–175)*.

Worth considering if you're staying in Sagone is a **boat trip** to Girolata and the Scandola reserve. Departing from the *Ancura* restaurant at 8.30am, the trips cost 200F (half-price for children) for a full day; the boats are narrow enough to penetrate several of the most impressive breaches in the red cliffs and sea caves around Porto, and return via the Calanche at around 5pm. Tickets should be reserved the day before (☎04 95 28 04 13).

Tiuccia

Continuing south from Sagone on the D81, after 6km you'll reach **TIUCCIA**, some 25km north of Ajaccio at the northern end of the Golfe de la Liscia, a half-moon bay set within the Golfe de Sagone. Consisting chiefly of a line of modern buildings bordering the main road, Tiuccia has a trio of minor historic sights – two seventeenth-century Genoese watchtowers and the ruined **Castello di Capraja**, seat of Giudice della Cinarca – but its strong point is **Plage de la Liscia**, a broad golden strand 500m to the south.

Tourist information is available from the *Hôtel Cinarca*, on the main street (☎04 95 52 21 39; ④), whose rooms afford a good view of the bay. You'll find the least expensive beds at *Le Bon Accueil* (☎ & fax 04 95 52 21 01; ③), a comfortable inn with ten rooms and a moderately priced restaurant specializing in Corsican food. Other options include the nearby *Beau Rivage* (☎04 95 52 21 09; ③), and the more upmarket *Hôtel Narval*, 3km south of Tiuccia at Liscia (☎04 95 52 25 35; ④; April–Oct), a luxurious modern complex near the beach, with tennis courts and a pool.

Autocars SAIB's Ajaccio–Porto **buses** (see p.184 for details) stop next to the **campsite** by the main road just outside the village. If you have your own vehicle, however, a better place to camp is the three-star *Les Couchants*, 3km out of Tiuccia on the D25 to Casaglione (☎04 95 52 26 60; May–Oct), which occupies an attractive site in fields overlooking the valley to the sea. Alternatively, head 3km south along the Ajaccio road to *La Liscia* (☎04 95 52 25 35; April–Oct), another large and well-equipped site with a disco, shop and snack bar.

Vico and around

Vico, a dismal outpost in one of the remoter parts of Corsica, crouches in the mountains 15km northeast of Sagone. Although there's not much to recommend the place itself, its single hotel is an ideal base for drives into the surrounding granite peaks. Close by you can visit the **Couvent St-François** on the way to the beautifully wild **Gorges du Liamone**, which extend to the south of the village. To the north, the **Col de Sevi** provides fine views across the mountains, or you can strike eastwards and visit the thermal springs at **Guagno-les-Bains**. Intrepid drivers can venture further up this way to the dramatically situated hamlets of **Soccia** and **Orto**, perched on a ledge in front of the crags of Monte Sant'Eliseo.

The only public transport in this region is Autocars R. Ceccaldi's **bus** between Ajaccio and Evisa (see p.194), which goes via Vico and the Col de Sevi.

Vico

Dominated by the dome of La Sposata, **VICO** lies at a crossroads amidst a high wooded valley, remaining invisible until the final approach. Its tough ambience is heightened by the tall dark houses and cold mountain air, but it does have the only **hotel** hereabouts, *U Paradisu*, on the outskirts of town along the road to Arbori (☎04 95 26 61 62, fax 04 95 26 67 01; ④, obligatory half-board July & Aug ⑦; April–Dec). Its rooms are quite plain, but it does good Corsican mountain food and has a pool. An alternative place to **eat** is the excellent *Auberge du Col*, at the junction of the D70 and D23 on the Evisa road (☎04 95 26 61 58). Don't be put off by its unpromising exterior: the restaurant serves variously priced, good-value set menus, including one with delicious *loup de mer* in cream sauce, and there's a choice of pungent local cheeses.

You can travel to Vico all year round by direct **bus** from Ajaccio, via Sagone; the service operates daily on Mondays to Saturdays (departs Ajaccio 7.45am & 3.30pm; 1hr 15min), with a slightly reduced service outside term time. For more information, contact Autocars R. Ceccaldi (☎04 95 21 01 24 or 04 95 21 38 06).

For two hundred years Vico was the residence of the bishops of Sagone after their settlement was destroyed by the Saracens in the tenth century. It went on to become the seat of the da Leca clan, a Cinarchesi family who ruled the district in the fifteenth century. One day in 1456, 23 members of this rebel family were put to death by the Genoese governor Spinola, who had their throats cut out on the slopes east of town, where they were left to die a lonely death. Gian' Paolo da Leca escaped this massacre and in 1481 founded the only surviving remnant of Vico's past: the **Couvent St-François**, a great white building encircled by vivid green woods and gardens, 1km along the road to Arbori. These days it's the headquarters of an old-style Roman Catholic missionary movement that culls converts from the poorer corners of the world. Worth a look here is the seventeenth-century church (daily 2–6pm), whose chief treasures are the carved **chestnut furniture** in the sacristy and the fifteenth-century wooden figure of Christ above the altar, thought to be the oldest in Corsica.

Col de Sevi

Aside from the obvious draw of the mountain views, a drive up to the **Col de Sevi** gives you an unadulterated taste of the rural Corsican way of life. By regaining the D70 north of Vico, you'll start the ascent along a high maquis-clad ridge. A detour 5km along will bring you to the apple-growing village of **RENNO**, spectacularly set amidst swathes of orchards and chestnut trees – be sure to taste the marvellous pippins that are sold in summer along the roadside. At first sight solely populated by pigs and chickens, the village hosts the annual **St-Roch fair** (August 16 to 18), a traditional country jamboree which involves selling livestock, honey- and chestnut-related products, as well as the usual pastis-imbibing.

Back on the D70 it's not far up to the **Col de Sevi** (1110m), the pass that links the Liamone basin with the Porto valley. From up here there's a tremendous **vista**, but for an even better view of the Golfe de Porto you can walk up to a spot called **L'Incinosa**, an easy-going

Hike to Lac de Creno

Surrounded by thick Laricio pine forest on the lower western slopes of the Rotondo massif, the **Lac de Creno** makes an ideal picnic spot if you're driving around the Vico area – easily accessible, well shaded and in the lap of the high mountains. The hike there and back takes around two hours; to pick up the trail, follow the recently tarmacked road up the valley from **Soccio**. After the second switchback you come to a car park with a large cross and information panel, from where the path strikes uphill across the northeast flank of Sant'Eliseo. En route you pass a couple of tumbledown *bergeries* and the little **Lac d'Arate**, and cross the trail leading to the lake from the village of **Orto**, on the far side of the Eliseo ridge. This latter route is harder and double the distance, but the scenery is more varied and the chestnut forest covering the lower part of the trail one of the healthiest and least spoilt on the island (for more on Corsica's chestnut forests, see p.318).

two-hour stroll there and back – just follow the path to the right of the road for 4km along the ridge until you reach the top. After the Col de Sevi, the road continues to rise for 1km before descending into the valley on the approach to Evisa.

Guagno-les-Bains, Soccia and Orto

A tedious winding route east of Vico passes goat enclosures and muddy green countryside before coming to **GUAGNO-LES-BAINS**, 12km along the D23. A couple of hot springs were first exploited here in the eighteenth century, when illustrious personages such as Pascal Paoli made the trip by mule to take a thermal bath. The spa was renovated quite recently and is open from May to October. Well-heeled visitors stay in the village's one hotel, the *Hôtel des Thermes* (☎04 95 28 30 68, fax 04 95 28 34 02; ⑤–⑥), the only three-star in central Corsica, boasting a pool, tennis court and gourmet restaurant.

Just beyond Guagno-les-Bains, a left turn up the unsignposted D123 to Poggiolo, followed by another left turn, will bring you to **SOCCIA**, where the *U Paese* (☎04 95 28 31 92 or 04 95 28 33 13; ③) provides comfortable **accommodation** for hikers attempting the **Lac de Creno** (see box). Its restaurant is popular, so if you want to take advantage of their good-value half-board deals book at least two days in advance. Perched on a high mountain shelf across the valley, **ORTO** is also only accessible from Poggiolo, from where a pitted track squirms up to the village. The attraction here is the forbidding proximity of **Monte Sant'Eliseo**, a peak crowned with a tiny chapel that is the object of a popular pilgrimage in August. Only masochists would take the road from Guagno-les-Bains to Guagno, 9km to the east.

The Gorges du Liamone and Arbori

South of Vico the D1 follows the River Liamone for 7km through the **Gorges du Liamone**, a gloriously remote landscape of sweeping valleys shrouded in chestnut trees, framed by shadowy ridges covered in patches of deep maquis. Wild pigs roam the route as far as **ARBORI**, an exquisite village of russet buildings strung out on a ledge jutting into the valley. Continuing south along here brings you to the hilly wine-producing region of the Cinarca.

The Cinarca

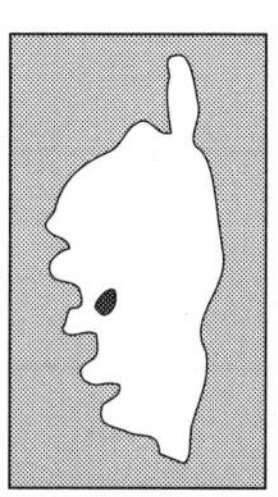

Contained within mountains approaching 1000m high to the north and south, the **Cinarca** forms the hinterland to the Golfe de Sagone north of Ajaccio. Once the seat of the powerful Cinarchesi, a family of corrupt self-titled nobles who ruled the country in the thirteenth century, the region is today renowned for its *appellation contrôlée*

> **WARNING**
>
> Over the past few years, the Cinarca has seen a worrying spate of armed robberies directed at tourists passing through the region. Cars have been stopped and their drivers relieved of valuables at gunpoint. The assailants wear black balaclavas (symbol of the Corsican separatist terrorists), but these incidents seem to have absolutely no political motive. Before venturing into the Cinarca, therefore, we recommend that you check at a tourist office to ensure the attacks are no longer taking place.

wine, produced near the banks of the River Liscia, in a cluster o sleepy villages along the **Route des Vins**. A tour of the Cinarca ca easily be made in about two hours, passing through **Calcatoggio** e route to the chief village of the region, **Sari d'Orcino**, an appealin little place set deep in the verdant countryside. From here you con tinue through the villages of **Casaglione** and **Ambiegna** befor returning to the coast road.

The villages

Two kilometres from the main D81, just over 20km north of Ajaccio **CALCATOGGIO**'s bleached houses rise from a jungle of vineyard and orchards, creating a scene that's typical of the Cinarca. The ter raced hillside location gives a pleasant view of the azure Golfe de l Liscia, and there are more marvellous views if you continue for abou 1km beyond the village and then turn right along the D101, descend ing to the sinuous corniche of the lush Liscia valley.

Passing through Sant'Andrea d'Orcino and Canelle, two village nestled close together amidst vines and fig trees, the road threads it way up to **SARI D'ORCINO**, a village composed of two hamlet stacked up the slopes of Punta San Damiano. In the second, Acqua i Giu, the parish church's terrace gives a panorama of the whole of th Cinarca, its green carpet of fruit trees sliced by the river, which yo can see flowing into the Golfe de la Liscia. Just beyond the village you can stop and **taste wine** at the *Clos d'Alzeto*, owned by Pasca Albertini (☎04 95 52 24 67; free); there are no set times, as a rule for visiting. North of Sari d'Orcino, the D1 skirts a high rocky wall fo 3km as far as **AMBIEGNA**, an elegant village bordering the Liamon valley and a soaring pine wood. Head south from here along the D2 for 3km to **CASAGLIONE**, an ancient cluster of silvery stone build ings grouped around a church that houses a painting of th Crucifixion dated 1505. From here it's a gentle meander back dow to the coast.

Giudice della Cinarca

The medieval **Cinarchesi**, a loose association of feudal lords, many of them distantly related, controlled wide tracts of the wilder southern half of Corsica, maintaining an especially tight grip on the Cinarca region. The most famous of these chieftains was Sinucello della Rocca, better known as **Giudice della Cinarca**, described by fifteenth-century historian Giovanni della Grossa as "one of the most extraordinary men who has ever existed on the island".

Born in Olmeto in 1219, Giudice began his career allied to the Genoese, but he refused to give up his feudal rights and become a vassal to the republic. Constantly battling against the rival Cinarchesi from his base in the castle of Istria, he managed to gain effective control of the whole of the south of the island, and at one point was able to summon all the region's lords and chieftains to form a national assembly before the Genoese eventually had him chased out of Corsica. Thereupon Giudice took up the Pisan cause, distinguishing himself at the Battle of Meloria in 1284, the naval engagement that was Pisa's downfall. After that he returned to the mountain fastnesses of Corsica to resume his war on Genoa and his neighbouring warlords.

It was during this period that Giudice (meaning "judge" or "governor") set himself up as a figure of public authority, arbitrating vendettas, forcing the rich to pay high taxes, and punishing wrongdoers and enemies with extreme brutality – blinding his adversaries was a favoured tactic. He consolidated his position by allowing a greater degree of freedom to the burgeoning peasant bourgeoisie than was accorded by other Cinarchesi tyrants, and married off his six daughters to local counts to ensure the continuation of his power. In 1289 and 1290 the Genoese launched two massive and unsuccessful attempts to overthrow Giudice, who by this time was nearly blinded by venereal disease, yet he was only captured when betrayed by one of his many illegitimate sons. Thrown into a common prison on the French mainland, he died of fever in 1307.

Dorothy Carrington, in her book *Granite Island*, recalls a popular folk tale concerning Giudice. According to the story, the mighty warlord, who started life miserably poor and hunchbacked, fell in love with a wealthy and beautiful widow named Sibilia, whom he asked to marry him. On receiving her refusal, Giudice threatened to abduct her, whereupon the lady asked him to her castle at Istria. But the invitation was a trap, and on arriving there the young suitor was imprisoned. To rub salt in the wound, it is said that Sibilia had him thrown into an iron cage in her dungeon and "paraded herself in front of him, in all her loveliness, stark naked". However, Giudice bribed the guards to set him free and soon exacted a cruel revenge. Capturing the castle, he took Sibilia in the same cage to a nearby mountain col and prostituted her to passers-by until she perished of hunger and humiliation. The story is mostly myth, but retains a few bones of historical truth: Giudice (neither poor nor hunchbacked) did indeed court a beautiful widow, Sibilia de Franchi, who had him thrown into prison for a reason that has been lost over time. When the insulted nobleman eventually escaped from her clutches, he restored his honour by committing Sibilia to a place that was, in the words of a chronicler, "less than honest".

Travel details

BUSES

The acronyms featured below refer to the following bus companies.

ARC = Autocars R. Ceccaldi (☎04 95 21 01 24 or 04 95 21 38 06).
SAIB = Autocars SAIB (☎04 95 22 41 99 or 04 95 21 02 07).

Evisa to: Ajaccio (ARC; Mon–Sat 1–3 daily; 1hr 45min); Sagone (ARC; Mon–Sat 1–3 daily; 1hr 20min); Tiuccia (ARC; Mon–Sat 1–3 daily; 1hr 30min); Vico (ARC; Mon–Sat 1–3 daily; 45min).

Porto to: Ajaccio (SAIB; Aug to mid-Sept Mon–Sat 2 daily, Sun 1 daily; rest of year Mon–Sat 2 daily; 2hr); Calvi (SAIB; mid-May to Oct Mon–Sat 1 daily; 3hr); Cargèse (SAIB; Mon–Sat 2 daily, summer Sun 3 daily; 1hr 15min); Col de la Croix (SAIB; mid-May to July Mon–Sat 1 daily; Aug 1 daily; 1hr); Curzo (SAIB; mid-May to July Mon to Sat 1 daily; Aug 1 daily; 40min); Galéria–Fango crossroads (SAIB; mid-May to July Mon–Sat 1 daily; Aug 1 daily; 2hr 20min); Ota (SAIB; Aug to mid-Sept Mon–Sat 2 daily, Sun 1 daily; rest of year Mon–Sat daily; 2hr); Partinello (SAIB; mid-May to July 1 daily Mon–Sat; Aug 1 daily; 30min); Piana (SAIB; 2 daily; 15min).

Vico to: Ajaccio (ARC; May–Oct Mon–Sat 2 daily; 1hr 15min).

Chapter 4

The Ajaccio region

Ajaccio is Corsica's largest town, capital of the *département* of Corse-du-Sud and seat of the island's Assemblée Régionale; yet – with its palm trees, street cafés and yacht-filled marina – the image it immediately projects is that of the classic French Mediterranean resort. Modern blocks are stacked up behind the town, but they do little to diminish the visual impact of its warm yellow-toned buildings and sturdy citadel, set in a magnificent bay and framed by a shadowy mountain range. Unlike Bastia, Ajaccio makes most of its money from tourism, a fact partly attributable to its own attractions, to its proximity to the west coast's wonderful beaches, and to its having been the birthplace of Napoléon Bonaparte. The prime Napoleonic sites – the Maison Bonaparte and the Salon Napoléonien – are not, however, the best of Ajaccio's cultural assets: that distinction goes to the Musée Fesch, which boasts France's most important collection of Italian paintings outside the Louvre.

The **Golfe d'Ajaccio**, an ethereal vista of mist-shrouded mountains by day, is transformed at night into a completely different but equally evocative scene by the lights of the bay's sprawling tourist developments. Flung out at the northern tip of the gulf, beyond the hotels, the islets known as the **Îles Sanguinaires** are perhaps the most popular excursion from the town, rivalled by **Porticcio** on the gulf's southern shore, a trendy outpost for weekending Ajacciens.

Accommodation Price Codes

Throughout this guide, hotel accommodation is graded on a scale from ① to ⑧. These numbers show the cost per night of the cheapest double room **in high season**, though remember that many of the cheap places will have more expensive rooms with en-suite facilities. In such cases we list two price codes, indicating the range of room rates offered.

① under 100F/under €15	⑤ 300–350F/€45–52.50
② 100–200F/€15–30	⑥ 350–400F/€52.50–60
③ 200–250F/€30–37.50	⑦ 400–500F/€60–75
④ 250–300F/€37.50–45	⑧ 500F and above/€75 and above

Of greater appeal to most visitors are the secluded beaches that punctuate this side of the bay towards **Capu di Muro**, ideal targets for a picnic and a swim. Inland from Ajaccio, the craggy **Gorges du Prunelli** edge the river as far as **Bastelica**, birthplace of Corsican freedom fighter Sampiero Corso, but an uninspiring village that owes its popularity to the nearby Val d'Èse ski station.

Apart from the train line to Bastia and a few long-distance bus connections, **public transport** in this region is confined to a few shuttle services past the holiday complexes of the Golfe d'Ajaccio.

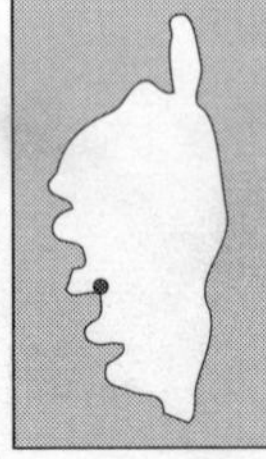

Ajaccio

Edward Lear claimed that on a wet day it would be hard to find so dull a place as **AJACCIO** (Aiacciu), a harsh judgement with an element of justice. The town has none of Bastia's sense of purpose and can seem to lack a definitive identity of its own, as if French domination has

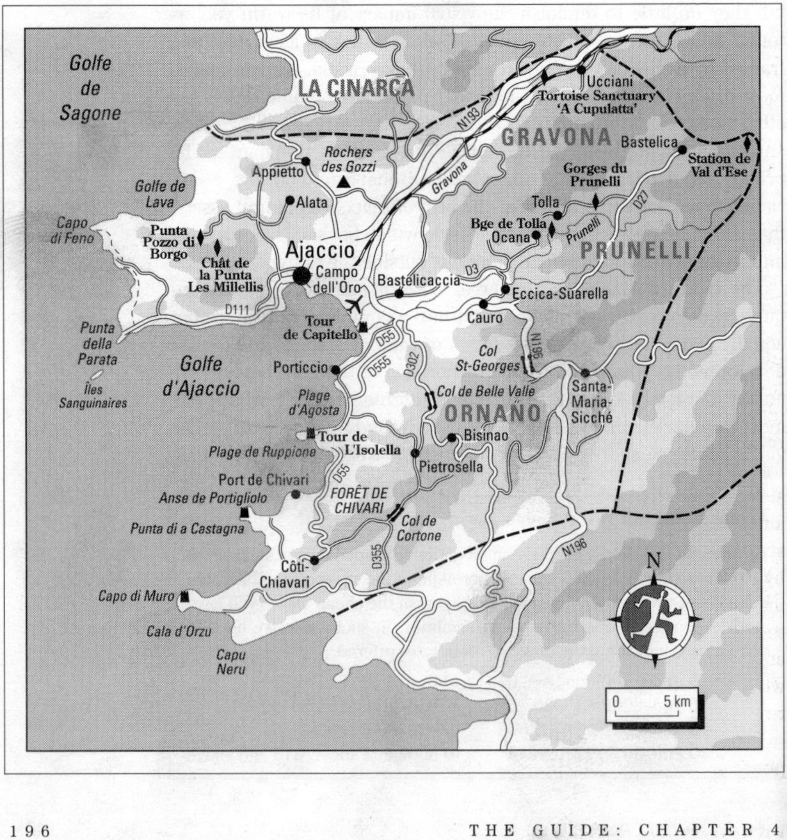

Golfe de Sagone
LA CINARCA
Ucciani
Tortoise Sanctuary 'A Cupulatta'
N193
GRAVONA
Bastelica
Station de Val d'Ese
Rochers des Gozzi
Appietto
Gravona
Gorges du Prunelli
Golfe de Lava
Alata
Tolla
D27
Capo di Feno
Punta Pozzo di Borgo
Bge de Tolla
Ocana
Prunelli
Châ̂t de la Punta Les Millellis
Ajaccio
Campo dell'Oro
PRUNELLI
D3
Bastelicaccia
Eccica-Suarella
D111
Cauro
Punta della Parata
Tour de Capitello
D55
N196
Col St-Georges
Golfe d'Ajaccio
Porticcio
D555
D302
Îles Sanguinaires
Plage d'Agosta
Col de Belle Valle
ORNANO
Santa-Maria-Sicché
Tour de L'Isolella
Bisinao
Plage de Ruppione
Pietrosella
Port de Chivari
D55
Anse de Portigliolo
FORÊT DE CHIVARI
Punta di a Castagna
Col de Cortone
N196
Côti-Chiavari
D355
N
Capo di Muro
Cala d'Orzu
Capu Neru
0 5 km

sapped its energy. On the other hand, it's a relaxed and good-looking place, with an exceptionally mild climate (the average temperature for the year is 17°C), a wealth of cafés, restaurants and chic shops.

Napoléon gave Ajaccio international fame, but though the self-designated Cité Impériale is littered with statues and street names relating to the Bonaparte family, you'll find the Napoleonic cult has a less dedicated following in his home town than you might imagine. The emperor is still considered by many Ajacciens as a self-serving Frenchman rather than as a Corsican, and from time to time their disapproval is expressed in a dramatic gesture – such as painting his statue yellow, as happened a few years ago. Napoléon's impact on the townscape of his birthplace wasn't enormous, either. Spacious squares and boulevards were laid out during Ajaccio's brief spell as island capital, but Napoléon's efforts did little to alter the intrinsic provinciality of the place, and Ajaccio remains memorable for the things that have long made it attractive – its battered old town, the pervasive scents of fresh coffee and grilled seafood, and the encompassing view of its glorious bay.

A brief history of Ajaccio

Although it's an attractive idea that Ajax once stopped here, the name of Ajaccio in fact derives from the Roman *Adjaccium* (place of rest), a winter stopoff point for shepherds descending from the mountains to stock up on goods and sell their produce. This first settlement, to the north of the present town in the area called Castelvecchio, was destroyed by the Saracens in the tenth century, and modern Ajaccio grew up around the citadel that was founded in 1492 by the **Bank of St George**, a Genoese military organization that handled the administration of Corsica. Built to intimidate the local nobility, who had been launching regular assaults on the oppressive Genoese, the citadel was packed with Ligurian immigrants and remained off limits to Corsican settlers for half a century. In 1553, the Corsican patriot Sampiero Corso took control of the citadel, having sided with the French, but within six years the former rulers had returned, inaugurating a period of expansion fuelled in part by an influx of people fleeing Moorish raids on the surrounding countryside. The town's population rose from 1200 to 5000 between 1584 and 1666, a period that saw the reinforcement of the citadel, the construction of a new cathedral and the improvement of the **port**, which by 1627 was doing better trade than Bastia, at that time a far more important military and political centre. Nonetheless, the infertility of the immediate hinterland kept many Ajacciens in extreme poverty and made the town reliant on imports of Genoese olive oil and wheat, while trading restrictions imposed on the town's merchants fostered resentment among the rising bourgeoisie.

Yet, when Pascal Paoli launched his first campaign for an independent republic in 1739, the Ajacciens stayed faithful to their

Genoese masters. In 1796, however, the **French** finally prevailed, and the ramparts were demolished on the orders of Napoléon. In its new role as capital of Corsica, Ajaccio expanded more rapidly than ever before and maintained its economic momentum right through the nineteenth century, largely due to the success of the wine trade. Since World War II – when Ajaccio, a centre for resistance fighters, was the first Corsican (and thus French) town to be liberated – the tourist industry has become the most important income-provider, yet Ajaccio continues to suffer from the malaise that afflicts the rest of the island, with many young people emigrating to France as soon as they leave school. It is the determination to reverse this trend that lies behind the success in elections to the Assemblée Régionale of **Corsica Nazione**, a union of politicians committed to the development of Corsica's economy and to the planning of future independence from France.

For more background to the Erignac murder, see the box opposite, and the essay on Corsican nationalism in Contexts, pp.376–383.

Traditionally confined to the south of the island, **nationalist violence** has also been on the increase here over the past couple of decades. In January 1980, the *Hôtel Fesch* was the scene of a tense standoff in which RPR militants from Bastelica held hostage three French Secret Service agents discovered on active service in their area. The siege ended peacefully, with the arrest and imprisonment of the Corsican activists involved, but since then the number of bombings and shootings has spiralled, mainly because of the intensifying feud between rival factions in the nationalist movement. The most infamous terrorist atrocity of recent years was the murder, in February 1998, of the French government's most senior official on the island, Claude Erignac, who was gunned down by nationalist terrorists while leaving the opera.

However, separatist violence rarely (if ever) affects tourists. The only outward signs of the unrest you're likely to come across are the heavily armed CRS police who routinely patrol the port and streets around the gendarmerie and Assemblée Régionale, and the façade of the Palais de Justice, which is periodically sprayed with automatic gunfire.

Arrival and information

Served by regular direct flights from France, northern Europe, and North and West Africa, Ajaccio's **airport**, Campo dell'Oro, is 6km southeast around the bay. All of the island's main car rental companies have offices lined up outside the terminal building (see "Listings", p.211), and metered taxis queue up here at flight times (the fare into town is around 150F). For budget travellers, three buses per hour provide a shuttle service into the centre, stopping on cours Napoléon, the main street – buy your ticket on the bus (20F one way) and stamp it in the machine behind the driver's cab. Long-distance buses pull in at the **bus station**, or terminal routière, next to the port de Commerce, a five-minute walk from the centre. Ferries

Death of a Prefect

Arguably the most shocking murder in over 25 years of nationalist violence took place in Ajaccio on February 6, 1998, when France's senior government representative, **Claude Erignac**, was gunned down outside the Kallysté theatre. The Préfet and his wife were leaving a classical music recital when gunmen shot him at close range.

Erignac's tough stance on organized crime and corruption earned him unparalleled popularity among Corsicans and he invariably walked around without a bodyguard. It may well have been this hardline stance, rather than his symbolic importance as chief official of the French state, that ultimately provoked his enemies.

Public reaction to the atrocity was one of outrage and distress. Three days after the attack, the province's trade unions and most of its political parties launched *Operation Île Morte* (Operation Dead Island), calling for a cessation of all non-essential activities for fifteen minutes. The silence was widely respected, even in nationalist strongholds.

At the time of writing, no one had been brought to justice for the murder, but following a fifteen-month enquiry police announced their principal suspect: a 39-year-old goatherd from Cargèse called Yvan Colonna. Protected by Corsica's infamous *loi du silence*, Colonna has evaded capture by hiding out in maquis and safe houses. He remains one of the most-wanted criminals in France. (See also our essay on Corsican nationalism in "Contexts", p.376).

from the mainland also dock in this gleaming modern complex, where you'll find Ajaccio's least expensive **left-luggage** facility (10F per article per day), a **bureau de change**, and the cleanest public toilets in town. The SNCF **train station**, however, lies almost 1km north along boulevard Sampiero, a continuation of the quai l'Herminier.

There are two free **car parks** flanking quai l'Herminier, close to the Hôtel de Ville. The **tourist office**, a short way further north on boulevard du Roi (May–Oct Mon–Sat 8am–8.30pm, Sun 9am–1pm; Nov–April Mon–Fri 8.30am–6pm, Sat 8.30am–1pm; ☎04 95 51 53 03), hands out large free glossy maps and posts up transport timetables for checking departure times. Anyone planning a long-distance hike should head for the office of the National Parks association, the **Parc Naturel Régional de Corse**, 2 rue Sergeant-Casalonga, around the corner from the Préfecture on cours Napoléon (Mon–Fri 8.15am–noon & 2–6pm; ☎04 95 51 79 00), where you can buy topo-guides, maps, guidebooks and leaflets detailing regional trail networks, and check the latest weather reports for the mountains. They are also a good source of advice on how to combine different stages of their long-distance footpaths, and will help you sort out gîte d'étape accommodation and transport to the trailheads.

Accommodation

Ajaccio suffers from a dearth of inexpensive **accommodation**, but there are a fair number of mid- and upscale places scattered around

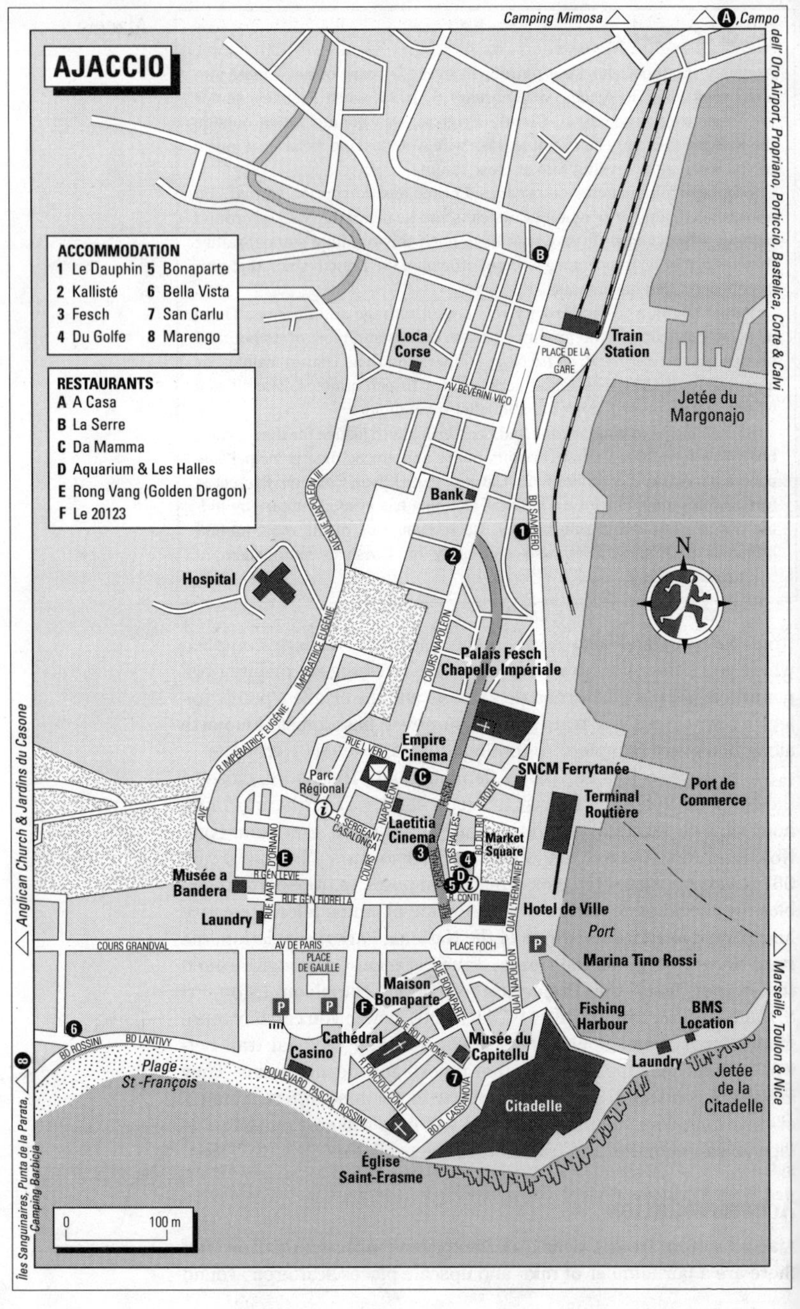
AJACCIO
ACCOMMODATION
1 Le Dauphin
2 Kallisté
3 Fesch
4 Du Golfe
5 Bonaparte
6 Bella Vista
7 San Carlu
8 Marengo
RESTAURANTS
A A Casa
B La Serre
C Da Mamma
D Aquarium & Les Halles
E Rong Vang (Golden Dragon)
F Le 20123
Camping Mimosa
Campo dell' Oro Airport, Propriano, Porticcio, Bastelica, Corte & Calvi
Train Station
PLACE DE LA GARE
Loca Corse
AV BEVERINI VICO
Jetée du Margonajo
Bank
BD SAMPIERO
AVENUE NAPOLEON III
Hospital
COURS NAPOLEON
IMPÉRATRICE EUGÉNIE
Palais Fesch Chapelle Impériale
R. IMPÉRATRICE EUGÉNIE
RUE L VERO
Empire Cinema
SNCM Ferrytanée
Port de Commerce
Parc Régional
Terminal Routière
R. SERGEANT CASALONGA
Laetitia Cinema
Market Square
RUE DES HALLES
BD DU ROI JEROME
RUE CARDINAL FESCH
Musée a Bandera
R GÉN LEVIE
RUE GÉN FIORELLA
RUE MAR D'ORNANO
Laundry
R. CONTI
Hotel de Ville
QUAI L'HERMINIER
Port
COURS GRANDVAL
AV DE PARIS
PLACE FOCH
Marina Tino Rossi
PLACE DE GAULLE
Maison Bonaparte
RUE BONAPARTE
QUAI NAPOLÉON
Fishing Harbour
BMS Location
Cathédral
RUE ROI DE ROME
Musée du Capitellu
BD ROSSINI
BD LANTIVY
Casino
Plage St-François
R. FORCIOLI-CONTI
Laundry
Jetée de la Citadelle
BOULEVARD PASCAL ROSSINI
BD D. CASSANOVA
Citadelle
Église Saint-Erasme
Anglican Church & Jardins du Casone
Îles Sanguinaires, Punta de la Parata, Camping Barbicja
Marseille, Toulon & Nice
0
100 m
N

town, chiefly along cours Napoléon and the coast road leading to the Îles Sanguinaires. Whatever your budget, it's a good idea to book ahead by telephone for June through to September, and bear in mind the numerous out-of-town hotels within thirty or forty minutes' drive of the centre, at Bastelicaccia and Porticcio. All those places listed below are open year-round unless specified otherwise.

Bastelicaccia's and Porticcio's hotels and campsites are reviewed on pp.222 and 220, respectively.

Hotels

Bella Vista, 20 bd Lantivy (☎04 95 21 07 97, fax 04 95 21 81 88). Large, rather imposing place slap on the seafront offering wonderful views of the gulf from its rooms at the front. Excellent value at this price, considering the location. ④.

Bonaparte, 1 rue Étienne-Conti (☎04 95 21 44 19). Rooms are small and a little overpriced, but immaculately clean, with views of the covered market; ask for one on the upper floor. Handy for the restaurants in the same lane. Closed Nov–March. ④–⑥.

Le Dauphin, 11 bd Sampiero (☎04 95 21 12 94, fax 04 95 21 88 69). Simple, clean and friendly place directly opposite the port de Commerce. They've a couple of budget rooms (②) in an adjacent building with shared showers and toilets. Bar downstairs is straight out of a French *policier*, complete with jukebox, pinball machine and old men sipping pastis under a cloud of Gauloise smoke. Tariff includes breakfast. ④.

Fesch, 7 rue Cardinal-Fesch (☎04 95 21 62 62, fax 04 95 21 83 36). Among the oldest-established hotels in Ajaccio, and famous thanks to the 1980 siege (see p.378). The sheepskin furnishings and medieval-style decor were designed by Corsicada, a group of local artisans, but the effect is rather sombre. All rooms have air-con and TVs; balconies cost extra. ⑥–⑦.

Du Golfe, 5 bd du Roi-Jérôme (☎04 95 21 47 64, fax 04 95 21 71 05). Popular with tour parties, this large, slick hotel has modern balconies overlooking the bay, and TVs in every room. ⑦.

Kallisté, 51 cours Napoléon (☎04 95 51 34 45, fax 04 95 21 79 00). Recently revamped third-floor hotel right in the centre, with parking space. Soundproofed rooms for up to four people, plus studios with kitchenettes (air-con 50F extra) and TVs; Internet facilties in lobby, and the proprietor speaks English. The best choice in this category. ④–⑥.

Marengo, 12 bd Mme-Mère (☎04 95 21 43 66, fax 04 95 21 51 26). 10min walk west of centre, up a quiet side-street off bd Mme-Mère. Slightly boxed in by tower blocks, but a secluded, quiet and pleasant, small hotel away from the city bustle. Open mid-March to mid-Nov. ④–⑥.

Mercure, 15 cours Napoléon (☎04 95 20 43 09, fax 04 95 22 72 44). New, very swish business-oriented place at the north end of town, with formula furnishings and central air-con. ⑦.

Du Palais, 5 av Bévérini-Vico (☎04 95 22 73 68). Recently refurbished mid-scale hotel, 10min walk north of the centre. The rooms are on the small side, but impeccably clean, and all have en-suite bathrooms. For more peace and quiet, ask for one at the rear of the building. Well placed for the train station. ④.

U San Carlu, 8 bd Danielle-Casanova (☎04 95 21 13 84, fax 04 95 21 09 99). Sited opposite the citadel and close to the beach, this three-star hotel is the poshest option in the old town. Well-appointed rooms, own parking facilities, and a special room for disabled guests in the basement. ⑦.

Campsites

Camping de Barbicaja, 4.5km west along the route des Sanguinaires (☎04 95 52 01 17). Crowded site, but close to the beach and easy to reach by bus (#5 from place de Gaulle). Open April–Sept.

Camping Les Mimosa, 3km northwest of town (☎04 95 20 99 85). A shady and well-organized site with clean toilet blocks, friendly management and fair rates, but rock-hard ground. It's a long trudge if you're loaded with luggage so take a taxi which should cost around 70F. Open May–Oct.

The town

The core of the old town holds the most interest in Ajaccio: a cluster of ancient streets spreading north and south of **place Foch**, which opens out onto the seafront by the port and the marina Tino Rossi. Nearby **place de Gaulle** forms the town centre and is the source of the main thoroughfare, **cours Napoléon**, which extends parallel to the sea almost 2km to the northeast. Lined with chic boutiques, stores and brassy cafés, this is Ajaccio at its posiest – an endless procession of designer clothes, clipped poodles and huge motorbikes. West of place de Gaulle is the town beach where Ajaccio's beau monde top up their tans, overlooked from the north by the honey-coloured citadel.

Around place de Gaulle and the new town

Place de Gaulle – otherwise known as place du Diamant, after the Diamanti family who once owned much of the property in Ajaccio – is the most useful point of orientation, even if it's not much to look at, being just a windy concrete platform surrounded by a shopping complex. The only noteworthy thing on the square is the huge **bronze statue** of Napoléon at the southern end: nicknamed *L'Encrier* (The Inkstand), this pompous lump was commissioned by Napoléon III in 1865, and shows Napoléon clad in Roman garb on horseback, surrounded by his four brothers.

The only museum in this part of town, **A Bandera**, is a short way north of the square, in rue Général-Levie, behind the *préfecture* (May–Sept Mon–Sat 10am–noon & 3–7pm; Oct–April Mon–Fri 9am–noon & 2–6pm; 20F). Scruffy and underfunded, this small military museum houses few objects of note, and is only likely to be of interest if your French is up to the lengthy written explanations that accompany the pictorial exhibits. A English guide may be borrowed from the desk when you buy your ticket, but this translates only a fraction of the material set out on the walls.

The first room is devoted to prehistoric times, with a model of a Bronze Age settlement or *castellu* alongside bronze daggers and pottery fragments; the more interesting second room deals with the

Moorish raids, displaying beautiful ivory-handled stilettos (small daggers) and several pictures of flamboyantly dressed corsairs. Among them is the notorious Dragut, a Moorish pirate who allied himself with the French during the campaign of 1553, when Sampiero Corso recaptured Corsica from the Genoese. The Wars of Independence are covered in the third room, featuring statutes drafted by Pascal Paoli and Sir Gilbert Elliot during the Anglo-Corsican alliance of 1794–96. The last room has a section on World War II and the Corsican resistance, though the highlights are the press cuttings and photos presenting the island's **bandits** as genial, popular, local heroes and showing notorious figures such as Spada hobnobbing with aristocratic ladies in forest glades.

Devotees of Napoléon should take a stroll 1km up cours Grandval, the wide street rising west of place de Gaulle and ending in a square, the **Jardins du Casone**, where gaudily spectacular son et lumière shows take place in summer. On the way you'll pass the **Assemblée Nationale**, an enormous yellow Art Deco building fronted by a jungle of palms and a couple of armoured police vans. An impressive **monument** to Napoléon dominates the square – a replica of the statue at Napoléon's burial place, Les Invalides in Paris, standing atop a huge pedestal inscribed with the names of his battles. Behind the monument lies a graffiti-bedaubed **cave** where Napoléon is supposed to have frolicked as a child.

Place Foch

Once the site of the town's medieval gate, **place Foch** lies at the heart of old Ajaccio. A delightfully shady square sloping down to the sea and lined with cafés and restaurants, it gets its local name – place des Palmiers – from the row of mature palms bordering the central strip. Dominating the top end, a fountain of four marble lions provides a mount for the inevitable statue of Napoléon, this one by Ajaccien sculptor Maglioli. A humbler effigy occupies a niche high on a wall south of the fountain, above a souvenir shop – a figurine of Ajaccio's patron saint, **La Madonnuccia**, her base bearing the text *Poserunt me custodem* ("They have made me their guardian"). The image dates from 1656, a year in which Ajaccio's local council, fearful of infection from plague-struck Genoa, placed the town under the guardianship of the Madonna in a ceremony that took place on this spot. Ajaccio was saved on this occasion and again in 1745, when *La Madonnuccia* was paraded around the ramparts to dispel the Anglo-Sardinian fleet that was bombarding the city – whereupon the enemy beat a miraculous speedy retreat. If you're here on March 18 you can witness Ajaccio's big event, the **Fête de la Miséricorde**, in which the statue is conveyed through the old town as a prelude to a big party and firework display.

Taking up the northern end of place Foch, the **Hôtel de Ville**, with its prison-like wooden doors, was built in 1826. The first-floor **Salon**

Napoléonien (June 15–Sept 15 Mon–Sat 9–11am & 2–5.45pm, Sept 16–June 14 Mon–Fri 9–11am & 2–4.45pm; 10F) consists of two rooms that are really only for dedicated Napoléon fans. A replica of the ex-emperor's **death mask** takes pride of place in a chamber bedecked with velvet, crystal chandeliers and a solemn array of Bonaparte family portraits and busts. Next door, the smaller medal room has a batch of minor relics – a fragment from Napoléon's coffin, some earth from his garden, and part of his dressing case – plus a model of the ship that brought him back from St Helena, and a picture of the house where he died.

South of place Foch

The **south side of place Foch**, the former dividing line between the poor district around the port and the bourgeoisie's territory, gives access to **rue Bonaparte**, the main route through the latter quarter. Built on the promontory rising to the citadel, the secluded streets in this part of town – with their dusty buildings, bistros and bar fronts lit by flashes of sea or sky at the end of the alleys – retain more of a sense of the old Ajaccio than anywhere else. Of the families who lived here in the eighteenth century, one of the most eminent was

Napoléon and Corsica

"M. de Choisel once said that if Corsica could be pushed under the sea with a trident it should be done. He was quite right. It is nothing but an excrescence." This sentiment, expressed by Napoléon to one of the generals who had followed him into exile on St Helena, encapsulates his bitterness about his birthplace. Corsica's opinion of its most famous citizen can be equally uncomplimentary.

The year of **Napoléon's birth**, 1769, was a crucial one in the history of Corsica, for this was the year the French took over the island from the Genoese. They made a thorough job of it, crushing Paoli's troops at Ponte Nuovo and driving the Corsican leader into exile. Napoléon's father, **Carlo**, a close associate of Paoli, fled the scene of the battle with his pregnant wife in order to escape the victorious French army. But Carlo's subsequent behaviour was quite different from that of his former leader – he came to terms with the French, becoming a representative of the newly styled Corsican nobility in the National Assembly, and using his contacts with the French governor to get a free education for his children.

At the age of 9, Napoléon was awarded a scholarship to the Brienne military academy, an institution specially founded to teach the sons of the French nobility the responsibilities of their status. The French were anxious to impress their values on the potential leaders of a now dependent territory, and with Napoléon they certainly appear to have succeeded. Give or take a rebellious gesture or two, this son of a Corsican Italian-speaking household used his time well, leaving Brienne to enter the exclusive École Militaire in Paris. At the age of 16, he was commissioned into the artillery. When he was 20, the Revolution broke out in Paris and the scene was set for a remarkable career.

the **Pozzo di Borgo** clan, whose house still stands at 17 rue Bonaparte, its façade adorned by trompe l'œil frescoes. Carlo Andrea Pozzo di Borgo was a distant cousin and childhood friend of Napoléon, but was later to become one of his bitterest enemies. A supporter of Paoli, he was elected to the Corsican legislature and became president of the Council of State under the short-lived Anglo-Corsican rule of 1794–96. Described as "a man of talent, an intriguer", Pozzo was not content with this domestic position and in 1803 he became the ambassador to Russia, later befriending Wellington, with whom he fought at Waterloo. He went on to become a favourite at the English court, where Queen Victoria referred to him affectionately as "Old Pozzo".

Maison Bonaparte

Napoléon was born in the colossal **Maison Bonaparte**, on place Letizia, just off the west side of rue Bonaparte (May–Sept Mon 2–6pm, Tues–Fri 9am–noon & 2–6pm, Sat 9–11.45am & 2–6pm, Sun 9am–noon; Oct–April Mon 2–6pm, Tues–Sat 10am–noon & 2–5pm, Sun 10am–noon; 22F). The Bonaparte family first appeared in the chronicles of Ajaccio in the fifteenth century, when they lived in a

Always an ambitious opportunist, he obtained leave from his regiment, **returned to Ajaccio**, joined the local Jacobin club and – with his eye on a colonelship in the Corsican militia – enthusiastically promoted the interests of the Revolution. However, things did not quite work out as he had planned, for Pascal Paoli had also returned to Corsica.

Carlo Bonaparte had died some years before, and Napoléon – though not the eldest son – was effectively the head of a family that had formerly given Paoli strong support. Having spent the last twenty years in London, Paoli was pro-English and had developed a profound distaste of revolutionary excesses (it was his determination to keep the guillotine out of Corsica that, as much as anything else, led him into the later failed experiment of union with Britain). Napoléon's French allegiance and his Jacobin views antagonized the older man, and his military conduct didn't enhance his standing at all. Elected second in command of the volunteer militia, Napoléon was involved in an unsuccessful attempt to wrest control of the citadel from Royalist sympathizers. He thus took much of the blame when, in reprisal for the killing of one of the militiamen, several people were gunned down in Ajaccio, an incident that engendered eight days of civil war. In June 1793, Napoléon and his family were chased back to the mainland by the Paolists.

Napoléon promptly renounced any special allegiance he had ever felt for Corsica. He Gallicized the spelling of his name, preferring "Napoléon" to his baptismal "Napoleone". And, although he was later to speak with nostalgia about the scents of the Corsican countryside, and to regret he did not build a grand house there, he returned only once more to the island (after being forced to dock here during his return voyage from Egypt) and put Ajaccio fourth on the list of places where he would like to be buried.

house that was demolished in 1555 by the French attack on the citadel. This later residence, acquired piecemeal over the years, passed to Napoléon's father Carlo in the 1760s and here he lived, with his wife Letizia and their family, until his death. Soon after, in May 1793, Letizia and her children were driven from the house by Paoli's partisans, who stripped the place down to the floorboards. Requisitioned by the English in 1794, Maison Bonaparte became an arsenal and a lodging house for English officers, amongst whom was Hudson Lowe, later Napoléon's jailer on St Helena. Though Letizia later paid for its restoration with an indemnity given to those Corsicans who had suffered at the hands of the English, her heart wasn't in the job – she left for the second and last time in 1799, the year Napoléon stayed here on his return from Egypt. Owned by the state since 1923, the house now bears few traces of the Bonaparte family's existence, and barely warrants the 20F admission charge unless you have a penchant for Napoleonic memorabilia.

The visit begins on the second floor, but before you go up look out for the wooden sedan chair in the hallway – Letizia was carried back from church on it when the prenatal Napoléon started giving her contractions, and it's one of the very few original pieces of furniture left in the house.

Upstairs, an endless display of portraits, miniatures, weapons, letters and documents gives the impression of having been formed by gathering together anything that was remotely connected with the family and unwanted by anyone else. Amongst the highlights of the first room are a few maps of Corsica dating from the eighteenth century, some deadly "vendetta" daggers and two handsome pairs of pistols belonging to Napoléon's father. The next-door Alcove Room was, according to tradition, occupied by Napoléon in 1799 when he stayed here for the last time, while in the third room you can see the sofa upon which the future emperor first saw the light of day on August 15, 1769. Adjoining the heavily restored long gallery is a tiny room known as the Trapdoor Room, whence Letizia and her children made their getaway from the marauding Paolists.

The Cathedral and St-Érasme

Napoléon was baptized in 1771 in the **Cathedral**, around the corner from Maison Bonaparte in rue Forcioli-Conti. Generally known as *A Madonnuccia*, it was built in 1582 on a much smaller scale than originally intended, due to lack of funds – an apology for its diminutive size is inscribed in a plaque inside, on the wall to the left as you enter. The interior is interesting chiefly for a few Napoleonic connections: to the right of the door stands the font where he was dipped at the age of 23 months; and his sister, Elisa Bacciochi, donated the great marble altar in 1811. Before leaving, take a look in the chapel to the left of the altar, which houses a gloomy Delacroix painting of the Virgin holding aloft the Sacred Heart.

Further down the same road stands **St-Érasme**, a Jesuit chapel built in 1617, then dedicated to the town's fishermen in 1815. Should you find it open, you can see inside some model ships, a statue of St Erasmus and a pair of wooden Christs.

Musée Capitellu and the Citadelle

A left turn at the eastern end of rue Forcioli-Conti brings you onto bd Danielle-Casanova. Here, opposite the citadel, an elaborately carved capital marks the entrance to **Musée Capitellu** (May–Oct Mon–Wed 10am–noon & 2–6pm; 25F), a tiny museum mainly given over to offering a picture of domestic life in nineteenth-century Ajaccio. The house belonged to a wealthy Ajaccien family, the Bacciochi, who were related to Napoléon through his sister's marriage, though he doesn't figure at all here. The collection will appeal to anyone with a special interest in art and antiques, but others may find the steep entrance fee poor value for money.

Watercolour landscapes of Corsica line the walls of the first room, which also contains a marble *Madonnuccia* whose head was cut off with a sabre during the French Revolution. A bust of Sampiero Corso, a common adornment of smart nineteenth-century households, dominates the second room, with some elegant copies of figures of Venus from Herculaneum. The glass display cases hold the most fascinating exhibits, however, which include a rare edition of the first history of Corsica, written by Agostino Giustiniani, a bishop of the Nebbio who drowned in 1536, and the 1796 *Code Corse*, a list of laws set out by Louis XV for the newly occupied Corsica. The last room contains a bronze bust of a chubby-cheeked Pascal Paoli, and a striking painting titled *Sunrise over Bavella*, attributed to Turner's nephew.

Opposite the museum, the restored **Citadelle**, a hexagonal fortress and tower stuck out on a wide promontory into the sea, is occupied by the military and usually closed to the public. Founded in the 1490s, the fort wasn't completed until the occupation of Ajaccio by Sampiero Corso and the powerful Marshal Thermes in 1553–58. During World War II it was taken by the Italians and used as a prison, whose most famous inmate was a young paratrouper captain called **Scamaroni**. Dispatched to Corsica from North Africa by de Gaulle in January 1943, he set up radio posts in the Ajaccio area (including one in the projection room of the largest cinema in town) and used them to broadcast information about enemy troop movements prior to the invasion later that year. But Scamaroni would never see the island's Liberation. Betrayed by the forced confession of a fellow radio operator, he was captured and incarcerated in the citadel. However, despite being subjected to days of appalling torture, the war hero did not divulge any names of his contacts. Instead, he ingested poison and strangled himself to death with wire extracted from the bars of his cell, although not before dragging himself over to the wall and writing in blood with the gnarled remains of his right hand *"Je n'ai pas parlé, vive la France. Ajaccio, 19 Mars, 1943"*. Like many martyrs of Corsica's Liberation from the Axis, Scamaroni's name has been immortalized in street and square names all over the island.

The citadel overlooks the town beach, **Plage St-François**, a short curve of yellow sand facing the expansive mountain-ringed bay. Several flights of steps lead down to the beach from bd Danielle-Casanova. To get a better view of the town, follow the waterfront back to the marina and walk to the end of the **Jetée de la Citadelle**, which juts into the sea under the shadow of the fortress.

North of place Foch

Immediately **north of place Foch** behind the Hôtel de Ville, **square César-Campinchi** is the venue for the island's largest fresh produce **market**, held here on weekday and Saturday mornings (9am–1pm) throughout the year, and an essential part of Ajaccien life. Alongside the usual array of cut flowers, vegetables and fruit laid out under colourful stripy awnings are stalls selling artisanal delicacies such as barbary fig jam, honey *aux fleurs du maquis*, wild boar sauces and ewe's cheese from the Niolo, as well as muscat wines and myrtle liqueurs. The goods on sale are not cheap, but the quality is consistently high, and the cafés lining the west side of the square are among the liveliest breakfast spots in town – ideal for crowd-watching after you've finished browsing.

Behind the market, the principal road leading north is **rue Cardinal-Fesch**, a delightful meandering street lined with boutiques, cafés and restaurants. Halfway along the street, set back from the road behind iron gates, stands the **Palais Fesch**, home of Ajaccio's best gallery, the **Musée Fesch** (April–June & Sept Mon 1–5.15pm, Tues–Sun 9.15am–12.15pm & 2.15–5.15pm; July & Aug Mon 1.30–6pm, Tues–Thurs 9am–6.30pm, Fri & Sat 10.30am–12.15pm, Sun 10.30am–6pm; Oct–March same hours, but closed Mon; 35F). Cardinal Joseph Fesch, whose image in bronze presides over the courtyard, was Napoléon's step-uncle and Bishop of Lyon, a lucrative position from which he invested in large numbers of paintings, many of them looted by the French armies in Holland, Italy and Germany. A highly cultured man with an eye for a bargain, he bequeathed a thousand paintings to Ajaccio on the condition that an academy of arts was created in the town. His wishes were contested by Napoléon's brother Joseph, who turned a quick profit by dispersing much of the collection on the art market. Luckily for Ajaccio, however, Renaissance art was less highly regarded in those days than in later years, so many of the more valuable works remained here.

The collection is housed on four storeys; if you're pushed for time, skip the basement – which harbours an uninspiring assortment of Napoleonic memorabilia – and head, via the temporary exhibition room on the ground floor, to **Niveau** (Level) **3** upstairs. where the cream of the sixteenth- and seventeenth-century Italian works are displayed. The paintings are ordered chronologically, starting in the gallery immediately to the right of the stairhead and progressing in an anticlockwise direction. In this first room hangs one of Fesch's greatest treasures, Sandro Botticcelli's exquisite *Virgin and Child*, painted when the artist was just 25 years old. Dating from a later period, Titian's smouldering *Man with a Glove*, at the end of the corridor, is shown opposite Veronese's *Leda and the Swan*, an uncompromisingly erotic work for its time. **Niveau 4** is given over primarily to seventeenth- and eighteenth-century paintings, where the absence of the Dutch masters sold off by Napoléon's brother is most keenly felt. Highlights here include Poussin's *Midas à la Source du Pactole*, in the first gallery on the right after the stairs, and a vibrant array of still lifes, notably Giuseppe Recco's *Ray on a Cauldron with Fish in a Basket*, noted for its subtle mix of silver-tinged hues. The largest gallery on this floor, **La Grande Galérie**, houses a collection of outsize canvases, of which Gregorio de Ferrari's *La Ste Famille* is the most famous.

You'll need a separate ticket for the **Chapelle Impériale** (same hours; 10F), which stands across the courtyard from the museum. With its gloomy monochrome interior the chapel itself is unremarkable; the interest lies in the crypt, which holds the remains of various members of the Bonaparte family. It was the cardinal's dying wish that all the Bonaparte family be brought together under one roof, so the chapel was built in 1857, and the bodies subsequently brought in – as recently as 1951, Charles Bonaparte was reburied here, alongside Letizia, Cardinal Fesch and half a dozen other Bonapartes.

Lucien Bonaparte laid the first stone of the adjacent **Bibliothèque Municipale**, which contains a huge collection of rare antique books. You're not allowed to handle any, but are welcome to browse and read periodicals and magazines on the long, polished table stretching down the middle of the chamber.

Eating, drinking and nightlife

Restaurants in Ajaccio vary from basic bistros to trendy pizzerias and pricy fish restaurants, the majority of which are found off rue Cardinal-Fesch. Rows of lookalike restaurants also crowd the narrow alleys of the old town along rue roi de Rome. Most compensate for unadventurous menus by an appealing location, with tables set outside in the thick of city life. **Bars** and **cafés** jostle for pavement space all over town but especially along cours Napoléon, which is generally lined with young people checking out the promenaders, and on place de Gaulle, where old-fashioned cafés and salons de thé offer a more sedate scene. If you fancy sipping a drink with a view of the bay, you can go to one of the flashy cocktail bars that line the seafront beyond the citadel on boulevard Lantivy, but expect to pay a lot more for the privilege. For **breakfast**, you can't beat the row of cafés along the west side of boulevard du Roi-Jérôme, which look onto the square César-Campinchi and the morning marketplace.

What **nightlife** there is in Ajaccio consists chiefly of eating and drinking, though there are two **cinemas** (see "Listings", p.211), a busy municipal **casino** on boulevard Lantivy, and a few Eurotrashy **discos**, whose only outstanding features are their extortionate entrance charges. Of these, *Pennies*, a kitsch and cavernous place in the old town at 13 rue Bonaparte, and *Ricantu*, Ajaccio's only gay club, out on the road to the airport, are the most promising.

North of the centre, in the district of Brasilia, the arts centre *A l'Aghjia*, 6 chemin de Biancarello (☎04 95 20 41 15), hosts theatre performances, world-music gigs and Corsican *polyphonie* singing, mostly on Friday and Saturday nights. It's hard to find, but is the only venue in town where you can escape synth maestros and "club-style" crooners; head for Brasilia bus stop and ask the way from there, or take a taxi (65F approximately). The tourist office usually has details of their programme.

Cafés and bars

Café Flore, 33 rue Cardinal-Fesch. Ersatz turn-of-the-century Parisian place, opposite the Musée Fesch, with Toulouse-Lautrec posters setting the tone. Renowned for its copious lunchtime salads.

L'Empéreur, 12 place de Gaulle. Elegant Art Nouveau salon de thé looking onto the main square.

Le Menestrel, 5 rue Cardinal-Fesch. Dubbed *le rendez-vous des artistes* because local musicians play here most evenings after 7pm; café jazz, traditional mandolin and guitar tunes, with the odd popular club-style singalong number.

La Rade, 1 place Foch. The most congenial of the cafés fronting the Port de Plaisance, and an ideal spot for crowd-watching over a chilled pastis.

Safari, 18 bd Lantivy. One of a row of lookalike cocktail bars next to the casino, overlooking the promenade. Good for a breezy coffee, and for watching Ajaccio's beau monde strut their stuff on Saturday nights.

Restaurants

Le 20123, 2 rue Roi-de-Rome (☎04 95 21 50 05). Decked out like a small hill village, complete with fountain and parked Vespa, the decor here's a lot more frivolous than the food: serious Corsican gastronomy (from charcuterie starter to chestnut-flour flan desserts) featured on a single 165F menu. Topnotch cooking, and organic wine at 65F per bottle.

L'Aquarium, rue des Halles. One of the best places in town for seafood – everything comes straight from the fish market across the square. Set menus 70–190F.

A Casa, 21 av Noel-Franchini, 2km north of the centre (☎04 95 22 34 78). Located in a dull part of town, but enduringly popular, as much for its unfussy, substantial cuisine as the eccentric *patron*, Frank, who doubles as a professional magician (right down to sawing his guests in half). Advance reservation essential. To find it, take the airport road and turn left at the end of bd Charles-Bonaparte. Menus at 76F, 125F and 180F.

Les Halles, rue des Halles. Open since 1920, and the favourite lunch venue for market stallholders and local office workers. They do a great-value 70F menu with wild boar, fresh fish of the day and a choice of omelettes.

Da Mamma, passage Guinghetta (☎04 95 21 39 44). Tucked away down a narrow passageway connecting cours Napoléon and rue Cardinal-Fesch. Authentic but affordable Corsican cuisine, such as *cannelloni al brocciu*, roast kid and seafood, on good-value set menus from 65F to 145F. Slick service, lively atmosphere, and the house wine's not bad, either. A sound budget choice.

La Serre, 91 cours Napoléon. Inexpensive, filling main meals – including moussaka, roast lamb, quiche, and imaginative salads – from a self-service counter in an Art Deco-style cafeteria, close to the train station. Good if you're on a tight budget.

Rong Vang (Golden Dragon), opposite the Bandera Museum on rue Maréchal-d'Ornano. One of Corsica's few Chinese restaurants, serving French-influenced Cantonese cuisine (frogs' legs *à la pékinoise* or with lemon curry); no set menus, but à la carte dishes are a reasonable 50–60F. Closed Sun.

Listings

Airlines Air France/Air Inter Europe, 1 bd du Roi-Jérôme, next to the *Hôtel du Golfe* (☎04 95 29 45 45; for reservations ☎0802/802802); Compagnie Corse Méditerranée (☎0802/802802); TAT /British Airways (☎04 95 71 00 22).

Airport enquiries ☎04 95 21 07 07.

Banks and exchange Most of the main banks have branches on place de Gaulle or cours Napoléon, while the BNP is near the marketplace, on bd du Roi-Jérôme; the Société Générale, just up from the Parc Naturel Régional office on rue Sergeant-Casalonga, changes Thomas Cook French-franc travellers' cheques without commission.

Bookshops Maison de la Presse, 2 place Foch (☎04 95 25 81 18), stocks Ajaccio's best selection of books on Corsica, as well as a good range of international newspapers, including the *Guardian*, *Independent*, *New York Times* and *Washington Post*. François Desjobert, on the opposite side of the square (☎04 95 23 30 17), is better for books in French, and sells audiocassettes by Corsican musicians.

Bus information ☎04 95 21 28 01 (see "Travel details", p.226, for details of bus companies).

Car rental A thoroughly dependable local company offering rock-bottom rates is Rent-a-Car's Ajaccio agent, ACL, based at the *Hôtel Kallisté*, 51 cours Napoléon (☎04 95 51 34 45; airport ☎04 95 23 56 36). Others include: Aloha (airport ☎04 95 23 57 19); Avis-Ollandini, 1 route d'Alata (☎04 95 23 92 50; airport ☎04 95 21 28 01); Citer, bd Lantivy (☎04 95 21 40 65; airport ☎04 95 20 52 32); Europcar, 16 cours Grandval (☎04 95 21 05 49; airport ☎04 95 23 18 73); Hertz-Locasud, 8 cours Grandval (☎04 95 21 70 94; airport ☎04 95 22 14 84).

Cinemas The Empire, 18 cours Napoléon (☎04 95 21 21 00), is a dowdy but fun 1930s-style cinema screening mainstream movies; in a similar vein is the

Bonaparte, at 10 cours Napoléon (☎04 95 51 27 98); while the Laetitia, 48 cours Napoléon (☎04 95 21 07 24), opposite the post office, shows mainly art-house and foreign films.

Diving Popular dive sites around Ajaccio include Les Dentis, a shallow shelf 200m offshore near the citadel; La Castagne, dramatic rock formations rich with underwater life on the southern extremity of the bay; and the Îles Sanguinaires, 12km west of town (see p.218). Winds and currents can be a problem in all three; for advice, transport and training, contact any of the following reputable diving clubs: Société Nautique d'Ajaccio, Fossé de la Citadelle (☎04 95 21 07 79); Homopalmus, 3 route d'Alata (☎04 95 22 68 12); Club les Calanques, route des Sanguinaires (☎04 95 52 09 37); or Aquasub Center, *Hôtel Stella di Mare* (☎04 95 52 01 07).

Hospital Centre Hospitalier, 27 av Impératrice-Eugénie (☎04 95 29 90 90); for an ambulance, dial ☎15.

Laundry Bottom of rue Maréchal-Ornano, off cours Grandval.

Left luggage In the terminal maritime; 10F per article per day (8.30am–7pm), or part thereof.

Motorbike rental Cheapest of the three companies in Ajaccio is Ajaccio Moto Location, at the *Hôtel Kallisté*, 51 cours Napoléon (☎04 95 51 34 45; airport ☎04 95 23 56 36), who also rent mountain bikes. Other places worth trying include: Locacorse, at 10 rue Bévérini (☎04 95 20 71 20), close to the train station, which rents mainly 80cc scooters; and BMS Locations, in the Port Tino Rossi (☎04 95 21 33 75). For trials bikes, try Moto Corse Évasion, Montée St-Jean (☎04 95 20 52 05).

Pharmacies Several large pharmacies on place Foch and cours Napoléon.

Police rue Général Fiorella (☎04 95 29 95 29); emergencies ☎17.

Post office 8 cours Napoléon (June–Aug Mon–Fri 9am–4.45pm, Sat 9am–noon; Sept–May Mon–Fri 9–11.45am & 2.30–4.45pm, Sat 9–11.45am).

Sports facilities The Complexe Municipal Pascal Rossi, on av Pascal-Rossini (☎04 95 21 08 30), is Ajaccio's largest public sports centre, with a pool, gym, weights room and running track. The municipal tennis courts are out of town, on route des Sanguinaires (☎04 95 52 00 25).

Taxis The main taxi rank is on the north side of place de Gaulle (☎04 95 21 00 87).

Telephones There are booths *(cabines téléphoniques)* all over the centre; phone cards are available in the post office, and at tobacconists and photography shops along cours Napoléon.

Train information Gare SNCF (☎04 95 23 11 03).

Travel agents Havas Kallistour Voyages, 11 place de Gaulle (☎04 95 21 17 36, fax 04 95 21 39 47); Nouvelles Frontières, 14 place Foch (☎04 95 21 89 16); Ollandini, 3 place de Gaulle (☎04 95 21 10 40, fax 04 95 51 05 54).

Moving on from Ajaccio

Ajaccio's ferry port is the second busiest on the island after Bastia, and its terminal routière on the quai l'Herminier forms the nexus of the long-distance bus network, so most independent travellers come here at some point to pick up onward transport.

By plane

Campo dell'Oro airport, 6km south of Ajaccio, is served by daily scheduled **flights** to cities on the French mainland, including Marseille, Nice and Paris on Air France/Air Inter, as well as weekly charter flights to northern Europe between April and October; Gatwick is the main destination for British charter operators, but there are also weekly departures to Birmingham and Manchester. Details of airline companies and travel agents in Ajaccio appear in "Listings", on pp.211–212. The cheapest way to get to the airport from town is on the shuttle bus that runs three times per hour from outside the terminal routière (20F); taxis cost around 150F.

By ferry

Most of the car and passenger **ferries** sailing out of Ajaccio go to Marseille, with less frequent departures to Toulon and Nice. SCNM operate one to two crossings to Marseille daily from July until mid-September, five to seven each week from then until the end of October and during late June, and three weekly for the rest of the year. The crossing takes seven hours by day and eleven hours on the night service, or four and a half hours on the superfast NGV 1, which only sails from June through October. Tickets cost 210–292F per person, depending on the destination and time of year, and are available up to two hours before departure time from SNCM's counter inside the arrivals hall of the terminal maritime (☎04 95 29 66 63), or in advance at their office directly opposite on the quai l'Herminier (Mon–Fri 8–11am & 2–6pm, Sat 8–11.45am; ☎04 95 29 66 99). You can also book through any of the travel agents named in "Listings" opposite. For more on ferry routes and ticket costs, see "Basics", p.8.

By train

The four-hour **train** trip from Ajaccio across the mountains to Bastia ranks among the island's most memorable journeys, taking in the wild valleys and pine forests of the interior around Corte, and a string of sleepy village stations. At Ponte Leccia the line forks, with a branch veering northwest along the coast to L'Île Rousse and Calvi; taking 4hr 35min through to Calvi with a change at the junction, this route is longer, but even more scenic, with the added attraction of panoramic seascapes along the way. Four trains leave Ajaccio daily in summer for Bastia (120F), and between two and four in winter, depending on the day; Calvi (140F) is served by two departures all year round, although the timetables change between September and June. You can check the times at the tourist office, or by telephoning the station direct (☎04 95 23 11 03).

By bus

Ajaccio is well connected by bus to other towns on the island, though finding out which one you need can be difficult, as the routes are all run by different companies. The tourist office on boulevard du Roi-Jérôme keeps a set of up-to-date timetables, and you can also get information at the terminal routière on quai l'Herminier, where all the operators have individual counters. Their destinations and departure times are displayed on boards, and you can pay for tickets in advance up to a couple of hours before the bus leaves; they'll also look after your luggage for free. A full list of destinations reachable by bus from Ajaccio, along with telephone numbers for their operators, appears in "Travel details" on p.226.

Around Ajaccio

The maquis-carpeted ridge of hills north of Ajaccio, known as **Les Crêtes**, holds a few interesting possibilities for a half-day excursion, as long as you have your own transport. Chief of these is the **Punta di Pozzo di Borgo**, which provides an excellent view of Ajaccio and its bay and is reached by a road that takes you close to **Les Millelli**, the country residence owned (but seldom visited) by the Bonapartes. Walkers can take the gentle stroll west of town to **Monte Salario** to see the **Fontaine de Salario**, or chance the more strenuous ascent up the pink-granite masses of the **Rochers des Gozzi**, a landmark in the Gravona valley northeast of town. A new attraction that's certain to appeal to children is the **tortoise sanctuary**, **"A Cupulatta"**, 17km northeast along the N193 (see opposite).

Les Millelli and Punta di Pozzo di Borgo

Situated 5km northwest of Ajaccio, off the D61, **Les Millelli** (daily except Tues 9am–noon & 2–6pm; 5F) came into the Bonaparte family in 1797, but was used rarely. In 1793, before it came into the family, Letizia was forced to hide out here on her way to the Tour du Capitello in her flight from the Paolists, and Napoléon stayed here with Murat in 1799 on his return from Egypt – but that's about the extent of its relevance. Nonetheless, the house is a firmly established stage on the Napoleonic trail. It's a stolid, plain, eighteenth-century building whose real attraction is the surrounding terraced olive grove that overlooks the gulf – a pleasant picnic spot. Inside, there's just a small and dreary ethnographical museum.

If, instead of taking the turn to Les Millelli, you go 6km further along the D61, you'll come to the Col de Pruno, where a left turn along a narrow twisting road will bring you after another 6km to the **Punta di Pozzo di Borgo** and its ruined **château**. Built by the Pozzo di Borgo family in 1886, the château was constructed with materials provided by the demolition of the Tuileries in 1871 and is the exact reproduction of one of the pavilions of that palace – an inscription on the wall states that it was built to preserve a precious souvenir of the home country. In the nineteenth century the Pozzo di Borgo family still owned everything round here, but virtually nothing remained of their native village, which was razed by pirates in 1594; a tower on the track up to the Punta is the sole remnant. From the terrace of the château you get fine **views** of the gulfs of Sagone and Ajaccio, and of Monte d'Oro and Renoso to the east.

La Fontaine de Salario

It's a 5km walk or drive from Ajaccio, or a ride on the #7 bus from place de Gaulle, to the **Fontaine de Salario** (or Funta Salamandra), a spring on a 300m hill at the base of Monte Salario. Named after the salamanders that once crawled all over this part of the country, the spring offers another magnificent view of the Golfe d'Ajaccio. From here a trail leads up to **Monte Salario**, a half-hour walk, and from the summit a rocky trail known as the Chemin de la Serra leads directly back down to town.

The Rochers des Gozzi

A solid pink-tinted clump of bare rock rising from the dense maquis and cultivated fields and vineyards northeast of Ajaccio, the **Rochers des Gozzi** provide the Ajaccio area's finest panorama of the mountains and the sea. The 10km hike should take between two and three hours from the village of **Appietto**, 20km from Ajaccio. From Ajaccio, take the **bus** to Listincone (16km), which drops you off in the village, just by the signposted turn-off for Appietto, another 4km up a narrow road. Drivers can take the car as far as Appietto.

The track to the summit begins by Appietto's cemetery, leading initially to the church standing on the facing ridge, and continuing as a goat track to the top of the ridge. Following the crest of the ridge, the track cuts through the maquis. After about 4km from the church you'll come to a fence that you can cross by means of a large boulder. Some 300m further, climb the crumbling stone wall that runs down the ridge, then continue to the right of this wall for a few metres before you reach a rocky platform, which affords tantalizing vistas and a place to catch your breath. Heading along the right-hand branch of the path, which skirts the hillside from the platform, you'll come to a faint trail that crosses the ridge over some difficult ground – follow it for 1km to another fork. Either branch will do, and you'll soon reach a trickle of a stream by a precipice facing a derelict stone building. You need to take care from now on as you walk along the wall and scramble down into the easily visible gap across the neck of the Rochers. After a stiff climb of 485m, with deep ravines dropping on either side, you'll reach the top.

A Cupulatta: the Tortoise Sanctuary

An essential destination for children and wildlife lovers is the new **Tortoise Sanctuary**, "**U Cupulatta**", at the hamlet of **Vignola**, 17km northeast of Ajaccio up the Vallée de la Gravona, on the N193, the main Corte road (daily: April, May & Sept–Nov 10am–5.30pm; June–Aug 9.30am–7pm; 30F). In the short time it has been open, this sensitively designed breeding and research centre has become the largest of its kind in Europe, boasting 125 different species and around 2000 animals from five continents. All the indigenous tortoises, terrapins and turtles are represented, along with a number of exotic types such as the gargantuan Alligator tortoise (*Macroclemys temminckii*) and the unfeasibly ugly Matamata (*Chelus fimbriata*) from the Amazon region, which looks like a cross between a rotten log and melting car tyre. The remaining species are considerably cuter, especially the newborns and the tiny terrapins you get to coo over on arrival.

U Cupulatta was the brainchild of **Philippe Magnan**, an accountant whose passion for reptiles nearly cost him his marriage, when the collection he started after the family dog brought a wounded tortoise home threatened to take over the house. Today, the whole family is involved in the management of the six-acre site, which has pioneered new breeding and feeding techniques.

The nearest **train** station to U Cupulatta is **Ucciani**, 2.5km northeast; you can also get here on any of the **buses** running between Ajaccio, Corte and Bastia.

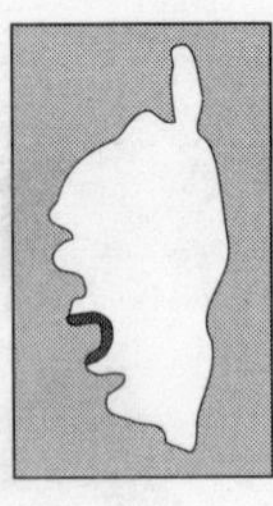

The Golfe d'Ajaccio

West of Ajaccio, the **route des Sanguinaires** (as the D111 is known) hugs the coast for 12km, passing a succession of tourist developments and sandy beaches before coming to an end at the northern tip of the gulf, the **Punta della Parata**. This headland faces the cluster of crumbling granite islets called the **Îles Sanguinaires**, a miniature archipelago ideally seen from the sea. **Boat excursions** from Ajaccio, run by the company Nave Va from their cabin at the marina, leave around 2pm each day from May to September, stopping for an hour on the largest of the islands, Mezzo Mare; tickets cost 110F.

Although the **beaches** along this stretch don't rate as highly as the more secluded strands of the southern gulf, they are more accessible to those without a vehicle. Regular **buses** from place de Gaulle follow the route: buses #1 and #2 go as far as Ajaccio's cemetery, whereas #5 will take you all the way to Punta della Parata, stopping at **Barbicaja**, **Scudo** and **Terre Sacré**.

The largest and most established resort along the southern arm of the Golfe d'Ajaccio – known as **La Rive Sud** – is **Porticcio**. Once a hangout for the rich and famous, the place nowadays has lost its elitist appeal and gets swamped by watersports enthusiasts and weekenders from Ajaccio as soon as summer sets in. Quieter spots are found beyond Porticcio, where the coast is less developed and the scent of the maquis takes over, the shrubland clearing at intervals to reveal superb sandy beaches such as **Plage de Verghia** and **Portigliolo**. Genoese watchtowers again feature on every headland, the most prominent being the **Tour de la Castagna** and the enormous construction on **Capu di Muro**, the southernmost point of the gulf.

An alternative to the coast road is the inland route from Pisciatella, crossing a series of lovely mountain passes surrounded by maquis and dense woodland, through the belvedere village of **Côti-Chiavari** and then down to Capu di Muro.

Route des Sanguinaires

The first landmark along the coast west of Ajaccio, the **Chapelle des Grecs**, lies 3km along the route. Built in 1632 by Artilio Pozzo di Borgo, it was allocated for the use of the Greeks in 1733, who settled in Ajaccio after being driven out of their small colony at Paomia by Corsican rebels (see p.187) and forced to take refuge here.

The **beaches** start about 1km beyond the cemetery with **Barbicaja**, a usually crowded sandy stretch close to a large campsite (see p.202). **Marinella**, another 2km on, is the next beach and the most popular, backed by bars and restaurants. About 4km further, **Terre Sacré** gets its name from the 1m-high stone urn, containing the ashes of soldiers killed in World War I, that stands on the beach. **Cala Lunga** is the last strand, stretching as far as **Punta della**

Walk to Capu di Feno from Punta Della Parata

A good way to reach the remote, southernmost point of the Golfe de Sagone is to walk north of **Punta della Parata** along the coast as far as **Capu di Feno**, a route that has the added attraction of giving access to some fine, relatively unfrequented beaches. The distance of 15km takes about five hours one way, but you can turn around before the headland at one of the coves, making an easy two- to three-hour amble from Parata. The route doesn't involve any steep climbs, but there is some quite thick maquis to plough through, particularly towards the end, so you'll need to cover your legs.

Around 500m before the restaurant at Punta della Parata, on the land side of the main road, the trailhead starts at some municipal tennis courts. Park (or jump off the bus) here and follow the dirt track above the courts as it skirts the disused rifle range along the hillside, at an easy gradient. Once past a row of makeshift weekend cabins, the path narrows and scales a low headland. From here the route is a very pleasant, gentle walk through the maquis, with lovely sea views. The path starts to drop downhill after around one hour, descending to a beautiful, steeply shelving sandy cove known as **Anse de Minaccia** (also reachable via the D111B from Ajaccio), where there's a small *buvette* (beach bar). The next beach, **Cala di Fico** thirty minutes walk further on, is just as beautiful and even quieter.

A wild promontory crowned by a Genoese watchtower, Capu di Feno is reached after another hour's walk along a rough path that keeps close to the rocky shoreline. From the top of the headland, a fine view extends north across the Golfe de Sagone to Cargèse, with the high peaks of the interior in the distance. Return by the same route.

Parata, the narrow, rocky headland that was once connected to the Îles Sanguinaires. Tremendous views of the gulf reward the ten-minute clamber up to the **Tour de la Parata**, a tall Genoese construction built in the sixteenth century to ward off Moorish pirates.

Îles Sanguinaires

Composed of four humps of red granite, the **Îles Sanguinaires** might be named after Sagone or after *Sagonarri* (Black Blood), from the colour they turn at sunset. A protected site, the islands harbour large colonies of gulls, and it's forbidden to pick flowers or take eggs from the land.

The largest islet, **Mezzo Mare** (or Grande Sanguinaire), is topped by a lighthouse, where Alphonse Daudet was inspired to write one of his *Lettres de Mon Moulin*, in which he waxed lyrical about the islet's "reddish and fierce aspect". Tufts of gorse, a ruined tower and crashing surf give the place a dramatic air, which is perhaps why Joseph Bonaparte wanted to be buried here, though his wish wasn't realized.

La Rive Sud: the southern gulf

Capped with crumbling Genoese watchtowers, the three headlands of the Golfe d'Ajaccio's southern shore – the **Rive Sud** – separate a succession of sheltered bays, each lined with large sandy beaches. Those closest to town, grouped around the charmless resort of **Porticcio**, are marred by modern holiday developments, but press on southwest down the D55, which keeps close to the convoluted coastline from its turning off the main N196 until the **Punta di a Castagna**, 22km south, and you'll soon escape the villa belt. Growing more spectacular at each bend in the road, the scenery culminates at **Capu di Muro**, the far southwestern extremity of the gulf, where a particularly impressive tower stands within walking distance of some gorgeous coves.

Buses along the Rive Sud depart more or less hourly from Ajaccio's terminal routière for Plage de Ricanto, near the airport. From July until mid-September, you can also catch Casanova Autocars' six daily services to Porticcio, a couple of which continue on to Isolella and Plage de Ruppione. However, to reach the most secluded beaches you'll need your own transport. To reach the inland route along the **southern gulf**, you need to follow the N196 from Ajaccio to the airport in the direction of Porticcio, until you reach Pisciatella, where you switch to the D302. There are no buses along this route.

Porticcio

Four kilometres before Porticcio, the massive **Tour du Capitello** appears at the end of a short track leading off to the right of the road across the bridge. The tower's cracks were the result of a famous siege in 1793, when Napoléon and fifty men from the French fleet were stranded waiting for backup in preparation for an attack on Ajaccio. With only one cannon to protect them from the army of Corsican patriots, they were holed up for three days. This was also the scene of Napoléon's reunion in 1793 with his mother and Cardinal Fesch, who sought refuge here after being chased out of town by Paolists before their flight to Toulon.

More background to these events appears on p.204.

PORTICCIO village, 18km south of Ajaccio, basically comprises a charmless loop of modern shops, banks, hotels and a post office fronting a large car park. The main road scythes straight through the middle and, come summer, the place is overwhelmed by a constant stream of cars, gleaming motorbikes, joggers, rollerbladers, windsurfers and lapdogs. The reason most of the Ajacciens drive out here is to visit the **Plage de La Viva**, a wide sandy stretch with a full-on watersports scene and great views of the gulf. Undeniably beautiful, but with finer and quieter stretches of coast only a half-hour's drive away, it's hard to think of a reason to linger here, unless you're staying at the Mark Warner complex on the edge of

The Mare e Monti Sud Trail

The recently inaugurated **Mare e Monti Sud** hiking trail runs from the south side of Plage d'Agosta, just south of Porticcio, to Propriano, divided into five relatively easy stages of between 3hr 45min and 6hr, and waymarked with orange splashes of paint. The scenery along the route, which winds southwest along the ridge dividing the Golfe d'Ajaccio from the Golfe de Valinco, is nowhere near as dramatic as on the original Mare e Monti trail (see p.146), but the gentle, maquis-covered hills and rocky coastline make it an enjoyable hike that will particularly appeal to less-experienced walkers. It also takes you within striking distance of the windswept beaches at Capu di Muro (covered on p.221), the prehistoric site at Filitosa (see p.232), and the picturesque resort of Porto Pollo (see p.230). The only real drawback is that, unlike most of the long-distance footpaths in Corsica, this one does not have gîtes d'étape at each stage, which means you have to shell out on hotels or campsites for at least three of the four or five nights.

Once again, the Parc Naturel Régional de Corse's **topo-guide** is an indispensable companion, giving contour maps and detailed descriptions of each stage; copies are available at most good bookshops on the island, and at the Parc Naturel Régional's office in Ajaccio (see p.199). You should also check the general introduction to hiking on p.30 of "Basics".

Mare e Monti Sud accommodation

The trail's only two gîtes d'étape are at Bisinao (☎04 95 24 21 66) and Burgo (☎04 95 76 15 05). Both are heavily booked during the summer, when you should reserve at least a couple of days in advance to ensure a bed. For reviews of hotels and campsites in Porticcio, Côti-Chiavari, Porto-Pollo, Olmeto and Propriano, check the relevant accounts on pp.220, 221, 231, 236 and 238.

the village, or at one of the many holiday villas scattered around the hills behind it.

Six daily **buses** (Casanova Autocars; ☎04 95 21 05 17) run between Ajaccio and Porticcio from July until mid-September (40min), with a reduced service onwards down the coast to Isolella and Ruppione.

A small **tourist office** in the shopping complex (May–Aug Mon–Sat 9am–1pm & 2.30–8pm, Sun 9am–1pm & 4–8pm; ☎04 95 25 01 01) can be helpful for finding somewhere to stay. Most of the **accommodation** hereabouts is very expensive during July and August, but tariffs are reasonable at *Hôtel de Porticcio*, although the location overlooking the crossroads in the centre of the village is unpromising (☎04 95 25 05 77; ⑥); breakfast is included in the price, rooms are light and airy, and the hotel has its own tennis courts. For **campers**, there's the well-equipped three-star *Camping Les Marines de Porticcio* (☎04 95 25 09 35; June–Sept), close to the beach and shops. For more accommodation along the south coast of the gulf, see below.

Beaches south of Porticcio

South of Porticcio the D55 narrows in its progress along the coast, a high bank of maquis screening expensive villas and private beaches from the passing cars. Some 5km along, you'll come to **Plage d'Agosta**, a popular, wide, sandy beach sheltered in the south by the Punta di Sette Nave, a narrow, rocky headland crowned by the **Tour de l'Isolella**. The best hotel in this area, the unpretentious *Kallisté* (☎04 95 25 54 19, fax 04 95 25 59 25; *www.cymos.com*; ⑦; May–Sept), stands on a hillside overlooking the bay (at the end of a badly rutted track). Located in a quiet spot with sweeping views, its rooms are light and airy and, off season, there are good discounts.

By far the finest beach along this stretch, and a less crowded spot than Plage d'Agosta, is **Plage de Ruppione**, a half-moon-shaped cove 8km south of Porticcio – perfect for sheltered swimming and snorkelling. Campers can stay here at the *Camping le Sud* (☎04 95 25 40 51, fax 04 95 25 47 39; May–Oct), one of the less expensive campsites along this coast, situated on a pine-shaded terrace beside the main road.

From here onwards, the coast becomes gradually less developed, with folds of woodland backing onto rocky headlands and golden coves. At **PORT DE CHIAVARI**, some 5km south of Ruppione, the beautiful **Plage de Verghia** has a handful of bars and a **campsite**, *La Vallée*, set back from the main road close to the beach (☎04 95 25 44 66; May–Oct). At this point the D55 narrows and turns sharply inland towards Côti-Chiavari. The road ahead deteriorates on the approach to the **Anse de Portigliolo**, a delightful, almost circular sandy cove. Around 500m up the steep lane leading inland from the sea, the *Hôtel Céline* (☎04 95 25 41 05, fax 04 95 25 50 36; ⑥) is a very pleasant two-star whose most outstanding feature is its pool, which has fantastic views across the bay.

The inland route

Some 10km from Pisciatella, where the D302 peels south off the main Ajaccio–Bonifacio road (N196), the **Col de Belle Valle** (522m) opens out with views of Ajaccio and the Îles Sanguinaires to the west. The right fork here will take you more directly to the Chiavari forest, but to get the most out of the landscape take the left fork, in the direction of Bisinao. This latter road twists through a dark rocky gorge, giving a great view of the Punta di Sette Nave, before reaching the **Col d'Aja Bastiano** (638m). At this point the D55 cuts south up the ridge at a gentle gradient amidst heavy scrubland of broom, mimosa, gorse and wild thyme, a mixture known as the *maquis dense*. Some 4km ahead, the **Col de Chenova** (629m) offers more expansive views, then the continuation of the D55 brings you into the eucalyptus-lined route shouldering the **Forêt de Chiavari**.

The **Col de Cortone** (523m) lies towards the southern edge of the forest, from where it's a short way to **CÔTI-CHIAVARI**, a pretty orange-stone village overlooking the Golfe d'Ajaccio. You can **stay** here at the *Hôtel Le Belvedère*, a family-run place just 1km below (south of) the village (☎04 95 27 10 32, fax 04 95 27 12 99; obligatory half-board in July & August, ④); it does excellent home cooking, served on a terrace overlooking the sea, and has a loyal following – so make sure you book ahead if you want to stay. Several people rent out apartments and rooms in the village; the *Belvedère* can point you in the right direction.

North of Côti-Chiavari, a road favoured by practising rally drivers hairpins down to the shore, while the D55 continues deeper into the headland. About 4km along the D55, a narrow track leading off to the right will take you almost as far as **Capu di Muro**, where a watchtower marks the southern limit of the Golfe d'Ajaccio. There's a magnificent **beach** on the south side of the promonotory called **Cala d'Orzu**, accessible along a rough but motorable dirt track, which is famous for its shack seafood **restaurant**, *Chez Francis* (☎04 95 27 10 39; April–Nov). Main dishes cost around 80F, or you could order a wonderful bouillabaisse for double that, washed down with some of the Ajaccio region's finest white wines.

The Gorges du Prunelli

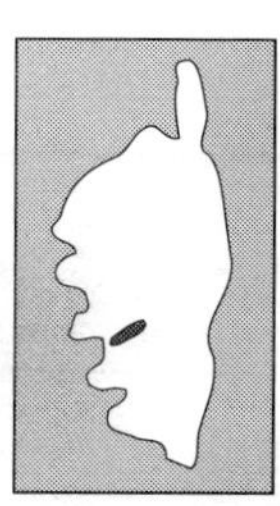

A drive up through the **Gorges du Prunelli** provides an easy but immensely varied excursion inland from Ajaccio, as the landscapes change dramatically from gardens and orchards to the bare jagged granite of the gorges themselves. Two roads climb the opposite flanks of the valley for 20km before converging on the run-up to **Bastelica**, a mountain village with restaurants and hotels that is the main gateway to the **Val d'Èse** ski station. The road on the north side of the valley, the D3, passes through the villages of **Bastelicaccia** and **Ocana** on its way to the dam at **Tolla**, where the route becomes increasingly hair-raising. To view the gorges from the other side, you can descend from Bastelica along the D27 via the **Col de Crichetto** and the attractive village of **Cauro**. The first route affords the best views, while the second is more easily negotiable by car; no public transport reaches these parts.

Bastelicaccia to Tolla

Fully cultivated since the nineteenth century in order to feed the growing population of Ajaccio, the plain around **BASTELICACCIA** has an air of cornucopian opulence, with its overflowing orchards of orange and lemon trees mingled with flower gardens and deep maquis. This is among the most pleasant places to stay within a short radius of Ajaccio, and one of the best local hotels is *L'Orangeraie* (☎04 95 20 00 09, fax 04 95 20 09 24; ⑥–⑦), situated 1km beyond the village amidst an orchard and a beautifully kept garden of palms and indigenous Mediterranean plants. In addition to rooms, you can rent well-equipped studios here, sleeping two to four people, by the night or the week; advance booking is essential.

Beyond Bastelicaccia the road threads through the maquis alongside the River Prunelli. Some 10km along you'll come to **OCANA**, a tiny village set in a small valley beneath a belt of fig trees, olive trees and cactus. Here they make *brocciu*, a milky cheese you'll find on sale in the market in Ajaccio – hence the abundant herds of ewes.

The scenery undergoes a dramatic change after Ocana, as high rock walls and pointed granite pinnacles begin to emerge from the greenery. **TOLLA**, a pretty village strung out on a ridge overlooking an immense reservoir of the **Lac de Tolla**, appears 2km further on. Trees abound: a bank of apple, walnut and chestnut orchards overhangs the valley in the approach to Tolla. Before you reach the village you can stop at the **Col de Mercuju** (716m), dominated by two great pyramids of rock rising from the circular hollow of the gorges. At the col, a Corsican **restaurant**, *Chez Baptiste*, is set back from the road and overlooks the gorges. Opposite the restaurant a path leads down to a platform above the dam, affording an impressive view across the lake, and various gentle forest paths thread through the woodland lining the banks.

Tolla itself is a lively place in summer, popular with Ajacciens who, returning to visit the family home, flock to the open-air pizzeria at the entrance to the village on the left. The only place to stay is a well-placed **campsite** down by the lake, *A Selva* (☎04 95 27 00 28; May–Oct), which also offers tasty Corsican cooking.

Once past Tolla, the landscape continues to be wild – rocky walls strewn with high maquis border the road, overlooked by the ragged crest of Punta di Forca d'Olmu to the south.

Bastelica

Set at 800m on the lower slopes of Monte Renoso, **BASTELICA** is a stark and unusually unprepossessing spot with a few rows of cold granite houses and an ugly modern church. It attracts a fair number of visitors, however, partly because the nearby **Val d'Èse** ski station, and partly because it is the birthplace of Sampiero Corso (see box overleaf), whose statue, dating from the 1890s, stands in the village centre. To visit the spot where Sampiero was born, walk up the road east of the church towards the adjoining hamlet of Dominicacci; take a left turn at the *U Renosu* restaurant, and then the first right up the lane running behind this building, which brings you to a T-junction; head right here and follow the backstreet for 20m or so; the house is on your right. The original building was burned down by the Genoese in 1554, but the façade of its replacement (1855) is adorned with an inscription that extols "the most Corsican of Corsicans, a famous hero amongst the innumerable heroes that love of the country, superb mother of male virtues, has nursed in these mountains and torrents".

For more background on Corsican nationalism, see "Contexts", p.376.

Bastelica has remained a hotbed of nationalism. In 1980, it witnessed one of the more dramatic encounters between Corsican activists and the State when, on January 6, a group of RPR militants discovered three undercover Secret Service agents operating in the village. The men were captured and taken at gunpoint to Ajaccio's *Hôtel Fesch*, where they were held to draw attention to the French government's covert activities on the island. Paris, however, refused to negotiate with the Bastelica nationalists, whom they dubbed "racketeers and hostage takers", and ordered the storming of the hotel. On January 12, armed police liberated the three agents and seized the militants, who were subsequently tried and imprisoned on the mainland. Coming only a few years after the siege at Aléria (see p.309), the event enraged the FLNC and plunged the island into a period of spiralling violence during the early 1980s.

Accommodation and eating

Bastelica has a few **hotels** open in summer. The most central is *Le Sampiero*, a large modern building opposite the church (☎04 95 28 71 99, fax 04 95 28 74 11; ④; closed Fri in winter), which, though lacking the character of its competitors, enjoys uninterrupted views of the mountains from most of its rooms, and has a friendly bar on the ground floor. More comfortable is *U Castagnetu*, past Sampiero's birthplace 1km north of the church (☎04 95 28 70 71, fax 04 95 28 74 02; half-board obligatory in July & August ⑧, otherwise ④), which has fifteen well-appointed rooms set amid chestnut trees, and stunning views over the valley from its sunny terrace. *Chez Paul*, 200m further along the same road (☎04 95 28 71 59; ④), is more modest but less pricy, and rents out apartments for longer stays; it also has an excellent little **restaurant** where you can enjoy traditional home cooking for around 120F per head. Bastelica is famous for its fine cheeses and charcuterie, and a good place to sample these is *Chez François Urbani*, next door to *Chez Paul*, which stocks a range of traditional local hams, sausages and ewe's cheese; the prices are high, but so is the quality.

Sampiero Corso

"The most Corsican of Corsicans", **Sampiero Corso** was born into a peasant family in 1498 and first took up arms in 1517, when he entered the service of the Medici as a mercenary – a career followed by many of his poorer compatriots. Gaining himself a reputation for audacious ambition – he is said to have put forward a plan to assassinate Charles V in 1536 – he arrived in France in the company of Catherine de' Medici, and went on to distinguish himself in several campaigns, becoming renowned as the most valiant captain in the French army. At Perpignan in 1543 he saved the life of the future Henry II, husband of Catherine de' Medici, thereby ensuring his promotion in 1547 to colonel of the Corsican infantry. He returned to Corsica a proud and popular figure, and promptly married a young noblewoman named Vannina d'Ornano. The match was not approved of by her brothers, who saw their inheritance about to slip from their fingers – and their enmity was to have dire consequences.

Around this time the Genoese, suspicious of Sampiero's prestige, decided to lock him up for a spell, accusing him of having plotted an uprising against the republic. Their action engendered a hatred of Genoa that Sampiero was to hold for the rest of his days. It was the French declaration of war against Genoa in 1553, and their attempt to "liberate" Corsica from the despotic republic, that established Sampiero's legendary status. Setting out with Marshal Thermes and an expeditionary force of seven thousand mercenaries, amongst them a Turkish contingent led by the notorious Dragut, he managed a rapid takeover of Bastia, Ajaccio and Corte. Bonifacio and Calvi weren't such an easy proposition, however, being populated primarily by Ligurian settlers and thus more firmly entrenched as Genoese strongholds. Long and relentless sieges ensued, with Turkish ships ruthlessly bombarding the towns in a prelude to massacre and pillage.

The subsequent Genoese alliance with the Spanish resulted in Sampiero's return to the continent in 1557, and two years later the treaty of Cateau-Cambresis gave Corsica back to Genoa. Sampiero passionately wanted independence for the island, but could not command the backing of France after strangling his wife, in Aix-en-Provence, after he found out she had betrayed him to the Genoese and sold most of his possessions. Escaping with some of her fortune, he returned to Corsica in 1564 to organize another revolt. He rapidly took over much of the island's interior but failed to take the ports, and enthusiasm for his cause soon diminished, a process doubtless hastened by the 2000-ducat price the Genoese put on his head. In 1567, Sampiero was decapitated in an ambush near Bastelica, a murder engineered by the Ornano brothers, who had never forgotten their grudge. His head was impaled on the town gate of Ajaccio, a warning to would-be rebels that ensured his martyr's status.

Bastelica to Cauro

On the way back down the main D27, there's the option of turning off the road 4km south of Bastelica to follow a parallel road which gives a stunning view of the gorges. If you're in a sturdy vehicle, you can enjoy even better views by taking the rough mountain track that branches off just before the junction at the **Col de Menta** (762m); this runs parallel to the D27, merging with it at the **Col de Crichetto**. The D27 is bordered by the **Forêt de Pineta**, whose carpet of Laricio pines, chestnut and beech trees makes it good place for a picnic. From the maison forestière, 3km along the same road, it's a ten-minute marked walk to the **Pont de Zipitoli**, a single arc of Genoese stone spanning the River Èse.

After regaining the D27 at the **Col de Marcuggio** (670m), you descend through an increasingly pastoral terrain of vineyards interspersed by fields and folds of woodland. About 6km along from the col, just before the hamlet of Radicale, a bridge on a sharp left bend marks the start of a fifteen-minute trail to the **Cascade de Sant'Alberto**, a high waterfall hidden amidst the forest. **CAURO**, a pleasant but unremarkable village at the junction of the D27 and N169, has a good **hotel** – *Sampiero*, in the centre opposite the post office (☎04 95 28 44 84; ④). Buses from Ajaccio to Bonifacio pass through here daily before crossing the **Col St-Georges**, 7km further south, where there's an excellent little roadside **restaurant**: in a small dining room behind a bar, the *Auberge du Col* serves traditional and tasty Corsican dishes such as cannelloni made with chestnut flour, and wild rabbit stew.

From Cauro, it's an easy 13km detour south to **SANTA MARIA SICCHÉ**, set amid dense swathes of coastal maquis just off the main road. The village would be a pretty but otherwise undistinguished place were it not for the fact that Sampiero Corso's wife, Vannina d'Ornano, was born here. The old stone house Sampiero built for her in 1554, the **Palazzo Sampiero**, still stands; follow the lane leading left around the village church for about 500m and you'll see it on your left, marked with a plaque. Its derelict state was caused by a fire in the forge that formerly occupied the ground floor. Vannina's family home, by contrast, has remained in fine condition, though it's harder to locate and unmarked: take the main road leading downhill past the church towards the highway for 300m – the house, a fifteenth-century tower, stands on the right, at the top of a black tarmac lane.

Travel details

TRAINS

Ajaccio to: Bastia (4 daily; 3hr); Bocognano (4 daily; 50min); Calvi (2 daily; 4hr 35min–5hr); Corte (4 daily; 1hr 40min); L'Île Rousse (2 daily; 4hr); Ponte Leccia (4 daily; 2hr 45min); Venaco (4 daily; 1hr 20min); Vizzavona (4 daily; 1hr).

BUSES

AR = Autocars Ricci (☎04 95 51 08 19).
ARC = Autocars R. Ceccaldi (☎04 95 21 01 24 or 04 95 21 38 06).
BE = Balési Évasion (☎04 95 70 15 55).
CA = Casanova Autocars (☎04 95 21 05 17).
EV = Eurocorse Voyages (☎04 95 21 06 30).
MM = M. Mordiconi (☎04 95 48 00 04).
SAIB = Autocars SAIB (☎04 95 22 41 99 or 04 95 21 02 07).

Ajaccio to: Aullène (BE; July & Aug Mon–Sat 1 daily; Sept–June Mon & Fri 2 weekly; 1hr 25min); Bastia (EV; Mon–Sat 2 daily; 3hr); Bavella (AR/BE; July to mid-Sept Mon–Sat 3 daily; mid-Sept to June Mon–Sat 1–2 daily; 2hr 5min–3hr 15min); Bonifacio (EV; July to mid-Sept 3 daily; mid-Sept to June 1 daily; 4hr); Cargèse (SAIB; July & Aug 2 daily; Sept–June Mon–Sat 1–2 daily; 1hr 10min); Corte (EV; Mon–Sat 2 daily; 1hr 45min); Evisa (ARC; Mon–Sat 1–3 daily; 2hr); Levie (AR; July to mid-Sept 1 daily; Sept–June Mon–Sat 1 daily; 2hr 45min); Olmeto (AR/EV; 4–6 daily; 1hr 35min); Porticcio (CA; 6 daily; 40min); Porto (SAIB; July & Aug 2 daily; Sept–June Mon–Sat 1–2 daily; 2hr 10min); Porto-Vecchio (BE/EV; 2–5 daily; 3hr 10min–3hr 45min); Propriano (AR/EV; 2–6 daily; 1hr 50min); Quenza (BE; July & Aug Mon–Sat 1 daily; Sept–June Mon–Fri 1 daily; 1hr 45min); Sagone (SAIB; July & Aug 2 daily; Sept–June Mon–Sat 1–2 daily; 40min); Sartène (AR/EV; 2–6 daily; 2hr 15min); Ste-Lucie-de-Tallano (AR; 1–2 daily; 21hr); Santa Maria Sicché (EV; 2 daily; 45min); Tiuccia (SAIB; July & Aug 2 daily; Sept–June Mon–Sat 1–2 daily; 35min); Vico (ARC; Mon–Fri 1 daily, 2 extra daily services in school-term times; 1hr 15min); Vizzavona (EV; Mon–Sat 2 daily; 1hr); Zonza (AR/BE; July to mid-Sept Mon–Sat 3 daily; mid-Sept to June Mon–Sat 1–2 daily; 2hr 15min–3hr).

Cargèse to: Ota (SAIB; July & Aug 2 daily; Sept–June Mon–Sat 1–2 daily; 1hr 30min); Piana (SAIB; July & Aug 2 daily; Sept–June Mon–Sat 1–2 daily; 30min); Porto (SAIB; July & Aug 2 daily; Sept–June Mon–Sat 1–2 daily; 1hr); Sagone (SAIB; July & Aug 2 daily; Sept–June Mon–Sat 1–2 daily; 15min); Tiuccia (SAIB; July & Aug 2 daily; Sept–June Mon–Sat 1–2 daily; 25min).

FERRIES

For ferry details, see "Basics" p.8.

GEOFFREY TAUNTON/CORBIS

Ajaccio Cathedral

KEVIN SCHAFER/CORBIS

Plage St. Francois, Ajaccio

DAVID ABRAM

War memorial, Propriano

ADAM WOOLFITT/CORBIS

Eroded rock, Îles Lavezzi

ADAM WOOLFITT/CORBIS

Home delivery, Bonifacio

CHARLES & JOSETTE LENARS/CORBIS

Neolithic menhir, Filitosa

ADAM WOOLFITT/CORBIS

Haute ville, Bonifacio

DAVID ABRAM

L'oriu de Cani

DAVID ABRAM

Bushfire art, Ospédale

DAVID ABRAM

Dolmen de Fontanaccia, Cauria

BOB GIBBONS/EYE UBIQUITOUS–CORBIS

North face of Monte Cinto

DAVID ABRAM

Dawn above Moltifao, with Capu a i Mori in the background

Chapter 5

The south

Some of the most enduring evocations of Corsica's varied landscapes and culture – from Edward Lear's eerie etchings, to Prosper Mérimée's vendetta-yarn, *Colomba*, and Dorothy Carrington's occult explorations in *Dream Hunters of the Soul* – were inspired by **the south**, and this remains the most quintessentially Corsican corner of the island. Sparsely populated by comparison with the Ajaccio region, its rugged, inhospitable coastline and sheltered valleys support scattered villages where the old ways are never far from the surface. Vendetta may have been officially stamped out, but its roots still run deep. In recent years, long-standing family rivalries have repeatedly erupted into violence, hiding behind the guise of nationalist-separatist score-settling, while organized crime, too, is rife, from petty racketeering of businesses in the resorts to high-level corruption.

An article on Corsica's recent troubles features on p.376.

However, the only evidence tourists tend to see of this malevolent undercurrent are the bullet-raked road signs, black FLNC graffiti and the odd bombed-out holiday home. It's the extraordinary landscapes that will leave the more lasting impression: the wild, maquis-backed coast beyond Campomoro, the striated chalk cliffs of Bonifacio, or the brooding, shadowy hinterland of Alta Rocca, with its vineyards, fragrant Laricio pine forests and backdrop of pale granite peaks.

The south is most famous, though, for its mysterious prehistoric standing-stone sites. Accorded World Heritage status by UNESCO,

Accommodation Price Codes

Throughout this guide, hotel accommodation is graded on a scale from ① to ⑧. These numbers show the cost per night of the cheapest double room **in high season**, though remember that many of the cheap places will have more expensive rooms with en-suite facilities. In such cases we list two price codes, indicating the range of room rates offered.

① under 100F/under €15	⑤ 300–350F/€45–52.50
② 100–200F/€15–30	⑥ 350–400F/€52.50–60
③ 200–250F/€30–37.50	⑦ 400–500F/€60–75
④ 250–300F/€37.50–45	⑧ 500F and above/€75 and above

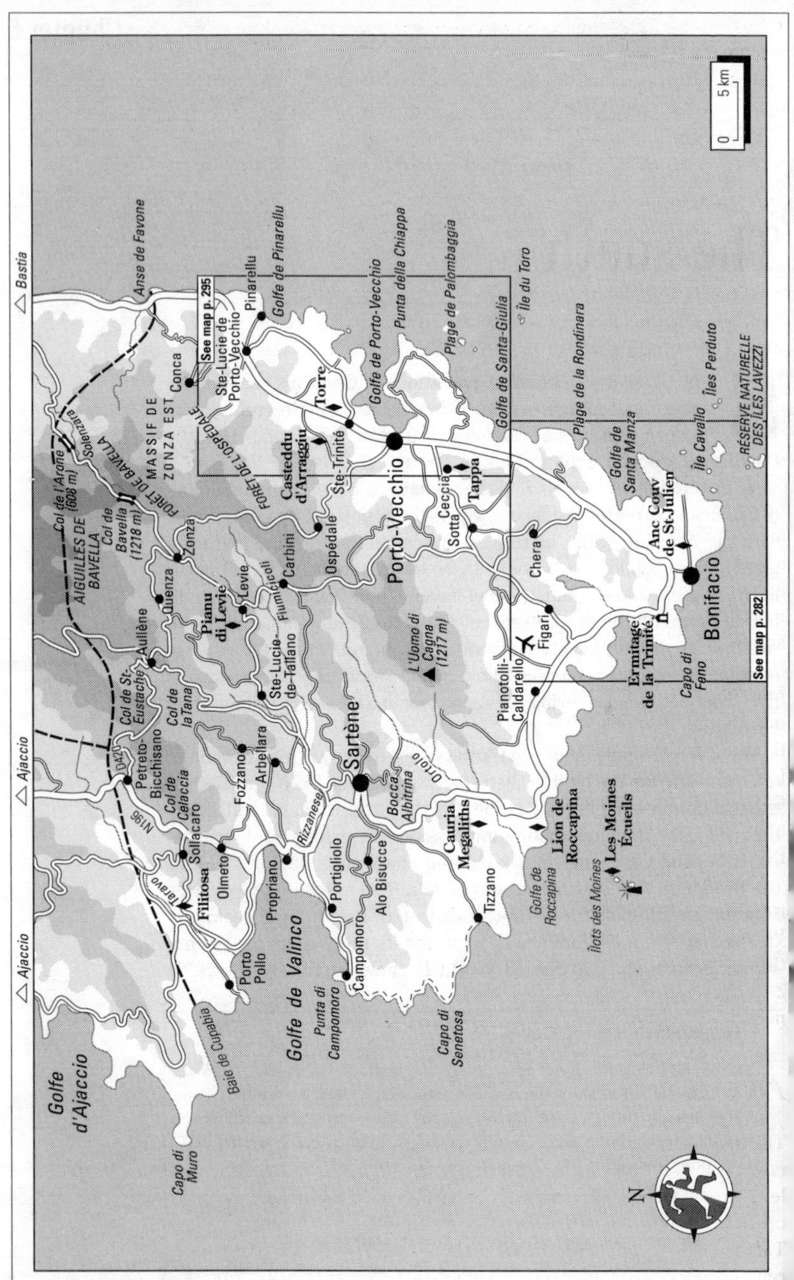

Bastia
Ajaccio
Ajaccio
Anse de Favone
Golfe de Pinarellu
Pinarellu
See map p. 295
Ste-Lucie de Porto-Vecchio
Conca
MASSIF DE ZONZA EST
Solenzara
Col de l'Arone (608 m)
AIGUILLES DE BAVELLA
Col de Bavella (1218 m)
FORÊT DE BAVELLA
FORÊT DE L'OSPÉDALE
Zonza
Quenza
Aullène
Pianu di Levie
Levie
Carbini
Fiumicicoli
Ospédale
Casteddu d'Araggiu
Torre
Ste-Trinité
Porto-Vecchio
Golfe de Porto-Vecchio
Punta della Chiappa
Plage de Palombaggia
Golfe de Santa-Giulia
Île du Toro
Ceccia
Tappa
Sotta
Chera
Plage de la Rondinara
Golfe de Santa Manza
Anc Couv de St-Julien
Bonifacio
Île Cavallo
Îles Perduto
RÉSERVE NATURELLE DES ÎLES LAVEZZI
See map p. 282
Ermitage de la Trinité
Capo di Feno
Figari
Pianotolli-Caldarello
L'Uomo di Cagna (1217 m)
Ste-Lucie-de-Tallano
Col de St-Eustache
Col de la Tana
Petreto-Bicchisano
D420
Fozzano
Arbellara
Sartène
Ortolo
Bocca Albitrina
Cauria Megaliths
Lion de Roccapina
Les Moines Écueils
Îlots des Moines
Golfe de Roccapina
Tizzano
Capo di Senetosa
Rizzanese
Col de Celaccia
Sollacaro
N196
Olmeto
Propriano
Portigliolo
Alo Bisucce
Campomoro
Punta di Campomoro
Golfe de Valinco
Filitosa
Taravo
Porto Pollo
Baie de Cupabia
Golfe d'Ajaccio
Capo di Muro
N
0
5 km

Filitosa is the best preserved of these, with carved menhirs strewn amid the ruins of three-thousand-year-old fortifications. A good base from which to visit Filitosa is **Porto-Pollo**, a secluded seaside village at the northern end of the vast **Golfe de Valinco**. Alternatively, there's **Propriano**, a livelier modern port in the centre of the bay, offering the widest choice of hotels, shops and restaurants in the area. From here you can also explore the southern section of the Golfe de Valinco as far as picturesque **Campomoro**, or roam into the island's richest wine-producing country, taking in **Fozzano**, famed for its blood feuds and stalwart granite tower houses. A bit deeper inland, the region of **Alta Rocca** has an abundance of historic villages and prehistoric sites – the architecture of **Sainte-Lucie-de-Tallano** pays testimony to the wealth of the area's former overlords, the della Rocca family, while a visit to the Bronze Age ruins of the **Pianu di Levie** is an essential complement to the Filitosa trip. In the heart of Alta Rocca, the village of **Zonza** stands on the threshold of the south's major natural attraction, the sublime granite "needles" of **Bavella**.

Moving southwest, **Sartène** is in many ways the quintessential Corsican town, its history saturated with stories of vendetta and its stark, fortified buildings redolent of the harshness of life in the not-so-distant past. South of Sartène, a weird landscape of thick maquis and eroded rock outcrops makes an appropriate background for the **megaliths of Cauria** and **Alignement de Palaggiu**, Corsica's largest arrays of prehistoric standing stones.

Marking the southern extremity of Corsica, **Bonifacio** is one of the most dramatically sited towns in the whole Mediterranean, its old quarter sitting atop vertiginous white cliffs and almost severed from the mainland by a deep natural harbour. It's a popular holiday centre for the island's wealthier tourists, as is **Porto-Vecchio**, a former Genoese citadel that's close to the island's most beautiful, and popular, beaches and to the majestic forest scenery of the **Massif de l'Ospédale**.

The area is reasonably well served by **public transport**, with buses running year-round, two to four times a day from Ajaccio to Porto-Vecchio, via Propriano, Bonifacio and Sartène. Daily buses also pass through the mountains from the west coast through Bavella and Zonza to Porto-Vecchio, but to visit all the prehistoric sites you will need your own vehicle.

Around the Golfe de Valinco

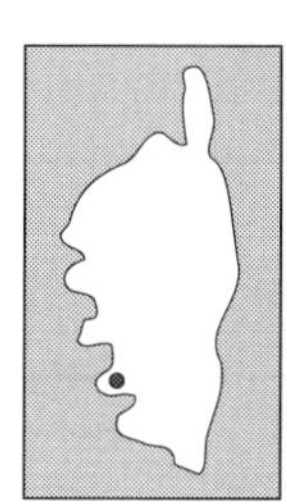

The most southerly of the four great bays indenting Corsica's west coast, the **Golfe de Valinco** gives easy sea access to two deep valleys – the Taravo and Rizzanese – that were among the first regions on the island to be settled. A stone's throw from the banks of the **Taravo River**, off the gulf's north shore, **Filitosa**'s prehistoric remains range from smoke-blackened early-Neolithic rock shelters to a fully developed Toréen castle, as well the carved menhirs for which the site is renowned. The Taravo twists through a fertile flat-bottomed valley to join the sea near **Porto-Pollo**, a former fishing village overlooking the river mouth that's among the quietest resorts in this region. By contrast, **Propriano**, at the far east end of the bay, can feel overwhelmed in summer, although its busy marina and dramatic setting warrant at least a short visit en route to idyllic **Campomoro**, at the far southwest corner of the gulf. Crowned by a large watchtower, its perfectly curved bay and sandy beach make this among the most photogenic villages in the south; moreover, beyond it lies a rugged stretch of coast accessible only on foot, and thus deserted save for the odd hiker.

Approaching the gulf from the north, most visitors travel along the N196, crossing the **Col de Celaccia** before dropping down to **Sollacaro** (en route to Filitosa) or to Olmeto (on the Propriano road). However, a much more scenic alternative is to take the coastal D155, threading its way around Capo di Muro in the Ajaccio region into the Golfe de Valinco. Aside from some amazing views of a totally unspoilt countryside, this badly potholed backroad passes close to beautiful **Cupabia beach** – a rarely visited gem.

Porto-Pollo

On the northwestern edge of the gulf is **PORTO-POLLO** whose name derives from the Corsican *Porti Poddu*, meaning "troubled port" – a legacy of the pirate raids that ravaged the island's coast in former times. Today, the little harbour in this cosy fishing village, 18km northwest of Propriano, provides sheltered moorings for yachts while a few fishermen still venture out to supply the local restaurants with fresh langoustine from the gulf. Development here has been limited: barely a handful of hotels line the road behind the village's narrow beach and traffic is minimal, making this a peaceful base from which to visit Filitosa, Alta Rocca and the Sartenais. In addition, the Golfe de Valinco's particularly clear waters ensure the village's popularity as a **diving** centre.

Beaches around Porto-Pollo

Porto-Pollo's beach isn't up to much, but the village lies close to two spectacular sandy bays that can be easily accessed by car, and by determined cyclists.

Just over the headland to the west, **Cupabia** lies 12km away by road: head out towards Propriano, but take the first left, along the D155; this snakes over a low pass and down the other side to a staggered crossroads where you should follow the D155A (marked "Plage de Cupabia"). The beach, a long curve of soft white sand, is undeveloped save for a scruffy, shadeless campsite and a solitary *buvette* (drinks stand) in summer. Although quite remote, the easy road access and proximity to the big holiday villages around

Propriano mean it does see visitors in the summer. To escape these, head right when you arrive at the beach and over the rocks at its far end to two secluded coves, where some driftwood structures and tall bushes provide more shade than you'll find on Cupabia proper.

Two kilometres east of Porto-Pollo lies a second enormous stretch of sand, **Plage de Taravo**. It's busier than Cupabia due to the presence of a couple of campsites behind it (see below), but the beach is large enough to absorb even the August deluge.

Practicalities

From June to September, **minibuses** provide the only public transport in the area, shuttling between Propriano and Porto-Pollo (Mon–Sat 1 daily; ☎04 95 74 05 58 or 04 95 74 01 88). They stop at various points along the road that runs behind Porto-Pollo's beach, which is dominated by a string of mid-range **hotels**. Of these, *Kallisté*, right in the centre of the village (☎04 95 74 02 38, fax 04 95 74 06 26; ⑤), is the best place to stay, with large rooms and modern fittings and furniture. Owned by a descendant of Pascal Paoli, it has an excellent restaurant, serving the best fresh seafood on this side of the gulf, though it's quite pricy, with set menus starting at 120F. Otherwise, try the equally central *Les Eucalyptus* (☎04 95 74 01 52, fax 04 95 74 06 56; ⑥; mid-May to Sept), with three good-value rooms, which are basic and don't have views, but are clean and affordable even in high season. *Le Golfe*, at the far end of the village (☎04 95 74 01 66; ③; May–Oct), is much the best budget option, with a handful of simple rooms overlooking the marina.

The only central option for **campers** is *Camping Alfonsi*, at the entrance to the village (☎04 95 74 01 80; June to mid-Oct), served by a cheap and cheerful pizzeria. With your own transport, however, two more peaceful and atmospheric alternatives lie 12km inland up the Taravo Valley at **Casalabriva**. Follow the Propriano road as far the bridge, just before which you should turn left onto the D757, which winds alongside the Taravo towards Petreto-Bicchisano. At the **Calzola crossroads**, head straight on for *Camping Kiesale* (☎04 95 74 63 73; open year round), a very secluded, clean and picturesque site, with its own small restaurant. A right turn at the crossroads takes you over the bridge, from where you'll see signs for *Camping A Miranda* (*Chez Marie-Jeanne Abbatucci*) (☎04 95 24 36 30), a tiny, farm campsite with simple but ample facilities for around 25 pitches.

Surfing and **windsurfing** equipment can be rented at the Centre Nautique de Porto-Pollo, at the entrance to the village. Divers are catered for by Porto-Pollo Plongeé (☎04 95 74 07 46), based in a Portakabin above the marina (accessible from the road). It runs dives to the spectacular Cathédrales, an underwater massif of rock pinnacles on the northern side of the gulf, as well as to some of the superb sites around Campomoro, on the opposite side of the gulf.

Filitosa

Eight thousand years of history are encapsulated by the extraordinary **Station Préhistorique de Filitosa** (daily Easter–Oct 9am–sunset, out of season by arrangement only; ☎04 95 74 00 91; 22F), 10km inland from Porto-Pollo. Little is known about the peoples who inhabited this spot, a fact that adds an element of mystery to **FILITOSA**'s statue-menhirs, which glare amid meadows, gnarled old olive groves and patches of wild mint – a scene little changed since their creation. The site remained undiscovered until **Charles-Antoine Cesari** came upon the ruins on his farmland in the late 1940s. He and **Roger Grosjean**, who was to become head of the centre for archeological research in Sartène, set about a full-scale excavation, discovering some menhirs lying face down in the maquis, others broken at waist level inside what is now known as the central monument (you can read an evocative firsthand account of the discovery in Dorothy Carrington's *Granite Island*; see p.390). When the digging was completed the menhirs were set into lines, and the site was opened to the public in 1954.

There's no public **transport** to Filitosa, but the Propriano to Porto-Pollo bus will take you as far as the D157/D57 junction, just before the Taravo bridge, from where you can hitch the remaining 6–7km; hitching is fairly reliable during the summer, when nearly all the traffic on these back roads is heading to or from the site.

A brief history of Filitosa

Filitosa was occupied from 6000 BC, when it was settled by **Neolithic** farming people who lived here in rock shelters. Flakes of obsidian, used to make arrowheads and only available from the Aeolian Islands and Sardinia, have been unearthed, indicating that the first Filitosans must have engaged in trade, but little else is known about them, other than the fact they were colonized some time between 3500 and 3000 BC by **megalithic** peoples from the East. Believed to have been missionary navigators, these early invaders came in search of converts to their faith, as well as land and metals, and were the creators of the first menhirs, the earliest of which were possibly phallic symbols worshipped by an ancient fertility cult. Later statues display stylized human features, making them quite distinct from nearly all other European menhirs of the megalithic period – such as those at Stonehenge and Avebury – which would seem to have been abstract expressions of devotion to a godhead rather than tributes to humankind. Most archeologists believe that the representational menhirs were memorials to dead chieftains and warriors. Grosjean, however, maintained that they were portraits of enemy **Torréens**, who – most people agree – arrived in the Golfe de Porto-Vecchio from the eastern Mediterranean around 1700 BC. To back up his theory, Grosjean cites Aristotle, who claimed the ancient Iberians used to raise stones around the tombs of slain enemies; moreover, very few knives or daggers like the ones depicted have ever been found in megalithic sites on the island, nor at the time of the invasions did the farmers of Filitosa have the technology to make them.

As they settled, the Torréens built conical structures known as **torri** (towers) all over the south of Corsica. Again, no one is absolutely certain of their function; it's generally agreed that the smaller of these beehive-like towers are likely to have been used as places of worship to some divinity, though traces of ashes and bones in the vicinity also suggest these could have been where the Torréens burned or buried their dead. The larger *torri*, too small for human habitation, are thought to have served as stores for weapons or food, or perhaps as refuges or lookout towers.

When the Torréens conquered Filitosa around 1300 BC, they destroyed most of the menhirs, incorporating the broken stones into the area of dry-stone walling surrounding the site's two *torri*. Around the towers, the remains of which are the central and western monuments, they constructed a village of Cyclopean stone shacks – a complex known as a **casteddu**. As such *casteddi* became more numerous, their inhabitants were forced into attacking neighbouring settlements in order to protect their land and livestock. Grosjean believed that competition between the *casteddi* forced Torréen expeditions to migrate to northern Sardinia, which would explain the existence on that island of **nuraghi**, larger and more technically advanced versions of *torri*. A rival theory, however, suggests that the Torréens were in fact indigenous Corsicans who simply acquired their technical expertise from the Sardinian *nuraghi* builders.

The site

Vehicles can be left in the small **car park** in the hamlet of Filitosa, where you pay the entrance fee; from here it's a five-minute walk to the site, which includes a small **museum** (best seen after the site) and a workshop producing reproduction prehistoric ceramics.

Filitosa V looms up on the right shortly after the entrance. The largest statue-menhir on the island, it's an imposing sight, with clearly defined facial features and a sword and dagger outlined on the body. Beyond a sharp left turn lies the oppidum or central monument, its entrance marked by the **eastern platform**, thought to have been a lookout post. The cave-like structure sculpted out of the rock is the only evidence of Neolithic occupation and is generally agreed to have been a burial mound.

Straight ahead, the Torréen **central monument** comprises a scattered group of menhirs on a circular walled mound, surmounted by a dome and entered by a corridor of stone slabs and lintels. Nobody is sure of its exact function.

Nearby **Filitosa XIII** and **Filitosa IX**, implacable lumps of granite with long noses and round chins, are the most impressive menhirs

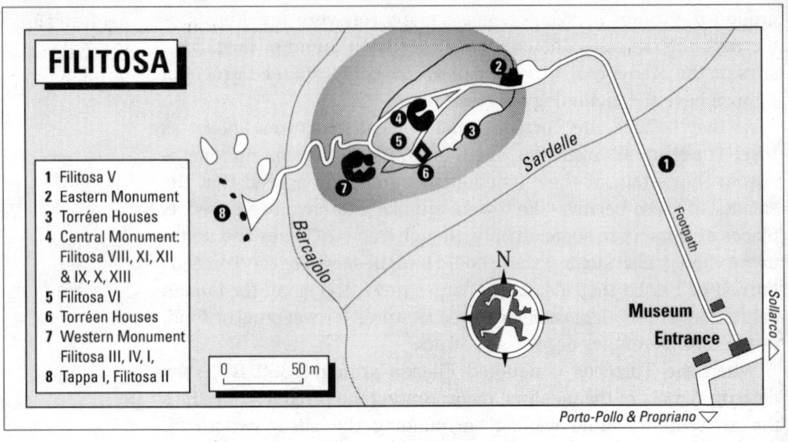

on the site – indeed Grosjean considered Filitosa IX to be the finest of all western Mediterranean megalithic statues. Filitosa XIII, the last menhir to be discovered here (the Torréens had built it into the base of the central monument), is typical of the figures carved just before the Torréen invasion, with its vertical dagger carved in relief – **Filitosa VII** also has a clearly sculpted sword and shield. **Filitosa VI**, from the same period, is remarkable for its facial detail. On the eastern side of the central monument stand some vestigial Torréen houses, where fragments of **ceramics** dating from 5500 BC were discovered; they represent the most ancient finds on the site, and some of them are displayed in the museum.

The **western monument**, a two-roomed structure built underneath another walled mound, is thought to have been some form of Torréen religious building. A steep flight of rough steps leads to the foot of this mound, where a tiny footbridge leads into the meadow, on the other side of which five statue-menhirs are arranged in a wide semicircle beneath a thousand-year-old olive tree. A bank separates them from a jumble of contorted, nobbly grey rocks – the **quarry** from which the megalithic sculptors hewed the stone for the menhirs. A granite block, marked ready for cutting, has been propped up on stakes to make a seat from which you can survey the site.

The **museum** is a shoddy affair, with poorly labelled exhibits and very little contextual information, but the artefacts themselves are fascinating. The major item here is the formidable **Scalsa Murta**, a huge menhir dating from around 1400 BC and discovered at Olmeto. Like other statue-menhirs of this period, this one has two indents in the back of its head, which are thought to indicate that these figures would have been adorned with headdresses like the horn that's been attached to Scalsa Murta. Other notable exhibits are **Filitosa XII** which has a hand and a foot carved into the stone, and **Trappa II**, a strikingly archaic face. Explanatory notes and photographs around the walls sketch the progression of the excavations.

Sollacaro and Olmeto

East of Filitosa, the D57 threads through hilly hedged-in pastures for about 8km before the village of **SOLLACARO** (Suddacaru) rises into view. A compact, reddish-toned collection of houses, the village boasts the distinction of having been the setting for the first meeting of James Boswell and Pascal Paoli on October 21, 1765 (see box) – a plaque opposite the post office commemorates the occasion.

Joining the coast road from Ajaccio and heading south, your first glimpse of the stunning Golfe de Valinco comes just below **Col de Celaccia** (583m), where a series of steep turns brings you down to **OLMETO**, situated 4km below the pass. With its grandstand view over Propriano, Olmeto was once a favourite spot with artists such as Edward Lear, and it remains a captivating place, close to the coast but far enough from Propriano to retain a village atmosphere,

Boswell in Corsica

Dr Johnson's biographer courted men of genius as assiduously as he pursued women, and one of his early conquests was the Corsican patriot **Pascal Paoli**. In 1765, at the age of 25, **James Boswell** contrived to make the acquaintance of the great French philosopher Rousseau in Switzerland. The Corsicans, struggling to formalize their independence, had asked the author of the *Social Contract* to give them a new set of laws. In certain circles Corsica had something of the appeal that Greece was to offer Byron's generation sixty years later, and Boswell promptly suggested that Rousseau make him his ambassador to the Corsicans. He duly received a letter of introduction, which he was able to present to Paoli the following year.

The meeting was a far more nerve-racking experience for Boswell than his encounter with the philosopher. "I had stood in the presence of many a prince but I never had such a trial as in the presence of Paoli," he wrote. "For ten minutes we walked backwards and forwards through the room hardly saying a word, while he looked at me with a steadfast, keen and penetrating eye, as if he searched my very soul." A student of physiognomy, Paoli also feared an attempt on his life, so the close scrutiny was scarcely surprising, and it didn't hinder the development of a friendship that was to hold throughout Paoli's later exile in London.

The success of Boswell's book about his visit, *An Account of Corsica – the Journal of a Tour to that Island and Memoirs of Pascal Paoli*, helped launch his social and literary career in London, and commemorated a passion that endured throughout his life. In 1769, the year of the book's publication, he attended the first annual celebration of Shakespeare's birthday in Stratford-on-Avon, an event organized by the actor David Garrick. Boswell appeared at the celebrations dressed in the Corsican national costume and wearing in his hat a card that read "Corsica Boswell".

A feature on piracy in Corsica appears on p.102.

For more background on Colomba and the Corsican vendetta, see p.244.

A short biography of Giudice appears on p.193.

compromised only by holiday traffic clogging up the main road through the centre in summer. Once off the road, however, you're instantly hemmed in by lofty buildings and sleepy back alleys.

Contrary to appearances, life in Olmeto has not always been peaceful. The village was actually established on this high, easily defensible site to provide protection from the constant pirate raids that menaced the gulf from the fifteenth to seventeenth centuries; in 1617, for example, some fifty villagers were abducted and taken as slaves to North Africa. The village is also renowned for its bloody **vendettas**, some of which carried on well into the twentieth century; in *Granite Island* (see p.390), Dorothy Carrington recalls meeting an old man who could name twenty people murdered there in his lifetime. Most famous of all the Corsican vendettas was the one instigated by **Colomba Carabelli**, the heroine of Merimée's novel *Colomba*, who died here in 1861, aged 96, in the forbidding mansion facing the mairie. Her reputation still attracts a few admirers, but what brings most tourists to Olmeto today are the incredible views from the village's two main streets, which are linked by steep stairways, with the foundations of the houses vanishing into a valley whose olive groves once sustained the local economy.

Just before you enter the village, you'll notice the ruined **Castello della Rocca** crowning an isolated peak. This inaccessible castle was inhabited in the fourteenth century by Arrigho della Rocca, the fiery great-grandson of Giudice della Cinarca. Exiled to Spain in 1362, Arrigho enlisted the support of the King of Aragon and returned to Corsica ten years later, intent on taking over the whole island. He virtually succeeded, with only Calvi and Bonifacio holding out against him, and as Count of Corsica ruled the island for four years until his death at Vizzavona in 1401, poisoned by one of his own vassals.

Practicalities

Straddling the busy N196, Olmeto is served by Eurocorse Voyages' regular **buses** between Ajaccio and Porto-Vecchio, which run via Propriano and Sartène (Mon–Sat 2–4 daily; for timetable information ☎04 95 21 06 30), as well as Autocars Ricci's Ajaccio–Alta Rocca service (1–2 daily, ☎04 95 51 08 19 or 04 95 76 25 59). The village's small **information office** (July & Aug daily 9am–noon & 2–6pm, Sept–June Mon–Fri 9am–noon; ☎04 95 74 65 87) can help you find **accommodation** in the area, but your best option is to try the old stone *U Santa Maria – Chez Mimi*, Overlooking the church square (☎04 95 74 65 59, fax 04 95 74 60 33; obligatory half-board in August; ④; open all year), it has smart comfortable rooms above an excellent little **restaurant**, whose set menus of classy Corsican cuisine range from 80F to 120F.

Propriano

Bracketed by the promontory of Scogliu Lungu, the fine natural harbour of **PROPRIANO**, 71km southwest of Ajaccio, was exploited by the ancient Greeks, Carthaginians and Romans, but became a prime target for pirate raids and by the eighteenth century had been largely destroyed. The port, developed at the beginning of this century, now handles **ferries** to the French mainland and Sardinia, but still has an unfinished appearance. This is due in part to terrorist bombs: the post office, a symbol of the French administration and especially targeted for its isolated position here, has had to be rebuilt four times over the last thirteen years after nationalist attacks.

The amount of building work going on here also bears witness to the pace of change in Propriano, which has, in a little over fifteen years, metamorphosed from a sleepy fishing village into a busy tourist resort capable of accommodating 23,000 visitors. Chief among the architects of this rapid transformation is the mayor, **Émile Mocchi**, who has led the local council for more than a decade. A second-generation Italian immigrant whose father made a fortune selling army surplus supplies after World War II, Mocchi owes his longevity to friends and family in high places, including a nephew who's one of the leaders of the nationalist group *A Cuncolta*. He's also a close associate of southern Corsica's most powerful godfather, Jean-Jérôme ("Jean-Jé") Colonna, veteran of

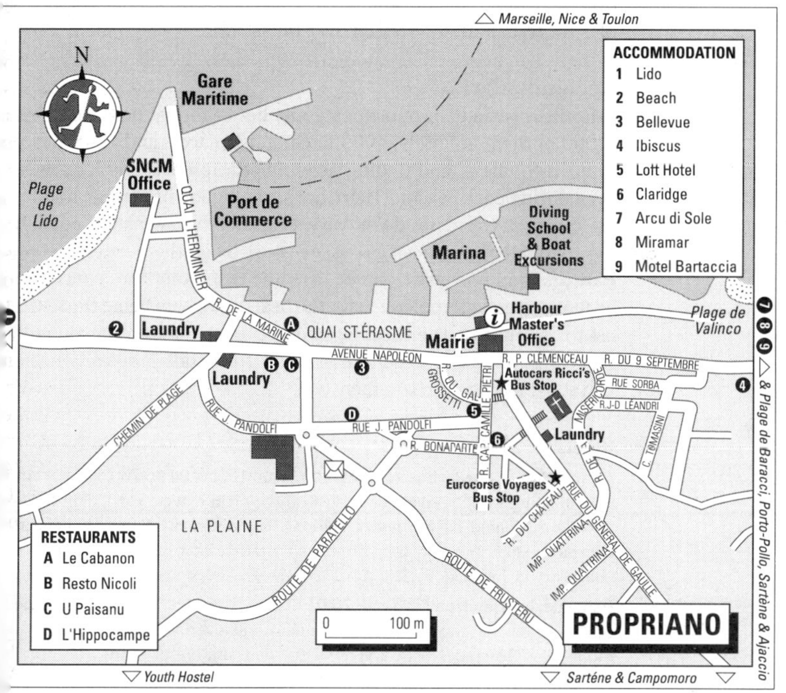

the infamous "French Connection" and the number-one tobacco smuggler on the island. Mocchi's influential connections, however, failed to protect him when the police investigated him for embezzlement of public funds (earmarked for development of the marina and welfare facilities in Propriano). At the ensuing trial in 1997, he was sentenced to a few years' imprisonment, but not even this has dented his ambition and, when this book went to press, he looked set to keep his job upon release.

Propriano's internal politics don't seem to deter the tourists, however, who come for the beaches, the sailing and watersports facilities. For people just passing through, the resort provides useful amenities (supermarkets and ATMs, for example) at the midway point between Ajaccio and Bonifacio.

Arrival and information

Ferries dock in the Port de Commerce, west of the town centre and ten minutes' walk from where the **buses** pull in at the top of rue Général-de-Gaulle, the town's main street, which runs at right angles to the water. The **tourist office** down in the marina (July & Aug daily 8am–8pm; June & Sept Mon–Sat 9am–noon & 3–7pm; Oct–May Mon–Fri 9am–noon & 2–6pm; ☎04 95 76 01 49) issues a glossy brochure with a plan of the town. They also have up-to-date timetables for transport services all over the island.

Accommodation

Propriano has a disproportionate number of tourist beds for its size (7000 of them in hotels, 4000 in camping places, and 12,000 more in holiday villas), and finding **accommodation** is rarely a problem, even during peak season. There are several good mid-range hotels in the centre of town, but if you have a car and the means you could try the more alluring places along the coast or on the quieter route de Baracci, 3km northeast. Cafés, bars and restaurants are concentrated along avenue Napoléon, with the best of the bars being those closest to the marina. The **theatre**, in the sports complex 1km along the road to Sartène (visit the tourist office for details), hosts concerts, plays and films in the summer.

Hotels

Arcu di Sole, route de Baracci (☎04 95 76 05 10, fax 04 95 76 13 36). A larg pink building with green shutters, just off the main Ajaccio road, 3km west c town (turn inland by the petrol station). No views, but there's a pool an gourmet restaurant, and they do excellent off-season discounts. Half-boar obligatory in July and August. April–Oct. ⑥–⑧.

Bellevue, av Napoléon (☎04 95 76 01 86, fax 04 95 76 38 94). The cheapes central hotel, halfway down av Napoléon and overlooking the marina; a rooms have balconies with a view of the gulf and are cheerfully decoratec downstairs there's a lively crêperie frequented by locals. ⑤.

Claridge, rue Bonaparte (☎04 95 76 05 54, fax 04 95 76 27 77). A modern building in the middle of town, with comfortable rooms but grim views. March–Oct. ⑥.

Ibiscus, route de la Grande-Corniche, just off rue du 9-septembre (☎04 95 76 01 56). A modern pink concrete block on the outskirts, whose front rooms have large balconies and good views over the gulf. Restaurant and parking. ⑤.

Beach Hôtel, av Napoléon (☎04 95 76 17 74, fax 04 95 76 06 54). A large four-storey block overlooking the Port de Commerce. Their rooms are spacious and comfortable, but a little bland and overpriced. ⑥.

Lido, Lido beach (☎04 95 76 06 37, fax 04 95 76 31 18). Peaceful but pricy hotel slap on the beach, with small rooms ranged around a cool courtyard and rear terraces jutting on the sand behind. Half-board obligatory in high season. 950F for a double room in August, dropping to 450F in June and Sept. ⑧.

Loft Hôtel, 3 rue Capitaine. Camille-Piétri (☎04 95 76 17 48, fax 04 95 76 22 04). Former wine and flour warehouse imaginatively converted into gleaming hi-tech hotel, with bright, clean rooms overlooking a car park. Good value. Closed Oct–April 15. ⑤.

Miramar Hôtel, route de la Grande-Corniche (a continuation of route de Baracci), 3km towards Ajaccio (☎04 95 76 06 13, fax 04 95 76 13 14). This four-star is the place to go if you want to splash out – a splendid luxury hotel with a huge swimming pool and sauna. May–Sept. ⑥.

Motel Bartaccia, 1km east of the centre off the Ajaccio road (☎04 95 76 08 02, fax 04 95 76 19 48). Inexpensive studios with fully equipped kitchenettes, tucked away in leafy gardens behind the *Miramar Hôtel*. Usually rented out by the week during July and August, but out of season they go for around 250F a night. ⑥.

Gîtes d'étapes and campsites

Centre Équestre Baracci, on the route de Baracci, 3km northeast of town (☎04 95 76 08 02, fax 04 95 76 19 48). The excellent gîte d'étape here is ideally situated if you're hiking around the long-distance trails in the area. Beds in their four-person dorms cost 85F. They also serve quality evening meals to order for 85F; bring your own sleeping bags (sheet rental 10F). See also p.36. ③.

Chez Angelini, further up the Baracci valley at Burgo, 7km northeast of Propriano (☎04 95 76 15 05). Run by the friendly and knowledgeable M. Angelini, this is one of the largest hikers' hostels in Corsica, with room for thirty people, though its proximity to the trailhead means advance booking is recommended during peak season.

Chez Antoine, in Marina d'Olmeto (☎04 95 76 06 06). Situated on the north side of the gulf, 5km from Propriano, this campsite is basic, but right next to one of the least-frequented beaches in the area.

Camping Colomba, 3km north along the route de Baracci (☎04 95 76 06 42). Take the right-hand turning off the main road by the Elf petrol station to reach this medium-sized, peaceful three-star with good facilities and plenty of shade – the best of the sites within walking distance of town.

Camping Lecci e Murta, on the Campomoro road (☎04 95 77 11 20). A good site near the beach, with a tennis court, pizzeria and store.

Around the Golfe de Valinco

Good beaches within driving distance of Propriano, however, are Plage de Cupabia, west of Porto-Pollo (see p.230), Campomoro (see p.246) and Roccapina (see p.269), off the main Bonifacio road.

A description of the Mare a Mare Sud trail, which starts in Propriano, features on p.242; for an account of the Mare e Monti Sud hike, which starts in Porticcio and ends here, see p.219.

Beaches and boat excursions

The nearest **beach** to Propriano, **Plage de Lido** lies a short way west of town, past the port de commerce and around the headland with the lighthouse. A steep crescent of yellow sand, it's surveyed by lifeguards during the summer.

Just north of Propriano, **Plage de Baracci**, a long, sheltered stretch of sand spanning the narrowest part of the gulf, is less than ideal: locals avoid it because of the strong undertow and unsightly heaps of rubbish littering the wasteland behind. Around 3km further north, the D157 branches off to the left and continues along the coast, which is built up with hotels and package-tour holiday blocks until **Olmeto Plage**, 10km west, where there's an abundance of campsites (see p.239). From June until September, you can travel all the way along this stretch by **minibus** from Propriano.

An alternative way of reaching some of the more scenic but less accessible stretches of the gulf is to take a **boat excursion** from Propriano marina. Particularly recommended are those on the catamaran *Big Blue* and its sister cruiser, *Valinco*, in their "Mer et Maquis" tour (140F). For bookings, go to their Portakabin at the far end of the marina past the tourist office. You are supplied with maps and photos for the walk up the coast from Campomoro (see box on pp.248–249), at the end of which they'll collect you at a remote bay, Cala d'Agulia, around 4.30pm. They also operate a cruise to the far-flung Senetosa tower, enlivened by underwater music recitals.

Restaurants

Le Cabanon, route de la Marine (☎04 95 76 07 76). Gourmet fish restaurant, with terrace, at the west end of the marina towards the port. Their special 85F lunch menu is excellent value, but the pricier options include more imaginative dishes such as ray's wing served with haricot beans and lemon sauce.

L'Hippocampe, rue Jean-Pandolfi (☎04 95 76 11 01). Tucked away behind the port, this is the best place for classy seafood at affordable prices, and their 98F set menu offers unbeatable value for Propriano. Dine inside, where nautical bits and bobs provide the decor, or outside on a flowery terrace.

Resto Nicoli, av Napoléon. An Italian-style budget restaurant near the port, and just about the cheapest place to eat; the excellent 65F menu features *beignets de courgettes* and a complimentary liqueur for "nice customers".

U Paisanu, av Napoléon. Rustic peasant place serving copious Corsican dishes, including mountain charcuterie, pigeon pâté, roast piglet and delicious vegetables *farcies à la Sarté* – a local speciality. Count on 150F per head, including wine.

Listings

Bus information Ollandini Valinco Voyages, 22 rue Général-de-Gaulle (☎04 95 76 00 76), for buses to Ajaccio. Autocars Ricci (☎04 95 51 08 19), who operate daily services between Ajaccio and Porto-Vecchio, via the villages of Alta Rocca and Bavella, work from an office at the bottom of the same road (tickets are sold on the bus).

Car rental Avis, 22 rue Général-de-Gaulle (☎04 95 76 00 76); Budget, rue Jean-Pandolfi (☎04 95 76 00 02); Citer, Location Valinco, 25 av Napoléon (☎04 95 76 11 84); Europcar, 2 rue Général-de-Gaulle (☎04 95 76 00 02).

Diving Valinco Plongée (☎04 95 76 31 01) and U Levante (☎04 95 76 23 83), both in the marina.

Doctors Dr Peninon, 11 av Napoléon (☎04 95 76 01 98); Dr Quilichini, 3 av Napoléon (☎04 95 76 00 96).

Horse riding The Centre Équestre de Baracci, 3km northeast on the route de Baracci, 5min walk from the Elf station (☎04 95 76 08 02, fax 04 95 76 19 48), offers rides for 100F per hour on beautiful horses. They also do longer trips from 500F per day, accompanied by an expert guide, across relatively unfrequented parts of the interior.

Hospital The nearest hospital with a casualty department is in Sartène.

Laundry Two self-service laundries (*laveries automatiques*): one just down from the tourist office on rue Général-de-Gaulle, the other opposite the Port de Commerce on av Napoléon.

Motorbike and mountain-bike rental Mountain bikes (*vtt*) and 50cc or 80cc scooters for rent through TCC, 25 rue Général-de-Gaulle (☎04 95 76 15 32), and Location Valinco, 25 av Napoléon (☎04 95 76 11 84); both also have a couple of 125cc trials bikes (350F per day).

Pharmacy Rue Général-de-Gaulle.

Taxis ☎04 95 76 11 03.

Fozzano

East of Propriano, the north flank of the Alta Rocca region (see p.248) is scattered with old stone villages, of which the best known is **FOZZANO**, 12km inland from Propriano and something of a tourist attraction due to its former reputation as a hotbed of vendetta. Its notoriety dates from the early eighteenth century, when the whole village became politically divided over the Corsican uprising against the Genoese, the lower village lining up behind the Carabelli and Bartoli families, the upper behind the Durazzo and Paoli clans. **Colomba Bartoli**, born a Carabelli, was a driving force within her faction and the most infamous example of the central role played by women in Corsican vendettas (see box on p.244).

In 1830, tension in Fozzano intensified after a quarrel outside the church culminated in three murders, with two victims coming from the

Ferries to France

Ferries depart from the Port de Commerce for Marseille and Toulon from the last week of March to the end of September. Contact the **SNCM**, quai l'Herminier, for bookings (☎04 95 76 04 36, fax 04 95 76 00 98). Ferries for: Marseille (March–May 1 weekly, June to mid-July 1 weekly, mid-July to Aug 5 weekly, Sept 4 weekly; 9hr 30min); Toulon (March–May 1 weekly, June to mid-July 1 weekly, mid-July to Aug 5 weekly, Sept 4 weekly; daytime 8hr 30min, overnight 10hr 30min). Prices for either destination start at around 256–292F, per passenger, plus another 215–615F for a car.

Carabelli clan. When, a year later, a confrontation led to the death of another Carabelli, Colomba plotted an ambush in the maquis to murder three of the enemy, but the plan backfired and her son was killed. The result of the mayhem was that Fozzano was thrown into a state of siege: houses were barricaded up and children kept from school. When **Prosper Merimée** came here in 1839, he talked to the ageing but fiercely rancorous Colomba, who had become something of a celebrity – Flaubert also paid homage to her. The Merimée novel that came out of their encounter, *Colomba*, made the gang leader famous throughout France as a youthful, cold-hearted and beautiful heroine, a character far removed from the more brutal and ugly reality.

The Mare a Mare Sud Trail

Crossing the rocky spine of the island between the Golfe de Porto-Vecchio and the Golfe de Valinco, the **Mare a Mare Sud trail** takes in the full cross-section of Corsican landscapes, from the deep-blue inlets of the coast to the pale-grey needle peaks of the Alta Rocca region, dusted for half the year in snow. Divided into five stages of between four and six hours, this hike can be attempted at any time of year, even high summer, thanks to the amount of tree cover along the route. Moreover, you rarely stray out of sight of a village, and every night halt has a good gîte d'étape, so it isn't necessary to carry more than a day's worth of food. The path is marked at regular intervals with signposts and splashes of orange paint, but you shouldn't rely solely on these: without the Parc Naturel Régional de Corse's essential **topo-guide** (see "Basics"), which contains the relevant sections of the IGN contour maps, you'll find yourself getting lost in dense maquis or wandering down dead-end game tracks, as the waymarks have faded along some stretches, and the path has become overgrown in others (notably between Loreto di Tallano and Burgo).

This is one of the most popular long-distance footpaths on the island, so if you want to avoid your fellow hikers walk it from west to east, beginning at Propriano. The trailhead is actually another 7km up the Baracci valley at **Burgo**; no buses run up this road, but if you're carrying a rucksack you shouldn't find it too hard to hitch a lift. Alternatively, walk along the road and spend the night in the gîte d'étape here (see opposite), which will allow you to get an early start the following day.

From Burgo, the trail drops down to the river through dense forest, before climbing up the other side of the valley to **Fozzano** (see p.241), where there's a small store. Rising southwest out of the village, it then veers north around the flank of Pointe de Zibo and begins the long haul up to the Punta d'Arja Vecchia pass, from where you get superb views of the interior mountains. A sharp descent via the ruined *bergeries* of Altanaria brings you out at some old quarry workings just outside the hamlet of Erbajolu. Turn left here and head up the road until you see a signpost pointing down to the Rizzanese River. Ascending steeply through lush old-growth forest, the final stretch up to **Sainte-Lucie-de-Tallano** (see p.249) is hard going, but you can break the walk at the Romanesque chapel of St-Jean-Baptiste, an account of which appears on p.249.

The second stage of this walk covers some of the most beautiful forest in the Mediterranean, between Sainte-Lucie and **Serra-di-Scopamène**. At

Fozzano's exceptionally high granite buildings and narrow streets are dominated by two towers: the fourteenth-century **Torra Vecchia**, on the left as you come from Arbellara, was the heavily fortified home of the Carabelli; **Torra Nova**, a Genoese construction built in 1548, was home to the Durazzo faction. It's possible to get inside the Torra Nova by asking for the key at the mairie in the main street, and at night the tower is dramatically lit.

At the edge of the village, south of Torra Nova, you'll find **Colomba's house** – the upstairs balcony is supposed to be where she heard the fatal gunshots far below in the maquis. Believing it to be only her enemies who had died, she gloated to the passing Durazzo

Around the Golfe de Valinco

Background on Corsica's distinctive Genoese towers appears on p.102.

the latter village is a superbly sited gîte d'étape, whose terrace looks south down the serene Rizzanese Valley. Stage three takes you up onto the Coscionu plateau (see p.256) – known by locals as *U Pianu* (The Plateau) – dominated by the summit of l'Alcudina (2136m) and by the needles of Bavella emerging to the east. Crisscrossed by numerous streams, this high, rocky basin formerly provided pasture for nomadic herders, and you'll come across several ruined *bergeries* punctuating the route to the picturesque mountain village of **Quenza**, one of the main settlements in the Alta Rocca. At this point, the trail swings south and follows a fairly level course to **Levie**, skirting the edge of the extraordinary Pianu di Levie archeological site (see p.252).

The penultimate day of the hike takes you south of Levie, through deep valleys carpeted with pine forests, to the lonely hamlet of **Carbini** (see p.253), and thence east towards the Col de Mela, reached via the hardest climb on the trail. From here, it's a gentle ascent through more old maritime pine forest around the Punta di a Vacca Morte (1314m) to the Foce Alta pass (1171m), which offers an awesome view of the Golfe de Porto-Vecchio, with the shadowy ridges of Sardinia clearly visible on the southern horizon. You can break this stage at **Cartalavonu**, an old stone herders' hamlet where there's a gîte d'étape, or continue on to **Ospédale**. Rather than complete the walk with a long zigzagging descent through the Ospédale forest, many hikers call it a day here and jump on the evening Autocars Balesi (1 daily: July & Aug Mon–Sat; Sept–June Mon & Fri only; ☎04 95 70 14 50 or 04 95 10 15 55) bus to **Porto-Vecchio**, which passes through between 6pm and 7pm.

Mare a Mare Sud gîtes d'étape

Excellent **gîtes d'étapes** mark all five stages of this walk. Dorm beds cost around 70F per night if you're cooking for yourself, and 180F for half-board. From June to September, it's essential to book ahead, especially if you require an evening meal.

Burgo (☎04 95 76 15 05).
Sainte-Lucie-de-Tallano (☎04 95 78 82 56).
Serra-di-Scapomène (☎04 95 78 64 90).
Quenza (☎04 95 78 64 05).
Levie (☎04 95 78 46 41).
Cartalavonu (☎04 95 70 00 39).

The Corsican Vendetta

Corsica has long been renowned for its **vendettas**, or blood feuds, which in the past affected nearly every family on the island, dividing dozens of villages and resulting in the kind of body counts normally reserved for civil wars. First alluded to by the Roman chronicler Diodorus Siculus, the institution probably predates the arrival in the early medieval era of the Vandals and Ostrogoths, who are most often blamed by local historians for introducing *vindetta*. The heyday of the Corsican feuds, however, was during the Genoese occupation, when an average of 900 murders were reported annually from a population of only 120,000 – a homicide rate triple that of contemporary Manhattan. Later, King Théodore tried to tackle the problem by decreeing that anyone found guilty of a vendetta killing be tortured to death and publicly quartered, while Paoli went further, executing murderers and levelling their family houses to erect special "pillars of national disgrace". Vendettas might be sparked off for all sorts of reasons, but rarely did the original offence bear much relation to the gravity of the ensuing feud. At Venzolasco in Casinca, for example, the Sanguinettis and the Paolis committed 36 murders after an argument over a chestnut tree; 14 deaths resulted from the theft of a cock in Castagniccia; and one of the most notorious and long-lasting feuds in the south was provoked by a stray donkey.

To understand how such seemingly trivial incidents could unleash years (or centuries) of violence, it's necessary to appreciate the traditional importance in Corsica of family **honour**. In close-knit peasant communities, the respect shown to members of a family depended less on its material wealth than on how closely its members adhered to unwritten codes of conduct and morality. Essential for basic survival, unsullied honour ensured the goodwill and economic cooperation of others. Without it, life could be miserable, as one individual's personal dishonour necessarily implicated his or her entire family.

The most common way of shaming a family was through its **women**, who, while they rarely committed violent acts themselves, often played a seminal role in vendettas. Rape, seduction or elopement were extreme causes, but a feud could easily result if a man merely went for a walk with a girl without the permission of her father. More often, however, vendettas were started on purpose, usually with an act of clear provocation, such as the public humiliation of a female family member outside the village church. In what became known as the **attacar**, a young woman's headscarf would be torn off while she was leaving Mass to cries of "Dishonorata!" from onlookers; this would be met with an on-the-spot stabbing or shooting.

Lost honour was not irredeemable, and could be atoned for with a revenge killing. Thus, following an *attacar*, a solemn vow to avenge the injury would be made before the assembled family. If a murder had been

"there's fresh meat for you down there", and received the retort that there was some for her, too. The tombs of Colomba and her murdered son, Francescu, are in the nearby chapel.

There's nowhere to stay up here, but Fozzano has an excellent **restaurant**, *U Pitraghju*, which serves Corsican food and pizzas, with a terrace on the hillside.

committed, the victim's shirt would be removed, smeared with blood from the wound and nailed to the wall of the house, to be left there until revenge had been exacted. Meanwhile, all windows would be boarded up – both a defensive and symbolic gesture – and the men would allow their beards and hair to grow to indicate their involvement in the feud. From this moment on, no member of either family could live in safety, for the declaration of a vendetta implicated all the relatives of any victims, from brothers and fathers to in-laws and third cousins.

Among the most emotionally persuasive means of inciting the menfolk to avenge the death was the **voceru**, an impassioned funerary rite in which close female relatives of the deceased would gather around the corpse, stretched out on the family table, to sing. While the chorus wailed and tore their hair and faces, the chief singer, or *voceratricci*, would improvise four- or six-line verses mourning the loss and stirring up vengeful zeal among the men, seated in a back room banging their gun butts in time with the dirge. Often, the *voceru* would be followed by a dance called the **caracolu**, in which the women would process around the table in darkness. And woe betide any of the men who failed to heed their wives' and daughters' call to arms. Cowards were subjected to **ribeccu** – cast out of their families and treated with looks of scorn and derision until they had settled scores with the enemy. In this way, vendettas could smoulder on indefinitely, only coming to an end if the murderer fled to the maquis to become a bandit (see box on p.246), or if a peace was brokered by the parish priest.

During the mid-nineteenth century, the Corsican vendetta excited the imagination of the French literary establishment, fuelled by a stream of lurid novels on the subject. The first of these was Balzac's *La Vendette* (1830), but it was Prosper Mérimée's phenomenally successful *Colomba*, inspired by the author's stay in the village of Fozzano (see p.241, that brought the subject to a mass reading public. Thereafter, a series of even more romanticized depictions of vendettas were penned by prominent writers – including Alexandre Dumas (*La Vendetta*; 1846) and Guy de Maupassant (*Un Bandit Corse*; 1877) – which over time actually provided role models for feuding Corsican villagers.

Officially, vendettas no longer exist in Corsica (the last one ended in a village near Ajaccio during the 1950s), but old habits die hard and family reputation and old rivalries still influence almost all major business deals, not to mention marriages and socializing in rural areas. Nationalist politics, too, have become increasingly vendetta-ridden. Reading the local press, you'll often come across the phrase *réglement de compte* ("settling of scores") to explain the politically motivated assassinations that have spiralled over the past few years. For more background on the recent upsurge in nationalist violence, see p.376.

Over the valley, some 2km away, the hamlet of **SANTA MARIA FIGANIELLA** boasts a twelfth-century church that's as pure an example of Romanesque as you'll find, with especially beautiful arcading under the roof and some fine carving on the door. The bell tower, set apart from the main body of the church, dates from a later period.

Les Bandits d'Honneur

The most romantic of all Corsican folk heroes is the bush bandit, or **bandit d'honneur**. Coined during the nineteenth century, the term was used to distinguish between common highway robbers and men who had taken to the maquis after committing a vendetta killing. Protected by impenetrable scrub and granite, these fugitives could survive for years in caves, ruins or makeshift shelters accessible only by a labyrinthine network of game trails.

The true *bandit d'honneur* never stole or murdered anyone except his sworn adversaries, and could rely on the support of local villagers in times of need. Wandering the maquis in a broad-brimmed hat, a gun slung over his shoulder and a dog at his heels, he was felt to epitomize the *âme corse*, or "Corsican soul" – the spirit of rugged defiance, pride and separateness with which islanders had traditionally regarded their colonial rulers. As such, the *bandits* were respected, and even revered: travellers, artists and famous authors would seek them out in their camps, wealthy women fell in love with them, and a spate of nineteenth-century novels romanticized their footloose lifestyles, steeped in the spirit of Jean-Jacques Rousseau's "noble savage". During a visit to the Lauretti brothers in their Fiumorbo hideout, for example, Flaubert wrote the following: "Great and valiant heart that beats alone in freedom in the woods . . . purer and nobler, no doubt, than most people in France" (quoted by Dorothy Carrington in *Granite Island*; see "Books", p.390).

While some *bandits* lived up to this ascetic ideal, many more took to drink, robbery, rape and murder, safe in the knowledge that they were

Campomoro

Isolated at the mouth of the Golfe de Valinco, **CAMPOMORO**, 17km southwest of Propriano, ranks among the most congenial seaside villages on the island. The main attraction here is the beach: 1km or so of gently curving golden sand and translucent sea, overlooked by an immense Genoese watchtower. In late July and August it's swamped by Italian families from the nearby campsites, but for the rest of the year Campomoro remains a sleepy place, with barely enough permanent residents to support a year-round post office. The village basically consists of one road, which turns left when it arrives at the beach and then runs in a curve around the bay, coming to a dead end below the promontory, which you can scale in ten or fifteen minutes to reach the **tower** (summer 9am–7pm; free), a stunning lookout point.

The rocks on the far side of the tower mark the beginning of a superb coastal walk, described in the box on *pp.248–249.*

Practicalities

You may have trouble finding a place to stay in July and August, as Campomoro possesses only two **hotels** and a couple of campsites. *Le Ressac*, about 100m behind the chapel (☎04 95 74 22 25, fax 04 95 74 23 43; ④; June–Sept), is a friendly family concern, where the rooms afford excellent views across the bay or over the olive trees beyond the reach of the *gendarmes*. In time, a new breed of outlaw emerged; one who adopted the wild life as a means to personal gratification rather than to escape the stringent ancestral code of vendetta. Playing on their reputation for ruthlessness, the new *bandits* – dubbed *bandits percepteurs*, or "tax-collecting bandits" – began to racket businesses and wealthy landowners. Far from being Corsican Robin Hoods, however, they sometimes amassed fortunes and large factions of followers, as well as widespread notoriety, and are these days regarded as the precursors of the modern Mafia.

Around the turn of the century, the atrocities committed by *bandits* such as the Bellacoscia brothers (an account of whose career appears on p.362) spurred the police to mount a sweeping crackdown. Hideouts were raided, outlaws rounded up and imprisoned and their protection rackets rumbled. Today, there are no longer any bona fide *bandits d'honneur* remaining in the Corsican maquis, but their racketeering tactics, heroic self-image and hold over the local population have become distinguishing traits of the FLNC paramilitaries, who regularly invite journalists to their hideaways in the dead of night to be photographed wearing black jumpsuits and balaclavas, brandishing automatic weapons. (For more on the FLNC, see pp.377–383).

A biography of one of the first, and most notorious, Corsican *bandits*, Théodore Poli ("Le Roi des Montagnes") appears on p.183, while the story of Muzarettu, among the only traditional *bandits d'honneur* to have lived in the postwar period, is featured in our account of Sartène on p.264.

behind; half-board (470F per head) is obligatory in peak season. *Le Campomoro*, overlooking the beach about 500m from the post office towards the tower (☎04 95 74 20 89; ⑥), is more expensive and less welcoming, but the rooms are adequate, if rather sparsely furnished. *Bar des Amis*, opposite the beach near the chapel, will also rent out rooms, but don't expect luxury (③–④). The more appealing of the two **campsites** in the village is *Camping Peretto Les Roseaux*, 300m from the post office in the direction of the tower (☎04 95 74 20 52; May–Oct); it's fairly basic, but a lot more peaceful than the other, which lies left of the road as you enter the village.

During the day there's a **snack bar** set up on the beach, where you can get the usual fast food as well as fresh salads and local charcuterie. By far the most popular lunchtime venue is *La Mouette*, opposite the church, which serves a selection of filling salads for around 50F, plus fresh fish from the gulf and local wild boar (when available). Their busy terrace makes the most of its situation overlooking the bay, and towards the end of the day fills up with boules players and spectators. For an evening meal, your best bet is *Le Ressac*'s excellent and rather pricy **restaurant**, whose superb bouillabaisse contains six or more different kinds of seafood. If you're on a tighter budget, try the pizzeria on the beach (open July & Aug only), which also serves fresh fish. Campomoro has two food **shops**: one is about five minutes' walk from the post office towards the tower (summer daily till 8pm); the other is behind the chapel (on your right as you arrive at the beach on the road) and has more erratic opening hours, though if it's shut you can ask to be served through the adjacent bar.

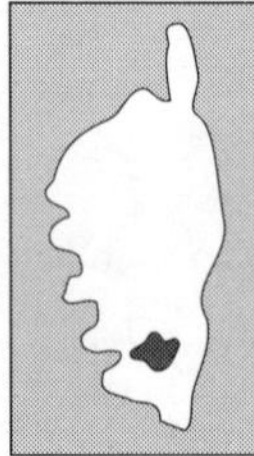

Alta Rocca and Bavella

A region of evocative prehistoric sites, delightful villages and stark mountain peaks, **Alta Rocca** also contains some of the most fertile parts of Corsica – **Vallée du Rizzanese**, in the south of the region, is cultivated with orchards and the most prolific vineyards on the island. In the upper part of the Rizzanese Valley the highlight is **Sainte-Lucie-de-Tallano**, an outstandingly attractive village, while high in the valley of the Fiumiccicoli tributary lies **Levie**, where you can clamber over a Bronze Age settlement and medieval castle. Many of the Alta Rocca villages have hotels, with the majority concentrated at **Zonza**, thanks to its proximity to the magnificent **Bavella**, whose granite needles and dense forests form one of the most celebrated Corsican landscapes.

If you're approaching Alta Rocca from Propriano, you can either follow the D19/119/69 from the village up to **Aullène**, or head south from Propriano along the N196, then turn onto the D69, which switches to the west bank of the Rizzanese River, leaving the D268 to continue to Sainte-Lucie. The approach from the other side of Corsica, via the Ospédale route, is covered on p.293. Two **buses** run

The Campomoro to Capu di Senetosa Coastal Hike

South of Campomoro stretches one of the wildest coastlines in Corsica: a windswept, sun-baked expanse of gently undulating maquis fringed by outlandish rock formations and empty pebble beaches. The absence of a road into the area, nowadays officially protected as a regional nature reserve, means the only way to explore it is on foot, though there exist enough 4WD tracks to make it accessible to intrepid mountain-bikers. This is also a stronghold of the Corsican *sanglier*, or wild boar, and a tangle of cartridge-strewn hunters' trails crisscrosses the deserted sea-facing slopes. Hikers, however, should stick to the recently inaugurated **coastal path**, which begins below the Campomoro watchtower and winds south through a string of flotsam-covered coves to Capo di Senetosa, crowned with a much-photographed Genoese tower. Before attempting this route, get hold of a copy of the area IGN **map**, without which you'll find it hard to judge distances between headlands.

The path, waymarked with splashes of paint and the occasional sign or cairn, is easy to follow for the first eighty minutes or so, as it threads through a series of dramatic granite outcrops eroded into phantasmagorical shapes. But once you've hit the **Anse d'Eccica**, an idyllic bottlenecked cove backed by a sheltered white-sand beach, the going gets markedly tougher. To pick up the trail again, head along the stream bed to this region: running year round Autocars Ricci's service from Ajaccio (1–2 daily; ☎04 95 51 08 19), goes as far as Bavella, via Sainte-Lucie, Levie and Zonza; while Baléssi's Évasion bus traverses the region en route to Porto-Vecchio (1 daily: July–Aug Mon–Sat; Sept–June Mon & Fri; ☎04 95 70 14 50).

Sainte-Lucie-de-Tallano

Perched high above the Vallée du Rizzanese, the exquisite village of **SAINTE-LUCIE-DE-TALLANO** has been wealthy since Rinuccio della Rocca made it his stronghold. An eminent patron of the arts as well as a fearsome warlord, Rinuccio donated many works of art to the parish church in between his desperate attempts to oust the Genoese in the first decade of the sixteenth century. Graceful balconied houses remain as a legacy of the illustrious families who once resided here, while the prosperity of many present-day residents is attested by the Mercedes lined up in the square. Some of the money comes from gangsterism, but there are two more legitimate sources of income: locally produced **Fiumiccicoli** wine, and an extremely rare rock called *diorite orbiculaire* – a greyish-blue stone with concentric rings of black and white, like a leopard pelt – which is quarried close by.

A wide street sweeps through the village in a loop, widening out in the centre to form **place des Monuments-aux-Morts**, whose terrace gives a glorious view of vineyards and verdant hills that is interrupted by the prominent red roof of **Chapelle St-Jean-Baptiste**, a few

that winds inland for around 200m until you reach a cairn, to the right of which lies a breach in a dry-stone wall. Beyond it, a hunters' trail plunges through dense maquis, climbing to a low pass over the ridge of the headland, and dropping down the other side to **Cala di Feru** and **Cala di Conca**, a secluded cove where *sanglier* hunters have cobbled together tables, chairs and bivouac sites from driftwood. Ten to fifteen minutes directly inland along the stream bed from the beach, a perennial **spring**, encased in stone and cement under an oak tree, provides a dependable source of water.

From Cala di Conca onwards, you need confidence and determination to make any progress, as the path gets mixed up with game trails at several points, forcing you onto the rocks at the shoreline. Once past the **Senetosa tower**, whose green lighthouse is still manned by two keepers, you're obliged to rock-hop for much of the way at sea level.

It's definitely possible to walk the whole 20km stretch from Campomoro to **Tizzano**, but allow a full day, and take plenty of food and water. As there is very little shade along the route, sunstroke can be a problem, so wear something on your head and rest often if you attempt this hike in hot weather. Note, too, that you can **camp** wild between the Punta d'Eccica and Capu di Senetosa, splitting the route into two more manageable stages.

kilometres to the south. Reached via a twenty-minute walk along the waymarked Mare a Mare Sud trail (follow the signposts for Fozzano), the floor of the monument, now used as a cattle shed, incorporates the local **diorite**, though it's hard to pick any out under the layer of straw and cow dung. Portable pieces of this strange stone can be bought for about 50F from Mme Françoise Renucci, just down the road from the *Hôtel Léandri* (look for the sign "pierre corse" outside her house), whose family own the only diorite mine in the area. It was closed fifteen or so years ago, but before sealing the shaft, Mme Renucci extracted four final tonnes of rock that she now keeps in a cellar, chipping chunks off from time to time to sell to tourists.

The anonymous **Église Paroissiale** has precursors going back to Roman times, but was rebuilt many times until its seventeenth-century Baroque incarnation that you see today. Inside, there's a marble font in the form of a hand, dating from the 1490s and bearing the della Rocca arms, but the real treasure is the finely worked marble bas-relief of the *Virgin and Child*, commissioned by Rinuccio della Rocca in 1498 – it's attached to a column, on the left inside the church entrance. The church's late fifteenth-century *Crucifixion*, attributed to the Catalan painter known as the Master of Castel Sardo, is now locked away in the mairie next door, where you can ask to see it.

Behind the church stands the **Maison Forte**, a huge, impenetrable, grey granite house built to shelter the population in times of danger. For a view of the village you could walk north for five minutes to the **Couvent St-François**, founded by Rinuccio in 1492 and set squarely on a plateau overlooking the valley. Another good **walk** takes you along the route of the Mare a Mare Sud footpath, which cuts between switchbacks in the road from the village centre to the hamlet of Altagène; from here, a motorable track hugs the shoulder of the hillside, bending northeast as it enters a dense and beautiful evergreen oak forest sliced by babbling streams. You can follow this easy trail through the woods for kilometres, but most people turn back as it begins the steep climb up to the **Col de Tarava** (reached after 2hr 30min; allow 4hr for the return trip to the pass, and take plenty of water with you).

Practicalities

Autocars Ricci's bus calls at Sainte-Lucie en route between Ajaccio and Porto-Vecchio, via Bavella, Zonza, Levie and Propriano (1–2 daily; ☎04 95 51 08 19). Tourist offices in the region have timetables for you to consult.

The village sees few overnight visitors and has just two places to **stay**, one of which is the attractively converted gîte d'étape *U Fragnonu*, on the north edge of the village (☎04 95 78 82 56 or 04 95 78 80 54; 70F per night, or 120F half-board), which serves copious, traditional and wholesome food. The other accommodation option is the *Léandri*, on the main street south of place des Monuments-aux-Morts (☎04 95 78 80 82; ③). This place is a creakingly old establishment trapped in a dilapidated time warp, with family portraits on the walls and old furniture in its three simple rooms; nothing at the front of the building suggests it's a hotel, except a handful of tatty green café tables.

For a **meal**, try the *Pizzeria Santa Lucia*, next to the monument, which turns out run-of-the-mill pizzas, salads and local cheeses, and whose terrace is the best place to watch the *pétanque* players next to the fountain. The streetside tables outside the village **bar**, the *Ortini*, provide another good vantage point from which to follow the comings and goings in the square, plus they serve fresh croissants and *pains au chocolat* for breakfast.

Levie

In the eighteenth century, **LEVIE** (Livia) was the capital of Alta Rocca, its Genoese families prospering from the fertile countryside and presiding over a village more populous than Sartène. Today the village is rather dour, its main attraction being the proximity of the **Pianu di Levie** (see p.252), whose prehistoric sites provide much of the substance of the **musée départementale** (July & Aug daily 10am–6pm; Sept–June Mon–Sat 10am–noon & 2–4.30pm; 10F), underneath the mairie off the main street. The star exhibit is the so-called *Dame de Bonifacio*, a human skeleton discovered near Bonifacio and dated around 6570 BC, making this the oldest found in Corsica. The remains are those of a woman in her mid-thirties whose legs were badly crippled by old fractures; to have lived to such an age, she must have been cared for by her community. The other noteworthy artefact on display here is a beautiful ivory statue of Christ by a pupil of Donatello, given to Levie in the 1580s by Pope Sixtus V.

Practicalities

In the summer, a small **tourist office** operates in the centre of the village on rue Sorba (July & Aug Mon–Fri 9am–noon & 3–6pm; ☎04 95 78 41 95). The most pleasant place to **stay** hereabouts is the small B&B-style guesthouse run by Annie de Peretti, above *Le Gourmet* restaurant at the entrance to the village (☎04 95 78 41 61; ③; open all year). As well as the simple rooms (with or without en-suite bathrooms), they have more expensive studios with kitchenettes to let. Walkers, however, usually head for the gîte d'étape, below the village centre beyond the gendarmerie (☎04 95 78 46 41; 65F per night); run by the local municipality, it's an untypically charmless place serving mediocre food.

You'll eat a lot better at the moderately priced *La Pergola* **restaurant** opposite the museum, which serves plain home cooking and will make charcuterie sandwiches on request. There's also a decent pizzeria, *Sorba*, on the main street, serving the usual range of inexpensive wood-baked pizzas from 40F plus plenty of salads. Lovers of quality regional cuisine, however, should note that one of the island's finest gourmet restaurants, *A Pignata* (☎04 95 78 41 90), lies close to Levie. Among the best-kept secrets of Corsican gastronomy, it's hidden deep in serene countryside near Cucuruzzu, 5km west. To find it, head 3km out of the village on the Sainte-Lucie road, turning right at the signpost for the Pianu de Levie archeological site. Roughly 1.5km further on the left you'll see a narrow, unsignposted lane marked by a couple of large rubbish bins; a short way up the lane lies the gateway to the auberge. They serve a single set menu, reasonably priced at 170F (plus wine), and the food is refreshingly unpretentious, with everything straight from the garden and prepared on the premises. Advance reservation is essential, especially if you want to stay in one of their very pleasant **rooms**, which are rented out on a half-board basis (a very reasonable 330F per head for bed, breakfast and evening meal).

The Pianu di Levie

The most interesting prehistoric site on Corsica after Filitosa, the **Pianu di Levie** (daily: July–Aug 9.30am–8pm; April–June & Sept–Oct 9.30am–7pm; 28F), is reached by taking the signposted road off the D268, 3km west of Levie. A further 4km will bring you to a field where you can park and buy your ticket – you get a ninety-minute cassette-guided tour of the site for no extra charge.

A fifteen-minute walk through a Tolkienesque tract of gnarled old oak trees brings you to the **Casteddu di Cucuruzzu**, the remains of a Torréen habitation dating from 1400 BC. Emerging from the forest and integrated into the chaos of eroded, moss-covered granite boulders, this is the best example of a *casteddu* in Corsica. The complex, dominated by a circular *torre* and surrounded by a thick high wall, was inhabited by Bronze Age artisans and farmers, who lived in the chambers surrounding the *torre* and in dry-stone shacks close by. The *casteddu* is entered by a steep and narrow stairway. Storerooms are ranged on the right, opposite a series of chambers with openings above to let the light in and the smoke out. Straight ahead, the *torre* has retained its vaulted roof of wide granite slabs, below which stones jutting out sideways from the walls suggest the existence of another floor. Stone tools, bronze belt links and domestic utensils, found in the course of excavations here, all point to the tower's having a functional rather than religious purpose. From the top you get a magnificent panoramic view of the region, from the needles of Bavella to the gulf of Propriano.

For more on the Torréens and their enigmatic towers, see p.232.

Another twenty minutes through the woods brings you to **Capula**, a site occupied from the Bronze Age until 1259, when its so-called **castle**, an impressive circular monument, was partly destroyed. Just below the entrance stands a headless menhir; other pieces of

Bronze and Iron Age stonework are incorporated into the monument, mixed with hundreds of small granite bricks from the medieval period. About 200m beyond the castle stands **Chapelle San Lorenzu**, a tiny thirteenth-century Romanesque building extensively restored this century.

Carbini

South of Levie, the D59 runs 8km through a twisting valley to **CARBINI**, whose isolated bell tower heads a straight road lined with lime trees and low cottages. Adjacent to the tower, which is all that remains of the Église St-Quilico, stands **San Giovanni**, built in the first half of the twelfth century and decorated with elegant early Romanesque arcading. In 1354, in the aftermath of the Black Death, this stately building saw the birth of a sect called the **Giovannali**, a bizarre Franciscan offshoot whose religious meetings were rumoured to end with orgies – their doctrine of the equal division of property extended to the sharing of wives as well as all worldly goods. Despite persecution, the Giovannali spread throughout the east of Corsica until, in 1362, Urban V dispatched an expedition that resulted in the massacre of a hundred people here. The village then had to be repopulated by families from Sartène.

Carbini does not have anywhere to stay or eat, nor even a café; the only facility for visitors is a small tap dispensing spring water – a welcome sight for hikers ambling through on the Mare a Mare Sud trail.

Aullène and around

Lush vegetation characterizes the region around the dispersed village of **AULLÈNE** (Auddé), 40km northeast of Sartène, whose inhabitants relied for centuries on the surrounding chestnut woods for survival. Set midway between the east and west coasts, at a crossroads of four main inland routes, the village makes a scenic place to stop. Its long-established *Hôtel de la Poste* **hotel**, rue Principal (☎ & fax 04 95 78 61 21; ②–③; May–Oct), is an old stone building fronted by lime trees, with sweeping views over the village rooftops. The rooms are modest but comfortable (some have shared toilets on the corridor), and very good value. Downstairs, a cosy restaurant, occupying a terrace that makes the most of the view offers two set menus (95F and 125F), both featuring superb local charcuterie, pork dishes and other mountain specialities, including home-made chestnut flour desserts.

If you're just passing through, pause at the seventeenth-century **church**, whose wood-carved pulpit is supported by twisting sea monsters emerging from a Moor's head. Ask at the reception of *Hôtel de la Poste* for the key.

West to Petreto-Bicchisano

Striking **west from Aullène** along the D420, a looping road rises through a spectacular rocky landscape, with enormous boulders dominating the road as far as the **Col de la Tana** (975m), situated some 7km along. Beyond this pass, a high narrow road hugs the mountainside above a belt of pinewood, overshadowed by the pink granite bulk of the Punta di Taccaluccjia. At the **Col de St-Eustache** (995m), a further 3km, the view extends north over the mountains to the Vallée du Taravo, its mass of greenery swamping the slopes.

A further 10km will bring you to **PETRETO-BICCHISANO**, an imposing sixteenth-century village overlooking the main Ajaccio–Propriano–Porto-Vecchio road (the N196). The church at Petreto is worth a look for its wooden statues representing St Francis of Assisi, St Claire and the Immaculate Conception.

East to Quenza

At the head of the Rizzanese valley, two charming hill villages straddle the main road midway between Aullène and Quenza, covered by Autocars Ricci's bus (Mon–Sat 1–2 daily; ☎04 95 51 08 19 or 04 95 76 25 59) but visited by surprisingly few outsiders. Hikers following the Mare a Mare Sud trail make up the majority of visitors to the first, **SERRA-DI-SCAPOMENA**, whose excellent gîte d'étape (☎04 95 78 64 90 or 04 95 78 60 13) enjoys glorious views across the pale-blue Bavella, Zonza and Ospédale massifs. If you are driving, a small car park in the middle of the village, with an equally dramatic panorama, makes a great picnic stop.

You can also **camp** here at the *Camping de l'Alta Rocca* (☎04 95 78 62 01; June 15–Sept 15), a rambling two-star site tucked away above the village under a chestnut wood; a stone's throw from the footpath to the Coscione plateau, it makes a great base for day-walks in the area.

The next village along the main road, **SORBOLLANO** marks the start of a spectacular, but rarely travelled, back route down the hidden **Rau di Codi valley**, a tributary of the Rizzanese. Twisting around a sharp spur, it veers north through dense woodland to cross the stream at Ponte de la Nova, where it switches south again. A short way beyond the bridge, at the hamlet of **Campu**, a Parc Naturel Régional signpost on the left of the road, marked "Santa Lucia", points the way to an idyllic **bathing place** at the confluence of two boulder-choked streams, a gentle ten-minute walk from the road. You'll know you've arrived when the path emerges from the woods at a dizzying footbridge across the river, underneath which a small coarse-sand beach makes a picturesque **picnic spot**.

Quenza and around

Set on a granite eminence smothered in pines and chestnut groves with Bavella as a spiky backdrop, **QUENZA** (13km east of Aullène,

An Alta Rocca Round-Walk: Quenza–Zonza–Quenza

A circular walk from **Quenza to Zonza** via the St-Antoine River bridge is a relatively easy, but hugely rewarding, hike (about 4hr 15min) offering glimpses of the mountains and opportunities for swimming in the crystal-clear rivers along the way. Don't attempt this route without a map, as the area is riddled with other trails confusingly marked with the same-coloured orange paint. Failing an IGN map of the region or a copy of the Parc Naturel Régional's topo-guide, try to get hold of the *Balades en Corse: Alta Rocca* leaflet from any tourist office, which has a black-and-white contour map of the area with the route marked on it.

The path begins about 600m from Quenza's eastern exit, signposted to the right. Dropping gently down through deciduous woodland, it crosses the **Rizzanese River** and steadily climbs the opposite side of the valley to meet the **D420**. Follow this into **Zonza** (1hr 45min); the onward trail is indicated 400m south of the village with a post marked "Quenza", on the right-hand side of the main road to Levie (D268). After crossing fairly level, open farmland, it enters the trees and zigzags sharply down, crossing onto the left (south) bank of the **de Rian stream**, which it follows through the woods for around forty minutes to rejoin the **St-Antoine River** (3hr). Once on the other side, you climb steeply through more beautiful oak and chestnut forest until the path runs alongside the tall fences of a **deer enclosure**. Deer were hunted out in Corsica by 1970, but have been reintroduced on the island from this fifty-acre farm, which releases five or six fawns into the woods each year. After following a motorable dirt track for 1km, bear left at the signpost for Quenza, reached after a gradual, hour-long ascent through broken plantations and grassy fields.

has a spectacular location and a fine Romanesque church, **Santa Maria**, which stands at the entrance to the village. Dating from 1000, it's built on a single-nave plan with a rounded apse, and retains some traces of its original frescoes. The church next door boasts a wooden pulpit supported by a couple of dragons and a Moorish head, as well as a curious fifteenth-century multicoloured wooden panel of the Virgin and Child, in a chapel to the left of the altar.

Lying within easy reach of Bavella and the Coscione plateau, Quenza is also a prime destination for **outdoor pursuits** enthusiasts. Corsica's most renowned mountaineer, the distinctively bearded Jean-Paul Quilicci, lives here. Dubbed "L'Homme de Bavella" because of his unrivalled knowledge of the local peaks, he leads **guided walks** into mountains during the summer (for more details, call ☎04 95 78 64 33).

Practicalities

Quenza lies along the route of Autocars Ricci's Ajaccio–Porto-Vecchio bus, which passes through daily in both directions. The village's only **hotel**, the *Sole e Monti*, is just past the centre along the road to Zonza (☎04 95 78 62 53, fax 04 95 78 63 88; half-board obligatory 450F per head). It's a large, recently converted granite building, with good food served in the small triangular garden out the front; non-residents can eat here for around 150F. Hikers passing through on the Mare a Mare Sud, however, tend to hole up in the more modest gîte d'étape, *I Muntagnoli Corsi* (☎04 95 78 64 05), which has an adjacent **campsite**. Located 1km north of the village at the end of an appallingly rutted dirt track, the gîte enjoys stunning views and has a congenial common room with easy chairs and a guitar.

To explore the country surrounding Quenza on **horseback**, contact Pierrot Milanini's stables (☎04 95 78 63 21 or 04 95 78 61 09), in the nearby village of **Jalicu**, 5km northwest. A day's pony trekking will set you back a steep 650F, but the horses are well looked after, and the landscape's superb. The Milaninis also run an independent **gîte**: a combination of budget dormitory accommodation and classy half-board cooking for the excellent all-in price of 200F per head.

The Plateau de Coscione

The **Plateau de Coscione**, known as *U Pianu* (The Tableland) in Corscian, is the rugged roadless region north of Quenza, west of the mighty Monte Incudine Massif (2136m). For centuries, this wilderness of rolling grassland and bog, which remains well watered throughout the summer by thousands of mountain streams, provided rich grazing for the pastoralist communities of the coast, who used to drive their immense flocks of sheep and goats up here each year after the spring snow melt. Between June and September, up to seven hundred men and their animals would live here in seasonal settlements of ramshackle stone huts. With the demise of transhumance, however, Coscione became a total backwater. Nowadays, barely a handful of shepherds follow in their forebears' footsteps, and those that do drive their animals up here in trucks for the summer, leaving them to their own devices until the autumn.

The rutted 4WD tracks used by today's shepherds and cattle rearers crisscross Coscione from north to south, but to experience the region properly you'll have to leave your car behind and set out on foot. Comprising areas of lumpy green marshland where mist and cloud frequently sweep in from the surrounding granite ridges, the landscape of the plateau will feel oddly familiar to British visitors. This is somewhere you'll want to walk more for the atmosphere than the views, although approaching the region via the GR20, which traverses Coscione en route between Zicavo and Bavella, affords some fine panoramas of the interior mountains and Alta Rocca. Probably the easiest way to get a quick taste of the plateau is to drive in **from Quenza**. A narrow single-track lane winds north along the west side of an otherwise roadless valley, around the flanks of Punta Grossa to a deserted outdoor pursuits complex that was built in the 1980s as a service centre for skiers; in winter, Coscione's undulating hills can be carpeted in deep snow for months – ideal for *ski de fond* (cross-country skiing). From the car park, you can set off on foot to follow a clearly defined jeep track into the heart of the plateau.

For a detailed description of the northern approach to the Coscione Plateau, via the village of Zicavo and the Mount Incudine path, see p.360.

Zonza

Set against the snow-dusted needles of the Bavella massif, **ZONZA** looks like something off the top of a chocolate box, and its prominence on postcard racks and brochure covers ensures that this picturesque granite village is transformed during summer by the annual influx of tourists – hikers, climbers and horse riders, as well as a steady stream of motorists and backpackers. Its most illustrious visitors, however, were probably Muhammed V, Sultan of Morocco, and his son, who turned up here with three limousines in October 1952 after the family had been deposed in a coup d'état. The French Ministry of the Interior had requisitioned the village's now-defunct *Mouflon d'Or* hotel to accommodate the royals during their two-year exile. But the winter snow and rain got the better of them, and after only five months the sultan demanded that the government find him a place on the coast. Another hotel was subsequently requisitioned: the palatial *Napoléon Bonaparte* in L'Île Rousse.

Situated within easy striking distance of the most dramatic mountain scenery in the south, Zonza is well placed to use as a base for day-walks in the Alta Rocca. It's also easy to reach by public transport, with daily bus connections to Porto-Vecchio, Ajaccio and other villages in the area.

Practicalities

Three scheduled **bus** services pass through Zonza during the summer. Autocars Ricci's coaches (☎04 95 51 08 19 or 04 95 76 25 59) leave from Ajaccio's terminal routière mid-afternoon via Propriano, Sainte-Lucie-de-Tallano and Levie, arriving here three hours later and returning early the next morning. From Porto-Vecchio Balési Évasion's daily minibus (☎04 95 70 15 55) leaves at 7am, and pulls in here an hour later en route to Ajaccio via Quenza and Aullène. Coming in the other direction, this service departs Ajaccio at 4pm, arriving in the village at around 6.15pm. Zonza's tiny **tourist office** (Mon–Fri 8am–noon & 1.30–5pm), just below the crossroads at the centre of the village (behind the war memorial), sells maps, topoguides and leaflets for the Alta Rocca walk described on p.255.

A cluster of **hotels**, all with more than decent **restaurants**, stand a stone's throw away from the centre. Pick of the bunch has to be the long-established *L'Aiglon*, in the village centre on the main road (☎04 95 78 67 79, fax 04 95 78 63 62; ③–④; April–Dec), which has comfortable, tastefully furnished rooms and a wonderful restaurant on the ground floor where you can sample classy local cuisine such as *fettuccini al brocciu* and smoked salmon, or melt-in-the-mouth kid stew, rounded off with cakes baked from chestnut flour. A slap-up à la carte meal here should cost you a little over 150F per head, plus wine, and they have a couple of less expensive fixed menus and dishes of the day to choose from. Roughly in the same price range is *Le Tourisme*, north of the village, set back on the west side of the Quenza road (☎04 95 78 67 72, fax 04 95 78 73 23; ④). Their pricier rooms have fine views over the valley, but the smaller, less expensive options are comfortable enough, if a little dark; and the restaurant is renowned throughout this area. Otherwise, there's the pleasantly old-fashioned *L'Incudine*, at the entrance to the village if you're coming from Ospédale (☎04 95 78 67 71; ④); affiliated to the Logis de France chain, it offers good value for money, with cosy en-suite rooms and a busy restaurant serving mountain charcuterie, cheeses and local game in season. The old-established *De la Terrasse*, just above the crossroads (☎04 95 78 67 69, fax 04 95 78 73 50; ⑤; April–Oct), is another comfortable option, with fine views from its popular restaurant terrace.

Zonza has two **campsites**. The nearest, *U Fuconu*, 1.5km out of the village centre, occupies a secluded spot just off the Quenza road. In addition to great views of the Aiguilles looming above the tree line, it has a pleasant on-site pizzeria. Set in a pine wood 4km out of the village on the D368, the main Ospédale/Porto-Vecchio road, is the somewhat less appealing *camping municipal* (☎04 95 78 62 74), which lays on complimentary minibuses for backpackers.

The route de Bavella

The D268 north from Zonza, known as the **route de Bavella**, is perhaps the most dramatic road in all Corsica. From Zonza it penetrates a dense expanse of pine and chestnut trees as it rises steadily to the **Col de Bavella** (1218m), marked by a towering statue of Notre-Dame-des-Neiges. An amazing panorama of peaks and forests surrounds the col: to the northwest the serrated granite ridge of the Cirque de Gio Agostino is dwarfed by the pinnacles of the **Aiguilles de Bavella**; behind soars Monte Incudine; and the east is dominated by the ruddy shades of Punta Tafonata and the distant sea.

The hamlet of **BAVELLA** itself, 9km northeast of Zonza, is a cluster of neatly painted tin- and stone-roofed huts and chalets just below the col, was built in the early nineteenth century for the inhabitants of the Conca commune, who were granted the land by Napoléon III as a refuge from the suffocating summer heat of the lowland. It's a lonely spot, especially in winter, but the proximity of the mountains and long-distance trails (the GR20 makes one of its rare descents to road level here) makes this is an ideal place to locate yourself for **hikes** in the area (see box). The *Auberge du Col* (☎04 95 57 43 87; April–Oct) offers clean and comfortable dormitory accommodation (70F per bed), with the option of good-

Walks from the Auberge du Col

A very enjoyable two-hour walk from the *Auberge du Col* in Bavella goes to the **Trou de la Bombe**, a circular opening that pierces the Paliri crest of peaks, between Punta Velaco (1483m) and Calanca Murata (1407m). From the auberge, follow the GR20 for 800m, then take the first path to the right, signposted "Trou de la Bombe". The track rises through a wood as far as a ridge, then drops gradually before beginning a short climb to the hole, which emerges to the right. Those with a head for heights should climb right into the hole for the dizzying view down the sheer 500m cliff on the other side.

Even more amazing views may be had from the summit of the adjacent peak, **Calanca Murata**, which you can scale after a steep, but technically straightforward haul from the head of the ravine just below Trou de la Bombe. Cairns mark the route, which threads its way up a sheer gulley immediately north of the main path, lined by gnarled pine trees. After ten minutes you emerge at a large natural balcony that makes a perfect **picnic place**. The pull to the top of the mountain through a narrowing chimney takes thirty to forty minutes. At no stage do you need to climb, and the views, which take in the entire Bavella massif to the west and a huge sweep of the eastern plains, are on a par with those from any of the island's major peaks.

value half-board (170F per person) in their restaurant, where you can tuck into groaning plates of local charcuterie and cheese on a sunny terrace.

From the auberge, it's a steep descent through what's left of the **Forêt de Bavella**, which suffered a devastating fire in 1960 but still boasts some huge Laricio pines. About 10km from the pass you'll come to the **Col de Larone** (608m), offering stunning vistas of the mountains and the **Forêt de Tova** in the north. Vast cliffs and rock falls tower on all sides as the road winds through a landscape reminiscent of the American Wild West, with dizzying drops to the River Solenzara full of smooth white rocks and turquoise pools. Towards the bottom of the gorge, you can pull over in several places for a dip.

The Sartenais

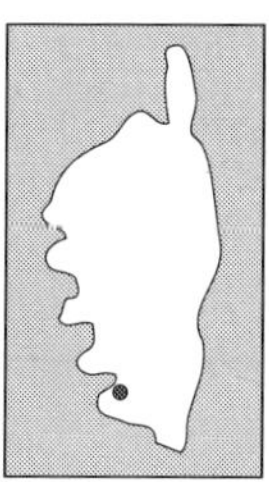

The wild and windswept **Sartenais**, in Corsica's far southwest, is the tract of dense maquis fanning seawards from of the district's main town, **Sartène**, which the French novelist Prosper Mérimée famously dubbed "la plus corse des villes corses" (the most Corsican Corsican town), famous for its feuds and austere, buttress-bottomed houses. Scattered with **standing-stone sites** and ghoulish rock formations, this is a region rich in folklore, much of it fragmented transmissions from ancient times, when the weird granite outcrops looming above the scrubland sheltered communities of hunter-gatherers and, later, Neolithic farmers. The settlements retained a healthy population until Saracen pirates made off with most of their inhabitants in the fifteenth and seventeenth centuries. Since then, the area has remained depopulated and desolate, save for the odd vineyard.

The writings of Dorothy Carrington did much to fix popular impressions of the Sartenais as a mysterious and somewhat forbidding corner of the island. Many of her most valuable informants – traditional healers, bards and *mazzeri* ("dream hunters"; see p.271) – were old folk from the region's most remote villages. Life has moved on since Lady Carrington first travelled here in the late 1940s, but this remains an area with a peculiarly loaded atmosphere, heightened by the shadowy forms that emerge from the rocks around sunset time. Crossed by comparatively few roads, it is also one of the least developed parts of Corsica. You can literally for walk for days along the Sartenais coast, between Tizzano and Campomoro, and not see a single inhabited building.

Public transport is frequent on the main road between Sartène and Bonifacio/Porto-Vecchio, but to reach the most interesting and atmospheric parts of the Sartenais you'll need your own vehicle, mountain bike or, best of all, sturdy walking boots.

Sartène

A "town peopled by demons" is how German chronicler Gregorovius described **SARTÈNE** (Sartè) in the nineteenth century, and the town hasn't shaken off its hostile image. Located near the coast and therefore vulnerable to foreign invaders, it was persistently attacked by pirates in the Middle Ages, and from the twelfth to the sixteenth centuries became the seat of the ferocious **Sgio** (from *signori*), feudal lords who preferred to implement justice without interference from the island's rulers and thus turned Sartène into an asylum for refugees from the law of the state. A bloody **vendetta** in the nineteenth century sealed the town's reputation and left a legacy of tall, grim fortress houses. An insular outlook continues to this day, and outsiders can be put off by the implacable ambience of the place, and by the heavy presence of gun-toting *chasseurs* (hunters). On the other hand it's a smarter, better-groomed town than most in Corsica, with a perfectly preserved medieval heart that's blissfully free of ferroconcrete. One of the main reasons for this is the communist mayor, who has passed laws banning unsightly buildings, neon signs, and even overhead cables. Another is the money brought in from the Sartène **wine** – the best on the island.

Despite its turbulent history, the town doesn't offer many diversions once you've explored the enclosed **vieille ville** and paid a visit to the **Musée de la Préhistoire Corse**. The only time of year Sartène teems with tourists is at Easter for **U Catenacciu**, its highly charged Good Friday procession (see p.266).

A brief history of Sartène

The Sartenais

Sartène was formed when, in the tenth century, the inhabitants of this region's agglomeration of hamlets were forced to congregate in one place by Saracen raids. In the twelfth century the **della Rocca** family held sway over the area with the consent of its Pisan governors, but when the Genoese took over in the thirteenth century, Sartène became a centre of discontent. The laws giving Genoa a monopoly on Corsica's trade were anathema to the local nobility, the **Sgio**, who continued to resist the Genoese until the final stand of Rinuccio della Rocca, defeated after a long struggle in 1502.

It was not until early in the sixteenth century that Sartène became a Genoese administrative centre, and even then their tenure was deeply troubled. In 1565 Sampiero Corso's army destroyed the town after a 35-day siege, then the Genoese took it back, only to lose it again in 1583 to **Hassan Pasha**, the mad king of Algiers, who ransacked the town and abducted four hundred of its inhabitants, a third of the population. Thereafter Sartène remained faithful to Genoa, so much so that Paoli had a struggle to win Sartène to his cause in the fight for a Corsican republic.

The nineteenth century saw the re-emergence of the Sgio: recognized as members of the nobility by the French monarchy, these powerful aristocrats prospered under privileges granted by

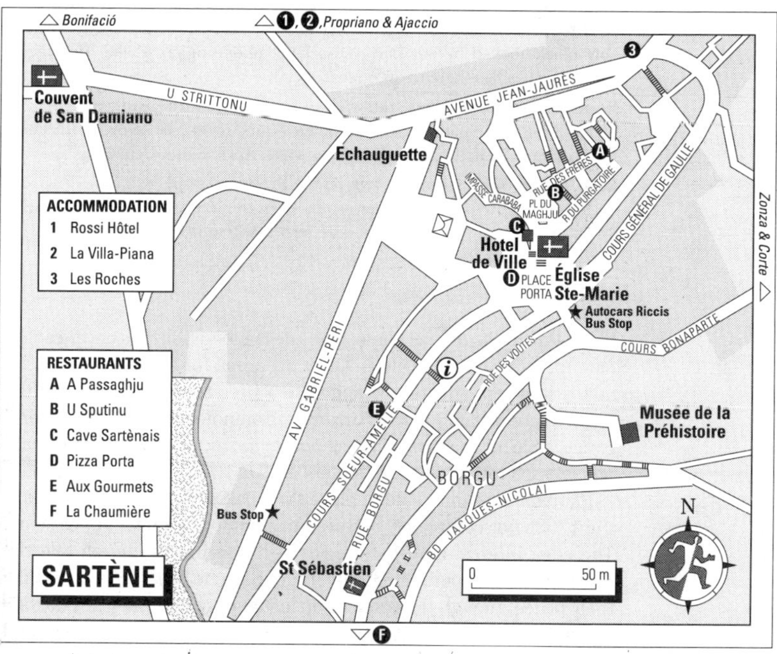

Napoléon III; and, whereas other parts of Corsica suffered depopulation and decline, the Sgio oversaw the development of a wine industry that still underpins the local economy. Today, as the *sous-préfecture* of southern Corsica – France's second-largest *commune* – Sartène is the most important town in the region after Ajaccio.

Arrival and information

If you're arriving in Sartène by **bus** you'll either be dropped at the top of avenue Gabriel-Péri (Eurocorse Voyages) or in the main square (Autocars Ricci). The **tourist office** is on rue Borgu (summer Mon–Fri 9am–noon & 2.30–6pm; ☎04 95 77 15 40), and can help you find accommodation in the area if the hotels listed below are full – only likely during U Catenacciu.

Accommodation

The nearest **campsite** to Sartène is the three-star *Camping Olva* (*Les Eucalyptus*), 5km out of town towards Castagna on the D69 (☎04 95 77 11 58, fax 04 95 77 05 68; May–Oct). Travellers without their own vehicle can telephone for a courtesy *navette* from the bus stop. Drivers are advised to park in cours Général-de-Gaulle or outside the Super U supermarket at the bottom of cours Sœur-Amélie, and walk up into town.

Les Roches, av Jean-Jaurès (☎04 95 77 07 61, fax 04 95 11 19 93). A large, family-run hotel on the edge of the old town, most of whose well-appointed en-suite rooms command panoramic views of the Vallée du Rizzanese. It's invariably block-booked by bus parties, so book phone or fax ahead. Half-board (680F per head) obligatory in August. ⑤.

Rossi Hôtel (Fior di Riba), 1km west of town on the Propriano road (☎04 95 77 01 80). Plain, modern place next to *La Villa-Piana* (see below), with smart rooms and furnished studios for longer stays. April to mid-Oct. ⑥.

La Villa-Piana, 1km west of town on the Propriano road (☎04 95 77 07 04, fax 04 95 73 45 65). The classiest option in this area, and good value, with lovely views from spacious front-side terraces, tennis court and a pool overlooking the Rizzanese. April–Oct 15. ⑤–⑦.

The Town

Place Porta – its official name, place de la Libération, has never caught on – forms Sartène's nucleus. Once the arena for bloody quarrels, it's now a well-kept square opening onto a wide terrace overlooking the rippling green valley of the Rizzanese. Somnolent by day, place Porta comes alive for the early-evening *passeggiata*, when it fills with snappily dressed townsfolk, and hunters in their green camouflage gear.

Flanking the south side of place Porta is **Église Ste-Marie**, built in the 1760s but completely restored to a smooth granitic appearance. The chief interest here is historical – it was in this church that the warring families of nineteenth-century Sartène were forced to make their peace, though the truce often lasted only until they got outside again. Inside the church you can see the weighty wooden cross and chain used in the Catenacciu procession (see p.266), but otherwise the only notable feature is the Baroque altar, a present from the town's Franciscan monastery, no longer in existence.

Formerly the palace for the Genoese governor, the nearby **Hôtel de Ville** serves as an archway into the Santa Anna district of the *vieille ville*; the building is not open to the public and its archives have been closed since the 1880s, due to the endemic corruption of local politics, it's said.

The vieille ville

A flight of steps to the left of the Hôtel de Ville leads past the Maison de la Culture and cinema to the post office, behind which stands the ruined **échauguette**, a small lookout tower which is all that remains of the town's twelfth-century ramparts. This apart, the best of the **vieille ville** is to be found behind the Hôtel de Ville in the **Santa Anna** district, a labyrinth of constricted passageways and ancient fortress-like houses reached via the archway directly beneath the Hôtel de Ville, which rarely harbours any signs of life. Featuring few windows and often linked to their neighbours by balconies, these houses are entered by first-floor doors, a necessary measure against unwelcome intruders; dilapidated staircases have replaced the ladders that used to provide the only access. The main "road" across Santa Anna is rue des Frères-Bartoli, to the left of which are the strangest of all the vaulted passageways, where outcrops of rock block the paths between the ancient buildings. Just to the west of the Hôtel de Ville, signposted off the tiny **place Maggiore**, you'll find the **impasse**

Vendetta in the Vieille Ville

In the villages of nineteenth-century Corsica it was common for blood feuds to start over something as trivial as the theft of a cockerel (see box on p.244), but Sartène's vendetta had its roots in a political dispute between the rich **Roccaserra** family of Santa Anna – supporters of the Bourbons – and the anti-monarchist Ortoli family of the poorer Borgo district. In 1830, on the occasion of the overthrow of the Bourbons in France, a group of Ortolis and their cohorts marched through Santa Anna to provoke the mayor, a royalist Roccaserra. In the ensuing fight Sebastien Pietri, a leading light in the Roccaserra clan, was killed and five of his comrades were wounded, which provoked an invasion of the town by a thousand Roccaserra allies from the mountains. The scene was witnessed by French chronicler A.C. Pasquin Valéry, who wrote, "The French are powerless against the nature, manners and passions of the Corsicans." After a series of violent confrontations in the maquis, where many members of both factions were killed, a mediator was brought in, a peace treaty drawn up and in 1834, at a Mass in Église Ste-Marie, the survivors of the vendetta were forced to swear to live in peace. Even then, street corners were guarded and windows bricked up, the feud only relaxing on the election of Napoléon III in 1848, when the children of the families were allowed to dance together at the celebrations.

Carababa, a remarkable architectural puzzle of a passageway cut through the awkwardly stacked houses. A few steps away, at the western edge of the town, **place Angelo-Maria-Chiappe** offers a magnificent view of the Golfe du Valinco.

Musée de la Préhistoire Corse

At the time of writing, plans are afoot to move the **Musée de la Préhistoire Corse** (June–Sept Mon–Sat 10am–noon & 2–6pm; Oct–May Mon–Fri 10am–noon & 2–5pm; 15F) to a new building across town (supposedly any time between 2000 and 2002). In the meantime, however, Corsica's largest collection of prehistoric archeological finds remains in a beautifully renovated old building a short way east of place Porta.

Spanning the period 6000 BC to 500 BC, the exhibition is dominated by dull fragments of terracotta pottery unearthed in Neolithic and Toréen sites across the island. Alongside these, however, are more accomplished fragments of decorated ceramics, obsidian arrowheads, polished granite axes and mattocks, gold jewellery and statuettes, as well as a pile of human bones deformed by fire, discovered near Bonifacio. In the main hall on the first floor, a model of Cucuruzzu gives a good idea of what a Bronze Age settlement looked like. Nearby, two **statue-menhirs**, one of them coloured red as it would have been during the megalithic era, stand opposite cases containing colourful bracelets, pendants and exquisite strings of beads from the Iron Age.

An account of the Cucuruzzu ruins, the most important archeological site in Corsica after Filitosa, appears on p.252.

Couvent de San Damiano

A ten-minute walk along the road to Bonifacio will take you to the **Couvent de San Damiano**, the building in which the Catenacciu penitent spends the night before the procession, when he has to be guarded from curious outsiders by police. One of the last of the old-style bandits, a formidable character called **Muzarettu**, died here in the 1940s at the age of 90, having been given refuge by the monks. Cast out from his village for killing a nephew who had slapped his face, Muzarettu took to the maquis, then proceeded to terrorize the neighbourhood from his cave hideout near Propriano, where he hosted wild parties for the fishermen who brought him food and drink. A few more murders along the way kept him outlawed for many years, but as an old man he developed cancer and came to this convent to die; repenting his sins right at the very end, he was visited by the chief of police on his deathbed. The convent is now home to a brotherhood of Belgian monks and is out of bounds to the public, but there's a fine view of the valley from the outside.

For a background feature on Corsican bandits, see p.246.

Eating and drinking

Hotels may be thin on the ground in Sartène, but there is no shortage of restaurants, most of them cosy, traditional places in old stone buildings. A handful of inexpensive snack bars and pizzerias also line the main square, and are ideal for a light lunch or ice cream.

La Cave Sartenais, place de la Libération. Directly beneath the Hôtel de Ville, and the most congenial place in town to taste and buy quality local wines.

La Chaumière, rue Capitaine-Benedetti. A cosy rustic restaurant specializing in local cuisine such as *tripettes sartenais*, river trout and wild pork. One of the few places open all year. Menus at around 100F.

Aux Gourmets, cours Sœur-Amélie. Small, unpretentious bistro just south of the main square, serving inexpensive omelettes and a good-value 85F set menu that includes wild-boar steaks and chips. Ask for a seat on the tiny terrace to the rear, which juts over the valley.

Transitus and Le Chœur d'Hommes de Sartène

On October 4, 1996, an extraordinary concert took place in Sartène's **Couvent de San Damiano**. In the crypt of the nineteenth-century Franciscan church, the newly formed male voice choir of the village, dressed in black and standing in a tight semicircle, celebrated St Francis of Assisi's day in truly traditional style by singing a choral work based on the saint's ascent to heaven. An original manuscript of the piece, **Transitus**, composed by the Italian friar **Pietro-Battista Farinelli da Falconara** in the late nineteenth century, had come to light two years before, enabling the Franciscans to revive a tradition that been dormant for over seventy years.

The concert was the consummation of a decade of work by Corsica's most famous singer and composer, **Jean-Paul Poletti**, who co-founded the hugely influential group **Canta U Populu Corsu** (The Corsican People Sing) in the mid-1970s. With their powerful renditions of traditional songs collected in the villages, Canta plucked *polyphonie* from near extinction and exploited its stirring harmonies and emotive associations as a rallying call for the nascent nationalist movement. Nine acclaimed albums later, however, the man dubbed "la plus belle voix de Corse" left the group to pursue formal music studies in Italy, where he became head chorister at the renowned Fiesole school in Siena.

More success followed Poletti's return from the continent, notably his formation of the platinum-disc selling *Nouvelles Polyphonies Corse* whose sublime harmonies opened the Winter Olympics at Albertville. But, away from the public eye, Poletti and the communist mayor of Sartène, Dominique Bucchini, were working to regenerate a grassroots choral tradition on their home patch. In 1987 they formed a school to promote what both regarded as an essential, but fast-disappearing, facet of village life. **Granitu Maggiore** ("granite" from the rock, and "major" after the chord) now boasts three choirs, the largest of them with 380 voices.

Transitus provided a perfect vehicle for the new choir formed from the cream of Granitu Maggiore's pupils, **Le Chœur d'Hommes de Sartène**. Since their recording of the long-lost score in 1996, the choir, comprising two local postmen, a Breton restaurateur and four students – in addition to Poletti himself – has toured all over Europe. Yet their most important gig remains the October 4 Mass at the convent of San Damiano, whose exceptional acoustics create the definitive setting for a piece of music that looks set to put Corsican choral music on the Classical map.

Pizza Porta, place Porta. *Paninis* (toasted sandwiches), fresh salads, crêpes and pizzas served at reasonable prices on tables in the vieille ville.

U Sputinu, 13 rue des Frères-Bartoli, in the *vieille ville*. Mostly salads and fresh pasta, with a fair choice of Corsican dishes such as stuffed courgettes, and local wines. Moderate.

Zia Paulina, at the end of rue des Frères-Bartoli, in the *vieille ville*. The perfect lunch venue, at the far end of an atmospheric narrow alleyway in the dead centre of the old town. Corsican specialities dominate both their good-value 75F and 95F menus, and there's a generous selection of local wines to choose from. Count on 150F for à la carte.

Around Sartène

You get captivating views of Sartène and the Golfe de Valinco by driving along the D50 southeast of Sartène, which descends into the Ortolo valley before reaching the tiny hamlet of **MOLA**. This nest of reddish houses lurks in the shadow of **L'Uomo di Cagna**, a gigantic globular rock perched on top of the mountain, which dominates the landscape of the southern Sartenais.

West of Sartène, the prehistoric monument of **Alo Bisucce** is reached by a lovely road that leads eventually to Campomoro (see p.246). To get there, take the N196 south as far as the Col de

U Catenacciu

Sartène's Good Friday ceremony of **U Catenacciu**, generally considered to be the most ancient ritual in Corsica, is a frighteningly authentic imitation of Christ's walk to Golgotha, despite a touch of exploitation in recent years. The nocturnal procession through candlelit streets is headed by the **Grand Pénitent** or Pénitent Rouge: dressed in a scarlet hooded robe which covers his face, he carries a heavy wooden cross and is chained on the ankle – *u catenacciu* means "chained one". In former times the penitent was usually a bandit whose identity was officially known only to the priest. Nowadays the Grand Pénitent is still anonymous and there's a waiting list of twelve years to take part, which means that some of the penitents are very old men. If the Grand Pénitent is too frail to shoulder the cross alone, he's helped out by the **Pénitent Blanc**, who follows behind, representing Simon of Cyrena. Behind him comes a troop of **Pénitents Noirs** bearing the statue of Christ on a bier. Accompanied by the continuous unearthly chanting of an ancient Corsican prayer, *Perdonu miu Diu*, the penitents pass slowly from Église Ste-Marie through the streets of the *vieille ville*, ending up three hours later in place Porta, where they receive benediction at midnight.

In the past it was a dangerous event, as the penitents were often known murderers at whom onlookers would fling stones – though this was one time of year when a truce was observed between sworn enemies, so nobody got killed. It's still a rough affair, with a lot of pushing and shoving to get the best view among the throng of tourists, and shots are often fired into the air at the end of the ceremony, by which time excitement is running high.

l'Albitrina, branching right towards Tizzano and then soon after veering along a sudden, unsignposted right turning that worms around the hillside in the direction of Grossa. After about 4km the unsignposted site emerges as a mound on the left-hand side of the road. Neolithic settlers occupied this rocky peak around 1700 BC, before the arrival of the Torréens, building a double wall of Cyclopean boulders surmounted by a structure measuring 8m across and centring on a hearth. East of here lies a rough platform, probably used for surveying the surrounding countryside for possible attackers.

For more background on the North African pirates who plagued the Corsican coast, see p.102.

The megalithic sites

Scattered across the southwest Sartenais is a bumper crop of **megalithic sites**, ranging from the famous **Dolmen de Fontanaccia** at Cauria, the best-preserved prehistoric tomb on the island, to the nearby alignments of **Stantari** and **Renaggiu**, an impressive congregation of statue-menhirs. Further northwest, 258 standing stones of various sizes lie strewn amid the maquis at **Palaggiu**. The coast hereabouts is equally wild, with deep clefts and coves providing some excellent spots for diving and secluded swimming.

The megaliths of Cauria

To reach the **Cauria** megalithic site you need to turn off the N196 about 2km southwest of Sartène, at the **Col de l'Albitrina** (291m), taking the D48 towards Tizzano. Four kilometres along this road a left turning brings you onto a winding road through vineyards, until eventually the **Dolmen de Fontanaccia** comes into view on the horizon, crowning the crest of a low hill amidst a sea of maquis. A blue sign at the parking space indicates the track to the dolmen, a fifteen-minute walk away.

Known to the locals as the *Stazzona del Diavolu* (Devil's Forge), a name that does justice to its enigmatic power, the Dolmen de Fontanaccia is in fact a burial chamber from the second phase of the megalithic era, around 2000 BC. This period was marked by a change in burial customs – whereas bodies had previously been buried in stone coffins in the ground, they were now placed above, in a mound of earth enclosed in a stone chamber. What you see today is the great stone table, comprising six huge granite blocks nearly 2m high topped by a stone slab, which remained after the earth rotted away.

The 22 "standing men" of the **Alignement de Stantari**, 200m to the east of the dolmen, date from the same period. All are featureless except the two distinctly phallic stones, which both have roughly sculpted eyes and noses, with diagonal swords on their fronts and sockets in their heads where horns would probably have been attached.

Across a couple of fields to the south you'll find the **Alignement de Renaggiu**, a gathering of forty menhirs standing in rows amid a small shadowy copse, set against the enormous granite outcrop of Punta di Cauria. Some of the menhirs have fallen, but all face north to south, a fact that seems to rule out any connection with a sun-related cult.

Palaggiu

To reach the **Alignement de Palaggiu**, the largest concentration of menhirs in Corsica, regain the D48 and head southwards past the Domaine la Mosconi vineyard (on your right, 3km after the Cauria turn-off), 1500m beyond which a green metal gate on the right side of the road marks the turning. From here a badly rutted dirt track leads another 1200m through to the stones, lost in the maquis, with vineyards spread over the hills in the half-distance. Stretching in straight lines across the countryside like a battleground of soldiers, the 258 menhirs include three statue-menhirs with carved weapons and facial features – they are amidst the first line you come to. Dating from around 1800 BC, the statues give few clues as to their function, but it's a reasonable supposition that proximity to the sea was important – the famous Corsican archeologist Roger Grosjean's theory is that the statues were some sort of magical deterrent to invaders.

Tizzano

TIZZANO (Tizza), at the end of the road 3km south of Palaggiu, is a secluded little marina tucked behind a sheltered inlet, surrounded by rocks and some exceptionally clear seas. The village consists of a handful of houses and a terraced **café** overlooking the yacht moorings. Just south of the village, a glorious **beach** of white sand draws increasing numbers of tourists every year. A string of even more enticing little coves – a short scramble over the rocks northwest of Tizzano – are overlooked by the ruins of a fifteenth-century **fort**. During World War II, this was used for attack and defence practice by a team of secret agents and Corsican patriots led by the maverick SOE commander, Andrew Croft, in preparation for landings in southern France. Having secretly landed in Calvi on October 3, 1943, Croft sailed to Tizzano in an ex-British fishing boat renamed the *Serinini*, and used the remote village as a training camp. While based in Corsica, he made 52 sorties and landed eighty agents on the island, many of them with the help of the submarine, the *Casabianca* (see p.70).

For more background on the SOE's role in the World War II Resistance struggle, see Contexts p.370.

The account of Corsica's most famous prehistoric site, Filitosa, on p.232, includes more background information on the Torréen invasions.

Self-reliant hikers in search of coastal wilderness may consider pressing on up the coast to the **Capo di Senetosa**, a remote headland crowned with a bleached white Genoese tower. The path peters out in dense maquis at several points, forcing you back to the rocks lining the shore, but the scenery is superb, and once beyond the tower the tangled wild-boar trails merge to form a more easily discernible path that you can follow all the way to Campomoro – a hike described in more detail on p.248. If you do decide to give it a try, start early in the day, take a sunhat, and carry plenty of food, water and a tent and/or sleeping bag in case you have to camp out. Count on three to three and a half hours to reach the tower, and the same to return.

The only **hotel** in the village, the swish *du Golfe* (☎04 95 77 14 76, fax 04 95 77 23 34; ⑦–⑧; open Easter–Oct), is ideally situated above a little cove on the outskirts of the village. The seventeen rooms are luxurious, with terraces and great views, but tariffs are decidedly ambitious, particularly in high season, when half-board is obligatory.

The road to Bonifacio

South of Sartène, the N196 undulates through a strange landscape of barren hills and vivid blue sea, dominated by the Uomo di Cagna. Once the road hits the coast, about 25km along, the huge roseate rock of the **Lion de Roccapina**, a lump of fawn-coloured granite bizarrely weathered into the shape of a lion's head, comes into view. Sheltered by crumbling cliffs, the **Golfe de Roccapina** below it is a dazzling turquoise-blue bay accessible to vehicles via a rocky and rutted track (look out for the turning at Asinaja, signposted "Camping Roccapina"). Shallow bathing, soft white sand and crystal-clear water make this a strong contender for the best beach in Corsica, though it's far from a secret. During the summer, large numbers of tourists from the campsite descend on the cove, designated a protected site – hence the fence safeguarding the dunes. To reach the old Genoese watchtower, head up the stony path that leads right off the main approach to the beach, and bear left when you reach a fork five minutes later (the right fork of this path will take you to the Lion de Roccapina, which is extremely dangerous to climb, claiming lives each year in spite of the warnings posted around it). From the ridge, the views south across the cove, and north over a stunning deserted bay, are superb; you can also follow the path downhill from the watchtower to the headland dividing the two bays, giving access to a wild and rocky shore that is great for diving, snorkelling and fishing.

If you want to camp at Roccapina, your only option is *Camping Municipal* (☎04 95 77 19 30, fax 04 95 77 10 60; mid-May to Sept), just behind the beach, though its tariffs are high. A friendlier and less crowded choice lies 5km further south along the Bonifacio road from the Roccapina turning. Calm and well shaded with oak trees, the *Camping de Pero-Longo* (☎04 95 77 10 74) has the additional attraction of a congenial little *ferme-auberge* restaurant, offering a very good-value three-course menu for under 100F.

Pianotolli-Caldarello

Back on the main road the first sign of civilization for kilometres comes at **PIANOTOLLI-CALDARELLO**, the largest settlement between Sartène and Bonifacio. Two hamlets make up the village, and their names tell you everything about the locale: Pianottoli, the northern half straddling the main road, is derived from the word for "plain", and Caldarello, 1.5km south, means "extreme heat". There's nothing much to see in either, but a handful of unfrequented coves lie within easy reach, and if you're catching a plane from nearby Figari airport the *Kevano Plage* **campsite**, 3km southeast on the Baie de Figari (☎04 95 71 83 22, fax 04 95 71 83 83; April to mid-Oct), is a convenient place to spend your last night on the island.

Figari

Cut through by the main Porto-Vecchio to Ajaccio road, the village of **FIGARI** sees a disproportionate amount of traffic thanks to its proximity to south Corsica's largest **airport** (☎04 95 71 10 31), spread over the floor of the valley below. Most charter and scheduled flights to northern Europe leave at civilized times of day, and visitors generally drive here on the day of their departure, depositing rental cars at the row of rental company offices outside the main terminal before checking in. If, however, you're travelling without the luxury of your own vehicle, and catching a morning flight from Figari, you'll have to get here by **bus** the night before. Two services per day pass through in both directions, from Ajaccio and Porto-Vecchio. Make sure you're dropped off in Figari village proper, not at the previous junction on the N196 (confusingly signposted "Aéroport"), from where the D22 branches inland to approach the airport from the far northeastern side, leaving you a very long walk along a disconcertingly quiet country road. From Figari, you can arrange a taxi at the one bar in the village, or hitch the remaining 5km. Note, too, that during the summer *navettes* run out here from opposite the marina in Porto-Vecchio to meet flights; more details of this service appear on p.292. There are, however, no eating or accommodation options in Figari.

Roccapina and the Queen-Emperor's Jewels

The Golfe de Roccapina witnessed one of the most notorious **shipwrecks** of the nineteenth century, when, on the night of April 17, 1887, the luxury P&O steam liner *Tasmania* ran aground onto the treacherous Des Moines rocks a short way out to sea. En route to Southampton from Bombay, she was carrying in her holds a trunk whose contents were worth an estimated eight times the value of the entire ship – precious gems sent by the rajahs of India to Queen Victoria on her jubilee. Once they learned of the cargo, rescuers began to search for the trunk, but it was eventually picked up by crew members of a salvage vessel, the *Stella*, three weeks later. Local legend has it, however, that some of the jewels found their way into the possession of the *bandit* **Barrittonu**, who used to hide out in the hollows around the Lion de Roccapina. No one has ever proven this rumour to be true, though it is known that a purse of Indian diamonds sent as part of the gift to the Queen-Emperor was never recovered; its whereabouts are still the subject of speculation in the bars of Sartène.

Mazzeri

Of all the occult phenomena recorded in Corsica – from vampire witches (*stregoni* and *strèga*), evil-eye (*occhiu*) healing, *orii* (see p.298), Christian sects and pagan cults – the strangest has to be the existence of **mazzeri**, dubbed by Dorothy Carrington in her book on the subject as "dream hunters". Also known as *colpadori* (from the Latin *culpi*, "to strike"), *mazzeri* (from the Corsican *ammazza*, "to kill") are those who possess the power to foresee death. They do this by slipping into the maquis in the dead of night and waiting silently, usually next to a stream, to kill the first living creature that passes. On retrieving the body, the *mazzeri* will recognize in its face, or hear in its death cries, the identity of a person they know well, usually someone from their own family or village, who will shortly die. If the *mazzeri* has only managed to wound the animal, the person concerned will suffer a grave illness, for the quarry temporarily harbours the spirit of the doomed individual.

Bizarrely, these nocturnal hunting expeditions rarely take place in the literal sense, for the *mazzeri's* realm is that of dreams. Nevertheless, records exist of *mazzeri* who were known to leave their house at night in a state of trance and return covered in scratches from the maquis – whence another of their Corsican names: *sunnambuli*, or "sleepwalkers". Despite the ambiguity surrounding the nature of the *mazzeri*'s hunting activities, the outcome is invariably unequivocal. Once the death of an individual has been foretold, it always occurs, usually within a week or two, and certainly before a year has passed.

Although the *mazzeri* may have predicted the event and performed a symbolic or dream killing of the deceased's spirit, he or she is not held directly responsible, nor regarded as a murderer. In some villages they are actually held in high esteem for the protective role they play in a former **pagan festival** marked on the last night of July. At this time it is said that *mazzeri* from different villages form teams (*milizia*) to wage phantom battles (*mandracho*) against each other on lofty mountain passes dividing districts. Using an armoury of traditional weapons – knives, axes, lances, human bones and asphodel plants (known in Corsica as *fiori di morti*, "flowers of death") – they fight the opposition until one side is forced to retreat. Once again, although the killing occurs in the dream world the outcome is real enough, and any *mazzeri* slain in a battle on July 31 is destined to die within twelve months. Moreover, the village whose side loses the ghost battle will sustain more unexpected deaths during the year. For this reason, villagers all over the island still light fires outside churches and place knives above doorways on the last night of July, to ward off evil spirits.

All this may sound like mere folk myth, but *mazzeri* still exist in many areas (notably the far south around Sartène and Figari), albeit in far smaller numbers than a century ago. Recent interest by local ethnologists has unearthed a wealth of lore surrounding the phenomenon, and several erudite books and papers have been published – well worth hunting out if you're interested in the esoteric side of island life. Of these, Dorothy Carrington's *The Dream Hunters of Corsica* (see p.390) is the most detailed, but if your French is up to it ask in any good bookshop for the special edition of *L'Origine* magazine devoted to Corsican *mazzeri* and related subjects.

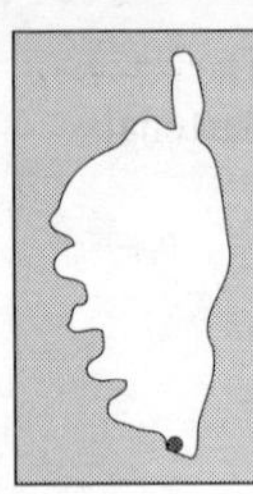

Bonifacio

BONIFACIO (Bonifaziu) enjoys a superbly isolated situation at Corsica's southernmost point, a narrow peninsula of dazzling white limestone creating a town site unlike any other on the island. The **haute ville**, a maze of narrow streets flanked by tall Genoese tenements, rises seamlessly out of sheer cliffs that have been hollowed and striated by the wind and waves, while on the landward side the deep cleft between the peninsula and the mainland forms a perfect natural harbour. A haven for boats for centuries, this harbour is nowadays a marina that attracts yachts from all around the Mediterranean.

Separated from the rest of the island by an expanse of maquis, Bonifacio has maintained a certain temperamental detachment from the rest of Corsica, and is distinctly more Italian than French in atmosphere. It has its own dialect based on Ligurian Italian, a legacy from the days when it was practically an independent Genoese town. The old town retains Renaissance features found only here and, with Sardinia just a stone's throw away, much of the property in the area is owned by upper-echelon Italians.

Such a place has its inevitable drawbacks: exorbitant prices, overwhelming crowds in August, and a commercial cynicism that's atypical of Corsica as a whole. However, the old town forms one of the most arresting spectacles in the Mediterranean, easily transcending the tourist frippery, and warrants at least a day-trip. If you plan to come in peak season, try to get here early in the day before the bus parties arrive at around 10am.

A brief history of Bonifacio

It could be that Bonifacio's first documented appearance is as the town of the cannibalistic Laestrygonians in **The Odyssey**; Homer's description of an "excellent harbour, closed in on all sides by an unbroken ring of precipitous cliffs, with two bold headlands facing each other at the mouth so as to leave only a narrow channel in between" fits the port well. The unploughed land that Odysseus comes across inland of the harbour could be a reference to the plain beyond the Bonifacio promontory, and it's also possible that the Neolithic tribes that once lived in this area were the barbaric attackers of Odysseus's crew.

In Roman times there was a village on this site, but the town really came into being in 828 AD, when **Count Bonifacio of Tuscany** built a castle on the peninsula. Like other settlements on the Corsican coast, this one suffered continuous pirate raids, but its key position in the Mediterranean made various powers covet the port. Subject of a dispute between Pisa and **Genoa** in

1187, Bonifacio eventually fell to the Genoese, who then proceeded to massacre the local population and replace them with Ligurian families, to whom they offered exemption from tax and customs duty in their ports. Two hundred and fifty families duly settled here, and soon the town developed into a mini-republic with its own constitution and laws, governed by elected magistrates called *Anziani*.

In 1420 **Alfonso V** of Aragon set his sights on Corsica, and for five months his fleet blockaded the port, hoping to starve the Bonifaciens into submission. Every citizen joined in the defence of the citadel, with clergymen, women and children flinging wooden beams, rocks and blinding chalk dust down on the attackers – they even tried to demoralize the enemy by pelting them with cheese, an action masterminded by one Marguerita Bobbia, whose ingenuity is commemorated by a street named after her in the old town. Eventually, a boat was built inside the citadel by the famished defenders, lowered onto the sea from the clifftop and dispatched to seek help from Genoa. Seven galleons were immediately sent to help the Bonifaciens, but they were delayed by contrary winds. Only by donning the armour of their dead soldiers, ringing all the church bells and parading around the town ramparts, were the last survivors of the siege able to buy the time needed for their Genoan rescuers to arrive. When the ships finally appeared, shortly after Christmas, the resolve of the Aragonese was decidedly weakened; they decamped shortly after. The Bonifacien bluff had turned the battle.

Another celebrated siege occurred in 1554, when the town was recovering from an outbreak of plague that had claimed two-thirds of the population. **Henri II** of France arrived with the Turkish fleet, led by the fearsome corsair Dragut. The town held on through eighteen days and nights of cannon fire, and then a member of the eminent Cattacciolo family was dispatched to Genoa to raise help. He was seized on his return by the Turks, who forced him to carry a forged letter refusing them the assistance of the republic, a ploy that brought about Bonifacio's surrender. The invaders pillaged the town, which was then rescued by Sampiero Corso. There followed a brief period of French rule, which came to an end when the Treaty of Cateau Cambrensis returned Corsica to Genoa in 1559.

Thereafter the Genoese port enjoyed relative prosperity until the late eighteenth century, when the French gained control of the island. No longer permitted their special autonomy, the merchants moved away and the town suffered a commercial decline that was really only reversed with the advent of tourism. Fishing, however, still brings in some income for a few Bonifaciens.

Arrival, information and accommodation

Arriving by plane, you'll land at **Figari** airport, 17km north of Bonifacio. There's no bus service from here, so you have to take a taxi into town – around 250F. If you're coming by **bus** you'll be dropped at the car park by the **marina**, close to most of the hotels. Drivers can either park here or head straight up avenue Général-de-Gaulle to the *haute ville*. This is where you'll find the **tourist office**, in the Fort San Nicro at the bottom of rue Fred-Scammoroni (July–Sept daily 9am–8pm; Oct–June Mon–Fri 9am–12.30pm & 2–5.15pm), which will check which hotels have vacancies for you.

Finding **accommodation** can be a chore, as Bonifacio's few hotels are quickly booked up in peak season; so if you want to stay centrally, ring in advance. Be prepared, too, for higher-than-average tariffs, though out of season it's usually possible to pick up a double room for around 230F. With the exception of the *Araguina*, the nearest **campsites** are all a drive away, along the road to Porto-Vecchio.

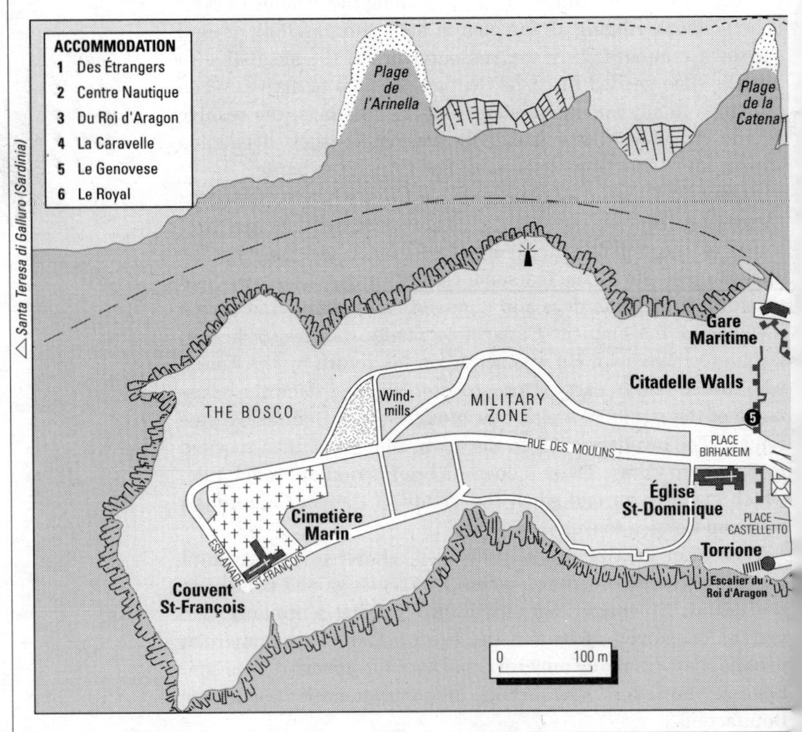

Hotels

La Caravelle, 37 quai J. Comparetti (☎ & fax 04 95 73 00 03). Stylish olde-worlde place whose excellent restaurant occupies a prime location on the marina. ⑥.

Centre Nautique, the marina (☎04 95 73 02 11, fax 04 95 73 17 47; *www.hotel.genovese.fr*). Chic but relaxed hotel on the waterfront, fitted out with wood and nautical charts. All rooms are tastefully furnished and consist of two storeys connected with a spiral staircase. The best upmarket option, although their prices (around 850F for a double in peak season) reflect the hotel's popularity among wealthy Americans. ⑧.

Des Étrangers, 4 av Sylvère-Bohn (☎04 95 73 01 09, fax 04 95 73 16 97). On the road to Ajaccio just past the port. A swish place whose (double-glazed) rooms are a bargain off season (250F), but rather pricy and too close to the main road for comfort during July and August. April–Oct. ⑦.

Le Genovese, the citadel (☎04 95 73 12 34, fax 04 95 73 09 03, *www.oda.fr/aa/genovese*). The only luxury hotel in the *haute ville*, hence the sky-high rates. No pool, but the views over the marina from some of the (priciest) rooms are great. ⑧.

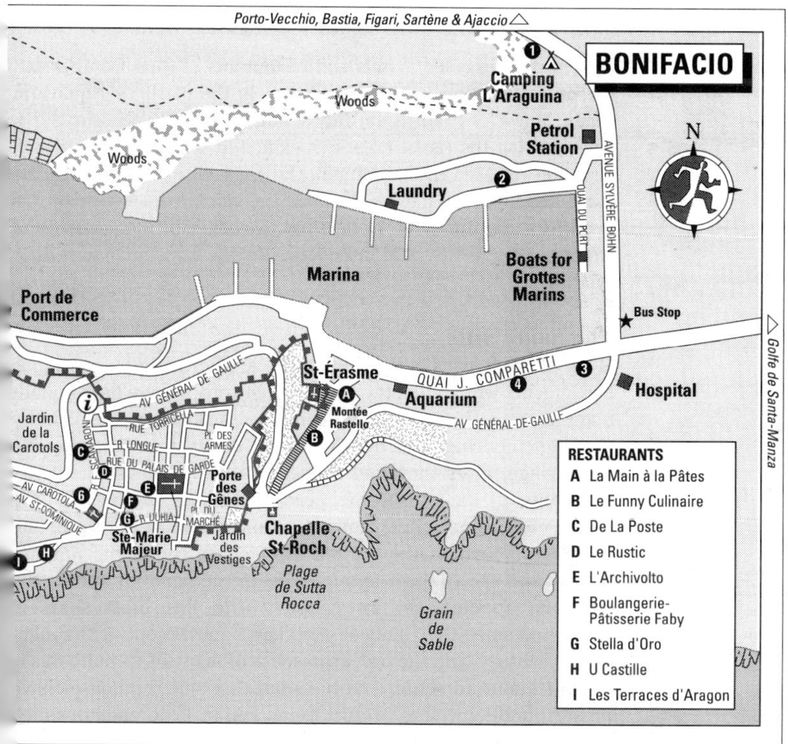

Le Roi d'Aragon, 13 quai J. Comparetti (☎04 95 73 03 99, fax 04 95 73 07 94). A stylish, recently renovated three-star overlooking the marina, with better-than-average off-season discounts. ⑦.

Le Royal, place Bonaparte/rue Fred-Scamaroni (☎04 95 73 00 51, fax 04 95 73 04 68). Above a modern bar-restaurant at the entrance to the *haute ville*. Bright, clean place with views of the citadel and the sea. Prices soar in high season but are reasonable (250–300F) at other times of the year. ⑧.

Campsites

L'Araguina, av Sylvère-Bohn, opposite the Total petrol station (☎04 95 73 02 96). Closest place to town and inexpensive for the location, but horrendously cramped and with inadequate washing and toilet facilities. Avoid unless desperate.

Campo di Liccia, 3km north towards Porto-Vecchio, opposite *U Farniente* (☎04 95 73 03 09). Well shaded and large, so you're guaranteed a place. June–Sept.

U Farniente, Pertamina, 3km along the road to Porto-Vecchio (☎04 95 73 05 47). Very flash four-star site with all mod cons, including a pool – essential to book in summer. June–Sept.

The Town

Apart from the cafés, hotels and restaurants of **quai Comparetti**, the only attraction in the lower town is the marina's **Aquarium** (daily: May–Oct 10am–8pm; July & Aug open until midnight; 22F), where all but the rarest creatures exhibited are caught fresh each year and released in the autumn, the giant blue lobster being the main highlight. At the far end lies the port, from which ferries depart for Sardinia and, in between, a cluster of restaurants and shops lies at the foot of **Montée Rastello**, the steps up to the *haute ville*.

The haute ville

Many of the houses in the **haute ville** are bordered by enormous battlements which, like the houses themselves, have been rebuilt many times – the most significant modifications were made by the French during their brief period of occupation following the 1554 siege, after they had reduced the town walls to rubble. Remnants of cannonshot-peppered buildings still scatter the *haute ville*, especially around the **Bosco** area at the tip of the promontory, where the barbed-wire fences round the military facility and the rubbish flying about in the wind all add to the war-torn appearance. The *haute ville* has been sparsely populated since the Genoese merchants moved out in the eighteenth century, and the precariousness of many of its buildings is no enticement to settle – on the southeast side the houses have no surrounding wall to protect them, and in 1966 one house fell into the sea, killing two people. Since then, various plans have been put forward to reinforce the cliff, but the state of the buildings is still a great problem.

From the top of the Montée Rastello steps, dubbed locally as the *grimpette* (literally "little climb"), you can cross avenue Général-de-Gaulle to **Montée St-Roch**, which gives a stunning view of the white limestone cliffs and the huge lump of fallen rock face called the **Grain de Sable**. At the **Chapelle St-Roch**, built on the spot where the last plague victim died in 1528, more steps lead down to the tiny beach of Sutta Rocca, which is great for snorkelling.

At the top of the Montée St-Roch steps stands the drawbridge of the great **Porte des Gênes**, once the only entrance to the *haute ville*. Through the gate and to the right, on place d'Armes, you can see the **Bastion de l'Étendard** (July & Aug daily 10am–9pm; April–June & Sept Mon–Sat 11am–5.30pm; 10F), sole remnant of the fortifications destroyed during the siege of 1554. Inside is a small museum whose only noteworthy exhibit, aside from some decidedly unlifelike mock-ups of historical scenes using dummies, is a facsimile of the *Dame de Bonifacio*, a remarkably intact prehistoric skeleton of a woman found in a cave shelter near the town. You can also climb over the battlements to the tiny **Jardin des Véstiges**, which affords the *haute ville*'s best views of the cliffs to the east.

Back in the square, a few paces from the bastion lies **rue des Deux-Empereurs**, where at no. 4 you'll see the flamboyant marble escutcheon of the Cattacciolo family, one of many such adornments on the houses of this quarter. In 1541, the emperor Charles V, having been caught in Bonifacio by a storm, stayed in this house as a guest of Filippo Cattacciolo; after the departure of his illustrious visitor, Cattacciolo shot the horse he had loaned to him, on the grounds that nobody else was worthy to ride the poor beast after it had supported the ruler of half the known world. Opposite stands the house in which Napoléon resided for three months in 1793.

Cutting down to rue Palais-du-Garde brings you to **Église Ste-Marie-Majeure**, originally Romanesque but restored in the eighteenth century, though the richly sculpted belfry dates from the fourteenth century. The façade is hidden by a **loggia** where the Genoese municipal officers used to dispense justice in the days of the republic. If you look up you can see buttresses connecting the houses in the adjoining streets to the roof of the church – these were vital not just as support but also for draining rainwater into a huge cistern underneath the porch, which provided the town with water in times of siege and during the dry summers. The church's treasure, a relic of the **True Cross** said to have been brought to Bonifacio by St Helena, the

The original Dame de Bonifacio *is housed in Levie's musée départementale;* *see p.251.*

mother of Constantine, was saved from a shipwreck in the Straits of Bonifacio; for centuries after, the citizens would take the relic to the edge of the cliff and pray for calm seas whenever storms raged. The relic is kept in the sacristy, along with an ivory cask containing relics of St Boniface, and you'll only be able to get a glimpse if you can find someone to open the room for you. In the main body of the church the highlight is the marble **tabernacle** to the left of the door; decorated with a bas-relief carving of Christ supported by eight glum-faced cherubs, it's thought to have been created by a north Italian sculptor in 1565. The holy water stoup below it is a third-century **sarcophagus**, the sole Roman item in town.

Rue du Palais-de-Garde, which runs alongside the church, is one of the most handsome streets in Bonifacio, with its closed arcades and double-arched windows separated by curiously stunted columns. The oldest houses along here did not originally have doors; the inhabitants used to climb up a ladder, which they would pull up behind them to prevent a surprise attack, while the ground floor was used as a stable and grain store.

South of here, rue Doria leads towards the Bosco (see opposite); at the end of this road a left down rue des Pachas will bring you to the **Torrione**, a 35m-high lookout post built in 1195 on the site of Count Bonifacio's castle. Descending the cliff from here, the **Escalier du Roi d'Aragon**'s 187 steps (daily June–Sept 11am–5.30pm; 10F) were said to have been built in one night by the Aragonese in an attempt to gain the town in 1420, but in fact they had already been in existence for some time and were used by the people to fetch water from a well.

The Bosco

To the west of the tower lies the **Bosco**, a *quartier* named after th wood that used to stand here in the tenth century. In those days community of hermits dwelt here, but nowadays the limeston plateau is open and desolate. The only sign of life comes from th military training camp, where young Corsicans sweat out thei national service. The entrance to the Bosco is marked by **Église St Dominique**, a rare example of Corsican Gothic architecture – it wa built in 1270, most probably by the Templars, and later hande over to the Dominicans.

Beyond the church, rue des Moulins leads onto the ruins c three mills dating from 1283, two of them decrepit, the thir restored. Behind them stands a memorial to the 750 people wh died when the troop ship *Sémillante* ran aground here in 185 on its way to the Crimea, one of the many disasters wreaked b the straits.

The tip of the plateau is occupied by the **Cimetière Marin**, its white crosses standing out sharply against the deep blue of the sea. Open until sundown, the cemetery is a fascinating place to explore, with its flamboyant mausoleums displaying a jumble of architectural ornamentations: stuccoed façades, Gothic arches and classical columns. Next to the cemetery stands the **Couvent St-François**, allegedly founded after St Francis sought shelter in a nearby cave – the story goes that the convent was the town's apology to the holy man, over whom a local maid had nearly poured a bucket of slops. Immediately to the south, the **Esplanade St-François** commands fine views across the bay to Sardinia.

Eating, drinking and nightlife

Eating possibilities in Bonifacio might seem unlimited, but it's best to avoid the chintzy restaurants in the marina, few of which merit their exorbitant prices – the places in the *haute ville* are less pretentious. The **bars** and **cafés** on quai Comparetti are the social focus for much of the day and in the evening, but the main nightspot is the *Amnésia* club, 10km north on the Porto-Vecchio road, which has an open-air stage, three bars and an over-the-top terrace with fountains. It's one of the island's main venues for live rock and dance music, and entrance costs 70–140F depending on who's on. You can get there in a free *navette* from the marina (☎04 95 72 12 22).

Restaurants

L'Archivolto, rue de l'Archivolto, just off the place de l'Église (☎04 95 73 17 48). Easily the most appealing place in the *haute ville*, with its candlelit, antique- and junk-filled interior. Prices are fair and the menu varied (plenty of choice for vegetarians), but the quality of the cuisine is patchy. Advance reservation recommended. Open Easter–Oct.

Boulangerie-Pâtisserie Faby, 4 rue St-Jean-Baptiste, *haute ville*. Tiny local bakery serving Bonifacien treats such as *pain des morts* (sweet buns with walnuts and raisins), *fugazzi* (*galettes* flavoured with eau de vie, orange, lemon and aniseed) and *migliaccis* (buns made with fresh ewe's cheese), in addition to the usual range of spinach and *brocciu bastelles*, baked here in the traditional way – on stone.

] Castille, rue Simon Varsi, *haute ville*. Two cosy, cavernous restaurants off place Fondaco-Montepagano: one is an upscale stone-walled pizzeria; the other specializes in pricy Italian-style dishes based mainly on lamb, veal and fresh seafood – try their wonderful *terrine de sanglier*, fresh pasta *à la carbonara*, or tomato and mozzarella salads steeped in fresh basil. The seafood menu at 120F is particularly commendable.

Le Funny Culinaire, Montée Rastello. Copious salads, crêpes and freshly squeezed fruit juices at reasonable prices. A good spot to break the haul up the steps to the *haute ville*.

La Main à la Pâtes, 1 place Bonaparte, at the bottom of the Montée Rastello. Three dozen different kinds of fresh pasta, including some imaginative concotions such as pasta with cocoa, mint or seaweed. Not cheap, but you get what you pay for here, which makes a change in Bonifacio.

De la Poste, 6 rue Fred-Scamaroni. A very popular pizza place serving some of the best-value food in the *haute ville*: oven-baked lasagne, spaghetti *al brocciu*, stuffed mussels and delicious pizzas.

Le Rustic, 16 rue Fred-Scamaroni. The town's most self-consciously Corsican restaurant, offering good-value set menus at 75F and 95F (for seafood). A great place to eat during the winter, when they keep a wood fire burning.

Stella d'Oro (Chez Jules), 23 rue Doria, near Église St-Jean-Baptiste. Pricy à la carte place with stone walls and wood beams, whose topnotch Corsican dishes include the definitive *merrizzane* (stuffed aubergine) – *the* local speciality.

Les Terraces d'Aragon, at the top of the Escalier du Roi-d'Aragon. A predictable mid-range terrace restaurant (set menus from 70F), whose main attraction is its stunning sea views. Open early, and a great breakfast venue.

Bars

Bar du Quai, marina. Run-of-the-mill café that's popular with locals, and an excellent spot for croissant and coffee breakfast, as its terrace catches the morning sun and breeze off the water.

Langoustier, quai Comparetti. Popular among young Bonifaciens, with midnight karaoke sessions.

Listings

Airport Figari, 17km north of town, off the D859 road (☎04 95 71 10 31).

Banks and exchange Societé Générale, 2 rue St-Érasme, at the foot of the steps to the *haute ville* has an ATM (as does the post office; see opposite). Avoid the bureaux de change dotted around town – they charge extortionate commission rates.

Bookshops There are a couple on the quai Comparetti, of which the Librairie-Papeterie Simoni is the largest, selling a range of imported newspapers, pulp fiction and guidebooks.

Car rental Avis, quai Banda-del-Ferro (☎04 95 73 01 28); Citer, quai Noel-Beretti (☎04 95 73 13 16); Hertz, quai Banda-del-Ferro (☎04 95 73 06 41). All of the above also have branches at Figari airport.

Diving Full information about the superb diving possibilities in the south of Corsica is available from Bonifacio's three accreditied schools: Atoll, at the *Auberge A. Cheda*, 2km north on the Porto-Vecchio road (☎04 95 73 02 83); Barakouda, 3km north on the same road (☎04 95 73 13 02); and Kallisté, in the harbour itself, reached via the roundabout 1km north of town – look for the sign by the Esso petrol station (☎04 95 73 53 66).

Hospital 1 route de Santa-Manza, at the entrance to town (☎04 95 73 95 73). For an ambulance, phone ☎04 95 73 06 95 or 04 95 73 06 94.

Laundry *Laverie automatique*, northeast side of the port.

Motorbike and mountain-bike rental Tam Tam, route de Santa-Manza (☎04 95 73 11 59); Corse Moto Services, quai Nova, on the north side of the port (☎04 95 73 15 16).

Pharmacy 17 quai Comparetti.

Police Route de Santa-Manza (☎04 95 73 00 17).

Post office On place Carrega in the *haute ville* (Mon–Fri 9am–noon & 2–5pm, Sat 9am–noon).

Taxis ☎04 95 73 19 08 (24hr).

Travel agent Voyages Gazano, quai Banda-del-Ferro, near the gare maritime (☎04 95 73 02 47).

Around Bonifacio

The views of the citadel from the cliffs at the head of the Montée Rastello (reached via a pathway running left from the top of the steps) are impressive enough, but they're not a patch on the spectacular panorama to be had from the sea. Throughout the day, a flotilla of excursion **boats** ferries visitors out to the best vantage points, en route to a string of caves and other landmarks only accessible by water, including the **Îles Lavezzi**, a scattering of small islets where the troop ship *Sémillante* was shipwrecked in 1855 and is now a nature reserve. The whole experience of bobbing around to an amplified running commentary is about as touristy as Bonifacio gets, but it's well worth enduring just to round the mouth of the harbour and see the *vieille ville* perched atop the famous chalk cliffs.

With more time, you can sidestep the crowds completely by heading off on one of the wonderful **cliff walks** from the town: southeast towards the lighthouse on **Capo Pertusato**, Corsica's southernmost point; or west to **Ermitage de la Trinité**, an old whitewashed convent with fine views across the straits to Sardinia.

With the notable exception of the horseshoe-shaped **Plage de Rondinara**, midway between Bonifacio and Porto-Vecchio, the **beaches** along this part of the coast are generally smaller and less appealing than most in southern Corsica, although those

Ferries to Sardinia

Ferries for Santa Teresa di Gallura, Sardinia, leave the gare maritime at the far southern end of the marina. Mobyline (☎04 95 73 00 29) and Saremar (☎04 95 73 00 96) operate ten to fourteen daily crossings between July 19 and September 1, reduced to between four and seven from March 3 to July 18 and September 2 to 29, with none for the rest of the year. The one-hour crossing costs 48–60F per passenger, plus 140–194F per car. You can get tickets for both operators from Agence Gazano, Port de Bonifacio (☎04 95 73 02 47).

fringing the **Golfe de Santa Manza**, to the north, are set amid some fine scenery. Over the past two decades, this whole area has become the preserve of an international jet set, whose luxury villas and helipads are sometimes the only blots on otherwise unspoilt islets and coves.

Ermitage de la Trinité

The **Ermitage de la Trinité**, 7km west of Bonifacio, off the N196, stands on a site that has been inhabited since prehistoric times and was a hermitage right at the beginning of the Christianization of the island. Heavily restored in the thirteenth century, the whitewashed convent sits beside a terrace of olive trees, a backdrop of gigantic boulders lending it a bizarre quality. There's a fine view of Bonifacio from here, and an even better one if you follow the track to the left before you reach the building, which arrives at the **Mont de la Trinité** after about 25 minutes' gentle climbing.

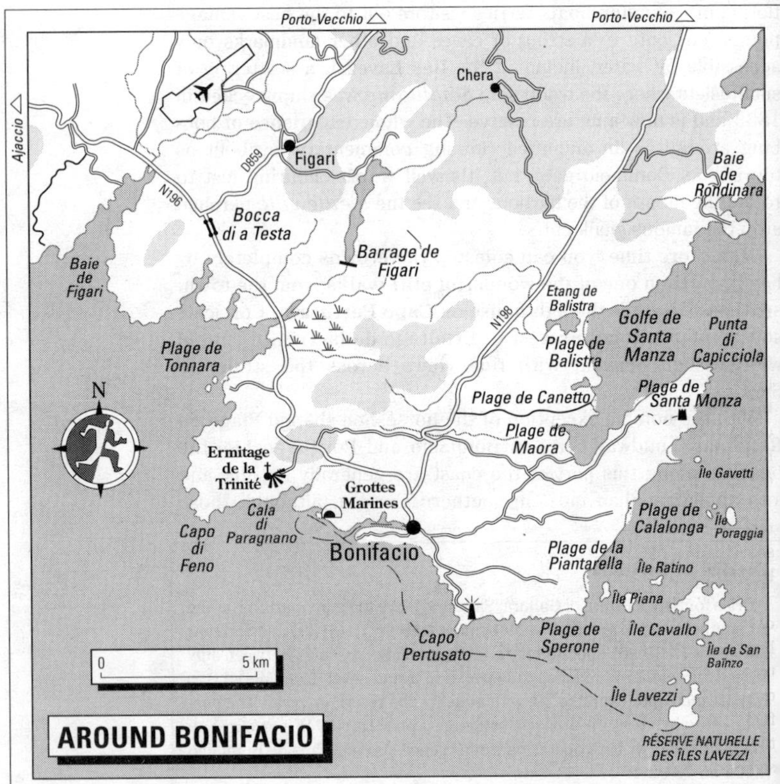

Capo Pertusato

The deeply scored limestone cliffs southeast of Bonifacio culminate in the wide headland of **Capo Pertusato** (Pierced Cape), a steepish climb of about 45 minutes from Bonifacio. At the end of the walk you'll be rewarded with an incredible seascape embracing Sardinia, the crested islands of Lavezzi and Cavallo, and Bonifacio itself, just discernible to the west. Leaving town along the D58, almost immediately bear right along the D260, a narrow road hugging the cliff side as far as the **Phare du Pertusato**, the lighthouse at the edge of

Boat Trips to the Grottes Marines and the Îles Lavezzi

From the moment you arrive in Bonifacio, you'll be pestered by touts from the many boat companies running excursions out of the harbour. There are more than a dozen of these, but they all offer more or less the same routes, at the same prices.

Lasting between thirty and forty-five minutes, the shorter trips take you out along the cliffs to the **grottes marines** (sea caves) and *calanches* (inlets) below the old town; tickets cost between 60F and 75F depending on the demand and how well you can haggle. The largest of the three caves, the **Grotte du Sdragonatu**, is worth the money on its own – a magnificent grotto where the water takes on an extraordinary violet luminosity and the rock walls, encrusted with stalactites and arches, glitter with the colours of amethyst, indigo and gold.

Longer excursions out to the **Îles Lavezzi**, part of the archipelago to the east of the straits of Bonifacio, cost around 100F. Most companies offer a shuttle (*navette*) service, allowing you to spend as much time as you like on the island before returning.

Having passed the Grain de Sable, the Phare du Pertusato and the heavily guarded private island of Cavallo, the boats moor at the main island of **Lavezzi**, beside the **cimetière Achiarino**. Buried here are the victims of the *Sémillante* shipwreck of 1855, in which 773 crew members and soldiers bound for the Crimean War were drowned after their vessel was blown on the rocks. The bodies were washed ashore over the following fortnight, but so disfigured were they that only one (that of the captain) could be identified; the rest are interred in unnamed graves. A stone pyramid on the western tip of the isle commemorates the tragedy, the worst ever shipwreck in the history of the Mediterranean.

Classified as a nature reserve since 1982, the island is home to several rare species of **wild flower**, such as the yellow-horned poppy, the white sea daffodil and the stonecrop, distinguished by its fleshy red leaves beneath heads of small blue flowers.

Further north, **Cavallo** and its adjoining islet, **San Bainzo**, were the sites of Roman quarries, which feature on most of the boats' half-day excursions; huge monolithic columns lie at the water's edge, cut from horizontal trenches in the rock nearby and discarded, seemingly in haste. The stone quarried here was not used in Corsica, but transported to the mainland to fuel the decadent building boom at the end of the Roman Empire. Most touching of the remains here is an image of Hercules Saxanus, the patron saint of hard labour, carved by slaves on the face of a large boulder.

the point. Driving is very dangerous, as there's no room for passing and no barriers at the side of the road.

Beaches around Bonifacio

Visible from the north side of the *haute ville*, the nearest accessible beach coves to Bonifacio, **Plage de la Catena** and **Plage de l'Arinella**, are small and picturesque but catch a lot of flotsam and oil pollution from the passing maritime traffic. However, the **walk** to them is very pleasant, beginning at a track just before *Camping L'Araguina* (see p.276).

On Corsica's southernmost tip, reached via a narrow but easily motorable road, a trio of small coves are the most popular beaches in this area. The first, **Plage de Pianterella**, is also the dullest, backed by an unsavoury swamp. Walk south around the headland for fifteen minutes and you'll reach the more pleasant **Plage de Sperone**, a pearl-white cove with calm, shallow water that's ideal for children. Overlooking the transparent waters of the straits, with Sardinia only 12km away, is the island's top **golf course**, 180 acres of immaculate turf installed with the help of huge subsidies from the regional assembly. In January 1997 it made headlines following the arrest of the nationalist leader François Santioni and his lawyer girlfriend, Marie-Hélène Mattei, who were accused of attempting to extort money from the golf club's owner, a Paris-based businessman called Jacques Dewez. Having refused to comply with the nationalists' demand for protection, Dewez's guardhouse was blown up on December 12 1996. Following the incident, however, Dewez did something almost unheard of in Corsica: he went to the police. All the evidence available suggested Santioni and his *Cuncolta* (the political wing of the FLNC-Canal historique) accomplices lay behind the blackmail, and aside from providing police with just the fi[illegible] they needed on one of the island's top political leaders, the new[illegible] also exposed *Cuncolta* as run-of-the-mill criminals. The scandal, however, has done little to dent the popularity of the golf course nor of the beach itself, which can get hopelessly crowded in summer. In this case, you may want to venture further around th[illegible] coast to **Plage de Calalonga**, where you stand a better chance o[illegible] escaping the masses at a string of sheltered coves. To get there head east of town on the D58, and take the first turning righ[illegible] after around 3km. Passing a series of heavily guarded militar[illegible] communications complexes, this narrows rapidly, deteriorating into a badly rutted *piste*, at the end of which lies a tiny bulldoze[illegible] car park.

The Golfe de Santa Manza

Marginally more enticing are the beaches lining the **Golfe d[illegible] Santa Manza**, northeast of Bonifacio along the D58. The first [illegible] these, **Plage de Maora**, lies at the far west end of the gulf, reached by a lane running north off the crossroads of the D60 and D58. A narrow curve of pink granite grit with a small *buvette*, it's frequented mainly by tourists from the surrounding *villages de vacances*. Further around the bay, the views improve and the coves, backed by the road, attract increasing numbers of watersports enthusiasts as you approach the **Plage de Santa Manza**, where the route ends. Again, the beach itself is a bit of a disappointment, but it does give access to a wild stretch of coast that has plenty of potential for walking. Don't follow the most obvious path along the shore; instead, head inland along a *piste* marked "Passage Privé" (it isn't private in fact), past the stone hut behind the beach and uphill for around twenty minutes as far as a fork. If you bear left here, you'll eventually come out, after around twenty to thirty minutes, at an old **watchtower**, from where the views along the coast and across to the Îles Lavezzi are wonderful.

Plages de Caneti and Balistra

Two of the least-frequented beaches in the Bonifacio region line the north coast of the Golfe de Santa Manza. With a backdrop of weathered chalk cliffs, **Plage de Caneti** is the most picturesque, but hard to reach. Heading north on the main Porto-Vecchio road, turn right directly opposite the *Camping di Liccia*, 3km out of town, and follow the signs for the luxury four-star *Hôtel Capu Biancu*, until you reach a fork after 4.5km. Bear left here (not right, which will take you to the hotel) and drop down the south bank of a stream; the beach lies a further 500m.

Plage de Balistra is the next beach up the coast, 5km north of the Caneti turning down an unsurfaced road (look for the signpost on the main road). The largest and least crowded in this area, it is strewn with seaweed and backed by an *étang* (brackish lagoon) that's a breeding ground for some particularly rapacious mosquitoes, but don't let this put you off. The sand is soft and white, and the views across the bay fine.

Rondinara

A perfect shell-shaped cove of turquoise water enclosed by soft dunes and a pair of twin headlands, **Rondinara** looks like most people's idea of a paradise Pacific lagoon, which is why you'll find it cropping up on postcard racks all over the island. Thankfully, it is also well off the beaten track, although the recent appearance of a surfaced road all the way to the beach could well change that. To see it at its most empty, get here early the morning. A large hoarding on the N198, 10km north of Bonifacio, indicates the way to "Camping Rondinara", 4km along the D158. Set back 300m or so behind the beach amid a scattering of (as yet) ineffectual saplings, the **campsite** (☎04 95 70 43 15, fax 04 95 70 56 79; mid-May to Sept) is spacious and well equipped, with its own pool. Tariffs are also low, considering the ideal location.

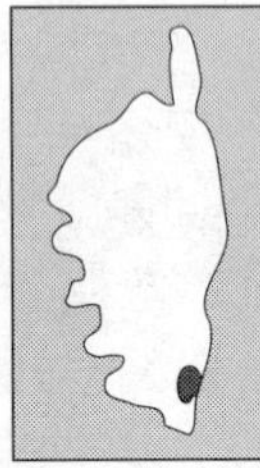

The Porto-Vecchio region

Nowhere on the island has been so thoroughly given over to tourism as the area around **Porto-Vecchio**, thanks to the wealth of white-sand beaches and turquoise bays that indent the coastline around this former Genoese port. Shaded by a canopy of pines, thousands of manicured holiday villas and *villages de vacances* carpet the headlands and hills behind the beaches, while the town itself, a seasonal ferry harbour, seems entirely populated by Italians in summer.

If you've wondered where those Seychelle-style beach shots might be that shine from every postcard rack on the island, head south from Porto-Vecchio to **Palombaggia**, Corsica's most-photographed beach, or to the translucent waters of **Santa Giulia**. Bear in mind, though, that these photos tend to be taken in winter, when the beaches are deserted, and that during the summer you won't be able to slot a postcard between the sun worshippers crammed onto them. The same goes for the bays north of Porto-Vecchio – **San Ciprianu** and **Pinarellu** – preludes to the near unbroken beach running from here all the way up the eastern plain to Bastia.

Most people make at least one trip to one of the many **prehistoric sites** dotted around Porto-Vecchio – north to the Bronze Age settlements of **Torre** and the **Casteddu d'Araggiu**, or south to the monuments at **Ceccia** and **Tappa**. To get right away from the sultry coast, you could head inland up to the cool **Forêt de l'Ospédale**, one of the highlights of southern Corsica.

Porto-Vecchio is connected by regular **buses** to Bastia, via the east coast highway. You can also get here on direct services from Ajaccio, either via the mountain route through Ospédale, Zonza and Bavella (see p.299), or on the Route Nationale that loops south through Propriano and Figari. In addition, *navettes* run throughout the busy summer months from the town to the most popular beaches in the area, including Santa Giulia and Palombaggia.

Porto-Vecchio

Set on a hill in the most sheltered corner of a deep gulf, **PORTO-VECCHIO**, in the southeast of the island, was rated by James Boswell as one of "the most distinguished harbours in Europe". Pleasure boats, yachts and international ferries still crowd the port

The Porto-Vecchio region

but trade has long given way to tourism as the town's *raison d'être*. Its popularity as a holiday centre derives more from the proximity of the island's most spectacular beaches, but you could do worse than spend an afternoon or evening here. Once beyond the unpromising outskirts – marred by roundabouts, light industry and patches of insalubrious marshland – things improve considerably as you approach the old **citadel** that still forms the hub of the town, with its leafy church square and picturesque backstreets, lined by restaurant terraces and designer boutiques.

Porto-Vecchio was founded in 1539 as a second Genoese stronghold on the east coast, Bastia being well established in the north. The location was perfect: close to the unexploited and fertile plain, the site benefited from secure high land and a sheltered gulf. Unfortunately, however, the Genoese hadn't counted on the mosqui-

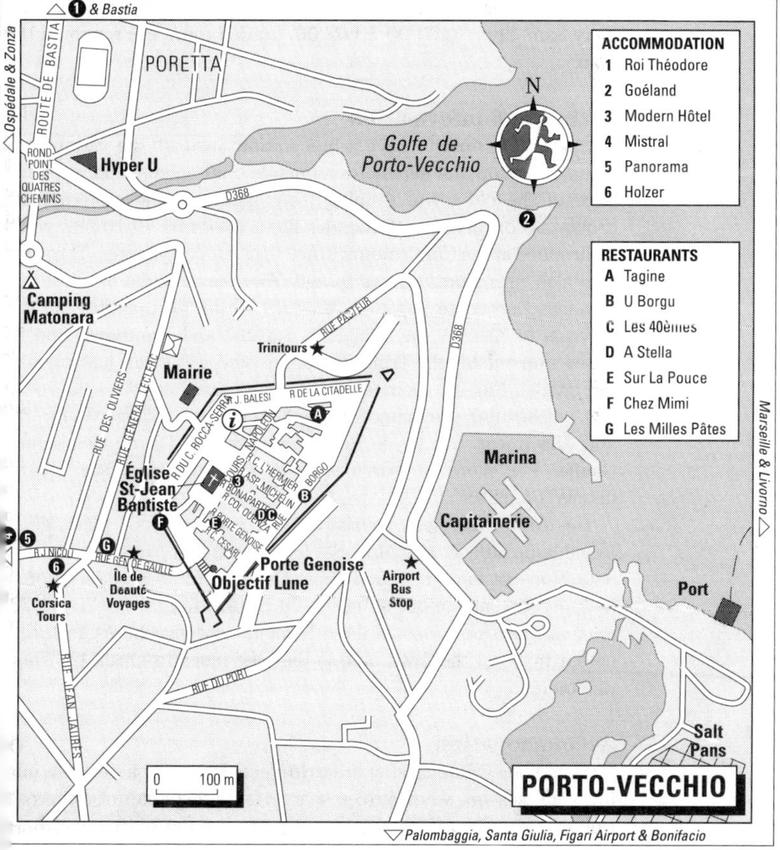

to problem, and within months malaria had wiped out the first Ligurian settlers. Sampiero Corso occupied the port for a brief period in 1564, having failed to take Ajaccio, but Genoa got it back a few months later, and things began to take off soon after, mainly thanks to the cork industry, which thrived until the twentieth century. Today a third of Corsica's wine is exported from here, but most revenue comes from the rich tourists who flock to the town each year, spending a fortune in Porto-Vecchio's flashy clothes shops.

Around the centre of town there's not much to see, apart from the well-preserved **fortress** and the small grid of ancient streets backing onto the main **place de la République**. East of the square you can't miss the **Porte Génoise**, which frames a delightful expanse of sea and through which you'll find the quickest route down to the modern **marina**, lined with cafés and hotels. Visible on the southern eastern fringes, a grid of shallow basins sporting rows of white mounds comprise the town's **salt pans**, or *salins*, which are open to visitors during the summer (mid-May to Sept daily 8am–8pm; ☎04 95 70 62 00; guided tours in French on the hour).

Arrival and information

Porto-Vecchio doesn't have a **bus** station; instead, the various bus companies stop and depart from outside their agents' offices on the edge of the old town. Coming from Bastia or the eastern plain (Solenzara or Aléria) with Rapides Bleus (☎04 95 70 10 36), you'll be dropped at the Corsicatours office on 7 rue Jean-Jaurès. The same firm also runs shuttle buses to and from Santa Giulia beach in the summer. Eurocorse Voyages (☎04 95 70 30 83) operates the fast services to Ajaccio via Bonifacio, Sartène and Propriano, and its buses stop outside the Trinitours office on rue Pasteur, just north of the citadel. Finally, the agents for Balési Évasion (☎04 95 70 15 55), whose minibus connects Porto-Vecchio with Ajaccio via Bavella and Alta Rocca, are Île de Beauté Voyages, at 13 rue Général-de-Gaulle. For more on services from Porto-Vecchio, see "Travel details" on p.299.

The town's efficient **tourist office**, just north of place de la République (July & Aug Mon–Sat 9am–8pm, Sun 9am–1pm; June & Sept Mon–Sat 9am–1pm & 3–6pm; Oct–May Mon–Fri 9am–noon & 2–6pm, Sat 9am–noon; ☎04 95 70 09 58, fax 04 95 70 03 72; *www.accueil-portovecchio.com*), hands out brochures featuring colour maps of the town, and is the best place to check transport timetables.

Accommodation

Finding somewhere to stay in Porto-Vecchio is only a problem during peak season, when prices soar even higher than elsewhere in Corsica. **Hotels** are grouped mostly around the old town, with a handful of more expensive places down in the marina, while **campsites** line the route north of the centre towards Pinarellu beach and Bastia, and along the road to Palombaggia.

Hotels

Goéland, port de Plaisance (☎04 95 70 14 15, fax 04 95 72 05 18; *hotel-goeland@wanadoo.fr*). Very pleasant and good value, in an excellent seaside location looking across the gulf; large rooms, convivial atmosphere. Tariff includes breakfast. ⑧.

Holzer, 12 rue Jean-Jaurès/rue Jean-Nicoli (☎04 95 70 05 93, fax 04 95 70 47 80). Labyrinthine place with airless, boxed-in rooms, but immaculately clean and very central. ⑦.

Mistral, rue Jean-Nicoli (☎04 95 70 08 53, fax 04 95 70 51 60). Comfortable mid-range hotel slightly removed from the noisy centre of town. Classier than the *Panorama* opposite, with the priciest rooms in a modern air-con block across the road. ⑦–⑧.

Modern, 10 cours Napoléon (☎04 95 70 06 36). Porto-Vecchio's best budget hotel, overlooking the square. Most rooms have shared toilets, but there are some en-suite options; particularly recommended are nos. 20 and 21 on the roof, which have gulf views. Tariffs are low even in high season and it's always popular, so book ahead. ④–⑦.

Panorama, 12 rue Jean-Nicoli (☎04 95 70 07 96, fax 04 95 70 46 78). Simple, family-run place with parking spaces, just above the old town. Somewhat spartan, but inexpensive for the area. ⑥.

Roi Théodore, route de Bastia, 500m north of Porto-Vecchio (☎04 95 70 14 94, fax 04 95 70 41 34). The best upmarket option: a splendid, tranquil hideaway boasting a gourmet restaurant, swimming pool, tennis courts and extensive grounds. ⑧.

Campsites

Asciaghju, Bocca di l'Oro (☎ & fax 04 95 70 37 87). Pick of the bunch within striking distance of the beaches to the south. Rock-hard ground, but plenty of shade, clean toilet blocks and only 300m from secluded Asciaghju beach (see p.294). Open mid-June to mid-Sept.

Arutoli, route de l'Ospédale (☎04 95 70 12 73). Large, well-equipped site located 2km northwest along the D368. Enormous swimming pool makes this a good option for families.

Îlots d'Or, Trinité de Porto-Vecchio, 5km north of town along the Bastia road (☎04 95 70 01 30). Very upmarket site with swimming pool and many more facilities.

Les Jardins du Golfe, 4km along the route de Palombaggia (☎04 95 70 46 92). One of a string of large, well-equipped sites lining the road to the area's most popular beach. This one's the closest to town and has a small shop and snack bar.

La Matonara, carrefour des Quatre-Chemins (☎04 95 70 37 05). A large site shaded by cork trees, with clean *sanitaires* blocks and washing machines. By far the best choice if you don't have your own vehicle, as it's within walking distance of the centre (see map, p.287), but don't come here without mosquito repellent.

Eating and drinking

On the whole, Porto-Vecchio's eating establishments are substandard tourist traps, but there are a couple of decent addresses where you can get quality fresh fish and seafood at affordable prices, and pizzerias and pasta places are found all over the centre. Cafés line place de la République and cours Napoléon, which runs along the east side of the square – *Au Bon Coin*, facing the church, is the nicest and least expensive. For quality, artisan-produced Corsican food, such as charcuterie, cheese, wine and liqueurs, pop into *L'Orriu*, 5 cours Napoléon – a member of the Authentica group (see p.40).

Les 40èmes, rue Bonaparte. Cosy, inexpensive *crêperie*, tucked away in the heart of the old town. Swathed in pot plants, their tables stand outside in the alleyway under awnings. Most crêpes 30–80F.

U Borgu, rue Borgo, parallel to cours Napoléon in the old town. Upscale pizzeria in the old town. The à la carte dishes are way overpriced, but the pizzas and salads are affordable and the views over the gulf sublime.

Les Milles Pâtes, 4 rue Général-de-Gaulle. Popular with locals for its wide variety of fresh pasta at reasonable prices. They offer three choices of three-course menus for under 100F, one featuring the delicious mixed seafood in cream of basil sauce.

Chez Mimi, 5 rue Général-Abbatucci. Run-of-the-mill streetside restaurant from the outside, but their 80F Corsican menu is one of the best deals in town, offering a choice of three or four dishes such as squid or the local speciality, stuffed aubergine. The portions are generous, too, and house wine is only 50F per litre.

A Stella, rue de colonel-Quenza. Tiny Spanish joint down a narrow alley in the old town, serving paella for a reasonable 75F, or paella *royale*, with lobster and crab for 110F, in addition to a range of inexpensive tapas.

Sur la Pouce, rue de la Porte-Genoise. Various *paninis* and other light snacks to take away for around 22F, many using quality local cheeses (try their delicious *panini "Corse"*, with real goat's cheese filling). A real find if you're on a tight budget.

Le Tagine, rue de la Citadelle. Authentic Moroccan cooking, based mainly on lamb, couscous and fresh vegetables, served from terracotta gratin dishes in an attractively decorated first-floor room. Most main dishes 85–115F.

Bars and nightlife

Apart from when the Italians swamp the town in August, **nightlife** is fairly low-key, revolving around the cafés in the square. The few bars and nightclubs that stand out are listed below. Admission to the clubs is free, but you're expected to shell out on at least a couple of exorbitantly priced drinks for the privilege.

L'Amnésia, nightclub situated on the road to Bonifacio. A large and posey place with an open-air dance floor and floodlit fountains.

Objectif Lune, on rue Jérôme-Léandri. Sports lively Tintin decor and hosts regular rock and jazz music sessions during the tourist season.

Pub de Bastion, opposite *Le Tagine* restaurant on rue de la Citadelle. Claiming to serve three hundred varieties of beer, this bar has one c

Corsica's only dartboards, and stages live music – cheesy local rock bands – most weekends.

Le Taverne du Roi, near the Porte Genoise, where you can hear more traditional music – a mixture of Corsican choral and folk tunes, and French standards, accompanied by guitar and piano.

Theatre d'Été, a small open-air stage down behind the marina. Hosts choral concerts and plays during the summer. Forthcoming events are advertised on posters around town, and in the tourist office.

Via Notte, on the south edge of town. One of the two most popular nightclubs in the area – a phenomenally kitsch Italian-oriented place.

Listings

Ambulance ☎15.

Banks and exchange All the big banks have branches in the town centre and will change travellers' cheques. Cash dispensers accepting Visa and other credit cards are available at the post office, Société Générale on the Quatre-Chemins crossroads near the Super U supermarket, and on the south wall of the Super U itself.

Car rental Budget, port de Plaisance (☎04 95 70 25 70); Citer, route de Bonifacio (☎04 95 70 16 96); Europcar, route de Bastia, Poretta (☎04 95 70 14 50); Hertz, Fillipi Auto, 1 quai Pascal-Paoli (☎04 95 70 28 04).

Diving CIP La Palanquée, Les Marines, 500m south of town on the Bonifacio road (☎04 95 70 16 53); Club Plongée Kallisté, Plage de Palombaggia (☎04 95 70 44 59); Hippocampe, Plage de la Chiappa, 11km southeast of town on the Palombaggia road (☎04 95 70 56 54). All the above can arrange trips to dive sites around the Îles Cerbicale, off Palombaggia, and the wreck of the *Pecorella*, lying 12m down at the north end of the gulf.

Internet access The tiny newsagents' directly opposite the tourist office on the square offers Internet access for 20F per 30 min.

Motorbike rental Garage Legrand, 3km south on the route de Bonifacio (☎04 95 70 15 84); Corse Moto Service, Yamaha Garage, route de Bastia, beyond the Géant supermarket (☎04 95 70 45 51); Suzuki Garage, route du Port-de-Plaisance (☎04 95 70 36 05).

Pharmacy on the corner of rue de Gaulle and rue Général-Leclerc.

Taxis ☎04 95 70 08 49.

Moving on from Porto-Vecchio

Porto-Vecchio's proximity to Figari airport means this is the first port of call for many independent travellers. Thankfully, it's well served by **public transport**, so you shouldn't have to spend more time here than you need in order to catch a bus somewhere else.

By plane

Figari airport, 28km southwest, is served by weekly charter **flights** to various destinations in northern Europe, including London Gatwick, and by domestic departures to several cities on the French mainland. During the summer there are also special helicopter flights for tourists around the gulf, costing 250–750F per person;

for more details, contact the Société Figari Aviation-Transports, on route du Port (☎04 95 72 07 12). **Getting to Figari** without your own vehicle is straightforward during the summer, when a bus leaves from opposite the *Capitainerie* (harbourmaster's) in the marina to connect with flights; tickets cost 50F single (for precise timetable information, contact Transports Rossi on ☎04 95 71 00 11). At other times of year, you'll have to take a taxi or catch the Ajaccio bus there.

By ferry

Car and passenger **ferry** services from Porto-Vecchio to Marseille and Livorno operate from mid-June to September, with none during the rest of the year.

Corsica Marittima, Port de Commerce (☎04 95 31 46 29). To Livorno (June–Sept 1–2 weekly; first week of Sept 3 weekly). The 7hr 30min–10hr 30min crossing costs 180–200F per passenger, 470–610F per car.

SNCM, Port de Commerce (☎04 95 70 06 03, fax 04 95 70 33 59). To Marseille (mid-June to Sept 3 1–3 weekly). The overnight crossing on the *Monte d'Oro* takes 14hr 30min and costs 256–292F per passenger, 214–614F per car.

For more general details on ferry services to Corsica, see "Basics," p.7.

By bus

Buses to **Ajaccio** via **Figari**, **Sartène** and **Propriano** are operated by Eurocorse Voyages (☎04 95 70 30 83), leaving two to three times daily (except Sun) from in front of the Trinitours travel agents on rue Pasteur (see map, p.287). From June through September you can also travel to the capital via a longer and more convoluted mountain route that takes you through **Ospédale**, **Zonza**, **Quenza** and **Aullène**; this service is run by Balési Évasion (July & Aug Mon–Sat; June & Sept to May Mon & Thurs; ☎04 95 17 15 55), and leaves from outside Île de Beauté Voyages, 13 rue Général-de-Gaulle, at 7am. For **Bonifacio**, there are one to four buses each day with Eurocorse Voyages, taking thirty minutes. Rapides Bleus (☎04 95 70 10 36) also run coaches up the east coast to **Bastia** (3hr) from outside the Corsicatours office, 7 rue Jean-Jaurès. Departure points for all of the above services are marked on the town plan on p.287.

Tickets for all bus services can be bought on the day from the driver. Note that in the winter timetables are scaled down slightly departure times may be checked at any of the travel agents in towr or at the tourist office.

Finally, if you're spending any time in the area and need transpor to the beaches south of Porto-Vecchio, it's worth knowing that dur ing July and August buses run out to **Santa Giulia** and **Palombaggia** leaving two to four times daily from the *Matonara* campsite; you ca also pick up the bus from the *Capitainerie* in the marina, or flag i down at various points along the N198.

Massif de l'Ospédale

Broadly covering the hinterland of the Golfe de Porto-Vecchio, limited in the northwest by the Massif de Bavella and in the southwest by the Montagne de Cagna, the **Massif de l'Ospédale** is a forested upland characterized by enormous granite boulders. Attractions up here include an impressive artificial **lake**, which makes an ideal picnic spot, and a magnificent beech forest, the **Forêt de l'Ospédale.** Although much of the woodland was devastated by fire four or five years back, enough remains on the higher slopes to make this a rewarding area for short hikes, with spellbinding views across the gulf.

Leaving Porto-Vecchio by the D368 northwest of town, a twisty drive of 19km up the slopes will soon get you to **OSPÉDALE**, a village that has long been used as a summer resort by the inhabitants of Porto-Vecchio. Plumb in the middle of the forest, within a backdrop of massive clumps of granite, it provides fine views through the trees across L'Alta Rocca and over the Golfe de Porto-Vecchio to Sardinia in the other direction. A great location from which to make the most of the views is the **restaurant** in the centre of the village, *Chez Paul – Le Vieux Lavoir*. It's a pricy place, serving fussy French-influenced Corsican food, but you can drop in for a coffee on the sunny terrace, from where the rippling hills and coast of Sardinia are clearly visible to the south. A less expensive place to eat lies just above the village, hidden among the giant pines and granite boulders of the massif. *Le Refuge*, above the village at the hamlet of Cartalaavonu, near the trailhead of the Mare a Mare Sud, is popular with tourists and locals alike for its fragrant home-made charcuterie and wild-boar pâté; a full four- or five-course meal, served in the rustic dining room, costs around 150F, plus wine. They also offer basic **accommodation** for hikers, at 60F per bed, in four- to six-bed dorms.

In the intense heat of summer, most people pass through Ospédale and head straight for the **lake**, which emerges a couple of kilometres up the road. A shimmering blue expanse backed by lines of spindly black trees, the lake is surrounded by marked forest trails in every direction. A particularly enjoyable walk goes to the **Piscia di Gallo** (Piss of the Cockerel) waterfall, a two-hour walk that provides plenty of opportunities to stop and bathe. The route begins about 1km past the dam on the right-hand side of the road, beyond the large parking area. From here the trail meanders through the pines and the maquis and crosses two streams before veering to the right. When you reach an opening in the pines, follow the stream for about 1km, keeping it on your right, and listen out for the sound of the waterfall about to come into view. Some 50m high, it's an impressive sight, plummeting between giant rocks into a swirling green pool.

North of the lake lies the **Forêt de Barocaggio-Marghèse**, a magnificent pine forest dominated by the pyramidal **Punta di u Diamante** (1227m); just past here the road crosses the **Col d'Illirata** (991m), 25km from Porto-Vecchio and 15km south of Zonza (see p.257).

Around Porto-Vecchio

Much of the coast of the **Golfe de Porto-Vecchio** and its environs is characterized by ugly development and dismal swampland, yet some of the clearest, bluest sea and whitest beaches on Corsica are also found around here. The most frequented of these can be reached by **bus** from town in the summer (see p.292); at other times of year you'll need your own transport.

South of Porto-Vecchio

Heading **south of Porto-Vecchio** along the main N198, take the turning signposted "Palombaggia" about 1km along and you'll find yourself on a narrow road leading to the hamlet of Picovaggia. Here you can veer left for the headland marking the southern limit of the Golfe de Porto-Vecchio, the **Punta di a Chiappa**, or keep going 3km south to **Plage de Palombaggia**, a golden semicircle of sand edged by short twisted umbrella pines and fantastically shaped red rocks. This might be the most beautiful beach in Corsica were it not for the crowds, which pour onto the beach in such numbers that a wattle fence has had to be erected to protect the dunes. A few kilometres further along the same road takes you to the **Golfe de Santa Giulia**, a sweeping sandy bay backed by a lagoon. Despite the presence of several holiday villages and facilities for windsurfing and other watersports, crowds are less of a problem here, and the shallow bay is an extraordinary turquoise colour.

A couple of equally beautiful, but somewhat less crowded, beaches lie **between Palombaggia and Santa Giulia**, backed by dunes and pine trees. The largest of them, **Plage d'Asciaghju** (sometimes spelt "Acciaju") has a small campsite (see "Accommodation" on p.289). Narrow access lanes and *pistes* peel off the main road around the headland at regular intervals, but the best way to enjoy these beaches is by walking along them; interpretative panels give detailed rundowns of the local flora, which includes a wealth of juniper species that conservationists are attempting to protect by fencing off areas of the dunes.

North of Porto-Vecchio

North of Porto-Vecchio, the coast has been intensively developed, much of it for upmarket tourism, with self-contained *villages de vacances* and sprawling villa complexes shielded from view by screens of recently planted pine trees. The first beach along this stretch, **baie de Stagnolu**, is the least appealing, backed by a large campsite, *Camping Golfo di Sogno* (☎04 95 70 08 98). Just around the headland, **Cala Rossa** is a beautiful bay of reddish sand and turquoise water. Large modern villas line up behind it, some of them very swish indeed, with landscaped gardens running right down to the beach, leaving little room for outsiders. Development is rather

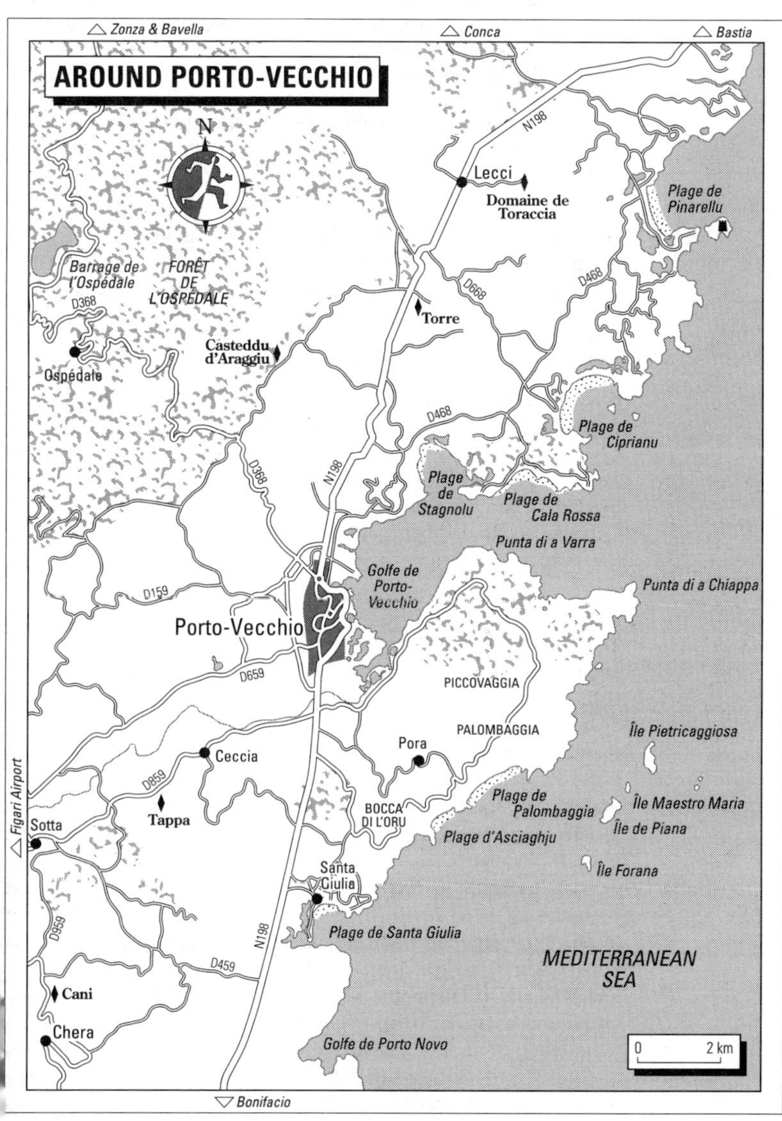

The Domaine de Torraccia

A short way inland from Pinarellu, the hamlet of Lecci, straddling the main Porto-Vecchio to Bastia Route Nationale, marks the turning for one of Corsica's finest vineyards, the **Domaine de Toraccia**. It was founded in the mid-1960s by viticulturalist Christian Imbert. Produced with traditional vine stock and labour-intensive organic cultivation methods, his wines have become renowned throughout the island, particularly the red, labelled "Oriu". You can visit the vineyard (Mon–Sat 8am–noon & 2–6pm; free) and taste the *domaine*'s range in its cellar, where there's an engaging exhibition of old Corsican photographs to peruse. Pick of the vintages currently on sale (at bargain prices, considering what you'd pay for these wines in the shops) is the 1998 Oriu, among the few quality local wines that ages well.

less obtrusive at **baie de San Ciprianu**, a half-moon of white sand, reached by turning left off the main road at the Elf garage. A few years back, the FLNC destroyed one of the largest holiday complexes here, having removed all the residents in minibuses during the middle of the night. The most promising beach for day-trips in this area, however, has to be the **Plage de Pinarellu**, 7km further up the coast, whose long sweep of immaculately clean, soft white sand is overlooked by a stately Genoese watchtower.

Beyond here, north of the village of Sainte-Lucie-de-Porto-Vecchio, the **Côte des Nacres** runs from Favone to Solenzara. The beaches at the **Anse de Favone** and **Canella** are pretty average by Corsican standards, but they gain immensely from the backdrop of towering crags behind.

Conca

The largest village inland from Pinarellu bay is **CONCA**, renowned among hikers as the traditional finishing (or starting) point of the GR20, France's toughest long-distance footpath (see pp.144–145). Scattered over a broad amphitheatre of maquis, with the crags of Punta d'Orto towering behind, it is livelier than most villages in Porto-Vecchio's depopulated, fire-scarred *arrière pays*, but holds nothing of sufficient interest to warrant a diversion from the nearby Route Nationale, beyond its role as walkers' gateway to the interior mountains.

Footsore GR20 veterans stagger straight to the gîte d'étape, *La Tonnelle* (☎04 95 71 46 55; ①–②), at the bottom of the village, run by an affable outdoor sports enthusiast who's also a good cook. Beds here cost between 70F and 100F depending on the size of the dorm, and you can camp in the garden for 30F. Breakfast (30F) and evening meals (70F; reserve in advance) are served in a cosy common dining room. For a small fee, the *gardien* will also run guests to and from **Sainte-Lucie-de-Porto-Vecchio**, on the Route Nationale, where you can pick up onward buses; this village also has a campsite that's handy if you pull in late from Bastia and intend to head off on the GR20 the following day.

If you fancy pampering yourself after a fortnight of rough refuges in the mountains, head for the *Hôtel San Pasquale*, at the top of the village (☎04 95 71 56 13; ⑥), which offers very comfortable studio apartments with large balconies, or smaller en-suite rooms, overlooking a sunny central courtyard. They don't do food, but the *U Chjosu* **restaurant**, a Corsican speciality place on Conca's main street, is only a short walk away.

Prehistoric sites around Porto-Vecchio

Torréen settlements are concentrated south of a line running from Ajaccio to Solenzara, with the majority located around Porto-Vecchio. The most fully preserved example is **Torre** itself, situated not too far to the north of Porto-Vecchio. Nearby **Casteddu d'Araggiu**, another Bronze Age settlement set higher on the mountain slopes above the gulf, is also worth a visit, and to complete the prehistoric tour you should go south of Porto-Vecchio to visit the sites of **Ceccia** and **Tappa**, also impressive legacies of the Torréen civilization. Finally, a worthwhile side-trip from the main Porto-Vecchio to Figari road takes you south to the tiny hamlet of Chera, where two enigmatic natural rock formations, known as **orii**, have become the objects of much local folklore.

Torre and the Casteddu d'Araggiu

Just follow the N198 north of Porto-Vecchio for 8km to reach **Torre**, which stands on its own a little way from the main road on the right-hand side. Built against a massive granite rock and covered in broad stone slabs, the semicircular construction, an impressive if small-scale Torréen edifice, crowns a granite hillock above a tiny farming hamlet, and is thought to have been used as a crematorium.

More background on the Torréens appears on p.232.

The **Casteddu d'Araggiu** lies on the other side of the main road, about 4km up the D759; from the site's car park it's a twenty-minute stiff climb through maquis and scrubby woodland, much of it burned out, along a well-defined path. Built in 2000 BC and inhabited by a community that lived by farming and hunting, the *casteddu* consists of a complex of chambers built into a massive circular wall of pink granite, splashed with vivid green patches of lichen. The site is entered via a 10m-long corridor covered in stone slabs. Immediately to the left you'll see a small triangular enclosure, in the centre of which would have been a clay fireplace, a forerunner of the *zidda* (hearth) found in traditional Corsican households. Continuing in a clockwise direction you come to the *torre* itself, comprising a central chamber, of which only the foundations remain. Past the tower, the next chamber – measuring 10m across – also harbours the remains of a fireplace, and a little further on it's possible to make out a well built into the thick walls, beyond which stands another small hut with fireplace.

Ceccia and Tappa

The **Ceccia** site lies about 5km southwest of Porto-Vecchio along the D859, a twenty-minute walk from the village of the same name. Set on a conspicuous spur, this isolated tower was raised around 1350 BC, possibly for scanning the surrounding countryside for invaders, or for cult purposes. Unlike other Torréen sites, no traces of dwellings remain here.

About 1km southwest of Ceccia down the D859, you'll find the **Tappa** *casteddu* signposted to the south of the road, opposite an abandoned farm building. Set on a granite mound about ten minutes' walk away, the site lies on private property and is approached on foot, passing through the gate and following the direction indicated. The surrounding wall is considered to be more recent than the rest of the *casteddu*, which was developed in the half-millennium prior to 1000 BC. A large *torre* at the southern end of the site consists of several small rooms around a central chamber. A ramp leads up to the main structure, entered by a narrow corridor, inside which another ramp winds up to a second level. The excavation of various clay pots, pounding implements and grindstones here has led archeologists to propose that this building was used for milling as well as storage.

The Orii of Chera and Cani

Amidst the chaos of rocks by the side of the roads in southern Corsica, you occasionally come across large boulders whose overhanging crevices have been bricked in with masonry. Known as **orii** (*oriu* in the singular), these distinctive rock formations, whose name is thought to derive from the Latin for "granary", *horreum*, have been used for centuries to store grain and hay, and to provide shelter for animals. They crop up with surprising frequency in old folk songs and legends, suggesting they were at one time central to the life of rural communities; some have even been "Christianized" and are the focus of religious rituals.

One such *oriu* stands in the far-flung hamlet of **CHERA**, roughly midway between Porto-Vecchio and Bonifacio (turn south off the D859 at Sotta). The most famous of its kind, it overlooks the village from the top of a rocky outcrop, crowned by a crucifix. Local people believe the artificial cave sheltered their pastoralist ancestors when they fled here centuries ago to escape a vendetta in the mountains, since when it has been revered as a kind of guardian spirit of the Culioli clan. Dorothy Carrington – who was shown the *oriu* by one of the island's most renowned bards, the long-white-bearded Jean-André Culioli – was told it was haunted by a phantom goat whose hoofsteps could occasionally be heard trotting over the rock in the dead of night.

Even spookier is the *oriu* of **CANI**, 4km north down the valley from Chera (look for a hand-painted sign on the right, or east, side of the road). Pull over outside the farmhouses where the road ends and follow the track as it bends right; once over two stiles, you come to a breach in a wall, from where a faint trail cuts uphill through the woods to the *oriu*, perched on a rock platform above the tiny hamlet. An unfeasibly contorted lump of granite with a strange high-pitched "roof", the structure looks like one of Salvador Dali's nightmares, and it's not hard to see why local people believe it was once inhabited by a witch. In fact, the last recorded resident was one Vinceguerra Pietri, the local landowner, who lived here until a ripe old age at the end of the nineteenth century.

Travel details

BUSES

AR = Autocars Ricci (☎04 95 51 08 19 or 04 95 76 25 59).
BE = Balési Évasion (☎04 95 70 14 50 or 04 95 70 15 55).
EV = Eurocorse Voyages (☎04 95 70 30 83).
RB = Rapides Bleus (☎04 95 31 03 79 or 04 95 70 10 36).

Bonifacio to: Ajaccio (EV; Mon–Sat 2 daily; 3–4hr); Olmeto (EV; Mon–Sat 2 daily; 1hr 55min); Porto-Vecchio (EV; Mon–Sat 1–4 daily; 30min); Propriano (EV; 2–4 daily; 1hr 40min); Roccapina (EV; Mon–Sat 2–4 daily; 45min); Sartène (EV; Mon–Sat 1–4 daily; 1hr 25min).

Levie to: Ajaccio (BE/AR; Mon–Sat 1–2 daily; 2hr 45min); Bavella (BE/AR; 1–2 daily; 30min); Sainte-Lucie-de-Tallano (BE/AR; 1–2 daily; 15min); Zonza (BE/AR; 1–2 daily; 15min).

Olmeto to: Ajaccio (EV; 2–4 daily; 1hr 30min); Bonifacio (EV; Mon–Sat 2–4 daily; 2hr 15min); Porto-Vecchio (EV; 2–4 daily; 1hr 45min); Propriano (EV; Mon–Sat 2–4 daily; 15min); Roccapina (EV; 2–4 daily; 45min); Sartène (EV; 2–4 daily; 40min).

Porto-Vecchio to: Ajaccio (EV/ BE/AR; 2–4 daily; 3hr 30min); Bastia (RB; 2 daily; 3hr); Bonifacio (EV; Mon–Sat 1–4 daily; 30min); Olmeto (EV; 2–4 daily; 1hr 45min to Figari); Propriano (EV/BE/AR; 2–4 daily; 2hr 10min); Roccapina (EV; 2–4 daily; 1hr); Sartène (EV; 2–4 daily; 1hr 55min).

Propriano to: Ajaccio (EV/BE/AR; 2–4 daily; 1hr 50min); Bonifacio (EV; 2–4 daily; 1hr 40min); Olmeto (EV/ BE/AR; 2–4 daily; 15min); Porto-Vecchio (EV/BE/AR; 2–4 daily; 2hr 10min); Roccapina (EV; 2–4 daily; 40min); Sartène (EV/ BE/AR; 2–4 daily; 20min).

Roccapina to: Ajaccio (EV; 2–4 daily; 2hr 30min); Bonifacio (EV; Mon–Sat 2–4 daily; 45min); Olmeto (EV; 2–4 daily; 45min); Porto-Vecchio (EV; 2–4 daily; 1hr); Propriano (EV; 2–4 daily; 40min); Sartène (EV; 2–4 daily; 30min).

Sainte-Lucie-de-Tallano to: Ajaccio (EV/BE/AR; 1–2 daily; 2hr 20min); Bavella (BE/AR; 1–2 daily; 45min); Levie (BE/AR; 1–2 daily; 30min); Zonza (BE/AR; 1–2 daily; 30min).

Sartène to: Ajaccio (EV/BE/AR; 2–4 daily; 2hr 10min); Bonifacio (EV; Mon–Sat 1–4 daily; 1hr 25min); Olmeto (EV; 2–4 daily; 40min); Porto-Vecchio (EV; 2–4 daily; 1hr 55min); Propriano (EV/BE/AR; 2–4 daily; 20min); Roccapina (EV; 2–4 daily; 30min).

Zonza to: Ajaccio (BE/AR; 1–2 daily; 2hr 45min); Bavella (BE/AR; 1–2 daily; 15min); Levie (BE/AR; 1–2 daily; 15min); Sainte-Lucie-de-Tallano (BE/AR; 1–2 daily; 30min).

FERRIES

Bonifacio to: Santa Teresa di Gallura, Sardinia (mid-July to Sept 10–14 daily; March to mid-July & Sept 4–7 daily; 1hr).

The Porto-Vecchio region

Porto-Vecchio to: Livorno (June–Sept 1–2 weekly; first week of Sept 3 weekly; 7hr 30min–10hr 30min); Marseille (mid-June to Sept 1–3 weekly; 14hr 30min).

Propriano to: Marseille (March–May 1 weekly, June to mid-July 1 weekly, mid-July to Aug 5 weekly, Sept 4 weekly; 9hr 30min); Toulon (March–May 1 weekly, June to mid-July 1 weekly, mid-July to Aug 5 weekly, Sept 4 weekly; 8hr 30min–10hr 30min).

Chapter 6

Eastern Corsica

Comprising a hundred and fifty square kilometres of vine-striped plains backed by rippling hills, the landscape of Corsica's **east coast** is restrained in comparison with the rest of the island. If you do visit the region, it'll probably be to take advantage of the smooth, straight N198, the island's main north–south artery, from which windier side-roads penetrate the more varied and rugged interior. That said, the *littoral oriental* does have its attractions, not least of which are several vast sandy beaches, where scattered resorts and a string of large self-contained campsites offer plenty of inexpensive accommodation. Solenzara, for example, is one of the area's more alluring small seaside towns, at the head of the spectacular road leading to the Col de Bavella. North of here, beyond the rather tired resort of **Ghisonaccia**, you move into the eastern plain, an enormous malaria-ridden swamp until the Americans sprayed it with DDT after World War II. Now enclosing kilometres of clementine orchards and vineyards, this patchwork of fields is punctuated by shimmering lagoons, of which the **Étang d'Urbino** and **Étang de Diane** are the largest, supplying plentiful oysters and seafood for the local restaurants. Set on a rise between these lagoons is the Roman capital of **Aléria**, which boasts an excellent museum, a beach close by, and a few hotels straddling the main road.

Inland, you could drive up to the terraced villages of the **Fiumorbo** region for a grand view of the plain and the Tuscan islands offshore,

Accommodation Price Codes

Throughout this guide, hotel accommodation is graded on a scale from ① to ⑧. These numbers show the cost per night of the cheapest double room **in high season**, though remember that many of the cheap places will have more expensive rooms with en-suite facilities. In such cases we list two price codes, indicating the range of room rates offered.

① under 100F/under €15	⑤ 300–350F/€45–52.50
② 100–200F/€15–30	⑥ 350–400F/€52.50–60
③ 200–250F/€30–37.50	⑦ 400–500F/€60–75
④ 250–300F/€37.50–45	⑧ 500F and above/€75 and above

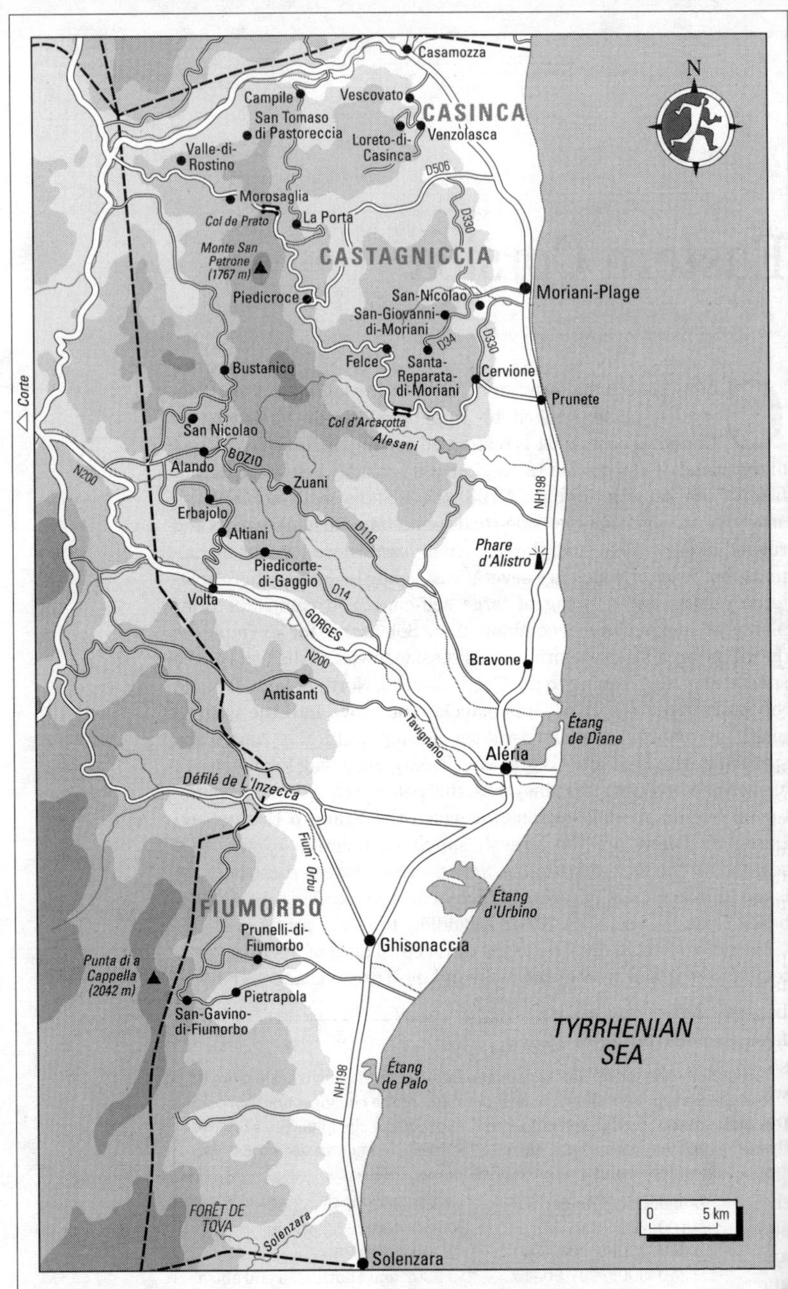
Casamozza
Campile
Vescovato
CASINCA
San Tomaso
di Pastoreccia
Loreto-di-
Casinca
Venzolasca
Valle-di-
Rostino
D506
Morosaglia
Col de Prato
La Porta
D330
Monte San
Petrone
(1767 m)
CASTAGNICCIA
Piedicroce
San-Nicolao
Moriani-Plage
San-Giovanni-
di-Moriani
D34
D330
Felce
Santa-
Reparata-
di-Moriani
Cervione
Bustanico
Prunete
Corte
Col d'Arcarotta
San Nicolao
Alesani
Alando
BOZIO
N200
Zuani
NH198
Erbajolo
Altiani
D116
Phare
d'Alistro
Piedicorte-
di-Gaggio
D14
Volta
GORGES
N200
Bravone
Antisanti
Tavignano
Étang
de Diane
Aléria
Défilé de L'Inzecca
Fium' Orbu
Étang
d'Urbino
FIUMORBO
Prunelli-di-
Fiumorbo
Ghisonaccia
Punta di a
Cappella
(2042 m)
Pietrapola
San-Gavino-
di-Fiumorbo
TYRRHENIAN
SEA
NH198
Étang
de Palo
FORÊT DE
TOVA
Solenzara
0
5 km
Solenzara
N

or venture into the craggy gorges and precarious villages of the **Vallée du Tavignano** and the **Bozio**, either as a diversion on the drive to or from Bastia or as a route into the core of the island. North of here, verdant **Castagniccia** is a fascinating region to explore, its tunnelled roads twisting past waterfalls and through an enormous forest of chestnut trees that shelters the highest concentration of highland villages in Corsica. A bed around here can be found at **Cervione**, the largest village in these parts, or **Piedicroce**, an old village occupying a fantastic location on the slopes of Monte San Petrone. North of the Castagniccia lies the **Casinca**, a more compact region of delightful villages such as **Vescovato** and **Venzolasca**, which could feasibly be seen on a day excursion from Bastia.

Transport around the east isn't too bad: Rapides Bleus' **bus** passes twice daily (June 15 to Sept 15 2 daily; mid-Sept to mid-June Mon–Sat 2 daily; ☎04 95 31 03 79) along the coast, stopping at Solenzara, Ghisonaccia and Aléria on its way between Bastia and Porto-Vecchio, but there's no service into the Fiumorbo and Tavignano valleys. For the Castagniccia you'll need a car, though the *micheline* train does pass through Casamozza, from where you can hitch into the region.

Solenzara, Ghisonaccia and Fiumorbo

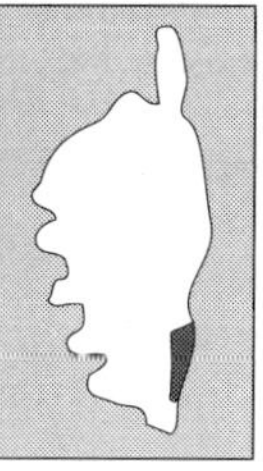

SOLENZARA might not be the most glamorous coastal resort in Corsica, but its endless sandy beach, hidden behind a strip of shops and busy marina, inspired Iggy Pop's French hit, *Sur la plage de Solenzara*, from the soundtrack of the movie *Arizona Dream*. The village's other claim to fame is that it lies at the junction of the **route de Bavella** (see p.258), one of the island's most spectacular mountain roads, whose lower reaches hug the river, giving access to numerous bathing and picnic spots.

There are a few **hotels** here as well: try the *Mare è Festa*, a pink-painted place at the southern end of the village (☎04 95 57 42 91, fax 04 95 57 43 23; ④), which rents cabins backing onto a small beach; or the *Maquis et Mer*, on the main street (☎04 95 57 42 37, fax 04 95 57 46 85; ⑤) – a huge old-fashioned three-star with a solemn Corsican restaurant and a swish bar (ask for a room in the old wing, which has flagstone floors, an original granite staircase and pale-blue shutters on the windows). The cheapest option is the family-run *Orsoni*, further up the main street, just past the tourist office (☎04 95 57 40 25; ②–③). *La Solenzara*, above the beach north of the village (☎04 95 57 42 18, fax 04 95 57 46 84; ⑦), is the most stylish place in the area, with high stucco ceilings, gilt candelabras and a gorgeous pool overlooking the sea; they also have a restaurant and do good off-season discounts.

The **tourist office**, on the main street opposite the Prisunic supermarket in the centre (June to Sept daily 9am–noon & 5–10pm; Sept to June Mon–Fri 9am–noon; ☎04 95 57 43 75), can provide additional addresses in the unlikely event that these hotels are booked up. For those intending to **camp**, there's *Camping de la Côte des Nacres*, set amid eucalyptus trees 1.5km north of Solenzara next to the river and beach (☎04 95 57 40 65; May–Oct), or the cheaper *U Rosumarinu*, 1.5km further up the main road (☎04 95 57 47 66; April–Sept).

Ghisonaccia

The one sizeable village between Solenzara and Aléria is dusty **GHISONACCIA**, whose pejorative "*accia*" suffix (meaning "bad") seems just as applicable today as it was when the town was a malarial bog. That said, the place has enjoyed a certain prosperity ever since the late 1950s, when pieds-noirs from Algeria bought much of the hitherto useless agricultural land in the area to plant vineyards. The wine they eventually produced became France's leading brand of cheap *vin de table*, stimulating a boom that lasted until the 1970s, when it was discovered that most of Ghisonaccia's farmers had been mixing sugar and dodgy chemicals into their wine to bump up production. Since then, the vines have been replaced by orchards of clementines, kiwis and other soft fruit, picked by the low-paid Arab agro-workers you'll see hanging around the main crossroads. The village's other main source of revenue, after tourism and farming, are the close-cropped national service lads from the nearby airforce base who fill the bars on weekends.

For more background on this scandal, and its violent repercussions, see box on p.309.

Practicalities

If you have to **stay** in Ghisonaccia, make for the welcoming *De la Poste*, an old-fashioned place just north of the crossroads on the Ghisoni road opposite the war memorial (☎ & fax 04 95 56 00 41; ④–⑤), whose pink and frilly restaurant has good-value 100F set menus featuring Corsican home cooking. Otherwise, there's the posher and pricier *Franceschini*, on the other side of the crossroads (☎04 95 56 05 32; ⑥).

The nearest **beach**, Plage de Tignale, lies 4km east; it's clean and large enough, but gets inundated during the summer by thousands of Germans and Italians from the enormous **campsites** behind it. These are all flashy four-star places complete with restaurants, shops, coin-operated fridges and the like. The most homely of the bunch is the *Arinella Bianca*, reached via a signposted turning off the main beach road (☎04 95 56 04 78, fax 04 95 56 12 54; May–Oct). A pleasant and relatively inexpensive place to **eat** at Plage de Tignale is *Les Deux Magots*, where you can enjoy locally caught seafood such as mussels and *loup de mer* on a breezy beachside terrace.

Making your way north from Ghisonaccia, you could turn off for the **Étang d'Urbino**, one of the half-dozen lagoons that break the monotony of the plain. Accessible via a dirt track, 10km along the main road from Ghisonaccia, this is a delightfully peaceful spot, fringed by reed beds.

The Mare a Mare Centre Trail

The **Mare a Mare Centre** footpath slices diagonally across the middle of Corsica, between Ghisonaccia on the eastern plain and Porticcio at the southern tip of the Golfe d'Ajaccio. Accessible to all from late April to November, it sees relatively few hikers, though the route is as varied and scenic as any on the island, with some particularly memorable stretches along remote ridges overlooking the sea. The trail is also punctuated at each of its seven stages by **gîtes d'étape**, and you can make several worthwhile side-trips to picturesque interior villages along the way.

Marked with orange splashes of paint, the Mare a Mare Centre starts 2.5km south of Ghisonaccia on the N198, near a bridge called Pont de l'Abatescu, which you can reach on any of the buses running between Bastia and Porto-Vecchio. From here the trail cuts across fruit orchards and vineyards, nurtured by the River Fium'orbu, from which this region takes its name, to begin a gradual ascent of the coastal range, peppered with red-roofed granite villages. Once over the snow-prone Col de Laparo (1525m), you enter the region of Haut Taravo, named after the river that drains into the Golfe de Valinco near Propriano, and thence head west via remote Cozzano and Tasso to Guitera-les-Bains, where the path climbs out of the Taravo valley and over a thickly forested ridge into Frasseto. Exposed ridges characterize the remaining few stages of the trail as it strikes north from Quasquara to scale the rocky Punta d'Urghiavari, before bending southwest to cross the main Ajaccio–Bonifacio road at the Col St-Georges. From here, another sharp ascent takes you onto a high ridge, and the path gives little ground until its junction with the Mare e Monti trail near the isolated village of Bisinao, where it swings northwest towards Porticcio.

Although it's divided into seven **stages** (of between 3hr and 6hr 30min), you can complete the route in six days by combining the first two stages, making a longer than average first day from Ghisonaccia to Catastaghju (7hr). Essential, as ever, is the Parc Naturel Régional's topo-guide *Corse: Entre Mer et Montagne*, which indicates the route on a full-colour contour map, with a description of the trail and its chief highlights in French.

Mare a Mare Centre gîtes d'étape

Ghisonaccia See p.304.
Serra-di-Fiumorbu Mme Guidicelli (☎04 95 56 75 48).
Catastaghju Mme Paoli (☎04 95 56 70 14).
Cozzano M. Pantalacci (☎04 95 24 41 59).
Zicavo See p.358.
Guitera les Bains M. Lafranchi (☎04 95 24 44 40).
Quasquara (☎04 95 53 61 21).
Col St-Georges Mme Renucci (☎04 95 25 70 06).
Porticcio See p.218.

Fiumorbo

The little-explored region of **Fiumorbo** (or Fium'orbo), immediately inland from Ghisonaccia, has been renowned for the independent spirit of its inhabitants ever since 1769, when a group of shepherds who had refused to ascribe to French laws were struck down in an ambush along the road to Corte. Thirty years later a coalition of royalist, Paolist and pro-British Corsican exiles organized another anti-French rebellion, which spread as far as the Sartenais before it was crushed by the French authorities. This tradition continued into the early nineteenth century, when an insurrection broke out and five thousand troops hired by Louis XVIII's government were unable to suppress the hordes of mountain people who seized control of the region. Eventually the ringleaders were either gunned down or deported to the French mainland by Général Morand, who was nevertheless obliged to accede to them an area of coastal land. By the end of the century the Fiumorbo had become notorious bandit country, ruled by outlaws who terrorized the villages, untouched by the police, but today this is one of the quietest, and most untroubled, parts of Corsica.

The region is reached by taking the D244 west off the main road 2km south of Ghisonaccia, then turning onto the D145, a route that takes you into the valley of the **River Albatesco**, a tributary of the River Fium'orbu ("Blind Waters") and location of the chief villages of the region. Once on the D145, you can either take the amazingly contorted sideroad up to **SERRA-DI-FIUMORBO**, which gives a fantastic view of the coastal plain, or continue to **PIETRAPOLA**, whose **thermal baths** attract sufferers from arthritis and rheumatic disorders throughout the year. The village is also thought to have been the site of an encounter between local bandits and a detachment of Roman soldiers en route from Sardinia in 231BC. Ambushed and relieved of their booty, the Romans pursued the Corsican robbers into the hills, only to nearly die of hunger and thirst trying to find a way down again. Eventually they discovered a spring at Pietrapola and survived, consecrating a special "Temple of the Spring" at the gates of Rome on their return. The façade of the village church, Santa Maria, sports a remnant of this era: an incongruous 4m column salvaged from a Jupiter-Saturn temple that once stood in a now deserted forest glade above the village.

Another column from the same ruin has been incorporated into the tower of **PRUNELLI-DI-FIUMORBO**'s church, 7km northeast uphill from Pietrapola along the D45. Approached along an avenue of oak trees, with the austere peaks of Monte Renoso looming behind, this beautiful village is clustered like an eagle's nest on top of a hill. Again, the views are superb, but an additional reason to make the drive up here is a little **museum** set up by local amateur historians (Mon–Fri 9.30am–noon & 3–5.30pm, Sat 9.30am–12.30pm; free). Situated in, and beneath, the mairie, it houses a modest but fascinating collection of Roman and other archeological artefacts, displayed alongside photographs of the ruined temples and Pisan chapels lost in the surrounding forest. In another room, is an array of World War II memorabilia, including evocative photos of the Liberation. If there's no one at the mairie to let you into the museum, ask at the *Café Buttéa* next door for the key.

The Défilé de l'Inzecca

Northwest of Ghisonaccia, the D344 scythes straight across a broad tract of fruit orchards and vineyards towards a narrow niche in the wall of coastal mountains. Formed by the fast-flowing Fium'orbu torrent, the **Défilé de l'Inzecca** is a sheer granite trench bounded in the south by the jagged needles of the Kyrie peaks, and in the north and west by the grey, snow-flecked Monte Renoso massif. The road that winds through the gorge, leading from the coast to the village of Ghisoni, provides one of the most spectacular approaches to the interior, cutting across dramatic pale-green serpentine cliffs speckled with stunted trees. Below, colossal boulders choke the river, which has been dammed to form a reservoir for a small hydroelectricity station.

Details of walks and accommodation in Ghisoni are featured on p.356.

A good place to break the trip through the *défilé* is the *U Sampolu* **restaurant**, 8km west of Ghisoni on the banks of the river (☎04 95 57 60 18; April–Oct Tues–Sat), where you can enjoy copious local cuisine at reasonable prices. The accent here is on meat, with grilled local lamb, veal and beef featuring prominently on both their 90F and 110F set menus. It's also very popular, so book a table in advance if you plan to lunch here.

Aléria

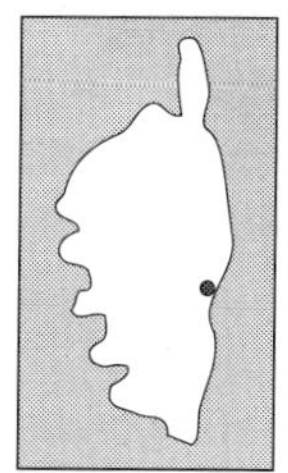

Built on the estuary at the mouth of the River Tavignano, **ALÉRIA** was the capital of the Corsican province during the Roman era, remaining the east coast's principal town and port right up until the eighteenth century. Little is left of the historic town except the **Roman ruins** and the Genoese fortress, which stand high against a background of chequered fields and green vineyards. A sizeable proportion of the local population is employed in farming oysters and mussels in the neighbouring **Étang de Diane**, formerly the Roman harbour. (During his exile on Elba, Napoléon kept in contact with his homeland by ordering boatloads of oysters from the lagoon.) To the south, a strip of modern buildings straddling the main road makes up the modern town, but it's the village set on the hilltop just west of here that holds most interest.

A brief history of Aléria

This area was first settled in 564 BC by a colony of Greek Phocaeans who had been chased from their land by the Persian invasion. Calling their new port Alalia, these Greeks initiated the island's trade routes around the Mediterranean, selling the copper and lead they mined from the land, and the wheat, olives and grapes farmed here. In 535 BC the settlers managed to survive a battle with the Carthaginians, but were left considerably weakened as a colony. Eventually fleeing to the mainland, the Phocaeans established a new capital at Massiglia (Marseille), retaining Alalia as a trading link between their colonies in southern Italy, Greece, Carthage and Spain.

In 259 BC the Romans arrived and conquered what was left of the port, which was by that time controlled by Carthaginians. It wasn't until around 80 BC, however, that they built up a naval base here, calling the town Aléria and re-establishing its importance in this part of the Mediterranean. As the only town of significant size, Aléria was named administrative capital of the province, and before long boasted a population of some thirty thousand. Under the orders of the emperor Augustus a fleet was harboured in the Étang de Diane and public buildings were constructed here, including baths, a forum and a triumphal arch, the remains of which are visible today. Light industries also flourished during this period as Aléria developed into a thriving crafts centre, producing jewellery, ceramics and clothes. Honey and wax were also marketed here, and seafood from the Étang de Diane found a ready trade with the continent.

Aléria's Roman days came to an end in 410 AD, when the city was struck by a fire that destroyed buildings and people alike. Malaria epidemics put paid to many of the survivors and the town was wiped out by Vandals later that century. Aléria was revived by the Genoese in the thirteenth century and was the seat of a bishopric for two hundred years thereafter. A fort was constructed in the sixteenth century, and when Theodor von Neuhof was received here in 1736 this was still one of the principal ports on the east coast.

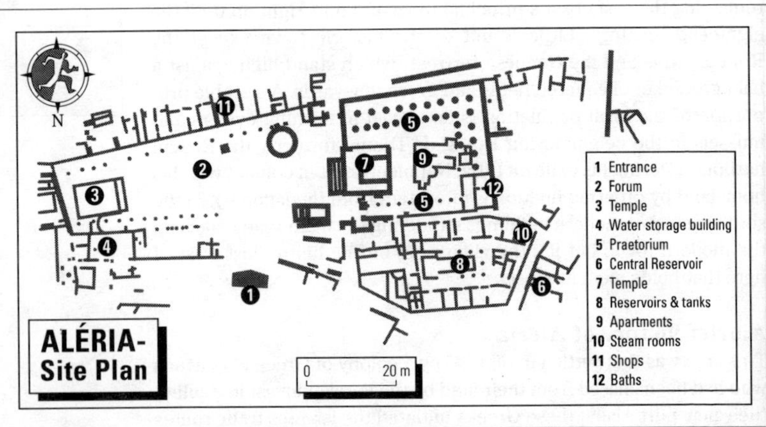

The Musée Jérôme Carcopino and ancient Aléria

The best place to begin your visit is the **Musée Jérôme Carcopino** (May 16–Sept daily 8am–noon & 2–7pm; Oct–May 15 Mon–Sat 8am–noon & 2–5pm; 5F), housed in **Fort Matra**. Pending the completion of building work on the ground floor, the collection – comprising remarkable finds from the Roman and Greek sites – is crammed into three interconnected rooms on the first storey of the fort, with ceramics, metal objects and jewellery forming the bulk of the exhibits.

The **first room** contains magnificent evidence of ancient Aléria's importance as a trading port. Hellenic and Punic rings and belt links are ranged alongside elaborate oil lamps decorated with Christian

The Aléria Siege

It may look little just another derelict, graffiti-covered ruin at the roadside, but the bombed-out Depeille wine cellar, 1.5km north of Aléria, was the site of the **Aléria siege**, an event seminal to the modern history of Corsica. On August 21, 1975, it was occupied by a group of armed nationalists, angry at its owners' part in a wine-adulterating scandal that threatened the livelihoods of many small-scale Corsican *viticultures*. Few of the militants, however, could have foreseen the violent outcome of their action, nor the dramatic impact it would subsequently have on the island's relations with the French government.

The **Depeilles** were one of around six hundred pied-noir families that settled on the east coast after Algerian independence in 1957, and who made sizeable fortunes from the vines they planted on newly reclaimed land in the area, helped by generous government subsidies. This and their North African origins made them unpopular with many locals, but the resentment never went beyond the odd piece of racist graffiti until it was discovered that many of the pied-noir farmers were doubling their wine output by illegally adding sugar and other chemicals to the grape juice. Frustrated by the government's apparent inability to stamp out the practice, armed commandos from the hitherto moderate nationalist organization the ARC (l'Action Régionaliste Corse), led by **Edmond Simeoni**, marched on the Depeilles's *cave*. With President Giscard d'Estaing on holiday, it fell to Michel Poniatowski, the Minister of the Interior and – unfortunately for the nationalists – a close associate of the Depeille family, to mount a response. Two days later, on August 23, 1250 police, four armoured cars and a couple of helicopters descended on the building, and in the ensuing shoot-out two police officers were killed. Afterwards Simeoni was arrested and imprisoned in Paris (the campaign for his release would become the cause célèbre of the nationalist movement for decades to come), and riots erupted in Bastia, where another gendarme died.

The Aléria siege, the first direct confrontation between armed nationalists and the French authorities, marked a turning point in the struggle for Corsican autonomy, leading to the inauguration of the FLNC (Fronte di Liberazione Nazionale di Corsica) in May 1976, and the first bombing campaign on the mainland. A full account of the nationalist armed struggle with the French state is featured in Contexts, p.376.

symbols, amphorae and some fragments of water pipes. In the first case on the left, a large Attic plate, depicting a faded red-grey elephant against a black background, takes up the middle of one display case, with various glazed dishes using the same painting method (red and black) ranged beneath. The real highlight of this first room, however, is a second-century marble bust of Jupiter Ammon, which was discovered near the forum.

Moving clockwise, the **second room** houses painted earthenware, Etruscan goblets, a number of exquisite Cretan-style vases from the fourth to third centuries BC, and more fine red and black ceramics in near-perfect condition. Among the latter are two remarkable drinking vessels or "rhytons", one representing the head of a mule and the other the head of a dog.

Most notable of the exhibits in the **third room** is a shallow-stemmed Attic bowl featuring a masturbating Dionysus, with twisting erotic figures on its rear face. Thought to date from 480 BC, this piece is attributed to master artist Panaitos and ranks among the museum's most treasured exhibits.

Finely worked Etruscan bronzes and delicate glasswork fill the longer **fourth room**, where you can also see jewellery from the fourth to the second centuries BC. There are also displayed objects discovered in the tombs of ancient Aléria, one of which, uncovered in 1966, revealed a priceless collection of elegantly curved Greek swords, lances and daggers from the fifth century BC. Iron weapons, armour and hundreds of finely painted cups called "craters", one of which features a picture of *Hercules and the Lion* and another which represents Dionysus, this time overseeing the grape harvest, are housed in this end room, near a ground plan of a fourth-century-BC tomb.

The Roman site

Scattered a short way up the hill from the fort you'll find the ruins of the **Roman site** (closes 30min before museum), where most of the excavation was done as recently as the 1950s, despite the fact that Merimée noticed signs of the Roman settlement during his survey of the island in 1830. Most of the site still lies beneath ground and is undergoing continuous excavation, but the *balneum* (bathhouse), the base of Augustus's triumphal arch, the foundations of the forum and traces of shops have been unearthed. The proximity of the sea, the strong scent of wild tarragon and the arresting view of snow-capped mountains and Fort Matra add to the atmosphere.

First discovered was the **arch**, which formed the entrance to the governor's residence – the praetorium – on the western edge of the **forum**. In the adjacent **balneum**, a network of reservoirs and cisterns, the **caldarium** bears traces of the underground pipes that would have heated the room, and a patterned mosaic floor is visible inside the neighbouring chamber. To the north of the site lie the foundation walls of a large house, while at the eastern end of the forum the foundations of the **temple** can be seen, alongside the foundations of the apse of an early Christian church.

Some traces of the Greek settlement, comprising the remains of an acropolis, have been discovered further to the east. It's believed that the main part of the town would have extended from the present site over to this acropolis and down to the Tavignano estuary. The port was located to the east of the main road, where the remnants of a second-century bathhouse have been found.

L'Étang de Diane and Plage de Padulone

A large saltwater lagoon, the **Étang de Diane** lies just north of Aléria. To get there, follow the main road north for 2km until you reach a turning on the right. A narrow dirt track leads down to *Le Chalet* restaurant (see below) and the banks of the lagoon, a glittering stretch of water dotted with fish-farm tanks, whose northeastern edge is marked by a lookout tower. The best places for swimming are the sandy eastern banks, which also make a pleasant picnic spot. **Plage de Padulone**, 3km due east of Aléria, is the most accessible beach in the area, reached via the narrow N200 from the Cateraggio crossroads. A row of modest seafood restaurants and downbeat cafés overlooks the sands, among them the old-style *Le Casabianca*, where groups of locals gather in the evenings to sing, play the accordion and cast fishing lines from the rear terrace.

Practicalities

Aléria has a handful of good-value **hotels**. *Les Orangers*, just off the crossroads on the road to the beach (☎04 95 57 00 31; ④; June–Sept), is the best place, with tariffs as low as 250F for a double room in high season. Alternatively, *L'Empereur*, a big chalet-style building around the corner just north of the crossroads on the highway (☎04 95 57 02 33; ③), is clean and comfortable, and a good deal, with large motel-style rooms opening onto a central garden. Another option is the slightly pricier two-star *L'Atrachjata*, a little further north (☎04 95 57 03 93; ③), which has a small restaurant – consider it as a fall-back. One of the most pleasant **campsites** on the east coast lies 3km east of the Cateraggio crossroads: the *Marina d'Aléria* (☎04 95 57 01 42, fax 04 95 57 04 29; Easter–Oct) backs onto the beach and is well equipped, with mod cons that include washing machines and refrigerated lockers. If it's full, try the smaller site at **Bravone Plage**, 12km further north of Aléria along the main road (☎04 95 38 84 08).

Those with a passion for **oysters** can sample them fresh from the lagoon at *L'Auberge le Chalet*, 500m north of the crossroads, which also serves other excellent seafood dishes. During the summer, you can enjoy the same high-class cuisine at *Le Chalet*'s lagoon cabin, a smart wooden shack on stilts in the Étang de Diane (see above for directions). It's pricy, with most main dishes costing around 100F, but the food, which according to the menu comes "fully furnished", is topnotch and the setting is wonderful; ask for a table on the rear terrace overlooking the lagoon.

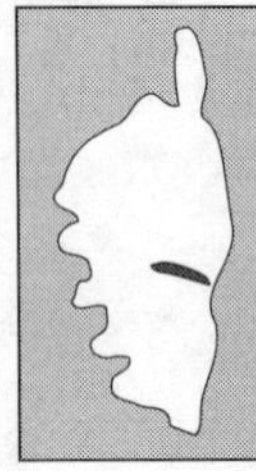

Vallée du Tavignano

Running northwest from Aléria, the **Vallée du Tavignano** forms an exhilarating approach to Corte, its craggy gorges and dark rocky slopes dotted with red-roofed villages. The N200, which tracks the river all the way, is the quickest route, but if you're in no hurry you could take the upland road through the **Bozio**, on the north flank of the valley. If, however, you've only got time for a detour on your way across the eastern plain, you might drive up to the village of **Antisanti**, which overlooks the coast and Corsica's mountainous spine from the south side of the valley.

Antisanti

Located at an altitude of 700m, **ANTISANTI**, 20km west of Aléria, offers views that more than reward anyone making the effort to get to it along the tortuous D43. In the twelfth century the village was an important stopoff point for merchants travelling between Corte and the coast. Resisting Pascal Paoli's revolution, the town was burned down in 1753. Today it consists of only one street, but there's a café from which, on a clear day, you can see all the main peaks of Corsica, the craggy needles of Bavella and Incudine rising to the south, Monte d'Oro to the west, while eastwards the islands of Elba, Capraia and Monte Cristo can be made out way beyond the plain.

The gorge route

Following the River Tavignano, one of the island's principal rivers, the main N200 road from Aléria to Corte (around 48km) provides a direct scenic route into the heart of the interior. The road meanders across the plain for about 10km, at which point it begins an ascent into the mountains, narrowing in the approach to a magnificent **gorge** a further 10km onwards. Slicing through the denuded schist walls of the valley, the route affords occasional glimpses of hilltop villages to the south, and after the same distance again you emerge from the gorge at the sparse hamlet of **VOLTA**, where a triple-arched Genoese bridge takes you across the river. Visible on the right bank is a tenth-century Romanesque chapel dedicated to John the Baptist, a tiny edifice built of patterned stones alternating with plain blocks of granite, now used as a shepherds' shelter.

The Bozio

Tucked between the Tavignano gorge and the Castagniccia, the **Bozio** is a grimly mountainous terrain, its maquis littered with

Romanesque churches and sombre villages that were hotbeds of Corsican nationalism in the eighteenth century. There are two routes through this region from Aléria: the D14, which leaves the N200 about 12km from town; or the D16/D116, which begins 5km north of Aléria, crossing the plain before rising to the north side of the Cursiglièse valley.

Vallée du Tavignano

If you take the former road, the landscape becomes really wild at **PIEDICORTE-DI-GAGGIO**, a protuberance of red roofs above the bleak rock, with a central square that gives you a panorama of the eastern plain plus a hazy view of the giant peaks on the opposite side of the valley. About 4km beyond lies **ALTIANI**, whose houses cluster around a huge lump of grey granite, and from here it's another 9km of switchback road to **ERBAJOLO**, which offers a fantastic view of the Tavignano valley, Monte d'Oro and Monte Renoso. From here you can take a walk to the remote Pisan chapel of **San Martino**, a gentle thirty-minute hike along a mule track through the maquis from the church in the centre of the village. A further twenty minutes from San Martino lies the ruined hamlet of **Casella**, another spectacular belvedere.

The alternative route becomes increasingly tortuous once you've joined the D116, winding through the flinty semi-derelict villages of **Tallone** and **Zuani** on its way to the **Col de San Cervone** (899m), where there's a fine view across the Tavignano in one direction and towards the distant sea in the other. Beyond here you could make a loop down to Erbajolo (see above) or continue to **ALANDO**, the birthplace of Sambucuccio d'Alando, a legendary fourteenth-century rebel. Leader of a popular movement against the region's despotic nobility, he is credited with the invention of the "Temps du Commun", an organization that from 1359 to 1362 united villages all over Corsica under one administrative body of elected magistrates.

From Alando you can head north through the stark hills as far as **BUSTANICO**, the village said to be the source of the War of Independence. It began in 1729 when an old man named Lanfranchi, or Cardone, sparked off a local rebellion against the Genoese after a tax collector threatened to carry off all his possessions. Outraged at such injustice, fellow villagers rose up in his defence, triggering riots and raids all over eastern Corsica, culminating in the sack of Bastia in 1730. The village church has a graceful wooden figure of Christ, sculpted by a local craftsman in the eighteenth century.

If you head west along the D441 you'll soon come to **SERMANO**, famous for *a paghjella* singing, which is performed once each year during the Jour des Morts festival at the Pisan chapel of **San Nicolao**. The chapel is fifteen minutes' walk from the church in the centre of the village, and is decorated with naive fifteenth-century frescoes of Christ, the Virgin, the Apostles and saints.

For more on a paghjella *singing, see p.336.*

No one, however, ventures up these windy roads without a Michelin map – the roads are simply too convoluted (see Michelin map 9° 15-20/5).

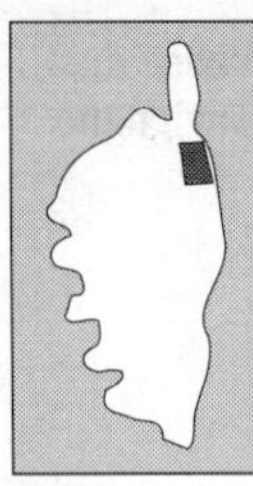

The Castagniccia

Famous for the herds of pigs that roam its sinuous backroads, **Castagniccia**, pronounced "Castan*ee*tch", takes its name from the dense forests of chestnuts (*castagna*) first cultivated here by the Genoese in the fifteenth century, which later made this the richest and most densely populated part of the island. Today, many of the beautiful grey-green and silver schist hamlets perched on its ribbon-thin ridges lie virtually deserted or derelict, but the region remains a rewarding one to explore – particularly during the autumn, when whole valleys are carpeted in vivid gold and russet, and in wet weather, when wisps of mist and cloud cling to the lush canopy.

Castagniccia covers roughly a hundred square kilometres, extending south of the River Golo as far as the Bozio, and westwards just beyond the shadowy crest of Monte San Petrone (1767m), its highest mountain. Fuelled by a lucrative trade in chestnut flour and fine woodcarving, the region's golden era occurred during the Genoese peace between 1569 and 1729, when the majority of its opulent Baroque churches, convents, chapels and lofty stone houses were built. In the eighteenth century the arms industry thrived here as well, and its products found a ready market during the Corsican Revolution, during which Castagniccia was a bastion of support for Pascal Paoli (see box overleaf), a native of **Morosaglia**. Decline only set in towards the end of the nineteenth century, with the completion of the railways through the interior of the island. Easing the transport of timber to the coast, this hastened the process of **deforestation**, which ultimately undermined the area's traditional agro-pastoral economy, and stimulated an exodus to the coastal towns and French mainland. These days, Castagniccia only comes alive during August, when families return from Marseille to visit their grandparents in their native villages.

Exploring the Castagniccia requires a vehicle and some caution: although there's a larger concentration of roads here than anywhere else on Corsica, routes are extremely winding and narrow, with the added hazard of roaming pigs, cows and goats. Daily **trains** from Bastia stop in Casamozza and Ponte Leccia, but unless you're prepared to walk or hitch this isn't much help for exploring the area. Furthermore, hotels and restaurants are to be found only at **La Porta**, **Piedicroce** and **Cervione** – though you could always stay on the coast at Moriani-Plage and see the Castagniccia on a day's tour. There's a choice of routes into the region: from the east coast via Prunete or Moriani-Plage; from the north, via Casamozza; or, from the west, through Ponte Leccia and Morosaglia.

Moriani-Plage and around

One of a string of virtually indistinguishable resorts along the coast north of Aléria, **MORIANI-PLAGE** is a bland strip of kitsch souvenir shops and cafés huddled around a crossroads on the N198. For a foray into Castagniccia, however, this is a convenient base, boasting the last decent beach before Bastia, a reasonable choice of accommodation, a large Champion supermarket (300m south of the crossroads), a Crédit Agricole cash dispenser (the only one for kilometres if you're heading inland), a self-service laundry (on the road leading to the beach) and a small **tourist office** (Mon–Fri 9am–noon & 2–5pm; ☎04 95 38 41 73).

A dependable budget **hotel** here is *L'Abri des Flots*, set back a little from the beach (☎04 95 38 40 76; ③), whose plain but clean rooms all have shower-toilets attached. For **campsites**, you've a choice between the flashy four-star *Camping Merendella*, 700m south of the crossroads (☎04 95 38 53 47; May–Oct), or the more modest *Camping Calamar*, 6.5km south at Prunete (☎04 95 38 03 54; May–Oct). The latter is situated right next to the beach amid an old olive grove, and ranks among the most congenial sites on the island; it's small, with only simple facilities, but is kept immaculately clean (the young *patronne* has even planted beds of aromatic herbs outside the toilet block), and has a sociable little snack bar that stays open late.

A great place to make the most of the stunning views available from the west-facing flanks of the coastal hills lies a short way **inland**

from Moriani-Plage along the D34. Signalled by the prominent bell tower of its church, the village of **SAN-NICOLAO** emerges after 6km of tight bends and dense chestnut woods. You could pull over here to admire the colourful decor and trompe l'œil in the seventeenth-century parish church, or continue 4km further uphill to the hamlet of **SAN-GIOVANNI-DI-MORIANI**, where the wonderful *Bar-Restaurant Cava* (☎04 95 38 51 14; June–Sept) serves wholesome Castagniccian specialities (including *migliacci*, goat's-cheese doughnuts, on the 100F set menu) on a terrace overlooking the Tyrrenean Sea. All the Tuscan islands are visible from here, and on a clear day you can even make out the Italian coast.

One of the most isolated villages in Castagniccia, **SANTA-REPARATA-DI-MORIANI**, lies at the end of the D34, which winds southwest from San-Giovanni-di-Moriani into a dense chestnut forest. A good reason to venture up here is the excellent gîte d'étape *Luna Piena* (☎04 95 38 59 48), which makes a perfect base from

Pascal Paoli

"He smiled a good deal when I told him that I was much surprised to find him so amiable, accomplished and polite," wrote Boswell on first meeting **Pascal Paoli** in 1765, "for although I knew I was to see a great man I expected to find a rude character, an Attila king of the Goths, or a Luitprand king of the Lombards." By this time Paoli was forty years old and famous throughout Europe, widely admired by the liberal intelligentsia of the time, among them Jean-Jacques Rousseau.

Paoli was born in **Morosaglia** (see p.324) with the cause of Corsican independence in his blood – his father, Giacinto, a doctor, was a first-generation rebel, one of the three primates elected in 1731 by the independent assembly. At the age of 14, Pascal accompanied his father into exile in Naples, where the boy became a keen student of political enlightenment. At the time of Gaffori's assassination, Pascal was a 29-year-old sublieutenant in a Neapolitan regiment, but his brother Clemente was in the thick of the rebellion. Appointed one of four regents after Gaffori's death, Clemente invited his younger brother to take over the position of **General of the Nation**, a title he accepted in **1755** and was to hold for the next fourteen years.

Paoli's intention was to drive out the Genoese by force of arms, but despite his military background he wasn't an experienced soldier, and was anyway always short of the necessary supplies. However, he proved to be adept in the art of government, giving the island a **democratic constitution** that anticipated that of the United States of America; founding the university at Corte; building a small navy that was strong enough to break the Genoese blockade; and establishing a mint, a printing press and an arms factory. Furthermore, the system of justice instituted by Pascal Paoli was effective enough to bring about a decline in vendetta killings.

Then in **1768** everything collapsed. The French moved in once more, this time intending to stay after having bought out the Genoese under the terms of the Treaty of Versailles. Determined to crush the rebels for good, the French overwhelmed the Corsican troops at **Ponte-Nuovo**, whereupon Paoli went into exile in London. However, his political life was not over.

which to explore a new network of **waymarked trails**. Three excellent round-walks of between two and a half and five hours begin at the village, taking in the old chapels, springs and *bergeries* (shepherds' huts) dotted about the surrounding forests and steep hillsides. Glossy leaflets giving details of the routes on a simple contour map are available free from the gîte. Beds in their two- or four-person dorms cost 65F, or 170F for half-board, which is a bargain considering the quality of the food served – Castagniccian specialities made entirely from local produce. Non-residents can also eat here by prior arrangement.

Cervione

From San-Nicolao, it's 5km south to the largest, busiest and most welcoming village of the Castagniccia, **CERVIONE**, whose houses, spread in an amphitheatre around the lower slopes of Monte Castello, tower over a sloping medieval square that's linked to the

In **1789**, at the start of the French Revolution, the people of Corsica were declared to be subject to the same laws as the revolutionary state, and it was in this changed political climate that Paoli returned triumphantly to the island in the following year. Initially he sympathized with the new republicanism, but the Corsican Jacobites – the Bonaparte family amongst them – owed too much to France to have much sympathy with separatist politics. Disagreements came to a head with Paoli's arraignment in June **1793**. His response was dramatic. Setting up an independent government in Corte, he approached the British government for help, who, having been driven out of Toulon by the French, were in search of a naval base in the area, and so there followed one of the more curious episodes of Corsican history.

The British sent **Sir Gilbert Elliot** to evaluate the situation, and agreement was quickly reached. English troops and naval forces moved in and after some fighting – during which the future Admiral Nelson lost the sight in one eye – the French moved out. A new constitution was drawn up that gave Corsica an attachment to the English Crown, but with a large degree of autonomy. It's questionable whether Paoli was ever entirely happy with the course of events, but he was in a difficult situation, as the guillotine was waiting for him if France ever regained control. There seems no doubt that he expected to be appointed viceroy of the island, and when Elliot was given the job things began to turn sour. The parliament of 1795 elected Paoli as president, but Elliot objected; soon after, rioting was provoked by a rumour that Paoli's bust had been deliberately smashed at a ball given in the viceroy's honour. When the English began talking again to the republican French, the game was over. In 1796 Paoli was persuaded to return to London, shortly before Elliot withdrew as Napoléon's army landed to secure the island for France.

Given a state pension, Paoli died in London in **1807** at the age of 82, a revered figure. He was initially buried in his place of exile – there's a bust of him in Westminster Abbey – but his body now lies in his birthplace.

A Castagna

The chestnut tree (*la chataîgnier* in French, **a castagna** in Corsican) grows in most areas of the island that lie between 500m and 800m, but only in Castagniccia – whose mild, moist climate and schist soils create the optimum environment – does it form such extensive forests. Planted in the fifteenth century by the Genoese, these were the linchpin of the local economy for more than four hundred years, providing fuel, carving and building material, pollen for bees and, most importantly of all, a ready source of food.

The first chestnut pods, or *pelous*, appear on the trees in mid-August, but the harvest doesn't usually start until two months later, while the leaves are falling. Removed from their spiky pods, the nuts are shelled and stored in special double-storey stone sheds called **sèchoirs**, where they dry over the winter. Traditionally, the largest and most succulent were eaten whole, while the rest were taken to watermills and ground

surrounding streets by a labyrinth of alleys and archways. Flanking the south side of the square is one of the first Baroque churches on Corsica, the **Cathédrale St-Érasme**, founded in 1578 by St Alexander Sauli, who was ordained bishop of Aléria in 1570 and soon transferred the bishopric to Cervione to escape the malaria-ridden swampland of the plain. Little remains of the old cathedral, which was restored in the nineteenth century, but the impressive black-and-white marble floor gives the place some appeal. Opposite the church stands the **bishop's palace**, once the residence of King Théodore (see box on p.321); its ethnographical **museum** (May–Sept Mon–Sat 9am–noon & 2.30–6pm; 5F) exhibits various geological specimens and farm implements.

The village's only **hotel is** the *St-Alexandre*, below the main road at the bottom of the village (☎04 95 38 10 83; ④), whose rooms have great views across the plains from their balconies. It's a stark, unfinished building with few frills, but the management is welcoming, and the pieces of old family furniture and antique memorabilia dotted around the corridors give the place a quirky air. You can **eat** at the lively *U Casone* pizzeria, through an archway off the square, and there's a good **bar** next door to the church.

The elegant Romanesque chapel of **Santa Cristina** is a forty-minute walk from Cervione – take the road down towards Prunete for about 600m, then a signpost shows the way. Marvellous **frescoes** dating from 1473 decorate the twin apses (you'll find the key on a ledge above the door): on the left side Christ is depicted with the Virgin, St Christina and a kneeling monk; on the right, Christ is surrounded by the symbols of the Evangelists; and over the arch between them is a portrayal of the Crucifixion. A more ambitious three-hour walk into the mountains starts from the west of the village: follow the signs to Notre-Dame-de-la-Scobiccia, a tiny Romanesque chapel about 2km up the slope, from where a mule into flour (*farina*). This formed the mainstay of the peasant diet in many areas of upland Corsica, where it was mixed with salt and water to make **pulenda**, a kind of polenta, or, on special occasions, baked into cakes and biscuits. Any surplus was bartered for olive oil and wine from the coastal villages.

During the late nineteenth century, the "chestnut economy" of regions such as Castagniccia went into free fall as acres of forest were felled for timber and to provide tannin for leather production. Still more trees died due to neglect as rural populations dwindled, while a virulent fungal disease has also taken its toll over the past decade. These days, *pulenda*- and chestnut-flour cakes, served as gourmet specialities in expensive restaurants and souvenir boutiques, have become more a symbol of the islanders' traditional identity than eaten as daily staples; emigrants, for example, are still often sent parcels of flour from their family land by older relatives. The only apparent beneficiaries of the chestnut's decline are Corsica's wild pigs, who gorge themselves on the ungathered windfalls.

track wends up into the maquis to the **Punta Nevera**, a rocky eminence overlooking much of the Castagniccia.

Cervione to Carcheto

South of Cervione, after about 12km of tormented hairpin bends (many with dizzying drops and no barriers), comes **Valle-d'Alesani**, from where it's a short detour up the D217 to the **Couvent d'Alesani** where King Théodore was crowned (see box on p.321). Founded in 1236, the Franciscan monastery is mostly a ruin, but its church holds a beautiful fifteenth-century Sienese painting known as the *Virgin and the Cherry*. The site is also associated with the infamous Giovannali sect, who sheltered here after the destruction of their monastery at Carbini.

More background on the Giovannalis, who were persecuted, and eventually exterminated, for their licentious religious practices, appears on p.253.

Back on the main road it's not long before you reach **FELCE**, whose Baroque church is decorated with simple yet arresting frescoes – on the ceiling you'll see the artist, palette in hand, floating among the clouds. Also of interest is the **tabernacle** above the altar, carved by a penitent bandit. Look out, too, for the wonderful local-produce shop, A Coualina, run by Christine Bereni, on the outskirts of the village, where you can buy home-grown chestnut-pollen honey, free-range eggs, charcuterie, jams, tasty goat's and ewe's cheese and locally made baskets.

Beyond Felce, the road winds slowly up to the **Col d'Arcarotta**, dividing the Alesani valley from the Caldone basin, the heartland of Castagniccia. Straddling the pass, *Auberge des Deux Vallées*, one of the area's few gîtes d'étapes (☎04 95 35 91 20; 60F per dorm bed), takes in the best of the views, with Monte San Petrone dominating the skyline to the northwest. Its convivial wood-lined bar makes a good place for a pit stop, or you can sample typical Castagniccian cuisine (such as *figatelle*, roast pork or trout in cream cheese) in the

The Mare a Mare Nord Trail

Begining at **Moriani-Plage** on the east coast, the principal **Mare a Mare Nord trail**, waymarked with orange paint splashes, winds west through the heart of the country's watershed to Cargèse. The route, which passes through the Bozio to Corte, and thence along the dramatic Tavignano valley into the Niolo, consists of ten stages (lasting 3hr 30min–6hr each), and is best attempted from late April to November, heading west.

A longer and more strenuous option is to turn off the trail at Sermano, three stages into the hike, where a **variante** (alternative) path peels south to begin an eight-day loop through the Vivario forest and up a series of cols en route to Guagno and the Incinosa massif. It rejoins the principal route at Marignana near Ota, where you follow the Mare e Monti trail for the final two days' walk to the west coast.

Accommodation along the main route is provided by a string of comfortable gîtes, but on the less-frequented *variante* you'll have to check into a hotel or refuge at the end of a couple of stages where no hikers' hostels have so far been built. In either case, advance booking is recommended, especially during high summer, when beds in the gîtes can be in short supply.

A stage-by-stage rundown of both routes is given in the Parc Naturel Régional de Corse's essential **topo-guide**, *Corse: Entre Mer et Montagne*, which you can buy at most good bookshops and tourist offices.

Mare a Mare Nord Principal accommodation

Santa-Reparata-di-Moriani (☎04 95 38 59 48).
Pianello (☎04 95 39 62 66 or 04 95 39 61 59).
Sermano M. Mariani (☎04 95 48 67 97).
Castellare di Mercurio M. Guiducekku (☎04 95 61 05 13).
Corte M. Gambini (☎04 95 46 16 85), see also p.345.
Calacuccia M. Mordiconi (☎04 95 48 00 04), see also p.339.
Albertacce M. Albertini (☎04 95 48 05 60), see also p.341.
Casamaccioli Reservation obligatory (☎04 95 48 03 31).
Evisa Mme Ceccaldi (☎04 95 26 21 28), see also p.340.

Mare a Mare Nord Variante accommodation

Poggio di Venaco M. Giorgetti (☎04 95 47 02 29).
Casanova Mme Casanova (☎04 95 47 03 73).
San-Petru-di-Venaco M. Hiver (☎04 95 47 07 29).
Vivario (☎04 95 47 22 00) see p.355.
Pastricciola Mairie (☎04 95 28 91 85 or 04 95 20 78 22).
Soccia *Hôtel U Paese* (☎04 95 28 31 92).
Guagno Mme Mariani (☎04 95 28 33 47), see also p.191.

restaurant. À la carte dishes cost around 60F, plus there's a good-value 80F "*menu corse*", served indoors or alfresco on the terrace (for a ten percent surcharge); wines cost 60F and upwards. Standing at a nexus of some immaculately waymarked local footpaths, the auberge is also well placed for **walks** in the area. Ask in the bar for the *sentiers du pays* leaflet (*dépliant*), which gives you a rough idea of the routes and distances of the various paths. From the col, much the most rewarding option is the five-hour round-walk to Stazzona and the mineral-water hamlet of Eaux d'Orezza (see p.322), taking in some of the region's best viewpoints and tracts of old chestnut forest.

The first sizeable settlement below the pass is **CARCHETO**, set amidst an ocean of chestnut trees and giving a good view of Piedicroce across the valley. Carcheto's dilapidated **Église Ste-Marguerite**, set by a wood on the edge of the hamlet, is an eighteenth-century edifice packed with decaying examples of local work – luridly painted stucco covers the walls, portraying scenes from the Crucifixion, with an alabaster statue of the Virgin and Child providing a restrained counterpoint. If the church is locked, you can pick up the key from the *Refuge* hotel in Piedicroce (see p.322). Outside the church, a sign for "La Fontaine" directs walkers through the wood to a **waterfall**, which cascades through an opening in the trees – a fine spot for a dip and a

Théodore von Neuhof

Scorned by Corsican historian Chanoine Casanova as an "operetta king", **Théodore von Neuhof** was crowned King of Corsica on April 15, 1736, a unique title he was to hold for just eight months.

Théodore was an ambitious nobleman with a very colourful past. Brought up in the court of France where he was page to the duchess of Orléans, mother of the Prince Regent, he travelled around England, Holland and Spain, killed his best friend in a duel, and acquired a fortune through some rather dubious financial speculations. Captured by Moors in Tunis in the early 1730s and put into slavery in Algiers, he managed to bribe his way to freedom, and was soon sending word to a group of Corsican exiles in Livorno that he would provide them with aid in return for the crown of their troubled island. Impressed by his royal connections and fancy talk, and desperate for money and arms, the Corsicans agreed. Soon after, Théodore landed at Aléria, decked out in full Turkish regalia with a retinue of French, Italian and Moorish attendants, and was taken in state to the Couvent d'Alésani to be crowned King Théodore I of Corsica. His powers were severely constrained – a council of 24 men was appointed to advise him, and he was answerable to a Corsican parliament – but Théodore had plenty of opportunities for kingly behaviour. Living it up at the bishop's palace in Cervione, he distributed titles among the wealthier Corsicans, made increasingly exaggerated promises of arms for the liberation of his people, and organized a few ineffectual sieges and pointless military manoeuvres against the Genoese.

Mistrust amongst his ministers increased as the emptiness of his promises became obvious, and in November 1736 the king was forced to flee the island via Solenzara, disguised as a priest. Théodore didn't give up entirely on the Corsicans, however – in 1739 he returned with a small fleet but was deterred from landing by the French. Eventually Théodore returned to England, where he died in 1756 having accumulated massive debts. A plaque in London's Soho Square commemorates him: "Fate poured its lessons on his living head, bestowed a kingdom and denied him bread."

picnic: follow the track indicated, heading straight on where the the main (motorable) trail switches sharply to the right (ignore the orange splashes of paint). You'll know you're going the right way when you pass a cemetery, followed by a spring.

Piedicroce

A cluster of hamlets belonging to the commune of **Orezza** lies to the north of Carcheto, strung along the lower slopes of Monte San Petrone. During the mid-nineteenth century, this was the most densely populated *commune* in the whole of France, with 91 inhabitants per square kilometre. Today, however, barely two hundred permanent residents live in **PIEDICROCE**, the area's principal village, whose **hotel**, *Le Refuge* (☎04 95 35 82 65, fax 04 95 35 84 42; ③; closed mid-Oct to Nov), is the sole place to stay in the valley. Perched on a steep terrace, the building itself is a pink monstrosity, but its restaurant does excellent Corsican food, including Castagniccian specialities such as chestnut fritters with *brocciu* cheese. Piedicroce's **Église St-Pierre-et-Paul**, built in 1691, harbours a handful of mediocre sixteenth- and seventeenth-century paintings, and a restored organ that is reputedly the oldest in Corsica.

Stazzona and Orezza

STAZZONA, 2km downhill along the D506 from Piedicroce, was the centre of arms manufacture during the War of Independence – its name means "forge" in Corsican. From the 1850s onwards, however, it has made its money from the **Eaux d'Orezza** spring: as the faded old hotel signs indicate, people used to come up here for the curative waters, among them Pascal Paoli, Napoléon Bonaparte, English aristocrats and colonialists from French Indochina. The local council, who own the springs, gave up the enterprise in 1995 because sales were poor, but the celebrated Eau d'Orezza made a comeback in 1999, relaunched by British designers, Claessens, with twenty million francs of public funding. The gradual decline in the water's popularity this century was mainly attributable to its foul metallic taste; for this reason, a large part of the grant was spent on a new bottling plant, where the iron content of the water is reduced and its bubbles made smaller. To reach the new factory, which churns out 2500 litres per hour, continue down the hill for a couple of kilometres and cross the bridge, where a sideroad turns right.

While you're on this side of the valley, you could follow the D46 past the spring another 4km to **Vallée d'Orezza**, where traditional smoking pipes and boxes are carved from olive and chestnut wood. Formerly this hamlet exported crafted wood objects all over Corsica, France and Italy; now only a handful of elderly artisans still live here, selling their work to visitors direct from tiny cottage workshops.

Heading back through Piedicroce, take the D71 north for the **Couvent d'Orezza**, which stands in a green glade in a bewitchingly

The Monte San Petrone Hike

Visible all over Castagniccia and central Corsica, the craggy summit of **Monte San Petrone** (1767m) is one of the most thrilling viewpoints on the island, and is accessible on a comfortable four-hour round-hike (2hr 30min ascent, 1hr 30min descent) along a clearly marked trail. Each year in August, hundreds of local villagers, including a fair number of old folk, climb to the top for a special Mass, so the route is relatively easy-going. That said, you'll definitely need sturdy footwear and a good pair of lungs, as the path gets steep towards the top.

The trailhead for the hike is at **Campodonico**, about 2km west of Couvent d'Orezza up a sideroad. Park your car in the lay-by at the entrance to the hamlet and head down the lane through the houses, turning right along the mule track that leads up the valley. From here, the trail – marked at regular intervals with splashes of orange or red paint – zigzags up to a scattering of **bergeries** (1hr 30min), where you should briefly quit the path and follow the hillside around to the north to get the best views of the mountains inland. All of Corsica's principal peaks are visible at this point, from the Cinto massif down to Monte Rotondo.

Once you've rejoined the marked trail, it takes around one hour to reach the summit, passing through beautiful birch woods and mossy boulders. The final thirty minutes are tough-going, but the 360-degree panorama from the top, marked with a crucifix and a serpentine-stone carving of St Peter, is breathtaking. In clear weather you can see from the coast of Tuscany to Cap Corse, and across the swathe of dramatic snow-capped mountains to the east.

Note that if you have the use of two vehicles or are happy to hitch, a good alternative descent leads north from the *bergeries* mentioned earlier along a clearly marked trail to the **Col de Prato**, a short way east of Morosaglia. Some hikers use this gentler, more shaded trail as an approach, but it isn't nearly as rewarding a route as the one described above (the beech cover obscures the views for most of the way).

silent spot. Reduced to a craggy ruin by the Germans in World War II, when it was temporarily used as a Resistance arms dump, the site has profound historic associations. In the eighteenth century the convent was a centre of resistance to the Genoese republic, and several *consulte* (rebel meetings) took place inside it – on April 20, 1731, twenty representatives of the clergy gathered to discuss whether violent rebellion was against the fundamental principles of Christian morality, and it was here that Paoli was voted commander-in-chief of the Corsican National Guard. Paoli also met Napoléon here in 1793 in an unsuccessful attempt to achieve a truce between their respective armies.

Campana and Croce

CAMPANA, 2km west of the Couvent d'Orezza, merits a stop for its Baroque church of **Sant'André**, which houses a fine *Adoration of the Shepherds* attributed to the Spanish seventeenth-century painter Zurbaran. Renowned for its beautiful light (and, bizarrely, for the faintly demonic expression on the face of the boy carrying the eggs), the painting was given to the parish by a wealthy local resident in 1895. The key to the church is kept by an old lady who lives in the last house on the left as you face the village. After Campana, head north for 2km, then veer right at the fork for the village of **CROCE**, which has Castagniccia's only **campsite** (☎04 95 39 21 33; May–Oct) – either phone the owner, M. Mattei, or ask at the mairie in the centre of the village.

La Porta and Col de Prato

Thanks largely to the gigantic five-storey bell tower rising from its terracotta and grey schist rooftops, **LA PORTA**, 6km up the hill from here, is the most distinctive village in Castagniccia. Swathed in lush chestnut forest, with the granite crags of Monte San Petrone looming behind, its centrepiece is the spectacular **Église St-Jean-Baptiste**, erected in 1720 and widely regarded as the high-watermark of Baroque architecture in Corsica. The church's grand façade gracefully unites all the principal features of Rococo, although a tasteless paint job recently submerged its former muted colours in gaudy yellow and white. Inside the building are several noteworthy art treasures, including a gory depiction of the beheading of St John the Baptist (to the left as you face the altar) and, opposite this, a sixteenth-century wood sculpture of the Crucifixion.

There is nowhere to stay in La Porta, but you can **eat** well in the *Restaurant de L'Ampigignani (Chez Elizabeth)*, down the road through the centre of the village from the church (☎04 95 39 22 00). This place looks unpromising from the outside, but is a light and airy dining hall with magnificent views down the valley. The food is superb, too, and reasonably priced (set menus from 100F, and pizzas from 35–45F) considering the quality; everything comes from the immediate vicinity, and is prepared according to traditional Castagniccian recipes.

Col de Prato marks the trail-head for the ascent of Monte San Petrone, a superb hike described in the box on p.323.

Heading uphill on the D205 out of La Porta will bring you to the **Col de Prato** (985m), the highest point on the roads of Castagniccia. From the col, a walk to the ruined **San Petrucolo** (a church founded as far back as the sixth century) can be done in half an hour. Follow the narrow track south in the direction of Monte San Petrone, then after 100m take the track on the right into the maquis – follow this for a few steps, then strike left, and you'll see the chapel straight in front of you.

Morosaglia

MOROSAGLIA, a short way north of Col de Prato, is known as the birthplace of Pascal Paoli. The **Maison de Pascal Paoli** (daily except Tues: April–Sept 9am–noon & 2.30–7.30pm; Oct–March 9am–noon & 1–5pm; 10F) is signposted east of the village in the hamlet of Stretta. A video primes you for the tour of the house, whose exhibits comprise a small collection of letters, portraits and other memorabilia, including the very first Corsican newspaper, printed in 1794. Paoli's ashes, brought back from England in 1807, are entombed in a chapel next door.

Paoli was baptized in the Pisan-founded but extensively rebuilt church of **Santa Reparata**, reached via a path that starts 400m down the hill, behind the large house on the right side of the road. His brother Clement, described by Dorothy Carrington as "a matchless marksman who prayed for his enemies' souls as he shot them down", lived out his retirement here, in the large mansion that's now the village school.

A couple of fine Romanesque chapels are to be found beyond Morosaglia. The nearer, **Santa Maria di Valle di Rostino**, stands to the west of the D15, 5km along the road. Passing the village on your right, continue for 500m to reach the ruined chapel, accessible via a rough track. Dating from the tenth century, the apse displays some fine Pisan stonework created by narrow blocks interspersed with green and grey schist, adorned with slender columns and harmonious arcading. Amongst the primitive sculpture along the external roof band, Adam and Eve on either side of the Tree of Life feature most prominently. **San Tommaso di Pastoreccia**, 10km north of Morosaglia at the end of the zigzagging route through Pastoreccia, is a half-ruined building of grey schist, dating from the tenth century, its interior enlivened by a series of sixteenth-century **frescoes.** Some are in very bad condition, but you won't have any difficulty picking out most of the Apostles and saints (a young St John stands out in a gold surround), or deciphering the scenes from the Passion and the Last Judgment.

The best **place to eat** in this area is an auberge called *A Stella di Rustino* (☎04 95 38 77 09) in the village of **Valle-di-Rostino**, reached via the windy backroad that turns right off the D71 at the Bocca a Serna, 2km below Morosaglia. Follow the D15B for 2km, and turn left at the first fork. The restaurant, recently opened in a new building at the entrance to the village, is run by a Basque who prides himself on his hospitality and delicious local speciality cooking. A set four-course meal here costs a very reasonable 80F per head, plus wine.

The Casinca

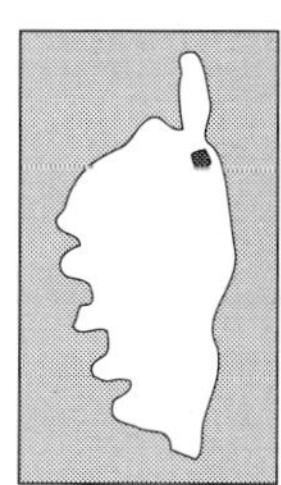

Bounded by the Golo and Fiumalto rivers, the **Casinca** covers the eastern slopes of Monte Sant'Angelo, an area swathed in olive and chestnut trees and embellished with stately villages. It's less popular with tourists than the Castagniccia, but is easier to get into if you haven't got your own transport, as there's a daily (except Sun) **bus** from Bastia to **Vescovato** and **Venzolasca** (Autobus Casinca ☎04 95 36 70 64), many of whose inhabitants earn their living in the city. There's no accommodation on offer, but it's a small area and easily coverable in half a day.

The Casinca

The Casinca villages

CASTELLARE-DI-CASINCA, just 1km up the D6 from the main coast road, about 15km north of Moriani-Plage, affords a wonderful view of the eastern plain and has a beautiful tenth-century church, **San Pancrazio**, notable for its triple apse. About 1km out of the village, a road off to the left leads to **PENTA-DI-CASINCA**, the second-largest village in the region. Its dark streets, crammed with lofty schist buildings dating principally from the fifteenth century, open out onto a large square, which gives a fine view across the plain.

Heading east for 1km along the D206 will bring you to a junction where an abrupt left turn leads onto the spectacular road flanking Monte Sant'Angelo. **LORETO-DI-CASINCA**, the next halt, and the area's most appealing village, perches on a spur overlooking all the villages of the Casinca, its long main street affording a panorama right across to Bastia – the terrace to the left of the church is the best place to make the most of it. A waymarked hike through the chestnut forest up **Monte Sant'Angelo** (1218m) starts 500m south of the village along a recently surfaced road, from the neighbouring hamlet of **Silvarecio** – it's about ninety minutes' fairly strenuous climbing to the summit.

Some 500m north of the village you can cut back east by taking a right turn and following the road across a ridge for 2km until you hit the D237 again. A right here will bring you to **VENZOLASCA**, a remote and lofty village whose slender, lance-like church spire is conspicuous from a long way off. Venzolasca is one of the few places in Corsica where you still see men dressed in traditional black corduroy, complete with silver studs and gun belt.

From here it's a short drive down to **VESCOVATO**, set amongst chestnut trees and olive groves. Capital of the Casinca, this was an important place in the thirteenth century when the bishopric of Mariana was transferred here in a move to escape the malaria-ridden plain (*vescovato* means "bishopric" in Corsican). The bishopric remained until 1570, when it was relocated to the more important town of Bastia. The village is livelier than most places hereabouts – its busy central square, shaded by lines of ancient plane trees, even has an outdoor café, a rare find in these parts.

On the south side of the square, a family coat of arms indicates the house of the historian Filippini, whose *Historia di Corsica* (1594) is a principal source of medieval Corsican history. A further wander through the village reveals various plaques commemorating eminent visitors such as Mirabeau, but Vescovato's main sight is the church of **San Martino**, reached by climbing a flight of steps north of the square. Enlarged by the bishops of Mariana in the fifteenth century, the church contains a fine marble tabernacle, carved by a Genoese sculptor in 1441 and portraying two Roman soldiers sleeping against the tomb.

Travel details

BUSES

Most of the buses along the east coast are operated by Rapides Bleus. Services run twice daily from June 15 until September 15; during the rest of the year, the Sunday buses are suspended.

AC=Autobus Casinca (☎04 95 36 70 64).
ACT=Autobus Cortenais (☎04 95 46 22 89).
AF=Autocars Figarella (☎04 95 31 07 80).
RB=Rapides Bleus (☎04 95 31 03 79 or 04 95 70 10 36).

Aléria to: Bastia (RB; 2 daily; 1hr 30min); Corte (ACT; Mon, Wed & Fri; 1hr 25min); Ghisonaccia (RB; 2 daily; 15min); Porto-Vecchio (RB; 2 daily; 1hr 20min); Solenzara (RB; 2 daily; 30min).

Ghisonaccia to: Aléria (RB; 2 daily; 15min); Bastia (RB; 2 daily; 1hr 45min); Porto-Vecchio (RB; 2 daily; 1hr); Solenzara (RB; 2 daily; 20min).

Moriani-Plage to: Bastia (RB/AF; 2–3 daily; 45min).

Solenzara to: Aléria (RB; 2 daily; 30min); Bastia (RB; 2 daily; 2hr 15min); Ghisonaccia (RB; 2 daily; 20min); Porto-Vecchio (RB; 2 daily; 45min).

Venzolasca to: Bastia (AC; Mon–Sat 1 daily; 50min); Vescovato (AC; Mon–Sat 1 daily; 10min).

Vescovato to: Bastia (AC; Mon–Sat 1 daily; 40min); Venzolasca (AC; Mon–Sat 1 daily; 10min).

Chapter 7

Central Corsica

Central Corsica is a non-stop parade of stupendous scenery, and the best way to immerse yourself in it is to get onto the region's ever-expanding network of marked trails and forest roads. The ridge of granite mountains forming the spine of the island is closely followed by the epic GR20, a trail that can be picked up from various villages and is scattered with refuge huts offering basic facilities. Other marked trails wind off the watershed to the surrounding summits. Of these, the island's two highest peaks – Monte Cinto and Monte Rotondo – provide the most popular routes, accessible in settled summer weather to anyone with sufficient stamina and a strong pair of boots. For less adventurous hikers, there are also plenty of lower-altitude trails to exquisite glacial lakes and viewpoints over the valleys, while the region's roads, though often in disrepair, penetrate deep into the forests that carpet the mountain slopes, crossing various lofty passes along the way.

For more on the GR20, see pp.144–145.

Corte, set in a dip at the centre of the island on the main road between Ajaccio and Bastia, provides the perfect base to begin exploring, as it's well placed to reach anywhere covered in this chapter and has the bulk of the region's accommodation – elsewhere, it's rare to find more than one basic hotel per village. Capital of independent Corsica in the eighteenth century, Corte is a fortress village *par excellence*, with its walled citadel, set atop a twisted pinnacle of rock, piercing the landscape of overlapping mountains and forests.

Accommodation Price Codes

Throughout this guide, hotel accommodation is graded on a scale from ① to ⑧. These numbers show the cost per night of the cheapest double room **in high season**, though remember that many of the cheap places will have more expensive rooms with en-suite facilities. In such cases we list two price codes, indicating the range of room rates offered.

① under 100F/under €15	⑤ 300–350F/€45–52.50
② 100–200F/€15–30	⑥ 350–400F/€52.50–60
③ 200–250F/€30–37.50	⑦ 400–500F/€60–75
④ 250–300F/€37.50–45	⑧ 500F and above/€75 and above

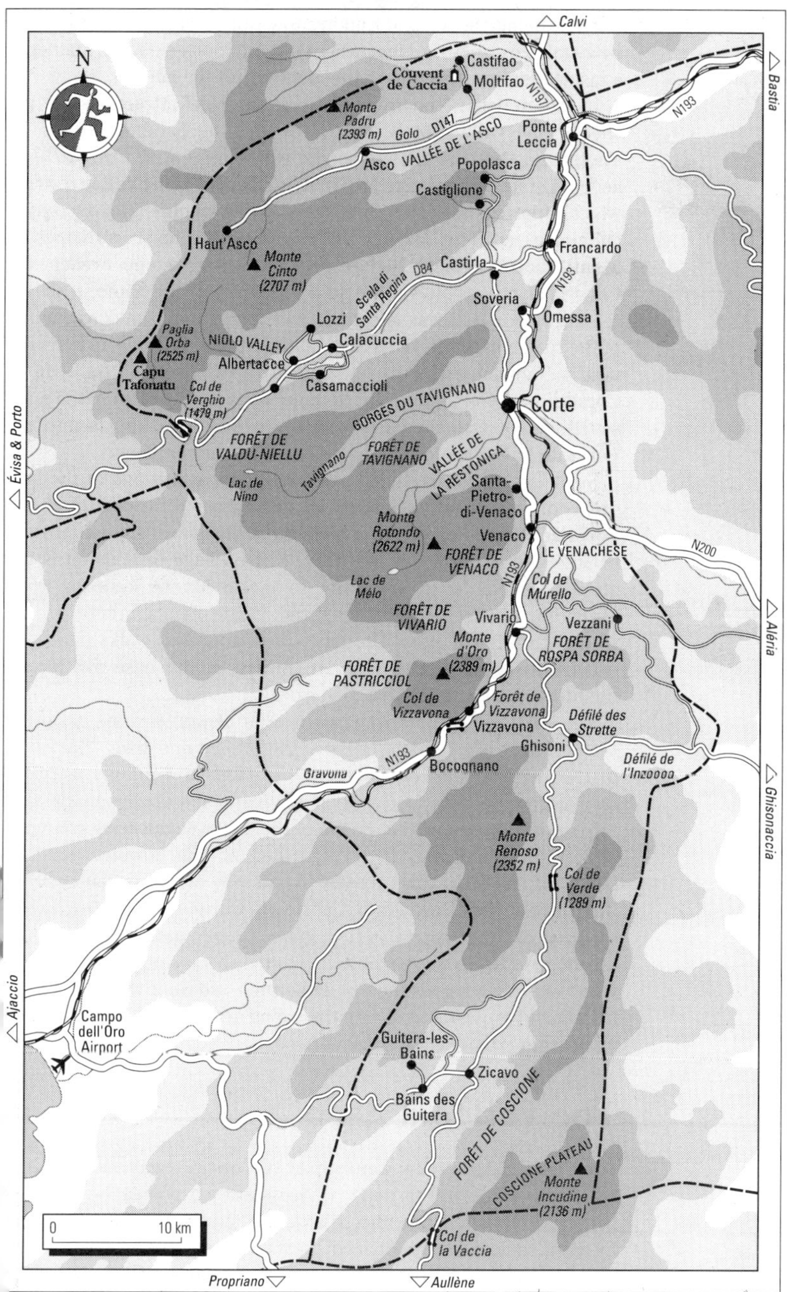
N
Calvi
Bastia
Évisa & Porto
Aléria
Ghisonaccia
Ajaccio
Propriano
Aullène
Castifao
Couvent de Caccia
Moltifao
N197
N193
Monte Padru (2393 m)
Golo
D147
VALLÉE DE L'ASCO
Ponte Leccia
Asco
Popolasca
Castiglione
Haut'Asco
Monte Cinto (2707 m)
Francardo
Castirla
D84
Scala di Santa Regina
Soveria
Omessa
Lozzi
Calacuccia
NIOLO VALLEY
Paglia Orba (2525 m)
Capu Tafonatu
Albertacce
Casamaccioli
Col de Verghio (1479 m)
GORGES DU TAVIGNANO
Corte
FORÊT DE VALDU-NIELLU
FORÊT DE TAVIGNANO
Tavignano
VALLÉE DE LA RESTONICA
Lac de Nino
Santa-Pietro-di-Venaco
Monte Rotondo (2622 m)
Venaco
FORÊT DE VENACO
LE VENACHESE
N200
Lac de Melo
Col de Murello
FORÊT DE VIVARIO
Vivario
Vezzani
Monte d'Oro (2389 m)
FORÊT DE ROSPA SORBA
FORÊT DE PASTRICCIOL
Col de Vizzavona
Forêt de Vizzavona
Vizzavona
Défilé des Strette
Ghisoni
Défilé de l'Inzoooo
Gravona
Bocognano
Monte Renoso (2352 m)
Col de Verde (1289 m)
Campo dell'Oro Airport
Guitera-les-Bains
Zicavo
Bains des Guitera
FORÊT DE COSCIONE
COSCIONE PLATEAU
Monte Incudine (2136 m)
0
10 km
Col de la Vaccia

Despite being the second-ranking town of northern Corsica, it's a peaceful, slow-moving place where old traditions die hard, making it a fascinating introduction to the mentality of the interior.

In the immediate environs of Corte the chief attractions are the spectacular **Vallée de la Restonica** and the parallel **Gorges du Tavignano**, but the most popular valley in central Corsica – on account of its comparative proximity to Bastia – is the **Vallée d'Asco**, which offers another superb gorge and rich wildlife. The Asco road culminates at **Haut'Asco**, a ski resort on the northern slopes of **Monte Cinto**, Corsica's highest peak. Access to the upper reaches of Cinto is also possible via the adjacent valley of the **Niolo**, a sheep-rearing region that was isolated for centuries until the construction of the road a hundred years ago. Like Corte, the Niolo is an essential visit for anyone eager to understand *l'âme corse* – "the soul of Corsica" – so you might want to linger for a night or two in the main settlement of **Calacuccia**, a centre for walks and drives into the **Forêt de Valdo-Niolo**, a dizzying forest of Laricio pines.

Such forests cover much of central Corsica, and one of the best drives on the island goes south of Corte from **Vivario** through the **Forêt de Rospa-Sorba**, the endless trees set against an omnipresent background of snowy peaks. The nearby village of **Ghisoni** is the place to make for if you want to tackle **Monte Renoso**, while **Vizzavona**, further south along the Bastia–Ajaccio route, is the springboard for Monte d'Oro, and offers countless walks into thick beech forest. Still further south, **Zicavo** is the base for **Monte Incudine**, the southernmost major peak.

The most memorable way to travel in central Corsica is on the *micheline* **train**, which crosses the mountains from Bastia to Ajaccio, with a main connection at Ponte Leccia. Four daily services stop at Ponte Leccia, Corte, Venaco, Vivario and Vizzavona, passing through a 4km tunnel that is one of the major engineering triumphs of the mountain railway. If you're pushed for time, however, you'll be better off travelling this route by **bus** on one of the regular coaches that run between Bastia and Ajaccio via Corte; the last stop before the descent to the capital is Bocognano. Public transport away from this main artery is more sporadic, limited to a seasonal summer service from Porto across the Col de Verghio and Niolo valley to Corte. In July and August and during the skiing season, you can also catch a bus from Ponte Leccia to Haut'Asco.

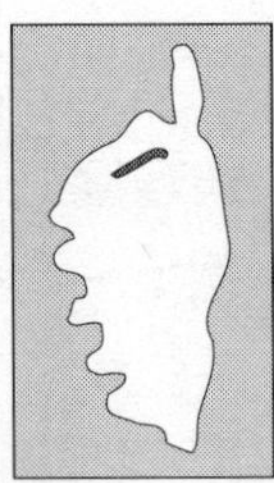

The Vallée d'Asco

The **Vallée d'Asco** – the wettest part of Corsica – was once a region of intensive pastoral farming, whose scattered population lived for centuries off small-scale cheese and wool production, supplemented by crops such as wheat, tobacco, linen and hemp. During the Genoese era, the *poix*, or pitch, made by the Aschesi from pine sap, caused the wholesale destruction of the area's forests, and today much of the landscape is denuded and bleak. Ringed by a string of 2000m peaks, the valley remains among Corsica's most remote enclaves; only in 1937 was Asco village connected to the road network, which was extended as far as the ski station by the French Foreign Legion in 1968. Today, the Aschesi, like most mountain communities, rely on the seasonal influx of hikers to make ends meet, along with modest sales of cheese and charcuterie, and their famously fragrant **honey**, produced in the ranks of ramshackle hives stacked up the hillsides.

The River Asco starts life as the Stranciacone, which rises at an altitude of 2556m on the lower slopes of **Monte Cinto**, Corsica's highest mountain, then flows through the village of Asco and on through a fantastic **gorge** before reaching the River Golo close to **Ponte Leccia**. In the upper valley, beyond Asco, the scenery is most alpine – up here mouflon roam in carefully protected zones, and bearded vultures and royal eagles are sometimes to be spotted in the magnificent **Forêt de Carozzica**. The road comes to an end 15km west of Asco at the semi-operational ski station at **Haut'Asco**, from where trails lead into the forest and up the flank of Cinto.

No buses run to Haut'Asco, so you'll need your own transport to make a tour of the valley. Starting at Ponte Leccia, it's a good idea to detour up to the delightful villages of **Moltifao** and **Castifao**, before returning to the gorge and the road up to Haut'Asco.

A description of the two main routes up Monte Cinto features on p.335.

Ponte Leccia, Moltifao and Castifao

Lying 19km north of Corte at the junction of road and rail routes to Bastia, Corte and the Balagne, **PONTE LECCIA** has nothing to recommend it except its supermarkets and service stations, where you might want to refuel before pressing on into the Vallée d'Asco or Castagniccia. A couple of kilometres north, the D47 leaves the N197 to follow the River Asco, initially along a flatland scattered with eucalyptus trees.

The Castagniccia region is covered on pp.314–325.

The best-value place to **stay** hereabouts is the *Cabanella*, just beyond the turning for Moltifao, 7km from the junction with N197 (☎04 95 47 80 29; ③): this modest, unpretentious auberge provides comfortable chambre d'hôte accommodation, with 90F meals of mixed French and Corsican dishes served in a downstairs dining room. Close by, the *Camping A Tizarella* (☎04 95 47 83 92; April–Oct) is a well-equipped two-star site with plenty of shade, a camping-gas bottle depot and pizzeria; it's easy to spot – look for the giant painted wooden flowers at the roadside.

A right along the D247 here will take you up the hillside to **MOLTIFAO**, an amphitheatre of old stone buildings set on a crest separating the valleys of the Tartagine and Asco. Moltifao's church houses a beautiful sixteenth-century **triptych** and some sacristy furniture, including a wooden retable incorporating a fine primitive painting of the Virgin on a gold background.

For a great view across to the Tartagine, carry on 3km north to **CASTIFAO**, a warm-toned settlement that once thrived on its copper mine and marble quarry. At the pass just before the village stands the ruined **Couvent de Caccia**, a former Franciscan convent built in the late Gothic style. Partially derelict, it nowadays serves as a cemetery for the nearby villages; the crucifixes, marble tombs, candles and flowers create an extraordinary atmosphere amid the exposed brick-work and lofty Gothic arches. Some of the tombstones outside the building bear the name "Stuart", which historians believe may have been brought to the area by Scottish mercenaries during the Wars of Independence. An ideal picnic spot from which to view the spectacular Mori massif, on the opposite side of the valley, is the grassy ledge below the ruin, reached by hopping through a gap in the fence where the road bends sharply towards the pass.

The Gorges de l'Asco and Haut'Asco

The valley proper begins at the **gorges de l'Asco**, where overhanging rock faces of orange granite soar to 900m. There isn't much to **ASCO** itself, an austere little place 22km west of Ponte Leccia, famed in the eighteenth century as home of the *paceri* (peacemakers), a tribunal of locally elected magistrates who mediated between families involved in vendettas. Its location, however, couldn't be better: built up the left bank of the river, the village lies at the base of a grandiose crest of mountains, with the crags of Monte Padro immediately to the northwest and the Monte Cinto massif and Capo Bianco to the southwest. You can stay here at the welcoming *Ferme-Auberge d'Ambroise et Nicole Vesperini*, on the way into the village (☎04 95 47 83 53; half-board for 250F per head obligatory in July and August; ④; May–Oct), which offers comfortable accommodation in small but cosy rooms, and excellent local cuisine in its **restaurant**, where a four-course meal will set you back around 120F.

A wonderful – if well-known – **swimming spot** can be found on the riverbank below Asco, at the renovated fifteenth-century **Genoese bridge**, a listed historical monument; follow the narrow one-way road west through the village until you reach a potholed lane running sharply downhill. The water on either side of the humpbacked stone bridge is transparent green and fairly deep, but pretty cold even in midsummer. On its far side, an ancient, paved mule track strikes up the **Pinara valley** towards the Col de Serra Piana – formerly the main line of communication with the Niolo valley to the south. Twenty minutes into the walk, you find yourself deep in a wilderness of scrub and towering rock, with only semi-wild goats for company.

Beyond Asco village the D147 widens as it passes through the **Forêt de Carozzica**, a magnificent forest of maritime and Laricio pines, which extend up the valley walls as far as the 2000m contour. Hugging the river, the road passes clearings and pools ideal for a picnic and a swim, then becomes increasingly difficult as it climbs to

HAUT'ASCO (or Asco La Neige), a ski station set amidst swathes of lush turf punctuated by stunted pines. Paid for largely by government grants, the unsightly chalet blocks and ski lifts would be more tolerable if they were used regularly, but over the past few years there has been so little snow up here that the station has remained closed. During the summer, however, the place is popular with hikers, who come to tackle the ice-flecked crags of the Cinto massif, looming menacingly to the south, and it serves as a major reprovisioning stop for long-distance walkers following the GR20.

Accommodation is provided by the large and impersonal *Le Chalet* (☎04 95 47 81 08, fax 04 95 30 25 59; ②–③; May–Sept), which, in addition to standard chalet-style rooms with balconies,

Mountain Walks from Haut'Asco

The road up the Asco valley takes you right into the heart of the mountains, and the ski station is a popular springboard for some exceptional high-altitude hiking, most notably the ascent of Monte Cinto. Nearly all of the trails in the area are well frequented and marked every 10m or so with paint splashes, but you should be prepared for sudden and dramatic changes of weather, particularly in August, when electric storms rip across the ridges most afternoons. An IGN **topo-map** of the area is also essential, although you could get by with the Parc Naturel Régional's topo-guide of the GR20, which passes within a stone's throw of the roadhead.

A line of broken crags marking the high point of the crest dividing the Niolo and Asco basins, **Monte Cinto** (2706m) is the loftiest, if not the most handsome, mountain in Corsica, and as such attracts greater numbers of hikers than any other peak on the island. Even so, it's a long hard slog to the summit, and you need to be in good shape to complete the climb in a day. The route from Haut'Asco, winding up the massif's wilder north face, is more varied and dramatic than the approach from the south (via the Niolo valley), and is a much better option except in May and early June, when patches of eternal snow clinging to sheltered crevices can be treacherous. A spray-painted rock and regular red spots indicate the way from the ski station car park, from where the trail crosses the Stranciacone torrent, hugging the true right bank before peeling left into the Cirque de Trimbolaccio. Eventually, you arrive at the foot of the gorge leading to the Col de Borba, at the head of the massif, where the trail plunges left into the huge boulder field below the summit. Count on five to six hours for the ascent, and up to four hours for the return trip to the ski station.

Five kilometres south of the station lies the challenge of the **Punta Minuta**, part of the Monte Cinto massif reached via the grandiose Cirque de la Solitude, or you might attempt **Monte Padro**, approached through the Vallée du Stranciacone. Probably the most straightforward option for a day-hike, however, is the ascent of the **Muvrella ridge** (Crête de la Muvrella), reached after a two-hour climb up a narrow rock corridor running west from the ski station. From the top, the views are superb, and on a clear day you should be able to pick out the Calvi coast and the needles of the Bonifatu massif. A further thirty minutes will bring you to the little lake on the northwest face of the mountain; allow a good two hours for the descent.

offers budget gîte d'étape rooms. Situated at the head of the valley, the hotel is perfectly placed for high-altitude hikes, lying within easy reach of a number of challenging routes, among them some of the most exciting stretches of the GR20. If you're **camping**, pull off the road 2km down the valley from Haut'Asco, where the two-star *Monte Cintu* campsite (☎04 95 47 85 88; May–Oct) has fairly level pitches under the pine trees, plus clean toilet blocks and electricity hook-ups for camper vans.

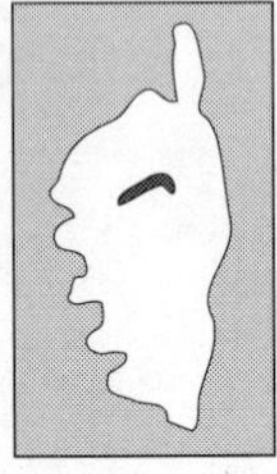

The Niolo

The Niolo – homeland of Corsican freedom, inviolable citadel from which the island's invaders have never been able to expel its mountain folk. This wild trench is unimaginably beautiful. Not a blade of grass, nor a plant; granite . . . nothing but granite.

Guy de Maupassant, *Un Bandit Corse* (1892)

The **Niolo** is the vast basin of the upper reaches of the **Golo**, a river that rises 2000m up in the mountains, is swelled by meltwater from the high peaks of Monte Cinto, Paglia Orba and Capo Tafonato, and expires to the south of Bastia, 80km from its source. The region's name – a corruption of the Corsican *Niolo*, meaning "sombre" or "afflicted" – is now more appropriate than ever, for fire has destroyed much of the Niolo's forested land (see p.115), leaving bleak landscapes of orange granite and shrivelled vegetation. Conifers and chestnut trees scatter the lower slopes of Monte Cinto, but of the great dark forest that once blanketed the whole basin all that remains is the **Forêt de Valdo-Niolo**, a majestic swathe of Laricio pines in the southwest of the district.

The forest extends east of the frequently snowbound Col de Verghio, the highest mountain pass in Corsica and one of two routes into the Niolo. The other one is the rocky corridor known as the **Scala di Santa Regina**, a vertiginous ravine some 21km long and 300m high, through which a road was built in the late nineteenth century. Until then, people had used hazardous goat and mule tracks (the *scala*) to get into this region, whose isolation and consequent inbreeding perpetuated the singularly tall, blond and blue-eyed appearance of the Neolithic tribes known as the Corsi, from whom the Niolins claim direct descent.

The Niolins have always made their living from the breeding o goats. Shepherds formerly lived a solitary, harsh existence, trekking over the mountains with their herds to the milder coastal plains fo winter – mainly to Galéria on the west coast, but sometimes as far as Cap Corse – and returning to the high ground with their flocks i summertime. Some of the old, bare stone dwellings still pepper th slopes, but are mostly abandoned these days. In addition, Niolo' craft industry has all but disappeared, though the production of loca

Niolo Hikes and Walks

The Parc Naturel Régional recently inaugurated an extensive network of marked footpaths in the Niolo, but by far the most popular mountain hike in the area remains the ascent of **Monte Cinto** (2706m), Corsica's highest mountain, via its southeast face. Although not nearly as dramatic as the approach from the Asco valley (see p.330), this route, boulder-strewn for much of its length, ranks among the island's most frequented trails between mid-June, when the snow melts, and mid-October, when it returns with a vengeance on the high ridges.

To drive as close to the mountain as possible, take the D218 north out of Calacuccia, then turn right along a rough track at the hairpin bend just beyond the hamlet of **Lozzi**, some 6km along. A short way above the village lie two good campsites (reviewed on p.339), from where a motorable dirt track winds via another series of sharp switchbacks to a small car park – the de facto trailhead. Another 35 minutes on foot will bring you to the **refuge de l'Ercu** (1600m), which is open all year but only staffed between July and mid-September. If you're hiking all the way from Lozzi, allow around three hours to reach the refuge. This is where the ascent proper starts, and you should aim to be here shortly after dawn, particularly during the summer, when electric storms and rain frequently force hikers off the mountain by mid-afternoon. The climb to the summit takes between three and four hours, depending on how fit you are, and the views are sublime, taking in both coasts, the Toscan islands and, even on very clear days, the Côte d'Azur and Alps.

For the best views of the Cinto massif itself, however, you have to scale the opposite, southern, side of the Niolo valley. An ancient mule track beginning at the Calacuccia dam cuts up a mountain spur to the **Col de l'Arinella** (1592m), a pass separating the Golo and Tavignano valleys, from which there's a magnificent vista of the surrounding summits. To pick up the trail – a section of the Mare a Mare Nord long-distance footpath – cross the dam and follow the right fork of the road peeling left off the D218. Cutting across the switchbacks, the path (marked with orange splashes of paint) is very steep, especially after the **bergeries de Casartine** (1169m), as it zigzags up to the col. Descend via the same route back to Calacuccia, or continue east to the **refuge de la Sega**, where you can spend the night. From here, the trail follows the Tavignano all the way to Corte, reached in around four hours from the refuge.

A good pair of boots is essential **equipment** for the latter climbs, and you should follow our advice regarding clothing and supplies given on p.34. For the Cinto hike, it's worth investing in a detailed IGN contour **map** of the massif; and if you plan to complete the whole of the Calacuccia–Corte route, the Parc Naturel Régional's topo-guide of the area, available at most tourist offices and bookshops on the island, is invaluable.

If you feel more like a leisurely **low-altitude walk** than a full-on mountain hike, call in at the Calacuccia tourist office for a free copy of the Parc Naturel Régional's excellent *Balades en Corse: Niolu* leaflet (*dépliant*), which outlines five routes (of between 3hr 30min and 7hr) on a monochrome topo-map. Some, like the "Tour des Cinque Frati", involve stiff ascents, but most are leisurely ambles along the valley floor.

The Mare a Mare Nord footpath is detailed on p.320.

For more on the role of song in the Corsican vendetta, see p.244.

Corsican Choral Music: Les Polyphonies Corse

Choral singing, known in French as *les polyphonies*, has for many centuries provided a crucial mode of entertainment and expression for the shepherds of poor and remote areas such as the Niolo and, though it is dwindling in its purest form, Corsican song remains an integral part of the island's traditional culture.

As recently as the 1960s, remote village streets would still occasionally echo with the wild, searing incantation of the **voceru**, an improvised song by a woman in mourning for a loved one. In the more distant past, when the death of a son or husband often stemmed from a vendetta, the song would register not only the pain of bereavement but also urgency of revenge, aimed at spurring the surviving men to retribution.

Death and separation have also provided inspiration for many shepherds' songs, often sung in the form of the three-part **a paghjella**, a form perhaps dating as far back as the megalithic age. It's performed by three male voices – the first (*a prima*) sets the pace for the chant, the second (*u boldu*) provides the base sound, while the third (*a terza*) sings the mesmerizing melody. Mass used to be sung this way in the more remote churches of the island; today you can hear *a paghjella* at its best at the Santa di u Niolu fair at Casamaccioli.

A third type of singing, known as **chiami e rispondi** (questions and answers), is also an important feature of the Santa di u Niolu. This takes the form of a competition in which two male contestants have to improvise a dialogue in strictly rhyming verse to a repetitive air. They may sing about anything, but it's popular to aim abuse at the assembled company or else proclaim about political issues. The one who first runs out of answers in this battle of wits is the loser.

In the course of this century, the drift of rural populations into the towns and to the French mainland nearly killed off folk singing, but the form enjoyed a dramatic revival during the nationalist upsurge of the 1970s, when young singers such as **Jean-Paul Poletti** and **Petru Guelficci** made a name for themselves performing patriotic songs at political rallies. Since then, several have formed **folk-rock** groups to spread the nationalist message, mixing modern guitar, keyboard and percussion sounds with

gastronomic specialities survives: a sharp goat's cheese and some renowned charcuterie, which cures particularly well at this altitude. Ancient traditions, however, have an extra vitality in the Niolo, and some of the finest *a paghjella* chanting can be heard here (see box). Improvised singing competitions are still held at Casamaccioli during the three-day **Santa di u Niolu**, a country fair that takes place around September 8.

These days tourism is making itself felt at the far-flung capital of the Niolo, **Calacuccia**, an exposed little place whose basic accommodation makes it a suitable base for exploring the area. Apart from a trip to **Casamaccioli**, you could pay a visit to **Albertacce**, which boasts a small ethnographic museum, to **Corscia**, an impressive stack of hillside hamlets, or to the southeast face of **Monte Cinto**. Southwest of Calacuccia, the glistening **Lac de Nino** makes a reward traditional harmonies. The most commercially successful of these is the band **I Muvrini**, who these days play to packed houses in Paris as well as Bastia and Ajaccio. Another name to look out for is **Les Nouvelles Polyphonies Corses**, a five-piece mixed-gender group of young singers who've collaborated with musicians from other parts of the world to forge a radically new, ambient reworking of traditional Corsican choral singing. Composed by Jean-Paul Poletti and produced by synth supremo Hector Zazou (of Voix Bulgares fame), their first album *Les Nouvelles Polyphonies Corse I* was an international "world music" bestseller, while their second offering, *Paradisu*, a collection of sacred music produced by ex-Velvet Underground violinist John Cale, with Patti Smith, has also been highly acclaimed. Perhaps the most outstanding albums to have come out of Corsica in the past few years, however, are those recorded by Jean-Paul Poletti's latest group, **Le Chœur d'Hommes de Sartène** (Audvis). Sombre and austere, the recordings represent a return to the traditional Christian context of choral music. For more on Poletti and the singing school he founded in Sartène, see p.265.

During the summer months, posters and banners advertise **gigs** by well-known nationalist-oriented bands – such as Chjami Aghalesi and Canta U Populu Corsu – at towns and resorts all over the island, and these are well worth attending. Rooting out pure, traditional *polyphonie* singing, however, can be more difficult. One occasion you're sure to encounter the *crème de la crème* of Corsican singers is the annual four-day **Rencontres Polyphoniques**, held in Calvi in mid-September. Regular recitals also take place at La Casa Musicale in Pigna, Balagne (see p.149), while during the **Santa di u Niolu** festival Casamaccioli's village bar bursts at the seams with exponents of most of the island's traditional choral forms.

Failing that, splash out on a **cassette** or **CD**. Recommended titles include *Voce di Corsica: Polyphonies* (Olivi Music/Sony), which features the island's six greatest living male voices recorded in a church in Bonifacio; *A Filetta: Una Terra ci hè* (Olivi Music), with the ethereal singing of Ghjuvan-Claudiu Acquaviva accompanied by traditional instruments such as the cittern (*cistre*); and anything by the all-women ensemble Donasulana (Silex/Auvidis), whose renditions of old *voceri* and *lamenti* are sublime.

ing hike from the Forêt de Valdo-Niolo, a magnet for walkers and tourists in search of some shade.

Calacuccia

A clutch of grim grey buildings, **CALACUCCIA** benefits from its unusual location – set high on a wide plain at the heart of the Niolo, in the shadow of the weird jagged ridge of the Cinque Frati mountains. West of the village stretches the Lac de Calacuccia, a large reservoir built in 1968 to supply Bastia and the eastern plain. Bathing and sailing on the lake are forbidden, and locals insist the water has caused undesirable climatic changes in the valley – notably an increase in mist and humidity – but its rippled surface, shimmering with reflections of snowy peaks, is an undeniably beautiful sight. The only historic monument here is the white-painted

Église de St-Pierre, built on an eminence at the western exit from the village; inside, a seventeenth-century wooden statue of Christ forms the principal attraction. The main reason visitors come to the village, however, is to access the network of trails that crisscross the surrounding mountainsides, affording wonderful views of the colossal massifs to the north and south.

Calacuccia practicalities

Calacuccia is served by daily **buses**, departing Bastia at 4pm and arriving in Calacuccia at 6.30pm run by Autocars Mordiconi (☎04 95 48 00 04). From July until mid-September, an additional service runs between Corte and Porto via Calacuccia and Col de Verghio (4 daily except Sun). Timetables are available at the village **tourist office**, 200m east of the centre on the Corte road, adjacent to the fire station (mid-June to Sept Mon–Fri 8am–noon & 2–7pm, Sat 8am–noon; ☎04 95 48 05 22), who can also give advice on hiking, climbing and kayaking in the area, and can put you in touch with qualified mountain guides.

Calacuccia has two **hotels** the most comfortable of which is *L'Acqua Viva*, overlooking the lake as you leave the village on the road to Col de Verghio (☎04 95 48 06 90 or 04 95 48 00 08, fax 04 95 48 08 82; ④); its dozen rooms are well appointed, with en-suite bathrooms and balconies, and the views of the mountain and lake are

La Forêt de Valdo-Niolo: Lac de Nino and Cascades de Radule

Two of the best hikes in Central Corsica begin southwest of Calacuccia, at the head of the Niolo valley. Crossed by the D84 on its way to Col de Verghio, this area is covered by the extensive **Forêt de Valdo-Niolo**, which comprises some of the island's finest Laricio pines, some of them more than 500 years old and 40m tall. For either of the routes below, we recommend you take along the relevant IGN topo-map, and are prepared and equipped for sudden changes in the weather.

The classic trail hereabouts leads from the **maison forestière at Poppaghia**, 10km southwest of Calacuccia, to Lac de Nino, an exquisite high-altitude lake reached after a strenuous three-hour climb from the road. The path is well waymarked and frequented, but it's a good idea to get hold of the IGN topo-map 25, #4251OT (ref A4/B4). The trail, marked with yellow splashes of paint, follows a mountain stream up to the **bergeries de Colga**, a gathering of stone shacks just above the tree line (1411m), then on – more steeply through a boulder-strewn landscape dotted with stunted elms – up to the **Col de Stazzona** (1762m), between Monte Tozzu (2007m) and Punta Artica (2327m). At the top of the pass there's a weird scattering of black, pointed rocks known as the **Devil's Oxen** – the story goes that the Devil was challenged by St Martin to plough a straight line and, upon failing, his oxen were turned to stone. The Devil hurled his ploughshare in a rage through the distinctively shaped red mountain known as **Capu Tafonatu** (Pierced Mountain), visible on the opposite side of the valley. It's only fifteen minutes further to the lake, superb. As a fall-back, the *Hôtel des Touristes*, in the centre of the village (☎04 95 48 00 04; ④; May–Oct), is a welcoming place despite its drab, grey façade, and has a popular restaurant. Of the village's two **gîtes d'étape**, the *Couvent St-François-di-Niolu*, 2km west, near the Musée Archéologique Licinoi (☎04 95 48 00 11; 60F per dorm bed; ③), is by far the most comfortable. *Chez Toussaint Mordiconi* (☎04 95 48 00 04; 60F per bed), Calacuccia's other gîte, is on the grubby side and nowhere near as pleasant as those in nearby Albertacce, 3.5km west (see p.340).

The two best **campsites** in the area – *Camping U Monte Cintu* (☎04 95 48 04 45) and *L'Arimone* (☎04 95 48 00 58) – lie next door to each other at the trailhead of the Monte Cinto hike, in the hamlet of Lozzi, 5km west. The latter also has a handful of inexpensive rooms, and a basic pizzeria.

To sample the best of the valley's renowned cuisine, head 2km west of the village along the road that skirts the lakeside to the *Auberge du Lac* (☎04 95 48 02 73), which enjoys a near-perfect location on the water's edge, and serves authentic Niolo cuisine at reasonable prices; set menus range from 76F to 128F, with home-made charcuterie and local cheeses featuring prominently. Alternatively, try the equally commendable *Auberge Casa Balduina*, opposite the convent 2km west of the village (☎04 95 48 08 57), where you should splash out on their top *menu berger*: local

which from June to September is thronged with flocks of sheep and goats; in autumn, with a dusting of snow on the peaks, the scenery is reminiscent of Tibetan plateau pastureland. The surrounding marshy turf declivities, known as *pozzi* (meaning "wells"), are the remnants of lakes gouged by glaciers, which subsequently filled up with sediment. To get back to the maison forestière, you can either retrace your steps (allow 5hr for the return-trip), or else follow the GR20 path marked with red and white paint splashes across the slopes of Monte Tozzu until it meets up with the Forêt de Valdo-Niolo round-route, which takes you back to the Colga valley, and thence through the pines to the road.

The other recommended hike in the forest is a much easier two-hour return-trip to the **Cascades de Radule**, where the River Golo, which has its source high up on Paglia Orba, plunges through a series of waterfalls, forming perfect natural pools. Although it is marked with red and white splashes, it's worth taking the IGN topo-map 25, #4250 OT (ref C1/D1). The trail (one of the rare easy-going stretches of the GR20) starts at the hairpin bend in the D84 known as *Fer à Cheval* (Horseshoe), 4km below the Col de Verghio. After around thirty minutes you emerge from the pine trees at the **bergeries de Radule**, from where the path descends to the river and falls. The GR20 proper continues north, winding up the stream valley, and is well worth following for another couple of hours as far as the **refuge Ciuttulu di i Mori** (1962m), the usual night halt for mountaineers attempting Paglia Orba (for a description of this ascent, see box on p.341).

charcuterie, white beans with cured ham, free-range veal steak with wild mushrooms, chestnut *fiadone* and coffee for 120F. Half *pichets* of local AOC wine cost 30F.

Around Calacuccia: Casamaccioli and Albertacce

Occupying the greenest part of the Niolo, **CASAMACCIOLI**, 5km from Calalcuccia, lies south of the lake in the middle of a chestnut forest. Its small square, edged by enormous chestnut trees, is the setting for the **Santa di u Niolu** (see box on p.336), Corsica's most important religious festival, when thousands of pilgrims and expatriate natives descend on the village to celebrate the Nativity of the Virgin. The focal point of the event is a statue of the Madonna, **Santa Maria della Stella**, which miraculously transported itself here by mule in the fifteenth century after the convent in which it originally resided was burned down by Turkish pirates. Now venerated for her miracle-working powers, she is carried in procession through the village, but the most visually striking feature of the festival is the famous **Granitola**, when dozens of white-robed and white-hooded penitents, drawn from the village's various religious brotherhoods, or *Cunfraterna*, wind and unwind in spirals around a cross (a similar procession takes place in Calvi; see p.126). La Santa has a strongly secular aspect, too. Formerly, the event, held at the end of the first week in September, provided the main opportunity of the year for Niolites from remote villages to buy, sell and barter; in exchange for wool, meat, milk, cheese and charcuterie, they would obtain hardware, hats, horse tack, woodcarving, textiles, shoes and anything else that could not be manufactured in the mountains. Gambling was also central, and remains so to this day, with serious round-the-clock card sessions held in unlicensed home casinos. Afterwards, the participants celebrate, or drown their sorrows, in the village bar – one of the few places in Corsica where you can still hear traditional improvised singing, or *chiami e rispondi* (see box on p.336). Outside festival time, however, the only noteworthy sight here is the small **Église de la Nativité**, where you can pay your repects to the crudely repainted and gold-crowned Santa Maria della Stella herself, and enjoy magnificent views of the Cinto massif to the northwest. In Casamaccioli's tiny **gîte d'étape** beside the church (☎04 95 48 03 47), dorm beds cost 60F per night. You can use their self-catering facilities or, if you book in advance, opt for an evening meal (80F).

The row of little cottages comprising **ALBERTACCE**, 3km west of Calacuccia, makes an interesting contrast with the fortress houses found throughout the rest of the island – people hereabouts thought the mountains were protection enough against uninvited guests. If you knock at the last house on the right coming from Calacuccia you'll be let into a small folk museum, the **Musée Archéologique Licinoi** (June–Sept Mon–Fri 10am–noon & 2–5pm, Sat 10am–noon

The Ascent of Paglia Orba

The great red wedge of **Paglia Orba** (2525m), rising like a giant dorsal fin beside the pierced peak of **Capu Tafonatu** (2343m), is the Corsican watershed's most distinctive mountain. Thanks to the dizzying drops into the Fangu Valley and Filosorma from its vast northwest face, it is also a more challenging proposition than nearby Cinto. In fine, dry weather you don't need ropes or any technical expertise to attempt the ascent, but a good head for heights is essential, as some sections are notoriously vertigo-inducing.

The traditional **approach** to the mountain via the **Cascades de Radule** at the head of the Golo Valley (described on pp.338–339) is itself a wonderful walk, passing stands of old Laricio pines, deep bathing pools, and eventually high Alpine-style pastureland where you can usually spot mouflon grazing on inaccessible ledges. However, you'd have to be a strong climber indeed to cover this, the ascent to the summit and descent back to the roadhead afterwards, in a single day. Instead, most people bivouac at the **refuge Ciuttulu di i Mori**, perched on a natural balcony at the head of the Golo, and set off for the top the following morning (thereby increasing the chances of clear skies and good views).

The **route** begins immediately behind the refuge, climbing steeply up a huge rock choke towards a ridge known as **Col de Maures**. A short way before the pass, cairns rising to your right (north) up a deep corridor indicate the way through a series of huge granite blocks. Once you've arrived at a large ledge after around twenty minutes, the route steepens, progressing through some tight chimneys as far as a false summit, the western edge of the giant Paglia Orba tabletop. From here you drop into a little hollow known as "La Combe de Chèvres", carpeted in deep *névés* during early summer, before tackling the final haul to the top. Because the sides of Paglia Orba fall away so steeply, the views from the summit are even more dramatic than from Monte Cinto, extending far out to sea and across the entire northwestern watershed. Allow a good three and a half hours for the ascent from the refuge, and don't attempt the route if the rock is wet.

free), where the exhibits include shepherds' implements and clothes, plus some evil-looking knives.

Housed in an old stone building at the roadside, Albertacce's little **gîte d'étape** (☎04 95 48 05 60; May–Oct) charges 60F for a bed in its four-person dorms, and around 170F for half-board. After the *Couvent St-François-di-Niolu* (see p.339), this is the nicest gîte in the area.

Corte (Corti) and around

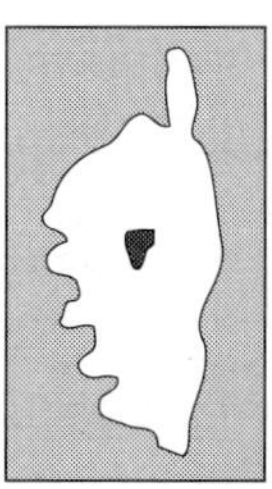

Stacked up the side of a wedge-shaped crag, against a spectacular backdrop of brooding granite mountains, **CORTE** (Corti) epitomizes *l'âme corse*, or "Corsican soul" – a small town marooned amid grandiose landscape, where a spirit of dogged defiance and patriotism is never far from the surface. This has been the home of

Corte (Corti) and around

Corsican nationalism since the first National Constitution was drawn up here in 1731, and was also where **Pascal Paoli**, "U Babbu di u Patria" (Father of the Nation), formed the island's first democratic government later in the eighteenth century. Self-consciously insular and grimly proud, it can seem an inhospitable place at times, although the presence of the island's only **university** lightens the atmosphere noticeably during term time, when the bars and cafés lining its long main street fill with students. For the outsider, Corte's charm is concentrated in the tranquil **haute ville**, where the forbidding **citadel** – home to the island's premier **museum**, the Museu di a Corsica – presides over a warren of narrow, cobbled streets. Immediately behind it, the Restonica and Tavignano gorges afford easy access to some of the region's most memorable mountain scenery, best enjoyed from the marked trails that wind through them.

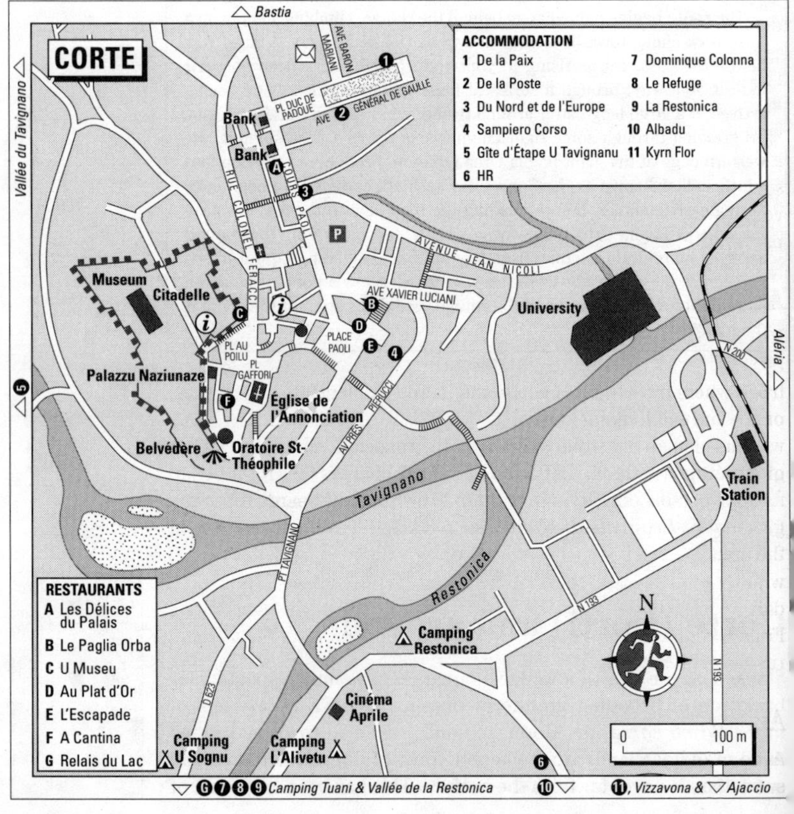

A brief history of Corte

Corte's reputation for belligerent independence was born in the ninth century, when the occupiers of the strategic post allegedly saw off a group of Saracen raiders. Later on, the Genoese rulers were constantly harried by the local nobles, culminating in 1419 with the takeover by **Vincentello d'Istria**, the king of Aragon's viceroy. After Vincentello's execution in 1434, Genoa ruled relatively undisturbed until the French expedition of 1553, when Corte happily succumbed to Sampiero Corso, though within six years the Genoese were back in charge, and were to stay in control for a long time.

By the early eighteenth century, Corsican nationalism was on the rise in Corte, its success due in part to the town's isolation from the occupied coastal towns. Following a local insurrection in 1731, a National Constitution was drawn up here at the first National Assembly, and in 1752 Gaffori was elected head of state in Corte. After Gaffori's assassination in 1753, Pascal Paoli returned from exile and from 1755 to 1769 made Corte the seat of his revolutionary government, which set up the first Corsican printing press and the **Università di Corsica**, the first university to be established on the island.

However, in 1768, under the terms of the Treaty of Versailles, France bought Corsica from the Genoese, and after the Battle of Ponte Nuovu the following year the period of Corsican independence was at an end. Under the French the town became insignificant, and it's only recently that it has acquired a slightly more exalted status as *sous-préfecture* of Haute-Corse and as the seat of the revived university, whose aims are to re-establish the value of Corsican culture, partly through the compulsory teaching of the indigenous language.

Arrival and information

Buses from Ajaccio and Bastia (Eurocorse Voyages; ☎04 95 21 06 30) stop in the centre of town on cours Paoli, the main street, and halfway along avenue Xavier-Luciani. The **train station** is at the foot of the hill near the university, from where it's a ten-minute uphill walk into town. If you're **driving**, the best place to park is at the top of avenue Jean-Nicoli, the road leading into town from Ajaccio.

Corte's swish new **tourist office** is situated just inside the main gates of the citadel, near the museum (May–Oct daily 9am–1pm & 2–7pm; Nov–April Mon–Fri 9am–noon & 2–6pm; ☎04 95 46 26 70), while the information office of the Parc Naturel Régional (June–Sept daily 9am–1pm & 4.30–7pm; ☎04 95 46 27 44) stands at the Fontaine des Quatre-Canons, a small square between cours Paoli and rue Colonel-Feracci.

Accommodation

Accommodation in Corte is plentiful and, with the exception of the smarter hotels hidden 2km southwest of town amid the lower reaches of the Restonica Valley, costs a lot less than on the coast. One reason for this is the huge *Hôtel HR*, whose unbeatable rates pin down tariffs throughout the town at the lower end of the scale; the other is that the majority of visitors to the area come here equipped for the outdoors and prefer to **camp**.

Hotels

If you're travelling without a vehicle, bear in mind that most of the hotels and guesthouses situated out of town, including *L'Albadu* and those up the Restonica Valley (but not *Kyrn Flor*), will provide a complimentary pick-up from the station if you let them know the day before.

L'Albadu, ancienne route d'Ajaccio, 2.5km southwest of town (☎04 95 46 24 55). Simply furnished rooms with showers (shared toilets) on a working farm-cum-equestrian centre. Warm family atmosphere, beautiful horses, fine views and top Corsican speciality food, served *en famille* so you get to practise your French (at 180F per head, the half-board is a bargain). Easily among the most congenial, and reasonably priced, *ferme-auberges* on the island. If you're driving, the easiest route is via the main Ajaccio road for 1500m, where a red-and-white sign points to the right. Advance reservation essential. ②.

Dominique Colonna, Vallée de la Restonica, 2km south of town (☎04 95 46 09 58, fax 04 95 61 03 91). A posh but rather overpriced three-star set in pine woods next to the stream. Owned by a retired football star, who bought it after winning the lottery. Half-board only July and August. Open April–Oct. ⑥.

HR, allée du 9-Septembre (☎04 95 45 11 11, fax 04 95 61 02 85). This converted concrete-block gendarmerie, 200m southwest of the SNCF train station, looks grim from the outside, but its 125 rooms are comfortable enough and its rates rock-bottom; bathroom-less options are the best deal (only 145F). No credit cards. ②–③.

Kyrn Flor (Chez M. et Mme Valentini), U San Gavina, 3km south on the N193 (☎04 95 61 02 88). Friendly bed and breakfast with very pleasant en-suite rooms and a leafy garden, although a little too close to the main road for comfort. You need a car to stay here. Evening meals 120F on request; breakfast included. ⑤.

Du Nord et de l'Europe, 22 cours Paoli (☎04 95 46 00 68). Pleasant, clean place right in the centre. The variously priced rooms are basic but huge, and the building has oodles of charm, with a marble-floored entrance hall and high stucco ceilings. Open all year. ②–③.

De la Paix, 1 av Général-de-Gaulle (☎04 95 46 06 72, fax 04 95 46 23 84). Large, smart and central, in an elegant part of town. Entirely refurbished in 1999, and now pitched primarily at tour groups. Their pricier rooms have large balconies and TVs. Open all year. ⑤.

De la Poste, 2 place du Duc-de-Padoue (☎04 95 46 01 37). The cheapest rooms in the centre (from 170F), in a huge old building that opens onto a quiet square just off the main drag. Comfortable enough, but on the gloomy side. ②–③.

Le Refuge, Vallée de la Restonica, 2.5km southwest of town (☎04 95 46 09 13, fax 04 95 46 22 38). Cosy, unpretentious hotel-restaurant at the roadside, with rooms overlooking the stream (the ones at the back are a touch noisy in spring, when the snow melt raises the water level, but fine in summer), and a sunny terrace. Half-board obligatory in summer (620F for two). Advance booking essential. ④.

La Restonica, Vallée de la Restonica, 2km southwest from town, (☎04 95 46 09 58, fax 04 95 61 03 91). Sumptuous comfort in a modern, riverside hotel with a pool. Pricy half-board (850F for two) is obligatory in season. April–Oct. ⑦.

Sampiero Corso, 1 av Président-Pierucci (☎04 95 46 09 76, fax 04 95 46 00 08). Good-value 1960s-style modern block, with spectacular views from the balconies. Breakfast included in the tariff. April–Sept. ④.

Gîtes d'étape and campsites

Albadu 2.5km southwest of town (☎04 95 46 24 55). Perfect little *camping à la ferme*, situated on a hillside above Corte. Basic, but much nicer than any of the town sites, and well worth the walk up here (the owners will show you a short cut that'll get you to the centre in 15min). For directions by road, see *Albadu*'s listing under "Hotels" opposite.

Gîte d'Étape U Tavignanu (Chez M. Gambini), behind the citadel (☎04 95 46 16 85). Run-of-the-mill hikers' hostel with small dorms and a relaxing garden terrace that looks over the valley. Peaceful, secluded, and the cheapest place to stay after the campsites. Follow the signs for the Tavignano trail (marked with orange spots of paint) around the back of the citadel. 80F per bed.

L'Alivetu, faubourg St-Antoine (☎04 95 46 11 09). One of two sites definitely to avoid (the other is the *Batho* behind the citadel): crowded, noisy and with dirty toilet blocks.

Restonica, 500m south of the town centre. Middle-sized site on the riverside, close to town, with low terraces, plenty of shade and its own café-bar.

U Sognu, route de la Restonica (☎04 95 46 09 07). At the foot of the valley, a 15min walk from the centre. Has a good view of the citadel, plenty of poplar trees for shade, and toilets in a converted barn. There's also a small bar (in summer) and a small restaurant (pizzas *au feu du bois* June–Sept).

Tuani, 7km southeast, Vallée de la Restonica (☎04 95 46 11 54). Too far up the valley without your own car, but the wildest and most atmospheric of the campsites around Corte, overlooking a rushing stream, deep in the woods. Ideally placed for an early start on Monte Rotondo. Basic facilities.

U Tavignanu, chemin de Balini, Vallée du Tavignano (☎04 95 46 16 85). The hiker's option: a tiny campsite next to the gîte d'étape of the same name, only accessible on foot. Follow the road around the back of the citadel, cross over the river bridge and bear right; the site lies another 10min walk up a path.

The Town

Corte is a very small town whose centre effectively consists of one long street – **cours Paoli**. Lined with shops, banks, restaurants and cafés, this busy thoroughfare runs alongside the **haute ville**, which is reached by climbing one of the cobbled ramps on the west side of the cours, or by taking the steep rue Scoliscia from place Paoli.

At the north end of the *cours* lies **place du Duc-de-Padoue**, an elegant square of nineteenth-century buildings that's strangely out of place in this rough mountain town. Its statue, a grim bronze lump by

Bartholdi, designer of the Statue of Liberty, is of Arrighi di Casanova, a general whose service under Napoléon earned him the title of Duke of Padua; his ancestral home can be seen in **place Poilu** in the *haute ville*. Apart from this square, there is only one spot where you might want to hang around: **place Paoli**, at the southern end of the main street in the lower town. A more tourist-friendly zone lined with relaxing cafés and restaurants, its centrepiece is a cumbersome statue of a rather self-satisfied-looking Pascal Paoli.

Place Gaffori

Place Gaffori, the hub of the old **haute ville**, is dominated by a statue of General Gian'Pietru Gaffori pointing vigorously towards the church. On its base a bas-relief depicts the siege of the Gaffori house by the Genoese, who attacked in 1750 when the general was out of town and his wife Faustina was left holding the fort. Faced with weakening colleagues, she is said to have brandished a burning torch over a barrel of gunpowder, threatening to blow herself and her soldiers to smithereens if they surrendered, a threat that toughened them up until Gaffori came along with reinforcements. The house stands right behind, and you can clearly make out the bullet marks made by the besiegers.

Opposite the house, the **Église de l'Annonciation**, built in 1450 but restored in the seventeenth century, is where Joseph Bonaparte, Napoléon's brother and future king of Spain, was christened. Inside, there's a delicately carved **pulpit** and a hideous wax statue of St Theophilus, patron of the town, on his deathbed. The saint's birthplace – behind the church in place Théophile – is marked by the **Oratoire St-Théophile**, a large arcaded building which commands a magnificent view across the gorges of Tavignano and Restonica. Born in 1676, Blaise de Signori took the name of Theophilus upon entering the Franciscan brotherhood, and went on to study in Rome and Naples, then to found numerous hermitages in Italy. In 1730 he returned to Corsica, where, after a few years' activity in the fight for independence, he died on May 9, 1740. He was canonized in 1930, the only Corsican to achieve sainthood, and on the anniversary of his death a commemorative Mass takes place in the oratory, followed by a procession from the Chapelle Ste-Croix, carrying a huge figure of Christ.

For the best view of the citadel, follow the signs uphill from place Gaffori to the viewing platform, aptly named the **Belvédère**, which faces the medieval tower, suspended high above the town on its pinnacle of rock and dwarfed by the immense crags behind. From here you can also admire the vista of the converging rivers and encircling forest – a summer bar adds to the attraction.

Just above place Gaffori, left of the gateway to the citadel, stands the **Palazzu Naziunale**, a great, solid block of a mansion that's the sole example of Genoese civic architecture in Corte. Having served as the seat of Paoli's government for a while, it became the **Università di Corsica** in 1765. Run by Franciscan monks, the island's first university offered free education to all (Napoléon's father studied here), and the monks taught the contemporary social thought of philosophers such as Rousseau and Montesquieu as well as traditional subjects such as theology, mathematics and law. The university closed in 1769, when the French took over the island after the Treaty of Versailles, not to be resurrected until 1981. Today several modern buildings have been added and it houses the Institut Universitaire d'Études Corses, dedicated to the study of Corsican history and culture.

The citadel and Museu di a Corsica

The monumental gateway just behind the Palazzu Naziunale leads from place Poilu into Corte's Genoese citadel, whose lower courtyard is dominated by the modern buildings of **Museu di a Corsica** (June 22–Sept 20 daily 10am–8pm; Sept 21–Oct 31 daily except Mon 10am–6pm; Nov–March Tues–Sat 10am–6pm; 35F). This state-of-the-art museum, designed by Turin architect Andréa Bruno, was inaugurated in 1997 to house the collection of ethnographer **Révérend Père Louis Doazan**, a Catholic priest who spent 27 years amassing a vast array of objects relating to the island's traditional transhumant and peasant past. Gifted to the state in 1972, the three thousand pieces he collected remained in storage for nearly a quarter of a century until a suitable site could be found to exhibit them. With its huge tinted windows and sweeping views, the building certainly makes the most of the location, but ultimately upstages the somewhat lacklustre exhibits inside it. On the first floor, old farm implements and peasant dress are the mainstay of the **Louis Doazan Gallery**, while the adjacent **Musée en train de se faire** (Museum in the Making) gallery explores aspects of contemporary Corsican society, including industry, tourism and religious brotherhoods. In addition, a couple of rooms at the head of the main staircase house themed temporary exhibitions of Corsica-related art and photography. If the amount of money lavished on the museum seems out of all proportion with its contents, bear in mind the importance of its symbolic value, at a time when the island as a whole is earnestly seeking to define what constitutes "Corsican culture". This may go some way to explaining the conspicuous absence of references to less palatable facets of the island's identity, such as vendetta and banditry.

The entry ticket to the museum also includes admission to the adjacent **Citadel**. The only such fortress in the interior of the island, it was founded in the fifteenth century and served as a military base for the Foreign Legion from 1962 until 1984. Reached by a huge staircase of Restonica marble, a medieval tower known as the **Nid d'Aigle** (Eagle's Nest) forms its highest point. The tower is the only original part of a complex built by Vincentello d'Istria in 1420; the barracks (*caserne*) were added during the reign of Louis-Philippe. These were later converted into a prison, in use as recently as World War II, when the Italian occupiers incarcerated Corsican resistance fighters in the tiny cells. Adjacent to these is the **échauguette**, a former watchtower which, at the time of Paoli's government, was inhabited by the hangman. This was a job no Corsican would take – accustomed to killing with guns and knives, they found the practice of hanging someone to death too demeaning and dishonourable. A Sicilian duly volunteered, and in 1766 James Boswell visited the poor reprobate: "a more dirty rueful spectacle I never beheld", he wrote of the wretched specimen he found cowering in the turret, with a "miserable bed and a little bit of fire" as his only comfort.

Eating and drinking

Corte has only a handful of restaurants worthy of note, plus the usual pizzerias and crêperies. As a rule of thumb, avoid anywhere fronted by gaudy food photographs and multilingual menus; their dishes may be cheap, but they offer poor value for money – for a few francs more, you'll eat a lot better in one of the places listed below. Cortenais specialities are trout, and lasagne with wild-boar sauce, but if you just want a hot snack try the pizza van parked opposite *Café de France* in place du Duc-de-Padoue. The **bars** along cours Paoli are patronized mainly by locals, while tourists hang out in those lining place Paoli. Students favour the bar in Corte's pint-sized **cinema**, the white building just over the Restonica bridge, next to the entrance of *L'Alivetu* campsite.

Cafés and bars

Bip's, on the square behind cours Paoli, facing av Xavier-Luciani. Cavernous bar with a small stage that hosts live music most nights, starting at 10.30pm. The bands are very ordinary rock cover outfits, and there's a 30F cover charge, but this is as lively as Corte gets.

Les Délices du Palais cours Paoli. Frilly little crêperie-cum-salon-de-thé whose bakery sells a selection of delicious Corsican patisserie: try their *colzone* (spinach pasties), or *brocciu* baked in flaky chestnut-flour pastry.

L'Escapade, place Paoli. Inexpensive crêpes from 10F to 30F, but best of all are their home-made ice creams: 24 flavours, including melt-in-the-mouth watermelon (*pastèque*) and pear (*poire*), served as single scoops or *coupes* of three.

De la Place, place Paoli. On the shady side of the main square, this is the most popular spot for crowd-watching, and a late-night watering hole for the locals

Restaurants

A Cantina, 20m south of place Gaffori, towards the Belvédère. Artisanal charcuterie and cheeses served in an attractive stone cellar, with a tasting counter and shop upstairs. Pricy (set menu 70F consisting of ham and cheese), but unbeatable quality.

Le Paglia Orba, 1 av Xavier-Luciani (☎04 95 61 07 89). Quality Corsican cooking at very reasonable prices, served on a raised terrace overlooking the street. Most people come for their succulent pizzas (40–50F), but they also offer plenty of choice à la carte, particularly for vegetarians (baked aubergine with chestnuts or stuffed onions), and do some imaginative salads (such as chicken in Cognac). Menus at 65F and 85F.

Au Plat d'Or, place Paoli (☎04 95 46 27 16). The classiest option in Corte: Corsican specialities made from locally produced ingredients, and served under awnings on the shady side of place Paoli. Meat and seafood dishes (such as brochettes of beef with fragrant wild mushrooms or river trout in Cap Corse liqueur) are their forte, but they also do pricier-than-average pizzas, pastas and home-made desserts. Menu at 110F (four courses), *plat du jour* 70F, or count on 150F à la carte. Closed Sun.

Relais du Lac, Pont de Tagone, Vallée de la Restonica, 10km southwest of Corte (☎04 95 46 14 50). A good way out of town, but this is a wonderful spot to round off a day's hiking, with set tables beside a rushing stream. Topnotch local cuisine of mostly meat and fish grilled on a wood fire, and served alfresco or inside the wooden cabin. Menus from 80F. Book ahead in summer.

U Museu, rampe Ribanelle in the *haute ville* at the foot of the citadel, 30m down the rue Colonel-Feracci. Congenial and well situated, with lots of choice on its mixed set menus. Try the 75F *menu corse*, featuring lasagne in wild-boar sauce, trout, and *tripettes* (imaginatively translated as "trips"). Their hot goat's cheese (*chèvre chaud*) salad, filling enough for two, comes on a groaning bed of richly flavoured potatoes. Great value for money, atmospheric terrace and the house wines are local AOC.

Listings

Banks All the main banks on cours Paoli have cash machines that accept Visa and Mastercard; the Société Générale stands halfway along, and changes French franc travellers' cheques free of charge.

Bookshop Maison de la Presse, 22 cours Paoli, has a good selection of books about Corsica, and occasional English-language newspapers.

Bus information Corte is the midway point for Eurocorse Voyages' Ajaccio to Bastia bus, which runs twice daily except Sun (☎04 95 46 01 09), tickets from Bar Colonna, av Xavier-Luciani. You can get to Bastia on Mon, Wed and Fri with Autocars Cortenais, 14 cours Paoli (☎04 95 46 22 89), who also operate services to Aléria from outside the train station on Tues, Thurs and Sat. During the summer, Corte is connected to Porto via Calacuccia and Évisa by Autocars Beaux Voyages's, four-daily services over Col de Verghio (Aug–Sept 15; ☎04 95 65 11 35), which leave from place Paoli.

Car rental Europcar, 9 cours Paoli (☎04 95 31 03 79); Hertz, c/o Cyrnea Tourisme, 9 av Xavier-Luciani (☎04 95 46 24 62).

Horse riding The Centre Équestre l'Albadu, ancienne route d'Ajaccio, 2.5km southwest of town (☎04 95 46 24 55), offer horse treks at 90F an hour, 160F for 2hr or 200F per half-day (with a stop to bathe and picnic by the Tavignano). In a complete day you can ride deep into the mountains (400F). This centre is among the best of its kind on the island and the rates are rock-bottom for Corsica.

Hospital av du 9-Septembre (☎04 95 46 05 36).

Outdoor equipment Omnisports Gabrielli, at the north end of cours Paoli (two doors up from the Société Générale bank) is the best-stocked outdoor equipment shop on the island.

Pharmacies Several on cours Paoli.

Police 4 av Xavier-Luciani (☎04 95 46 04 81).

Post office Av du Baron-Mariani, off place du Duc-de-Padoue.

Taxis Taxis Corte (☎04 95 46 07 90 or 04 95 61 01 41).

Train information At the SNCF station (☎04 95 46 00 97).

Travel agents Corte Voyages, 14 cours Paoli, next to the gendarmerie (☎04 95 46 00 35); Cyrnea Tourisme, 9 av Xavier-Luciani (☎04 95 46 24 62).

Around Corte

The **Gorges du Tavignano**, virtually on the town's doorstep, offer an exhilarating hike from Corte but are only accessible on foot. The less energetic can simply drive southwest to the **Vallée de la Restonica**. A torrent of jade-green water punctuated with enormous boulders, the Restonica is followed closely by the road out of Corte, which comes to a stop within striking distance of the stunning **Lac de Mélo**, the **Lac de Capitello** and **Monte Rotondo** – a sprawling mountain that may not be much to look at from a distance but is a superb sight close up, with its ring of crags encircling a cluster of blue glacial lakes.

Gorges du Tavignano

A deep cleft of ruddy granite 5km to the west of Corte, the **Gorges du Tavignano** offer one of central Corsica's great walks, marked in yellow paint flashes alongside the broad cascading River Tavignano. You can pick up the trail, a stage of the Mare a Mare Nord long-distance footpath (covered on p.320), from the bottom of rue col-Feracci, below the citadel, and follow it as far as the Col de l'Arinella, some 30km west of the town, where it drops into the Niolo valley. There's a **refuge**, *A Sega*, situated 15km along the route, but check first at the tourist office to make sure it's open, as nationalist terrorists blew the place up in 1995.

The hike from Calacuccia to the Arinella pass is described on p.335.

From the trailhead, an old mule track steadily climbs the steep left bank of the river across a bare hillside scarred with the remains of old farming terraces. Massive rocks, fringed by dense vegetation, border the river below, which you can scramble down to in places for a secluded swim. Some 5km into the walk, the gorge proper begins and the scenery becomes wilder, with bare rock faces surging up on each side and boulders cluttering the path. Passing through patches of dense maquis interspersed with evergreen oak and chestnut trees, you gradually rejoin the river crossed at the **Passarelle de Rossolino** footbridge after around two and a half hours. Once you're on the true right bank, the mountainside grows steeper as the path skirts the **Ravin de Bruscu**, then winds gently along the stream to the refuge, reached after five and a half hours from Corte. From here, you can press on the next day over the **Col de l'Arinella** pass (1592m) – which affords one of the best views of the Cinto massif and Paglia Orba – return by the same route to Corte (a 4hr hike), or cross into the Vallée de la Restonica via the plateau d'Alzo (see box). Either way, you should invest in an IGN contour **map** of the area (IGN topo-map 25, #4251 OT; map reference A7/A10), available at the Parc Naturel Régional office in Corte (see p.343) and at the bookshop mentioned in "Listings", p.349.

Vallée de la Restonica

Dividing the barren wastes of the Rotondo massif and the cloud-swept plateau d'Alzo, the **Vallée de la Restonica** is lined with some of the most spectacular glacier-moulded gorges in the Mediterranean – a riot of twisted granite cliffs lapped by thick Laricio pine forest and a translucent green torrent. Unfortunately, it is also among the few motorable routes into the wild heart of the Corsican watershed, which, along with its proximity to Corte, means the entire 15km stretch from town to the *bergeries* de Grotelle can get hideously congested in high summer, so avoid the area completely between July and early September, or else take it in from the marked forest trail that winds all the way to the *bergeries* along the riverbank.

The **gorges** begin after 6km, just beyond where the route penetrates the **Forêt de la Restonica**, a glorious forest of chestnut,

The Lost Arch Hike and Alzo Eclipse

Connecting the Restonica and Tavignano valleys via the plateau d'Alzo, one of the best day-hikes in the Corte region begins 10.5km up the Vallée de la Restonica, from a car park under some chestnut trees on the right (north) side of the road, known as **parking de Frasseta**. As this route ends in town and there are no bus services up the valley, you'll have to hitch a ride as far as the trailhead, marked by a sign board. From here, the path climbs northeast through dense forest along a series of switchbacks. Just after the **Funtana Bianca** spring (1450m), it emerges from the tree cover to begin a long ascending traverse to the **plateau d'Alzo**. Each year on July 26–28, this high pastureland, scattered with old stone *bergeries*, witnesses one of the island's weirder natural phenomena, when the sun disappears behind the red mass of Paglia Orba to the west, only to reappear moments later through the pierced peak of Capu Tafonatu. The plateau d'Alzo also has its own strange rock archway, the **arche de Padule**, passed by the trail before it begins a long descent to the **refuge de la Sega**, on the floor of the Vallée du Tavignano. For more details of this route, consult topo-map IGN 25, #4251 OT (ref A8/B8).

Allow three hours to reach the refuge from parking de Frasseta, and another four to walk down the valley to Corte (along the route described on p.350).

Laricio pine and the tough maritime pine endemic to Corte, recognizable by its conical shape. Not surprisingly, it's a popular place to walk, picnic and bathe – the many pools fed by the cascading torrent of the Restonica River are easily reached by scrambling down the rocky banks.

The **bergeries de Grotelle**, 15km from Corte, mark the end of the road, with an outsize car park that barely accommodates the summer crowds. From here, a well-worn path winds along the valley floor to a pair of beautiful glacial lakes. The first and largest, **Lac de Melo**, is reached after a fairly strenuous hour's hike through the rocks. Particularly steep parts of the path have been fitted with stanchion chains and vertical iron ladders, causing some visitors to freeze with vertigo halfway up. If you're attempting this walk in early spring, you should also expect to encounter deep snow patches in places, especially once you've past Lac de Melo, where a steeper trail over a moraine climbs up to the second lake, **Lac de Capitello** – the more spectacular of the pair. Hemmed in by vertical cliffs, the deep, turquoise-blue pool affords fine views of the Rotondo massif on the far side of the valley, and in fine weather you can spend an hour or two exploring the surrounding crags, scoured by rock pipits. Beyond here, the trail climbs higher to meet the GR20, and should only be attempted by experienced and well-equipped mountain walkers.

Hike to Monte Rotondo and the Lac d'Oriente

A jagged-topped arc of granite splashed with small blue lakes, **Monte Rotondo** (2622m), Corsica's second highest mountain, looms southwest of Corte at the head of the Restonica valley. The peak can be scaled from two directions, but the most common approach is from the north, via the beautiful Lac d'Oriente. Though technically straightforward between July and late September, this route is a long hard slog involving 3360m of ascent and descent, much of it across steep and boulder-choked terrain. Don't consider attempting it unless you're in good shape and properly equipped (see p.32), and check the weather forecast carefully before you set off. Of the many hikers that tread the Rotondo trail during the summer, most only aim to reach the lake, a rewarding return-trip (4hr 30min) in itself.

The **trailhead** lies 11km up the Restonica valley, 700m beyond the Tagone bridge (where the road crosses from the north to the south side of the gorge) – look for the red spray-painted sign on a rock to the right. From here, a wide forestry track strikes steeply up the side of a stream valley, zigzagging through fragrant pine woods to the **bergeries de Timozzo** (1hr 15min), where it levels out briefly before climbing a long ridge. Follow the red and yellow splashes of paint rather than the cairns (which mark a less well-defined path that gets lost in maquis), crossing the stream near the head of the valley.

Enfolded by the Rotondo massif, the **Lac d'Oriente** (2hr 30min) is a great place to picnic before pressing on to the summit. From here, the

South of Corte

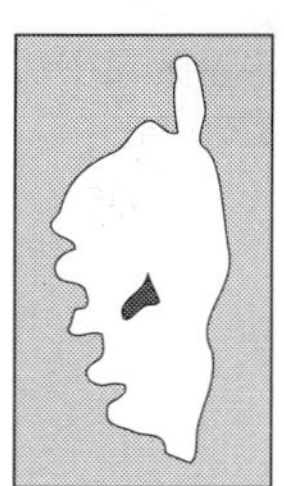

The main road south of Corte, the N193, slices into the heart of the Corsican mountains, tracked by the railway through Venaco, Vivario, Vizzavona and Bocognano – a rattling ride that's worth taking even if you have your own vehicle. East from **Vivario** there's an incredible drive through the **Forêt de Rospa-Sorba** to **Vezzani**, while to the southeast lies **Ghisoni**, a mountain base dominated by the peaks of **Kyrie-Eleison** and the craggy **Monte Renoso**. You have a choice of spectacular exits from Ghisoni: east through the **Défilé de l'Inzecca**, a short cut down to the eastern plain; or south along the zigzagging route to **Col de Verde**, offering incredible views of the peaks. South of the col, **Zicavo** gives access to **Monte Incudine**, the southernmost high summit of the island.

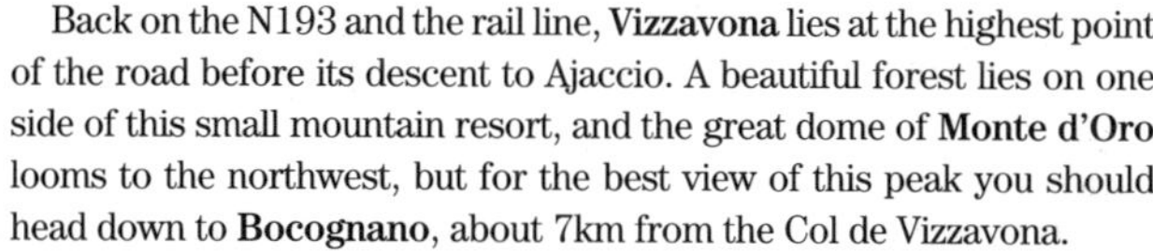

Back on the N193 and the rail line, **Vizzavona** lies at the highest point of the road before its descent to Ajaccio. A beautiful forest lies on one side of this small mountain resort, and the great dome of **Monte d'Oro** looms to the northwest, but for the best view of this peak you should head down to **Bocognano**, about 7km from the Col de Vizzavona.

Aside from the handful of hikers' refuges that punctuate the region's footpaths, **accommodation** is very limited in these parts, with the odd hotel at Vezzani, Vivario and Vizzavona.

trail, which restarts at the south side of the lake, is marked every 10m or so by cairns; as long as you keep close to these, the ascent across the moraine that follows is safe and enjoyable. However, things get a little trickier towards the top, where patches of snow and ice can be hazardous, particularly during early summer (an ice axe or snow stick is recommended if you're attempting this route before August); keep an eye out, too, for loose rocks, as these can be lethal for anyone ascending below you. The last stretch of the climb is a very steep clamber up a narrow corridor; patches of ice are more common on the left side of this, so pick a route up the right (sunnier) side. From the **ridge** (4hr 15min), drop down slightly to the left and follow the cairns to a cleft that leads up the crow's-nest **summit** (4hr 30min). On a clear day, the views from the top are sublime, taking in all of the island's major peaks, both coasts, the shores of Tuscany and, if you're lucky, the distant Alps. If you have an all-season sleeping bag, it is possible to bivouac in the tiny tin-roofed **Helbronner refuge** just below the summit and enjoy the spectacle at dawn.

Return by the same route, or down the south side of the mountain, via the beautiful **Lac de Bellabone**, to the **Petra Piana refuge**. Note that times given do not take into account rest breaks; allow a total of eight hours for the return-trip to the top from the Restonica valley and back (5hr 15min ascent and 2hr 45min descent), and aim to start walking by 7am, which will get you to the summit well before the clouds blister up at around 2pm.

South of Corte

The Venachese

The mountainous region immediately south of Corte, known as the **Venachese**, was once an important corridor for transhumant pastoralists, who would drive their flocks through here en route between *a piaghja e a muntagna*, (the plains and the mountains). These days, the shepherds' and old drovers' trails have been superceded by the smooth N193 and rail line, winding in tandem between Bastia and Ajaccio.

Swathed in chestnut forest, the first sizeable village you come to along the road is **SANTO-PIETRO-DI-VENACO**, 7.5km south of Corte. It boasts a better-than-average **hotel**, *Le Torrent* (☎04 95 47 00 18; ③; June–Oct), a stylishly old-fashioned place with panoramic views and a restaurant tucked beneath a tree-shaded terrace by the river. Also in the village is a welcoming **gîte d'étape** (☎04 95 47 07 29), a night halt on the Mare a Mare Nord (*variante*) footpath, where you can opt for dorm beds (50F) or more comfortable chambre d'hôte accommodation (250F for two).

The Mare a Mare Nord trail and its variant is outlined on p.320.

Venaco

A couple of kilometres south of Santo-Pietro, the road sweeps through **VENACO**, an elegant village emerging from the verdant lower slopes of Monte Padro. You might want to halt here to admire the **vistas** – from the terrace of the Baroque church there's a spectacular view of the lower Vallée du Tavignano to the east – or to **hike** one of the Parc Naturel Régional's waymarked trails mentioned earlier (see box). Six routes start from, or near, the village, the most challenging being the path straight up the mountain to the Uboli ridge, via the *bergeries* de Tatarellu. Afterwards, you could recover over a meal at the *Restaurant de la Place* on the main square (☎04 95 47 01 30), which offers a good-value 75F *menu fixe* featuring spinach pie and red mullet stuffed with ewe's cheese, rounded off by home-made walnut flan.

Venaco also harbours one of the area's few good **campsites**, the *Camping Peridundellu* – take the D43 towards the Tavignano valley and you'll see it after 4km on your right (☎04 95 47 09 89; April–Oct). It's very cosy, with room for a couple of dozen tents, and the farmhouse doubles up as a simple restaurant (fixed four-course menu at 90F) serving local dishes prepared from home-grown ingredients. Much the most congenial **hotel** in this area lies 5km southeast on the D43 towards Aléria. Making the most of the views across the Vallée du Tavignano, the *Hôtel Paesotel E Caselle* (☎04 95 47 39 00, fax 04 95 47 06 65; ⑥) has spacious, comfortable rooms ranged around a small pool, as well as self-catering *pavillons* (1900F–2885F per week depending on the time of year). Facilities here include a restaurant (offering good-value half-board for residents), gym, Jacuzzi, sauna and mountain-bike rental. The hotel's easy to find: follow the signs for Aléria, and turn right off the D43 where you see a large sign on the roadside.

Hikes in the Venachese

Some of the old shepherds' trails in the Venachese have recently been cleared and waymarked by the Parc Naturel Régional. Six return-routes of varying length and difficulty feature in their excellent leaflet *Balades en Corse: Venachese*, which you can pick up at the park office in Corte, and in most tourist offices. For an easy four-hour ramble, try the route from Venaco village to **Pont de Noceta**, which passes a couple of pleasant bathing spots and old dry-stone grain storage huts known as *aghja*. More experienced walkers have a choice of *boucles sportives* (strenuous routes), such as the steep five-hour climb from Venaco to the **Uboli ridge** via the **bergeries de Tatarellu**. In settled weather, the park leaflet, which includes a black-and-white contour **map** of the area with the trails marked on it, is adequate for reference, as the paths are all regularly marked with splashes of orange paint.

Vivario

Gustave Eiffel (of Eiffel tower fame) built the dizzying **Pont de Vecchiu** railway bridge at the foot of Monte Rotondo, 5km south of Venaco. Alongside it, the even more impressive new road bridge, opened in 1999, spans the 222m-wide gorge at a height of 137.5m. Beyond the bridges, a series of tortuous switchbacks brings you to **VIVARIO**, located at the junction of the routes to the Forêt de Rospa-Sorba and the Col de Verde. Straddling a nexus of the area's principal long-distance footpaths, this large village makes a good base if you're planning to hike in the area. Most visitors arriving by train head straight for the small *Hôtel Macchje e Monti* (☎04 95 47 22 00; half-board compulsory mid-June to mid-September; ③), but a better place to stay if you have your own vehicle is *U Sambuccu*, 11km further east (for a review of this hotel, see p.356).

Vivario's attraction lies in its forest setting, which once supported its own **wild man**, dubbed by folk chroniclers as *un Mowgli corse*. In 1800 a 10-year-old boy went missing here after an argument with his parents, and stayed missing for twenty years until a group of hunters ensnared him by the Vecchiu. The unfortunate soul was carted off to be reunited with his parents but, unable to adapt to his new life, perished after a few months. The only traversable spot across the Gorge du Vecchiu, a three-hour walk west of Vivario, is a 3m jump still known as the **Saut du Sauvage**, or "Wild Man's Leap". Vivario's other claim to fame is as the birthplace of the infamous **Bartolomeo brothers**, who were abducted by pirates here in the sixteenth century and went on to lead highly eventful lives. Shipwrecked off the coast of Italy, they escaped the clutches of their Saracen captors and swam to safety at Talamona on the Tuscan shore, where they subsequently settled. The elder of the two, later known as Bartolomeo de Talamone, rose to become an admiral in the local navy, and used his position to exact revenge on the pirates who had kidnapped him in his youth, ruthlessly pillaging the Mytilena region of Algeria, home of the dey of Algiers – the Red Beard, or Barbarossa, of pirate legends. It is said that the sultan was so incensed at Bartolomeo's behaviour that he attacked Talamona in 1544, only to find his adversary dead and buried, whereapon he exhumed the Corsican's corpse and burned and scattered what was left by way of retribution. The other brother, Bartolomeo de Vivario, eventually returned home from Talamona and worked for the Genoese for a while, before defecting to Sampiero Corso's side in the Wars of Independence, in the course of which he was mortally wounded.

If you feel like a **short walk** from Vivario, head 1km south of the village to a stony car park on the side of the main road, from where a clear path leads to the **Fort de Pasciolo**, an evocative ruin set high on rounded hilltop 1km or so west of the N193. Facing a great circle of peaks above the deep gorge of the Vecchiu, the fort was built around 1770 by the French, and later transformed into a prison to incarcerate the rebels of Fiumorbo (see p.306).

Vezzani

For most of the year, distant snowy mountain tops tower above the main road and rail line as they sweep in a wide semicircle towards **VEZZANI**. Fantastically located under the high ridge of Punta di a Ringhella, this mountain village has a couple of **hotels**, of which the best is *U Sambuccu*, 3km south on the Pietrosi road (☎04 95 43 03 38; ③). Set deep in the pine woods, the hotel has comfortable en-suite rooms with views over the valley and forest, and an excellent **restaurant** where you can enjoy local mountain cuisine, such as home-made charcuterie, goat stew and wild boar, at reasonable prices. This is also one of the few places in the region that stays open all year round.

Ghisoni

Nestling in a huge hollow at the head of the Vallée du Fiumorbo, **GHISONI** is hidden from the main Corte–Ajaccio artery by a 1500m-high ridge crossed at the **Col de Sorba**. The D69, which wriggles south from the pass to the village, affords tantalizing glimpses of the Renoso massif, and the majority of the people who come here do so to climb the peak (see box). Ghisoni's only **hotel** is the unsightly mustard-coloured *Kyrié*, close to the centre of the village (☎04 95 57 60 33; ③). It's an unexciting place, but the rooms are clean (the cheaper ones on the top floor enjoy the best views of the valley) and there's a cosy, unpretentious little bar-**restaurant**. Your only other option for food is *U Sampolu*, a down-to-earth *ferme-auberge* 8km east across the river (☎04 95 57 60 18; May–Oct daily except Mon). Renowned locally for its fresh mountain cuisine, this place does a brisk trade in the summer, in spite of its off-track location, so if you want to eat here phone ahead for a table. Set menus range from 90F to 120F.

South of Corte

Hugging the sinuous Fium'orbo River, the road running **east from Ghisoni** plunges steeply downhill through the **Défilé des Strette** gorge, affording spectacular views of the two peaks on the far side of the valley: **Kyrie** (1535m) and **Christe Eleison** (1260m). It was at the foot of these mountains that the last group of **Giovanalanis**, devotees of a breakaway Franciscan sect whose rituals were rumoured to include mass orgies, were massacred at the behest of Pope Urban V in 1362. Hounded to this remote spot, they were captured and bound for burning, but just at the point when the wood was to be set alight, an old priest took pity on the heretics and administered their last rites. The assembled crowd is then said to have taken up the last line of the prayer – *Kyrie eleison, Christe eleison* – which echoed through the gorge and across the mountains, giving the peaks the names by which they are known to this day. Further east, the main road skirts the Sampolo reservoir before penetrating the spectacular **Défilé de l'Inzecca**, a sheer trench slicing the coastal range (see p.307). The gorge forms a little-frequented short cut from the interior to the fertile eastern plains, and after the shattered rock formations, cuttings and tunnels marking the road, the lush orange groves and vineyards around Ghisonaccia come as something of a shock.

For coverage of Aléria and Ghisonaccia, the two east coast settlements nearest the mouth of the Défilé de l'Inzecca, see pp.307 and 304, respectively.

Monte Renoso

The easiest and most popular ascent of **Monte Renoso** (2352m) is up the north side, a relatively straightforward, although strenuous, nine-hour circular walk from the **Campanelle refuge**. You get to the refuge by following the D69 south of Ghisoni for 6.5km as far as the Pont de Casso, where you turn right onto an excessively windy road that traverses the **Forêt de Ghisoni**, a dense forest of pines, beech and alders. The refuge – once a shepherd's hut – lies 500m west of the spot where the road comes to an end, next to a makeshift ski station that rarely sees enough snow to function.

From here the track is marked with cairns, leading off to the southwest across the stream beneath the ski lift. Passing the idyllic **Pizzolo springs**, the track skirts the west shore of the **Lac de Bastiani**, a grey expanse of water framed intermittently by snowdrifts, before following the ridge to the **summit**. Here you'll be treated to one of Corsica's most amazing views – the panorama embraces the whole of the south of the island, taking in the Golfe d'Ajaccio and Golfe de Valinco on the west coast, and extending even as far as Sardinia.

If you carry on south along the waymarked track past the **Punta Orlandino**, you'll gain the **Col de Pruno** (2262m) in another thirty minutes or so. From here the path descends to the **bergeries des Pozzi**, then strikes east to the Plateau de Gialgone, after which it joins the **GR20**. At this point, you can either follow the GR20 north, hugging the contours of Renoso for another three and a half hours to get back to Campanelle refuge, or take the quicker and easier route east via **Col de la Flasca** to rejoin the D69 where it crosses **Col de Verde** – a section of the route described in more detail in the box on p.358.

Walks from Col de Verde

Dividing the Fiumorbo and Taravo valleys, **Col de Verde** (1289m) marks the start of some rewarding forest trails, among them the one leading to the **sites des Pozzi**, a string of high-altitude lakes and pools gouged from the slopes of Monte Renoso. A section of the GR20 footpath, most of the route is marked at regular intervals by splashes of red and white paint. Using the indispensable IGN **map** of the area, follow these west from Col de Verde to **Col de la Flasca**, and thence through the **Vallon de Marmano**, site of some immense pine trees, the largest of which towers to 55m and is thought to be the tallest in Europe. Around an hour and a half from the Col de Verde, you arrive at a clearing, the **Clairière de Gialgone**, where you should turn left off the GR20 and follow the orange waymarks up to the **bergeries des Pozzi**. Beyond here the trail emerges to patches of open marshy ground scattered with lakes and winding watercourses interconnecting at different levels. Allow roughly two and a half hours for the ascent, and an hour and a half for the walk back down by the same path.

Zicavo

One of the least travelled roads on the island winds **south from Ghisoni** along the banks of the Fium'Orbo to **Col de Verde** (see box), where the GR20 makes another of its rare dips to road level. Forest cover continues uninterrupted almost all the way to **ZICAVO**, 20km beyond the pass. Ringed by high ridges and impenetrable chestnut forests, this area is the definitive *Corse profonde*, where the ageing human population is far outstripped by that its semi-wild pigs, and where you're almost guaranteed not to meet another tourist. Zicavo is also well placed for hikes into its mountainous hinterland, notably the trail southeast to the **plateau du Coscione** (covered in more detail on p.256), and the long ascent of Monte Incudine, the most southerly of the island's high peaks.

Autocars Santoni's daily **bus** service from Ajaccio (year round Mon–Sat; 1hr 15min; ☎04 95 22 64 44 or 04 95 24 51 56) connects the village with the coast, providing one of the most convenient and dependable means of access to the deep interior of the island. In addition to its well-stocked stores, Zicavo has two very good **hotels**, both with satisfying little **restaurants**: the *Tourisme*, in the centre of the village (☎04 95 24 40 06; ②–③) and the *Florida*, just north of the village on the Col de Verde road (☎04 95 24 43 11; 180F per person for half-board; ②; May–Sept). Hikers, however, generally hole up in Zicavo's tiny **gîte d'étape**, *Le Paradis* (☎04 95 24 41 20), just down the road from the *Tourisme*, which charges 50F per dorm bed and 60F per person for beds in self-contained apartments; you can also put up a tent for 40F, which includes the use of hot showers. Excellent-value home cooking is available on request (half-board 180F per head, or *menus fixes* at 50F or 80F), and the *gardienne* serves breakfasts of fresh bread, jam and coffee (25F).

Vizzavona and around

Monte d'Oro dominates the route south of Vivario to **VIZZAVONA**, 30km beyond Corte. Shielded by trees, the village is invisible from the main road, so keep your eyes peeled for a couple of lanes dropping down on the right, one of them signposted for the train **station** – the place where the bandit Bellacoscia surrendered to the police at the age of 75 (see p.362). Marking the midway point of the GR20, Vizzavona is always crowded with walkers during summer, and those on a modest budget are well catered for by the handful of **gîtes d'étape**, hotels and hikers' cafés grouped around the railhead.

Top of the range here is *I Laricci* (☎ & fax 04 95 47 21 12; ③; April–Oct), a recently converted red-and-white alpine-style building with pitched roofs and charming Moroccan carpets decorating the walls of its dining room. Rooms here are invariably booked up well in advance, but you can nearly always get a bed in their annexe, which houses a handful of six-person dorms (150F per bed for half-board). More conventional gîte d'étape accommodation is offered at *Resto-Refuge-Bar "De la Gare"* (☎04 95 47 21 19, fax 04 95 47 22 20; June–Oct), directly opposite the station, a small but lively family-run place offering good home cooking in a cosy restaurant with an open fire. Hot showers are included in the price (70F per person, or 165F with half-board) but they don't have self-catering facilities.

For more atmosphere, head 3km further south along the main road to the hamlet of **LA FOCE**, where the venerable old *Monte d'Oro* (☎04 95 47 21 06; *www.sitec.fr/monte.oro*; ⑤–⑥) occupies a prime spot overlooking the valley. With its period furniture and fittings, *fin-de-siècle* feel and magnificent terrace looking out onto the mountain, this ranks among the most congenial hotels in Corsica. It was originally built in 1880 as a guesthouse for government engineers and has altered little since. Considering the location and charm of the place, the tariffs are also very reasonable. Adjacent to the *Monte d'Oro*, slap on the main road, is a little gîte d'étape (☎04 95 45 25 27) that's nowhere near as gloomy as it looks and makes a handy fall-back if the places down in the village are fully booked.

For **campers**, there's the small and well-shaded *Camping Le Soleil* at **SAVAGGIO**, 4km north of Vizzavona village on the N193 (☎04 95 47 22 14), which also offers inexpensive gîte d'étape-style dorms. Arriving by train, ask to be dropped at the request stop just before (north of) Vizzavona, which is closer to the site than the main village station.

Forêt de Vizzavona

A glorious forest of beech and Laricio pine, the **Forêt de Vizzavona** is the most popular walking area in Corsica, thanks to the easy access by main road or train. A lot of people come here to tackle the ascent of Monte d'Oro (see box on p.362), but there are many less

Zicavo to Bavella via Monte Incudine

Taking its name from the massive anvil-shaped rock just below its summit, the 4km hump of **Monte Incudine** (2136m), south Corsica's highest mountain, is crenellated by numerous peaks, the highest of which can be climbed from Zicavo via waymarked paths. The route poses no technical difficulties, but you'll need plenty of stamina and an early start to reach the top and then press on further than the refuge d'Asinao, just below the summit, from where it is possible to reach Bavella or Quenza in a long day. With a car, you might consider cutting short the first section of this route by driving as far as the chapelle de San Petru, or hitching a ride to the refuge des Bergeries de Basetta, also on the D428; a grocer in the village and the *gardien* of the refuge both do the journey daily in summer, which could save you a long slog over the dullest stretch of the walk. Wherever you decide to start, take along a copy of the GR20 topo-guide (pp.70 and 74 of which map the routes described below) and read our advice on hiking in "Basics" (p.30).

The classic approach to Monte Incudine begins with a long ascent of the east side of the vallée du Taravo, via a link section of the GR20 that joins the main path with Zicavo. Follow the yellow waymarks south out of the village along the D69 for around 1km, at which point the path turns off the road and climbs southwards through dense beech and chestnut forest. Having emerged from the woods and rounded the shoulder of **Punta de l'Erta**, it then keeps to largely level ground to cross the **ruisseau de Tinturaio** at the head of a small valley, climbing to briefly join the winding D428, which it leaves soon after en route to the **chapelle de San Petru**, reached after roughly two and a half hours. From here, a generally easy two hours takes you past the **refuge de Matalza** (neither staff nor water) and across the northern fringes of the atmospheric and beautiful **plateau de Coscione** (an account

demanding trails to follow. One of the most frequented of these is the walk to the **Cascade des Anglais**, which is connected to Vizzavona by a waymarked path but is more commonly approached from La Foce, 3km south of the village. Some 200m north of the hamlet, you turn right (north) onto a forest *piste* that plunges through the woods to the river; follow the green waymarks for a little over a quarter of an hour until they merge with the red-and-white ones of the GR20, which passes a stone's throw from the falls, where the River Agnone crashes into emerald-green pools. These are perfect for bathing, but the site is far from a secret (there's even a drinks stall there).

Less than 1km west of La Foce lies the highest pass on the Ajaccio–Bastia road, the **Col de Vizzavona** (1163m), which is usually jammed with picnickers, most of whom take a postprandial stroll along one of the various short walks laid out from here. Fifteen minutes south of the col along the forest trail you come to a magnificent **viewpoint** over the forested peaks, with the ruins of the Genoese **Fort de Vizzavona** prominent on a rise in the valley below. You can reach the fort itself in just fifteen minutes along a wide path north of the picnic tables. A walk to **La Madonnuccia** – a mound of scrambled of which appears on p.256) to the **junction with the GR20**, at 1450m. A sign points the way west from the intersection to the **Auberge de la Passerelle**, the half-way stage. Throughout the summer, this privately run refuge dishes up hearty Corsican stews and pasta to hungry hikers, and sells energy-rich food, as well as shots of local *anis* to steel you for the stiff ascent ahead.

From the *auberge*, a thirty-minute climb following the red-and-white waymarks of the GR20 brings you to the ruins of the **refuge de Pedinieddi**, now disused, beyond which the path rises gradually, with fine views over the plateau de Coscione. This is where the final ninety-minute haul to the summit starts, with an initial steep climb along a stream gully to the **Col de Luana**, followed by a wonderfully exposed, rocky ridge walk to the top (2134m), marked with a large crucifix.

You can either descend by the same route, or else continue southwest to the Bocca Stazzunara pass (2025m), where the GR20 veers east and drops very steeply down the exposed east side of the Vallée d'Ainao to the **refuge d'Asinao** (reached after 1hr 20min from the summit). Most hikers call it a day here, but from an intersection twenty minutes below the refuge, routes lead down the valley to Quenza and Bavella (4hr 30min). The best option of the three paths off the mountain is the "**Variante Alpine**" of the GR20, marked with yellow splashes, which strikes steeply uphill around an hour and a quarter after the refuge. Crossing the heart of the Bavella needles massif, this ranks among the most challenging, and spectacular, sections of the GR20, and shouldn't be missed if you have a head for heights (certain pitches involve loose scrambles and crossing steep, smooth boulders). Don't, however, attempt this route if the rock is wet. From the refuge d'Asinao to Bavella, allow four and a half hours for the "Variante Alpine" and around five hours for the standard route.

An account of Bavella appears on p.258.

rocks that's supposed to look like the Virgin – takes about thirty minutes from the col, following the trail signposted "Bergeries des Pozzi", which branches off southeast. Another marked path from the col takes you to the **Fontaine de Vitulo**, the source of the Foce stream, which joins the River Gravona further down the mountain.

To get the best out of the forest, though, you should walk to **Col de Palmente** (1645m), a relatively strenuous four-hour there-and-back hike along the GR20 from the maison forestière just south of Vizzavona on the main road. The path winds through magnificent woodland before rising to the col, which affords fantastic views of Monte Renoso and the Forêt de Vizzavona.

Bocognano

From the Col de Vizzavona, the route winds southwards for 6km before reaching the appealing ochre cottages of **BOCOGNANO** (Bucugnanu). Set on a plateau amidst a chestnut forest, the village gives a perfect panorama of Monte d'Oro's pale-grey needles, and is well placed for walks to the **Cascade du Voile de la Mariée**, where the River Gravona crashes from a height of 150m in a series of cascades.

Monte d'Oro

The fifth highest peak on Corsica, **Monte d'Oro** (2389m) stands on the edge of the island's interior range and thus affords superb views not only of the other four big mountains – Cinto, Rotondo, Renoso and Incudine – but also Ajaccio and the southwest coast. The route up it is well frequented, but involves some slightly tricky climbing towards the top and you should be prepared to cross the odd nevé (patches of deep ice or snow), until late June. The exposed position of the peak also means it is particularly vulnerable to sudden and extreme changes in weather, so check the forecast before you set off.

There are two ways to the summit from Vizzavona. We recommend you ascend the easier one, via the Cascade des Anglais and the main route of the GR20 along the River Agnone, and then follow the 'Variante' of the GR20 over the summit and down the east flank of the mountain via the bergeries de Pozzatelli – a fine round walk that should take you about eight hours. Take along a copy of the FFRP's topo-guide for the GR20, which clearly maps the route, or IGN Top 25, #4251 OT (ref D9/D10).

From Vizzavona, follow the red-and-white- waymarks of the GR20 for 30min until the **Cascade des Anglais**. Once across the ruisseau d'Agnone, the path climbs northeast along the left bank of the stream, zigzagging steeply up pastureland strewn with elms and, later, denuded rocky terrain to the **crête de Muratellu** (2020m). At this point, you leave the waymarked section of the GR20 and follow its cairned variant northeast towards **Bocca di u Porcu** (2159m). The final leg to the summit involves some climbing for which you'll need a head for heights but not ropes.

The **descent** to Vizzavona is well cairned. Head north and northeast from the summit, past a small grassy plateau known as **Bratu Scampicciolo**, and down the steep zigzags of **La Scala** to the distinctively shaped rock dubbed **Le Cafetière**. Shortly after, you should veer due east and drop down the side of a stream gulley, penetrating the treeline just above the **bergeries de Pozzatelli**. The remaining leg keeps to the forest, much of it damaged by fire and clear cutting. Allow at least two-and-a-half hours to reach Vizzavona from the summit.

The best approach to the falls is 3km along the main road south of Bocognano, just before the Pont de Vitiluccia, from where they're a thirty-minute walk. Another worthwhile stroll from the village is to **La Clue de la Richiusa**, where the stream surges through 60m cliffs, emerging at a chain of beautiful deep pools. Further upstream lies the so-called **Glacier de Busso**, site of what is reputedly Corsica's only eternal snow; avalanches collect and compact so tightly here during the winter that they are able to endure the spring melt. To pick up the trail to the falls, follow the signs for the restored chestnut mill (*moulin*) and cross the Gravona via the footbridge near the electricity substation car park.

Bocognano is indissolubly associated with Antoine and Jacques **Bellacoscia**, born here in 1817 and 1832, fathered by a man who earned the family surname – meaning "beautiful thigh" – by also fathering eighteen daughters by three sisters with whom he lived simultaneously. Antoine, the elder son, took to the maquis in 1848, having killed the mayor of the village after an argument over some land. With his brother he went on to commit several more murders in full view of the hapless *gendarmes*, yet remained at liberty thanks to the support of the local population. In 1871 Antoine and Jacques managed to gain a safe pass into Ajaccio to organize an expedition to fight for the French in the war with Prussia. They returned from the war with their reputations restored, and took up residence in the family home, from where they continued to flaunt the law. In 1888 the police finally succeeded in ousting them from their house, which was converted into a prison. Antoine eventually surrendered when he was 75, at Vizzavona station on June 25, 1892, whereupon he was acquitted and exiled to Marseille in true Corsican tradition. The fate of Jacques is unknown.

Travel details

TRAINS

Bocognano to: Ajaccio (4 daily; 45min); Bastia (4 daily; 2hr 10min); Calvi (2 daily, via Ponte Leccia; 3hr 35min); Corte (4 daily; 50min); L'Île Rousse (2 daily, via Ponte Leccia; 3hr 5min); Ponte Leccia (4 daily; 1hr 30min); Venaco (4 daily; 35min); Vivario (4 daily; 25min); Vizzavona (4 daily; 12min).

Corte to: Ajaccio (4 daily; 2hr); Bastia (4 daily; 1hr 30min); Bocognano (4 daily; 1hr); Calvi (2 daily; 2hr 30min); L'Île Rousse (2 daily; 1hr 55min); Ponte Leccia (4 daily; 30min); Venaco (4 daily; 13min); Vivario (4 daily; 20min); Vizzavona (4 daily; 40min).

Ponte Leccia to: Ajaccio (4 daily; 2hr 5min); Bastia (4 daily; 50min); Bocognano (4 daily; 1hr 25min); Calvi (2 daily; 3hr); Corte (4 daily; 30min); L'Île Rousse (2 daily; 1hr 50min); Venaco (4 daily; 40min); Vivario (4 daily; 1hr); Vizzavona (4 daily; 1hr 10min).

Venaco to: Ajaccio (4 daily; 1hr 20min); Bastia (4 daily; 1hr 35min); Bocognano (4 daily; 40min); Calvi (2 daily; 3hr 50min); Corte (4 daily; 15min); L'Île Rousse (2 daily; 2hr 20min); Ponte Leccia (4 daily; 45min); Vivario (4 daily; 15min); Vizzavona (4 daily; 30min).

Vivario to: Ajaccio (4 daily; 1hr 5min); Bastia (4 daily; 1hr 50min); Bocognano (4 daily; 30min); Calvi (2 daily; 3hr 5min); Corte (4 daily; 30min); L'Île Rousse (2 daily; 2hr 35min); Ponte Leccia (4 daily; 1hr); Venaco (4 daily; 10min); Vizzavona (4 daily; 15min).

Vizzavona to: Ajaccio (4 daily; 55min); Bastia (4 daily; 2hr); Bocognano (4 daily; 15min); Calvi (2 daily; 4hr); Corte (4 daily; 1hr); L'Île Rousse (2 daily; 2hr 50min); Ponte Leccia (4 daily; 1hr 10min); Venaco (4 daily; 35min); Vivario (4 daily; 15min).

BUSES

AM = Autocars Mordiconi (☎04 95 48 00 04).
EV = Eurocorse Voyages (☎04 95 21 06 30).

Corte to: Ajaccio (EV; 2 daily; 2hr); Bastia (EV; 2 daily; 1hr 15min); Calacuccia and the Niolo (AM; July to mid-Sept Mon–Sat 4 daily; 1hr 30min); Évisa (AM; July to mid-Sept Mon–Sat 4 daily; 2hr); Porto (AM; July to mid-Sept Mon–Sat 4 daily; 2hr 30min).

Ponte Leccia to: Calvi (ABV; Mon–Sat 1 daily; 1hr).

Part 3

The Contexts

The Historical Framework

Invasion and resistance are recurring themes throughout Corsica's history. This has always been an island of particular strategic and commercial appeal, with its sheltered harbours and protective mountains, set on the western Mediterranean trade routes within easy reach of several colonizing powers. Greeks, Carthaginians and Romans came in successive waves, landing on the eastern coast, driving native Corsicans into the high interior and battling against new predators in their turn. The Romans were ousted by Vandals, and for the following thirteen centuries the island was attacked, abandoned, settled and sold as nation-states and empires squabbled over Europe's territories, and generations of islanders fought against foreign rule and against each other. In the light of this turbulent past, it seems inevitable that Corsica's early history, unexplored until this century, should have its own pattern of invasion and occupation.

Beginnings

For thousands of years the relics of Corsica's **Stone Age** were simply accepted as an inexplicable aspect of the island's landscape. In 1840 Prosper Mérimée, then Inspector of Historic Monuments, described the simple **menhirs** (from the Celtic *maen hir* – "long stone") of the southwest and tabulated various primitive stone monuments elsewhere in Corsica, but the origins and functions of these stone slabs and figures remained unknown until 1954, when French archeologist Roger Grosjean set about excavating and recording the megalithic sites. Only when his excavations started in earnest did a picture emerge of a complex prehistoric society that developed its religious and cultural framework over several millennia.

The First Settlers

It's now believed that Corsica's **original inhabitants** arrived from northern Italy in the **seventh millennium BC**, long before the monument-building era. Making their shelters in caves and under cliffs, they survived by hunting, gathering and fishing. A thousand years later came new settlers with new skills, building villages, planting crops and herding cattle. The practice of **transhumant pastoralism** – driving sheep to graze on the uplands in summer, then down to coastal pastures in the winter – may have been started in this era, and is still followed by Corsican shepherds to this day. In the **fourth millennium**, the creators of the island's **megalithic** buildings migrated into the Mediterranean area from Asia Minor and the Aegean. There are numerous interpretations of the stone monuments and tombs that were erected during the next 2000 years, but the most widely held opinion is that they were connected with the veneration of ancestors and the spirits of the dead, and perhaps centred on an Earth Deity or Mother.

At first the dead were buried in underground tombs or **cists**, and were represented, commemorated or maybe guarded by single menhirs placed nearby. Clusters of these tombs and menhirs have been found in the southwestern Sartenais region and near Porto-Vecchio. Cist burial later gave way to the custom of setting stone sarcophagi or **dolmens** (table stones) above ground and covering them with earth; about a hundred of these, measuring about 2m by 2.5m, have been discovered (now exposed after the erosion of the soil), one of the best examples being at **Fontenaccia**. At a later stage the menhirs acquired human forms and features: some were given swords or daggers, some were carved with rudimentary shoulder blades or ribs, and no two statues were the same. The function of these eerie warrior figures, most of which were found at **Filitosa** (see pp.232–235), can only be imagined. Suggestions range from representations of dead spirits to trophies of war, each one marking a defeated invader.

The Torréens

The culture embodied by these carved menhirs reached its peak towards 1500 BC, when new aggressors – portrayed, perhaps, by the stone warriors – landed in the south and made their first base near Porto-Vecchio. Naming this civilization the **Torréens**, after the dry-wall **torri** (towers) they raised in various parts of the island, Roger Grosjean posited that they were the same people as the seagoing Shardana who are known to have attacked Egypt in the late second millennium BC, and that the bronze weapons with which they subdued the islanders were the weapons depicted on the sword-bearing menhirs of Filitosa.

Their towers, each one built around a central cavity with smaller chambers to the sides, were found to contain remnants of fires, and may have been used to cremate the dead or even sacrifice the living. Fragments of the earlier, Neolithic structures, perhaps destroyed as the Torréens advanced along the island, were incorporated in their walls. Grosjean has traced the invaders' progression to the west, as they drove the megalithic natives further into the interior and finally to the north, where the natives were left to pursue their own beliefs and practices in peace. Stone menhirs were still being created in northern Corsica as the Iron Age got under way, centuries after the Torréen invasion, while in the south of the island – according to Grosjean – rivalry between Torréen settlements precipitated another migration, this time south to the island of Sardinia.

Greeks, Romans and Saracens

In 565 BC, Corsica's first major colony was founded at Alalia (Aléria) by Greek refugees from **Phocaea**. For a few decades these settlers made a successful living, planting vines and olive trees and enjoying a brisk trade in metals and cereals, but within thirty years they were fighting off an invading fleet of **Carthaginians** and **Etruscans**. By 535 BC, devastated by their losses in battle, the Greeks had abandoned Alalia to the Etruscans, who in turn were briefly succeeded by Carthaginian settlers in the third century BC.

By now Corsica had attracted the attention of the **Romans**, who sent in troops under the command of Lucius Cornelius Scipio in 259 BC. The indigenous islanders, enslaved or driven into the mountains by each successive invading power, joined forces with the Carthaginians and their leader Hanno to resist Roman occupation. Although the east coast was soon conquered and settled, it took another forty years before Corsica (together with Sardinia) could be brought within Roman administration, and another century of rebellion passed before the island's interior was overpowered.

For more than 500 years Corsica remained a province of the Roman Empire. A string of ports was established along the south coast – subsequently flattened by invasion and malaria – and a settlement built at **Mariana**, to the south of present-day Bastia, though Aléria remained the largest settlement. From the third century AD onwards, **Christianity** was introduced to the island and bishoprics were established at Mariana, Aléria, the Nebbio, Sagone and Ajaccio.

This comparatively stable period in Corsican history came to an end as the Roman Empire disintegrated and the **Vandals** started to harass the coast. By 460 AD the Vandals were established on the island, only to be defeated by Belisarius and his Byzantine forces in 534, but absorption into the Byzantine empire did little to protect Corsica from the Ostrogoths and later from the **Lombards**, who managed to annex Corsica in 725 – by which time the coastal settlements were suffering frequent raids by the Saracens (or Moors). In 754 Pépin the Short, King of the Franks, agreed to hand Corsica over to the **papacy** once it was free of the Lombards; when the Lombards were driven out twenty years later, Pépin's son, Charlemagne, honoured the promise.

Within thirty years of its transfer to papal sovereignty, parts of Corsica were being overrun by the **Saracens**. These invaders retained their grip for another two centuries, despite the brief triumph of **Ugo della Colonna**, reputedly a Roman aristocrat sent to "liberate" the island by Pope Stephen IV, but more likely a semi-legendary figure based on Count Boniface of Lucca, who gained a foothold on the island in 825, building the fortress of Bonifacio on its southern tip.

Whatever the facts may be, Ugo della Colonna became a useful point of reference for the local Corsican families, who began to assert their authority as the Moors retreated under pressure from an allied force of Pisans and Genoese at the start of the eleventh century. During the Saracens' rule, the native islanders had been confined to the interior, where they had developed a system of administration based on mountain communities, with elected leaders who took every opportunity to make their status hereditary. This period saw the rise of such mighty clans as the **della Rocca** and **Istria** families, the dominant dynasties among the feudal lords known as the **Cinarchesi**, most of whom claimed descent from Ugo della Colonna. As their feuds and rivalries intensified, some swore allegiance to the pope, who in 1077 placed Corsica under Pisan protection; others turned for support to the Genoese, who claimed their own right to the island.

The Pisan Period

In 1133, Pope Innocent II split Corsica's bishoprics between Pisa and Genoa, an action that did nothing to stem the enmity of the two republics. For two centuries, while Corsica remained **officially governed by Pisa**, the Genoese stayed on the offensive, capturing Bonifacio in 1187 and Calvi in 1268. Nevertheless, the Pisans were able to impose a framework of government built around the local parish or **piève**. A massive programme of church-building got under way, each church providing the focus for its *piève*, which in turn linked several village communities.

In the meantime, the Corsican nobles continued to flex their muscles. **Sinucello della Rocca**, a vassal of Pisa who held lands in the southwest, took advantage of the running dispute with Genoa and made his own bid for power, taking arms against other Corsican nobles and switching his loyalties between Pisa and Genoa as necessary. He eventually gained control of almost the whole island, drawing up a constitution and earning the name **Giudice** (Judge) for his sense of justice, but his success had made him few friends, and the rival *signori* soon turned against him. When Genoa defeated the Pisan fleet at **Meloria in 1284** and finally took control of the island, della Rocca retreated to his original base in the southwest and was eventually betrayed by his own illegitimate son. Captured by the Genoese, he died in prison in 1306.

The Genoese Period

Despite **Genoa**'s decisive victory at Meloria, the republic's struggle to control Corsica was by no means over. In 1297, the island, along with Sardinia, was handed by Pope Boniface VIII to the **Kingdom of Aragon**, setting off yet another territorial war – one that was to rumble on for two hundred years more. While Genoa held fast against Aragonese attempts to realize their claim to Corsica, the *signori* continued to fight it out among themselves. A people's revolt led by **Sambocuccio d'Alando** drove out the battling nobles of the northeast, and led to a political split between two areas of the island. In the northeast, the area known as *Diqua dai Monti* (This Side of the Mountains), the ancestral lands were taken over by village communities to form the **terra di commune**, officially protected by the Genoese, who founded and fortified Bastia in 1380. The southwest – *Dila dai Monti* – remained the **terra dei signori**, ruled in effect by the Cinarchesi, who looked to the more distant power of Aragon for support.

Generations of *signori* kept up a relentless effort to bring the whole island under their rule. Backed by Aragon, **Arrigo della Rocca** gained considerable successes against the Genoese in 1376, and then his nephew, **Vincentello d'Istria**, gained control of most of the island as viceroy of the King of Aragon from 1420 until 1434, when he was captured by Genoese forces and publicly beheaded. In 1453, in a bid to overcome such ambitious nobility, Genoa put Corsica into the hands of the **Bank of Saint George**, a powerful financial corporation with its own army. For ten years the bank imposed a tough military government, building a series of coastal watchtowers, restoring battered fortifications and containing the fractious warlords.

Sampiero Corso

Events in Europe brought this era to an end: **Henry II of France**, at war with Charles V, struck a blow against the Hapsburg emperor's Genoese allies by sending a fleet to capture Corsica. Leading the invasion was mercenary **Sampiero Corso**, who took possession of the entire island except Calvi and Bastia. French rule lasted all of two years, before Corsica was passed back to Genoa under the Treaty of Cateau Cambresis in 1559. Corso, however, was rather less inclined to relinquish his supremacy, and led a successful uprising against the Genoese in 1564, again securing control of most of the island. He was finally defeated by a vicious Corsican custom – the **vendetta** – according to which any act of violence or dishonour had to be avenged by the victim's relations. Corso was murdered in 1567 by the brothers of his wife Vannina d'Orso, whom he had strangled in the belief that she had betrayed him to his Genoese enemies. His killers were heftily rewarded by the Genoese.

Genoese Consolidation

In the late **sixteenth century** the Corsican population was reeling from years of war, pirate attacks, famine and malaria. The Genoese republic, now governing the island directly, was finally able to impose an administration of sorts. A governor was installed in Bastia to oversee the network of provinces and parishes, leaving local government to the Corsican communities and their assemblies (*consulta*). Attempts were even made to clamp down on the vendetta, but with no success – hundreds of murders were committed each year in the name of honour.

Nevertheless, in comparison with the previous pattern of civil war and invasion, the 170 years of direct Genoese rule were relatively peaceful. Corsicans enjoyed a certain degree of freedom to run their own affairs, and the rural economy developed and prospered – factors that were eventually to undermine the Genoese supremacy. Influential families, beneficiaries of the boom in agricultural trade, formed an articulate and ambitious new class. Excluded from the top ranks of government and resentful of Genoa's trade monopolies and high taxes, they provided the leadership for a Corsican society growing in political maturity and aspirations. Circumstances came to a head in the early eighteenth century, when discontent exploded into armed rebellion.

The Wars of Independence

The hated Genoese taxes were the trigger for **revolt in 1729** when, having suffered a series of failed harvests, one village near Corte refused to pay. Its defiance developed into a full-scale uprising and the reinforcements sent in to suppress it were soon overpowered. Rebellion spread quickly across the island and was formalized in **1731**, when a popular assembly declared **national independence**, adopting a constitution and forming a parliament with a representative from each village. The Genoese, besieged in their coastal fortresses, turned for help to Emperor Charles VI, who responded with six battalions, which helped recapture St-Florent and Algajola from the insurgents. Under pressure from the emperor's troops, the Corsicans agreed to a settlement in 1732, winning several concessions from the Genoese, including access to public office.

The fighting resumed as soon as the emperor's soldiers had withdrawn, but the rebels made little progress, being short of resources and blockaded by a Genoese fleet. Salvation arrived in 1736 in the bizarre form of **Theodor von Neuhof**, a Westphalian adventurer brought up in the French royal court, who had spotted in Corsica's chaos an opportunity for glory. Having persuaded Tunisian financiers to back his venture, von Neuhof sailed into Aléria with ample supplies of money, arms and ammunition. The rebels had little choice but to accept his offer of support and they crowned him **King of Corsica**, though his authority was severely restricted by a new constitution, an executive council and an elected legislature. King Theodor's reign lasted eight months, by which time a lack of military success and depleted funds had provoked the hostility of many Corsicans; in November 1736 their monarch left the island, promising to find new allies.

Still the Corsicans and Genoese were in stalemate, each side unable to raise enough funds or forces to influence events decisively – until, in 1738, Genoa appealed to Louis XV of France and received several regiments commanded by the Comte de Boisseux. The following year, after the deployment of a further detachment of French troops, a thousand Corsicans were forced to flee the island. Among the refugees was **Giacinto Paoli**, one of the first leaders of the revolt, who went into exile in Naples with his teenage son Pascal.

The French pulled out of Corsica in 1741 but before long the major European powers were fighting over the island again, hoping for a strategic advantage in the War of the Austrian Succession. A British fleet carrying Austrian and Sardinian troops joined forces with the Corsican patriots, who elected **Gian'Pietru Gaffori** their commander. The 1748 Treaty of Aix-la-Chapelle marked an end to British involvement in the struggle, but the Corsicans continued their campaign, drawing up a new constitution in 1752. Gaffori led a determined drive against the Genoese, eventually capturing their stronghold at Corte, despite the fact that his son had been abducted and held hostage within the city walls. His heroic reputation among the Corsicans was matched by that of his wife, who prevented her household from surrendering to enemy troops by threatening to light a barrel-load of gunpowder and blow them and herself to smithereens.

Paoli's Independent Corsica

The rebels lost their dynamic commander in 1753, when Gaffori was assassinated, and in 1754 **Pascal Paoli**, son of the exiled Corsican leader, was called back to Corsica to take over leadership of the rebellion.

Paoli returned with a keen sense of constitutional theory and a thorough political education. Having been elected leader of the nation in 1755, he introduced a constitution according to which every man over 25 had a vote and every parish could send representatives to the public Assembly, which in turn elected an executive council of state. Paoli himself was in charge of military and foreign matters, but all other policies required the Assembly's agreement. Rapid steps were taken to boost the islanders' flagging morale and pitiful resources: schools were built and a university was founded in Corte; a mint and a printing press were established; mines and an arms factory were put into production. The death penalty was rigorously enforced for vendetta killings, which finally began to decline. Under Paoli's command the Corsican patriots and their enlightened system of government found admirers among the liberals and radicals of Europe. Jean-Jacques Rousseau toyed with the idea of moving to the island and writing its history; James Boswell came to meet Paoli and sang his praises in his Journal of the visit, published in 1768 (see p.390).

In the meantime, events were overtaking the Corsicans. French forces occupied five coastal towns in 1764, and in **1768** the **Genoese ceded their rights** to the island, selling their claim to France under the Treaty of Versailles. An invading force landed within a month of the treaty's being signed, taking possession of Cap Corse. Paoli's men – and women – kept up the pressure, hiding out in the maquis and launching guerrilla attacks on the French, but when a new detachment of troops was sent in there was little hope for the Corsicans, who suffered a terrible defeat at the **Battle of Ponte-Nuovo** in May 1769. Pascal Paoli was obliged to flee to England.

French Rule to the Twentieth Century

Though sporadic resistance continued even after Paoli's departure, Corsica was brought fairly painlessly within the monarchy as a Pays d'État, with its own biennial gathering of churchmen, nobles and commoners. As part of its programme of assimilation, the French offered Corsica's noble families scholarships to its prestigious military schools. Among the successful applicants was the son of Paoli's ex-secretary – **Napoléon Bonaparte**.

During the twenty years of rule by the French monarchy, the drive for independence gradually subsided and, when the revolutionaries ousted Louis XVI in 1789, Corsica urged the Assembly to make the island a fully integrated part of the French State. The royal ban imposed on political exiles was lifted, and Paoli returned to be elected President of the Corsican Conseil-Général. His authority was at first accepted by the Paris Convention, but soon Paoli fell out of favour after a Paris-instigated campaign to conquer Sardinia ended in failure. When it became known that Paoli was to be arrested, the Corsican Assembly came to his defence, naming him **Father of the Nation**. Paoli's supporters turned on the French and pro-French on the island; the Bonaparte family, who had long since transferred their loyalty to France, left their Ajaccio home to the looters and were hastened to Toulon by Napoléon, by then serving in the French army.

The Anglo-Corsican Interlude

Aware of the superior strength of French forces, Paoli called on his old English allies for help, and in 1794 **Sir Gilbert Elliot** arrived with reinforcements who quickly captured St-Florent, Bastia and Calvi (where Nelson lost the use of one of his eyes). In return for this intervention, Britain demanded a stake in the island's government, and in June **1794** an **Anglo-Corsican kingdom** was proclaimed.

To the bitter disappointment of Paoli and his supporters, Sir Gilbert was made viceroy of the new kingdom, with the power to dissolve parliament, nominate councillors and appoint the highest officers of state. When the Corsican members of parliament responded by electing Paoli their president, Sir Gilbert threatened to pull out his troops, and they were forced to back down. A series of riots followed, and a nervous Sir Gilbert persuaded the king to exile Paoli once again – this time for good. But the damage was already done: Paoli loyalists joined the French in their attacks on British soldiers, and in September 1796 Sir Gilbert and his troops sailed away, leaving the island to be retaken by France.

The Napoleonic Era and its Aftermath

Apart from a brief stay in Ajaccio in 1799, **Napoléon** paid scant attention to his homeland during his period of power. A number of uprisings on the island during the 1790s were put down with brutal force, and opposition to

Corsica in World War II

Corsica was first annexed by 80,000 of Mussolini's troops in 1940, while the Nazis were busy invading France. Regarded as strategically vital for control of the Mediterranean's seaways, the island was also one of the most obvious points from which to launch an Allied invasion of continental Europe. The Allies had in fact settled upon southern Italy as their landing site, but to throw the Axis armies off the scent they stepped up resistance and reconnaissance activities in Corsica.

That their mission in Corsica was in essence one big diversionary tactic would presumably not have been made clear to members of the Special Operations Europe (or **SOE**), the covert British military outfit charged with marshalling the local resistance. In December 1942, SOE began dispatching agents from Algiers to link up with the Corsican partisans, led by a local gendarme, **Colonna d'Istria** (or "Cesari"). Code-named "Balaclava", its private navy in Corsica was headed by Oxbridge graduate and former polar explorer, **Andrew Croft**, whose mission was to establish a network of radio operators, and to harass the enemy forces as much as possible. From a secret camp in Calvi and store in St-Florent, he helped equip and train resistance fighters in sabotage techniques and guerrilla warfare. Arms, ammunitions and agents were sent direct from SOE in North Africa via the submarine *Casabianca*, commanded by **Capitaine Jean l'Herminier** (see p.70).

SOE's campaign, codenamed **Operation Firebrand**, was highly effective. In all, 52 missions were mounted by Croft, around half of them successful. Once active, however, the agents found it increasingly difficult to keep one step ahead of the Gestapo and Italian secret police. Many were captured, tortured and shot, among them a captain sent by General de Gaulle himself, **Fred Scamaroni**, who committed suicide in his cell in Ajaccio rather than divulge the names of his comrades.

By 1943, the Corsican Resistance, now entirely dominated by the left-wing Front National, boasted 12,000 men. For the most part, they targeted the Germans (based in the south of the island around Bonifacio and Porto-Vecchio), attacking convoys then melting back in the maquis (the term "**Maquis**" was subsequently taken up by the Allies to refer to the entire French Resistance).

The turning point in Corsica's war was the capitulation of Mussolini's successor, Marshal Badoglio after Eisenhower's landing at Salerno in early September 1943. The surrender placed the Italian occupying forces in an awkward position. Reviled by the islanders and no longer allied to the Germans many Italian troops regarded Corsican retribution as less of a risk than Nazi justice, and mutinied o fled to the mountains to fight with the Maquis.

On the same day the armistice was announced, German **General Von Sengen und Etterlin**, flew int Corsica to oversee the withdrawal of the troops from Sardinia which, with the Allies advancing steadil through Italy, were now needed on the mainland. His plan was to form a bridgehead in the south an press northwards up the east coast to Bastia, where a mass evacuation to Leghorn (Livorno) could tak place. This huge troop movement gave the Allies a golden opportunity to destroy Marshal Kesselring' Ninth Panzer Division as it lumbered unprotected by air support along the exposed, flat shoreline of th east coast. They, however, had their hands full at Salerno. Instead, the job of forestalling the Germa retreat fell to the Corsican Maquis, beefed up by a French colonial force from North Africa.

Meanwhile, the Italians' uneasy standoff with the Germans erupted into a fight for control of Bast (the two powers were by this stage technically enemies). Angered by the obstinacy of his former allie

Napoleonic rule led to widespread revolt by an alliance of Royalists, Paolists and British supporters in 1799. This, too, was stamped out and its leaders executed. In 1801 the constitution was suspended and Général Morand arrived to administer a harsh military rule. His reign of terror lasted until 1811, when the almost equally unpopular Général César Berthier took his place. In the same year the island was made a single *département* of France (it had been divided into two in 1796), with its capital in Ajaccio. Resistance to the French continued, and in 1814 the citizens of Bastia appealed to Britain to intervene on their behalf. A detachment of British troops was sent, but in April of that year Napoléon abdicated and the soldiers were recalled.

After 1815 and the **restoration of the French monarchy**, the governing state made some attempts to develop the island's economy,

Hitler personally ordered the execution of the Italian officers captured in the battle. Von Sengen, however, ignored the *Führer*'s instructions, sending the prisoners directly to Livorno where no such orders existed.

By mid-September, the German evacuation was proceeding at pace, with 3000 troops per day being airlifted or shipped off the east coast, while the Maquis and Free French army (newly dispatched by Général Giraud from Algiers and now numbering some 6600 men) closed in from the hills behind. Bombed by the Allied air forces, and torpedoed by British submarines in the Ligurian Sea, the retreating German army was effectively surrounded by October 2, when Von Sengen informed his commanding officer that he could only hold the beachhead at Bastia for another twenty-four hours. By the time the General stepped onto his launch to leave that night, approximately 27,000 German troops and up to 100 tanks had been removed to safety, for the relatively cheap price of 17,000 tonnes of shipping (and one million litres of top Corsican wine, which rampaging German troops poured down the drains before they left).

Corsica was officially "liberated" on September 16, 1943, but was not yet out of trouble. Due to crossed wires in Allied Command, American bombers mounted a devastating broad-daylight high-altitude raid on October 4 – as most of Bastia was partying in the streets. Hundreds were killed, and the Vieux Port, in particular, took a dreadful pounding. This fatal error soured celebrations on the island, and did little to calm the nerves of de Gaulle, who was already in a fury. Credit for the Liberation had gone to his arch rival, **Général Giraud**, who had dispatched the Free French troops without consulting the Committee of National Liberation, or CFLN (the de facto government in exile) in Algiers. Much to his right-wing adversary's chagrin, Giraud had also allowed the communist-dominated Front National to take control of communications and local government on the island, setting a potentially undesirable (from de Gaulle's point of view) precedent for the future recapture of French territories. ("He has stolen my Corsica!" de Gaulle is said to have cried).

Backed by Roosevelt, Giraud was much more popular than de Gaulle – according to one eminent British historian, not least because "he grew a very large moustache and laughed at other people's jokes, whereas de Gaulle wasn't much of a success at either". Ultimately, however, charm proved powerless in the face of the future French president's wiliness, and within six months an outmanoeuvred Giraud was sacked from the CFLN and consigned to political obscurity.

De Gaulle's anger at the way Corsica had been liberated may go some way to explaining why this key episode in the history of World War II rarely occupies the place it deserves in the history books. But the Liberation provided an important platform for the ensuing invasion of southern France – codenamed **Operation Anvil**. Corsica became the Allies' key maritime and secret service base in 1944, and a vital staging post for landing craft bound for Italy. An additional fact, often overlooked by more racist Corsican nationalists, is that the Liberation of the island could not have been achieved without the help of several thousand Arab and West African soldiers, hundreds of whom died in battle alongside Corsican partisans. A memorial on the **Col de Teghime** honours their bravery in the face of a considerably larger and better-equipped German army.

opening mines and foundries, setting up a railway, introducing an education act, and building roads and schools. But most of their schemes had little success, and Corsica remained a marginal and largely neglected part of the country. For Corsicans, the real opportunities lay in France, and young islanders began to turn away from the old villages, seeking their careers and education on the mainland. The romance and drama that visitors such as Edward Lear and Prosper Mérimée discovered in mid-nineteenth-century Corsica veiled a grim picture of poverty, malaria and violence – vendetta, though on the decline, was still claiming up to 160 victims a year (see p.244). In the last half of the century, **emigration** surged so dramatically that within sixty years the population had been halved.

The Twentieth Century

In 1909, as a result of a commission set up by Georges Clemenceau, French Minister of the Interior, the French government promised more investment and development for Corsica. This plan was set aside with the outbreak of **World War I**, which itself reduced Corsica's population still further, taking over twenty thousand lives.

During the 1920s and 1930s Mussolini set his sights on Corsica, and World War II brought occupation by eighty thousand Italians and ten thousand German troops – almost half the number of the island's inhabitants. Once more, Corsican rebels took to the maquis, earning worldwide fame for their relentless guerrilla activity against the Axis powers (see box on p.372). In 1943 the Italians surrendered, and in the following year Corsica was the first French *département* to be liberated by the Allied forces. American soldiers moved in and began the process of real change in Corsica's economy, chiefly by using DDT to clear the east coast of malarial mosquitoes.

In the postwar years, Corsica was earmarked by the French government as a target for development, and in 1957 two State-sponsored organizations were set up to exploit its potential: **SOMIVAC** – the Société pour la Mise en Valeur Agricole de la Corse – introduced modern agricultural techniques; **SETCO** – the Société pour l'Équipement Touristique de la Corse – provided funds to build a tourist industry. Both organizations met with considerable distrust, seen as threats to an ancient way of life that had evolved and survived during centuries of hostile occupation. Nevertheless, the development gathered pace and, after 1962, when Algeria gained its independence, the situation was complicated by a massive influx of pieds-noirs refugees from the ex-French colony. Over 15,000 settlers poured into Corsica during the next twenty years, many of them buying up the newly developed land and hotels, adding to Corsican fears of losing control of their resources. Summer **tourists** began to arrive in steadily rising numbers, topping the half-million mark in the early 1970s (and now heading for 1.5 million).

Calls for Autonomy

It was against this background of insecurity and mounting frustration with the ineffectiveness of Paris's half-hearted economic policies that demands for greater administrative power were increasingly voiced from the 1960s. Led by the **Simeoni brothers**, Max and Edmond, a party of nationalist students known as L'Action Régionaliste Corse (**ARC**) started to call for decentralized government, for restrictions on the east coast tourist developments, for a Corsican university (Paoli's had been closed by the French), and for compulsory schooling in Corsican language and history.

A number of more radical **autonomist movements**, varying in tactics and demands, entered the political scene, and from the mid-1970s these won substantial support for their manifesto of a national assembly and demand for investment in controlled development and protection of the land. Meanwhile, following the **Aléria siege** of 1975, when two policemen died in a shoot-out with armed separatists (see p.378), a group of activists operating as the **FLNC** (Fronte di Liberazione Naziunale di a Corsica) embarked on a programme of bombing campaigns, targeting the tourist villages and foreign-owned properties that they believed were destroying Corsica's land and culture.

In the early 1980s the autonomists profited from a change of policy in France favouring increased decentralization. A Corsican university was re-established in 1981, providing a channel for the ambitions and political ideas of the younger generation. In the following year, Corsica was the first of the French regions to be granted a National Assembly, with limited powers over policy, administration and finance. Nonetheless, benefiting from close links with the IRA, a mo ruthless and efficient FLNC intensified its paramilitary activities. Dozens of explosions heralded the **election** of 1984, as allegations of fraud and corruption were levelled against the politicians.

In 1987, **Charles Pasqua**, the (then) Minister of the Interior, mounted a clampdown on the FLNC. Nevertheless, nationalist political parties continued to poll around seventeen percent of the vote in elections, though a crisis was brewing that would inflict considerably more damage to the nationalist movement than any of Pasqua's heavy-handed tactics. Following a period of deepening political divisions, in 1990 the movement split into two opposing factions: **Cuncolta** and their armed wing, the FLNC Canal Historique; and the **MPA**, whose paramilitary group dubbed itself the FLNC Canal Habituel. Soon an all-out blood feud erupted between the two, which has since claimed dozens of lives on both sides.

In spite of – or, some would argue, because of – the violence, the past twenty years have seen a slow progression towards a re-evaluation of Corsican culture and the island's attainment of increasing control over its own affairs. A statute passed in 1990 gave a greater degree of autonomy to Corsica, and in 1992 the nationalists won 13 of the 61 seats in the Regional Assembly. Since then their share of the vote has diminished, but they remain a significant political force on the island (see p.376). Though many young Corsicans still seek jobs and education on the mainland, those who stay can now study the language and customs that once appeared to be dying out, and enjoy a standard of living that has risen markedly since the 1950s, largely as a result of the tourist boom. Parts of the island may seem in danger of becoming bland international-style holiday resorts, and the abandonment and spoliation of large tracts of agricultural land presents a real problem, but the revival of a strong Corsican identity has led to a reassessment of the island's future – which is guaranteed to be as controversial and unyielding as its past.

David Abram and Nia Williams

The Corsican Troubles: An Overview

To the outsider, Corsica may seem peaceful enough. But you don't have to look too hard to find signs of the 25-year conflict being waged between local nationalist extremists and the French State. On the outskirts of larger villages are fortified gendarmeries, surrounded by high walls; bullet marks mar the façades of many post offices, banks and government buildings; black graffiti defaces most road signs; and the rubble of bombed-out holiday villas dots coastal landscapes from Cap Corse to the Bouches de Bonifacio.

Spawning more than five hundred bombings, arson and machine-gun attacks annually, the conflict, which in recent years has descended into factional infighting among the islanders themselves, has left few families unscathed. Since 1986, the murder rate in Corsica has run at an average of forty per year – for a population of 256,000.

The chances of your getting caught up in any violence while on holiday are virtually nil, but the Corsican troubles remain a defining feature of island life, as integral to local society as the sectarian war of Northern Ireland or the mafia's presence in Sicily, with which *le problème corse*, as the troubles are euphemistically dubbed on the mainland, shares many similarities.

The Roots of Nationalism

Although Corsica has always maintained its own culturally distinct way of life, the conviction that the islanders' unique language and customs should form the basis of an individual nation is a relatively new phenomenon. Not until the Wars of Independence and rise of **Pascal Paoli** (see p.317) in the mid-eighteenth century did nationalism gather any momentum, inspired by widespread outrage at the atrocities perpetrated by the French in the wake of the Genoese withdrawal in 1768. Before this time, any seeds of nationalist consciousness that may have taken root were stifled by instability or foreign oppression. Since the time of the Romans, Corsica has witnessed nineteen changes of overlords, thirty-seven popular revolts and seven spells of outright anarchy.

The other force that has traditionally mitigated against the emergence of a unified Corsican nation has been **clannism**. In common with many Mediterranean societies, the island has always been riven by internal divisions: between families, hamlets, villages, valleys, and between coastal peoples and shepherds in the mountains. All too often, these differences were perpetuated by **vendettas** resulting from some kind of perceived slight to an individual or family's honour (see p.244). The prevalence of such feuds, which were commonplace until the end of the nineteenth century, ensured that mutual mistrust, suspicion and the readiness to resort to violence became firmly ingrained in the Corsican psyche.

Economic Decline

The **revival** of Corsican nationalism in the twentieth century emerged essentially as a response to the island's steady economic decline under French rule. Whereas the Genoese had instigated a coherent and productive agricultural policy (whence the vast chestnut forests of Castagniccia and olive groves of the Balagne) the only distinguishing feature of their French successors' approach to the island's economi woes was **neglect**. With its agricultural produce no longer in demand, Corsica's crops literally withered on the vine.

Emigration, to the cities of the mainland and French colonies in Africa and the Americas, left whole regions perilously underpopulated by the start of the twentieth century. The world wars took their toll, too. Per capita, Corsica lost more of its menfolk on the battlefields of Europe than any other *département* in France. Experience of the wider world also encouraged those who survived to emigrate after demobilization. Between 1937 and 1956, census figures show the island's population dropped to a little under 76,000, while during the 1960s port records registered 10,000 more annual departures than arrivals.

The effect of such widespread emigration on the Corsican economy was devastating. Not only were there now fewer hands to work what little land remained under cultivation, but the drop in population also meant a much smaller labour pool, discouraging potential investors. By the mid-1960s, the island was officially the poorest *département* in France, importing six times what it exported, yet with a cost of living thirty percent higher than the average on the mainland.

The response of the French government to such poverty, however, continued to lack vision, while makeshift decisions issued by Paris throughout this era compounded Corsica's economic problems. Eager to put it on a par with the rest of the country, **de Gaulle** whittled away at the island's special fiscal exemptions, which had been in place since 1811, imposing duties on public transport and gambling, as well as tobacco and alcohol. As a result, transport costs of goods to Corsica increased, further worsening the balance of payments and contributing to inflation. To Corsicans, it seemed as if France was actively penalizing the island for being an island. To rub salt into the wound, neighbouring Sardinia, which also had become depopulated and poor, began to thrive from the 1950s on, thanks to massive investment and dispensations from the Italian government, which had put its economy on a level playing field with that of the mainland.

The Rise of the FLNC

The adoption of violence by Corsican nationalists arose out of a widespread sense of frustration and powerlessness in the face of continued French indifference. Peaceful protests had consistently failed to galvanize Paris. Strikes called by an increasingly militant workforce in the early 1960s proved little more than a shot in the foot: when dockers downed tools in 1961, the resulting disruption provoked two major Italian shipping firms to remove their operations from the island altogether.

The mounting dissatisfaction may have rumbled on without erupting for another decade, had it not been for a string of controversies that struck in quick succession during the early 1960s. The first was the arrival, in 1962, of 15,000 pieds-noirs. The influx of newcomers provoked alarm among Corsican traditionalists that the island was being used as a "dumping ground" at the cost of indigenous culture and was losing control of its resources. Fears of exploitation were whipped up further the following year, when the government announced it wanted to export cheap **electricity** generated in Corsica to Sardinia. Considering Paris's long-term economic neglect, the plans were regarded as adding insult to injury.

The gravest insult to Corsican pride around this time, however, came direct from de Gaulle himself. When world opinion made it impolitic to stage **nuclear tests** in the French-occupied Sahara, de Gaulle and his team of military advisers chose **Argentella**, southwest of Calvi, as a potential atom-bomb-testing site. News of the plans were greeted with public outrage in Corsica. An island-wide general strike and referendum showed unanimous opposition to the proposals, and thirty thousand demonstrators took to the streets of Ajaccio and Bastia (the largest crowds to gather on the island since Liberation day in 1943). De Gaulle, however, refused to back down.

At this point, local "vigilance committees", monitoring government surveyors on the northwest coast, lost patience with peaceful protest and took the law into their own hands. Armed patrols located a couple of engineers, and nearly killed them (even though, as it turned out, the men had nothing to do with the nuclear tests). The remaining government technicians were immediately recalled to Paris and the Argentella project was shelved.

Aside from being a rare example of how – at a time when anti-nuclear protesters were in prison in both the US and UK – a small population was able to reverse the nuclear policy of a national government, the Argentella episode marked a watershed in the island's history: it was effectively the first time since the Wars of Independence that Corsicans had taken up arms against the French State.

ARC and the Aléria Siege

The impetus Corsica needed to finally launch a nationalist political party came with the return from the mainland of radicalized students after the university-led revolution in Paris of **May 1968**. In its infancy, the nationalist political scene was dominated by two groups: right-wing conservatives from established bourgeois families, and a smaller contingent of young Maoist and Trotskyists. The latter emerged as the dominant force in the **ARC** (L'Action Régionaliste Corse), founded in 1967. Regaled by the stirring, newly revived **polyphony** singing of groups like Canta U Populu Corsu, its conferences resounded with the rallying cry "*I Francesi fora!*" (French Out!).

Direct conflict with the French government, however, didn't come until 1975, when the radical armed wing of the ARC, led by the **Simeoni brothers**, occupied a wine cellar near **Aléria** on the east coast to voice their anger at Paris's lack of action over a wine-adulteration scandal. A 1250-strong force of armed police were dispatched by Giscard d'Estaing to break the siege, and during the shoot-out that followed two policemen were killed.

In the wake of Aléria, on the anniversary of the Battle of Ponte Novu (when Pascal Paoli's army was routed by the French) a clandestine nocturnal press conference – or *nuit bleue* – was held by balaclava-wearing nationalist gunmen to announce the formation of the Fronte di Liberazione Naziunale di a Corsica, or **FLNC**. The stated aim of the (then) poorly equipped, poorly trained paramilitary group was total freedom from French dominion.

The Early Years of Armed Struggle: 1976–82

The first two years of **armed struggle** were relatively restrained, with attacks directed against strategic government targets, such as Ajaccio airport, where an Air France Boeing 707 became an early casualty of the conflict. But after 1978 the tone became more militant. A right-wing anti-separatist group, **SAC** (Service d'Action Civique), believed to have been covertly funded by the government, was attempting to infiltrate and sabotage the FLNC, who responded by setting up a unit called **Secteur V**, charged with mounting bomb attacks on the mainland.

Proof that Paris and the SAC were in cahoots came in 1980 with the capture of three active French secret service agents in **Bastelica** (see p.223). The men were taken at gunpoint to the *Hôtel Fesch* in Ajaccio, and held until the building was stormed six days later. No one was killed, but the nationalists involved were seized and sent to swell the growing ranks of Corsican prisoners in mainland France.

The debacle infuriated the FLNC rank and file, and plunged the island into its worst spell of nationalist violence to date. This period also saw the spread of **racketeering** as the FLNC's principal means of raising funds. Protection money was increasingly demanded of hotels, restaurants and other tourist-oriented businesses across the island, while hold-ups and armed robberies proliferated.

By the beginning of the 1980s, however, it was clear that small-time villains had started to cash in on the troubles by running rackets behind a veneer of FLNC "respectability". In order to differentiate the *pur et dur* (pure and hard) from the *truands et petits voyous* (crooks and little yobs), the leadership imposed what it called **impôt revolutionnaire** (revolutionary tax). "Contributors" were notified when their payments were due in the magazine *Ribombu*, mouthpiece of the FLNC's newly formed political wing, **A Cuncolta di i Cumitati Naziunalisti**, or Cuncolta.

With the election of François Mitterrand and his Socialist government in 1981, hopes were high that some kind of solution to *le problème corse* may at last be attainable. Corsica was granted its own **Assemblée Régionale** the following year (months ahead of any other region in France), and behind-the-scenes talks were held with the FLNC. Despite this, nationalist attacks continued to spiral, with 800 in 1982 alone.

The Pasqua Crackdown

The situation seemed to have reached a stalemate by 1985, when Jacques Chirac's Gaull home affairs minister, **Charles Pasqua**, instigated a crackdown on nationalist activities under the slogan "*Terroriser les terroristes!*" ("Terrorize the terrorists!"). Journalists who didn't tow the government line were purged, overtly nationalist music groups such as I Muvrini were banned and "Wanted" posters stuck everywhere. Suspected FLNC activists were rounded up and tension rose to a new high.

Meanwhile, in a bid for greater respectability, the FLNC declared a **war on drugs**. "*A droga fora!*" replaced anti-French invective as the graffiti writers' preferred slogan, and brutal summary justice awaited anyone identified as a dealer. But the campaign looked to be running out of control when two Tunisian immigrants accused of trafficking were gunned down in January 1986, provoking outrage both on the island and in mainland France.

From this point on, the **bombing of holiday villas** became the FLNC's prime propaganda ploy. Justified by the nationalists' claims that Corsica needed to be protected from foreign "influences" in general and modern architecture in particular, the nationalists' destruction of second homes on the island was, and continues to be, a vote winner. No islanders like to see ugly new buildings appearing along the coast, least of all ones only occupied for a couple of months each year, so when the FLNC reduce them to rubble they are regarded by many Corsicans, even those who may not otherwise support nationalist terrorism, as providing a much-needed service. Of course, house bombing also provides potent lever with which to extract "revolutionary tax" from holiday-home owners.

Break-up of the FLNC

The late 1980s saw a marked softening of the French government's line on Corsica. With the backing of Mitterrand and his new socialist prime minister, Michel Rocard, home affairs minister **Pierre Joxe** visited the island nineteen times during his tenure. For the first time, recognition of *un peuple corse* (a Corsican people) and special status for the region, such as that enjoyed by former colonies L'Île de la Réunion and Martinique, were mooted.

The FLNC, however, procrastinated about how to respond to the new initiative, paralysed by mounting divisions between its hard- and softliners. Joxe began to lose patience as the disputes over his proposals intensified. Eventually, the strain exploded with the departure of one of the Front's key military leaders, **Pierrot Poggioli**, to form a rival nationalist party, L'Accolta Naziunale Corsa, or **ANC**. One of the most-respected old guard of the early FLNC era, Poggioli condemned the "Mafia-ization" of the separatist movement, and the corrosive effects of "revolutionary tax".

Intelligence reports, meanwhile, hinted at a massive **build-up of arms** in Corsica, but with the nationalists in apparent disarray, an all-out internecine feud rather than an intensification of violence against the State seemed the more likely outcome.

The Ribombu Incident

The catalyst for the **break-up of the FLNC**, and the ensuing war between its respective factions, came at the end of 1990. Bastiais hardliners, marshalled by one of Cuncolta's leaders, **Charles Pieri**, tried to forcibly take over the movement's paper and main mouthpiece, **Ribombu**. When its editor realized what was happening, he telephoned the head of Secteur V in Ajaccio, charismatic Aléria veteran **Alain Orsoni**, who immediately travelled north to intervene. The two factions traded insults, but it was Pieri and his men who were left humiliated after Orsoni accused them of betraying FLNC activists while in police custody. The gauntlet had been thrown down.

Ripples from the "*Ribombu* incident" rocked the movement to its grass roots. Within a few months, the FLNC had split into three groups, each with its own political wing: Led by Alain Orsoni, the **MPA** (Mouvement Pour l'Autodétermination) lined up alongside **FLNC-Canal Habituel**, while **Cuncolta** aligned itself with the **FLNC-Canal Historique** The rogue element in the equation was Pierrot Poggioli's ANC and its small *bras armé* (armed faction), **Resistenza**, who initially sided with the Canal-Historique but would later switch to Orsoni's camp.

The lines were now drawn for a bloody vendetta-like feud. Murders multiplied across the island as activists were picked off in tit-for-tat killings and reprisals, known as *règlements de compte* (settling of scores). Each faction's business interests were also targeted in a protracted bombing campaign.

One of the major flash points in the conflict occurred in May 1995, when the 35-year-old leader of Cuncolta, former primary schoolteacher **François Santoni**, and his friend, Gallo, ran into an ambush while motorcycling on the outskirts of Ajaccio. Gallo was killed in the encounter, but Santoni escaped. The next day, FLNC-Canal Historique vowed to track down all seven members of the hit squad involved, suspected to be from the MPA/FLNC-Canal Habituel. Consequently, the summer of 1995 was the bloodiest in living memory. Fifteen key figures, and dozens of minor activists in the nationalist movement, would be murdered, while those that survived were forced into hiding.

1996: Tralonca and the Bastia Bombing

President Chirac and Prime Minister Juppé's public response to the relentless violence in Corsica was to initiate another law-and-order crackdown, declaring that it was "unacceptable for there to be one set of laws for Corsica and another for mainland France". Meanwhile, their junior ministers – as it later transpired – pursued secret negotiations with the terrorist groups, striking deals to secure an uneasy peace.

The most tangible result of these covert talks was the now famous *nuit bleue* at **Tralonca**, near Corte, when, on a freezing January night in 1996, six hundred FLNC-Canal Historique commandos gave a press conference to announce a temporary **ceasefire**. Armed to the teeth with Kalashnikovs, Israeli sub-machine guns, grenades, new flame throwers and AK47s stolen from the UN in Bosnia, the balaclava army presented a chilling photo opportunity for invited journalists. The promised truce, however, didn't last long.

Six months later it was broken in the most dramatic fashion, with the explosion of a **car bomb in Bastia**. The intended target was Charles Pieri, Cuncolta's national secretary. Timed to detonate in broad daylight as he was leaving the headquarters of his security firm in the Vieux Port, the device killed one Cuncolta member, Pierre-Louis Lorenzi, and injured fourteen innocent passers-by. Pieri himself sustained extensive injuries, but survived.

This was the first occasion in the history of Corsica's recent troubles that a large bomb had exploded during the day in a busy public place. The prime suspects were Orsoni's MPA/FLNC-Canal Habituel, but they moved swiftly to deny responsibility, raising suspicions that the attack had been an act of "outside provocation". One prominent MPA activist said it was "inconceivable" that such indiscriminate violence could have been perpetrated by Corsican paramilitaries. The finger of blame thus shifted towards the government, or some kind of anti-separatist group.

Contrary to expectations, the Bastia bombing did not spark off a spate of reprisal killings. The possibility that the attack may have been the work of *agents provocateurs* rather than merely another *règlement de compte* seemed to jolt the paramilitaries into realizing the extent to which their factional infighting was playing into the hands of their enemies. For a while, it seemed as if the attack on Pieri might shock the warring wings of the FLNC into another ceasefire.

Apart from costing the paramilitaries dozens of their best men, six years of intense internecine war had left the political process in disarray. No one seemed to know any longer who was negotiating with whom, or why, or what the ultimate aims of the armed struggle were.

Part of the problem lay in the fact that many o the sources of conflict back in the early 1970s nc longer existed. Since the inauguration of the FLNC, the government had shown itself willing tc address the island's problems: two genera amnesties had been called, Corsican had beer recognized as an official language and the uni versity at Corte resurrected.

Vast sums had also been poured int developing the island, to reduce unemploy ment and promote a sustainable economy Corsica today boasts four international ai ports, eight maritime ports, high-specificatio trunk roads and ample, inexpensive air an sea links with the mainland, bankrolled b 950 million francs of government money eac year. It also receives roughly 7 billion franc annually (27,000F per head of population) national and EU subsidies, making it the mo heavily subsidized region in France. Corsica are also exempt from social security contrib tions, and the island as a whole enjoys pre erential tax status.

The majority of islanders benefit directly fro this special treatment, and from State emplo ment (one third of the total workforce is employed by the government or government-funded local councils), as well as welfare handouts of various kinds. It's hardly surprising, therefore, that public support for independence has gradually diminished over the past two decades. These days only the hardest of hardliners in the movement favour complete secession.

The new pragmatism is most vividly reflected in the agendas of Corsica's myriad nationalist parties, who have consistently polled between 15 and 25 percent of the vote in regional elections. The most moderate among them is the UPC – direct successor to the original autonomist party, the ARC. While the dust was still settling after the Bastia bomb, its annual convention in Aléria set out a list of **key demands** from the French government. These ranged from greater tax-raising and legislative powers for the *assemblée régionale*, to a lower rate of VAT on the island, mandatory teaching of language in schools, a special Corsican *carte d'identité* and recognition of *le peuple corse* as a "national minority".

Juppé's Revenge

In late 1996, during a period when France's new right-wing Gaullist government was constantly reaffirming its refusal to negotiate with terrorists, an unexpected twist came about when the prime minister himself, Alain Juppé, became embroiled in a scandal after the Cuncolta leader, François Santoni, claimed he had had secret talks with the government.

The most sensational of Santoni's accusations centered on the *nuit bleue* at Tralonca, which, he claimed, had been staged with the full connivance of the government. The prime minister had allegedly wanted a big turnout to ensure that the FLNC's rank and file would not later be able to disassociate themselves from the ensuing ceasefire. Juppé vociferously denied the charges, but the mud stuck.

Santoni's revelations had apparently been prompted by the prime minister's orders that participants of the Tralonca *nuit bleue* should be arrested – regarded by the FLNC as a flagrant betrayal of the covert agreement. Soon after, the city hall in Bordeaux, where Juppé is mayor, was bombed, and death threats issued to the French premier. But the FLNC clearly underestimated the prime minister's stomach for a fight. The personal attacks merely seemed to steel Juppé's resolve to defeat the terrorists.

Within a couple of months, he ordered a massive **crackdown** on lawlessness and corruption in Corsica, during which police raids netted all but one of Cuncolta's leaders, most of whom were charged with extortion offences after the owner of the **Sperone golf course**, near Bonifacio, had gone to the police about protection threats he'd received (a story described in more detail on p.284). To everyone's amazement, the response from the paramilitaries was muted. The rate of attacks on mainland France dropped, and no general strike was called on the island itself, where there seemed to be a tangible shift in public mood away from the nationalist cause.

The Erignac murder

The general election in June 1997 of a Socialist government under **Lionel Jospin** coincided with the announcement by FLNC-Canal Historique of yet another **ceasefire**, this time allegedly to encourage concessions from the new administration. When these failed to materialize, however, the truce was called off and bombings resumed.

Thus it was initially the FLNC-Canal Historique who were to be held responsible for the brutal murder of the French government's most senior representative in Corsica, **Claude Erignac**, gunned down in front of his wife while leaving a classical music concert in Ajaccio on February 6, 1998. The FLNC-Canal Historique, however, surprised everyone by condemning the attack. That no one admitted responsibility for the highest-profile assassination in the island's history was widely regarded as symptomatic of the indiscipline and confusion that had overtaken the separatist struggle.

After a fifteen-month investigation, police announced that their prime suspect for the murder was a goatherd from Cargèse called **Yvan Colonna**, an activist from one of Corsica's more militant breakaway terrorist groups. When this book went to press, Colonna, officially France's most-wanted criminal, was still thought to be hiding out in a safe house somewhere on the island, protected by Corsica's implacable *loi du silence*.

Erignac's successor, meanwhile, is serving a prison sentence after it was revealed that he had sanctioned an arson attack by undercover police agents on a nationalist-owned beach café in Ajaccio. In the wake of this scandal at the end of 1999, Paris remained divided about what to do next. While the prime minister, Lionel Jospin, makes robust statements about "firmness and intransigence" in the face of the terrorist threat, his home affairs minister strikes a more placatory tone, offering "dialogue", "justice" and "greater autonomy in exchange for peace". In practice, as nationalist commentators point out, Paris comes up with little more than carefully chosen words. Meanwhile, the bombings, arson attacks and machine-gun strafings of government buildings continue at a steady rate of around five hundred per year on the island, with occasional explosions on the mainland.

The reality is that the French government, while happy to dole out huge subsidies to Corsica, remains reluctant to concede any real ground to the autonomists. If they did, Basques, Bretons, Savoyards and a host of smaller minorities in the country would, the government fears, demand the same devolutionary powers, and eventually self-government.

Prospects for Peace

At the start of the 21st century, the prospects of Corsica's armed nationalists renouncing violence seem as distant as they have at any point in the past 25 years. Few would deny that the State, while lavishing funds and tax exemptions on the island, has failed to devise an effective and lasting economic strategy. But this does not explain why so many initiatives by a string of successive administrations have failed, nor why violence continues to be the island's predominant response to its political differences with the motherland.

To understand the real roots of *le problème corse* you have to look to Corsica's traditional culture. As Nicolas Giudici, one of the most-respected commentators on the troubles, has pointed out, "Corsica is an ancient Mediterranean society, convinced of the legitimacy of its ways of doing things – which means factions, clans, infighting and vendettas".

Compounding the persistence of clannism in Corsica is the fact that nowadays the potential pickings of patronage and corruption are richer than ever before. It is no secret that the lion's share of government money and subsidies diverted to Corsica gets "misappropriated", as much by corrupt mayors as paramilitary movements. The internecine war being waged between the various feuding families and groups is in essence a struggle to control this money.

Another, more nefarious, element in the whole equation is **organized crime**. The Corsican **Mafia**, which dominates the underworlds of Marseille and Paris, has traditionally limited its activities to the mainland. But in recent years, the mob, or *milieu* as it's known in French, has moved in on the extortion rackets being run by the paramilitaries at home. In the process, the dividing line between nationalist and Mafia violence has become blurred.

"Manifeste pour la Vie"

Among the few local voices courageous enough to speak out against nationalist violence has been that of **Manifeste pour la Vie** (Manifesto for Life), a women's movement launched in Ajaccio in January 1996. One of its founder members was Laetitia Sozzi, whose husband, Robert, a former paramilitary, was shot after denouncing links between the FLNC and corruption in the building industry. At the core of the movement is its rejection of what it calls "the establishment of a system based on terror".

Manifeste's demonstrations consistently attract crowds of more than a thousand – an impressive statistic, given that any woman who marches behind the banner of "*Non à la loi des armes*" ("No to the rule of the gun") knows that by doing so she is opening herself to intimidation from the paramilitaries. Anonymous phone calls, letters and death threats have been directed against Manifeste activists, while Cuncolta's newspaper *Ribombu*, has several times indulged in vitriolic attacks on the movement, subsequently condemned by *La Ligue des Droits de l'Homme* (League of Human Rights) as "shameful and archaically misogynistic".

After 25 years, the nationalist movement seems less dominated by political ideology and visions of a better future than by the macho, violent culture of the island's past. Adherence to the old ways, however, is not going to be relin quished overnight on an island where clan rivalries and mistrust of government are firmly rooted, nor where anyone who openly opposes the paramilitaries effectively risks their life. As the French satirical newspaper, *Le Canard Enchaîné* recently commented, "A sick Corsica needs emergency treatment. No one, however, wishes to wield the lancet [because] in Corsica any surgical operation places the surgeon's life in danger. Recovery is not around the corner."

Corsican Wildlife

The Parc Naturel Régional de la Corse, established in 1972, now embraces about a third of Corsica, largely down the mountain spine but reaching the sea in the northwest. Managing important sites such as Scandola, the Restonica valley, the Finocchiarola isles in the north and the Îles Lavezzi in the south, the park authorities ensure the survival of the mouflon and other endangered species, and increase the accessibility of the wildlife of Corsica, through the publication of excellent books and booklets and through the maintenance of footpaths. The ruggedness of Corsica's heartland naturally restricts intensive exploitation, but even in areas where human intervention has occurred the island's terrain is extraordinarily rich. The lush chestnut woodland of the Castagniccia, for example, is the result of plantation, and the tangled, headily scented maquis which clothes more than half of Corsica might seem a natural cover, but is in fact what comes in after fire or on abandoned grazing land.

The Habitat Zones

Corsica's landscape has three well-defined **habitat zones**, the lowest of which is the Mediterranean zone, which runs from the sea to an altitude of 1000m. Corsica is noted for its clean seas and varied marine life. At places along the coast you'll find pristine sand dunes, lagoons and estuaries, all three of which are now hard to find elsewhere in the Mediterranean. Trees sometimes grow right at the edge of the beach: the highly resinous **Aleppo pine** prefers rocky ground at this level, while the **stone pine** (or umbrella pine) is often seen growing singly but sometimes in groves – some of the best specimens are at Palombaggia beach near Porto-Vecchio. Stands of tall Australian **eucalyptus** can also be found in many places, planted in the late eighteenth century to rid localities such as Porto in the northwest, of malaria.

However, the typical indicator of the Mediterranean climate is the **olive tree**. Solitar specimens can be found everywhere in Corsica' Mediterranean zone (the oldest giant is near th deserted convent below Oletta at the foot of Ca Corse), while the largest groves are in th Balagne and near Propriano. At these lower alti- tudes erect "funeral" cypresses are often plante alongside family tombs. Three species of oa also identify this zone – the **cork oak** (its trur dusky red when newly stripped), the evergree **holm oak** (which has spiny leaves on suck shoots and is found in both shrub and tree form and the **kermes oak** (rarely tree-sized, and wi holly-like leaves).

Introduced shrubs and trees that thrive in th Mediterranean climate include **orange** a **lemon** in groves and gardens, red or purp **bougainvillea** in gardens, **palms** in tov squares, pink and white **oleanders** and t gigantic cactus-like **Mexican agave** on roadsid

Another characteristic of the Mediterrane zone is that the **maquis** springs up after fire when fields or open grazings are abandoned. most easily recognized plants are the shrubs the **cistus** family, carrying pink or white flow with crumpled petals, which are shed at the e of each day. Some cistus have highly scen gummy stems and leaves – the Montpellier tus, which likes acid granite soils and has ma es of small white flowers, is perhaps the m fragrant of all.

Cistus bushes often indicate open, new maquis, which in time will grow into an all- impenetrable scrub, with yellow-flowe

brooms (some of which are wickedly thorny), the taller **strawberry tree** (the red strawberry-like fruits are edible but pappy), the pungent **mastic** and **myrtle**, **rosemary** and white-flowered **tree heather**, which grows 2m tall or more. In the "tall" maquis, cork, holm oaks and other trees come in, and as their crowns broaden they begin to shade out the shrubs below them, until eventually woodland or forest results.

Towards the top of the Mediterranean zone these trees might be joined by **maritime pine**, which unusually keeps large cones of different ages on its branches, and it retains those branches even when they are starkly dead – the Restonica valley has many examples. **Sweet chestnut** also makes an appearance (it is most widespread between 500m and 800m), as does bracken. Groves of ancient chestnuts can be found near most of the hill villages, where the production of chestnut flour used to play an important part in the economy. Nowadays the chestnuts are given over to pigs (and patisseries), and many of the trees display dead antler-like branches as a result of attacks of mildew and parasites.

At around 1000m, the **mountain zone** succeeds, as oaks and chestnuts give way to forests of the native, tall-trunked **Laricio** (or Corsican) **pine**, maybe mixed with **beeches** and **firs**. The Aïtone, Valdo-Niello, Bonifato and Tartagine are among the most magnificent of these forests, featuring centuries-old Laricio pines reaching up to 40m that are the tallest conifers in Europe.

Above 2000m stretches the **alpine zone** – open and largely rocky, perhaps with scatters of ground-hugging bushy alders, and often with a wonderful variety of flowers.

Wild Flowers

Many Corsican plants are distinctive of the island - of the 2000 species of **wild flowers** found here, ight percent are native to Corsica or shared only y Corsica and Sardinia. Which species you'll see vill depend on the soil, the bedrock, the altitude nd, of course, the time of year. Spring is glorious, vith wild flowers everywhere, and many species elebrate a "second spring" after the summer rought: **cyclamens** and **autumn crocus** appear vith the autumn rains, for example, and the andsome **bush spurges** of Cap Corse are in vivid een leaf in winter and spring, but reduced to are twigs in summer.

Flowers of the Mediterranean Zone

On the seashore in summer, the dramatic **yellow-horned poppy** is worth looking for, with its very long curved seed pods. Colourful **sea stocks** and **sea lavender** grow on shingle and on rocks, where carpets of **stonecrop** – with fleshy red leaves and heads of small blue flowers – also make a handsome showing. The **sea holly**, one of the most beautiful of all wild plants with its grey-green spiny leaves and blue flower heads, sometimes forms low mats a couple of metres across – you'll see it on the open sands at Cargèse, for example. Here and at the back of other sandy beaches you can also find the white **sea daffodil** flowering in August, and almost anywhere you might come across carpets of **Hottentot fig**, with its brilliant lilac or yellow-orange flowers.

In spring, various wild flowers brighten the clearings among the colourful **maquis** shrubs. If the maquis is invading old grazing land, or if the open patch is overgrazed and impoverished, there will probably be **asphodel** growing; its delicate white flowers are withered husks by summer, although the tall spikes remain. Many of Corsica's fifty or so species of **wild orchid** flower in the maquis: one of the most handsome is the pink **butterfly orchid**, and there are always a good number of the unmistakable hooded **serapias** group, which are purple or dark red. French **lavender** is common, its small, almost black flowers carried below striking purple sails, and in some areas wild **gladiolus** can be seen along the roads or even as a weed in the ploughed fields – it has smaller flowers than the garden hybrids but is easily recognizable.

The verges and rocky cuttings of roads and lanes through the maquis and between the fields are home to **wild pinks** (some of the mountain pinks are endemic to the island), **ferns**, **honeysuckle** and **eglantine** (a wild white rose looking rather like cistus). Wild **asparagus** is often found growing around the olive groves, while in spring **tassel hyacinths** and white **Florentine iris**, the original fleur-de-lis, flower on open soil (the iris is also popular in gardens).

Flowers of the Mountain and Alpine Zones

In the chestnut woods and amongst the pines of the mountain zone grow the handsome green tufts of the **Corsican hellebore**, a poisonous species endemic to Corsica and Sardinia.

Foxgloves may be found here, and in spring scatters of **cyclamen** mix with **violets** along the stream-sides, together with hosts of delicate white or lilac **anemones** in some areas. **Autumn crocus** and **squill** also flower here and elsewhere towards the end of the year. Wherever you find beech trees at this height, you might look for wild red **peony**.

Although the mountain zone is harsh, there can be a surprising variety of flowers when the snow melts, many of them endemic – indeed, half of those you see might grow only in Corsica and Sardinia, such as a Corsican alpine groundwort and a blue mountain columbine. And many common enough in the Alps are not found here, suggesting that these two islands separated from mainland Europe at a far-distant time in the past.

Birds

As a result of the closed breeding of its resident island populations, Corsica's **birds** often display certain differences from those of mainland Europe. Songbirds such as the blackbird have a song that's distinct from that of related European species, and the birds' normal habitats are in many instances extended in some way. In Corsica the blackbird ranges from coastal maquis to the high mountains, while the explosive "chet-ti" call of the small brown **Cetti's warbler** is heard not only in the reed beds around the coastal lagoons but also in the maquis up to 500m. The most-renowned Corsican example is the elusive **Corsican nuthatch** of the Aïtone and other high pine forests. The **treecreeper** is another, while there are also forms of **great spotted woodpecker** and **wren** shared with Sardinia. Corsica is the place to add the **Dartford warbler** to your list – it is a localized and rare resident in the south of Britain; here it is common in the coastal maquis but as a darker, smaller subspecies.

Because of its position, Corsica is probably visited by the majority of trans-Mediterranean **migrants**, many of which make landfalls on the headlands or lagoons. The **spring** and **autumn** list includes common and curlew sandpiper (the latter is the commonest migrant wader here), reed bunting, marsh and Montague's harriers, pied flycatcher, grey heron, black kite and tree pipit. Of the birds that come to **winter** on the island, the sparrow-like dunnock is one of the commonest in the maquis, and amongst the other regulars are snipe, cormorant, common starling, gannet, pochard, tufted duck, teal, black-necked grebe, redwing and song thrush. Others such as the wood pigeon are resident, but numbers swell in winter, when incomers fly in to gorge on the plentiful crops of acorns.

Seabirds and Wetland Species

In general most **coastal birdlife** is centred on remote headlands and islands. Scandola, for example, has osprey, peregrine, rock dove and blue rock thrush (which also nest on bare slopes inland to 1800m). Shearwaters nest in some places, but you'll see fewer **gulls** than you might expect. Herring gulls nest at Scandola and Capo Rossu and other remote sites, and you may spot the Mediterranean gull (black-headed in summer) and the slim-winged Audouin's gull, which nest on several offshore islands. Shags, too, nest on rocky shores and are often seen flying low over the sea.

Despite widespread drainage for vineyards, fruit and other crops, the string of lagoons off the east coast remain one of the most extensive wetland units of the whole Mediterranean, attracting great crested and little **grebes**, pochard and mallard, and the water rail with its incredible pig-like cry. Reed, moustached, Cetti's and other **warblers** call from the reed beds, while marsh harrier and hobby hunt across them. In winter, Biguglia and the other lagoons are an important station for ducks, grey heron, wintering kingfisher and others

Maquis Species

The **maquis** in its various forms offers ideal nesting for **warblers** and birds such as red-backe shrike, pipits, buntings and even the highl colourful bee-eater. The **linnet** picks out mor open areas, as does the **stonechat** and the red legged **partridge** (the grey has been introduce for shooting in some places). These birds all fo low the maquis as it spreads up the valleys an slopes inland, but where it grows tall and invaded by holm oak and other trees (as seen the Fango valley, for example) the scrub warble such as Dartford and Sardinian leave, while th blackcap and subalpine remain. Being evergree the maquis maintains its insect larder in wint when many of its resident birds are joined b migrant cousins.

Kestrel and buzzards (widespread but nowhe very common) patrol above the maquis, as do red kite, which prefers the lower scrubby maqu to the taller growth. At night the clear bell-like notes of the **Scops owl** and the call of the nightjar echo across the maquis, mingling with the constant croaking of frogs.

The chestnut groves are comparatively empty of birdlife, but look for the endemic **tree creeper** here, and also the **mistle thrush** and the **wryneck**, the last now rare almost everywhere.

Mountain Species

In the **mountain** and alpine levels, grey wagtail and dipper forage in the spray of the torrents, where the crag martin is often seen as well. The pine forests have **goldcrest**, **coal tit** and the endemic **nuthatch** – this last, found from the Tartagine in the north to Ospédale in the south, is smaller than its mainland cousins and is more often heard than seen. Sparrowhawk and goshawk have a presence in these pine woods, as does the crossbill.

A feature of some parts of the **high mountains** are *pozzines* – small tablelands of peaty turf cut by meandering streams. Here **lark** and **wheatear** are often seen, with even blackbird and chaffinch if there are scrubby alders for cover. The blue rock thrush, though nesting on the coast at Scandola and elsewhere, can be met as high as 1500m. The central mountains are the domain of the yellow-beaked **alpine chough** and the rare **lammergeier** and **golden eagle**. Bonelli's eagle is reported from the Asco valley, but it is not known if it nests.

Garden Species

Gardens attract many birds, such as blackbird, warblers, hooded crow and turtle dove – the latter are widely shot when they fly in in spring, but there are always some to be heard in summer. The collared dove is a recent colonist and still uncommon.) Gardens also attract the spotted flycatcher – the Corsican form scarcely lives up to its name, with few if any speckles, but it is quickly recognized by its lively fly-catching sorties, usually returning to the same post. In the Nebbio and a few other spots, the **hoopoe** (with its dramatic crest) is also seen in gardens at dawn. The towns attract **house martin** and **swifts** – both the familiar Eurasian swift and the similar pallid swift.

Mammals

Woodmouse, shrew, rabbit, brown hare, weasel and hedgehog are as familiar in Corsica as elsewhere in Europe, but there are no squirrels. Squirrel-like nests in shrubs or low trees may be those of the black rat, while a sighting of a small brownish animal with squirrel-like bushy tail would be the **fat dormouse**, though it is shy and nocturnal. The slimmer **garden**, (or **oak**) **dormouse**, with white underside to body and tail, is also resident. Both these animals may search houses for a hibernation den in autumn, and you often hear them scratching around in the attic. Bats are common everywhere: in the gorge of the Bonifato forest behind Calvi, for example, they swarm out at sunset.

The fox is seen, and there are reports of a wild cat in remote parts of the island such as the Aïtone forest – it may turn out to be a tribe of striped feral cat, domestic stock now living wild. There are similar indecisive reports of pine marten in these forested areas.

Around five hundred **mouflon** – a wild sheep, the males sporting massive curved horns – are found in two main areas: at Asco and at Bavella. They might be the relic of an original wild population that began to be domesticated in Neolithic times, or they may be the descendants of escapees from those first domestic flocks.

The **sanglier** (wild boar) is found throughout the maquis and in the lower mountains, and has something of a cult status in Corsica. Many villages organize weekly hunts over the winter, culling an estimated 10,000 each year from an average population of 30,000. Even though the males are smaller than their continental cousins, the Corsican boar can still reach 80kg, and is a formidable animal, being armed with tusks for rooting and grubbing – you'll come across the disturbed ground during walks in the maquis. It is a Corsican habit to let domestic **pigs** roam free in the chestnut and beech woods on the mountain flanks, so there is certainly interbreeding between boar and pig, yet about forty percent of the wild-boar stock remains untainted.

The native **red deer** – the smallest of all red deer – became extinct only a few decades ago, but some Sardinian stock can be seen in a paddock near Quenza in the south, from where they are released into the surrounding forest.

Offshore, the common and striped **dolphins** and the common **porpoise** patrol, if no longer as regularly or in the numbers that were once seen. The endangered monk seal of the Mediterranean was last seen in Corsican waters in 1982. The **fin whale**, however, is often seen with young off Cap Corse in springtime.

Reptiles and Insects

Corsica's hot rocky landscape suits reptiles, and **lizards** are always seen scuttling across walls and rocks. The **Tyrrhenian wall lizard** is a sometimes abundant species found only in Corsica and Sardinia, and the mountain lizard is also endemic, but their variable colouring makes identification of lizard species difficult. Their cousins, the plump but flattened **geckos**, are most often noticed high on room walls and ceilings, which they patrol after sunset, dealing with mosquitoes and other irritations.

There are no poisonous snakes on the island. The **grass snake** is seen in damp places, while the **whip snake** – a slender snake often with a barred pattern – is found on sunny hillsides and other dry habitats. It will attempt to bite if annoyed – its French name is *coléreuse*, "quick-tempered one".

Hermann's tortoise is a fairly common sight in some areas, and a centre for tortoise breeding and release has recently been created near Ajaccio. The European pond **terrapin** might be seen in secluded pools and other still waters that have overgrown banks.

Endemic to the island is the **brook salamander**, olive-grey and brown and with a clear yellow stripe down its spine, found near running water up to 2000m. The rather larger **fire salamander**, with dramatic black and yellow skin, might also be seen.

Most piercingly vocal are the **edible frog** and the **common tree frog**, which has enormous vocal sacs for its small size. The **green toad**, with spotted green and white skin and shrill warbling call, is also reasonably common.

The frog chorus takes over from the summer daytime chorus of the **cicadas**, especially loud in the vicinity of their favourite umbrella pines. The cicadas are just one of a host of grasshoppers, bushcrickets, beetles, bees and **butterflies** that make Corsica so fascinating for anyone with any interest in natural history. Some butterflies will be familiar from

A Checklist of Wildlife Sites

Forests

Aïtone – magnificent specimens of Laricio pine; in the remoter reaches (towards Monte Cinto), wild boar, eagle and mouflon. See p.180.

Bavella – impressive though fire-damaged hunting reserve; chance of sightings of mouflon and eagle. See p.258.

Bonifato – classic "chaos" of rocks and forest, pines and maquis. See pp.272–281.

Castagniccia – chestnut woods. See p.314–325.

Ospédale – pines and other trees. See p.293.

Tartagine – bat caves and magnificent pines. See p.113.

Valdo-Niolo – the largest of the island's forests, with fine examples of Laricio pine. See p.338.

Vizzavona – some of the finest pines and beech. See p.359.

Other Wildlife Zones

Asco valley – possible sightings of mouflon, eagle, lammergeier; Laricio and maritime pines. See p.332.

Biguglia and the east coast lagoons – birdlife. See p.77.

Bonifacio – limestone cliffs with rare flowers. See pp.272–281.

Calanche – flowers and coastal birds. See p.175.

Cap Corse – remote maquis, good for birds (maybe eagles attracted by remoteness); nature reserve on Finocchiarola isles. See pp.78–96.

Désert des Agriates – a largish area of thin maquis growing on rocky, impoverished terrain; good for flowers and nesting birds. See p.108.

Fango valley – good walking through mix of maquis and forest habitats. See p.161.

Îles Sanguinaires – distinctive island vegetation. See p.218.

Îles Lavezzi – nature reserve off Bonifacio. See p.283.

Niolo – alpine choughs and other mountain birds. See pp.334–341.

Restonica – Corsican and maritime pine. See p.351.

Scandola – supreme nature reserve of international importance; classic lava-column geology; osprey and other birds; marine life. See p.137.

northern Europe, such as the migrant painted lady and the red admiral. Of the Mediterranean species, one of the most handsome is the large and strong **two-tailed pasha**, which feeds on the strawberry tree of the maquis. **Hummingbird hawk moths** of various kinds are commonly seen in gardens, hovering in front of the flowers.

Damselflies and mayflies are a common sight dancing over the streams, and the dramatic and fierce **hawker dragonflies** – a birdwatcher's insect if ever there was one – may spend the day hunting across the maquis, far from water.

Geoffrey Young

Books

Very few books about Corsica have been written in English, and the great majority of them are out of print, so you'll have to resort to secondhand book shops or libraries if you want to get stuck into most of the titles listed below. Out-of-print titles are marked "o/p" in the listings that follow. For those few that are in print, the UK publisher is given first, followed by the publisher in the US, unless the title is available in one country only, in which case we have specified the country concerned. If the same publisher produces the book in the UK and US, the publisher is simply named once. For the benefit of fluent French readers, we've also included a handful of French titles, which you can buy in any good bookshop in Corsica and mainland France or order via the Internet at *www.fnac.co.fr*. In the UK, virtually any French title in print may be ordered from The European Bookshop, 5 Warwick St, London W1R 5RA (☎020/7734 5259; *www.eurobooks.co.uk*).

Travel Books and Journals

James Boswell, *An Account of Corsica - the Journal of a Tour to that Island and Memoirs of Pascal Paoli* (In Print Publishing, UK). Typically robust and witty account of meetings with a broad cross-section of Corsican people, including absorbing insights into the psychology of local hero Pascal Paoli. Following his eventful trip to the island in 1765, Boswell became famous as an advocate of Corsican independence.

Thomasina Campbell, *Southward Ho!* (o/p). Jolly account of the island as seen through the eyes of a Victorian walker, with plentiful descriptions of wild flowers and scenery – but little on the inhabitants.

Dorothy Carrington, *Granite Island* (Penguin). A fascinating and immensely comprehensive book, combining the writer's personal experiences with an evocative portrayal of historical figures and events. By far the best study of Corsica ever written in English. Her most recent offering, *The Dream Hunters of Corsica* (Phoenix), covers some of the same ground, but is well worth reading too, focusing on the occult phenomena unique to the island, notably *mazzeri* (see p.271) and the evil eye.

Maurice Choury, *Tous Bandits d'Honneur!* (La Marge Éditions, France). Short, accessible history of Corsica's liberation from the Axis forces, June 1942 to October 1953, focusing on the Front National (left-wing) contribution to the Resistance.

A. Dugmore-Hardie, *Corsica the Beautiful* (o/p). Gushing eulogy of Corsica's landscapes, flora and fauna.

Emma Eleanor Elliot, *The Life and Letters of Si Gilbert Elliot* (o/p). Observations on Corsica from the British viceroy's office (1794–96), compiled by his granddaughter.

Gustave Flaubert, *Voyage dans les Pyrénées e en Corse* (Flammarion, France). Flaubert's parent promised him a trip to Corsica if he passed hi baccalaureate, and this book is an account of th trip the young novelist-to-be subsequently mad in the summer of 1840. Full of freshness, sensu ality and evocative descriptions of the island' landscape and people, it follows the 19-yea old's progress across the Pyrenees to th Mediterranean, with a poignant interlude descrit ing his secret love affair with a beautiful Peruvia woman in Marseille.

Capitaine Jean L'Herminier, *Casabianca* (Franc Empire, France). Definitive account of the subma rine *Casabianca*'s adventures in 1942–43, by i redoubtable commander. If you can handle th obscure nautical vocabulary, this makes a engrossing read and brings into sharp relief th nuts and bolts – and sheer perilousness – of th Resistance struggle during World War II.

Edward Lear, *Journal of a Landscape Pain* (Century, UK, o/p). Account of a Corsican visit the 1860s, augmented by beautifully atmospheric engravings.

Carola Oman, *Nelson* (The Reprint Society, UK, o/p). The definitive biography of Britain's most illustrious admiral, whose misadventures in Corsica nearly cost him his life. Published in 1947, but written in a nautical style reminiscent of Nelson's own era.

Alan Ross, *Time Was Away – A Journey Through Corsica* (Collins Harvill, UK, o/p). Gloomy impressionistic account of a visit to postwar Corsica, with drawings by John Minton.

Paulo Silvani, *Et la Corse fut Libérée* (La Marge Éditions, France). Written as recently as 1993, this prize-winning history of the Liberation quickly established itself as the classic version, drawing on recently released records and firsthand accounts to reconstitute the dramatic events of 1942–43.

Geoffrey Wagner, *Elegy for Corsica* (Cassell/Southern Illinois UP, both o/p). A highly readable miscellany drawn from an American's extended sabbaticals on the island in the 1960s. Portraits of local people (from Calenzana pimps to Niolu shepherds) are woven together with historical anecodote, descriptions of festivals, contemporary issues and a host of literary snippets to give a slice of island life at this formative point in Corsica's history. Well worth hunting out.

Archeology

Roger Grosjean, *La Corse Avant L'Histoire* (Klincksiek, France). The most influential discussion of the island's prehistoric sites, from the man who excavated most of them. The explanations are clear and precise, and aided by photographs.

Jean Jehasse, *Aléria Grecque et Romaine* (o/p). Heavy-going in-depth study of the Roman site of Aléria.

Geneviève Moracchini-Mazel, *La Corse Romane* (o/p). The island's Pisan Romanesque architecture discussed with drawings and descriptions of building techniques.

Geneviève Moracchini-Mazel, *Les Monuments Préchrétiens de la Corse* (o/p). An important work on Bronze Age Corsica, including an interpretation of the statue-menhirs of Filitosa.

History and Society

Philippe Alfonsi, *Les Chemins d'Orgueil* (Plon, France). The background to the rise of the FLNC, explored through the family history of one of its founder members. Based on solid journalistic research, but written in a fictional style.

Corelli Barnett, *Bonaparte* (Allen & Unwin/Hill & Wong, both o/p). An anti-Napoléon biography with vivid insights into his life in Corsica – good pictures as well.

Dorothy Carrington, *Napoleon and his Parents on the Threshold of History* (Viking/Nal-Duhon, both o/p). Lucid study of Napoléon's early years in his native country, from the Battle of Ponte-Nuovo until the death of his father in 1785, based on the archives of Prince Napoléon and other previously unconsulted private collections. The most thorough work on this period, with facsimiles of little-known documents and an exhaustive bibliography.

Vincent Cronin, *Napoleon* (Fontana/Harper-Collins). Enthusiastic and accessible biography; you might still find copies of the recently deleted Penguin edition on the shelves.

Peter Geyl, *Napoleon – For and Against* (Penguin, o/p). A compendium of various French scholars' views on Napoléon.

M. Maclaren, *Corsican Boswell* (o/p). Places Boswell's reactions to Corsica within their historical context; an amusing read, but difficult to find.

Elie Papadacci, *Les Bandits Corses: Honneur et Dignité* (Éditions Almar, France). The life histories of Corsica's most infamous *bandits* (see p.246), sympathetically written by the island's top historian.

Valerie Pirie, *His Majesty of Corsica* (o/p). An illuminating biography of Corsica's ephemeral king, Theodor von Neuhof.

Patrick Whinney, *Corsican Command* (Patrick Stephens, UK). Wittily written memoirs of clandestine operations in Corsica between 1943 and 1944, from the Allies' perspective. Of particular interest is the author's description of Bastia in the wake of the German withdrawal, illustrated with evocative photos.

Literature

Gabriel Xavier Culioli, *La Terre des Seigneurs* (Lieu Commun, France). Phenomenally successful novel following the evolution of a family through a century in Corsica. Full of fascinating background on island politics and village life.

Alphonse Daudet, *Letters from my Windmill* (Penguin). Daudet's tale of a lonely Corsican lighthouse keeper on the Îles Sanguinaires, near Ajaccio, has become a literary classic, and is studied by schoolchildren throughout the country.

Alexandre Dumas, *Les Frères Corses* (La Marge Éditions, France). Far-fetched yarn about two outlaw brothers in nineteenth-century Corsica.

Gustave Flaubert, *Memoires d'un Fou* (Flammarion, France). Flaubert romanticizes the *bandits*, the maquis, the mountains and the sea in letters to his sister.

Guy de Maupassant, *Un Bandit Corse et Autres Contes* (Marzocchi, France). Maupassant, France's most illustrious short-story author, spent two months in Corsica in 1880, and the lively tales in this anthology were all inspired by his visit. The *Bandit Corse* has become a classic, and is said to have been avidly read by the *bandits* themselves after its publication.

Prosper Mérimée, *Colomba* (Hachette, France). Short novel loosely based on a real-life blood feud that divided the village of Fozzano in the 1830s. A son returns to Corsica and is expected to avenge the death of his father. Though far from historically accurate, the story vividly evokes the violent spirit of the times and was a roaring success for Mérimée, inspiring a mini tourist invasion in Fozzano.

Walking and Climbing

Alan Castle, *The Corsican High Level Route* (Cicerone, UK). Detailed, day-by-day description of the GR20, with plenty of photographs and solid information, but no topo-maps.

Robin G. Collomb, *Corsica Mountains* (West Co, UK). Covers all the principal mountain peaks, with information on different approaches and ascents, backed up with diagrams.

Institut Géographique National, *Corse* (Les Guides IGN, France). Arguably the best all-round outdoor-pursuits guide currently in circulation (if you can read French). Thoroughly reliable route descriptions for climbs, hikes, canoe courses, horse and mountain-bike rides; illustrated with quality photos and schematic topo-maps. Available at most bookstores in Corsica, or through *www.ign.co.fr.*

Walks in Corsica (Robertson McCarta, UK, o/p). The cream of Corsica's long-distance hiking trails described in translation from the French hiking association's essential topo-guides, including colour 1:50,000 maps overlaid with the routes. Essential for serious walkers, although you might have to rely on the French version as this English translation has been out of print for some years.

Language

Since 1974 it has been compulsory for schoolchildren to learn Corsican up to the level of the baccalaureate, and at Corte University all students are obliged to study the language. Corsican nationalists use the language for their campaign literature, folk singers always sing in Corsican, and there's a newscast in Corsican on television every evening. Yet the language is struggling to survive in competition with French, the official language of the island, which is spoken and understood everywhere in Corsica.

The Corsican Language

Corsican (see pp.398–399), originally a Latin-based language with resemblances to Romanian, developed an Italianate vocabulary and syntax during Pisan and Genoese occupation. Arabic and French influences have added to the complexity of Corsican, which for centuries was predominantly an oral tongue until around two hundred years ago – hence the confusing variety of spellings for place-names, despite attempts at standardization. The commonest variants come about through the transposition of *ll* and *dd* – as in *casteddu* and *castellu*. Buildings and monuments are often labelled in different languages (San Pietro/San Pietru), and on maps you'll find mountain passes, rivers and regions marked in a mixture of Italian, French and Corsican – the *u* ending (pronounced as in English "zoo") is a frequent indicator of Corsican usage. Deep in the country, many old people are still easier with Corsican than French, so a few phrases will be met with surprise and pleasure. Pronunciation is generally as for Italian, but look out for two tricky clusters of consonants – *chj/chi* and *ghj/chi*, pronounced "ty" or "dy".

French Pronunciation

One easy rule to remember is that **consonants** at the ends of words are usually silent. *Pas plus tard* (not later) is thus pronounced "pa-plu-tarr". But when the following word begins with a vowel, you run the two together: *pas après* (not after) becomes "pazaprey". **Vowels** are the hardest sounds to get right. Roughly:

a	as in h**a**t	*eu*	like the u in h**u**rt	*ou*	as in f**oo**d
e	as in g**e**t	*i*	as in mach**i**ne	*u*	as in a pursed-lip version of **u**se
é	between g**e**t and g**a**te	*o*	as in h**o**t		
è	between g**e**t and g**u**t	*o, au*	as in **o**ver		

More awkward are the **combinations** *in/im*, *en/em*, *an/am*, *on/om*, *un/um* at the ends of words, or followed by consonants other than *n* or *m*. Again, roughly:

in/im	like the **an** in **an**xious	*on/om*	like the d**on** in D**on**caster said by someone with a heavy cold
an/am, en/em	like the d**on** in D**on**caster when said with a nasal accent	*un/um*	like the **u** in **u**nderstand

Consonants are much as in English, except that: *ch* is always "sh", *c* is "s", *h* is silent, *th* is the same as "t", *ll* is like the *y* in "yes", *w* is "v", and *r* is growled (or rolled).

French Words and Phrases

Learning Materials

Rough Guide French Phrasebook (Rough Guides). Mini dictionary-style phrasebook with both English–French and French–English sections, along with cultural tips for tricky situations and a menu reader.

Breakthrough French (Pan; book and two cassettes). Excellent teach-yourself course.

French and English Slang Dictionary (Harrap/Prentice Hall); **Dictionary of Modern Colloquial French** (Routledge). Both volumes are a bit large to carry, but they are the key to all you ever wanted to understand.

French Experience (BBC Books). Crammed with authentic, modern material and learning practices, the BBCs latest French self-tutor, accompanied by audiocassettes, CDs and a TV series (on video), makes the competition look dowdy and dated. A particularly upbeat volume 2 includes sections on French from around the Francophone world. Easily the best choice for beginners and intermediate learners.

Mini French Dictionary (Harrap/Prentice Hall). French–English and English–French, plus a brief grammar and pronunciation guide.

Verbaid (Verbaid, Hawk House, Heath Lane, Farnham, Surrey GU9 0PR). CD-sized laminated paper "verb wheel" that gives you the tense endings for the regular verbs.

Basic Words and Phrases

French nouns are divided into masculine and feminine. This causes difficulties with adjectives, whose endings have to change to suit the gender of the nouns they qualify. If you know some grammar, you will know what to do. If not, stick to the masculine form, which is the simplest – it's what we have done in this glossary.

today	*aujourd'hui*	that one	*celà*
yesterday	*hier*	open	*ouvert*
tomorrow	*demain*	closed	*fermé*
in the morning	*le matin*	big	*grand*
in the afternoon	*l'après-midi*	small	*petit*
in the evening	*le soir*	more	*plus*
now	*maintenant*	less	*moins*
later	*plus tard*	a little	*un peu*
at one o'clock	*à une heure*	a lot	*beaucoup*
at three o'clock	*à trois heures*	cheap	*bon marché*
at half past ten	*à dix heures et demie*	expensive	*cher*
at midday	*à midi*	good	*bon*
man	*un homme*	bad	*mauvais*
woman	*une femme*	hot	*chaud*
here	*ici*	cold	*froid*
there	*là*	with	*avec*
this one	*ceci*	without	*sans*

Numbers

1	*un*	9	*neuf*	17	*dix-sept*	50	*cinquante*
2	*deux*	10	*dix*	18	*dix-huit*	60	*soixante*
3	*trois*	11	*onze*	19	*dix-neuf*	70	*soixante-dix*
4	*quatre*	12	*douze*	20	*vingt*	75	*soixante-quinze*
5	*cinq*	13	*treize*	21	*vingt-et-un*		
6	*six*	14	*quatorze*	22	*vingt-deux*	80	*quatre-vingts*
7	*sept*	15	*quinze*	30	*trente*	90	*quatre-vingt-dix*
8	*huit*	16	*seize*	40	*quarante*		

95	*quatre-vingt-quinze*	101	*cent-et-un*	500	*cinq cents*	5000	*cinq milles*
100	*cent*	200	*deux cents*	1000	*mille*	1,000,000	*un million*
		300	*trois cents*	2000	*deux milles*		

Days and Dates

January	*janvier*	Wednesday	*mercredi*
February	*février*	Thursday	*jeudi*
March	*mars*	Friday	*vendredi*
April	*avril*	Saturday	*samedi*
May	*mai*		
June	*juin*	August 1	*le premier août*
July	*juillet*	March 2	*le deux mars*
August	*août*	July 14	*le quatorze juillet*
September	*septembre*	November 23	*le vingt-trois novembre*
October	*octobre*		
November	*novembre*	1997	*dix-neuf-cent quatre-vingt-dix-sept*
December	*décembre*		
		2000	*deux mille*
Sunday	*dimanche*	2001	*deux mille un*
Monday	*lundi*	2010	*deux mille dix*
Tuesday	*mardi*		

Talking to People

When addressing people you should always use *Monsieur* for a man, *Madame* for a woman, *Mademoiselle* for a girl. Plain *bonjour* by itself is not enough. This isn't as formal as it seems, and it has its uses when you've forgotten someone's name or want to attract someone's attention.

Excuse me	*Pardon*	please	*s'il vous plaît*
Do you speak English?	*Vous parlez anglais?*	thank you	*merci*
How do you say it in French?	*Comment ça se dit en Français?*	hello	*bonjour*
		goodbye	*au revoir*
What's your name?	*Comment vous appelez-vous?*	good morning/ afternoon	*bonjour*
My name is ...	*Je m'appelle ...*	good evening	*bonsoir*
I'm English/	*Je suis anglais[e]/*	good night	*bonne nuit*
Irish/	*irlandais[e]/*	How are you?	*Comment allez-vous?/ Ça va?*
Scottish/	*écossais[e]/*		
Welsh/	*gallois[e]/*	Fine, thanks	*Très bien, merci*
American/	*américain[e]/*	I don't know	*Je ne sais pas*
Australian/	*australien[ne]/*	Let's go	*Allons-y*
Canadian/	*canadien[ne]/*	See you tomorrow	*A demain*
a New Zealander	*néo-zélandais[e]*	See you soon	*A bientôt*
yes	*oui*	Sorry	*Pardon, Madame/ Je m'excuse*
no	*non*		
I understand	*Je comprends*	Leave me alone! (aggressive)	*Fichez-moi la paix!*
I don't understand	*Je ne comprends pas*		
Can you speak slower please?	*S'il vous plaît, parlez moins vite*	Please help me	*Aidez-moi, s'il vous plaît*
OK/agreed	*d'accord*	Help!	*Au secours!*

Continues overleaf

French Words and Phrases continued

Finding the Way

bus	*autobus/bus/car*	What time does it arrive?	*Il arrive à quelle heure?*
bus station	*gare routière*	a ticket to . . .	*un billet pour…*
bus stop	*arrêt*	single ticket	*aller simple*
car	*voiture*	return ticket	*aller retour*
train, taxi, ferry	*train, taxi, ferry*	validate your ticket	*compostez votre billet*
boat	*bâteau*	valid for	*valable pour*
plane	*avion*	ticket office	*vente de billets*
train station	*gare (SNCF)*	how many kilometres?	*combien de kilomètres?*
platform	*quai*	how many hours?	*combien d'heures?*
What time does it leave?	*Il part à quelle heure?*	straight on	*tout droit*
hitchhiking	*autostop*	on the other side of	*à l'autre côté de*
on foot	*à pied*	on the corner of	*à l'angle de*
Where are you going?	*Vous allez où?*	next to	*à côté de*
I'm going to . . .	*Je vais à . . .*	behind	*derrière*
I want to get off at . . .	*Je voudrais descendre à . . .*	in front of	*devant*
the road to . . .	*la route pour . . .*	before	*avant*
near	*près/pas loin*	after	*après*
far	*loin*	under	*sous*
left	*à gauche*	to cross	*traverser*
right	*à droite*	bridge	*pont*

Questions and Requests

The simplest way of asking a question is to start with *s'il vous plaît* (please), then name the thing you want in an interrogative tone of voice. For example:

Where is there a bakery?	*S'il vous plaît, la boulangerie?*
Which way is it to the Genoan watchtower?	*S'il vous plaît, la route pour la tour génoise?*

Similarly with requests:

We'd like a room for two.	*S'il vous plaît, une chambre pour deux.*
Can I have a kilo of oranges?	*S'il vous plaît, un kilo d'oranges.*

Question words

where?	*où?*	why?	*pourquoi?*
how?	*comment?*	at what time?	*à quelle heure?*
how many/how much?	*combien?*	what is/which is?	*quel est?*
when?	*quand?*		

Accommodation

room for one/two people	*chambre pour une/deux personnes*	for one/two/three nights	*pour une/deux/trois nuits*
double bed	*lit double*	Can I see it?	*Je peux la voir?*
room with a shower	*chambre avec douche*	room on the courtyard	*chambre sur la cour*
room with a bath	*chambre avec salle de bain*	room over the street	*chambre sur la rue*
		first floor	*premier étage*

second floor	*deuxième étage*
with a view	*avec vue*
key	*clef*
to iron	*repasser*
do laundry	*faire la lessive*
sheets	*draps*
blankets	*couvertures*
quiet	*calme*
noisy	*bruyant*
hot water	*eau chaude*
cold water	*eau froide*
Is breakfast included?	*Est-ce que le petit déjeuner est compris?*
I would like breakfast	*Je voudrais prendre le petit déjeuner*
I don't want breakfast	*Je ne veux pas de petit déjeuner*
Can we camp here?	*On peut camper ici?*
campsite	*camping/ terrain de camping*
tent	*tente*
tent space	*emplacement*
youth hostel	*auberge de jeunesse*

Cars

service station	*garage*
service	*service*
to park the car	*garer la voiture*
car park	*un parking*
no parking	*défense de stationner/ stationnement interdit*
petrol station	*poste d'essence*
fuel	*essence*
(to) fill it up	*faire le plein*
oil	*huile*
air line	*ligne à air*
to put air in the tyres	*gonfler les pneus*
battery	*batterie*
the battery is dead	*la batterie est morte*
plugs	*bougies*
to break down	*tomber en panne*
gas can	*bidon*
insurance	*assurance*
green card	*carte verte*
traffic lights	*feux*
red light	*feu rouge*
green light	*feu vert*

Health Matters

doctor	*médecin*
I don't feel well	*Je ne me sens pas bien*
medicines	*médicaments*
prescription	*ordonnance*
I feel sick	*Je suis malade*
I have a headache	*J'ai mal à la tête*
stomachache	*mal à l'estomac*
period	*règles*
pain	*douleur*
it hurts	*ça fait mal*
chemist	*pharmacie*
hospital	*hôpital*

Other Needs

bakery	*boulangerie*
food shop	*alimentation*
supermarket	*supermarché*
to eat	*manger*
to drink	*boire*
camping gas	*camping gaz*
tobacconist	*tabac*
stamps	*timbres*
bank	*banque*
money	*argent*
toilets	*toilettes*
police	*police*
telephone	*téléphone*
cinema	*cinéma*
theatre	*théâtre*
to reserve/book	*réserver*

Corsican Words and Phrases

Basics

yes, no, OK	*iè, nò, và bé*
please, thank you	*fate u piacè, a' ringraziavvi*
where, when	*induve, quandu*
what, how much	*chi, quantu*
here, there	*custi, custà*
this, that	*quellu/quella, quessu/quessa*
now, later	*ora, dopu*
open, closed	*apertu, chiusu*
with, without	*cù, senza*
good, bad	*bonu, male*
big, small	*grande/maio, piccola/chjucu*
cheap, expensive	*bonu mercatu, cara*
hot, cold	*caldu, fredda*
more, less	*piu, menu*
nothing	*nulla/nunda/nudda*
today, tomorrow	*oghje, dumane*
day	*ghjurnu*
week	*simana*
month	*meze*
yesterday	*ieri*
day before	*avant'ierisera*
night	*a notte*
car	*a vittura*
girl, boy	*zitella, zitellu*
it's good	*he bonu*
something	*qualcosa*
I want	*vogliu*
next week	*simana'dopu*
next month	*meze'dopu*
morning	*a mane*
evening	*a sera*

Greetings and Responses

hello, goodbye	*bonghjornu, a'vedeci*
good evening	*bona sera*
goodnight	*bona notte*
sorry	*me dispiace*
excuse me	*scusame*
How are you?	*Comu sì?*
I (don't) understand	*(nò) capiscu*
Do you speak English?	*Parla inglese?*
My name is . . .	*Me chjamanu . . .*
What's your name?	*Cumu a chjamanu?*
I am English	*Sò Inglese*
Let's go	*Andemu*

Questions and Requests

Do you have?	*Avetene?*
Give me (one like that)	*Datemi*
That's enough	*Basta*
What would you like to drink?	*Chi vulete beie?*
I'd like a lemonade/coffee	*A me una limnata/caffè*
How much?	*Quantu costanu?*
Is there . . .?	*C'he . . .?*
. . . a room	*. . . una camera*
. . . with two beds	*. . . cù duie letti*
. . . with shower/bath	*. . . cùillad uscia/bag narola*
It's for one person/two people	*Ci ne vole una/duie persona*
How long are you staying?	*Quantu ci avete da stà?*
for one night/one week	*. . . pé una notte/una semana*
It's fine – how much is it?	*Và bé – quantu costanu?*
It's too expensive	*He troppu caru*

Directions

Where is . . ?	*Induv'é . . .?*
It's near	*He vicinu*
It's far	*He lontana*
left, right, straight on	*sinistra, dritta, sempredrittu*

How long will it take to get to Ponte Leccia?	*Quantu ci vole à ghjunghje à u Ponte à a Leccia?*	What's the time ?	*Chi ora he?*
		It's three o'clock	*Sò trè ore*

Months and Seasons

January	*Ghjennaghju*	October	*Ottobre*
February	*Febbraghju*	November	*Novembre*
March	*Marzu*	December	*Dicembre*
April	*Aprile*		
May	*Maghjiu*	winter	*imbernu/ ingnernu*
June	*Ghjiugnu*		
July	*Ghjugliu*	spring	*veranu*
August	*Aostu*	summer	*estate*
September	*Sittembre*	autumn	*auturnu*

Numbers and Days

1	*unu (una)*	21	*vintunu*
2	*dui (duie)*	22	*vintidui*
3	*trè*	30	*trenta*
4	*quattru*	40	*quaranta*
5	*cinque*	50	*cinquanta*
6	*sei*	60	*sessanta*
7	*sette*	70	*settanta*
8	*ottu*	80	*ottanta*
9	*nove*	90	*novanta*
10	*dece*	100	*centu*
11	*ondeci*	101	*cent'e unu*
12	*dodeci*	102	*cent'e dui*
13	*tredeci*	Monday	*luni*
14	*quattordeci*	Tuesday	*marti*
15	*quindeci*	Wednesday	*mercuri*
16	*sedeci*	Thursday	*ghjovi*
17	*dicessette*	Friday	*venneri*
18	*diciottu*	Saturday	*sabatu*
19	*dicennove*	Sunday	*dumenica*
20	*vinti*		

Words of the countryside

bird	*acellu*	plateau	*pianu*
mountain	*montane*	cliff	*scuglialu*
mountain pass	*bocca, foce*	bridge	*ponte*
mountain peak, summit	*capu, cima, monte, punta*	river	*fiume*
		tree	*arburu*
forest, wood	*furesta, valdu*	beach	*a marina*
lake	*lavu*	village	*u paese*

Index

Stay in touch with us!

ROUGH*NEWS* is Rough Guides' free newsletter. In four issues a year we give you news, travel issues, music reviews, readers' letters and the latest dispatches from authors on the road.

I would like to receive ROUGH*NEWS*: please put me on your free mailing list.

NAME . . . .

ADDRESS . . . .

Please clip or photocopy and send to: Rough Guides, 62–70 Shorts Gardens, London WC2H 9AB, England or Rough Guides, 375 Hudson Street, New York, NY 10014, USA.

ROUGH GUIDES: Travel

Amsterdam
Andalucia
Australia

Austria
Bali & Lombok
Barcelona
Belgium & Luxembourg
Belize
Berlin
Brazil
Britain
Brittany & Normandy
Bulgaria
California
Canada
Central America
Chile
China
Corfu & the Ionian Islands
Corsica
Costa Rica
Crete
Croatia
Cyprus
Czech & Slovak Republics
Dodecanese & the East Aegean
Dominican Republic
Ecuador
Egypt
England
Europe
Florida
France
French Hotels & Restaurants 1999
Germany
Goa
Greece
Greek Islands
Guatemala
Hawaii
Holland
Hong Kong & Macau
Hungary
India
Indonesia
Ireland
Israel & the Palestinian Territories
Italy
Jamaica
Japan
Jordan

Kenya
Lake District
Laos
London
Los Angeles
Malaysia, Singapore & Brunei
Mallorca & Menorca
Maya World
Mexico
Morocco
Moscow
Nepal
New England
New York
New Zealand
Norway
Pacific Northwest
Paris
Peru
Poland
Portugal
Prague
Provence & the Côte d'Azur
The Pyrenees
Rhodes & the Dodecanese
Romania
St Petersburg
San Francisco
Sardinia
Scandinavia
Scotland
Scottish highlands and Islands
Sicily
Singapore
South Africa
South India
Southwest USA
Spain
Sweden
Syria

Thailand
Trinidad & Tobago
Tunisia
Turkey
Tuscany & Umbria
USA
Venice
Vienna
Vietnam
Wales
Washington DC
West Africa
Zimbabwe & Botswana

AVAILABLE AT ALL GOOD BOOKSHOPS

AITO

ATOL
2770